Frommer's®

Sweden
4th Edition

by Darwin Porter & Danforth Prince

Here's what the critics say about Frommer's:

"Amazingly easy to use. Very portable, very complete."

—*Booklist*

"Detailed, accurate, and easy-to-read information for all price ranges."
—*Glamour Magazine*

"Hotel information is close to encyclopedic."

—*Des Moines Sunday Register*

"Frommer's Guides have a way of giving you a real feel for a place."
—*Knight Ridder Newspapers*

WILEY
Wiley Publishing, Inc.

About the Authors

As a team of veteran travel writers, **Darwin Porter** and **Danforth Prince** have produced numerous titles for Frommer's, including best-selling guides to Italy, France, the Caribbean, England, and Germany. Porter, a former bureau chief of the *Miami Herald,* is also a Hollywood biographer. His most recent releases are *The Secret Life of Humphrey Bogart* and *Katherine the Great,* the latter a close-up of the private life of the late Katherine Hepburn. Prince was formerly employed by the Paris bureau of the *New York Times* and is today the president of Blood Moon Productions and other media-related firms.

Published by:

Wiley Publishing, Inc.

111 River St.
Hoboken, NJ 07030-5774

ISBN-13: 978-0-7645-7827-4
ISBN-10: 0-7645-7827-8

Editor: Marc Nadeau
Production Editor: M. Faunette Johnston
Cartographer: Roberta Stockwell
Photo Editor: Richard Fox
Production by Wiley Indianapolis Composition Services

For information on our other products and services or to obtain technical support, please contact our Customer Care Department within the U.S. at 800/762-2974, outside the U.S. at 317/572-3993 or fax 317/572-4002.

Wiley also publishes its books in a variety of electronic formats. Some content that appears in print may not be available in electronic formats.

Manufactured in the United States of America

5 4 3 2 1

Contents

List of Maps

An Invitation to the Reader

In researching this book, we discovered many wonderful places—hotels, restaurants, shops, and more. We're sure you'll find others. Please tell us about them, so we can share the information with your fellow travelers in upcoming editions. If you were disappointed with a recommendation, we'd love to know that, too. Please write to:

Frommer's Sweden, 4th Edition
Wiley Publishing, Inc. • 111 River St. • Hoboken, NJ 07030-5774

An Additional Note

Please be advised that travel information is subject to change at any time—and this is especially true of prices. We therefore suggest that you write or call ahead for confirmation when making your travel plans. The authors, editors, and publisher cannot be held responsible for the experiences of readers while traveling. Your safety is important to us, however, so we encourage you to stay alert and be aware of your surroundings. Keep a close eye on cameras, purses, and wallets, all favorite targets of thieves and pickpockets.

Other Great Guides for Your Trip:

Frommer's Scandinavia
Frommer's Denmark
Frommer's Norway
Frommer's Europe
Europe For Dummies

Frommer's Star Ratings, Icons & Abbreviations

Every hotel, restaurant, and attraction listing in this guide has been ranked for quality, value, service, amenities, and special features using a **star-rating system.** In country, state, and regional guides, we also rate towns and regions to help you narrow down your choices and budget your time accordingly. Hotels and restaurants are rated on a scale of zero (recommended) to three stars (exceptional). Attractions, shopping, nightlife, towns, and regions are rated according to the following scale: zero stars (recommended), one star (highly recommended), two stars (very highly recommended), and three stars (must-see).

In addition to the star-rating system, we also use **seven feature icons** that point you to the great deals, in-the-know advice, and unique experiences that separate travelers from tourists. Throughout the book, look for:

Finds	Special finds—those places only insiders know about
Fun Fact	Fun facts—details that make travelers more informed and their trips more fun
Kids	Best bets for kids, and advice for the whole family
Moments	Special moments—those experiences that memories are made of
Overrated	Places or experiences not worth your time or money
Tips	Insider tips—great ways to save time and money
Value	Great values—where to get the best deals

The following **abbreviations** are used for credit cards:

AE	American Express	DISC	Discover	V	Visa
DC	Diners Club	MC	MasterCard		

Frommers.com

Now that you have the guidebook to a great trip, visit our website at **www.frommers.com** for travel information on more than 3,000 destinations. With features updated regularly, we give you instant access to the most current trip-planning information available. At Frommers.com, you'll also find the best prices on airfares, accommodations, and car rentals—and you can even book travel online through our travel booking partners. At Frommers.com, you'll also find the following:

- Online updates to our most popular guidebooks
- Vacation sweepstakes and contest giveaways
- Newsletter highlighting the hottest travel trends
- Online travel message boards with featured travel discussions

What's New in Sweden

Sweden, unlike much of the rest of Europe, remains fairly stabilized. It is not a land of violent upheavals and changes, and has maintained more or less the same hotels and sightseeing attractions as it did at the turn of the 20th century.

Although part of the European Union, Sweden has opted—at least for the moment—to keep its time-honored currency, the Swedish *krona,* going along with the policies set by its neighbors, Norway and Denmark. Of all the Scandinavian countries, only Finland has opted to abandon the Finnish mark and go under the euro umbrella.

The one event that has had the greatest impact on Sweden as it moves deeper into the 21st century is the opening of the Øresund Bridge, that 16km (10-mile) motor and railway link that links Sweden to Denmark. Of course, pre-bridge Swedes who wanted to visit Denmark could easily take a trip over there by boat—perhaps via a link between Helsingborg, a west coast Swedish city, and Helsingør in Denmark (famed for its so-called Hamlet's Castle).

Somehow the water caused a psychological barrier greater than it actually was. As one resident of Malmö, Selma Linden, told us, "There is something about being able to get in your own car and drive over to Denmark that's different from traveling by boat. This past summer my family and I made frequent trips to the Tivoli Gardens in Copenhagen whereas in the past we went over there only once a year."

The opening of the bridge has brought Sweden closer to the heart of the Continent as never before. Many foreign visitors rent cars in Germany and, after seeing that country, drive through Denmark all the way to Stockholm without having to take a car ferry, a feat once thought impossible.

Although not earth-shaking, here are some late-breaking developments in the far northern country of Sweden.

GOTHENBURG In Sweden's second city, **Quality Hotel 11,** Maskingatan 11 (© **031/779-11-11**), has burst onto the scene at a harborfront location lying west of the center at Eriksberg. It's worth the trek over to spend the night. The owners took a 19th-century warehouse and successfully converted it into this winning choice with multi-level terraces. Each room opens onto a vista of the water. Furnishings are in the attractive modern Scandinavian mode, with wooden floors and pastel fabrics.

In dining, Chef Stefan Karlsson has become a media darling in the wake of his opening of **Fond,** Götaplatsen (© **031/81-25-80**). Each dish is prepared with market-fresh ingredients. Memorable taste sensations and flavors have created a steady stream of devoted foodies who are putting Fond on the Gothenberg culinary map.

Among night clubbers, no one ever accused Gothenburg of being Las Vegas, but it does have a casino with the opening of **Casino Cosmopol** at

Packhusplatsen 7 (© **031/333-55-00**). In a building that dates from 1865, this amusement palace offers games of chance but also food, drink, and entertainment. You can also have an elegant dinner here at the second-floor Casanova with its panoramic views of the harbor. See chapter 5.

GOTLAND On this Baltic island, **Villa Alskog** (© **0498/49-11-88**), is undergoing an important expansion and improvement and is in line to become the choice address on this windswept but historical island. The core building is from 1840, but improvements, including full spa treatments, are keeping the well-run establishment up with the times.

In other developments on the island, **Donners Brunn,** Donners Plats 3 (© **0498/27-10-90**) has become the number one choice for dining in the wake of Bo Nilsson's arrival. He was the former chef at Stockholm's **Operakällaren,** hailed as one of the greatest restaurants in Sweden. He has taken his skill and imagination to Visby where he fashions a premier French-inspired Swedish cuisine. Based on fresh ingredients, his dishes often reach the sublime. See chapter 8.

HELSINGBORG In this western coast port city across the sound from Denmark, **SS Swea,** Kungstorget (© **042/131516**) is bringing some culinary excitement to this staid old city. The restaurant is installed on a permanently docked ship furnished like a luxury liner. It doesn't rely just on this gimmick for its sudden success. Its fresh seafood and Swedish specialties are among the best in Helsingborg. See chapter 6.

KARLSTAD In the capital of the ancient province of Värmland, **Comfort Hotel Bilan,** Karlbergsgatan 3 (© **054/100300**), has been converted into a 68-room hotel of coziness and taste. But back in the 1800s it was a dreaded address—the local prison for

convicts. The rooms are a bit small (just ask Martha Stewart what these are like) but otherwise it's a first-class address. See chapter 10.

LULEÅ Most tours of the north of Sweden begin at the port city of Luleå on the east coast at the northern end of the Gulf of Bothnia, 113km (70 miles) south of the Arctic Circle and a long 930km (578 miles) north of Stockholm. Once you arrive here, the chillingly named **Arctic Hotel,** Sandviksgatan 80 (© **0920/109-80**), warms considerably once you go inside its inviting precincts. Both functional and stylish, the restored hotel is becoming more and more the point of choice for visitors who are using it as their first night's stopover before heading even farther north into the bone-chilling Lapland of Sweden. The first-class cuisine served in the hotel's on-site restaurant makes the Arctic even more of a desired stopover. See chapter 12.

MALMÖ Sweden's third city, the port of Malmö, has seen the opening of **Salt & brygga,** Sundspromenade 7 (© **040/611-59-40**), serving an inspired cuisine based on cues from both the Swedish and Mediterranean kitchens. This is the most successful of the post-millennium restaurants in the city. A local food critic hailed Salt & brygga as "the restaurant of the moment." Built at quayside, its courtyard tables open onto a panoramic view of the Öresund.

SKARA This town, 350km (217 miles) southwest of Stockholm, makes one of the best stopovers between Karlstad (capital of Värmland) and the western port city of Gothenburg for motorists touring Sweden. The Skara Stadshotellet in the center of town has long been one of the best hotels in the area. Recent improvements in its restaurant, **Rosers Salonger,** Järnvägsgatan 5 (© **0511/240-50**), have made an overnight visit more interesting than ever. A finely honed Swedish and international cuisine is served, featuring thoughtful menus of well-prepared dishes served with style and flair and based on the highest quality of raw ingredients available in the area. See chapter 9.

STOCKHOLM   Hotel grand openings are scarce in Stockholm, then along comes **Hotel Rival,** Mariatorget 3 (© **08/545-789-00**), which originally opened in 1937 as a hotel-cafe-bakery-cinema. After a massive dose of money from Benny Andersson, former member of ABBA, the hotel has been given a new lease on life. Today its restored Art Deco styling and luxury makes it one of the most charming of the boutique hotels of Stockholm. It lies on the gentrified island of Södermalm in southern Stockholm and is creating a lot of press excitement in Sweden. It has also become the favorite hotel for visiting pop or rock stars because of the ABBA connection.

In dining, Stockholm has a heavenly new restaurant serving the finest Italian food in the city. It's the aptly named **Divino,** Karlavägen 28 (© **08/611-02-69**). Backed up by an excellent

selection of vintages from a mammoth wine cellar, the cuisine is never dull. Chefs create unusual variations of the classics, and do so exceedingly well. Wait until you try their guinea fowl with morels.

Other press excitement is being generated by Johan Lindqvist's new restaurant, **Spring,** Karlavägen 110 (© **08/783-15-00**). East meets West in this showcase of fusion cuisine, mostly blending the finest recipes of Scandinavia with trendy Asian-influenced dishes. Dishes arrive on your plate in delicate hues and brimming with flavor. Where else in Stockholm can you order Japanese eel with foie gras and maki tempura?

Another fashionable eatery has opened: **Vassa Eggen,** Birger Jarlsgatan 29 (© **08/21-61-69**), serving one of the city's most cutting-edge international cuisines. Its chefs borrow gastronomic ideas from around the globe to concoct a cuisine pleasing to both eye and palate. The Swedish edition of *Gourmet* magazine raves about the oxtail tortellini with mascarpone cheese served in consommé. See chapter 3.

1

The Best of Sweden

Sweden presents visitors with an embarrassment of riches, everything from sophisticated cities to medieval towns, to Europe's last untamed wilderness. To help you decide how best to spend your time in Sweden, we've compiled a list of our favorite experiences and discoveries. In the following pages, you'll find the kind of candid advice we'd give our close friends.

1 The Best Travel Experiences

- **Shopping in the "Kingdom of Crystal":** Many visitors come to Sweden just to shop for glass. In the "Kingdom of Crystal," which stretches some 112km (69 miles) between the port city of Kalmar and the town of Växjö in Småland province, some of the world's most prestigious glassmakers, including Kosta Boda and Orrefors, showcase their wares. At least 16 major glassworks welcome visitors to this area and offer cut-rate discounts in the form of "seconds"—goods containing flaws hardly noticeable except to the most carefully trained eye. Visitors can see glass being blown and crystal being etched by the land's most skilled craftspeople. See section 2, "Växjö," in chapter 7.

- **Exploring the High Coast:** The Höga Kusten is the most panoramic stretch of the Bothnian Coast along the northern regions of eastern Sweden. It stretches between the towns of Härnösand and Örnsköldsvik, a land of rolling mountains and forested valleys that at times seem to plunge into the Gulf of Bothnia itself. Along the coast, you can cross Höga Kusten Bridge, the seventh-longest in the world, spanning the Ångermanalv River, and encounter dramatic coastal scenery in every direction. In America, only the coasts of Maine and northern California compete in general magnificence. See section 5, "Härnösand," in chapter 11.

- **Viewing the Awe-Inspiring Northern Lights:** In the darkest of winter in the north of Sweden (called Lapland or Norrbotten), you can view the shimmering phenomenon of the northern lights on many clear nights, usually from early evening until around midnight. The sun and solar winds create this amazing light show when electrons from the sun collide with atmospheric atoms and molecules. See chapter 12.

- **Touring the Land of the Midnight Sun:** Above the Arctic Circle, where the summer sun never dips below the horizon, you have endless hours to enjoy the beauty of the region and the activities that go with it—from hiking to white-water rafting. After shopping for distinctive wooden and silver handicrafts, you can dine on filet of reindeer served with cloudberries. You can even pan for gold with real-life pioneers in Lannavaara, or climb rocks and glaciers in Sarek's National Park. See chapter 12.

2 The Best Active Vacations

- **Fishing:** Sweden offers some of the world's best fishing—its pristine lakes and streams are crystal clear, and many of them are extremely well stocked. Many varieties of fresh- and saltwater fish are available in Sweden's waters. See especially chapters 5, 9, 11, and 12.

- **Golfing:** Many Swedes are obsessed with golf. Most courses, from the periphery of Stockholm to Björkliden (above the Arctic Circle), are open to the public, and enthusiasts can play under the midnight sun. Halland, south of Gothenburg, is called the Swedish Riviera, and it's the golf capital of the country. Båstad is the most fashionable resort in Halland, and you can play a game of golf here at two prestigious courses: the **Båstad Golf Club** at Boarp (© 0431/783-70), and the **Bjåre Golf Club** at Solomonhög (© 0431/36-10-53), both located right outside the center of Båstad. See section 8, "Easy Excursions to the Bohuslän Coast & Halland," in chapter 5.

- **White-Water Rafting:** Sweden has some of Europe's best white-water rafting. Trips run the gamut from short and comfortable rides through peaceful landscapes, to heart-stopping races on fast-running rivers. In Dalarna, the best white-water rafting is on the Västerdalälven River rapids, which are rated moderately difficult. In northern Värmland, 5km (3 miles) south of Höljes, you can take easy white-water trips in paddle boats. See chapter 10.

- **Hiking:** The Kungsleden (Royal Trail) may provide the hike of a lifetime, as it takes you through the mountains of Lapland, including Kebnekaise, which, at 2,090m (6,855 ft.), is the highest mountain in Sweden. This 500km (310-mile) trail cuts through the mountains of Abisko National Park to Riksgränsen on the Norwegian frontier. See section 4, "Tärnaby & Hemavan," in chapter 12.

- **Skiing:** In Lapland, you can enjoy both downhill and cross-country skiing year-round. In Kiruna, serious skiers head for the Kebnekaise mountain station, where skiing can be combined with dog-sledding and other winter sports. South of the city of Gällivare, you arrive at Dundret, or "Thunder Mountain," for some of the finest skiing in the north. The hotel to stay at here also is called **Dundret** (© 0970/145-60), and its staff possesses all the expertise needed to link you up with both cross-country skiing and skiing on the downhill slopes. Inaugurated in 1955, its chairlift to the top of the slopes was the first of its kind in Sweden. For Dundret, see section 7, "Gällivare," in chapter 12.

3 The Best Ways to Spend Time on the Water

- **Exploring the "Garden of Skerries" Around Stockholm:** Few cities enjoy a marinescape as dramatic as Stockholm's. The city is surrounded by some 24,000 islands and islets (some no more than skerries or rocks jutting out of the water), and the water is dotted with colorful yachts. You can easily explore the archipelago in summer, using the car ferries and bridges that connect it. The highlight of the journey is taking a boat trip from the center of Stockholm to the town of Sandhamn, a ride that will introduce you to the scenic highlights of a place many Stock-holmers call home in summer. See section 7, "Side Trips from Stock-holm," in chapter 4.

- **Riding Along the Göta Canal:** This canal, known as Sweden's "blue ribbon," links Stockholm in the east with Gothenburg in the west, and is one of Scandinavia's major tourist attractions. As boats travel along the canal, some of the most beautiful panoramas in Swe-den unfold. The canal dates from 1810 and covers 565km (350 miles) of beautiful scenery. Artifi-cial canals, lakes, and rivers are linked by a series of 65 locks, some of them rising 90m (295 ft.) above sea level. Any travel agent can book you on this trip. See sec-tion 1, "The Göta Canal," in chapter 9.

- **Angling on the Göta Älv:** The southwestern sector of Lake Vän-ern, which is part of the Göta Canal (see above), has been called an angler's El Dorado, especially in the valley of the River Göta. The Göta Älv's well-stocked trout waters make for some of Scandi-navia's finest spinning and fly-fish-ing. More than 30 different species of fish live in Lake Vänern, especially perch, pike, and differ-ent types of carp. Some 35,000 young salmon and trout are released annually to keep the waters well stocked. See section 5, "Skara," in chapter 9.

- **Sailing the *Gustaf Wasa:*** The best way to go between the lake-side resorts of Mora and Leksand in Dalarna—the province most steeped in Swedish folklore—is by boat. This way you can see and experience this most traditional of Swedish provinces from a seascape, as the scenery along the shoreline unfolds before you. Lek-sand itself is the doorway to the province's most scenic lake, Siljan. No less an authority than Hans Christian Andersen pronounced this trip idyllic. After a panoramic trip, you arrive in Mora, a provin-cial town in Upper Dalarna, where passengers disembark to see the Santa complex (Santa's house and factory). See section 5, "Lek-sand," in chapter 10.

- **Viewing the Hudiksvall Archi-pelago:** The islands around the small town of Hudiksvall on the Bothnian Coast are the most beautiful in the north of Sweden. At one time, there were 50 fishing villages and harbors in this archi-pelago, but today what formerly were fishermen's homes serve as summer cottages for vacationers. Wander and explore this natural-ist's paradise at your leisure. It has such unique species of flora and fauna that it was made a nature reserve and is protected by the government. See section 3, "Hudiksvall," in chapter 11.

4 The Most Scenic Towns & Villages

- **Sigtuna:** Sweden's oldest town, founded at the beginning of the 11th century, stands on the shores of Lake Mälaren, northwest of Stockholm. High Street, with its low-timbered buildings, is believed to be the oldest street in Sweden. Traces of Sigtuna's Viking and early Christian heritage can be seen throughout the town. See

section 7, "Side Trips from Stock-holm," in chapter 4.

- **Uppsala:** Located northwest of Stockholm, Uppsala is Sweden's major university city and boasts a celebrated 15th-century cathedral. Nearby Gamla Uppsala (see below) also is intriguing, built on the site of Viking burial grounds where both humans and animals were sacrificed. See section 7, "Side Trips from Stockholm," in chapter 4.

- **Lund:** This town, situated 18km (11 miles) northeast of Malmö, rivals Uppsala as a university town. It, too, is ancient, having been founded by Canute the Great in 1020. The town is filled with centuries-old buildings, winding passages, and cobblestone streets; a major attraction is its ancient cathedral, one of the finest expressions of Romanesque architecture in northern Europe. See section 3, "Lund," in chapter 6.

- **Visby:** On the island of Gotland, this once was a great medieval European city and former Viking stronghold. For 8 days in August, this sleepy Hanseatic town awakens for the annual Medieval Week, which features fire-eaters, belly dancers, and tournaments. Visby's ruins of 13th- and 14th-century churches and memories of a more

prosperous period are intriguing in any season. See section 2, "Gotland & Visby," in chapter 8.

- **Rättvik:** This is a great resort bordering Lake Siljan in the heart of Dalarna, a province known for its regional painting, handicrafts, and folk dancing. Timbered houses reflect Dalarna's old-style architecture, and on summer nights, fiddle music evokes the long-ago past. See section 7, "Rättvik," in chapter 10.

- **Jokkmokk:** Located just north of the Arctic Circle, this is the best center for absorbing Lapp (or Sami) culture. The Lapps hold their famous "Great Winter Market" here in early February, a tradition that is centuries old. You can visit a museum devoted to Sami culture in the center of town and then go salmon fishing in the town's central lake. See section 5, "Jokkmokk," in chapter 12.

5 The Best Places to Go Back in Time

- **Gamla Uppsala** (Uppsala): Gamla Uppsala, 5km (3 miles) north of the city center, is one of the most revered historic spots in Sweden. Some 1,500 years ago, the Kingdom of the Svea (Swedes) was ruled from a spot outside the modern university city of Uppsala, north of Stockholm. Here Viking life dominated, and both animals and humans were sacrificed to pagan gods. It is suspected, although not authenticated, that three Swedish kings dating from the 6th century were entombed here. See section 7, "Side Trips from Stockholm," in chapter 4.

- **Skansen** (Djurgården, Stockholm): Called "Old Sweden in a Nutshell," this is the best open-air museum in all of Sweden in terms of numbers of dwellings and authenticity. Some 150 structures

were moved from places ranging from the château country in southwest Sweden to as far north as Lapland. From manor houses to windmills, they're all here, giving visitors an idea of how Sweden used to look. This is an especially valuable stop for visitors who see only Stockholm and don't have time to visit the rest of the country. Folk dancing and concerts enliven the atmosphere, and young Swedes demonstrate the creation of handicrafts from the 17th and 18th centuries. See p. 96.

- **Kivik Tomb** (Bredaror): In the château country of Sweden, the Kivik Tomb was discovered in 1748 north of the coastal town of Simrishamn. It immediately became the most important Bronze Age discovery in the country. One of the former members of the discovery team compared it to being "invited into the living room of a Bronze Age family." Not only were the usual bronze fragments uncovered, but also some grave carvings and, most notably, tomb furniture. A total of eight runic slabs depict scenes from everyday life, including horses and a sleigh, plus a bit of prehistoric humor in what appears to be a troupe of dancing seals. See p. 210.

- **Eketorp Ring-Fort** (Öland): This fortified village, built inside of a ring-shaped enclosure for defensive purposes, is the most important of more than a dozen prehistoric forts known to have existed on Öland in prerecorded times. It appears that the heavily protected village was inhabited by various settlers from A.D. 300 to 1300. Swedish archaeologists have filled the settlement with the Iron Age–style houses that once existed here, and they have reconstructed a massive wall along its edges. Although it is a reconstruction, it is believed to be an authentic replica of what the ring fort and village once looked like, giving an amazing insight into life in the Sweden of ages ago, when prehistoric people fought to survive in an inhospitable terrain. See p. 253.

- **A Visit to Gamlia** (Umeå): Along the Bothnian Coast, Umeå is called "the city of birch trees" because hundreds of these trees grow here. In this leafy setting lies a museum complex called Gamlia, less than a kilometer (½ mile) northeast of the city center, but centuries into the past. At the original museum, Friluftsmuseet, you can view 20 old-fashioned buildings, many of them dating from the 17th century. Guides dressed up in clothing like that worn 200 or 300 years ago will show you around while answering questions about how the people lived and worked. On the same site is the Västerbottens Museum, with a repository of artifacts— some prehistoric—discovered in the area. See section 6, "Umeå," in chapter 11.

6 The Best Museums

- **Millesgården** (Lidingö, outside Stockholm): Sweden's foremost sculptor, Carl Milles (1875–1955), lived here and created a sculpture garden by the sea that now has been turned into a museum. Milles relied heavily on mythological themes in his work, and many of his best-known pieces are displayed here. See p. 98.

- **Nationalmuseum (National Museum of Art)** (Stockholm): One of the oldest museums in the world (it celebrated its 200th birthday in 1992), the National Museum houses Sweden's treasure trove of rare paintings and sculpture. From Rembrandt to Rubens, and from Bellini to van Gogh, a panoply of European art unfolds before your eyes. In addition to paintings, you'll find antique porcelain, furniture, and clocks. See p. 96.

- **Vasamuseet (Royal Warship *Vasa*)** (Stockholm): In the Djurgården, this 17th-century man-of-war, which is now a museum, is a popular tourist attraction. The *Vasa* is the world's oldest known complete ship. It capsized and sank on its maiden voyage in 1628 before horrified onlookers. The ship was salvaged in 1961 and has been carefully restored; 97% of its 700 original sculptured decorative motifs were retrieved. See p. 97.

- **Göteborgs Konstmuseum** (Gothenburg): This is the city's leading art museum, a repository of modern paintings that's strong on French Impressionists, including van Gogh and Bonnard. Modern artists such as Picasso and Edvard Munch also are represented, as are sculptures by Milles. See p. 151.

- **Åjtte** (Jokkmokk): In true Lapp country, this is the best repository of artifacts of the Sami culture. Integrating nature with culture, the museum is the largest of its kind in the world. It depicts how the Lapps lived and struggled for survival in a harsh terrain, and features the houses they lived in as well as the animals and weapons needed for their livelihood. See p. 354.

7 The Best Castles & Palaces

- **Drottningholm Palace and Theater** (Drottningholm): Lying 11km (6¾ miles) from Stockholm on an island in Lake Mälaren, Drottningholm, or "Queen's Island," has been dubbed the Versailles of Sweden. It is a magnificent royal residence, a gem of baroque architecture with a palace, gardens, a Chinese pavilion, and one of the most remarkable court theaters in Europe. Since 1981, Sweden's royal family has occupied the south wing. See p. 98.

- **Kungliga Slottet** (Stockholm): One of the few official residences of the royal family that is open to the public, this palace in Gamla Stan (Stockholm's Old Town) dates back 700 years. Encompassing 608 rooms, today it is used by the Swedish king and his family mainly for ceremonial occasions. The 18th-century Royal Apartments, with their painted ceilings, glittering chandeliers, and heirloom tapestries, are the highlight of any visit. See p. 116.

- **Castle of Bosjökloster** (Lund): The origins of this former Benedictine convent date from 1080. Closed in the 1500s, at the time of the Reformation, it fell into disrepair but has since been restored to some of its former glory. Situated on the shores of Lake Ringsjö, today the castle is surrounded by a recreation area with beautiful gardens. The great courtyard here is one of high drama, with thousands of flowers and exotic shrubs. You can bring along a picnic lunch to enjoy on the grounds. See p. 206.

- **Kalmar Slott** (Kalmar): Once called "the key to Sweden," this historic castle was the setting for the Kalmar Union that temporarily united the thrones of Denmark, Norway, and Sweden in 1397. The original keep dates from the 12th century, but in the 16th century, King Gustav Vasa rebuilt the castle, and his sons eventually transformed it into a Renaissance palace. The castle is the major site in this port city in southern Sweden, which also makes a good base for exploring the "Kingdom of Crystal," the bargain-filled concentration of glassworks. See p. 225.

- **Läckö Slott** (Lidköping): Lying in the vicinity of the pleasant little town of Lidköping, this castle on the waters of Lake Vänern often has been likened to a fairy-tale setting. Between 1298 and 1681, 250 rooms were built, many quite large; only the royal palace in Stockholm is larger than Läckö.

As you approach from a distance, its distinctive white walls, towers, and turrets seem to rise out of the water. The palace furnishings eventually were carted off and the rooms left bare, but over the years many of the original furnishings have been reclaimed and returned. A visit here and a walk through the once royal grounds is a highlight of any trip to the waters of Lake Vänern. See p. 281.

8 The Best Cathedrals & Abbeys

- **Riddarholm Church** (Stockholm): Evoking pre-Reformation Sweden, this is one of the best-preserved Franciscan churches left in northern Europe. After being consecrated at the dawn of the 14th century, it served for centuries as the mausoleum for Swedish royalty. The church's cast-iron steeple, which dates from 1841, remains one of the most distinctive landmarks of the Stockholm skyline. The interior is especially impressive; coats of arms of knights of the Order of Seraphim, founded in 1336, cover the walls. The floor is paved with gravestones. After you visit the church, you can walk through Stockholm's Gamla Stan, or Old Town. See p. 97.
- **Uppsala Domkyrka** (Uppsala): This twin-spired Gothic structure, nearly 120m (394 ft.) tall, was constructed in the 13th century. Today the silhouette of this largest cathedral in Scandinavia dominates the landscape, affording Uppsala the status of ecclesiastical capital of Sweden. Its layout is simple compared with other major European cathedrals, yet its high Gothic aura is nevertheless impressive. In one of the chapels on the south aisle, you can visit the tomb of the philosopher Emanuel Swedenborg (1688–1772). See p. 126.
- **Domkyrkan (Cathedral of Lund)** (Lund): The apex of Romanesque architecture in Sweden, this imposing twin-towered gray sandstone cathedral is one of the most ancient in Sweden. It was consecrated in 1145, although actually launched sometime in the 1080s by King Canute II. Some of the sculptural details of its architecture evoke Lombardy or other parts of Italy. This is especially evident in its apse, which dates from the 1130s. See p. 225.
- **Vadstena Abbey** (Vadstena): Sweden's greatest abbey is dedicated to its patron saint, St. Birgitta, who has brought lasting fame to this charming little town on the shores of Lake Vättern. In the Middle Ages, the abbey was at the center of a pilgrimage, which earned it the appellation of "Rome of the North." One of the most important stopovers for those taking the Göta Canal trip, Vadstena is dominated by its Klosterkyrkan, or Abbey Church, built between the mid–14th and 15th centuries to the specifications of its founder, St. Birgitta herself. This Gothic church is rich in art and relics from the Middle Ages. See p. 244.
- **Kiruna Kyrka** (Kiruna): This church in the far north of Sweden in the midst of Lapland would hardly make it in the grand cathedral circuit of northern Europe. It is, however, one of the most unusual churches in the world and raises a lot of eyebrows at first sight. It was constructed in 1912 like a stylized Sami tent, with an origami design of rafters and wood beams. In Lapland, it is hailed as "the Shrine of the Nomadic people." A free-standing

bell tower in front is supported by props and the tombstone of the founder of Kiruna. The altarpiece scene representing Paradise as a

Tuscan, not Lappish, landscape is the only incongruous note. See section 8, "Kiruna," in chapter 12.

9 The Best Hotels

- **Grand Hotel** (Stockholm; ✆ **800/ 223-5652** in the U.S., or 08/679-35-00): Opposite the Royal Palace, this is the most prestigious hotel in Sweden; many well-known people have stayed here, from actress Sarah Bernhardt to Nobel Prize winners. Set on the waterfront, it dates from 1874 but is continuously renovated to keep it in state-of-the-art condition. The rooms have been luxuriously redecorated, and the bathrooms are made of Italian marble with under-floor heating. See p. 66.
- **Nordic Hotel** (Stockholm; ✆ **800/ 337-4685**): Unique for the Swedish capital, this two-in-one hotel is as modern and dramatic as the 21st century itself. Turning to the cold Arctic waters of the north and the northern lights for its architectural inspiration, the hotel creates an "only-in-Sweden" aura that definitely makes you feel like you're in the far north of Europe. See p. 67.
- **Victory Hotel** (Stockholm; ✆ **08/ 506-400-00**): In the Old Town, this small but stylish hotel ranks among the top in Sweden. Famous for the treasure once buried here (part of which can be seen at the Stockholm City Museum), the hotel was originally built in 1642. The well-furnished bedrooms with modern beds typically have exposed beams and pine floors. On a small rooftop terrace, tables are arranged around a fountain. See p. 73.
- **Radisson SAS Park Avenue Hotel** (Gothenburg; ✆ **800/333-3333** in the U.S., or 031/758-40-00): Since its opening in 1950,

Gothenburg's premier hotel has hosted everybody from the Beatles to David Rockefeller. Located on Gothenburg's attractive main boulevard, near the cultural center, it's a cosmopolitan hotel with a fresh and contemporary ambience. The best double rooms are quite spacious and decorated in a semi-modern, sleek style; about a quarter of the guest rooms are equipped with balconies. See p. 142.
- **Elite Plaza** (Gothenburg; ✆ **031/ 720-40-00**): This is not only the newest, but one of the very best hotels to open in Gothenburg in recent years. A 19th-century insurance company was gutted and recycled into a superior first-class hotel with many of its original architectural features intact. The building not only got a new lease on life, but visitors to Gothenburg today have a place to stay that's as good as some of the most superior hotels in Stockholm. See p. 140.
- **Elite Marina Plaza** (Helsingborg; ✆ **042/19-21-00**): This is the most innovative hotel in this port city, which faces the eastern coast of Denmark across from "Hamlet's Castle." A nautical decor prevails, and large glass windows are typical of the sleek, contemporary architecture of Sweden. With its rock gardens, abundant flowers, and fountains, it is a lovely place to spend the night in grand comfort and style. See p. 184.
- **Scandic Stadshotellet** (Kalmar; ✆ **0480/496-900**): With very reasonably priced rooms, at times less than 900SEK ($100) a night in a double, this is an exceptional

choice for lodgings in this historic port city in southeastern Sweden. A landmark hotel constructed in 1906 but completely modernized in 1999, it still retains its look of romanticized architecture, with gables and a bell tower. Many Art Nouveau embellishments remain, including cut-glass chandeliers and an Edwardian-style library. Its bedrooms are the largest and most comfortable in town. See p. 226.

- **Halltorps Gästgiveri** (Borgholm; ✆ **0485/850-00**): On the Baltic Island of Öland, you can stay at an inn that dates from 1850. It has been a restaurant longer than it has been a hotel, but is an ideal place to stay on this historic island. Bedrooms are light and airy and frequently renovated, ensuring a good night's sleep in comfort and style. Its restaurant, Bakfickan, or "hip pocket" in English, is one of Öland's best. See p. 258.

- **Park Inn Ronnums Herrgård** (Vargön; ✆ **0521/223270**): One of the most idyllic stopovers along the Göta Canal is in Vargön, which a poet once labeled "Little Paris." In this setting of charm and grace, you can enjoy life in a restored 18th-century manor house with yellow clapboards and a red roof, standing in its own parklike grounds. Surrounded by 19th-century antiques, you can enjoy life as it was lived in old Sweden, all at a very reasonable price. See p. 279.

- **Elite Stadshotellet Karlstad** (Karlstad; ✆ **054/293-000**): In the heart of the folkloric province of Värmland, this hotel, behind its neo-baroque facade, is one of the most impressive of the 19th-century hotels remaining in Sweden. If you like old-fashioned style but modern comfort, this is for you. From its British-inspired pub to its gourmet restaurant, it's a winner. See p. 295.

- **The Ice Hotel** (Jukkasjärvi; ✆ **0980/668-00**): Surely there is no hotel in all of Europe as curious as this one deep in the heart of Swedish Lapland. Every winter the hotel is carved out of the ice at a point 200km (124 miles) north of the Arctic Circle. Come spring, this igloo-shaped hotel literally melts away. In its glacial setting, guests can check in for an icy night—hopefully with a good bed partner. If you've ever dreamed of living like an Eskimo, here is your chance. See p. 364.

10 The Best Restaurants

- **Ben Lloc** (Stockholm; ✆ **08/660-6060**): The culinary rage of Stockholm is the domain of the capital's finest chef, Mathias Dahlgren, who turns out Mediterranean cuisine. In the kitchen, the chef marches to his own drummer, creating original, imaginative dishes that are influenced by other recipes but given a distinctly original touch at this temple of gastronomy. See p. 78.

- **Paul & Norbert** (Stockholm; ✆ **08/663-81-83**): With only eight tables on the fashionable Strandvägen, this exclusive restaurant is set in a patrician residence dating from 1873. The most innovative restaurant in Stockholm, it's the creation of German owner Norbert Lang. In winter, the Swedish game served here is without equal in the entire country—just try the pigeon with Calvados sauce. And you can always count on something tempting and unusual; sautéed sweetbreads in nettle sauce, anyone? See p. 78.

- **Gripsholms Värdshus Restaurant** (Mariefred; ℂ **0159/34750**): If you're seeking traditional Swedish food with French overtones, this is the best dining choice on the periphery of the capital. Local game dishes, including wild grouse, are featured in autumn, and marinated salmon with a mild mustard sauce is a year-round favorite. Tastings also can be arranged in the wine cellar. See p. 129.

- **Sjömagasinet** (Gothenburg; ℂ **031/775-59-20**): By far the most intriguing and interesting restaurant in town, this is one of the finest places to go for seafood on the west coast of Sweden. Lying in the western suburb of Klippan, this converted 1775 warehouse serves an array of fresh fish whose flavor never diminishes, regardless of the sauce or preparation. The fish and shellfish pot-au-feu with a chive-flavored crème fraîche is worth the trek. See p. 147.

- **Hipp** (Malmö; ℂ **040/97-40-30**): Even the Danes are flocking across the new Øresund Bridge to dine at Malmö's "hip" Hipp Restaurant. Its blend of Swedish and French cuisines is so successful that so far it's attracted everybody from Scandinavian prime ministers to Hollywood actors. In a Belle Epoque setting, menu items are the freshest in town, each platter a creation from the kitchen. See p. 196.

- **Anna Kock** (Helsingborg; ℂ **042/18-13-00**): "Anna the Cook" was known all over this port city across from the eastern coast from Denmark. She's gone now, but her relatives carry on, offering inexpensive Swedish food with style and flair. In this cozy enclave, feast on such dishes as filet of reindeer with lingonberry sauce or breast of wild duck with rhubarb chutney. See p. 185.

- **Kalmar Hamn Krog** (Kalmar; ℂ **0480/411-020**): Since its 1988 establishment, this international restaurant has quickly moved to the front of the line. Hailed as the best in this historic port city, it prepares reasonably priced food with flair, using only market-fresh ingredients deftly handled by a trained kitchen staff. The chefs borrow freely from the world's larders, using spices or ingredients from any country where their culinary imaginations wander. See p. 228.

- **Halltorps Gästgiveri** (Borgholm; ℂ **0485/850-00**): On the historic Baltic island of Öland, this dining room serving Swedish food takes you back to the good old days. Here you can feast on the dishes beloved by your great-grandparents—provided they came from Sweden. Herbs and vegetables come from suppliers who grow them right on the island, and the local fishers bring in their catch of the day. The place is charming, a bit stylish, and it occupies one of the oldest manor houses on the island. See p. 258.

- **Stek Huset** (Karlstad; ℂ **054/56-00-80**): Deep in the heart of the province of Värmland, made famous by the great international writer Selma Lagerlöf, you can dine on refined Swedish and international cuisine, some of the best in the area. Patrons arrive from miles around to enjoy the fare, all for a reasonable price. Fresh fish and steaks often are flambéed at the table with high drama. See p. 297.

- **Restaurant Kriti** (Skellefteå; ℂ **0910/77-95-35**): Along the Bothnian coast of eastern Sweden, across from Finland, this restaurant in a port city of the far north is acclaimed for—of all things—its Greek food. A taste of the

Mediterranean cheers devoted local diners during the long, dark, Swedish winter nights of snow and ice. Dig into their stuffed grape leaves, souvlaki, or moussaka, and you may think you're looking at the Acropolis instead of a wintry landscape. Their pizzas also are known as the best along the coast. See p. 341.

2

Planning Your Trip to Sweden

In the pages that follow, we've compiled everything you need to know about how to handle the practical details of planning your trip in advance—airlines, a calendar of events, details on currency, and more.

1 The Regions in Brief

GÖTALAND The southern part of Sweden takes its name from the ancient Goths. Some historians believe they settled in this region, which is similar in climate and architecture to parts of northern Europe, especially Germany. This is the most populated part of Sweden and includes eight provinces—Östergötland, Småland (the "Kingdom of Crystal"), Västergoütland, Skåne, Dalsland, Bohuslån, Halland, and Blekinge—plus the islands of Oüland and Gotland. The Goüta Canal cuts through this district. **Gothenburg** is the most important port in the west, and **Stockholm,** the capital, is the chief port in the east. Aside from Stockholm, **Skåne,** the château district, is the most heavily visited area. Its dunes, moors, and pasturelands are often compared to the Danish countryside. Many seaside resorts line the west and east coasts.

SVEALAND The central region encompasses the folkloric province of Dalarna (**Dalecarlia** in English) and **Värmland** (immortalized in the novels of Selma Lagerloüf). These districts are the ones most frequented by visitors. Other provinces include Våstmanland, Uppland, Soüdermanland, and Nårke. Ancient Svealand often is called the cultural heart of Sweden. Some 20,000 islands lie along its eastern coast.

NORRLAND Northern Sweden makes up Norrland, which lies above the 61st parallel and includes about 50% of the landmass. It's inhabited by only about 15% of the population, including Lapps and Finns. Norrland consists of 24 provinces, of which **Lapland** is the most popular with tourists. It's a land of thick forests, fast-flowing (and cold) rivers, and towering mountain peaks. Lapland, the home of the Lapp reindeer herds, consists of tundra. **Kiruna** is one of Norrland's most important cities because of its iron-ore deposits.

2 Visitor Information

In the **United States,** contact the **Scandinavian Tourist Board,** 655 Third Ave., 18th floor, New York, NY 10017 (© **212/885-9700;** www.go scandinavia.com), at least 3 months in advance for maps, sightseeing information, ferry schedules, and other advice and tips.

In the **United Kingdom,** contact the **Swedish Travel & Tourism Council,** 11 Montague Pl., London W1H 2AL (© **020/7870-5600**).

You also can try the website **www. visit-sweden.com.**

If you get in touch with a travel agent, make sure the agent is a member

Destination: Sweden—Red Alert Checklist

- Citizens of E.U. countries can cross into Sweden for as long as they wish. Citizens of other countries must have a passport.
- If you purchased traveler's checks, have you recorded the check numbers and stored the documentation separately from the checks?
- Did you pack your camera and an extra set of camera batteries, and pur-chase enough film? If you packed film in your checked baggage, did you invest in protective pouches to shield film from airport X-rays?
- Do you have a safe, accessible place to store money?
- Did you bring your ID cards that could entitle you to discounts such as AAA and AARP cards, student IDs, and so on?
- Did you bring emergency drug prescriptions and extra glasses and/or contact lenses?
- Do you have your credit card PINs?
- If you have an e-ticket, do you have documentation?
- Did you leave a copy of your itinerary with someone at home?
- Do you have the address and phone number of your country's embassy with you?

of the **American Society of Travel Agents (ASTA).** If a problem arises, you can complain to the society's Consumer Affairs Department at 1101 King St., Suite 200, Alexandria, VA 22314 (© **703/739-2782;** www.asta net.com).

3 Entry Requirements & Customs

ENTRY REQUIREMENTS

U.S., Canadian, U.K., Irish, Australian, and New Zealand citizens with a **valid passport** don't need a visa to enter Sweden if they don't expect to stay more than 90 days and don't expect to work there. If after entering Sweden you want to stay more than 90 days, you can apply for a permit for an extra 90 days, which as a rule is granted immediately. Go to the nearest *questura* (police headquarters) or to your home country's consulate. If your passport is lost or stolen, head to your consulate as soon as possible for a replacement.

CUSTOMS

WHAT YOU CAN BRING INTO SWEDEN Foreign visitors can bring along most items for personal use duty-free, including fishing tackle, a pair of skis, two tennis racquets, a baby carriage, two hand-held cameras with 10 rolls of film, and 400 cigarettes or a quantity of cigars or pipe tobacco not exceeding 500 grams (1 lb.). Strict limits exist on importing alcoholic beverages. However, for alcohol bought tax-paid, limits are much more liberal than in other countries of the European Union.

WHAT YOU CAN TAKE HOME Rules governing what you can bring back duty-free vary from country to country and are subject to change, but they're generally posted on the Web.

Returning **U.S. citizens** who have been away for at least 48 hours are allowed to bring back, once every 30 days, $800 worth of merchandise duty-free. You'll be charged a flat rate of 10% duty on the next $1,000

Sweden

0   100 mi
0   100 km

FINLAND

Narvik

Abisko
Kiruna

Saltoluokta

ATLANTIC OCEAN

Gällivare

Kvikkjokk   Jokkmokk

ARCTIC CIRCLE

Lule River

Boden   E4

LAPLAND

Pite River

Luleå

Arvidsjaur

Piteå

Skellefteå

NORRLAND   Umeå

Trondheim

E14

Indals River

Östersund

E4

Härnösand

FINLAND

Sundsvall

Gulf of Bothnia

NORWAY   SWEDEN

Mora   Rättvik   Söderhamn

DALARNA   Gävle

Falun   E4

Oslo   Filipstad

E18   SVEALAND   Uppsala

VÄRMLAND   Sigtuna

Karlstad   Stockholm

E20

Vänern

ESTONIA

E18   Skara

Vättern

Lidköping   Vadstena

E22

North Sea

GÖTALAND   Visby

GOTLAND

Gothenburg   E4

Växjö

DENMARK   Kalmar

ÖLAND   LATVIA

Helsingborg

SKÅNE   *Baltic Sea*

Copenhagen   Malmö

Ystad

worth of purchases. Be sure to have your receipts handy. On mailed gifts, the duty-free limit is $200 or less. You cannot bring fresh foodstuffs into the United States; tinned foods, however, are allowed. For more specific guidance, contact the **Customs & Border Protection (CBP),** 1300 Pennsylvania Ave., Washington, DC 20229 (© 877/287-8667; www.cbp.gov), and request the free pamphlet *Know Before You Go.* For a clear summary of Canadian rules, request the book *I Declare* from the **Canada Revenue Agency,** 1730 St. Laurent Blvd., Ottawa, KIG 4KE (© 800/461-9999 in Canada, or 204/983-3500; www.ccra-adrc.gc.ca). If you're a citizen of the United Kingdom, contact **HM's**

Customs and Excise Office, National Advise Service, Dorset House, Stamford Street, London SE1 9PY (© 0845/010-9000; www.hmce.gov.uk). Australian citizens should contact the **Australian Customs Service,** GPO Box 8, Sydney NSW 2001 (© 1300/363-263 in Australia, or 02/6275-6666; www.customs.gov.au). New Zealanders should contact **New Zealand Customs,** 50 Anzac Ave., P.O. Box 29, Aukland, NZ (© 09/359-66-55; www.customs.govt.nz). And citizens of Ireland should contact the **Revenue Commissioner,** Dublin Castle (© 01/679-27-77; fax 01/679-3261; www.revenue.ie), or write the Collector of Customs and Excise, The Custom House, Dublin 1.

4 Money

THE SWEDISH KRONA Sweden's basic unit of currency is the **krona (or SEK).** Note that the Swedes spell the plural kronor with an *o* instead of an *e* as in the kroner of Denmark and Norway. One krona is divided into 100 **oüre.** Banknotes are issued in denominations of 20, 50, 100, 500, 1,000, and 10,000 SEK. Silver coins are issued in denominations of 50 oüre and 1SEK and 5SEK.

TRAVELER'S CHECKS Although regarded as old-fashioned by today's ATM users, traditionalists still like to carry traveler's checks as a safe means of carrying cash abroad. Most banks will give you a better exchange rate for traveler's checks than for cash. Checks denominated in U.S. dollars or British pounds are accepted virtually anywhere; sometimes you also can get these checks in a local currency.

Each of the agencies in the following list will refund checks if lost or stolen, provided that you produce documentation. When purchasing checks, ask about refund hot lines. American Express has the largest number of offices around the world.

Issuers sometimes have agreements with groups to sell traveler's checks commission-free. For example, the American Automobile Association (AAA) clubs sell American Express checks in several currencies without commission.

American Express (© 800/221-7282; www.americanexpress.com in the U.S. and Canada) is one of the largest and most immediately recognized issuers of traveler's checks. No commission is charged to members of the American Automobile Association and holders of certain types of American Express cards. For questions or problems arising outside the United States or Canada, contact any of the company's many regional representatives. We'll list locations throughout this guide.

Citicorp (© 800/645-6556, toll-free in U.S., collect from anywhere else in the world; www.citibank.com) issues checks in several different currencies.

Thomas Cook (© 800/223-7373, toll-free in U.S., collect from anywhere else in the world; www.thomascook.com) issues MasterCard traveler's

The Swedish Krona

For American Readers   At the time of this writing, $1 US = approximately 7.7 krono (or 1 krona = .13 US cents). This was the rate of exchange used to calculate the dollar values given in this edition. Bear in mind that throughout the context of this book, dollar amounts less than $10 are rounded to the nearest nickel, and dollar amounts greater than $10 are rounded to the nearest dollar.

For British Readers   At this writing, £1 = approximately 13.7 kronor (or 1 krona = approximately 7 pence). This was the rate of exchange used to calculate the pound values in the table below.

Regarding the Euro   At the time of this writing, 1€ = 9.18SEK, or, stated differently, 1SEK = 11 eurocents. But these relationships can and probably will change during the lifetime of this edition. For more exact ratios between these and other currencies, check an up-to-date source at the time of your arrival in Sweden.

SEK	US$	UK £	Euro €	SEK	US$	UK £	Euro €
1.00	0.13	0.07	0.11	75.00	9.75	5.25	8.25
2.00	0.26	0.14	0.22	100.00	13.00	7.00	11.00
3.00	0.39	0.21	0.33	125.00	16.25	8.75	13.75
4.00	0.52	0.28	0.44	150.00	19.50	10.50	16.50
5.00	0.65	0.35	0.55	175.00	22.75	12.25	19.25
6.00	0.78	0.42	0.66	200.00	26.00	14.00	22.00
7.00	0.91	0.49	0.77	225.00	29.25	15.75	24.75
8.00	1.04	0.56	0.88	250.00	32.50	17.50	27.50
9.00	1.17	0.63	0.99	275.00	35.75	19.25	30.25
10.00	1.30	0.70	1.10	300.00	39.00	21.00	33.00
15.00	1.95	1.05	1.65	350.00	45.50	24.50	38.50
20.00	2.60	1.40	2.20	400.00	52.00	28.00	44.00
25.00	3.25	1.75	2.75	500.00	65.00	35.00	55.00
50.00	6.50	3.50	5.50	1000.00	130.00	70.00	110.00

checks denominated in several currencies; not all currencies are available at every outlet—call ℂ **800/223-9920.**

Visa Travelers Checks (ℂ **800/732-1322;** toll-free in U.S., collect from most other parts of the world; www.visa.com) sells Visa checks denominated in several major currencies.

CREDIT & CHARGE CARDS American Express, Diners Club, and Visa are widely recognized throughout Sweden. Discover cards are not accepted. If you see a Eurocard or Access sign, it means that the establishment accepts MasterCard. With an American Express, MasterCard, or Visa card, you also can withdraw currency from cash machines (ATMs) at various locations. Always check with your credit or charge card company about this before leaving home.

ATM NETWORKS Plus, Cirrus, and other networks connect with automated teller machines throughout Scandinavia. If your credit card has been programmed with a PIN (personal identification number), you can probably use your card at Scandinavian ATMs to withdraw money as a cash advance on your card. Always

What Things Cost in Stockholm	US$
Taxi from the airport to the city center	45.00
Basic bus or subway fare	1.95
Local telephone call	0.30
Double room at the Grand Hotel (very expensive)	403.00
Double room at the Kung Carl Hotel (moderate)	244.00
Double room at the Långholmer (inexpensive)	150.00
Lunch for one at Eriks Bakfica (moderate)	30.00
Lunch for one at Cattelin Restaurant (inexpensive)	8.95
Dinner for one, without wine, at Operakällaren (very expensive)	104.00
Dinner for one, without wine, at Prinsens (moderate)	36.00
Dinner for one, without wine, at Magnus Ladulås (inexpensive)	22.00
Pint of beer (draft pilsner) in a bar	4.30
Coca-Cola in a cafe	3.50
Cup of coffee in a cafe	3.10
Admission to Drottningholm Palace	7.80
Movie ticket	11.00
Budget theater ticket	13.00

determine the frequency limits for withdrawals and check to see if your PIN code must be reprogrammed for usage on your trip abroad. Also, be aware that you will most likely be able to access only your checking account from ATM machines overseas. For **Cirrus** locations abroad, call © **800/424-7787** or visit **www.mastercard.com**. For **Plus** usage abroad, check the Plus site on the Web at **www.visa.com** or call © **800/843-7587.**

5 When to Go

THE CLIMATE Sweden's climate is hard to classify because temperatures, influenced by the Gulf Stream, vary considerably from the fields of Skåne to the wilderness of Lapland (the upper tenth of Sweden lies north of the Arctic Circle).

The country as a whole has many sunny days in summer, but it's not superhot. July is the warmest month, with temperatures in both Stockholm and Gothenburg averaging around 64°F (18°C). February is the coldest month, when the temperature in Stockholm averages around 26°F (–3°C). Gothenburg is a few degrees warmer.

It's not always true that the farther north you go the cooler it becomes. During summer, the northern parts of the country—from Halsingland to northern Lapland—may suddenly have the warmest weather and the bluest skies. Check the weather forecasts on television and in the newspapers. (Swedes claim these forecasts are 99% reliable.)

SUMMER Regarding weather, the ideal time to visit Sweden is from June to August. At this time, all its cafes and most attractions, including open-air museums, are open and thousands

Fun Fact **The Midnight Sun**

In summer, the sun never fully sets in northern Sweden; even in the south, daylight can last until 11pm and then the sun rises around 3am.

In Sweden, the best vantage points and dates when you can see the thrilling spectacle of the midnight sun are as follows: **Bjoürkliden,** from May 26 to July 19; **Abisko,** from June 12 to July 4; **Kiruna,** from May 31 to July 14; and **Gällivare,** from June 2 to July 12. All these places can be reached by public transportation.

Remember that although the sun may be shining brightly at midnight, it's not as strong as at midday. Bring along a warm jacket or sweater.

flock to the north of Sweden to enjoy the midnight sun. Inclement weather can close attractions at other times of the year. However, summer also is the most expensive time to fly to Sweden, as this is peak season. To compensate, hotels sometimes grant summer discounts (it pays to ask).

SPRING & FALL The months of spring and autumn, notably May through June and the month of September, are almost prettier than a Swedish summer. When spring comes to the Swedish countryside and wild flowers burst into bloom after a long dark winter, it is a joyous time in the country.

WINTER Scandinavia's off season is winter (about Nov 1–Mar 21). Many visitors, except those on business, prefer to avoid Sweden in winter. The cold weather sets in by October, and you'll need to keep bundled up heavily until long past April. However, other, more adventurous tourists go to Sweden in spite or even because of the winter. Students have returned to such university cities as Stockholm and Lund, and life seems more vibrant then. Cultural activities also abound. Except for special festivals and folkloric presentations, the major cultural venues in Sweden, including opera, dance, ballet, and theater, shut down in summer. Skiers also go to Sweden in winter, but we don't recommend it. It is pitch dark in winter in the north of Sweden, and the slopes have to be artificially lit. You'd be better off soaking up the alpine sun in Germany, Switzerland, or Austria.

Of course, one of the most eerie and fascinating experiences available in Europe is to see the shimmering northern lights, which can be viewed only in winter.

Sweden's Average Daytime Temperatures (°F/°C)

	Jan	Feb	Mar	Apr	May	June	July	Aug	Sept	Oct	Nov	Dec
Stockholm	27/–3	26/–3	31/–1	40/4	50/10	59/15	64/18	62/17	54/12	45/7	37/3	32/0
Karesuando	6/–14	5/–15	12/–11	23/–5	39/4	54/12	59/15	51/11	44/7	31/–1	9/–13	5/–15
Karlstad	33/1	30/–1	28/–2	37/3	53/12	63/17	62/17	59/15	54/12	41/5	29/–2	26/–3
Lund	38/3	36/2	34/1	43/6	57/14	63/17	64/18	61/16	57/14	47/8	37/3	37/3

HOLIDAYS Sweden celebrates the following public holidays: New Year's Day (Jan 1); Epiphany (Jan 6); Good Friday, Easter Sunday, Easter Monday; Labor Day (May 1); Ascension Day (mid-May); Whitsunday and Whitmonday (late May); Midsummer Day (June 21); All Saints' Day (Nov 1); and Christmas Eve, Christmas Day, and Boxing Day (Dec 24, 25, and 26). Inquire at a tourist bureau for the actual dates of the holidays that vary from year to year.

SWEDEN CALENDAR OF EVENTS

The dates given here may in some cases be only approximations. Be sure to check with the tourist office before you make plans to attend a specific event. For information on Walpurgis night and midsummer celebrations, call the local tourist offices in the town where you plan to stay. (See individual chapters for the phone numbers.)

April

Walpurgis Night, nationwide. Celebrations with bonfires, songs, and speeches welcoming the advent of spring. These are especially lively celebrations among university students at Uppsala, Lund, Stockholm, Gothenburg, and Umeå. April 30.

May

Drottningholm Court Theater. Some 30 opera and ballet performances, from baroque to early romantic, are presented in the unique 1766 Drottningholm Court Theater, Drottningholm, with original decorative paintings and stage mechanisms. Call ✆ **08/660-82-25** for tickets. Take the T-bana to Brommaplan, then bus no. 301 or 323. A steamboat runs in the summer; call ✆ **08/411-7023** for information. Late May to late September.

June

Midsummer, nationwide. Swedes celebrate Midsummer Eve all over the country. Maypole dances to the sound of the fiddle and accordion are the typical festive events of the day. Dalarna observes the most traditional celebrations. Mid-June.

July

Falun Folk Music Festival. International folk musicians gather to participate in and attend concerts, seminars, lectures, exhibitions, and films on folk music. Events are conducted at various venues; contact the **Falun Folk Music Festival,** S-791 13 Falun (✆ **023/233-79;** www.falufolk.com), for more information. Mid-July.

Around Gotland Race, Sandhamn. The biggest and most exciting open-water Scandinavian sailing race starts and finishes at Sandhamn in the Stockholm archipelago. About 450 boats, mainly from Nordic countries, take part. Call the Stockholm tourist office for information. Two days in mid-July.

Rättviksdansen (International Festival of Folk Dance and Music), Rättvik. Every other year for some 20 years, around 1,000 folk dancers and musicians from all over the world have gathered to participate in this folkloric tradition. Last week in July.

August

Medieval Week, Gotland. Numerous events are held throughout the island of Gotland—tours, concerts, medieval plays, festivities, and shows. For more information, contact the Office of Medieval Week, Hästgatan 4, S-621 56 Visby (✆ **0498/29-10-70;** www.medeltid sveckan.com). Early August.

Stockholm Waterfestival. A tradition since 1989, this weeklong festival around the city's shores offers entertainment such as fireworks, boat races, and concerts, as well as information about the care and preservation of water. An award of $150,000 is given to an individual or organization that has made an outstanding contribution to water preservation. Call the Stockholm tourist office for information. Begins second week in August.

Minnesota Day, Utvandra Hus, Växjöü (Småland). Swedish-American relations are celebrated at the House of Emigrants with speeches, music, singing, and dancing; the climax is the election of the

Swedish-American of the year. Call ℂ **0470/201-20** for information. Second Sunday in August.

December

Nobel Day, Stockholm. The king, members of the royal family, and invited guests attend the Nobel Prize ceremony for literature, physics, chemistry, medicine, physiology, and economics. Attendance is by invitation only. The ceremony is held at the concert hall and followed by a banquet at City Hall. December 10.

Lucia, the Festival of Lights, nationwide. To celebrate the shortest day and longest night of the year, young girls called "Lucias" appear in restaurants, offices, schools, and factories, wearing floor-length white gowns and special headdresses, each holding a lighted candle. They are accompanied by "star boys"—young men in white with wizard hats covered with gold stars, each holding a wand with a large golden star at the top. One of the "Lucias" is eventually crowned queen. In olden days, Lucia was known as "Little Christmas." December 13.

This celebration is observed nationwide. Actual planned events change from year to year and vary from community to community. The best place for tourists to observe this event is at the open-air museum at Skansen in Stockholm.

6 The Active Vacation Planner

BIKING Much of Sweden is flat, which makes it ideal for cycling tours. Bicycles can be rented all over the country, and country hotels sometimes make them available free of charge. A typical rental is 200SEK ($26) per day. For more detailed information, contact the **Svenska Turistfoürening (Swedish Touring Club),** P.O. Box 25, Amiralitetshuset 1, Flagmansvägen 8, S101 20 Stockholm (ℂ **08-463-21-00**; www.stfturist.se).

FISHING In Stockholm, within view of the king's palace, you can cast a line for what are some of the finest salmon in the world. Ever since Queen Christina issued a decree in 1636, Swedes have had the right to fish in waters adjoining the palace. Throughout the country, fishing is an everyday affair; it has been estimated that one of every three Swedes is an angler.

If you'd like to fish elsewhere in Sweden, you'll need a license; the cost varies from region to region. Local tourist offices in any district can give you information about this. Pike, pike-perch, eel, and perch are found in the heartland and the southern parts of the country.

GOLFING With about 400 rarely crowded courses, Sweden may have more golf enthusiasts than any other country in Europe after Scotland. Visitors are often granted local membership cards, and greens fees vary, depending on the club. Many golfers fly from Stockholm to Boden in the far north in the summer months to play by the light of the midnight sun at the **Björkliden Arctic Golf Course,** which opened in 1989 some 240km (149 miles) north of the Arctic Circle. It's not only the world's northernmost golf course, but it's one of the most panoramic, set against a backdrop of snow-capped peaks, green valleys, and crystal lakes. The narrow fairways and small greens of this 9-hole, par-36 course offer multiple challenges. For details, contact the **Björkliden Arctic Golf Club,** Kvarnbacksvägen 28, Bromma S-168 74 (ℂ **09/80-40040**). For general information on courses in Sweden, contact the **Svenska Golffoürbundet,** P.O.

Box 84, Daneered S-182 11 (© **08/ 622-15-00;** www.golf.se).

HIKING   Sarek, in the far north, is one of Europe's last real wilderness areas; Swedes come here to hike in the mountains, pick mushrooms, gather berries, and fish. The **Svenska Turist- foürening (Swedish Touring Club),** P.O. Box 25, Amiralitetshuset 1, Flag- mansvägen 8, S101 20 Stockholm (© **08/463-21-00;** www.stfturist.se), provides accommodations in the area in mountain huts with 10 to 30 beds. The staff knows the northern part of Sweden well and can advise you about marked tracks, rowboats, the best excursions, the problems you're likely to encounter, communications, and transportation. The company also sells trail and mountain maps.

HORSEBACK   RIDING   Many opportunities for overnight horseback pack trips exist in such wilderness areas as the forests of Värmland or Norrbotten, where reindeer, musk oxen, and other creatures roam. The most popular overnight horseback trips start just north of the city of Karlstad in Värmland. Covered- wagon trips with overnight stopovers also exist. A typical horseback trip begins in the lakeside village of Torsby and follows a forested trail up a moun- tain. An average of 4 hours a day is spent on the horse, with meals cooked over an open fire.

In northern Sweden, two popular starting points are Funäsdalen, close to the Norwegian border, and Ammarnäs, not far from the Arctic Circle and the midnight sun. These trips begin in June. Local tourist offices can provide further information.

Sweden also has many riding stables and riding schools. Ask about them at local tourist offices. One of the most popular excursions is a pony trek through the region surrounding Swe- den's highest mountain, Knebnekaise.

In sites convenient to Stockholm, you might try a ride or two around the

rinks at **Djurgärdens   ridskola,** Kaknäs, Djurgården (© **08/660-21- 11**), or a bit farther afield at **Boügs Gård AB,** in Sollentuna (© **08/96- 79-71**), which maintains a comple- ment of Icelandic ponies, which thrive throughout the region's frigid winters. Both sites can help arrange overnight treks through the surrounding fields and forests, even though most of their business derives from rink-riding and improvement of equestrian forms.

One more unusual choice is explor- ing the *Orsa* (outback) by horse and covered wagon. In the province of Dalarna, you can rent a horse and wagon with space for up to five peo- ple. The outback is an almost unpop- ulated area of wild beauty, and the route goes past beautiful summer pas- tures, small lakes in the midst of forests, and panoramic views. Rides are available June through August. Clients cover about 16km (10 miles) a day, sleeping in or beside the covered wagon, following a preselected itiner- ary, and usually overnighting beside lakes or rivers. For more information, contact **Häst och Vagn,** Torsmo 1646, S-794 91 Orsa (© **0481/531-00**).

If you prefer to make your horse- back riding arrangements before your departure from the United States, per- haps as part of an organized bus, rail, or self-drive tour, **Passage Tours of Scandinavia,** 239 Commercial Blvd., Fort Lauderdale, FL 33308 (© **800/ 548-5960** or 954/776-7070; www. passagetours.com), can custom-design a suitable tour for you, usually config- ured with visits to Sweden's cultural, architectural, or historical highlights en route.

RAFTING   White-water rafting and river-rafting are the two major forms of this sport. For white-water rafting, you go in a fast riverboat, the trip made all the more exciting by a series of rapids. Throughout the country, visitors can take advantage of both short trips and those lasting a week or so. In Värmland, contact **Branäs Sport AB,** Branäs Fritidsanläggnin, Gondolvägem 1, S-680 60 Syssleback (℃ **564/475-50;** www.branas.se).

River rafting is much tamer because you go gently down a slow-moving river in Sweden's heartland. For information about the best river rafting in Sweden, contact **Kukkolaforsen-Turist & Konferens,** P.O. Box 184, S-593 91 Haparanda (℃ **922/310-00;** www.kukkolaforsen.se). If you want to try log-rafting, we recommend a lazy trip down the Klarälven River, winding through beautiful and unspoiled valleys between high mountains, with sandy beaches where you can swim if temperatures and river conditions allow. There also is excellent fishing for pike and grayling. You will travel through northern Värmland at a speed of 2km (1¼ miles) per hour from the mouth of the Vinguümngssjoün Lake in the north to Ekshärad in the south, a distance of 110km (68 miles) in 6 days. Overnight accommodations are arranged either on the moored raft or ashore. Each raft can accommodate between two and five people, and the trips are available from May to August. For a 6-day tour, adults pay 2,350SEK ($306); for a 3-day tour, 1,960SEK ($255). Rental of a tent and kitchen equipment costs an additional 380SEK to 480SEK ($49–$62)

per person. Participants supply their own food and fishing equipment. Contact **Branäs Sverigeflotten,** Klara Strand 66, S-680 63 Likenäs (℃ **564/402-27;** www.sverigeflotten.se).

SAILING & CANOEING Canoes and sailing boats can be rented all over the country; you can obtain information about this from the local tourist office. Often hotels situated near watersports areas have canoes for rent.

SWIMMING If you don't mind swimming in cool water, Sweden has one of the world's longest coastlines—plus some 100,000 lakes—in which you can take the plunge. The best bathing beaches are on the west coast. Both the islands of Oüland and Gotland have popular summer seaside resorts. Beaches in Sweden are generally open to the public, and nude bathing is allowed on certain designated beaches. Topless bathing for women is prevalent everywhere. If a Swedish lake is suitable for swimming, it's always signposted.

WALKING & JOGGING Sweden is ideal for either activity. Local tourist offices can provide details and sometimes even supply you with free maps of the best trails or jogging paths. In Stockholm, hotel reception desks often can tell you the best places to go jogging nearby.

7 Travel Insurance

Because Sweden is far from home for most of us, and a number of things could go wrong—lost luggage, trip cancellation, a medical emergency—consider the following types of insurance.

Check your existing insurance policies before you buy travel insurance to cover trip cancellation, lost luggage, medical expenses, or car rental insurance. You're likely to have partial or complete coverage already. But if you need some, ask your travel agent about a comprehensive package. The cost of

travel insurance varies widely, depending on the cost and length of your trip, your age and overall health, and the type of trip you're taking. Insurance for extreme sports or adventure travel, for example, costs more than coverage for a European cruise. Some insurers provide packages for specialty vacations, such as skiing or backpacking. More dangerous activities might be excluded from basic policies.

TRIP-CANCELLATION INSURANCE Trip-cancellation insurance helps you get your money back if you have to back out of a trip, if you have to go home early, or if your travel supplier goes bankrupt. Allowed reasons for cancellation can range from sickness to natural disasters, to the State Department declaring your destination unsafe for travel. (Insurers usually won't cover vague fears.) In this unstable world, trip-cancellation insurance is a good buy if you're getting tickets well in advance—who knows what the state of the world, or of your airline, will be in 9 months? Insurance policy details vary, so read the fine print—and especially make sure that your airline or cruise line is on the list of carriers covered in case of bankruptcy. A good resource is "Travel Guard Alerts," a list of companies considered high-risk by Travel Guard International (see website below). Protect yourself further by paying for the insurance with a credit card—by law, consumers can get their money back on goods and services not received if they report the loss within 60 days after the charge is listed on their credit card statement.

Note: Many tour operators, particularly those offering trips to remote or high-risk areas, include insurance in the cost of the trip or can arrange insurance policies through a partnering provider, a convenient and often cost-effective way for the traveler to obtain insurance. Make sure the tour company is a reputable one, however: Some experts suggest you avoid buying insurance from the tour or cruise company you're traveling with, saying it's better to buy from a "third party" insurer than to put all your money in one place.

For information, contact one of the following insurers: **Access America** (© 866/807-3982; www.access america.com); **Travel Guard International** (© 800/826-4919; www.travel guard.com); **Travel Insured International** (© 800/243-3174; www.travel insured.com), or **Travelex Insurance Services** (© 888/457-4602; www. travelex-insurance.com).

MEDICAL INSURANCE For trav-el overseas, most health plans (including Medicare and Midicaid) do not provide coverage, and the ones that do often require you to pay for services upfront and reimburse you only after you return home. Even if your plan does cover overseas treatment, most out-of-country hospitals make you pay your bills up front, and send you a refund only after you've returned home and filed the necessary paperwork with your insurance company. As a safety net, you may want to buy travel medical insurance, particularly if you're traveling to a remote or high-risk area where emergency evacuation is a possible scenario. If you require additional medical insurance, try **MEDEX Assistance** (© 800/527-0218 or 410/453-6300; www.medex assist.com) or **Worldwide Assistance** (© 800/821-2828; www.worldwide assistance.com). This latter company is the oldest and most experienced travel-assistance network in the world.

LOST-LUGGAGE INSURANCE On international flights (including U.S. portions of international trips), baggage coverage is limited to approximately $9.07 per pound, up to approximately $635 per checked bag. If you plan to check items more valuable than the standard liability, see if your valuables are covered by your homeowner's policy, get baggage insurance as part of your comprehensive travel-insurance package, or buy Travel Guard's BagTrak product. Don't buy insurance at the airport, as it's usually overpriced. Be sure to take any valuables or irreplaceable items with you in your carry-on luggage, as many valuables (including books, money, and electronics) aren't covered by airline policies.

If your luggage is lost, immediately file a lost-luggage claim at the airport,

> **Tips   Quick ID**
>
> Tie a colorful ribbon or piece of yarn around your luggage handle, or slap a distinctive sticker on the side of your bag. This makes it less likely that someone will mistakenly appropriate it. And if your luggage gets lost, it will be easier to find.

detailing the luggage contents. For most airlines, you must report delayed, damaged, or lost baggage within 4 hours of arrival. The airlines are required to deliver luggage, once found, directly to your house or destination free.

CAR RENTAL INSURANCE (LOSS/DAMAGE WAIVER OR COLLISION DAMAGE WAIVER)

If you hold a U.S. private auto insurance policy, you probably are covered in the United States but not abroad for loss or damage to the car and liability in case a passenger is injured.

The credit card you used to rent the car also might provide some coverage.

Car rental insurance probably does not cover liability if you caused the accident. Check your own auto insurance policy, the rental company policy, and your credit card coverage for the extent of coverage. Is your destination covered? Are other drivers covered? How much liability is covered if a passenger is injured? (If you rely on your credit card for coverage, you might want to bring a second credit card with you: Damages might be charged to your card, and you could find yourself stranded with no money.)

Car rental insurance costs from $20 a day.

8 Health & Safety

STAYING HEALTHY

Sweden is viewed as a "safe" destination, although problems, of course, can and do occur anywhere. You don't need to get shots; most foodstuff is safe and the water in cities and towns potable. If you're concerned, order bottled water. It is easy to get a prescription filled in towns and cities, and nearly all hospitals in Sweden have English-speaking doctors and well-trained medical staffs.

In other words, Sweden is part of the civilized world. In fact, it's one of the most advanced countries on the planet.

WHAT TO DO IF YOU GET SICK AWAY FROM HOME

If you worry about getting sick away from home, consider purchasing **medical travel insurance** and carry your ID card in your purse or wallet. In

most cases, your existing health plan will provide the coverage you need. See the section on insurance above for more information.

Pack **prescription medications** in your carry-on luggage, and carry prescription medications in their original containers. Also bring along copies of your prescriptions in case you lose or run out of your medications. Carry the generic name of prescription medicines, in case a local pharmacist is unfamiliar with the brand name.

And don't forget sunglasses and an extra pair of contact lenses or prescription glasses.

Contact the **International Association for Medical Assistance to Travelers (IAMAT)** (© 716/754-4883, or in Canada 416/652-0137; www.iamat. org) for tips on travel and health concerns in Sweden and lists of local,

English-speaking doctors. The United States **Centers for Disease Control and Prevention** (© 800/311-3435; www.cdc.gov) provides up-to-date information on necessary vaccines and health hazards by region or country. (Its booklet, *Health Information for International Travel,* is $25 by mail; on the Internet, it's free.) Any foreign consulate can provide a list of area doctors who speak English. If you get sick, consider asking your hotel concierge to recommend a local doctor—even his or her own. You can also try the emergency room at a local hospital; many have walk-in clinics for emergency cases that are not life-threatening.

STAYING SAFE

Sweden has a relatively low crime rate, with rare but increasing instances of violent crime. Most crimes involve the theft of personal property from cars or residences. Pickpockets might be a problem in public areas. Beware of pickpockets and purse-snatchers who often work in pairs or groups, with one distracting the victim while another grabs valuables. They often operate in or near major tourist attractions like Stockholm's Old Town, restaurants, amusement parks, museums, bars, buses, and subway trains. Hotel breakfast rooms and lobbies attract professional, well-dressed thieves who blend in with guests and target purses and briefcases left unguarded by unsuspecting tourists and business travelers. Valuables should not be left unguarded in parked vehicles.

The loss or theft abroad of a U.S. passport should be reported immediately to the local police and the nearest U.S. Embassy or Consulate. If you are the victim of a crime while overseas, in addition to reporting it to local police, contact the nearest U.S. Embassy or Consulate for assistance. The Embassy/Consulate staff can, for example, assist you by finding appropriate medical care, contacting family members or friends, and explaining how funds can be transferred. Although the investigation and prosecution of the crime is solely the responsibility of local authorities, consular officers can help you to understand the local criminal justice process and to find an attorney, if needed.

U.S. citizens may refer to the Department of State's pamphlet, *A Safe Trip Abroad,* for ways to promote a trouble-free journey. The pamphlet is available by mail from the **Superintendent of Documents, U.S. Government Printing Office,** Washington, DC 20402; via the Internet at www.gpoaccess.gov; or via the Bureau of Consular Affairs home page at http://travel.state.gov.

9 Specialized Travel Resources

A number of resources and organizations in both North America and Britain exist to assist travelers with special needs in planning their trips to Sweden.

TRAVELERS WITH DISABILITIES

Laws in Sweden have compelled rail stations, airports, hotels, and most restaurants to follow a stricter set of regulations about **wheelchair accessibility** to restrooms, ticket counters, and the like. Even museums and other attractions have conformed to the regulations, which mimic many of those presently in effect in the United States. Always call ahead to check on accessibility in hotels, restaurants, and sights you want to visit.

Many travel agencies offer customized tours and itineraries for travelers with disabilities. **Flying Wheels Travel** (© 507/451-5005; www.flyingwheelstravel.com) offers escorted tours and cruises that emphasize sports and private tours in minivans with lifts. **Access-Able Travel Source** (© 303/232-2979; www.access-able.com) offers extensive access information and advice for traveling around the world with disabilities. **Accessible Journeys** (© 800/846-4537 or 610/521-0339; www.disabilitytravel.com) caters specifically to slow walkers and wheelchair travelers and their families and friends.

Organizations that offer assistance to travelers with disabilities include **MossRehab** (www.mossresourcenet.org), which provides a library of accessible-travel resources online; **SATH** (Society for Accessible Travel and Hospitality) (© 212/447-7284; www.sath.org; annual membership fees: $45 adults, $30 seniors and students), which offers a wealth of travel resources for all types of disabilities and informed recommendations on destinations, access guides, travel agents, tour operators, vehicle rentals, and companion services; and the **American Foundation for the Blind (AFB)** (© 800/232-5463; www.afb.org), a referral resource for the blind or visually impaired that includes information on traveling with Seeing Eye dogs.

For more information specifically targeted to travelers with disabilities, the community website **iCan** (www.icanonline.net/channels/travel/index.cfm) has destination guides and several regular columns on accessible travel. Also check out the quarterly magazine *Emerging Horizons* ($15 per year, $20 outside the U.S.; www.emerginghorizons.com); **Twin Peaks Press** (© 360/694-2462), offering travel-related books for travelers with special needs; and *Open World Magazine,* published by SATH (see above; subscription: $13 per year, $21 outside the U.S.).

FOR BRITISH TRAVELERS The **Royal Association for Disability and Rehabilitation (RADAR),** Unit 12, City Forum, 250 City Rd., London EC1V 8AF (© 020/7250-3222; www.radar.org.uk), publishes three holiday "fact packs" for £2 each or £5 for all three. The first provides general information, including tips for planning and booking a holiday, obtaining insurance, and handling finances; the second outlines transportation available when going abroad and equipment for rent; and the third deals with specialized accommodations. Another good resource is **Holiday Care Service,** 7th floor, Sunley House, 4 Bedford Park, Croydon, Surrey CR0 2AP (© 0845/124-9971; www.holidaycare.org.uk), a national charity advising on accessible accommodations for the elderly and persons with disabilities. Annual membership is £37.

IN SWEDEN About two million people in Sweden have a disability; as a result, Sweden is especially conscious of their special needs. In general, trains, airlines, ferries, and department stores and malls are accessible. For information about wheelchair access, ferry and air travel, parking, and other matters, your best bet is to contact the Scandinavian Tourist Board (see "Visitor Information," earlier in this chapter). For information on youth hostels with special rooms for those with disabilities, contact **Svenska Turist Foreningen,** P.O. Box 25, S-101 20 Stockholm (© 08/463-21-00; www.stfturist.se).

GAY & LESBIAN TRAVELERS

Stockholm is the gay capital of Scandinavia, and Sweden ranks along with Norway, Denmark, and The Netherlands as among the most tolerant and gay-friendly nations on earth. Even gay marriage is now legal in this enlightened, sophisticated country. The age of consent is almost uniformly the same as for heterosexuals, usually 15 or 16. However, outside Stockholm and Gothenburg you'll find few gay bars.

Many gay and lesbian organizations in Stockholm welcome visitors from abroad. Foremost among these is the **Federation for Gay and Lesbian Rights (RFSL),** Sveavägen 57 (Box 350), S-10126 Stockholm (📞 **08/457-13-00;** www.rfsl.se), open Monday through Friday from 9am to 5pm. Established in 1950, the group has headquarters on the upper floors of the biggest gay nightlife center in Stockholm. Meetings are held weekly—a Wednesday 3pm meeting for gay men over 60 and a twice-monthly meeting of "Golden Ladies" (yes, they use the English expression) for lesbians over 50, plus a Monday-night youth session for those 18 to 21. They also operate a **Gay Switchboard** (📞 08/457-13-00), staffed with volunteers; call daily from 8am to 11pm for information. The biggest event of the year is **Gay Pride Week,** usually held the first week in August. Call or write the RFSL for information.

The **International Gay and Lesbian Travel Association (IGLTA)** (📞 **800/448-8550** or 954/776-2626; www.iglta.org) is the trade association for the gay and lesbian travel industry, and offers an online directory of gay- and lesbian-friendly travel businesses; go to their website and click on "Members."

Many agencies offer tours and travel itineraries specifically for gay and lesbian travelers. **Above and Beyond Tours** (📞 **800/397-2681;** www.abovebeyondtours.com) is the exclusive gay and lesbian tour operator for United Airlines. **Now, Voyager** (📞 800/255-6951; www.nowvoyager.com) is a well-known San Francisco–based gay-owned and operated travel service. **Olivia Cruises & Resorts** (📞 **800/631-6277** or 510/655-0364; www.olivia.com) charters entire resorts and ships for exclusive lesbian vacations and offers smaller group experiences for both gay and lesbian travelers.

The following travel guides are available at most travel bookstores and gay and lesbian bookstores, or you can order them from **Giovanni's Room** bookstore, 1145 Pine St., Philadelphia, PA 19107 (📞 **215/923-2960;** www.giovannisroom.com): *Frommer's Gay & Lesbian Europe,* an excellent travel resource; *Out and About* (📞 **800/929-2268;** www.outandabout.com), which offers guidebooks and a newsletter ($35 per year; 12 issues) packed with solid information on the global gay and lesbian scene; *Spartacus International Gay Guide* (Bruno Gmünder Verlag; www.spartacusworld.com/gayguide) and *Odysseus: The International Gay Travel Planner* (Odysseus Enterprises Ltd.), both good annual English-language guidebooks focused on gay men; the *Damron* guides (www.damron.com), with separate, annual books for gay men and lesbians; and *Gay Travel A to Z: The World of Gay & Lesbian Travel Options at Your Fingertips,* by Marianne Ferrari (Ferrari International, Box 35575, Phoenix, AZ 85069), a great gay and lesbian guidebook series.

SENIOR TRAVEL

Mention the fact that you're a senior when you first make your travel reservations. All major airlines and many Swedish hotels offer discounts for seniors.

Members of **AARP** (formerly known as the American Association of Retired Persons), 601 E St. NW, Washington, DC 20049 (📞 **888/687-2277;** www.aarp.org), get discounts on hotels, airfares, and car rentals. AARP offers members a wide range of benefits, including *AARP The Magazine* and a monthly newsletter. Anyone over 50 can join.

Many reliable agencies and organizations target the 50-plus market. **Elderhostel** (📞 877/426-8056; www.elderhostel.org) arranges study programs for those ages 55 and over (and

Traveling with Minors

It's always wise to have plenty of documentation when traveling in today's world with children. For changing details on entry requirements for children traveling abroad, keep up-to-date by going to the U.S. State Department website: http://travel.state.gov/foreignentryreq.html. To prevent international child abduction, E.U. governments have initiated procedures at entry and exit points. These often (but not always) include requiring documentary evidence of relationship and permission for the child's travel from the parent or legal guardian not present. Having such documentation on hand, even if not required, facilitates entries and exits. All children must have their own passport. To obtain a passport, the child **must** be present—that is, in person—at the center issuing the passport. Both parents must be present as well. If not, then a notarized statement from the parents is required. Any questions parents or guardians might have can be answered by calling the **National Passport Information Center** at ℭ **877/487-2778** Monday to Friday 8am to 8pm Eastern Standard Time.

a spouse or companion of any age) in the U.S. and more than 80 countries around the world, including Sweden. Most courses last 2 to 4 weeks abroad, and many include airfare, accommodations in university dormitories or modest inns, meals, and tuition. **ElderTreks** (ℭ **800/741-7956;** www. eldertreks.com) offers small-group tours to off-the-beaten-path or adventure-travel locations. Restricted to travelers 50 and older.

Recommended publications offering travel resources and discounts for seniors include: the quarterly magazine *Travel 50 & Beyond* (www.travel 50andbeyond.com); *Travel Unlimited: Uncommon Adventures for the Mature Traveler* (Avalon); *101 Tips for Mature Travelers,* available from Grand Circle Travel (ℭ **800/221-2610** or 617/350-7500; www.gct. com); *The 50+ Traveler's Guidebook* (St. Martin's Press); and *Unbelievably Good Deals and Great Adventures That You Absolutely Can't Get Unless You're Over 50* (McGraw-Hill), by Joann Rattner Heilman.

IN SWEDEN Visitors over age 65 can obtain 30% off first- and second-class train travel (except Fri and Sun) on the Swedish State Railways. Seniors get discounts on the ferries crossing from Denmark to Sweden, and on certain attractions and performances. However, you may have to belong to a seniors' organization to qualify for certain discounts. **In Stockholm,** there are discounts on transportation, concert, theater, and opera tickets.

FAMILY TRAVEL

The family vacation is a rite of passage for many households, one that in a split second can devolve into a *National Lampoon* farce. But as any veteran family vacationer will assure you, a family trip can be among the most pleasurable and rewarding times of your life.

Most Swedish hoteliers will let children 12 and under stay in a room with their parents for free, although some do not. Sometimes this requires a little negotiation at the reception desk.

Swedes like kids but don't offer a lot of special amenities for them. For example, a kiddies' menu in a restaurant is a rarity. You can, however, order a half-portion, and most waiters will oblige.

At attractions—even if it isn't specifically posted—inquire if a kids' discount is available. European Community citizens under 18 are admitted free to all state-run museums.

Look for our child-friendly icons throughout the guide.

Babysitting services are available through most hotel desks or by applying at the Tourist Information Office in the town where you're staying. Many hotels have children's game rooms and playgrounds.

Throughout the guide, look for our child-friendly "Kids" icons.

Familyhostel (℡ 800/733-9753; www.learn.unh.edu/familyhostel) takes the whole family, including kids ages 8 to 15, on moderately priced domestic and international learning vacations. Lectures, field trips, and sightseeing are guided by a team of academics.

Recommended family travel Internet sites include **Family Travel Forum** (www.familytravelforum.com), a comprehensive site that offers customized trip planning; **Family Travel Network** (www.familytravelnetwork.com), an award-winning site that offers travel features, deals, and tips; **Traveling Internationally with Your Kids** (www. travelwithyourkids.com), a comprehensive site offering sound advice for long-distance and international travel with children; and **Family Travel Files** (www.thefamilytravelfiles.com), which offers an online magazine and a directory of off-the-beaten-path tours and tour operators for families.

STUDENT TRAVEL

If you're planning to travel outside the U.S., you'd be wise to arm yourself with an International Student Identity Card (ISIC), which offers substantial savings on rail passes, plane tickets, and entrance fees. It also provides you with basic health and life insurance and a 24-hour help line. The card is available for $22 from **STA Travel** (℡ 800/781-4040 in North America; www.sta.com or www.statravel.com), the biggest student travel agency in the world. If you're no longer a student but are still under 26, you can get an International Youth Travel Card (IYTC) for the same price from the same people, which entitles you to some discounts (but not on museum admissions). (**Note:** In 2002, STA Travel bought competitors Council Travel and USIT Campus after they went bankrupt. It's still operating some offices under the Council name, but it's owned by STA.) **Travel CUTS** (℡ 800/667-2887 or 416/614-2887; www.travelcuts.com) offers similar services for both Canadians and U.S. residents. Irish students may prefer to turn to **USIT** (℡ 01/602-1600; www.usitnow.ie), an Ireland-based specialist in student, youth, and independent travel.

SINGLE TRAVELERS

Single travelers are often hit with a "single supplement" to the base price. To avoid it, you can agree to room with other single travelers on the trip, or you can find a compatible roommate before you go from one of the many roommate locator agencies.

Note: Travel Companion Exchange is not currently operating due to an extended family emergency. **Travel Buddies Singles Travel Club** (℡ 800/998-9099; www.travelbuddiesworld wide.com), based in Canada, runs small, intimate, single-friendly group trips and will match you with a roommate free of charge and save you the cost of single supplements. **TravelChums** (℡ 212/787-2621; www.travelchums.com) is an Internet-only travel companion matching service with elements of an online personals-type site, hosted by the respected New York–based Shaw Guides travel service. **The Single Gourmet Club** (www.singlegourmet. com/chapters.php) is an international social, dining, and travel club for singles of all ages, with club chapters in 21 cities in the U.S. and Canada. Annual membership fees vary from city to city.

Many reputable tour companies offer singles-only trips. **Singles Travel International** (℡ 877/765-6874; www.singlestravelintl.com) offers singles-only trips to places like London, Fiji, and the Greek Islands. **Backroads** (℡ 800/462-2848; www.backroads. com) offers more than 160 active-travel trips to 30 destinations worldwide, including Bali, Morocco, and Costa Rica.

For more information, check out Eleanor Berman's latest edition of *Traveling Solo: Advice and Ideas for More Than 250 Great Vacations* (Globe Pequot), a guide with advice on traveling alone, whether on your own or on a group tour.

10 Planning Your Trip Online

SURFING FOR AIRFARES

The "big three" online travel agencies, Expedia.com, Travelocity.com, and Orbitz.com, sell most of the air tickets bought on the Internet. (Canadian travelers should try expedia.ca and Travelocity.ca; U.K. residents can go for expedia.co.uk and opodo.co.uk.) Each has different business deals with the airlines and may offer different fares on the same flights, so it's wise to shop around. Expedia and Travelocity will also send you e-mail notification when a cheap fare becomes available to your favorite destination. Of the smaller travel agency websites, Side-Step (www.sidestep.com) has gotten the best reviews from Frommer's authors. It's a browser add-on that purports to "search 140 sites at once," but in reality beats competitors' fares only as often as other sites do.

Also remember to check **airline websites,** especially those for low-fare carriers, whose fares are often misreported or simply missing from travel agency websites. Even with major airlines, you can often shave a few bucks from a fare by booking directly through the airline and avoiding a travel agency's transaction fee. But you'll get these discounts only by **booking online:** Most airlines now offer online-only fares that even their phone agents know nothing about. For the websites of airlines that fly to and from your destination, go to "Getting There," p. 37.

Great **last-minute deals** are available through free weekly e-mail services provided directly by the airlines. Most of these are announced on Tuesday or Wednesday and must be purchased online. Most are valid for travel only that weekend, but some can be booked weeks or months in advance. Sign up for weekly e-mail alerts at airline websites or check megasites that compile comprehensive lists of last-minute specials, such as **Smarter Travel** (www. smartertravel.com). For last-minute trips, **lastminute.com** in Europe often has better air-and-hotel package deals than the major-label sites. A website listing numerous bargain sites and airlines around the world is **www.itravel net.com**.

If you're willing to give up some control over your flight details, use what is called an **opaque fare service** like **Priceline** (www.priceline.com; www.priceline.co.uk for Europeans) or its smaller competitor, **Hotwire** (www.hotwire.com). Both offer rock-bottom prices in exchange for travel on a "mystery airline" at a mysterious time of day, often with a mysterious change of planes en route. The mystery airlines are all major, well-known carriers. The airlines' routing computers have gotten a lot better than they used to be. But your chances of getting a 6am or 11pm flight are pretty high. Hotwire tells you flight prices before you buy; Priceline usually has better deals than Hotwire, but you have to play their "name our price" game. If you're new at this, the helpful folks at **BiddingForTravel** (www. biddingfortravel.com) do a good job of demystifying Priceline's prices and strategies. Priceline and Hotwire are great for flights between the U.S. and Europe. *Note:* In 2004 Priceline added non-opaque service to its roster. You now have the option to pick exact flights, times, and airlines from a list of offers—or opt to bid on opaque fares as before.

For much more about airfares and savvy air-travel tips and advice, pick up a copy of *Frommer's Fly Safe, Fly Smart* (Wiley Publishing, Inc.).

SURFING FOR HOTELS

Shopping online for hotels is generally done one of two ways: by booking through the hotel's own website or thorough an independent booking agency (or a fare-service agency like Priceline; see below). These Internet hotel agencies have multiplied in mind-boggling numbers of late, competing for the business of millions of consumers surfing for accommodations around the world. This competitiveness can be a boon to consumers who have the patience and time to shop and compare the online sites for good deals—but shop they must, for prices can vary considerably from site

to site. And keep in mind that hotels at the top of a site's listing may be there for no other reason than that they paid money to get the placement.

Of the "big three" sites, **Expedia** offers a long list of special deals and "virtual tours" or photos of available rooms so you can see what you're paying for (a feature that helps counter the claims that the best rooms are often held back from bargain booking websites). **Travelocity** posts unvarnished customer reviews and ranks its properties according to the AAA rating system. Also reliable are **Hotels.com** and **Quikbook.com**. An excellent free program, **TravelAxe** (www.travelaxe.net), can help you search multiple hotel sites at once, even ones you may never have heard of—and conveniently lists the total price of the room, including taxes and service charges. Another booking site, **Travelweb** (www.travelweb.com), is partly owned by the hotels it represents (including the Hilton, Hyatt, and Starwood chains) and is therefore plugged directly into the hotels' reservations systems—unlike independent online agencies, which have to fax or

---

Frommers.com: The Complete Travel Resource

For an excellent travel-planning resource, we highly recommend Frommers.com (www.frommers.com). We're a little biased, of course, but we guarantee that you'll find the travel tips, reviews, monthly vacation giveaways, and online-booking capabilities thoroughly indispensable. Among the special features are our popular Destinations section, where you'll get expert travel tips, hotel and dining recommendations, and advice on the sights to see for more than 3,500 destinations around the globe; the Frommers.com Newsletter, with the latest deals, travel tends, and money-saving secrets; our Community area, featuring Message Boards, where Frommer's readers post queries and share advice (sometimes even our authors show up to answer questions); and our Photo Center, where you can post and share vacation tips. When your research is done, the Online Reservations System (www.frommers.com/book_a_trip) takes you to Frommer's preferred online partners for booking your vacation at affordable prices.

e-mail reservation requests to the hotel, a good portion of which get misplaced in the shuffle. More than once, travelers have arrived at the hotel, only to be told that they have no reservation. To be fair, many of the major sites are undergoing improvements in service and ease of use, and Expedia will soon be able to plug directly into the reservations systems of many hotel chains—none of which can be bad news for consumers. In the meantime, it's a good idea to **get a confirmation number** and **make a printout** of any online booking transaction.

In the opaque website category, **Priceline** and **Hotwire** are even better for hotels than for airfares; with both, you're allowed to pick the neighborhood and quality level of your hotel before offering up your money. Priceline's hotel product even covers Europe, though it's much better at getting five-star lodging for three-star prices than at finding anything at the

bottom of the scale. On the down side, many hotels stick Priceline guests in their least desirable rooms. Be sure to go to the BiddingforTravel website (see above) before bidding on a hotel room on Pricelilne; it features a fairly up-to-date list of hotels that Priceline uses in major cities. For both Priceline and Hotwire, you pay upfront, and the fee is nonrefundable. *Note:* Some hotels do not provide loyalty program credits or points or other frequent-stay amenities when you book a room through opaque online services.

SURFING FOR RENTAL CARS

For booking rental cars online, the best deals are usually found at rental car company websites, although all the major online travel agencies also offer rental car reservations services. Priceline and Hotwire work well for rental cars, too; the only "mystery" is which major rental company you get, and for most travelers, the difference among Hertz, Avis, and Budget is negligible.

11 The 21st-Century Traveler

INTERNET ACCESS AWAY FROM HOME

Travelers have any number of ways to check their e-mail and access the Internet on the road. Of course, using your own laptop—or even a PDA (personal digital assistant) or electronic organizer with a modem—gives you the most flexibility. But even if you don't have a computer, you can still access your e-mail and even your office computer from cybercafes.

WITHOUT YOUR OWN COMPUTER

It's hard nowadays to find a city that doesn't have a few cybercafes. Although there's no definitive directory for cybercafes—these are independent businesses, after all—three places to start looking are at www.cybercaptive.com, www.netcafes.com, and www.cybercafe.com. See "Fast

Facts," under various cities such as Stockholm for cybercafes.

Aside from formal cybercafes, most **youth hostels** nowadays have at least one computer you can get to the Internet on. And most **public libraries** across the world offer Internet access free or for a small charge. Avoid **hotel business centers,** unless you're willing to pay exorbitant rates.

Most major airports now have **Internet kiosks** scattered throughout their gates. These kiosks, which you'll also see in shopping malls, hotel lobbies, and tourist information offices around the world, give you basic Web access for a per-minute fee that's usually higher than cybercafe prices. The kiosks' clunkiness and high price means they should be avoided whenever possible.

To retrieve your e-mail, ask your **Internet service provider (ISP)** if it has a Web-based interface tied to your existing e-mail account. If your ISP doesn't have such an interface, you can use the free **mail2web** service (www. mail2web.com) to view and reply to your home e-mail. For more flexibility, you may want to open a free, Web-based e-mail account with **Yahoo! Mail** (http://mail.yahoo.com). (Hotmail is another option, but it has severe spam problems.) Your home ISP may be able to forward your e-mail to the Web-based account automatically.

If you need to access files on your office computer, look into a service called **GoToMyPC** (www.gotomypc. com). The service provides a Web-based interface for you to access and manipulate a distant PC from anywhere—even a cybercafe—provided your "target" PC is on and has an always-on connection to the Internet (such as with Road Runner cable). The service offers top-quality security, but if you're worried about hackers, use your own laptop rather than a cybercafe to access the GoToMyPC system.

WITH YOUR OWN COMPUTER

Wi-fi (wireless fidelity) is the buzzword in computer access, and more and more hotels, cafes, and retailers are signing on as wireless "hotspots" where you can get a high-speed connection without cable wires, networking hardware, or a phone line (see below). You can get a wi-fi connection one of several ways. Many laptops sold in the last year have built-in wi-fi capability (an 802.11b wireless Ethernet connection). Mac owners have their own networking technology, Apple AirPort. For those with older computers, an 802.11b/Wi-fi card (around $50) can be plugged into your laptop. You sign up for wireless access service much as you do cellphone service, through a plan offered by one of several commercial companies that have made wireless

service available in airports, hotel lobbies, and coffee shops.

Increasingly, travelers can find places that provide **free wireless networks** in cities around the world. To locate these free hotspots, go to **www. personaltelco.net/index.cgi/Wire lessCommunities**.

Most business-class hotels throughout the world offer dataports for laptop users, and a few thousand hotels in Europe offer free high-speed Internet access using an Ethernet network cable. You can use your own cables, but most hotels rent them for about $10. **Call your hotel in advance** to explore your options.

In addition, major Internet service providers (ISPs) have **local access numbers** around the world, allowing you to go online by simply placing a local call. Check your ISP's website or call its toll-free number and ask how you can use your current account away from home, and how much it will cost.

Wherever you go, bring a **connection kit** of the right power and phone adapters, a spare phone cord, and a spare Ethernet network cable—or find out whether your hotel supplies them to guests.

USING A CELLPHONE
OUTSIDE THE U.S.

The three letters that define much of the world's wireless capabilities are GSM (Global System for Mobiles), a big, seamless network that makes for easy cross-border cellphone use throughout Europe and dozens of other countries worldwide. In the U.S., T-Mobile, AT&T Wireless, and Cingular use this quasiuniversal system; in Canada, Microcell and some Rogers customers are GSM, and all Europeans and most Australians use GSM.

If your cellphone is on a GSM system and you have a world-capable multiband phone such as many (but not all) Sony Ericsson, Motorola, or Samsung models, you can make and receive calls across civilized areas on much of the globe. Just call your wireless operator and ask for "international roaming" to be activated on your account. Unfortunately, per-minute charges can be high—usually $1 to $1.50 in Western Europe.

That's why it's important to buy an "unlocked" world phone from the get-go. Many cellphone operators sell "locked" phones that restrict you from using any other removable computer memory phone chip (called a **SIM card**) other than the ones they supply. Having an unlocked phone allows you to install a cheap, prepaid SIM card (found at a local retailer) in your destination country. (Show your phone to the salesperson; not all phones work on all networks.) You'll get a local phone number—and much, much lower calling rates. Getting an already locked phone unlocked can be a complicated process, but it can be done; just call your cellular operator and say you'll be going abroad for several months and want to use the phone with a local provider.

For many, **renting** a phone is a good idea. While you can rent a phone from any number of overseas sites, including kiosks at airports and at car rental agencies, we suggest renting the phone before you leave home. That way you can give loved ones and business associates your new number, make sure the phone works, and take the phone wherever you go—especially helpful for overseas trips through several countries, where local phone-rental agencies often bill in local currency and may not let you take the phone to another country.

Phone rental isn't cheap. You'll usually pay $40 to $50 per week, plus airtime fees of at least a dollar a minute. If you're traveling to Europe, though, local rental companies often offer free incoming calls within their home country, which can save you big bucks. The bottom line: Shop around.

Two good wireless rental companies are **InTouch USA** (© **800/872-7626;** www.intouchglobal.com) and **Road-Post** (© **888/290-1606** or 905/272-5665; www.roadpost.com). Give them your itinerary, and they'll tell you what wireless products you need. InTouch will also, for free, advise you on whether your existing phone will work overseas; simply call © **703/222-7161** between 9am and 4pm EST, or go to http://intouchglobal.com/travel.htm.

For trips of more than a few weeks spent in one country, **buying a phone** becomes economically attractive, as many nations have cheap, no-questions-asked prepaid phone systems. Once you arrive at your destination, stop by a local cellphone shop and get the cheapest package; you'll probably pay less than $100 for a phone and a starter calling card. Local calls may be as low as 10¢ per minute, and in many countries incoming calls are free.

12 Getting There

BY PLANE

Flying in winter—Scandinavia's off season—is cheapest; summer is the most expensive. Spring and fall are in between. In any season, midweek fares (Mon–Thurs) are the lowest.

THE MAJOR AIRLINES

Travelers from the U.S. East Coast usually choose **SAS** (© **800/221-2350** in the U.S.; www.scandinavian.net).

Another major competitor is **American Airlines** (© **800/433-7300** in the U.S.; www.aa.com), which offers daily flights to Stockholm from Chicago, and excellent connections through Chicago from American's vast North American network. Between November and March (excluding the Christmas holidays), American offers round-trip fares as low as $540 for weekday departures from Chicago.

There's a supplemental charge of $50 for travel on a Friday, Saturday, or Sunday. This fare, matched for the most part by SAS, requires a stay abroad of between 7 and 60 days, as well as several other restrictions. Although these fares probably will have changed by the time you make your vacation plans, the new prices are likely to be somewhat similar. Travelers from Seattle usually fly SAS to Copenhagen, then connect to one of the airline's frequent shuttle flights into Stockholm.

Other airlines fly to gateway European cities and then connect to other flights into Stockholm. **British Airways** (© **800/247-9297** in the U.S.; www.britishairways.com), for example, flies from almost 20 North American cities to London/Heathrow, and then connects with onward flights to Stockholm. **Northwest** (© **800/225-2525** in the U.S.; www.nwa.com) also flies at frequent intervals to London, from which ongoing flights to Stockholm are available on either SAS or British Airways. Finally, **Icelandair** (© **800/223-5500** in the U.S.; www.icelandair.com) has proved to be an excellent choice for travel to Stockholm, thanks to connections through its home port of Reykjavik.

People traveling **from Britain** can fly **SAS** (© **0870/6072-7727** in London) from London's Heathrow to Stockholm on any of five daily nonstop flights. Flying time is about 2½ hours each way. Likewise, SAS flies daily to Stockholm from Manchester, making a brief stop in Copenhagen en route. Flight time from Manchester to Stockholm is about 3½ hours each way.

A NOTE FOR BRITISH TRAVELERS A regular fare from the United Kingdom to Stockholm is extremely expensive, so call a travel agent about a charter flight or special air-travel promotions. If this is not possible, then an APEX ticket (described below) might be the way to trim costs. You might also ask the airlines about a "Eurobudget ticket," which carries restrictions or length-of-stay requirements.

British newspapers are always full of classified ads touting "slashed" fares from London to other destinations. One good source is *Time Out,* a magazine filled with cultural information about London. The *Evening Standard* maintains a daily travel section, and the Sunday editions of virtually any newspaper in the British Isles will run ads.

Although competition among airline consolidators is fierce, one well-recommended company is **Trailfinders** (© **0845/05-05-891** in London; www.trailfinder.com). Buying blocks of tickets from such carriers as British Airways, SAS, and KLM, it offers cost-conscious fares from London's Heathrow or Gatwick airports to Stockholm.

In London, many bucket shops around Victoria and Earl's Court offer low fares. Make sure that the company you deal with is a member of the IATA, ABTA, or ATOL. These umbrella organizations will help you if anything goes wrong.

CEEFAX, a British television information service, airs on many home and hotel TVs and runs details of package holidays and flights to Stockholm and beyond. Just switch to your CEEFAX channel, and you'll find a menu of listings that includes travel information.

Make sure that you understand the bottom line on any special deal. Ask if all surcharges, including airport taxes and other hidden costs, are included before committing. Upon investigation, some of these "deals" are not as attractive as advertised. Also ask about penalties if you're forced to cancel at the last minute.

GETTING THROUGH THE AIRPORT

With the federalization of airport security, security procedures at U.S.

airports are more stable and consistent than ever. Generally, you'll be fine if you arrive at the airport 2 hours before an international flight; if you show up late, tell an airline employee and she'll probably whisk you to the front of the line.

Bring a **current, government-issued photo ID** such as a driver's license or passport. Keep your ID at the ready to show at check-in, the security checkpoint, and sometimes even the gate. (Children under 18 need government-issued photo IDs for international flights.)

Passengers with e-tickets can still beat the ticket-counter lines by using airport **electronic kiosks** or even **online check-in** from your home computer. Online check-in involves logging on to your airline's website, accessing your reservation, and printing out your boarding pass—and the airline may even offer you bonus miles to do so. If you're using a kiosk at the airport, bring the credit card you used to book the ticket or your frequent-flier card. Print out your boarding pass from the kiosk and simply proceed to the security checkpoint with your pass and a photo ID. If you're checking bags or looking to snag an exit-row seat, you will be able to do so using most airline kiosks.

If you have trouble standing for long periods of time, tell an airline employee; the airline will provide a wheelchair. Speed up security by **not wearing metal objects** such as big belt buckles. If you've got metallic body parts, a note from your doctor can prevent a long chat with the security screeners. Keep in mind that only **ticketed passengers** are allowed past security, except for folks escorting children or passengers with disabilities.

Federalization has stabilized **what you can carry on** and **what you can't**. The general rule is that sharp things are out, nail clippers are okay, and food and beverages must be passed through the X-ray machine—but that security screeners can't make you drink from your coffee cup. Bring food in your carry-on rather than checking it, as explosive-detection machines used on checked luggage have been known to mistake food (especially chocolate) for bombs. Travelers are allowed one carry-on bag, plus a "personal item" such as a purse, briefcase, or laptop bag. Carry-on hoarders can stuff all sorts of things into a laptop bag; as long as it has a laptop in it, it's still considered a personal item. The Transportation Security Administration (TSA) has issued a list of restricted items; check its website (www.tsa.gov/public/index.jsp) for details.

Airport screeners may decide that your checked luggage needs to be searched by hand. You can now purchase luggage locks that allow screeners to open and relock a checked bag if hand-searching is necessary. Look for Travel Sentry certified locks at luggage or travel shops and Brookstone stores (you can buy them online at www.brookstone.com). These locks, approved by the TSA, can be opened by luggage inspectors with a special code or key. For more information on the locks, visit www.travelsentry.org. If you use something other than TSA-approved locks, your lock will be clipped if a TSA agent needs to hand-search your luggage.

FLYING FOR LESS: TIPS FOR GETTING THE BEST AIRFARE

Passengers sharing the same airplane cabin rarely pay the same fare. Travelers who need to purchase tickets at the last minute, change their itinerary at a moment's notice, or fly one-way often get stuck paying the premium rate. Here are some ways to keep your airfare costs down:

- Passengers who can book their ticket long in advance, who can stay over Saturday night, or who fly midweek or at less-trafficked hours may pay a fraction of the full fare. If your schedule is flexible, say so, and ask if you can secure a cheaper fare by changing your flight plans.

- **APEX,** or advance-purchase booking fares, are often the key to getting the lowest fare. You generally must be willing to make your plans and buy your tickets as far ahead as possible. The **21-day APEX** is seconded only by the **14-day APEX,** with a stay in Sweden of 7 to 30 days. Because the number of seats allocated to APEX fares is sometimes less than 25% of the airplane's capacity, the early bird gets the low-cost seat. There's often a surcharge for flying on a weekend, and cancellation and refund policies can be strict.
- You can also save on airfares by keeping an eye out in local newspapers for promotional specials or fare wars, when airlines lower prices on their most popular routes. You rarely see fare wars offered for peak travel times, but if you can travel in the off-months, you may snag a bargain.
- Search the Internet for cheap fares (see "Planning Your Trip Online").
- Consolidators, also known as bucket shops, are great sources for international tickets, although they usually can't beat the Internet on fares within North America. Start by looking in Sunday newspaper travel sections; U.S. travelers should focus on the *New York Times, Los Angeles Times,* and *Miami Herald.* For less-developed destinations, small travel agents who cater to immigrant communities in large cities often have the best deals. *Beware:* Bucket shop tickets are usually nonrefundable or rigged with stiff cancellation penalties, often as high as 50% to

75% of the ticket price, and some put you on charter airlines, which may leave at inconvenient times and experience delays. Several reliable consolidators are worldwide and available on the Net. STA Travel is now the world's leader in student travel, thanks to its purchase of Council Travel. It also offers good fares for travelers of all ages. **ELTExpress** (Flights. com) (℗ 516/228-4972; www. eltexpress.com) started in Europe and has excellent fares worldwide, but particularly to that continent. It also has "local" websites in 12 countries. **FlyCheap** (℗ **800/FLY-CHEAP;** www.1800flycheap.com) is owned by package-holiday megalith MyTravel and so has especially good access to fares for sunny destinations. **Air Tickets Direct** (℗ **800/778-3447;** www.airtickets direct.com) is based in Montreal and leverages the currently weak Canadian dollar for low fares.
- Join frequent-flier clubs. Accrue enough miles, and you'll be rewarded with free flights and elite status. It's free, and you'll get the best choice of seats, faster response to phone inquiries, and prompter service if your luggage is stolen, your flight is canceled or delayed, or you want to change your seat. You don't need to fly to build frequent-flier miles—frequent-flier credit cards can provide thousands of miles for doing your everyday shopping.

BY CAR FROM CONTINENTAL EUROPE

FROM GERMANY You can drive to the northern German port of Travemünde and catch the 7½-hour ferry to the Swedish port of Trelleborg, a short drive south of Malmö. This route saves many hours by avoiding transit through Denmark. If you want to visit Denmark before Sweden, you can take the 3-hour car ferry from

Travemüünde to Gedser in southern Denmark. From Gedser, the E64 and the E4 express highways head north to Copenhagen. After a visit here, you can take the Øresund Bridge from Copenhagen to Malmö.

FROM NORWAY From Oslo, E18 goes east through Karlstad all the way to Stockholm. This is a long but scenic drive.

BY TRAIN FROM COPENHAGEN OR OSLO

Copenhagen is the main rail hub between the other Scandinavian countries and the rest of Europe. Seven daily trains run between Copenhagen and Stockholm, six between Copenhagen and Gothenburg. All connect with the Danish ferries that operate to Sweden via Helsingør or Frederikshavn.

At least three trains a day depart from Oslo to Stockholm (travel time: about 6½ hr.). One of the trains leaves Oslo around 11pm. Three trains run from Oslo to Gothenburg daily (travel time: about 4 hr.).

RAIL PASSES FOR NORTH AMERICAN TRAVELERS

If you plan to travel extensively on the European and/or British railroads, it would be worthwhile for you to get a copy of the latest edition of the *Thomas Cook European Timetable of Railroads.* It's available online at www.thomascooktimetables.com.

EURAILPASS If you plan to travel extensively in Europe, the **Eurailpass** may be a good bet. It's valid for first-class rail travel in 17 European countries. With one ticket, you travel whenever and wherever you please; more than 100,000 rail miles are at your disposal. Here's how it works: The pass is sold only in North America. A Eurailpass good for 15 days costs $588, a pass for 21 days is $762, a 1-month pass costs $946, a 2-month pass is $1,338, and a 3-month pass goes for $1,654. Children under 4

travel free if they don't occupy a seat; all children under 12 who take up a seat are charged half-price. If you're under 26, you can buy a **Eurail Youthpass,** which entitles you to unlimited second-class travel for 15 days ($414), 21 days ($534), 1 month ($664), 2 months ($938), or 3 months ($1,160). Travelers considering buying a 15-day or 1-month pass should estimate rail distance before deciding whether a pass is worthwhile. To take full advantage of the tickets for 15 days or a month, you'd have to spend a great deal of time on the train. Eurailpass holders are entitled to substantial discounts on certain buses and ferries as well. Travel agents in all towns and railway agents in such major cities as New York, Montreal, and Los Angeles sell all of these tickets. For information on Eurailpasses, and other European train data, call RailEurope at ☎ **800/438-7245,** or visit them on the Web at **www.rail europe.com**.

Eurail Saverpass offers 15% discounts to groups of three or more people traveling together between April and September, or two people traveling together between October and March. The price of a Saverpass, valid all over Europe for first class only, is $498 for 15 days, $648 for 21 days, $804 for 1 month, $1,138 for 2 months, and $1,408 for 3 months. Even more freedom is offered by the **Saver Flexipass,** which is similar to the Eurail Saverpass, except that you are not confined to consecutive-day travel. For travel over any 10 days within 2 months, the fare is $592; any 15 days over 2 months, the fare is $778.

Eurail Flexipass allows even greater flexibility. It's valid in first class and offers the same privileges as the Eurailpass. However, it provides a number of individual travel days over a much longer period of consecutive days. Using this pass makes it possible to stay longer in one city and not lose a single day of travel. There are two Flexipasses: 10 days of travel within 2 months for $694, and 15 days of travel within 2 months for $914.

With many of the same qualifications and restrictions as the Eurail Flexipass, the **Eurail Youth Flexipass** is sold only to travelers under 25. It allows 10 days of travel within 2 months for $488 and 15 days of travel within 2 months for $642.

SCANRAIL PASS If your visit to Europe will be primarily in Scandinavia, the Scanrail pass may be better and cheaper than the Eurailpass. This pass allows its owner a designated number of days of free rail travel within a larger time block. (Presumably, this allows for days devoted to sightseeing scattered among days of rail transfers between cities or sites of interest.) You can choose a total of any 5 days of unlimited rail travel during a 2-month period, 10 days of rail travel within a 2-month period, or 21 days of unlimited rail travel. The pass, which is valid on all lines of the state railways of Denmark, Finland, Norway, and Sweden, offers discounts or free travel on some (but not all) of the region's ferry lines as well. The pass can be purchased only in North America. It's available from any office of **RailEurope** (© **800/848-7245**) or **ScanAm World Tours,** 108 N. Main St., Cranbury, NJ 08512 (© **800/545-2204;** www.scandinaviantravel.com).

Depending on whether you choose first- or second-class rail transport, 5 days out of 2 months costs $291, 10 days out of 2 months costs $390, and 21 consecutive days of unlimited travel costs $453. Seniors get an 11% discount, and students receive a 30% discount.

RAIL PASSES FOR BRITISH TRAVELERS

If you plan to do a lot of exploring, you may prefer one of the three rail passes designed for unlimited train travel within a designated region during a predetermined number of days. These passes are sold in Britain and several other European countries.

An **InterRail Pass** is available to passengers of any nationality, with some restrictions—they must be under age 26 and able to prove residency in a European or North African country (Morocco, Algeria, and Tunisia) for at least 6 months before buying the pass. It allows unlimited travel through Europe, except Albania and the republics of the former Soviet Union. Prices are complicated and vary depending on the countries you want to include. For pricing purposes, Europe is divided into eight zones; the cost depends on the number of zones you include. The most expensive option, £295, allows 1 month of unlimited travel in all eight zones and is known to BritRail staff as a "global." The least expensive option £119, allows 12 days of travel within only one zone.

Passengers age 25 and older can buy an **InterRail 26-Plus Pass** which, unfortunately, is severely limited geographically. Many countries—including France, Belgium, Switzerland, Spain, Portugal, and Italy—do not honor this pass. It is, however, accepted for travel throughout Denmark, Finland, Norway, and Sweden. Second-class travel with the pass costs £223 for 12 days or £415 for 22 days. Passengers must meet the same residency requirements that apply to the InterRail Pass (described above).

For information on buying individual rail tickets or any of the just-mentioned passes, contact **National Rail Inquiries,** Victoria Station, London (© **08705/848-848** or 0845/748-4950). Tickets and passes also are available at any of the larger railway stations as well as selected travel agencies throughout Britain and the rest of Europe.

BY SHIP & FERRY

FROM DENMARK   Ferries ply the waters for the brief run from Helsingoür, a short drive north of Copenhagen, and Helsingborg, Sweden, just across the narrow channel that separates the countries. The 25-minute trip on a conventional ferry (not a catamaran) runs at 10- to 40-minute intervals, 24 hours a day. Operated by **Scandlines** (✆ **33-15-15-15** in Copenhagen; www.scandlines.dk), it's one of the most popular ferry routes in Europe. Round-trip passage costs 460DKK ($77) for a car with up to nine passengers; the ticket is valid for up to 2 months. Pedestrians pay 34DKK ($5.70) round-trip, regardless of when they return.

FROM ENGLAND   Two English ports, Harwich (year-round) and Newcastle-upon-Tyne (summer only), offer ferry service to Sweden. Harwich to Gothenburg takes 23 to 25 hours, Newcastle to Gothenburg, 27 hours. Boats on both routes offer overnight accommodations and the option of transporting cars. Prices are lower for passengers who book in advance through the company's U.S. agent. For details, call **Sea Europe Holidays,** 6801 Lake Worth Rd., Suite 103, Lake Worth, FL 33467 (✆ **800/533-3755** in the U.S.; www.seaeurope.com).

FROM GERMANY   **Stena Line Ferries** (✆ **031/704-00-00;** www.stenaline.com) sails daily from Kiel to Gothenburg. The trip takes 14 hours and costs 690SEK to 1,690SEK ($90–$220) for a one-way passage.

13 Escorted General & Special-Interest Tours

Sweden's various regions, especially Dalarna and Lapland, offer such a variety of sights and activities that you may want to take an organized tour. The following tours are just a small sample of what's available. Contact your travel agent to learn about tours of interest to you or to design a special one for you.

ESCORTED TOURS

ScanAm World Tours (✆ **800/545-2204;** www.scanamtours.com) offers a tour of the folkloric Dalarna region by rail. "Mora and the Folklore District" includes round-trip train fare from Stockholm to Mora and 2 nights at the First Resort Mora. The 3-day tour is available May through September; prices start at $565 per person. The company also offers a "Kalmar and the Swedish Glass District" rail tour. The 3-day excursion includes round-trip train fare from Stockholm to Kalmar and 2 nights at the Kalmar Stadshotell; prices start at $675 per person.

The tour is available May through September.

"Gotland Island and the City of Roses" is a cruise on the Gotland Line from Stockholm to Nynäshamn or from Oskarshamn to Visby, including 2 nights at the Visby Hotel or Hotel Solhem. The 3-day tour is available May through September.

Scantours (✆ **800/223-7226;** www.scantours.com) offers the most widely diverse tours of Sweden, ranging from a 2-day "Taste of Sweden's Best" tour by steamboat and vintage train to a 2-day canal cruise. One of the best of the tours is a 3-day journey through the folkloric province of Dalarna and along the shores of Lake Siljan.

Passage Tours (✆ **800/548-5960**) offers trips to both Stockholm and the "Kingdom of Crystal," with stopovers in such glass factories as Kosta Boda and Orrefors. Trips to the port of Kalmar on the Baltic Sea are also included, as well as visits to the island of Oland.

SPECIAL-INTEREST VACATIONS

ADVENTURE TOURS In the U.S. For overall adventure travel, including skiing, hiking, and biking, the best bet is **Borton Overseas,** 5412 Lyndale Ave. S., Minneapolis, MN 55419 (© **800/843-0602** or 612/822-4640; www.bortonoverseas.com), which offers sea kayaking and backpacking expeditions in Sweden. Tours should be arranged before you go. **Backroad Travel in Sweden, Inc.,** 18 Lake Shore Dr., Arlington, MA 02474 (© **888/648-3522** or 781/646-2955; www.backroadtravel.com), offers bicycle and walking tours off the beaten paths in Sweden, especially in Gotland and the Stockholm archipelago.

In the U.K. The oldest travel agency in Britain, **Cox & Kings,** Gordon House 10, Greencoat Place, London SW1P 1PH (© **020/7873-5000;** www.coxandkings.co.uk), was established in 1758; at that time, the company served as the paymasters and transport directors for the British armed forces in India. Today the company sends large numbers of travelers from Britain throughout the rest of the world and specializes in unusual—if pricey—holidays. Scandinavian tours include cruises through the region's spectacular fjords, bus and rail tours through sites of historic and aesthetic interest, and visits to the best-known handicraft centers, Viking burial sites, and historic churches. The company's staff focuses on tours of ecological and environmental interest.

Those who would like to cycle their way through the splendors of Scandinavia should join Britain's oldest and largest association of bicycle riders, the **Cyclists' Touring Club,** Cotterell House, 69 Meadow, Godalming, Surrey GU7 3HS (© **0870/873-0060;** www.ctc.org.uk). Founded in 1878, it charges £30.50 ($50) a year for membership, which includes information, maps, a subscription to a newsletter packed with practical information and morale boosters, plus recommended cycling routes through virtually every country in Europe. The organization's information bank on scenic routes through Scandinavia is especially comprehensive. Membership can be arranged over the phone with an appropriate credit card (such as MasterCard, Visa, Access, or Barclaycard).

In Sweden The archipelago that fronts Stockholm's harbor is one of the most frequently visited wilderness areas in northern Europe, thanks to its convenience to the Swedish capital. An outfitter that can help you appreciate the archipelago's resources in any season is **30,000 Oüar (30,000 Islands),** Fågelbrouhus, S-13960 Väumrmdoü (© **0707-59-01-00).** Owner Bengt Kull will propose a range of activities. For example, how about midwinter ice-skating in the environs of Stockholm? During mild winters, the venue would be on the frozen surface of Lake Malaren; during very cold winters, you might join the dozens of skaters who fly in regularly from Holland for Hans Brinker–style skating excursions on the frozen sea between some of the islands of the archipelago. (*Warning:* We emphatically urge you not to try this without a guide because pockets of warm water from undersea springs can make the ice treacherously thin in some spots.) Warm weather hiking and boating, and midwinter cross-country skiing, are all part of this outfit's areas of expertise. Trips are organized individually and, for some upscale gatherings, can even include a string quartet to greet you with a concert of Beethoven sonatas in a lakeside chalet after your hiking or waterborne excursions.

LEARNING VACATIONS An international series of programs for persons over 50 who are interested in combining travel and learning is offered by **Interhostel,** developed by the University of New Hampshire.

Each program lasts 2 weeks, is led by a university faculty or staff member, and is arranged in conjunction with a host college, university, or cultural institution. Participants may stay longer, if they wish. Interhostel offers programs consisting of cultural and intellectual activities and including field trips to museums and other centers of interest. For information, contact the **University of New Hampshire,** Interhostel/Familyhostel, 11 Garrison Ave., Durham, NH 03824 (© **800/313-5327** or 603/862-2015; www.learn.unh.edu).

Another good source of information about courses in Sweden is the **American Institute for Foreign Study (AIFS),** River Plaza, 9 W. Broad St., Stamford, CT 06902 (© **800/727-2437** or 203/399-5000; www.aifs.org). This organization can set up transportation and arrange for summer courses, with room and board included.

The biggest organization dealing with higher education in Europe is the **Institute of International Education (IIE),** 809 United Nations Plaza, New York, NY 10017 (© **800/445-0443** or 212/883-8200; www.iie.org). A few of its booklets are free, but for $46.95, plus $6 for postage, you can purchase the more definitive *Short Term Study Abroad.* Visitors to New York can use the resources of its Information Center, which is open to the public Tuesday through Thursday from 11am to 4pm. The institute is closed on major holidays.

One recommended clearinghouse for academic programs throughout the world is the **National Registration Center for Study Abroad (NRCSA),** 823 N. 2nd St., P.O. Box 1393, Milwaukee, WI 53201 (© **414/278-0631;** www.nrcsa.com). The organization maintains language-study programs throughout Europe.

HOME STAYS   Friendship Force International (FFI), 34 Peachtree St., Suite 900, Atlanta, GA 30303 (© **404/522-9490;** www.friendshipforce.org), is a nonprofit organization that fosters and encourages friendships among people worldwide. Dozens of branch offices throughout North America arrange en masse visits, usually once a year. Because of group bookings, the airfare to the host country usually is less than the cost of individual APEX tickets. Each participant spends 2 weeks in the host country—one as a guest in the home of a family, and another traveling throughout the country.

Servas, 11 John St., Room 505, New York, NY 10038 (© **212/267-0252;** www.usservas.org), is an international nonprofit, nongovernmental, interfaith network of travelers and hosts whose goal is to help promote world peace, goodwill, and understanding. (Its name means "to serve" in Esperanto.) Servas hosts offer travelers hospitality for 2 days. Travelers pay an $85 annual fee and a $25 list deposit after filling out an application and being approved by an interviewer (interviewers are located across the United States). They then receive Servas directories listing the names and addresses of Servas hosts.

HOME EXCHANGES   One of the most exciting breakthroughs in modern tourism is the home exchange. Home exchanges cut costs: You don't pay hotel bills, and you also can save money by shopping in markets and eating in. Sometimes even the family car is included. Of course, you must be comfortable with the idea of having strangers in your home, and you must be content to spend your vacation in one place. Also, you may not get a home in the area you request.

Intervac, U.S. & International, 30 Corte San Fernando, Tiburon, CA 94920 (© **800/756-HOME** or 415/435-3497; www.intervacus.com), is part of the largest worldwide exchange network. It publishes four catalogs a year, containing more than 10,000 homes in more than 36 countries. Members contact each other directly. The cost is $65 plus postage, which includes the purchase of three of the company's catalogs (which will be mailed to you), plus the inclusion of your own listing in whichever one of the three catalogs you select.

The Invented City, 41 Sutter St., Suite 1090, San Francisco, CA 94104

(© **415/252-1141;** www.invented-city.com), publishes home exchange listings three times per year. For the $50 membership fee, you can list your home with your own written descriptive summary.

Home Link International (© **800/ 638-3841;** www.homelink.org), will send you five directories per year—one of which contains your listing—for $75.

14 Getting Around Sweden

BY PLANE

WITHIN SWEDEN For transatlantic flights coming from North America, Stockholm is Sweden's major gateway for Scandinavia's best-known airline, **SAS** (Scandinavian Airlines System). For flights arriving from other parts of Europe, the airport at Gothenburg supplements Stockholm's airport by funneling traffic into the Swedish heartland. In the mid-1990s, SAS acquired **LIN Airlines (Linje-flyg);** thus, it now has access to small and medium-size airports throughout Sweden, including such remote but scenic outposts as Kiruna in Swedish Lapland. Among the larger Swedish cities serviced by SAS are Malmö, capital of Sweden's château country; Karlstad, center of the verdant and folklore-rich district of Värmland; and Kalmar, a good base for exploring the glassworks district.

During the summer, SAS offers a number of promotional "minifares," which enable one to travel round-trip between two destinations for just slightly more than the price of a conventional one-way ticket on the same route. Children 11 and under travel free during the summer, and up to two children 12 to 17 can travel with a parent at significantly reduced rates. Airfares tend to be most reduced during July, with promotions almost as attractive during most of June and August. A minimum 3-night stopover at the destination is required for these

minifares, and it must include a Friday or a Saturday night. When buying your tickets, always ask the airline or travel agency about special promotions and corresponding restrictions.

Those under 26 can take advantage of SAS's special **standby fares,** and seniors over 65 can apply for additional discounts, depending on the destination.

WITHIN SCANDINAVIA The best way to get around the whole of Scandinavia is to take advantage of the air passes that apply to the entire region or, if you're traveling extensively in Europe, to use the special European passes. The vast distances of Scandinavia encourage air travel between some of its most far-flung points. One of the most worthwhile promotions is SAS's **Visit Scandinavia Airpass.** This pass, available only to travelers who fly SAS across the Atlantic, includes up to eight coupons, each of which is valid for any SAS flight within or between Denmark, Norway, and Sweden. Each coupon costs 69€ ($80), a price that's especially appealing when you consider that an economy-class ticket between Copenhagen and Stockholm can cost as much as $250 each way. The pass is especially valuable if you plan to travel to the far northern frontiers of Sweden; in that case, the savings over the price of a regular economy-class ticket may be substantial. For information on purchasing the pass, call **SAS** (*C* **800/221-2350**).

BY TRAIN

The Swedish word for train is *tåg,* and the national system is the Statens Järn-vägar, the Swedish State Railways.

Swedish trains follow tight schedules. Trains leave Malmö, Helsingborg, and Gothenburg for Stockholm every hour throughout the day, Monday through Friday. Trains depart every hour, or every other hour, to and from most big Swedish towns. On *expresståg* runs, seats must be reserved.

Children under 12 travel free when accompanied by an adult, and those up to age 18 are eligible for discounts.

BY BUS

Rail lines cover only some of Sweden's vast distances. Where the train tracks end, buses usually serve as the link to remote villages. Buses usually are equipped with toilets, adjustable seats, reading lights, and a telephone. Fares depend on the distance traveled; for example, the one-way fare for the 525km (326-mile) trip from Stockholm to Gothenburg is 260SEK ($34) Monday to Thursday, 370SEK ($48) Friday to Sunday. **Swebus** (*C* **036/ 290-80-00;** www.swebusexpress.se), the country's largest bus company, provides information at the bus or railway stations in most cities. For travelers who don't buy a special rail pass (such as Eurail or ScanRail), bus travel can sometimes be cheaper than traveling the same distances by rail. It's a lot less convenient, however—except in the far north, where there isn't any alternative.

BY CAR FERRY

Considering that Sweden has some 100,000 lakes and one of the world's longest coastlines, ferries play a surprisingly small part in the transportation network.

After the car ferry crossings from northern Germany and Denmark, the most popular route is from the mainland to the island of Gotland, in the Baltic. Service is available from Oskar-shamn and Nynäshamn (call *C* **0771/ 22-33-00,** Destination Gotland, for more information). The famous "white boats" of the Waxholm Steamship Company (*C* **08/679-58-30;** www. waxholmsbolaget.se) also serve many destinations in the Stockholm archipelago.

BY CAR

Sweden maintains an excellent network of roads and highways, particularly in the southern provinces and in the central lake district. Major highways in the far north are kept clear of snow by heavy equipment that's in place virtually year-round. If you rent a car at any bona-fide rental agency, you'll be given the appropriate legal documents, including proof of adequate insurance (in the form of a "Green Card") as specified by your car rental agreement. Current driver's licenses from Canada, the United Kingdom, New Zealand, Australia, and the United States are acceptable in Sweden.

RENTALS The major U.S.-based car rental firms are represented throughout Sweden, both at airports and in urban centers. The companies' rates are aggressively competitive, although promotional sales will favor one company over the others from time to time. Prior to your departure from North America, it will be advantageous to phone around to find the lowest available rates. Membership in AAA or another auto club may enable you to get a moderate discount. Be aware that you may avoid a supplemental airport tax by picking your car up at a central location rather than at the airport.

Avis (*C* **800/331-1212;** www.avis. com) offers a wide variety of cars. If you pay before you leave North America, the least expensive, a Ford Ka, rents for around $179 a week. Avis's most expensive car, a Swedish-made Saab 905, goes for around $476 a week.

If you pay before your departure from the United States, **Hertz** (© **800/ 654-3131;** www.hertz.com) offers a Ford Focus for $277 a week.

An auto supplier that might not automatically have come to mind is **Kemwel** (© **800/678-0678;** www. kemwel.com), an auto rental broker that accumulates into one database the availability of rental cars in markets across Europe, including Sweden. Originally established in 1908, and now operating in close conjunction with its sister company, **Auto Europe** (© **800/223-5555;** www.autoeurope. com), it offers convenient and prepaid access to thousands of cars from a variety of reputable car rental outfits throughout Europe, sometimes at rates a bit more favorable than those you might have gotten if you had gone through the hassle of contacting those companies directly. Car rentals are prereserved and prepaid, in dollars, prior to your departure for Europe, thereby avoiding the confusion about unfavorable currency conversions and government tax add-ons that you might have discovered after your return home. You're given the option at the time of your booking whether you want to include collision damage and other forms of insurance. Most car rentals can be picked up at either the airport or in the downtown offices of cities throughout Sweden, and there's usually no penalty for one-way rentals.

15 Suggested Itineraries

If You Have 1 Week

Day 1   Settle into Stockholm and relieve your jet lag.

Days 2 and 3   Explore Stockholm's attractions, including the raised royal flagship *Vasa*. One afternoon should be reserved for a boat trip through the archipelago and another for exploring Drottningholm Palace, on an island in Lake Mälaren.

Day 4   Take a day trip north to Sweden's oldest town, Sigtuna, on the shores of Lake Mälaren, and to the nearby 17th-century Skokloster Castle, which houses one of the most interesting baroque museums in Europe. Then it's on to the university city of Uppsala, and also to the neighboring Gamla Uppsala ("Old Uppsala") to see Viking burial mounds.

Day 5   Begin a fast 3-day excursion through the most interesting folkloric provinces of Sweden: Dalarna and Värmland. Arrive first at the mining town of Falun to visit the Falun Copper Mine and the home of Carl Larsson, the famous Swedish painter. Spend the night here or in one of the smaller resort towns such as Tällberg, Rättvik, Mora, or Leksand.

Day 6   Visit the Lake Siljan towns just mentioned. This blue glacial lake, ringed by lush forests, is one of the most beautiful in Europe. Take a boat tour leaving from Rättvik. On the outskirts of town you can visit Gammelgården, an old farmstead, for a glimpse into the past; stay overnight again in one of the lakeside villages or towns.

Day 7   From Falun, Route 60 heads south to Karlstad. You'll pass through the heart of Selma Lagerlöuf country (Sweden's most famous novelist). Have lunch at Filipstad, the birthplace of John Ericsson, who designed the ironclad-ship *Monitor* during the U.S. Civil War. Spend the night in Karlstad.

If You Have 2 Weeks

Days 1–7 Spend the first week as described above. But instead of cutting your trip short in Karlstad, extend it another night and then use the following itinerary.

Day 8 Spend another night in Karlstad; explore its attractions and branch out into its environs, including Rottneros Manor.

Day 9 In the morning, head south along the eastern shore of Lake Vänern. After lunch in charming lakeside Lidköping, head for Gothenburg, Sweden's second-largest city.

Day 10 Explore Gothenburg and make a side trip to such places as Kungälv or Marstrand, a former royal resort.

Days 11–13 From Gothenburg, take the Goüta Canal excursion, a distance of 560km (347 miles) to Stockholm. As you pass through its 58 locks, you'll have a chance to see the heartland of Sweden.

Day 14 Arrive in Stockholm and prepare for your return flight.

If You Have 3 Weeks

Days 1–14 In addition to the 2-week itinerary outlined above,

you may want to explore Sweden's southern region.

Days 15 and 16 Head south (by air or ferry) to Sweden's largest island, Gotland, whose capital is Visby. Spend the next day exploring the island's attractions.

Day 17 Return to the mainland and continue south to the old city of Kalmar, where you can explore Kalmar Castle and other attractions.

Day 18 Visit the glassworks district, which is centered at Växjoü. Within less than an hour's drive from Växjoü are several glassworks, including Orrefors and Kosta Boda, both of which offer guided tours. You can purchase "seconds" in their workshops.

Days 19–21 Skåne, Sweden's southernmost region, is often called the "château district." Malmö, Sweden's third-largest city, makes an ideal base because of its many attractions. The university city of Lund, northeast of Malmö, also is a good bet, and Ystad is a favorite stop on the southern coastline. From Helsingborg, north of Malmö, you can cross into Denmark and see Hamlet's Castle.

16 Recommended Books

ART & ARCHITECTURE The most comprehensive survey of Swedish art is found in *A History of Swedish Art,* by Mereth Lindgren (Signum i Lung), published in 1987. For architecture buffs, *Sweden: 20th-Century* (Prestel Publishing), was published in 1998, so it's current almost to the dawn of the 21st century. You can see the emergence of Swedish modern in this opus.

HISTORY & MYTHOLOGY *The Early Vasas: A History of Sweden, 1523–1611,* by Michael Roberts (CUP), covers one of the most dra-

matic and action-filled eras in Sweden's long history.

Scandinavian Folk & Fairy Tales, edited by Claire Booss (Avenel), is an extraordinary collection filled with elves, dwarfs, trolls, goblins, and other spirits of the house and barnyard.

BIOGRAPHY *Sweden in North America (1638–1988),* by Sten Carlsson (Streiffert & Co.), follows the lives of some of the 2% of the North American population that has some sort of Swedish background—from Greta Garbo to Charles Lindbergh.

Alfred Nobel and the Nobel Prizes, by Nils K. Ståhle (Swedish Institute), traces the life of the 19th-century Swedish industrialist and creator of the coveted awards that bear his name.

Garbo: Her Story, by Antoni Gronowicz (Simon & Schuster), is a controversial, unauthorized memoir based on a long and intimate friendship; it goes beyond the fabulous face, with many candid details of this most reluctant of movie legends.

LITERATURE & THEATER *A History of Swedish Literature,* by Ingemar Algulin (Swedish Institute), is the best overview on the subject—from the runic inscriptions of the Viking age up to modern fiction.

The Story of Gösta Berling, by Selma Lagerlöf (in various international editions), is the acclaimed work—originally published in 1891—that Garbo filmed.

Three Plays: Father, Miss Julie, Easter, by August Strindberg (Penguin), provides an insight into the world of this strange Swedish genius who wrote a number of highly arresting dramas, of which these are some of the best known.

FILM *Ingmar Bergman: The Cinema as Mistress,* by Philip Mosley (Marion Boyards), is a critical study of Bergman's *oeuvre* dating from his earliest work as a writer/director in the late 1940s up to *Autumn Sonata.*

Swedish Cinema, from Ingeborg Holm to Fanny and Alexander, by Peter Cowie (Swedish Institute), covers the complete history of Swedish films, from the emergence of the silent era, to the rise of Ingmar Bergman, up to the most recent wave.

PIPPI LONGSTOCKING TALES The world was saddened to learn of the death in 2002 of Astrid Lindgren, the Swedish writer of the Pippi Longstocking tales, who died at the age of 94 at her home in Stockholm. One of the world's most widely translated authors, Lindgren horrified parents but captivated millions of children around the globe with her whimsical, rollicking stories about a carrot-haired *enfant terrible.* In 1999 she was voted the most popular Swede of the century, having produced more than 70 books for young people. The best known is *Pippi Longstocking* (Seafarer Book), first published in 1945.

FAST FACTS: Sweden

Area Code The international country code for Sweden is **46.** The local city (area) codes are given for all phone numbers in the Sweden chapters.

Business Hours Generally, **banks** are open Monday through Friday from 9:30am to 3pm. In some larger cities, banks extend their hours, usually on Thursday or Friday, until 5:30 or 6pm. Most **offices** are open Monday through Friday from 8:30 or 9am to 5pm (sometimes to 3 or 4pm in the summer); on Saturday, offices and factories are closed, or open for only a half-day. Most **stores and shops** are open Monday through Friday between 9:30am and 6pm, and Saturday from 9:30am to somewhere between 1 and 4pm. Once a week, usually on Monday or Friday, some of the larger stores are open from 9:30am to 7pm (July–Aug to 6pm).

Camera & Film Cameras (especially the famed Hasselblad), film, projectors, and enlarging equipment are good values in Sweden. Practically all the world's brands are found here. Photographic shops give excellent service, often developing and printing in 1 day.

Dentists For emergency dental services, ask your hotel or host for the location of the nearest dentist. Nearly all dentists in Sweden speak English.

Doctors Hotel desks usually can refer you to a local doctor, nearly all of whom speak English. If you need emergency treatment, your hotel also should be able to direct you to the nearest facility. In case of an accident or injury away from the hotel, call the nearest police station.

Drug Laws Sweden imposes severe penalties for the possession, use, purchase, sale, or manufacture of illegal drugs ("illegal" is defined much like in the U.S.). Penalties are often (but not always) based on quantity. Possession of a small amount of drugs, either hard or soft, can lead to a heavy fine and deportation. Possession of a large amount of drugs can entail imprisonment from 3 months to 15 years, depending on the circumstances and the presiding judge.

Drugstores Called *apotek* in Swedish, drugstores generally are open Monday through Friday from 9am to 6pm and Saturday from 9am to 1pm. In larger cities, one drugstore in every neighborhood stays open until 7pm. All drugstores post a list of the names and addresses of these stores (called *nattapotek*) in their windows.

Electricity In Sweden, the electricity is 220 volts AC (50 cycles). To operate North American hair dryers and other electrical appliances, you'll need an electrical transformer (sometimes erroneously called a converter) and plugs that fit the two-pin round continental electrical outlets that are standard in Sweden. Transformers can be bought at hardware stores. Before using any American-made appliance, always ask about it at your hotel desk.

Embassies & Consulates All embassies are in Stockholm. The Embassy of the **United States** is at Daj Hammarskjölds Väg 31, S-115 89 Stockholm (© 08/783-53-00); **United Kingdom,** Skarpoügatan 6-8, S-115 93 Stockholm (© 08/671-30-00); **Canada,** Tegelbacken 4, S-103 23 Stockholm (© 08/453-30-00); and **Australia,** Sergels Torg 12, S-103 86 Stockholm (© 08/613-29-00). **New Zealand** does not maintain an embassy in Sweden.

Emergencies Call © 90-000 from anywhere in Sweden if you need an ambulance, the police, or the fire department *(brandlarm)*.

Language The national language is Swedish, a Germanic tongue, and many regional dialects exist. Some minority groups speak Norwegian and Finnish. English is a required course of study in school and is commonly spoken, even in the hinterlands, especially among young people.

Liquor Laws Most restaurants, pubs, and bars in Sweden are licensed to serve liquor, wine, and beer. Some places are licensed only for wine and beer. Purchases of wine, liquor, and imported beer are available only through the government-controlled monopoly *Systembolaget*. Branch stores, spread throughout the country, are usually open Monday through Friday from 9am to 6pm. The minimum age for buying alcoholic beverages in Sweden is 21.

Mail Post offices in Sweden are usually open Monday through Friday from 9am to 6pm and Saturday from 9am to noon. Sending a postcard to North America costs 5.50SEK (70¢) by surface mail, 10SEK ($1.30) by airmail. Letters weighing not more than 20 grams (⅞₀ oz.) cost the same.

Mailboxes can easily be recognized—they carry a yellow post horn on a blue background. You can buy stamps in most tobacco shops and stationers.

Maps Many tourist offices supply routine maps of their districts free of charge, and you also can contact one of the Swedish automobile clubs. Bookstores throughout Sweden also sell detailed maps of the country and of such major cities as Gothenburg and Stockholm. The most reliable country maps are published by Hallweg. The best and most detailed city maps are those issued by Falk, which have a particularly good and properly indexed map to Stockholm.

Newspapers & Magazines In big cities such as Stockholm and Gothenburg, English-language newspapers, including the latest editions of the *International Herald Tribune* and *USA Today,* and *The London Times* are usually available. At kiosks or newsstands in major cities, you also can purchase the European editions of *Time* and *Newsweek.*

Passports **For Residents of the United States:** Whether you're applying in person or by mail, you can download passport applications from the U.S. State Department website at **http://travel.state.gov.** For general information, call the **National Passport Agency** (© 202/647-0518). To find your regional passport office, either check the U.S. State Department website or call the **National Passport Information Center** (© 877/487-2778, toll-free) for automated information.

For Residents of Canada: Passport applications are available at travel agencies throughout Canada or from the central **Passport Office, Department of Foreign Affairs** and International Trade, Ottawa, ON K1A 0G3 (© 800/567-6868; www.ppt.gc.ca).

For Residents of the United Kingdom: To pick up an application for a standard 10-year passport (5-year passport for children under 16), visit your nearest passport office, major post office, or travel agency, or contact the **United Kingdom Passport Service** at © 0870/521-0410 or search its website at www.ukpa.gov.uk.

For Residents of Ireland: You can apply for a 10-year passport at the **Passport Office,** Setanta Centre, Molesworth Street, Dublin 2 (© 01/671-1633; www.irlgov.ie/iveagh). Those under age 18 and over 65 must apply for a €25 5-year passport. You can also apply at 1A South Mall, Cork (© 021/272-525), or at most main post offices.

For Residents of Australia: You can pick up an application from your local post office or any branch of Passports Australia, but you must schedule an interview at the passport office to present your application materials. Call the **Australian Passport Information Service** at © 131-232, or visit the government website at www.passports.gov.au.

For Residents of New Zealand: You can pick up a passport application at any New Zealand Passports Office or download it from their website. Contact the **Passports Office** at © 0800/225-050 in New Zealand or 04/474-8100, or log on to www.passports.govt.nz.

Police In an emergency, dial © 90-000 anywhere in the country.

Radio & TV In summer, Radio Stockholm broadcasts a special program for English-speaking tourists, "T-T-T-Tourist Time," on 103.3 MHz (FM) from 6 to 7pm daily. Swedish radio transmits P1 on 92.4 MHz (FM) and P2 on 96.2

MHz (FM) in the Stockholm area. P3 is transmitted on 103.3 MHz (102.9 MHz in southern Stockholm), a wavelength shared by Radio Stockholm and local programs.

The two most important TV channels, STV1 and STV2, are nonprofit. Three major privately operated stations—Channel 4, TV3, and TV5—operate, as well as several minor stations.

Restrooms The word for toilet in Swedish is *toalett,* and public facilities are found in department stores, rail and air terminals, and subway (T-bana) stations. DAMER means women and HERRAR means men. Sometimes the sign is abbreviated to D or H, and often the toilet is marked WC. Most toilets are free, although a few have attendants to offer towels and soap. In an emergency, you can use the toilets in most hotels and restaurants, although, in principle, they're reserved for guests.

Shoe Repairs Shoe-repair shops rarely accommodate you while you wait. If all you need is a new heel, look for something called *klackbar* in the stores or shoe departments of department stores. They'll make repairs while you wait.

Taxes Sweden imposes a "value-added tax," called MOMS, on most goods and services. Visitors from North America can beat the tax, however, by shopping in one of the 15,000 stores with the yellow-and-blue tax-free shopping sign. To get a refund, your total purchase must cost a minimum of 200SEK ($26). Tax refunds range from 14% to 18%, depending on the amount purchased. MOMS begins at 19% on food items but is 25% for most goods and services. The tax is part of the purchase price, but you can get a tax-refund voucher before you leave the store. When you leave Sweden, take the voucher to a tax-free Customs desk at the airport or train station you're leaving from. They will give you your MOMS refund (minus a small service charge) before you continue on to your next non-Swedish destination. Two requirements: You cannot use your purchase in Sweden, and it must be taken out of the country within 1 month after purchase. For more information, call **Global Refunds** at ✆ **0410/48606.**

Telephone, Telex & Fax Information on these facilities in Stockholm is found in "Fast Facts: Stockholm," in chapter 3. The same rules apply to calling from public phones elsewhere in the country. Avoid placing long-distance calls from your hotel, where the charge may be doubled or tripled on your final bill.

Time Sweden is on central European time—Greenwich mean time plus 1 hour, or Eastern Standard Time plus 6 hours. The clocks are advanced 1 hour in summer.

Tipping Hotels include a 15% service charge in your bill. Restaurants add 13% to 15% to your tab. Taxi drivers are entitled to 8% of the fare, and cloakroom attendants usually get 6SEK (80¢).

Water The water is safe to drink all over Sweden. However, don't drink water from lakes, rivers, or streams, regardless of how clean it appears.

3

Settling into Stockholm

Stockholm, a city of 1.8 million people, is built on 14 islands in Lake Mälaren, which marks the beginning of an archipelago of 24,000 islands, skerries, and islets stretching all the way to the Baltic Sea. A city of bridges and islands, towers and steeples, cobblestone squares and broad boulevards, Renaissance splendor and steel-and-glass skyscrapers, Stockholm also has access to nature just a short distance away. You can even go fishing in the downtown waterways, thanks to a long-standing decree signed by Queen Christina.

Although the city was founded more than 7 centuries ago, it did not become the official capital of Sweden until the mid–17th century. While today it reigns over a modern welfare state, and the medieval walls of the Old Town (Gamla Stan) no longer remain, the old winding streets have been preserved.

1 Orientation

ARRIVING

BY PLANE   You'll arrive at **Stockholm Arlanda Airport** (© **08/797-61-00** for information on flights), about 45km (28 miles) north of the city on the E4 highway. A long, covered walkway connects the international and domestic terminals.

The fastest and the cheapest way to go from the airport to the Central Station within Stockholm is on the **Arlanda Express** train, which takes only 20 minutes and is covered by the Eurailpass. This high-speed line is the finest option for the rail traveler. Trains run every 15 minutes daily from 5am to midnight. If you don't have a rail pass, the cost of a one-way ticket is 180SEK ($23) for adults and 90SEK ($12) for seniors and students (those under 8 ride free). For more information, call © **020/22-22-24.**

A bus outside the terminal building will also take you to the **City Terminal,** on Klarabergsviadukten, about a 40-minute trip, for 89SEK ($12).

A taxi to or from the airport is expensive, costing 400SEK to 500SEK ($52–$65) or more. (See "Getting Around," later in this chapter, for the name of a reputable taxi company.)

BY TRAIN   Trains arrive at Stockholm's **Centralstationen (Central Station;** © **07/717-57-575** in Sweden) on Vasagatan, in the city center where connections can be made to Stockholm's subway, the T-bana. Follow the TUNNELBANA sign.

Only large towns and cities can be reached by rail from Stockholm's Centralstationen.

BY BUS   Buses also arrive at the Centralstationen city terminal, and from here you can catch the T-bana (subway) to your final Stockholm destination. For bus

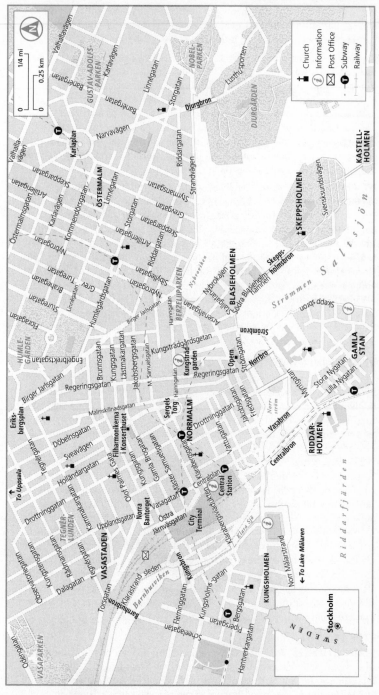

information or reservations, check with the bus system's **ticket offices** at the station (✆ **08/440-85-70**). Offices in the station labeled BUS STOP sell bus tickets. For travel beyond Sweden, call **Euroline** (✆ **08/762-5960**).

BY CAR   Getting into Stockholm by car is relatively easy because the major national expressway from the south, E4, joins with the national expressway, E3, coming in from the west, and leads right into the heart of the city. Stay on the highway until you see the turnoff for Central Stockholm (or Centrum).

Parking in Stockholm is extremely difficult unless your hotel has a garage. Call your hotel in advance and find out what the parking situation is, as most hotels do not offer parking. However, if you're driving into the city, you can often park long enough to unload your luggage; a member of the hotel staff will then direct you to the nearest parking garage.

BY FERRY   Large ships, including those of the **Silja Line,** Kungsgatan 2 (✆ **08/22-21-40**), and the **Viking Line,** Centralstationen (✆ **08/452-40-00**), arrive at specially constructed berths jutting seaward from a point near the junction of Södermalm and Gamla Stan. This neighborhood is called Stadsgården, and the avenue that runs along the adjacent waterfront is known as Stadsgårdshamnen. The nearest T-bana stop is Slussen, a 3-minute walk from the Old Town. Holders of a valid Eurailpass can ride the Silja ferries to Helsinki and Turku at a reduced rate.

Other ferries arrive from Gotland (whose capital is Visby), but these boats dock at Nynäshamn, south of Stockholm. Take a Nynäshamn-bound bus from the Central Station in Stockholm or the SL commuter train to reach the ferry terminal at Nynäshamn.

VISITOR INFORMATION

The **Tourist Center,** Sweden House, Hamngatan 27, off Kungsträdgården (Box 7542), S-103 93 Stockholm (✆ **08/789-24-00** or 08/789-24-90), is open June to August Monday to Friday from 9am to 7pm, Saturday 9am to 5pm, and Sunday 10am to 4pm; September to May Monday to Friday from 9am to 6pm, and Saturday and Sunday from 10am to 4pm. Maps and other free materials are available.

The largest organization of its kind in all of Sweden is the **Kulturhuset,** Sergels Torg 3 (✆ **08/508-31-400**). It was built in 1974 by the city of Stockholm as a showcase for Swedish and international art and theater. There are no permanent exhibits; instead, the various spaces inside are allocated to a changing array of paintings, sculpture, photographs, and live performance groups. Kulturhuset also serves as the focal point for information about other cultural activities and organizations throughout Sweden and the rest of Europe. Inside are a snack bar, a library (which has newspapers in several languages), a reading room, a collection of recordings, and a somewhat bureaucratic openness to new art forms. Admission is 50SEK ($6.50) for adults. Those 18 and under are admitted free. Open Tuesday to Friday 11am to 7pm, Saturday and Sunday 11am to 5pm.

CITY LAYOUT

MAIN STREETS & ARTERIES   Stockholm's major streets—**Kungsgatan** (the main shopping street), **Birger Jarlsgatan,** and **Strandvägen** (which leads to Djurgården)—are on Norrmalm (north of the Old Town). **Stureplan,** which lies at the junction of the major avenues Kungsgatan and Birger Jarlsgatan, is the commercial hub of the city.

About 4 blocks east of Stureplan rises **Hötorget City,** a landmark of modern urban planning, which includes five 18-story skyscrapers. Its main traffic-free artery is **Sergelgatan,** a 3-block shopper's promenade that eventually leads to the modern sculptures at the center of Sergels Torg.

About 9 blocks south of Stureplan, at **Gustav Adolfs Torg,** are both the Royal Dramatic Theater and the Royal Opera House.

A block east of the flaming torches of the opera house is the verdant north-to-south stretch of **Kungsträdgården**—part avenue, part public park—which serves as a popular gathering place for students and a resting spot for shoppers.

Three blocks to the southeast, on a famous promontory, are the landmark Grand Hotel and the National Museum.

Most visitors to Stockholm arrive at either the SAS Airport Bus Terminal, the Central Station, or Stockholm's Central (Public) Bus Station. Each of these is in the heart of the city, on the harbor front, about 7 blocks due west of the opera house. **Kungsholmen (King's Island)** lies across a narrow canal from the rest of the city, a short walk west from the Central Station. It's visited chiefly by those who want to tour Stockholm's elegant Stadshuset (City Hall).

South of **Gamla Stan (Old Town),** and separated from it by a narrow but much-navigated stretch of water, is **Södermalm,** the southern district of Stockholm. Quieter than its northern counterpart, it's an important residential area with a distinctive flavor of its own.

To the east of Gamla Stan, on a large and forested island completely surrounded by the complicated waterways of Stockholm, is **Djurgården (Deer Park).** The summer pleasure ground of Stockholm is the site of many of its most popular attractions: the open-air museums of Skansen, the *Vasa* man-of-war, Gröna Lund's Tivoli, the Waldemarsudde estate of the "painting prince" Eugen, and the Nordic Museum.

FINDING AN ADDRESS   All even numbers are on one side of the street and all odd numbers are on the opposite side. Buildings are listed in numerical order but often have an A, B, or C after the number. In the very center of town, numbered addresses start from Sergels Torg.

MAPS   Free maps of Stockholm are available at the tourist office, but if you want to explore the narrow old streets of Gamla Stan, you'll need a more detailed map. The best, published by **Falk,** is a pocket-size map with a street index that can be opened and folded like a wallet. It's sold at most newsstands in central Stockholm and at major bookstores, including **Akademibokhandeln,** Mäster Samuelsgatan 32 (© **08/613-61-00**).

NEIGHBORHOODS IN BRIEF

As you'd expect of a city spread across 14 major islands in an archipelago, there are many neighborhoods, but those of concern to the average visitor lie in central Stockholm.

Gamla Stan (Old Town)   The "cradle" of Stockholm, Gamla Stan lies at the entrance to Lake Mälaren on the Baltic. Its oldest city wall dates from the 13th century. The Old Town, along with the *Vasa*, is the most popular attraction in Stockholm. This is our favorite place to spend our nights in Stockholm. The hotels here are in general the most evocative of 18th-century Stockholm, built in romantic architectural styles. The downside of this area is that there are few hotels, and they tend to be expensive; there are, however, dozens of restaurants. Gamla Stan's major shopping street is Västerlånggatan, but many artisans' galleries and antiques stores abound on its small lanes. Its main square, and the heart of the ancient city, is Stortorget.

Norrmalm North of Gamla Stan, what was once a city suburb is now the cultural and commercial heart of modern Stockholm. Chances are, your hotel will be in this district, as the area is generously endowed with hotels in all price ranges; it's also the most convenient location for most visits, as it encompasses the City Terminal and the Central Station. Hotels here are not the most romantic in town, but they're generally modern, up-to-date, and well run.

The most famous park in Stockholm, Kungsträdgården (King's Garden), also is in Norrmalm. In summer, this park is a major rendezvous point. Norrmalm also embraces the important squares of Sergels Torg and Hötorget, the latter a modern shopping complex. Norrmalm's major pedestrian shopping street is Drottninggatan, which starts at the bridge to the Old Town.

Vasastaden As Norrmalm expanded northward, the new district of Vasastaden was created. It's split by a trio of main arteries: St. Eriksgatan, Sveavägen, and Odengatan. The area around St. Eriksplan is called "the Off-Broadway of Stockholm" because it has so many theaters. Increasingly, this district has attracted fashionable restaurants and bars and has become a popular residential area for young Stockholmers who work in fields such as journalism, television, and advertising.

Vasastaden is slightly more removed from the scene of the action, but it's still a good bet for hotels. In New York City terms, Norrmalm would be like staying in the Times Square area, whereas Vasastaden would be equivalent to staying on the Upper East Side. Hotels in Vasastaden come in a wide range of price categories.

Kungsholmen Once known as "Grey Friars Farm," Kungsholmen (King's Island), to the west of Gamla Stan, is the site of City Hall. Established by Charles XI in the 17th century as a zone for industry and artisans, the island now has been gentrified. One of its major arteries is Fleminggatan. Along Norrmälarstand, old Baltic cutters tie up to the banks. Stockholm's newspapers have their headquarters at Marieberg on the southwestern tip of the island.

Södermalm South of Gamla Stan, Södermalm (where Greta Garbo was born) is the largest and most populated district of Stockholm. Once synonymous with poverty, today this working-class area is becoming more fashionable, especially with artists, writers, and young people. If you don't come here to stay in one of the moderately priced hotels or to dine in one of its restaurants, you might want to take the Katarina elevator, at Södermalmstorg, Slussen, for a good view of Stockholm and its harbor. Admission is 10SEK ($1.30), free for ages 6 and under.

Östermalm In central Stockholm, east of Birger Jarlsgatan, the main artery, lies Östermalm. In the Middle Ages, the royal family used to keep its horses, and even its armies, here. Today it's the site of the Army Museum. There are wide, straight streets, and it also is home to one of the city's biggest parks, Humlegården, dating from the 17th century.

This is another area of Stockholm that's a hotel district. Östermalm doesn't have quite the convenience of Norrmalm and Vasastaden, but it still is not so far removed from the action as to be called inconvenient. In summer, when visitors from all over the world are in town, this is a good place to hunt for a room. Because Norrmalm and Vasastaden are located close to the Central Station, hotels in those neighborhoods tend to fill up very quickly.

Djurgården To the east of Gamla Stan (Old Town) is Djurgården (Deer Park), a forested island in a lake that's the summer recreation area of Stockholm. Here you can visit the open-air folk museums of Skansen, the *Vasa* man-of-war, Gröna Lund's Tivoli (Stockholm's own version of the Tivoli), the Waldemarsudde estate and gardens

of the "painting prince" Eugen, and the Nordic Museum. The fastest way to get here is over the bridge at Strandvägen/Narvavägen.

Skeppsholmen On its own little island, and reached by crossing Skeppsholmsbron, a bridge from the Blasieholmen district, Skeppsholmen is like a world apart from the rest of bustling Stockholm. Although it makes for a pleasant stroll, most people visit it to see the exhibits at the Moderna Museet (see chapter 4, "Discovering Stockholm"). Skeppsholmen also is home of *af Chapman,* Sweden's most famous youth hostel, a gallant tall ship that, with its fully rigged masts, is a Stockholm landmark.

2 Getting Around

BY PUBLIC TRANSPORTATION

You can travel throughout Stockholm county by bus, local train, subway (T-bana), and trams, going from Singö in the north to Nynäshamn in the south. The routes are divided into zones, and one ticket is valid for all types of public transportation in the same zone within 1 hour of the time the ticket is stamped.

REGULAR FARES   The basic fare for public transportation (in Stockholm this means subway, tram/streetcar, or bus) requires tickets purchased from the agent in the toll booth on the subway platform, not from a vending machine. Each ticket costs 15SEK ($1.95). To travel within most of urban Stockholm, all the way to the borders of the inner city, requires only two tickets. The maximum ride, to the outermost suburbs, requires five tickets. You can transfer (or double back and return to your starting point) within 1 hour of your departure free of charge.

SPECIAL DISCOUNT TICKETS   Your best transportation bet is to purchase a **tourist season ticket.** A 1-day card, costing 95SEK ($12) for adults and 65SEK ($8.45) for children 7 to 17 and seniors, is valid for 24 hours of unlimited travel by T-bana, bus, and commuter train within Stockholm. It also includes passage on the ferry to Djurgården. Most visitors probably will prefer the 3-day card for 180SEK ($23) for adults and 110SEK ($14) for children 7 to 17 and seniors, valid for 72 hours in both Stockholm and the adjacent county. The 3-day card also is valid for admission to Skansen, Kaknästornet, and Gröna Lund. Kids up to 7 years of age can travel free with an adult. These tickets are available at tourist information offices, in subway stations, and at most news vendors. Call ✆ **08/600-1000** for more information.

Stockholmskortet (Stockholm Card) is a personal discount card that allows unlimited travel by bus, subway, and local trains throughout the city and county of Stockholm (except on airport buses). You can take a sightseeing tour with City Sightseeing, where you can get on and off as often as you please. These tours are available daily from mid-June to mid-August. In addition, the card

Subway Art

In 1950 two women came up with the idea of commissioning artists to decorate the subway stations of Stockholm. Some of the country's finest artists were asked to participate; their work now is displayed in "the longest and deepest art gallery in the world," some 100 stations stretching all the way from the center of Stockholm to the suburbs.

---

enables you to take a boat trip to the Royal Palace of Drottningholm for half-price. Admission to 70 attractions is also included in the package.

You can purchase the card at several places in the city, including the Tourist Center in Sweden House, Hotell Centralen, the Central Station, the tourist information desk in City Hall (in summer), the Kaknäs TV tower, SL-Center Sergels Torg (subway entrance level), and Pressbyrän newsstands. The cards are stamped with the date and time at the first point of usage. A 24-hour card costs 260SEK ($34) for adults and 100SEK ($13) for children 7 to 17 and seniors; a 48-hour card is 390SEK ($51) for adults and 140SEK ($18) for children and seniors; and a 72-hour card is 540SEK ($70) for adults and 190SEK ($25) for children and seniors.

BY T-BANA (SUBWAY)   Before entering the subway, passengers tell the ticket seller the destination, then purchase tickets. Subway entrances are marked with a blue *T* on a white background. For information about schedules, routes, and fares, phone ℂ **08/600-1000.**

BY BUS   Where the subway line ends, the bus begins; therefore, if a subway connection doesn't conveniently cover a particular area of Stockholm, a bus will. The two systems have been coordinated to complement each other. Many visitors use a bus to reach Djurgården (although you can walk) because the T-bana doesn't go there.

BY CAR

If you're driving around the Swedish capital, you'll find several parking garages in the city center as well as on the outskirts. In general, you can park at marked spaces Monday through Friday from 8am to 6pm. Exceptions or rules for specific areas are indicated on signs in the area. At Djurgården, parking is always prohibited, and from April to mid-September it's closed to traffic Friday through Sunday.

BY TAXI

Taxis are expensive—in fact, the most expensive in the world—with the meter starting at 36SEK ($4.70). A short ride can easily cost 100SEK ($13). It costs around 200SEK ($26) to reach most destinations within the city limits. Those that display the sign LEDIG can be hailed, or you can order one by phone. **Taxi Stockholm** (ℂ **08/15-00-00**) is one of the city's larger, more reputable companies.

BY FERRY

Ferries from Skeppsbron on Gamla Stan (near the bridge to Södermalm) will take you to Djurgården if you don't want to walk or go by bus. They leave every 20 minutes Monday through Saturday, and about every 15 minutes on Sunday, from 9am to 6pm, charging 30SEK ($3.90) for adults, seniors, and children 7 to 12; passage is free for children 6 and under.

BY BICYCLE

The best place to go cycling is on Djurgården. You can rent bicycles from **Djurgårdsbrons Skepp o Hoj,** Djurgårdsbron (℡ **08/660-57-57**), for about 250SEK ($33) per day. It's open May through August daily from 9am to 9pm.

FAST FACTS: Stockholm

American Express For local 24-hour customer service, call ℡ **08/429-56-00**.

Area Code The international country code for Sweden is **46**; the city code for Stockholm is **08** (if you're calling Stockholm from abroad, drop the 0). You do not need to dial 8 within Stockholm; only if you're outside the city.

Babysitters Stockholm hotels maintain lists of competent babysitters, nearly all of whom speak English. There is no official agency; rather, it's a word-of-mouth system. Your hotel reception desk can assist you.

Bookstores For a good selection of English-language books, including maps and touring guides, try **Akademibokhandeln,** Mäster Samuelsgatan 32 (℡ **08/613-61-00**), open Monday through Friday from 10am to 7pm, Saturday from 10am to 4pm, and Sunday from noon to 4pm.

Car Rentals See section 14 in chapter 2. In Stockholm, some of the big car rental companies include **Avis,** Ringvägen 90 (℡ **08/644-99-80**), and **Hertz,** Vasagatan 24 (℡ **08/24-07-20**).

Currency Exchange There's a currency exchange office, **Forex,** at the Central Station (℡ **08/411-67-34**), open daily from 7am to 9pm. It's fully approved by both the Bank of Sweden and the Swedish tourist authorities, offers some of the best exchange rates in town, and takes some of the lowest commissions for cashing traveler's checks. Several other offices are scattered throughout the city.

Dentists Emergency dental treatment is offered at **Sct. Eriks Hospital,** Fleminggatan 22 (℡ **08/545-51220**), open daily from 8am to 5pm.

Doctors If you need 24-hour emergency medical care, check with **Medical Care Information** (℡ **08/320-100**). There's also a private clinic, **City Akuten,** at Apelberg Sq. 48, 1st floor (℡ **08/412-29-61**).

Drugstores A pharmacy that remains open 24 hours a day is **C. W. Scheele,** Klarabergsgatan 64 (℡ **08/454-81-00**).

Embassies & Consulates See "Fast Facts: Sweden," in chapter 2.

Emergencies Call ℡ **112** for the police, ambulance service, or the fire department.

Eyeglasses **The Nordiska Kompaniet,** Hamngatan 18–20 (℡ **08/762-80-00**), a leading Stockholm department store, has a registered optician on duty at its ground-floor service center. The optician performs vision tests, stocks a large selection of frames, and makes emergency repairs.

Hospitals Call **Medical Care Information** at ℡ **08/320-100** and an English-speaking operator will inform you of the hospital closest to you 24 hours a day.

Internet Cafe A convenient cybercafe is **Dome House,** Sveavägen 108 (℡ **08/612-61-10**), open daily 11am to 3am, charging 15SEK ($1.95) per hour. An alternative choice is **Internet Café Stockholm,** Krukmakargatan

33b (📞 **08/669-09-99**), open daily 1 to 9pm, charging 20SEK ($2.60) per hour.

Laundry & Dry Cleaning **City Kemtvatt,** Drottningsholmsvägen 9 (📞 **08/654-95-34**), does dry cleaning and also laundry by the kilo for same-day delivery if it's brought in before 10am. It's open Monday through Friday from 7am to 7pm and Saturday from 10am to 2:30pm. Note that the system of coin-operated launderettes is pretty much outmoded in Sweden. The cost for doing laundry is 50SEK ($6.50) per kilo (2.2 lb.). Your clothes will be neatly folded for you as part of the price.

Libraries **The Stockholms Stadsbibliotek,** Sveavägen 73 (📞 **08/508-310-60**), is the biggest municipal library in Sweden, with 2.5 million books (many in English) and audiovisual materials. It also subscribes to 1,500 newspapers and periodicals (again, many in English). Open June 21 to August 15 Monday to Friday 9am to 7pm, Saturday noon to 4pm. Otherwise hours are Monday to Thursday 9am to 9pm, Friday 9am to 7pm, and Saturday and Sunday noon to 4pm.

Lost Property If you've lost something on the train, go to the Lost and Found office in the Central Station, lower concourse (📞 **08/771-315-315**). The police also have such an office at the police station at Bergsgatan 39 (📞 **08/401-07-88**). The Stockholm Transit Company (SL) keeps its recovered articles at the Klaraostra Kyrkogata 6 (📞 **06/6862650**).

Luggage Storage & Lockers Facilities are available at the Central Station on Vasagatan, lower concourse (📞 **08/762-25-95**). Lockers also can be rented at the ferry stations at Värtan and Tegelvikshamnen, at the Viking Line terminal, and at the Central Station.

Photographic Needs Photo shops are plentiful in Stockholm. One of the most centrally located is the **Kodak Image Center,** at Hamngatan 16 (📞 **08/21-40-42**). Open Monday to Friday 10am to 7pm, Saturday 10am to 4pm, and Sunday noon to 4pm.

Police Call 📞 **112** in an emergency.

Post Office The main post office is at Centralstationen 10126 (📞 **08/781-24-25**), open Monday to Friday 7am to 10pm, and Saturday and Sunday 10am to 7pm. If you want to pick up letters while you're abroad, they should be addressed to your name, c/o Post Restante, Post Center, Central Station 11120, Stockholm, Sweden.

Radio & TV Sweden has two TV channels and three national radio stations, plus a local station for Stockholm, broadcasting on 103.3 MHz (FM). Many hotels are equipped to receive English-language TV programs broadcast from England, and many of the more expensive hotels have 24-hour CNN news broadcasts in English.

Restrooms Public facilities are found in the Central Station, in all subway stations, and in department stores, as well as along some of the major streets, parks, and squares. In an emergency, you also can use the toilets in most hotels and restaurants, although generally they're reserved for patrons.

Shoe Repair In the basement of **Nordiska Kompaniet,** Hamngatan 18–20 (📞 **08/762-80-00**), a leading Stockholm department store, there is a shoe repair place, which also may be able to repair broken luggage.

Taxis See "Getting Around," earlier in this chapter.

Telephone, Telex & Fax Instructions in English are posted in public phone boxes, which can be found on street corners. Very few phones in Sweden are coin operated; most require a phone card, which can be purchased at most newspaper stands and tobacco shops. You can send a telegram by phoning ✆ **00-21** anytime.

Post offices throughout Stockholm now offer phone, fax, and telegram services. Of course, most guests ask their hotels to send a fax. All but the smallest boarding houses in Stockholm today have fax services.

Transit Information For information on all services, including buses and subways (T-bana) and suburban trains *(pendeltåg)*, call ✆ **08/600-10-00**. Or, visit the SL Center, on the lower level of Sergels Torg. It provides information about transportation and also sells a map of the city's system, as well as tickets and special discount passes. Open Monday to Friday 7am to 9pm, and Saturday and Sunday 10am to 9pm.

3 Where to Stay

By the standards of many U.S. or Canadian cities, hotels in Stockholm are very expensive. If these high prices make you want to cancel your trip, read on. Dozens of hotels in Stockholm offer reduced rates on weekends all year, and daily from around mid-June to mid-August. For further information, inquire at a travel agency or the tourist center (see "Orientation," earlier in this chapter). In summer it's best to make reservations in advance, just to be on the safe side.

Most of the medium-priced hotels are in Norrmalm, north of the Old Town, and many of the least expensive lodgings are near the Central Station. There are comparably priced inexpensive accommodations within 10 to 20 minutes of the city, easily reached by subway, streetcar, or bus. We'll suggest a few hotels in the Old Town, but these choices are limited and more expensive.

Note: In most cases, a service charge ranging from 10% to 15% is added to the bill, plus the inevitable 21% MOMS (value-added tax). Unless otherwise indicated, all of our recommended accommodations come with a private bathroom.

BOOKING SERVICES   Hotell Centralen, Vasagatan (✆ **08/789-24-56**), on the lower level of the Central Station, is the city's official housing bureau; it can arrange accommodations in hotels, pensions (boarding houses), and youth hostels—but not in private homes. There's a 60SEK ($7.80) service fee. It's open Monday to Friday 9am to 6pm, and Saturday and Sunday noon to 4pm.

The least expensive accommodations in Stockholm are rooms in private homes. The best way to get booked into a private home is by going to the **Hotell Tjänst AB,** Nybrogatan 44 (✆ **08/10-44-37** or 08/10-44-57; fax 08/21-37-16). Here, Mr. Gustavsson and his staff will book you into a private double room, without breakfast, from 600SEK ($78), including the reservation fee. There is a two-night minimum stay requirement. From June 15 to August 15, this agency also can book you into Stockholm's major hotels at a big discount.

Mr. Gustavsson asks that you avail yourself of these bargains only upon your arrival in Stockholm. He's confident of booking you into a room because of his long "secret" list of private addresses; he doesn't answer letters requesting reservations. Hotell Tjänst is open Monday through Friday from 9am to noon and 1 to 5pm. Advance booking is rarely accepted; however, if you're going to arrive

Stockholm Accommodations

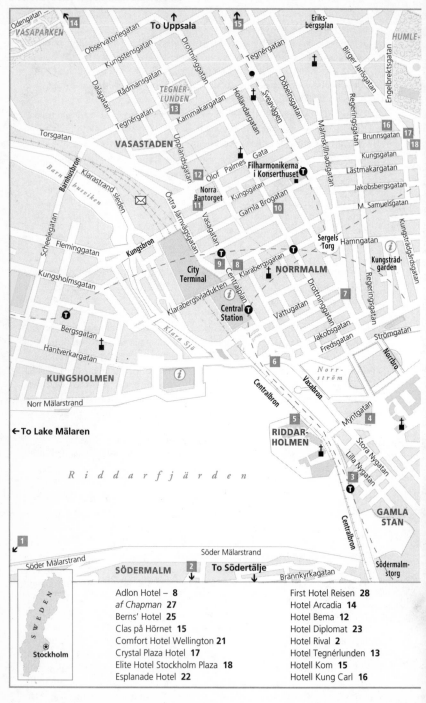

Adlon Hotel – **8**
af Chapman **27**
Berns' Hotel **25**
Clas på Hörnet **15**
Comfort Hotel Wellington **21**
Crystal Plaza Hotel **17**
Elite Hotel Stockholm Plaza **18**
Esplanade Hotel **22**

First Hotel Reisen **28**
Hotel Arcadia **14**
Hotel Bema **12**
Hotel Diplomat **23**
Hotel Rival **2**
Hotel Tegnérlunden **13**
Hotell Kom **15**
Hotell Kung Carl **16**

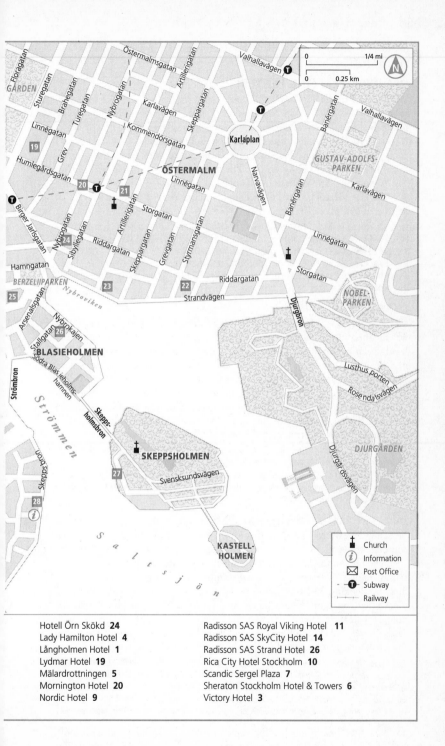

0	1/4 mi
0	0.25 km

Church
Information
Post Office
Subway
Railway

Hotell Örn Skökd **24**
Lady Hamilton Hotel **4**
Långholmen Hotel **1**
Lydmar Hotel **19**
Mälardrottningen **5**
Mornington Hotel **20**
Nordic Hotel **9**

Radisson SAS Royal Viking Hotel **11**
Radisson SAS SkyCity Hotel **14**
Radisson SAS Strand Hotel **26**
Rica City Hotel Stockholm **10**
Scandic Sergel Plaza **7**
Sheraton Stockholm Hotel & Towers **6**
Victory Hotel **3**

in Stockholm on a weekend, when the office is closed, call or fax the office and maybe Mr. Gustavsson will bend the rules.

IN NORRMALM (THE CENTER)
VERY EXPENSIVE

Grand Hotel ★★★ Opposite the Royal Palace, this hotel—a bastion of elite hospitality since 1874—is the finest in Scandinavia. The most recent restoration was in 1996, but its old-world style has always been maintained. Guest rooms come in all shapes and sizes, all elegantly appointed with traditional styling. Some feature an air-cooling system. The bathrooms are decorated with Italian marble and tiles, and have heated floors and tub/showers. The priciest rooms overlook the water. The hotel's ballroom is an exact copy of Louis XIV's Hall of Mirrors at Versailles.

Södra Blasieholmshamnen 8, S-103 27 Stockholm. © **800/223-5652** in the U.S. and Canada, or 08/679-35-00. Fax 08/611-86-86. www.grandhotel.se. 310 units. 3,100SEK–4,400SEK ($403–$572) double; 5,500SEK–8,200SEK ($715–$1,066) suite. Rates include breakfast. AE, DC, MC, V. Parking 390SEK ($51). T-bana: Kungsträdgården. Bus: 46, 55, 62, or 76. **Amenities:** 2 restaurants; bar; fitness center; sauna; 24-hr. room service; laundry service; dry cleaning; nonsmoking rooms; rooms for those w/limited mobility. *In room:* TV, data-port, minibar, hair dryer, safe.

EXPENSIVE

Berns Hotel ★★ During its 19th-century heyday, beginning in 1863, this was the most elegant hotel in Sweden, with an ornate Gilded Age interior that was the setting for many a legendary rendezvous. In 1989, following years of neglect, it was rebuilt in the original style, and the restaurant facilities were upgraded. Although the dining and drinking areas are usually crowded with club kids and bar patrons, the guest rooms are soundproof and comfortably isolated from the activity downstairs. Each room offers a good-size bathroom sheathed in Italian marble and neatly maintained shower units. The Red Room is the setting and namesake of Strindberg's novel *Röda Rummet*.

Näckströmsgatan 8, S-111 47 Stockholm. © **08/566-32-200.** Fax 08/566-32-201. www.berns.se. 65 units. 1,650SEK–3,900SEK ($215–$507) double; 2,950SEK–4,700SEK ($384–$611) suite. Rates include breakfast. AE, DC, MC, V. Parking 375SEK ($49). T-bana: Östermalmstorg. **Amenities:** 2 restaurants; 4 bars; sauna; 24-hr. room service; babysitting; laundry service; dry cleaning; nonsmoking rooms; rooms for those w/limited mobility. *In room:* TV, minibar, hair dryer.

Hotel Diplomat ★ Well-managed, discreet, and solid, this hotel is a dignified and conservative operation that knows how to handle business clients and corporate conventions. Built in 1911, it retains hints of its original Art Nouveau styling. Public areas are more streamlined. The individually conceived guest rooms are decorated with well-crafted furniture. Many rooms contain bay windows overlooking the harbor; most of the less expensive accommodations face a quiet inner courtyard. Rooms range in size from cramped singles to spacious doubles with sitting areas. All have good beds and average-size bathrooms, with tiled vanities, bidets, and both tubs and hand-held showers. At least once, take the circular stairs for views of the hotel's antique stained-glass windows.

Strandvagen 7C, Östermalm, S-104-40 Stockholm. © **08/459-68-00.** Fax 08/459-68-20. www.diplomat hotel.com. 128 units. Mon–Thurs 1,895SEK–3,045SEK ($246–$396) double; Fri–Sun 1,795SEK–2,245SEK ($233–$292) double; from 3,955SEK ($514) suite. AE, DC, MC, V. Rates include breakfast on weekends. Parking 390SEK ($51). T-bana: Storeplan. **Amenities:** Restaurant; 2 bars; 24-hr. room service; babysitting; laundry service; dry cleaning; nonsmoking rooms; rooms for those w/limited mobility. *In room:* TV, minibar, hair dryer.

Lydmar Hotel ★ Opposite the garden of the King's Library, in what looks like an office building, the Lydmar opened in 1930 (as the Eden Terrace). The guest rooms are cozy and traditionally furnished, and come in many shapes and sizes. Although the rooms aren't large, they are exceptionally well maintained. The bathrooms are well appointed and contain tub/showers. The hotel has a large dining room and a rooftop terrace where guests can enjoy drinks in the summer. In recent years, its Matsalen restaurant has become ever so chic.

Sturegatan 10, S-114 36 Stockholm. ℭ **08/566-11-300**. Fax 08/566-11-301. www.lydmar.se. 62 units. 2,400SEK–2,600SEK ($312–$338) double; 3,950SEK ($514) junior suite. Rates include buffet breakfast. AE, DC, MC, V. Parking nearby 300SEK ($39). T-bana: Östermalmstorg. Bus: 1 or 46. **Amenities:** 2 restaurants; bar; limited room service; babysitting; laundry service; dry cleaning. *In room:* TV, dataport, minibar, hair dryer.

Nordic Hotel ★★ *Finds*   There's nothing in Scandinavia quite like this hotel, which was voted "The World's Sexiest Hotel" by *Elle* magazine. It definitely has a split personality—its astrological sign is Gemini. You're given a choice of a room of "watery calm" in the 367-room Nordic Sea or "post-minimalist luminescence" in the 175-room Nordic Light. Lying on either side of a new square, Vasaplan, the hotel stands adjacent to the express rail link with the airport, or the central rail station.

Each hotel has its own individual design. Nordic Sea, of course, turns to the ocean for its inspiration and features a 2,400-gallon aquarium and steel walls constructed from ship hulls. Rooms have a certain elegant simplicity with excellent comfort and beautiful bathrooms with tub/showers. These accommodations range in size from extra small to extra large. Approached by an underground walkway, Nordic Light is filled with sun-shape projections that guarantee bright light even on the darkest winter's day. Surprisingly for a hotel, the lobby emits sounds and lightning effects when it senses the presence of a guest. The suggestive light patterns projecting from the walls re-create the ever-changing patterns of the lights of the north. This hotel is not just about gimmicks and offers real comfort with rooms boasting the best sound insulation in town.

4–7 Vasaplan. ℭ **800/337-4685** in the U.S., or 08/217-177. Fax 08/505-630-30. www.nordichotels.se. 367 units in Nordic Sea, 175 units in Nordic Light. 2,900SEK–3,600SEK ($377–$468) double Nordic Sea; 2,400SEK–3,600SEK ($312–$468) double Nordic Light. AE, DC, MC, V. T-bana: Centralen. **Amenities:** Restaurant; 2 bars; steam bath; sauna; some spa treatments; mini-gym; limited room service at Nordic Sea, 24-hr. room service Nordic Light; laundry service; dry cleaning; nonsmoking rooms; rooms for those w/limited mobility. *In room:* TV, dataport, minibar, coffeemaker, iron/ironing board, safe.

Radisson SAS Strand Hotel ★   In stark contrast to the angular modernity of many other SAS hotels in Scandinavia, this one has a traditional and charming exterior. Originally built in 1912 with a hint of Art Nouveau styling, it lies at the edge of a complicated network of canals and waterways, in a prosperous and conservative neighborhood near the Royal Palace. As part of the hotel's renovation and modernization in the early 1980s, all the antique detailing was ripped out and replaced with a blandly international modernist style. Much of the hotel's clientele consists of business travelers from other parts of northern Europe. The bedrooms are outfitted with solid furniture and light pastel colors. Rooms are available in a wide range of sizes, with those at the lowest end of the spectrum being rather small and containing smallish, not particularly comfortable beds. The more expensive rooms are considerably larger and plusher, and have the large beds more suited to North American tastes. All rooms have neatly kept bathrooms equipped with tub/showers.

Nybrokajen 9, S-103 27 Stockholm. ℭ **800/333-3333** in the U.S., or 08/50-66-40-00. Fax 08/50-66-40-01. www.radisson.com. 152 units. Mon–Thurs 2,380SEK–2,580SEK ($309–$335) double, from 3,500SEK ($455) suite; Fri–Sun 1,395SEK–1,695SEK ($181–$220) double, from 1,895SEK ($246) suite. AE, DC, MC, V. Parking

390SEK ($51) per night. T-bana: Kungsträdgården. **Amenities:** Restaurant; bar; sauna; 24-hr. room service; babysitting; laundry service; dry cleaning. *In room:* A/C, TV, dataport, minibar, coffeemaker, hair dryer, safe, trouser press.

Scandic Sergel Plaza ★★   This hotel opened in 1984 at the entrance to Drottninggatan, the main shopping street. Designed as living quarters for parliament members, improvements have made it one of the city's leading hotels. The elegant decor includes 18th-century artwork and antiques. The beautifully decorated guest rooms are done in modern but traditional style. The average-size tiled bathrooms have tub/showers. Maintenance is first rate, and there are some accommodations for nonsmokers and wheelchair users. A special executive floor offers enhanced luxuries and several electronic extras, such as dataports.

Brunkebergstorg 9, S-103 27 Stockholm. ✆ **800/THE-OMNI** in the U.S., or 08/517-26-300. Fax 08/517-26-311. www.scandic-hotels.com. 403 units. 1,250SEK–2,300SEK ($163–$299) double; from 5,400SEK ($702) suite. Rates include breakfast. AE, DC, MC, V. Parking 250SEK ($33). T-bana: Centralen. Bus: 47, 52, or 69. **Amenities:** Restaurant; bar; limited room service; laundry service; dry cleaning; nonsmoking rooms; rooms for those w/limited mobility. *In room:* TV, dataport, minibar, hair dryer, trouser press (in some).

MODERATE

Adlon Hotell   This 1884 building was redesigned by brothers Axel and Hjalmar Jumlin in the 1920s. Upgraded and improved many times since, including in 2003, it lies near the Central Station (and the subway) and is convenient to buses to and from Arlanda Airport. All the rather small rooms have been renovated and are comfortably furnished; 70% of them are designated for nonsmokers. The small bathrooms have tub/showers.

Vasagatan 42, S-111 20 Stockholm. ✆ **08/402-65-00.** Fax 08/20-86-10. www.adlon.se. 83 units. 1,895SEK–2,495SEK ($246–$324) double. Rates include breakfast. AE, DC, MC, V. Parking 250SEK ($33) in garage 1 block away. T-bana: Centralen. **Amenities:** Bar; lounge; laundry service; dry cleaning; nonsmoking rooms. *In room:* TV, minibar, hair dryer.

Clas på Hörnet ★★   Built in the 1730s as a private house, this small, upscale, and very charming inn is less than a kilometer (about ½ mile) north of the commercial heart of Stockholm. Its attention to period detail—whose installation was supervised by the curators of the Stockholm City Museum—gives a distinctive country-inn ambience that's enhanced with bedrooms outfitted in the late-18th-century style of Gustavus III. Each of the bedrooms is outfitted in a different color scheme and motif, usually with cheerful colors, wide floorboards, antiques, and all the amenities you'd expect from a well-managed and intimate hotel, including good beds and medium-size bathrooms with well-kept shower units. Many have four-poster beds. The in-house restaurant, Clas på Hornet (Clas on the Corner), is recommended separately under "Where to Dine."

Surbrunnsgatan 20, S-113 48 Stockholm. ✆ **08/16-51-36.** Fax 08/612-53-15. 10 units. Mon–Thurs 1,795SEK ($233) double, 2,395SEK ($311) suite; Fri–Sun 1,095SEK ($142) double, 1,995SEK ($259) suite. Rates include breakfast. Parking 200SEK ($26). Bus: 46 or 53. **Amenities:** Breakfast room; lounge; nonsmoking rooms. *In room:* TV.

Crystal Plaza Hotel   In the 1990s, a charming, richly detailed, turn-of-the-20th-century hotel, the Karelia, was transformed after several large-scale renovations. Many aspects of the building's original grandeur were retained, including the soaring Romanesque entranceway, the decorative double staircase, and the copper-capped tower. Renovations improved the rooms with renewed bathrooms equipped with tub/showers, yet retained some old-fashioned touches, including high, ornate ceilings, and some of the old-world detailing.

Birger Jarlsgatan 35, S0111 45 Stockholm. © **08/406-8800.** Fax 08/24-15-11. 112 units. Sun–Thurs 2,025SEK–2,325SEK ($263–$302) double; Fri–Sat 1,250SEK–1,550SEK ($163–$202) double; 2,925SEK–39,25SEK ($488–$655) suite. Rates include breakfast. AE, DC, MC, V. Parking 300SEK ($39). T-bana: Östermalmstorg. Bus: 46. **Amenities:** Restaurant; bar; laundry service; dry cleaning; nonsmoking rooms; rooms for those w/limited mobility. *In room:* TV, dataport, minibar, hair dryer.

Elite Hotel Stockholm Plaza ★

Built on a triangular lot that might remind some visitors of New York's Flatiron Building, this first-class hotel is a well-run and inviting choice in the city center. From the time of its construction in 1884 until its complete overhaul in 1984, the building had many uses—a run-down rooming house, private apartments, and offices. The light, fresh guest rooms have firm beds and tiled bathrooms with tub/showers.

Birger Jarlsgatan 29, S-103 95 Stockholm. © **08/566-22-000.** Fax 08/566-22-020. www.elite.se. 151 units. 1,796SEK–1,995SEK ($233–$259) double; 2,675SEK–4,095SEK ($348–$532) suite. Rates include breakfast. AE, DC, MC, V. Parking 200SEK ($26). T-bana: Hötorget or Östermalmstorg. **Amenities:** Restaurant; bar; dance club; sauna; limited room service; laundry service; dry cleaning; nonsmoking rooms; rooms for those w/limited mobility. *In room:* TV, dataport, minibar (in some), hair dryer.

Esplanade Hotel ★

This informal hotel, next to the more expensive Diplomat, attracts representatives from the nearby embassies and others who like its comfortable charm and traditional atmosphere. Constructed in 1910, it became a family-style hotel in 1954. Many of the rooms, furnished in old-fashioned style, have minibars. Single rooms are minuscule. Most doubles have double-glazed windows, extra-long beds, and well-kept, decent-size tile bathrooms with tub/showers. Four rooms have a water view, and the English lounge features a balcony with a view of Djurgården. Only breakfast is served.

Strandvägen 7A, S-114 56 Stockholm. © **08/663-07-40.** Fax 08/662-59-92. www.hotelesplanade.se. 34 units. Mon–Thurs 1,995SEK–2,295SEK ($259–$298) double; Fri–Sun 1,695SEK ($220) double. Rates include breakfast. AE, DC, MC, V. Parking nearby 250SEK ($33). T-bana: Östermalmstorg. Bus: 47 or 69. **Amenities:** Breakfast room; lounge; sauna; limited room service; laundry service; dry cleaning; nonsmoking rooms. *In room:* TV, dataport, minibar, hair dryer.

Hotell Kung Carl ★

Discreet, tasteful, and quietly glamorous, this hotel in the heart of Stockholm was built in the mid-1800s by a religious group that offered lodgings to women newly arrived in Stockholm from the country. It's one of the longest-operating hotels in the city. Transformed into a hotel in the 1870s, and elevated to four-star status thanks to many improvements, it retains an old-fashioned charm. The conservatively furnished guest rooms were expanded and renovated in 1998. The bathrooms, although small, are well maintained and equipped with tub/showers. There's no restaurant on the premises, but the lobby bar sells pizza and sandwiches.

Birger Jarlsgatan 21, S-11145 Stockholm. © **08/463-50-00.** Fax 08/463-50-50. www.hkchotels.se. 112 units. Mon–Thurs 1,875SEK–2,145SEK ($244–$279) double; Fri–Sun 1,250SEK–1,500SEK ($163–$195) double; 5,500SEK ($715) suite. Rates include breakfast. AE, DC, MC, V. Parking 120SEK–300SEK ($16–$39). T-bana: Östermalmstorg. **Amenities:** Restaurant; bar; lounge; Jacuzzi (in some); limited room service; laundry service; dry cleaning; nonsmoking rooms; rooms for those w/limited mobility. *In room:* A/C (in some), TV, dataport, minibar, hair dryer, safe, iron (in some), sauna (in some).

Radisson SAS Royal Viking Hotel ★

This airline-affiliated hotel in a nine-story tower is in a commercial neighborhood near the railway station and the Stockholm World Trade Center. It has a soaring, plant-filled atrium. Especially popular in summer with organized tours and conventioneers, it offers rooms with stylized modern furniture and good, firm beds. Bathrooms are on the small side, but big enough for tub/showers and phones. Some rooms are reserved for

---

Kids Family-Friendly Hotels

af Chapman (p. 74) Although there are no family rooms, kids will delight in staying in one of the staterooms (two to eight beds) aboard an authentic three-mast schooner.

Hotel Tegnérlunden (p. 71) Twenty big, airy rooms are ideal for families on a budget.

Sheraton Stockholm Hotel & Towers (p. 70) This well-run chain has always pampered children. The spacious rooms are comfortably shared with parents.

---

nonsmokers, and others are wheelchair accessible. Many units are minisuites, well accessorized with electronic extras.

Vasagatan 1, S-101 24 Stockholm. ⓒ 800/333-3333 in the U.S., or 08/506-54000. Fax 08/506-54001. www.radissonsas.com. 459 units. 1,120SEK–2,495SEK ($146–$324) double; 4,000SEK ($520) suite. Rates include breakfast. AE, DC, MC, V. Parking 350SEK ($46). T-bana: Centralen. **Amenities:** Restaurant; 3 bars; indoor pool; fitness center; Jacuzzi; sauna; 24-hr. room service; laundry service; dry cleaning; nonsmoking rooms; rooms for those w/limited mobility. *In room:* TV, minibar, hair dryer, trouser press.

Sheraton Stockholm Hotel & Towers ⭐ *Kids* Sheathed with Swedish granite, this eight-story hostelry is within view of Stockholm's City Hall (Rådhuset). Short on Swedish charm, it's excellent by chain hotel standards, attracting many business travelers and families, both foreign and domestic. The guest rooms are the largest in the city, with one king or two double beds with bedside controls and closets with mirrored doors. A family of three or four can fit comfortably into most of them. Medium-size tile bathrooms have tub/showers and heated towel racks, and some units have bidets. Most units offer sweeping views of the city, many over Gamla Stan.

Tegelbacken 6, S-101 23 Stockholm. ⓒ 800/325-3535 in the U.S. and Canada, or 08/412-34-00. Fax 08/412-34-09. www.sheratonstockholm.com. 462 units. 1,250SEK–2,900SEK ($163–$377) double; from 4,000SEK ($520) suite. AE, DC, MC, V. Parking 300SEK ($39). T-bana: Centralen. **Amenities:** 2 restaurants; bar; fitness center; indoor pool; sauna; 24-hr. room service; babysitting; laundry service; dry cleaning; nonsmoking rooms; rooms for those w/limited mobility. *In room:* TV, dataport, minibar (in some), hair dryer.

INEXPENSIVE

Comfort Hotel Wellington ⭐ A longtime favorite with frugal travelers, the nine-story Wellington sounds like something you'd find in London. Built in the late 1950s, it maintains some English decorative touches and lies in a quiet but convenient neighborhood less than a kilometer (about ½ mile) east of Stockholm's commercial core. The public rooms are filled with engravings of English hunting scenes and leather-covered chairs. Some of the small but stylish guest rooms overlook a flower-filled courtyard. Some rooms on higher floors have panoramic views. Beds are firm, and the small bathrooms are well equipped, including tub/showers combinations. Two floors are reserved for nonsmokers.

Storgatan 6, S-11451 Stockholm. ⓒ 08/667-09-10. Fax 08/667-12-54. www.wellington.se. 60 units. Summer and Fri–Sat year-round 1,395SEK–1,495SEK ($181–$194) double; rest of year 2,245SEK–2,445SEK ($292–$318) double. Rates include breakfast. AE, DC, MC, V. Parking 280SEK ($36). T-bana: Östermalmstorg. **Amenities:** Breakfast room; bar; sauna; limited room service; laundry service; dry cleaning; nonsmoking rooms; rooms for those w/limited mobility. *In room:* TV, hair dryer, iron (in some), trouser press (in some).

Hotel Bema   When it was constructed in 1905, this building was an apartment house, lying within a 10-minute walk of Stockholm's railway station. Today it's been converted into a small and intimate hotel, just battered enough to relieve the inhibitions of anyone who fears formality. The decor and amenities date from 1987, when the owners radically upgraded the place in a contemporary style. Most of the clients here are backpackers, students, and cyclists who appreciate the youthful ambience and the good-natured reception. The rooms are not exactly plush, but are all nonsmoking, and the bathrooms are neatly maintained and come with tub/showers. Housekeeping generally is adequate, despite the functional, no-frills atmosphere.

Upplandsgatan 13, S-11123 Stockholm. © **08/23-26-75.** Fax 08/20-53-38. hotell.bema@stockholm.mail. telia.com. 12 units. Mon–Thurs 910SEK–1,010SEK ($118–$131) double; Fri–Sun 700SEK–800SEK ($91–$104) double. Rates include breakfast. AE, DC, MC, V. Parking 150SEK ($20) in nearby garage. Bus: 69. **Amenities:** Breakfast service in rooms,. *In room:* TV.

Hotell Kom *Value*   In a residential neighborhood scattered with stores and private apartments, this small 1910 hotel, a former youth hostel, has been considerably improved and upgraded over the years. The present building dates from 1972. You get good value and a warm welcome here. Rooms, although small, are tastefully and comfortably furnished in the latest Swedish modern. The building itself is well maintained and up-to-date. Many of the rooms open onto good views of the cityscape. Bathrooms are well organized and a bit tiny, but each with modern plumbing such as showers. A number of simple and rather small budget rooms are also rented on the ground floor, each with two bunk beds in each room. These bargains can accommodate up to four guests. Readers tend to like this one, which is owned by the YWCA and YMCA.

17 Döbelnsgatan, S-11140 Stockholm. © **08/412-23-00.** Fax 08/412-23-10. www.komhotel.se. 99 units. Mon–Thurs 1,720SEK–1,950SEK ($224–$254) double; Fri–Sun 1,180SEK–1,380SEK ($153–$179) double; budget rooms 600SEK ($78) double, 800SEK ($104) quad. Rates include breakfast. AE, DC, MC, V. Parking 160SEK ($21). T-bana: Rådmansgatan. **Amenities:** Breakfast room; lounge; fitness center; sauna; laundry service; dry cleaning; nonsmoking rooms; rooms for those w/limited mobility. *In room:* TV, dataport, minibar, hair dryer, safe.

Hotell Örnsköld   The five-story building that contains this hotel was built in 1910, and today the nearby Royal Dramatic Theater uses most of it for prop storage and staff housing. The hotel is situated on the second floor. High-ceilinged rooms have simple, contemporary furnishings, and more expensive units are big enough to hold extra beds, if necessary. All units contain well-kept bathrooms with shower units. A few cubicle rooms—called "cabins"—are rented for 475SEK ($62); they contain no windows.

Nybrogatan 6, S-11434 Stockholm. © **08/667-02-85.** Fax 08/667-69-91. www.hotelornskold.se. 27 units. 1,375SEK–1,975SEK ($179–$257) double; "cabin" 475SEK ($62). Rates include breakfast. AE, MC, V. Parking 250SEK ($33) in nearby public garage. T-bana: Östermalmstorg. **Amenities:** Lounge; laundry service; dry cleaning. *In room:* TV, dataport, minibar, hair dryer, iron/ironing board.

Hotel Tegnérlunden *Kids*   In a 19th-century building at the edge of a city park, this hotel has a few public rooms, a lobby, and a bar. The best feature is the tasteful, functionally furnished rooms, many suitable for families. They're blissfully quiet, especially those opening onto the rear. The rooms vary in size and shape, and those we inspected were well maintained. The hotel offers comfort but not a lot of style. The bathrooms equipped with shower units are small but beautifully kept.

Tegnrlunden 8, S-113 59 Stockholm. © **08/5454-5550.** Fax 08/5454-5551. www.hoteltegnerlunden.se. 102 units. Sun–Thurs 1,560SEK ($203) double, 1,895SEK ($246) suite; Fri–Sat 990SEK ($129) double, 1,395SEK

($181) suite. Rates include breakfast. AE, DC, MC, V. Parking 150SEK ($20) in nearby garage. Bus: 47, 53, or 69. **Amenities:** Breakfast room; bar; sauna; laundry service; dry cleaning; nonsmoking rooms. *In room:* TV, dataport, hair dryer, iron (in some).

Mornington Hotel ⭐ Proud of its image as an English-inspired hotel, this effi-cient modern establishment has a concrete exterior brightened with rows of flower boxes. It was built in 1956 and has been renovated several times, most recently in 1997. Most rooms have standard decor, and many are quite small. Each unit con-tains well-kept bathrooms with tub/showers. The lobby contains a small rock gar-den. The hotel offers rooms for nonsmokers and guests with disabilities.

Nybrogatan 53, S-102 44 Stockholm. © **800/780-7234** in the U.S. and Canada, or 08/663-12-40. Fax 08/ 507-33-039. www.morningtonhotel.com. 141 units. Sun–Thurs 2,227SEK–2,337SEK ($290–$304) double; Fri–Sat 1,731SEK ($225) double; 3,350SEK ($436) suite. Rates include breakfast. AE, DC, MC, V. Parking 150SEK–220SEK ($20–$29). T-bana: Östermalmstorg. Bus: 49, 54, or 62. **Amenities:** Restaurant; bar; sauna; 24-hr. room service; laundry service; dry cleaning; nonsmoking rooms; rooms for those w/limited mobility. *In room:* TV, dataport, hair dryer, iron.

Rica City Hotel Stockholm Set in a desirable location between two of Stockholm's biggest department stores (PUB and Åhléns City), Rica City Hotel has small but clean, comfortable guest rooms. They have been elegantly refur-bished using mirrors, hardwood trim, carpeting, and tile. All units have neatly kept bathrooms with tub/showers. Although the hotel doesn't serve alcohol, it maintains a simple restaurant that's open Monday to Friday from 6:30am to 3pm, and Saturday and Sunday from 7:30am to 3pm. There's also a sauna.

Slöjdgatan 7 (at Hötorget), S-111 81 Stockholm. © **08/723-72-00.** Fax 08/723-72-09. www.rica.se. 283 units. Mon–Thurs 1,900SEK ($247) double, 2,170SEK ($282) suite; Fri–Sat 1,320SEK ($172) double, 1,620SEK ($211) suite. Rates include breakfast. AE, DC, MC, V. Parking 225SEK ($29). T-bana: Hötorget. **Amenities:** Restaurant; lounge; sauna; nonsmoking rooms; rooms for those w/limited mobility. *In room:* TV, minibar, hair dryer.

ON GAMLA STAN (OLD TOWN)
EXPENSIVE
First Hotel Reisen ⭐⭐ Just three alleyways from the Royal Palace, this hotel faces the water. Dating from the 17th century and begun as a coffeehouse, the three-building structure attractively combines the old and the new. The rooms are comfortably furnished in a stylish modern fashion inspired by traditional designs. Beds are frequently renewed, and the bathrooms are excellent, with deep tubs, massaging showerheads, scales, marble floors, heated towel racks, and phones. Some suites have Jacuzzis. Some units for nonsmokers are available, and the top-floor accommodations open onto small balconies.

Skeppsbron 12, S-111 30 Stockholm. © **08/22-32-60.** Fax 08/20-15-59. www.firsthotels.com. 144 units. Mon–Thurs 2,399SEK–3,199SEK ($312–$416) double, from 3,999SEK ($520) suite; Fri–Sun 1,200SEK– 1,700SEK ($156–$221) double, from 2,000SEK ($260) suite. Rates include breakfast. AE, DC, MC, V. Parking 395SEK ($51). Bus: 43, 46, 55, 59, or 76. **Amenities:** Restaurant; bar; indoor pool; sauna; limited room serv-ice; laundry service; dry cleaning; nonsmoking rooms. *In room:* TV, dataport, minibar, hair dryer, iron/ironing board, trouser press.

Lady Hamilton Hotel ⭐ *Finds* This hotel, consisting of three connected buildings, stands on a quiet street surrounded by antiques shops and restau-rants—a very desirable location, indeed. Dozens of antiques are scattered among the well-furnished guest rooms. Most rooms have beamed ceilings. The beds (queen or double) are of high quality. Bathrooms are tiled but vary in size from spacious to cramped. All have heated towel racks, heated floors, and tub/show-ers. Top-floor rooms have skylights and memorable views over the old town.

Some rooms for nonsmokers are available. You'll get a sense of the 1470 origins of this hotel when you use the luxurious sauna, which encompasses the stone-rimmed well that formerly supplied the building's water. The ornate staircase wraps around a large model of a clipper ship suspended from the ceiling.

Storkyrkobrinken 5, S-111 28 Stockholm. ⓒ **08/506-40-100.** Fax 08/506-40-110. www.lady-hamilton.se. 34 units (some with shower only). 2,390SEK–3,190SEK ($311–$415) double. Rates include buffet breakfast. AE, DC, MC, V. Parking: 375SEK ($49). T-bana: Gamla Stan. Bus: 48. **Amenities:** Bistro; bar; sauna; limited room service; babysitting; laundry service; dry cleaning; nonsmoking rooms. *In room:* TV, dataport, minibar, hair dryer.

Victory Hotel ⭐⭐   A small but stylish hotel, the Victory offers warm, inviting rooms, each named after a prominent sea captain. They sport a pleasing combination of exposed wood, antiques, and 19th-century memorabilia. Many rooms are smoke-free, and the beds are comfortable, with firm mattresses. The average-size bathrooms are tiled and have heated floors and shower units. Only the suites have tubs. The hotel rests on the foundations of a 1382 fortified tower. In the 1700s, the building's owners buried a massive silver treasure under the basement floor—you can see it in the Stockholm City Museum. There's a shiny brass elevator, but from the stairs you'll see one of Sweden's largest collections of 18th-century nautical needlepoint, much of it created by sailors during their long voyages.

Lilla Nygatan 5, S-111 28 Stockholm. ⓒ **08/506-400-00.** Fax 08/506-40-010. www.victory-hotel.se. 49 units (some with shower only). 2,590SEK–4,290SEK ($337–$558) double; 3,990SEK–6,190SEK ($519–$805) suite. Rates include buffet breakfast. AE, DC, MC, V. Valet parking 375SEK ($49). T-bana: Gamla Stan. Bus: 48. **Amenities:** Restaurant; bar; indoor pool; sauna; 24-hr. room service; babysitting; laundry service; dry cleaning; nonsmoking rooms. *In room:* TV, dataport, minibar, hair dryer, safe.

MODERATE

Mälardrottningen ⭐ *Finds*   During its heyday, this was the most famous motor yacht in the world, the subject of gossip columns everywhere, thanks to the complicated friendships that developed among the passengers and, in some cases, the crew. Built in 1924 by millionaire C. K. G. Billings, it was the largest motor yacht in the world (72m/236 ft.), and was later acquired by the Woolworth heiress, Barbara Hutton. The below-deck space originally contained only seven suites. The yacht was converted into a hotel in the early 1980s and permanently moored beside a satellite island of Stockholm's Old Town. The cabins are now cramped and somewhat claustrophobic. Most have bunk-style twin beds. All units have neatly kept bathrooms with tub/showers. Considering the hotel's conversation-piece status and its location close to everything in the Old Town, it might be worth an overnight stay.

Riddarholmen, S-11128 Stockholm. ⓒ **08/545-187-80.** Fax 08/24-36-76. www.malardrottningen.se. 60 units. Mon–Thurs 1,220SEK–2,150SEK ($159–$280) double; Fri–Sun 1,030SEK–2,150SEK ($134–$280) double. Rates include buffet breakfast. AE, DC, MC, V. Parking 200SEK ($26) per hour. T-bana: Gamla Stan. **Amenities:** Restaurant; bar; sauna; laundry service; dry cleaning; nonsmoking rooms. *In room:* TV, hair dryer.

ON LANGHOLMEN
INEXPENSIVE

Långholmen Hotel   Beginning in 1724, on the little island of Langholmen, this structure was a state penitentiary for women charged with "loose living." The last prisoner was released in 1972 and today it's a newly restored and reasonably priced hotel, which, in addition to comfortable but small rooms, also houses a museum of Sweden's prison history and one of the best restaurants in the country. Instead of a prison induction area, you get the hotel's reception area and a 24-hour snack bar. Accommodations were carved from some 200 cells, creating cramped but serviceable rooms equipped with small showers and toilets.

Ten of the bedrooms are suitable for persons with disabilities, and 91 are reserved for nonsmokers. This is one of the best hotels in Stockholm for the single visitor on a budget, as 89 rooms are rented only to solo travelers. Just 13 rooms are large enough to accommodate two people.

Långholmsmuren 20, S-102 72 Stockholm. © **08/668-05-00.** Fax 08/720-85-75. www.langholmen.com. 102 units. Sun–Thurs 1,495SEK ($194) double; Fri–Sat 1,155SEK ($150) double; extra bed 215SEK ($28) per person. AE, MC, V. Rates include breakfast. T-bana: Hornstul. Bus: 4, 40, or 66. **Amenities:** Restaurant; bar; laundry service; dry cleaning. *In room:* TV, dataport, hair dryer.

ON SKEPPSHOLMEN
INEXPENSIVE
af Chapman *Kids*   Moored off Skeppsholmen, this authentic three-masted schooner has been converted into a youth hostel ideal for families. Staterooms have two, four, six, or eight beds; there are no single cabins. Each section—one for men, one for women—has showers and washrooms. Personal lockers are available. The gangplank goes up at 2am, with no exceptions, and there's a 5-day maximum stay. The rooms are closed from 11am to 3pm. Smoking is not allowed. A summer cafe operates on the ship's deck. Breakfast, at an extra charge, is available in the self-service coffee bar and dining room. International Youth Hostel Association cards can be obtained on the *af Chapman.*

Västra Brobänken, Skeppsholmen, S-111 49 Stockholm. © **08/463-22-66.** Fax 08/611-98-75. www.stf chapman.com. 136 beds in 36 cabins, none with bathroom. Members 140SEK–210SEK ($18–$27); nonmembers 185SEK–255SEK ($24–$33). MC, V. Closed Dec 16–Apr 1. Bus: 65. **Amenities:** Lounge. *In room:* No phone.

ON SÖDERMALM
EXPENSIVE
Hotel Rival *★★★* *Finds*   Originally opened in 1937, this hotel-cafe-baker-cinema has received a new lease on life, with a lot of the money supplied by Benny Andersson, former member of the musical group Abba. Reinvented and given a new life in the 21st century, this exciting boutique hotel on the Stockholm scene reeks of Art Deco evocative of the era of the great Swedish cinema actress Greta Garbo. Lying on the rapidly gentrified island of Södermalm in southern Stockholm, the hotel generates a lot of excitement in Stockholm. Because of the tie-in with Abba, it is the favorite of visiting pop or rock stars.

Bedrooms aren't old-fashioned at all, but are imbued with sleek, contemporary Swedish styling, with wooden floors and some of the most comfortable beds in the city. All the modern amenities are here, including wall-mounted TVs and DVD players. Try for a room opening onto the Mariatorget—one of Stockholm's loveliest squares—and not fronting a rather uninspired courtyard. The designer opted for classical rather than trendy, comfortable rather than luxurious. The bathrooms are elegant, with marble floors and special details such as colored knobs. A scene from a classic Swedish film hangs over every bed.

The on-site Bistro is the trendy place to dine on Södermalm, and the Cocktail Bar is a seductive place to have a drink. In addition to a first-class bakery and cafe, on site is the Rival Cinema, originally opened before World War II and now fully restored to its former glory. What a venue this would be for a Garbo festival.

Mariatorget 3, S-11891 Stockholm. © **08/545-789-00.** Fax 08/545-789-24. www.rival.se. 99 units. Sun–Thurs 2,290SEK–2,990SEK ($298–$389) double; from 3,890SEK ($506) suite; Fri–Sat 1,340SEK–1,790SEK ($174–$233) double, from 2,690SEK ($350) suite. AE, DC, MC, V. T-bana: Mariatorget. **Amenities:** 2 restaurants;

3 bars; gym; 24-hr. room service; laundry service; dry cleaning; rooms for those w/limited mobility; nonsmoking rooms. *In room:* A/C, TV, dataport, minibar, hair dryer, iron/ironing board, safe.

NORTH OF THE CENTER
INEXPENSIVE
Hotel Arcadia   This angular-looking five-story hotel has gone through several administrations and name changes since its original construction as a student dormitory in the 1960s. Its present role as an uncomplicated, unpretentious tourist-class hotel began in 1975 when it was renovated and upgraded. In 1998, bedrooms on the second floor were renovated as part of a process that will eventually encompass most of the rooms in the hotel. It's located on a tree-lined boulevard, on a hillside with a good view, a 5-minute walk from the railway station. The hotel has a restaurant, Babylon, serving Swedish and international food, and there is an outdoor terrace for sunbathing and reading. Be warned in advance that bedrooms here are not particularly plush, but they are clean and well maintained, with good beds and small but adequate bathrooms equipped with tub/showers.

Kärnbärsvagen 1, S-114 89 Stockholm. © **08/566-215-00.** Fax 08/566-21-501. www.arcadia.elite.se. 84 units. Sun–Thurs 1,395SEK ($181) double; Fri–Sat 845SEK ($110) double. Rates include breakfast. AE, DC, MC, V. Parking 100SEK ($13). T-bana: Tekniska Högskolan. **Amenities:** Restaurant; bar; lounge; laundry service; dry cleaning; nonsmoking rooms. *In room:* TV.

NEAR THE AIRPORT
EXPENSIVE
Radisson SAS SkyCity Hotel ⋆   This three-story hotel lies at Stockholm's Arlanda airport, 39km (24 miles) north of the city. Built in 1993, it's a part of the sprawling SkyCity airport complex that includes banks, travel agencies, restaurants, cafes, souvenir shops, and the busiest of the airport's terminals (nos. 4 and 5). Bedrooms are outfitted in one of three distinct styles: Scandinavian modern, Oriental/Chinese, and business-class units with slightly upgraded extras. All units contain neatly kept bathrooms with tub/showers. The staff is multilingual, well trained, and hardworking, contributing to the successful day-to-day administration of this minicity where visitors wing in at all times of the day and night from practically everywhere. The hotel's SkyCity Bar and Restaurant is the best within the airport complex.

SkyCity, P.O. Box 82, S-19045 Stockholm-Arlanda. © **08/50-67-40-00.** Fax 08/50-67-40-01. www.radisson. com. 230 units. 2,100SEK–2,400SEK ($273–$312) double; 3,300SEK ($429) suite. Rates include breakfast. AE, DC, MC, V. Parking 240SEK ($31). Airport bus departs at 10-min. intervals for the city center, 80SEK ($10) each way. **Amenities:** Restaurant; bar; fitness center; Jacuzzi; sauna; limited room service; laundry service; dry cleaning. *In room:* A/C, TV, dataport, minibar, coffeemaker (in some), hair dryer, safe (in some), trouser press (in some).

4 Where to Dine

Increasingly, visitors are viewing Sweden as a culinary citadel of renown. Part of this derives from the legendary freshness of Swedish game and produce; part derives from the success of Sweden's culinary team at cooking contests everywhere. Some social pundits claim that the fame of Sweden's culinary team now rivals that of its national hockey team. There are today an estimated 1,500 restaurants and bars in Stockholm alone.

Food is expensive in Stockholm, but those on a budget can stick to self-service cafeterias. At all restaurants other than cafeterias, a 12% to 15% service charge is added to the bill to cover tipping, and the 21% value-added tax also is included in the bill. Wine and beer can be lethal to your final check, so proceed

Stockholm Dining

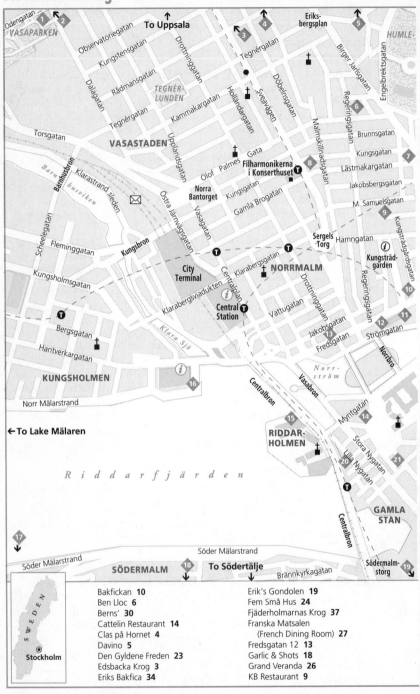

Bakfickan **10**
Ben Lloc **6**
Berns' **30**
Cattelin Restaurant **14**
Clas på Hornet **4**
Davino **5**
Den Gyldene Freden **23**
Edsbacka Krog **3**
Eriks Bakfica **34**

Erik's Gondolen **19**
Fem Små Hus **24**
Fjäderholmarnas Krog **37**
Franska Matsalen
   (French Dining Room) **27**
Fredsgatan 12 **13**
Garlic & Shots **18**
Grand Veranda **26**
KB Restaurant **9**

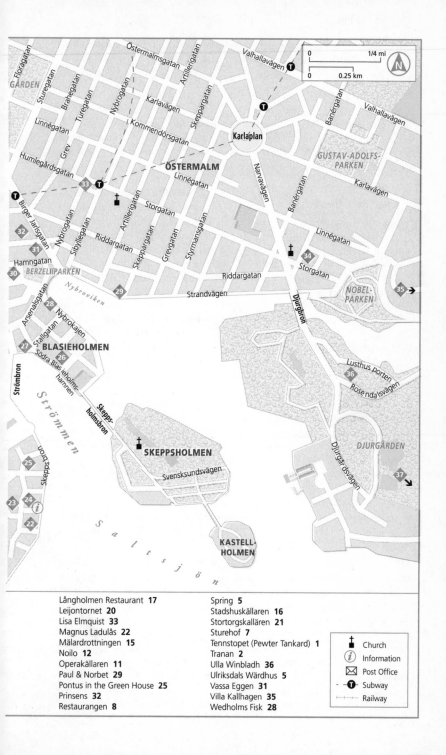

Långholmen Restaurant 17
Leijontornet 20
Lisa Elmquist 33
Magnus Ladulås 22
Mälardrottningen 15
Noilo 12
Operakällaren 11
Paul & Norbet 29
Pontus in the Green House 25
Prinsens 32
Restaurangen 8

Spring 5
Stadshuskällaren 16
Stortorgskällären 21
Sturehof 7
Tennstopet (Pewter Tankard) 1
Tranan 2
Ulla Winbladh 36
Ulriksdals Wärdhus 5
Vassa Eggen 31
Villa Kallhagen 35
Wedholms Fisk 28

✝ Church
ⓘ Information
✉ Post Office
- ◉ Subway
├──┼──┤ Railway

77

carefully. For good value, try ordering the *dagens ratt* (daily special), also referred to as dagens lunch or dagens menu, if available.

IN THE CENTER
VERY EXPENSIVE

Ben Lloc ★★★ MEDITERRANEAN   This is a Swedish temple of gastronomy. Chef Mathias Dahlgren is a darling of food critics and is hailed by some of his admirers as the finest chef in Sweden. Bon Lloc in Catalan means "good luck," and you'll need it to get a table here. The interior looks like a sophisticated blend of the best of contemporary Swedish and post-Movida Spanish decors. There's a bar at the entrance and an intensely contemporary-looking dining room on two tiers (something like a stage set at an opera). The room is sheathed in massive amounts of oak (on the floor and in the wood trim), with occasional touches of reddish stone, gray walls, and minimalist furniture.

Tips **Bar Food**

One tip to save you a little inconvenience: Don't rush into a bar in Stockholm for a pick-me-up martini. "Bars" in Stockholm are self-service cafeterias, and the strongest drink that many of them offer is apple cider.

Some members of the press call Dahlgren's cuisine "nouveau euro-Latino." His actual cuisine is hard to define. Even though Mediterranean in inspiration, dishes are prepared with such skill and imagination that they seem to merit a category of their own. His style balances delicacy and richness. This is not overly fussy cookery, but it makes a tremendous impact.

An oven-roasted cod comes with a lobster *brandade* and a gazpacho salsa, and it was as good as this dish gets. Out of the same oven popped the most delicious oven-roasted ham with apple cider glaze we've ever had. Who would have thought that Dahlgren could take such a lowly ingredient as a pig's foot and turn it into a platter of such flavorful, crispy joy? The free-range pork glazed with white pepper and served with plum vinegar gravy was exciting and original at the same time. We could make a meal of the creamy Roquefort served here. Its secret: The cheese is made only from nursing cows.

Regeringsgatan 111. Ⓒ 08/660-6060. Reservations required. Main courses 345SEK–375SEK ($45–$49); 4-course fixed-price menu 545SEK ($71); 7-course tasting menu 1,150SEK ($150). Mon–Sat 6–11pm. T-bana: Rådmansgatan.

Operakällaren ★★★ FRENCH/SWEDISH   Opposite the Royal Palace, this is the most famous and unashamedly luxurious restaurant in Sweden. Its elegant decor and style are reminiscent of a royal court banquet at the turn of the 20th century. The service and house specialties are impeccable. Many come here for the elaborate fixed-price menus; others prefer the classic Swedish dishes or the modern French ones. A house specialty that's worth the trip is the platter of northern delicacies, with everything from smoked eel to smoked reindeer, along with Swedish red caviar. Salmon and game, including grouse from the northern forests, are prepared in various ways. There's a cigar room, too.

Operahuset, Kungsträdgården. Ⓒ 08/676-58-00. Reservations required. Main courses 400SEK–500SEK ($52–$65); 3-course fixed-price menu 800SEK ($104); 4-course fixed-price menu 900SEK ($117); 7-course menu dégustation 1,300SEK ($169). AE, DC, MC, V. Daily 6–10pm. Closed July. T-bana: Kungsträdgården.

Paul & Norbert ★★★ CONTINENTAL   In a patrician residence dating from 1873, adjacent to the Hotell Diplomat, this is the finest and most innovative restaurant in Stockholm. Seating only 30 people, it has vaguely Art Deco decor, beamed ceilings, and dark paneling. Chef Norbert Lang prepares a tantalizing terrine of scallops in saffron sauce. The foie gras is the finest in town. Perfectly prepared main dishes include sautéed medallion of fjord salmon, scallops, and scampi in lobster sauce; crisp breast of duck with caramelized orange sauce; and juniper-stuffed noisettes of reindeer immersed in caraway sauce with portabella.

Strandvägen 9. ✆ 08/663-81-83. Reservations required. Main courses 250SEK–310SEK ($33–$40); 9-course *grand menu de frivolit* 1,100SEK ($143); 5-course fixed-price menu 650SEK ($85); 6-course fixed-price menu 990SEK ($129). AE, DC, MC, V. Mid-Aug to June Tues–Fri noon–2pm, Mon–Sat 6–10pm; July to mid-Aug Mon–Sat 6–10pm. Closed Dec 24–Jan 6. T-bana: Östermalmstorg.

EXPENSIVE

Divino ⭐ ITALIAN   It's a long way from sunny Italy to this far northern capital city, but the aptly named Divino manages to travel the distance with its Mediterranean flavors intact. Many local food critics hail Divino as Stockholm's finest Italian restaurant. In a setting attracting an elegant clientele, the restaurant boasts a mammoth wine cellar with some of Italy's best vintages to go with your meal. The cookery is rarely marred by a misstep. Too often the antipasti selection is dull in many Italian eateries. Here the chefs work overtime to come up with unusual variations of the classics, including sweetbreads flavored with lemon and fresh thyme, or a tantalizing carpaccio with rocket and Parmesan. A starter of scallops is perfectly cooked and flavored with fresh tomatoes and basil. Monkfish and lobster are served on one platter and flavored with vanilla bean along with fresh fennel, or else sea bass is another delight with crispy fresh vegetables and a luxury offering of truffles. Among the meat and poultry courses, we highly endorse the guinea fowl with morels, duck liver, and green asparagus, or else the veal entrecote with prosciutto, sage, and a flavoring of Marsala.

Karlavägen 28. ✆ 08/611-02-69. Reservations required. Main courses 245SEK–275SEK ($32–$36). AE, MC, V. Mon–Sat 6–11pm. Closed Mon in July. T-bana: Östra Station or Rädmansgatan.

Franska Matsalen (French Dining Room) ⭐⭐ FRENCH   Widely acclaimed as one of the greatest restaurants in Stockholm, this elegant establishment is on the street level of the city's finest hotel. The dining room is appointed with polished mahogany, ormolu, and gilt accents under an ornate plaster ceiling. Tables on the enclosed veranda overlook the Royal Palace and the Old Town. Begin with a cannelloni of foie gras with cèpes, or perhaps mousseline of scallops with Sevruga caviar. Main dishes include seared sweetbreads served with artichokes, langoustines, and frogs' legs with broad beans, and veal tartare with caviar. Fresh Swedish salmon is also featured. The chefs—highly trained professionals working with the finest ingredients—have pleased some of Europe's more demanding palates.

In the Grand Hotel, Södra Blasieholmshamnen 8. ✆ 08/679-35-84. Reservations required. Main courses 225SEK–495SEK ($29–$64); 7-course tasting menu 1,200SEK ($156); 5-course Scandinavian menu 895SEK ($116). AE, DC, MC, V. Mon–Fri 6–11pm. T-bana: Kungsträdgården. Bus: 46, 55, 62, or 76.

Fredsgatan 12 ⭐⭐⭐ SWEDISH/INTERNATIONAL   In the Royal Academy of Arts Building, this is one of the premier restaurants of Stockholm. The decor is ultrasophisticated and hip, almost nightclubish in aura with its use of mauve walls, gold chairs, and long, shimmering curtains. Since it's near the parliament and various government ministries, it draws officials at lunch, but a far trendier and classier crowd in the evening. Danyel Couet and Melker Andersson combine their talents to create dishes with clear, robust flavors. For our latest meal here, we dined with a Swedish food critic. In translation, his verdict was "confident, generous, and brilliantly handled," and we concur. For an appetizer, you're faced with such imaginative choices as bleak roe coming in a Mexican-style taco with cream laced with lemon zest. One member of our party found the anise-flavored black bread and the salty butter so enticing he was unable to tackle his main course. A pity, really, since the main courses here are even more delectable than the starters, including, for example, a perfectly cooked turbot with an amusing salmon "pastrami" and a very good rendering of sweet and sour venison (not always available). Among the more successful desserts is a blood-orange sorbet with a citrus salad.

Fredsgatan 12. ℂ 08/248-052. Reservations required. Main courses 265SEK–325SEK ($34–$42). AE, DC, MC, V. Mon–Fri 11:30am–2pm; Mon–Sat 5–10:30pm. T-bana: Kungsträdgården.

Restaurangen ★★ INTERNATIONAL   Come here for a high-ceilinged decor whose angularity might remind you of an SAS airport lounge, and for combinations of cuisine that many cosmopolitan Swedes have found absolutely fascinating. Owner and chef Malker Andersson divides his menu into "fields of flavor" as defined by unexpected categories. These include, among others, lemon-flavored themes or coriander-flavored themes, which can be consumed in any order you prefer. If you want a "taste of the lemon," for example, it might appear to flavor fresh asparagus and new potatoes. Freshly chopped coriander is used to flavor a delectable shellfish ceviche. The chef roams the world and doesn't try to duplicate classical international dishes, but to take the flavor of one country and combine its traditional dish with the time-honored dish of another country. An amazing and very tasty example of this is tacos from Mexico combined with foie gras of France and caviar from Russia. Since none of the portions are overly large, some diners interpret a meal here like something akin to a series of tapas, each permeated with flavors that linger on your palate after you consume them.

Oxtorgsgatan 14. ℂ 08/220-952. Reservations recommended. 3-course fixed-price menu 250SEK ($33); 5-course fixed-price menu 350SEK ($46); 7-course fixed-price menu 450SEK ($59). AE, DC, MC, V. Mon–Fri 11:30am–2pm and 5pm–1am; Mon–Sat 5pm–1am. T-bana: Hörtorget.

Spring ★ ASIAN/SCANDINAVIAN   East meets West in Johan Lindqvist's showcase of trendy fusion cuisine. The key is not only skill in the kitchen, but a carefully chosen list of ingredients that is fresh and of high quality. The decor is minimalist, the severity broken by the colors of Asia. Blond ash wood of northern Sweden is combined with colorful furniture from Asia. Lots of upwardly mobile young people form most of the patronage and have made Spring a hit since the day it opened. "We view it as 'in' to dine here," one of the young Stockholmer patrons told us. "Or is it 'in' to say 'in' anymore in English?" Our party of eight took delight in what we were served. In delicate hues and brimming with flavor, dishes such as steamed chicken dumplings appeared, followed by Japanese eel with foie gras and a maki tempura. There was more to come, and we know why the chef takes pride in the poached cod in ginger bouillon with shiitake mushrooms and bok choy, or the grilled veal entrecote with sea urchin butter including sweetbreads seasoned with five spices. The confit of turbot with a crab and tadish terrine was an unusual taste sensation. For dessert, we found nothing more soothing than the crème brûlée.

Karlavägen 110. ℂ 08/783-15-00. Reservations required. Main courses 195SEK–295SEK ($25–$38). AE, MC, V. Mon–Fri 11:30am–2pm; Tues–Sat 6–11pm. T-bana: Östra Station or Rädmansgatna.

Vassa Eggen ★ *Finds* INTERNATIONAL   One of the most cutting-edge cuisines is served at this fashionable eatery in the center of the city. Gastronomic influences from all over the world are revealed in this light, airy dining room accented by a beautiful glass dome. Using only the finest products, the young chefs concoct a cuisine pleasing to both eye and palate. The Swedish editions of *Gourmet* magazine put Vassa Eggen on the culinary map with raves about its oxtail tortellini with mascarpone cheese served in a consommé, finding it "a masterful balance of acidity, salt, sweetness, and spices." Other raves were to follow, including our own. The melon soup with Serrano ham immediately won us over, as did the fried herring with a potato purée. A duck terrine with a truffle polenta flavored with sherry showed a masterful touch, as did the main course of char in a creamy lobster juice. A perfectly prepared brill was cooked in brown butter and flavored with horseradish. The desserts are also worthy, especially the succulent chocolate truffle dish and the raspberry sorbet.

Birger Jarlsgatan 29. © **08/21-61-69**. Reservations required. Main courses 95SEK–295SEK ($12–$38). Tasting menu 895SEK ($116). AE, DC, MC, V. Mon–Sat 11:30am–2pm and 5pm–1am. Closed in July. T-bana: Östermalmstorg.

Wedholms Fisk ✦✦✦ SWEDISH/FRENCH   This is one of the classic—and one of the best—restaurants in Stockholm. It has no curtains in the windows and no carpets, but the display of modern paintings by Swedish artists is riveting. You might begin with marinated herring with garlic and *bleak* (a freshwater fish) roe, or tartare of salmon with salmon roe. The chef has reason to be proud of such dishes as perch poached with clams and saffron sauce, prawns marinated in herbs and served with Dijon hollandaise, and grilled filet of sole with Beaujolais sauce. For dessert, try the homemade vanilla ice cream with cloudberries. The cuisine is both innovative and traditional—for example, chevre mousse accompanies simple tomato salad. On the other hand, the menu features grandmother's favorite: cream-stewed potatoes.

Nybrokajen 17. © **08/611-78-74**. Reservations required. Lunch main courses 175SEK–225SEK ($23–$29); dinner main courses 265SEK–535SEK ($34–$70). AE, DC, MC, V. Mon–Fri 11:30am–11pm; Sat 5–11pm. Closed for lunch in July. T-bana: Östermalmstorg.

MODERATE

Bakfickan ✦ *Finds* SWEDISH   Tucked away behind the Operakällaren, the "Back Pocket" is a chic place to eat for a moderate price. It shares a kitchen with its glamorous neighbor, Operakällaren (see "Very Expensive," above in this section), but its prices are more bearable. Main dishes are likely to include salmon in several varieties, including boiled with hollandaise and salmon roe. You might also try beef Rydberg (thin-sliced tenderloin). In season, you can order reindeer and elk. In the summer, nothing's finer than the rich ice cream with a sauce of Arctic cloudberries. Many patrons prefer to eat at the horseshoe-shape bar.

Jakobs Torg 12. © **08/676-58-09**. Reservations not accepted. Main courses 98SEK–200SEK ($13–$26). AE, DC, MC, V. Mon–Sat noon–11:30pm. T-bana: Kungsträdgården.

Berns ✦ SWEDISH/INTERNATIONAL   Built in 1860, this "pleasure palace" was one of Stockholm's most famous restaurants and nighttime venues. It was dramatically renovated in 1999 and is now one of the most attractive restaurants in the capital. Three monumental chandeliers light the main hall. August Strindberg frequented the Red Room (*Röda Rummet*) and described it in his novel of the same name. It's still there—plush furniture and all—and is used by guests at Berns' Hotel. Each day a different Swedish specialty is featured, including fried filet of suckling pig with fresh asparagus. You might also try calves' liver with garlic and bacon, or grilled tournedos. More innovative main

dishes include cuttlefish with black pasta and tomato sauce, and filet of ostrich
with mushroom cannelloni and Marsala sauce. More and more exotic dishes are
appearing on the menu—tandoori-marinated lamb with mango, curry sauce,
and couscous, for example.

Näckströmsgatan 8. ℭ **08/566-32-222.** Reservations recommended. Main courses 165SEK–350SEK
($21–$46). AE, DC, MC, V. Mon–Fri 11:30am–2:30pm; Tues–Sat 5–11pm; Sun 11:30am–11pm. T-bana: Östermalmstorg.

Clas på Hornet ⚘ SWEDISH/CONTINENTAL   Decorative touches evocative of the late 1700s adorn these five cream-colored dining rooms, within the
previously recommended hotel. This restaurant is owned by the entrepreneur
who made Nils Emil (also recommended) into one of the capital's most
acclaimed restaurants. Homage to the place has even appeared in the poetic verse
of one of Sweden's most valued poets, Carl Michael Bellman. There's a sometimes crowded bar area that many clients visit regularly, in some cases even those
who have no interest in dining. No one will mind if you come just for a drink,
but the true value of the place emerges only at the table. Here menu items
change with the seasons but are likely to include an "Archipelago Platter,"
named after the islands near Stockholm that provide many of its ingredients. It
contains assorted preparations of herring, a medley of Swedish cheeses, and
homemade bread. Other delectable choices include blinis stuffed with bleak roe,
trout roe, and onions; cream of wild-mushroom soup with strips of reindeer;
grilled char that's served with a hollandaise sauce enriched with fish roe; baked
turbot in horseradish sauce; and roasted venison with a timbale of chanterelles.

Surbrunnsgatan 20. ℭ **08/16-51-30.** Reservations recommended. Main courses 155SEK–255SEK
($20–$33). AE, DC, MC, V. Mon–Fri 11:30am–10:30pm; Sat–Sun 5–10:30pm. Bus: 46.

Eriks Bakfica 𝘝𝘢𝘭𝘶𝘦 SWEDISH   Although other restaurants in Stockholm
bear the name Eriks, this one is relatively inexpensive and offers particularly
good value. Established in 1979, it features a handful of Swedish dishes from the
tradition of *husmanskost* (wholesome home cooking). A favorite opener is toast
Skagen, with shrimp, dill-flavored mayonnaise, spices, and bleak roe. There's
also a daily choice of herring appetizers. Try the tantalizing "archipelago stew,"
a ragout of fish prepared with tomatoes and served with garlic mayonnaise. Marinated salmon is served with hollandaise sauce. You might also try Eriks's cheese-
burger with the special secret sauce, but you have to ask for it—the secret
specialty is not on the menu.

Fredrikshovsgatan 4. ℭ **08/660-15-99.** Reservations recommended. Main courses 110SEK–295SEK
($14–$38). AE, DC, MC, V. Tues–Fri 11:30am–midnight; Sat 5pm–midnight; Sun 5–11pm. Bus: 47.

Grand Veranda ⚘ 𝘒𝘪𝘥𝘴 SWEDISH   On the ground floor of Stockholm's most
prestigious hotel, and fronted with enormous sheets of glass, this restaurant
opens onto a stunning view of the harbor and the Royal Palace. The Veranda is
famous for its daily buffets, which occasionally feature a medley of shellfish,
including all the shrimp and lobster you can eat. Many foreign families like to
patronize this place because of the lavishness of its buffets. Try such a la carte
dishes as filet of reindeer marinated in red wine, or braised wild duck and deep-
fried root vegetables served with an apple-cider sauce. Here is your chance to
sample the offerings of the most famous hotel in Sweden, to enjoy wonderful
food, and to have one of the best views in town—all for a reasonable price.

In the Grand Hotel, Södra Blasieholmshamnen 8. ℭ **08/679-35-86.** Reservations required. Main courses
115SEK–295SEK ($15–$38); Swedish buffet 350SEK ($46). AE, DC, MC, V. Daily 7am–11pm. T-bana:
Kungsträdgården. Bus: 46, 55, 62, or 76.

KB Restaurant SWEDISH/CONTINENTAL A traditional artists' rendezvous in the center of town, KB Restaurant features good Swedish food as well as continental dishes. Fish dishes are especially recommended. You might begin with salmon trout roe and Russian caviar, followed by boiled turbot or lamb roast with stuffed zucchini in thyme-flavored bouillon. Dishes usually come with aromatic, freshly baked sourdough bread. Desserts include sorbets with fresh fruits and berries, and a heavenly lime soufflé with orange-blossom honey. There's also a relaxed and informal bar.

Smålandsgatan 7. ℂ 08/679-60-32. Reservations recommended. Main courses 170SEK–295SEK ($22–$38); fixed-price 2-course dinner 295SEK ($38). AE, DC, MC, V. Mon–Fri 11:30am–11:30pm; Sat noon–midnight. Closed June 23–Aug 7. T-bana: Östermalmstorg.

Lisa Elmquist ★ *Kids* SEAFOOD Under the soaring roof, amid the food stalls of Stockholm's produce market (the Östermalms Saluhall), you'll find this likeable cafe and oyster bar. Because of its good, affordable food, this is the most popular choice for Stockholm families visiting the market. It's owned by one of the city's largest fish distributors, so its menu varies with the catch. Some patrons come here for shrimp with bread and butter for 100SEK to 160SEK ($13–$21). Typical dishes include fish soup, salmon cutlets, and sautéed filet of lemon sole. It's not the most refined cuisine in town—it's an authentic "taste of Sweden," done exceedingly well. The establishment looks like a pleasant bistro under the tent at a country fair.

Östermalms Saluhall, Nybrogatan 31. ℂ 08/553-404-10. Reservations recommended. Main courses 70SEK–500SEK ($9.10–$65). AE, DC, MC, V. Mon–Fri 11am–5pm; Sat 10am–3:30pm. Closed at 2pm on Sat in July–Aug. T-bana: Östermalmstorg.

Noilo SWEDISH Located at the corner of this landmark square at the opera, this restaurant overlooks the Royal Palace. It has rustic, old-fashioned charm and satisfies different tastes and pocketbooks. You might begin with a selection of herring washed down with a glass of aquavit, or smoked salmon with Swedish red caviar. Seafood selections include filet of perch-pike with basil, fresh asparagus, and lobster sauce; or such meat dishes as filet of beef with potato hash. If you're arriving late, you might prefer the late-night menu, whose offerings range from cheeseburgers to a chicken drumstick with potato salad. Although a lunch-only place during the week, on Saturday this becomes your best bet for late-night dining in the capital.

Gustav Adolfs Torg 20. ℂ 08/10-27-57. Reservations recommended. Main courses 200SEK–300SEK ($26–$39); fixed–price lunch 237SEK ($31). AE, DC, MC, V. Mon–Sat 11:30am–3pm and 5–10pm. T-bana: Kungsträdgården.

Prinsens SWEDISH A 2-minute walk from Stureplan, this artists' haunt has become increasingly popular with foreign visitors. It has been serving people since 1897. Seating is on two levels, and in summer some tables are outside. The fresh, flavorful cuisine is basically Swedish food prepared in a conservative French style. It includes such traditional Swedish dishes as veal patty with home-made lingonberry preserves, sautéed fjord salmon, and roulades of beef. For dessert, try the homemade vanilla ice cream. Later in the evening, the restaurant becomes something of a drinking club.

Mäster Samuelsgatan 4. ℂ 08/611-13-31. Reservations recommended. Main courses 139SEK–316SEK ($18–$41). AE, DC, MC, V. Mon–Fri 11:30am–11pm; Sat 1–10:30pm; Sun 5–10pm. T-bana: Östermalmstorg.

Sturehof SWEDISH This seafood restaurant in the center of town was founded in 1897. Tasty and carefully prepared specialties include Swedish or

Canadian lobsters and oysters, fried plaice, boiled salmon with hollandaise, and fresh shrimp. A daily changing menu of genuine Swedish *husmanskost* (home cooking) is a bargain. Sample, for example, boiled salted veal tongue or potato and beet soup with sour cream. Try the famous *sotare* (grilled small Baltic herring served with boiled potatoes) if you want to sample a local favorite. Many locals come here to make an entire meal from the various types of herring—everything from tomato herring to curry herring.

Stureplan 2. (℃) **08/440-57-30.** Main courses 100SEK–350SEK ($13–$46). AE, DC, MC, V. Mon–Fri 11am–2am; Sat noon–2am; Sun 1pm–2am. T-bana: Östermalmstorg.

Tranan *Value* SWEDISH A real local restaurant, this 1915 tavern serves very good food and draws a friendly crowd attracted by affordable prices and the kitchen's deft handling of fresh ingredients. Its decor gives clues to the place's former role as a blue-collar beer tavern. The menu is only in Swedish, but the waiters speak English and will help guide you through an array of traditional Swedish dishes that often have French overtones. Nothing is more typical than the filet of beef served with fried potatoes, egg yolk, and horseradish. One Swede told us he comes here at least twice a week to order the Swedish meatballs and mashed potatoes. Other menu items are conservative and flavorful, in many cases virtually unchanged since the day the restaurant was founded. Examples include Swedish pork and lard sausage served with mashed potatoes and pickled beets, herring platters, toast "Skagen" piled high with shrimp, and beef "Rydberg" style: cubes of sautéed filet steak served with braised onions, sautéed potatoes, egg yolk, cream, and horseradish. Later you can go downstairs to enjoy an authentic local bar, where DJs spin the latest hits on Friday and Saturday nights. Patrons must be 23 or older to enter the bar.

Karlbergsvagen 14. (℃) **08/527-281-02.** Main courses 95SEK–285SEK ($12–$37). AE, DC, MC, V. Mon–Fri 11:30am–11:45pm; Sat–Sun 5–11:45pm. Cellar bar until 1am. T-bana: Odenplan.

ON GAMLA STAN (OLD TOWN)
VERY EXPENSIVE

Pontus in the Green House ★★ FRENCH/SWEDISH/ASIAN Set within a building whose foundations date back to the 16th century, this is a well-orchestrated and elegant restaurant that attracts some of the most powerful figures in Stockholm. Your dining experience will begin with a drink or aperitif in the ground-floor bar and cocktail lounge, where a staff member will explain the menu and record your choices. You'll then be ushered upstairs to a gold-and-green

---

(Kids) Family-Friendly Restaurants

Lisa Elmquist (p. 83) Because this restaurant is found in the produce market, Östermalms Saluhall, having lunch here is a colorful adventure. One favorite food item is a portion of shrimp with bread and butter. Families can dine under a tent, which evokes a country fair setting.

Solliden Near the top of the Skansen compound, a Williamsburg-type park dating from 1891, Solliden ((℃) **08/662-93-03**) is a cluster of restaurants set in a sprawling building. This all-purpose dining emporium has an array of dining facilities, which is attractive to families. Solliden offers a lunch smorgasbord.

dining room with high arched windows and an undeniable sense of respect for the presentation of food. Chef Pontus Frithiof was inspired by two of the grand francophile chefs of England, Marco Pierre White and Gordon Ramsay. Their influence is seen in dishes that include garlic-sautéed turbot with sweetbreads; tender veal tongue with Jerusalem artichokes; steamed turbot with horseradish, prawns, and brown butter; and citrus-glazed *Challonais* duck breast served with foie gras, shiitake mushrooms, spring onions, and teriyaki sauce. In our view, the herring with vinegar-and-onion marmalade is the Old Town's tastiest. It's worth the trek across town to sample the creamy Roquefort made from the first milk nursing cows produce. After tasting this cheese, you'll never go back—except with regret—to that store-bought stuff again.

Österlånggatan 17. ✆ 08/23-85-00. Reservations recommended. Main courses 485SEK–495SEK ($63–$64); 8-course fixed-price menu 745SEK ($97). AE, DC, MC, V. Mon–Fri 11:30am–3pm and 6–11pm; Sat 1–11pm. T-bana: Gamla Stan.

EXPENSIVE

Den Gyldene Freden ✪ SWEDISH   "Golden Peace" is said to be Stockholm's oldest tavern. The restaurant opened in 1722 in a structure built the year before. The Swedish Academy owns the building, and members frequent the place on Thursday night. The cozy dining rooms are named for Swedish historical figures who were patrons. Today it's popular with artists, lawyers, and poets. You get good traditional Swedish cooking, especially fresh Baltic fish and game from the forests. Herring is a favorite appetizer. More imaginative appetizers include a creamy artichoke soup, Jerusalem artichokes with a dollop of caviar, and an especially intriguing consommé of oxtail with tiny ravioli stuffed with quail breast. Notable main courses are fried breast of wild duck in Calvados sauce, and roast of reindeer in juniper-berry sauce. A particular delight is homemade duck sausage with three kinds of mushrooms in black pepper sauce. Want something different for dessert? How about warm rose hip soup with vanilla ice cream? Of course, if you order that, you'd be denying yourself the "symphony" of lingonberries or the longtime favorite: Stockholm's best chocolate cake.

Österlånggatan 51. ✆ 08/24-97-60. Reservations recommended. Main courses 115SEK–395SEK ($15–$51). AE, DC, MC, V. Mon–Fri 5pm–midnight; Sat 1pm–midnight. Closed on Mon July–Aug. T-bana: Gamla Stan.

Fem Små Hus ✪ SWEDISH/FRENCH   This historic restaurant, with cellars that date from the 17th century, is furnished like a private castle, with European antiques and oil paintings. The nine rooms in the labyrinthine interior hold candlelit tables. You can order assorted herring, slices of fresh salmon in Chablis, braised scallops with saffron sauce, terrine of duckling with goose liver and truffles, filet of beef with herb sauce, and sorbets with seasonal fruits and berries. The best ingredients from Sweden's forests and shores appear on the menu. The cuisine and staff are worthy of the restaurant's hallowed reputation.

Nygränd 10. ✆ 08/10-87-75. Reservations required. Main courses 235SEK–295SEK ($31–$38); 3-course fixed-price menu 450SEK–531SEK ($59–$69). AE, DC, MC, V. Daily 5–11pm. T-bana: Gamla Stan.

Leijontornet ✪✪ SWEDISH/INTERNATIONAL   This is one of the Old Town's most stylish and fashionable restaurants, noted for its fine food and the quality of its service. From the small, street-level bar where you can order a before-dinner drink, patrons descend into the intimately lit cellar (the restaurant was built around a medieval defense tower). To reach this restaurant, you need to negotiate a labyrinth of brick passageways through the Victory Hotel.

You might begin with grilled, marinated calamari with eggplant and paprika cream, or a salad with roast deer and curry dressing, or perhaps a potato crepe with bleak roe vinaigrette and fried herring. Main courses include roast lamb with moussaka and basil; grilled salmon with tomato, spinach, and lime taglierini; and risotto with pumpkin and flap mushrooms. Dishes often arrive at your table looking like works of art, and some of the country's finest produce appears on the menus here.

In the Victory Hotel, Lilla Nygatan 5. © 08/14-23-55. Reservations required. Main courses 195SEK–295SEK ($25–$38); 7-course tasting menu 695SEK ($90). AE, DC, MC, V. Mon–Sat 6pm–midnight. Closed July and bank holidays. T-bana: Gamla Stan.

MODERATE

Erik's Gondolen *Finds* INTERNATIONAL/FRENCH This monument from the 1930s offers one of the more panoramic views in Stockholm. Partially suspended beneath a pedestrian footbridge that connects the island of Gamla Stan with the island of Södermalm, it requires access through a (free) private elevator from the Stadtsgården. This elevator will haul you up the equivalent of 11 stories to a restaurant with a decor that hasn't changed much since it was built as an engineering oddity in 1935.

The bar is cozy, and the dining room is well managed and very popular; gentlemen usually wear jackets and ties. Menu items reflect a mixture of French and Swedish cuisine. For appetizers, take delight in such servings as bleak roe with a warm onion and cauliflower sauce, or else risotto with truffles. From the grill emerges such sublime dishes as red trout or filet of Swedish lamb, served with tarragon butter. Grilled filet of pike-perch is one of the chef's special dishes, as is breast of corn-fed chicken with a sherry sauce and a side of grilled vegetables. The talent of the kitchen keeps local habitués returning, and hotel concierges often recommend this restaurant to guests seeking excellent fare at a reasonable price.

Stadtsgården 6. © 08/641-7090. Reservations required. Lunch main courses 95SEK–175SEK ($12–$23); dinner main courses 250SEK–325SEK ($33–$42); fixed-price lunch 95SEK ($12). AE, DC, MC, V. Mon–Fri 11:30am–2:30pm and 5–11pm; Sat noon–2:30pm and 5–11pm. T-bana: Slussen.

Mälardrottningen ★ *Finds* SEAFOOD/INTERNATIONAL This upscale floating restaurant occupies the showplace deck of a motor yacht, built by industrialist C. K. G. Billings in 1924, that's now a hotel (see "Where to Stay," earlier in this chapter). Admittedly, a lot of its allure derives from its novelty, but the food is well prepared, with some of the flair associated with the ship's heyday. Menu items change with the seasons but might include imaginative offerings such as salmon-filet spring roll with pepper-garlic vinaigrette, pear-and-goat-cheese salad with thyme-flavored honey, and skewered scampi served with Parmesan cheese and chutney made from pesto and bananas. One of the least expensive main courses—appropriate for foggy days beside the harbor—is a heaping portion of marinated mussels in white wine and butter sauce, served with french fries. More formal dishes include a parfait of chicken livers with an apricot and oregano brioche, cream of chanterelle soup with a pumpkin- and sage-flavored gnocchi, prosciutto-wrapped tiger prawns, grilled Dublin Bay prawns with a fennel-flavored butter sauce, and fried filets of pike-perch with crisp-fried paella, red peppers, and lobster sauce.

Riddarholmen. © 08/545-187-80. Reservations recommended. Main courses 150SEK–255SEK ($20–$33). AE, DC, MC, V. Mon–Fri 11:30am–2pm and 3–10pm; Sat 5–10pm. T-bana: Gamla Stan.

Stortorgskällaren SWEDISH In the winter, this restaurant occupies medieval wine cellars whose vaulted ceilings date from the 15th century. Old walls and chandeliers complement plush carpeting and subtle lighting. In summer, seating is on the outdoor terrace, beside a charming square opposite the Stock Exchange, or, in bad weather, in the street-level dining room.

The menu changes often. You might begin with pâté of wild game with blackberry chutney and pickled carrots, or cured salmon and white bleak roe served with crème fraîche and onions. There's also fried salmon with mushroom sauce. Another specialty is a casserole of Baltic fish seasoned with saffron. After you've sampled some of these dishes, you'll know why Stockholmers have long cited this restaurant as one of their most reliable. You don't get fireworks, but you do get a cheerful atmosphere, lots of flavor, and a hearty menu.

Stortorget 7. © 08/10-55-33. Reservations required. Main courses 200SEK–400SEK ($26–$52); 3-course fixed-price dinner 309SEK–380SEK ($40–$49). AE, DC, MC, V. Mon–Fri 11am–midnight; Sat 11am–11pm; Sun noon–11pm. T-bana: Gamla Stan.

INEXPENSIVE

Cattelin Restaurant *Value* SWEDISH   This restaurant on a historic street opened in 1897 and continues to serve fish and meat in a boisterous, convivial setting. Don't expect genteel service—the clattering of china can sometimes be almost deafening, but few of the regular patrons seem to mind. First-rate menu choices include various preparations of beef, salmon, trout, veal, and chicken, which frequently make up the daily specials that often are preferred by lunch patrons. This restaurant has survived wars, disasters, and changing food tastes, so it must be doing something right. It remains a sentimental favorite—and not just for the memories. In a city where people have been known to faint when presented with their dining tabs, it has always been a good, reasonably priced choice. The fixed-price lunch is served only Monday through Friday from 11am to 2pm for 59SEK ($7.65).

Storkyrkobrinken 9. © 08/20-18-18. Reservations recommended. Main courses 159SEK–210SEK ($21–$27); dagens (daily) menu 69SEK ($8.95); 3-course fixed-price dinner 245SEK ($32). AE, DC, MC, V. Mon–Fri 11am–11pm; Sat 11am–3pm; Sun noon–11pm. T-bana: Gamla Stan.

Magnus Ladulås SWEDISH/INTERNATIONAL   This is a pleasant restaurant converted from a vaulted inner room of a 12th-century weaving factory. You can enjoy a drink at the bar before your meal, which might include a mixed seafood plate with lobster sauce, fresh salmon from Lapland, or filet of beef in puff pastry with a deviled sauce. A specialty is steak cooked as you like it on a hot stone placed on your table. The cookery is first rate, and the quality of the ingredients is always high. It's a local favorite, and deservedly so.

Österlånggatan 26. © 08/21-19-57. Reservations recommended. Main courses 129SEK–182SEK ($17–$24). AE, DC, MC, V. Mon–Fri 11am–3pm and 5pm–midnight; Sat–Sun 5pm–midnight. Closed for lunch in July. T-bana: Gamla Stan.

ON KUNGSHOLMEN
EXPENSIVE

Stadshuskällaren SWEDISH/INTERNATIONAL   Near the harbor, in the basement of the City Hall, you'll find two dignified restaurants. After passing through a beautiful carved wooden doorway, you'll enter an interior that is divided into two sections: the Skänken, which serves lunch only, and the Stora Matsalen, where chefs prepare the annual banquet for the Nobel Prize winners; you can actually sample a Nobel menu. Dining here is like taking a culinary trip through Sweden. To go truly local, you'll want to try the elk or reindeer dishes (in season). Swedish salmon is our all-time favorite, and here it's prepared with consummate skill. Lately the chefs have become more imaginative, preparing such dishes as marinated filet of chicken breasts with avocado pesto (yes, avocado pesto), or perhaps almond-fried catfish with olives and mushrooms. Our vote for the finest dish offered on recent Nobel menus goes to roast pigeon breast with cèpe and pigeon meat ragoût, flavored with tart raspberry vinegar and accompanied by onion and potato compote.

Stadshuset. ℂ **08/650-54-54.** Main courses 120SEK–260SEK ($16–$34); 2-course fixed-price lunch 235SEK ($31); 3-course fixed-price dinner 475SEK ($62). AE, DC, MC, V. Skänken Mon–Fri 11:30am–2pm. Stora Matsalen Mon–Fri 11:30am–11pm; Sat 2–11pm. T-bana: Rådhuset. Bus: 3 or 62.

ON DJURGÅRDEN
EXPENSIVE

Ulla Winbladh ✿ SWEDISH   Since it opened in 1994, this restaurant has impressed even the most jaded of Stockholm's foodies. It's in a white stone structure, built as part of Stockholm's International Exposition of 1897. There's a large dining room decorated with works by Swedish artists, and a summer-only outdoor terrace laced with flowering plants. The menu focuses on conservative Swedish cuisine, all impeccably prepared. (Patrons who agree with this assessment include members of the Swedish royal family and a bevy of well-known TV, theater, and art-world personalities.) Menu choices include tender steak with artichokes and a perfectly prepared rack of Swedish lamb flavored with bacon. Fish selections might be platters of herring (marinated and fried), whitefish or pike-perch in white-wine sauce, divine turbot with saffron sauce, the inevitable salmon with dill sauce, and others that vary with the season.

Rosendalsvägen 8. ℂ **08/663-05-71.** Reservations required. Main courses 195SEK–265SEK ($25–$34). AE, DC, MC, V. Mon 11:30am–10pm; Tues–Fri 11:30am–11pm; Sat 1–11pm; Sun 1–10pm. Bus: 47.

Villa Kallhagen ✿ SWEDISH   Only a 5-minute ride from the city, this inn nonetheless gives you a feeling of dining in the Swedish countryside. This is one of the most popular restaurants in Stockholm during the summer months, when locals stroll along the park's canal, called Djurgårdkanalen. It's a lovely choice for either lunch or dinner. The crowd-pleasing bill of fare has typically Swedish dishes that are fresh and well prepared, including such favorites as Dijon mustard fried herring with mashed potatoes, or grilled salmon with creamy chanterelles in a red-wine sauce. Other dishes are more innovative, including lightly smoked breast of duck with an Asian salad and orange vinaigrette, or fried roast of veal with lemon and rosemary flavoring, served in a port wine sauce. Swedes adore a carpaccio of beets with goat cheese and lemon olive oil, and perhaps you will, too. Here's your chance to try the amber-colored cloudberries, which are picked in Lapland in the midnight sun. The rose hip soup might even be better than dear old mom made.

Djurgårdsbrunnsvagen 10. ℂ **08/665-03-00.** Reservations required. Main courses 195SEK–345SEK ($25–$45). AE, DC, MC, V. Mon–Fri 11:30am–2pm and 5–11pm; Sat noon–11pm. Closed in July. Bus: 69 from Central Station.

NEAR VASAPARKEN
INEXPENSIVE

Tennstopet (Pewter Tankard) SWEDISH   A well-known pub and restaurant, Tennstopet is in the northern part of town, near the Hotel Oden. It's the oldest pub in Sweden, adjacent to a classic dining room. Main dishes might include a ragout of fish and shellfish, salmon schnitzel, and plank steak. At lunch, you can dine on pork chops, vegetables, bread, butter, and coffee. Or just

Picnic Fare & Where to Eat It

Fast-food eateries and fresh food markets abound in Stockholm, especially in the center of the city, around Hötorget. Here you can visit **Hötorgs Hallen,** a fresh food market where you can buy the makings of an elegant picnic. Recently arrived immigrants sell many Turkish food products here, including stuffed pita bread.

For the most elegant fare of all, however, go to **Östermalms Hallen,** at the corner of Humlegårdsgatan and Nybrogatan, east of the center. Here, stall after stall sells picnic fare, including fresh shrimp and precooked items that will be wrapped carefully for you.

With your picnic fixings in hand, head for **Skansen** or the wooded peninsula of **Djurgården.** If you like to picnic with lots of people around, go to **Kungsträdgården,** "the summer living room of Stockholm," in the center of town.

order a draft beer, toss some darts, and admire the setting. This is the type of food that accompanies heavy drinking—it's good, hearty, and filling, but nothing more. The place prides itself on serving genuine English pints.

Dalagatan 50. ✆ **08/32-25-18.** Reservations recommended. Main courses 98SEK–230SEK ($13–$30). AE, DC, MC, V. Mon–Fri 4pm–1am; Sat–Sun 1pm–1am. T-bana: Odenplan. Bus: 54.

AT SÖDERMALM
INEXPENSIVE
Garlic & Shots MEDITERRANEAN/INTERNATIONAL   This theme restaurant follows two strong, overriding ideas: Everyone needs a shot of garlic every day, and everything tastes better if it's doctored with a dose of the Mediterranean's most potent ingredient. The no-frills setting is artfully spartan, with bare wooden tables that have hosted an unexpectedly large number of rock stars. Expect garlic in just about everything, from soup (try garlic-ginger with clam) to such main courses as beefsteak covered with fried minced garlic and Transylvania-style vampire steak, drenched in horseradish-tomato-and-garlic sauce. Dessert might be a slice of garlic-laced cheese or garlic-honey ice cream garnished with honey-marinated cloves of garlic. An appropriate foil for all these flavors? Garlic ale or garlic beer, if you're up to it.

Folkungagatan 84. ✆ **08/640-84-46.** Reservations recommended. Main courses 79SEK–229SEK ($10–$30). MC, V. Daily 5pm–1am. T-bana: Medborgarplatsen.

ON LANG HOLMEN
MODERATE
Långholmen Restaurant INTERNATIONAL   This premier dining venue is housed within the Långholmen Hotel, the former-state-penitentiary-turned-hotel. From the windows of the old-fashioned dining room, you can still see the high brick walls and the paraphernalia of what caused a lot of inmates a great deal of mental distress—small doors with heavy bolts, and bars on the windows. Ironically, within the establishment's new venue, these mementos are showcased rather than concealed—even the paintings, many in gentle pastels, reflect the workhouse drudgery that used to prevail here. Come here for an unusual insight

Cheap Eats

While touring Djurgårdsvagen, you can enjoy lunch at **Café Blå Porten,** Djurgårdsvagen 64 (© **08/663-8759**), a cafe/cafeteria that often draws patrons of the Lilijevalch art gallery next door. Soups, salads, sandwiches, and hot meals are served. Take the ferry from Slussen or Gamla Stan. At Nybrogatan, **Stockholm Bar and Restaurant,** Smalandsgatan 12 (© **08/611-31-95**), lies in the vicinity of the Royal Dramatic Theater. It serves international fare at very reasonable prices. Meals begin at about 79SEK ($10). Take the T-bana to Östermalmstorg.

Also at Östermalmstorg, you can patronize the well-known **Örtagården,** Nybroatan 31 (© **08/662-17-28**). This eatery on the second floor of the Östermalms food hall allows you to help yourself to a small smorgasbord of both hot and cold Swedish fare. It is increasingly rare to find the typical Swedish smorgasbord in Stockholm these days, and Örtagården is a holdout of the old culinary tradition at a bargain price.

into the hardships of the 19th century, and menu items that change with the seasons. Examples include a carpaccio of shellfish, smoked breast of duck with a walnut-cranberry vinaigrette, a combination of lobster and turbot stewed with vegetables in a shellfish bouillon, and tournedos of venison with juniper-berries, smoked ham, pepper sauce, and Swedish potatoes. This is hardly prison food—in fact, the most dedicated devotees of the restaurant hail it as one of the finest in Stockholm. Only market-fresh ingredients are used, and the staff here is clearly dedicated to pleasing your palate.

Kronohäktet. © **08/720-85-50.** Reservations recommended. Lunch main courses 92SEK–185SEK ($12–$24); dinner main courses 150SEK–290SEK ($20–$38); 3-course fixed-price dinner 390SEK ($51). AE, DC, MC, V. Mon–Fri 11:30am–10pm; Sat noon–10pm; Sun 11am–7pm. T-bana: Hornstul. Bus: 4, 40, or 66.

AT SOLNA
EXPENSIVE
Ulriksdals Wärdshus ★ *Finds* SWEDISH   This out-of-town establishment serves the best smorgasbord in Sweden. On the grounds of Ulriksdal's Royal Palace on Edviken Bay, you can dine in the all-glass Queen Silvia Pavilion, which opens onto gardens owned by the king and queen. The smorgasbord, featuring 86 delicacies (both shellfish and meat), is accompanied by beer or aquavit. Most people eat the smorgasbord in five courses, beginning with herring that comes in 20 varieties. They follow with salmon and then meat dishes, including *frikadeller* (meatballs) or perhaps reindeer, then a choice of cheese, and finally dessert. Some dishes are based on old farm-style recipes, including "Lansson's Temptation," which blends anchovies, heavy-cream potatoes, and onions. Over the Christmas season, the almost-doubled buffet is lavishly decorated in a seasonal theme and costs 550SEK ($72) per person.

Ulriksdals Royal Park, S-170 79 Solna. © **08/85-08-15.** Reservations required. Main courses 225SEK–375SEK ($29–$49); fixed-price menus 550SEK–675SEK ($72–$88). AE, DC, MC, V. Mon–Fri noon–11pm; Sat 2–11pm; Sun 12:30–7pm. Closed Dec 24–26. Take Sveavägen toward Arlanda Airport (Exit E18), 5km (3 miles) north of Stockholm.

AT SOLLENTUNA
EXPENSIVE
Edsbacka Krog ★ *Finds* SWEDISH/FRENCH   In a historic, thick-walled building from 1626, this was the first licensed inn in Stockholm. Ten minutes by taxi from the town center, you'll find dining rooms with an upscale country atmosphere. Menu items include combinations you're not likely to find in many other restaurants. Examples include whitebait roe with marinated halibut and avocado; boiled lobster in vegetable terrine; scallops with smoked cod in duck liver sauce; terrine of duck liver served with fried sweetbreads; and a platter that combines oxtail and beef tongue with duck liver and duck liver sauce. Chef Christer Lindström's dishes attract visitors from around the district. He is dedicated to sturdy continental cooking served with immaculate taste.

Sollentunavägen 220, Sollentuna. ✆ **08/96-33-00**. Reservations recommended. Main courses 295SEK–425SEK ($38–$55); fixed-price menus 585SEK–1,300SEK ($76–$169); 2-course business lunch 345SEK ($45). AE, DC, MC, V. Tues–Fri 11:30am–2:30pm and 5:30pm–midnight; Sat 2pm–midnight. May–June and Dec Sun–Mon 11:30am–2:30pm and 5:30pm–midnight. T-bana: Sollentuna.

AT FJÄDERHOLMARNA
EXPENSIVE
Fjäderholmarnas Krog ★ *Finds* SWEDISH   Just a 25-minute ferry ride from the center of Stockholm, this discovery is reached by going to the closest island in the archipelago. Part of the Fjäderholm islands, this restaurant is worthy not only because of its sublime cuisine, but as an excuse to visit the beautiful archipelago that lies at the doorstep to Stockholm. The restaurant is in a red house from 1985 that lies on the east peak of Fjäderholmarna. You have a choice of dining on the veranda (ideal in summer), at a table in the loft, or in the traditionally decorated main dining room. Backed up by a good wine list, the menu offers dishes well balanced in flavors, and chefs show an impeccably sharp technique. The *carte* is strongest on fish dishes, including such delights as steamed halibut in a butter sauce with trout roe, or roasted filet of salmon with sweet peppers, artichokes, and walnuts. A whole fried lemon sole is sautéed in brown butter and served with fresh chanterelles. Meat courses feature the likes of Swedish meatballs with cream sauce and lingonberries (how Swedish can you get?). Appetizers are also imaginative, including spinach salad with fried oysters and shallot vinaigrette.

Stora Fjäderholmarna. ✆ **08/718-33-55**. Reservations required. Main courses 115SEK–335SEK ($15–$44); fixed-price menus 405SEK–545SEK ($53–$71). AE, DC, MC, V. May–Sept and first 3 weeks in Dec Mon–Fri 11:30am–midnight, Sat–Sun noon–11:30pm. Take ferry to Fjäderholmarna.

4

Discovering Stockholm

Regardless of your age, interests, or the time of year, Stockholm is loaded with interesting sights and activities. If the *Vasa* Ship Museum doesn't pique your interest, perhaps the changing of the guard at the Royal Palace or the Gröna Lunds Tivoli amusement park will. Even window shopping for beautifully designed Swedish crafts can be an enjoyable way to spend an afternoon. And after dark, Stockholm becomes one of the livelier cities in the north of Europe.

SUGGESTED ITINERARIES

If You Have 1 Day

It's far too short, but take a ferry to Djurgården and visit the *Vasa* Ship Museum, Stockholm's most famous attraction, and explore the open-air Skansen folk museum. In the afternoon, take our walking tour of Gamla Stan (Old Town) (see later in this chapter) and have dinner at one of its restaurants.

If You Have 2 Days

On your first day, follow the previous suggestions.

On Day 2, get up early and visit the Kaknästornet television tower for a panoramic view of the city and its archipelago. Go to the Museum of Nordic History for a review of 5 centuries of life in Sweden. After lunch, visit the Millesgården of Lidingö, the sculpture garden, and former home of Carl Milles.

If You Have 3 Days

For the first 2 days, follow the itinerary given earlier.

On the third morning, take our "Walking Tour 2" (see later in this chapter). At noon (Sun 1pm), return to Gamla Stan to see the changing of the guard at the Royal Palace. View this French-inspired building that has been the residence of Swedish kings for more than 700 years. In the afternoon, visit the National Museum.

If You Have 4 or 5 Days

For Days 1 to 3, follow the suggestions given earlier.

On Day 4, take one of the many available tours of the Stockholm archipelago. Return to Stockholm and spend the evening at the Gröna Lunds Tivoli amusement park on Djurgården.

For your last day, visit Drottningholm Palace and its 18th-century theater. In the afternoon, go to Uppsala, which is easily reached by public transportation (see "Side Trips from Stockholm," later in this chapter).

1 Seeing the Sights
THE TOP ATTRACTIONS
GAMLA STAN & NEIGHBORING ISLANDS
Kungliga Slottet (Royal Palace) & Museums ★★   Kungliga Slottet is one of the few official residences of a European monarch that's open to the public. Although the king and queen prefer to live at Drottningholm, this massive 608-room showcase remains their official address. Severe, dignified, even cold-looking on the outside, it has a lavish interior designed in the Italian baroque style and built between 1691 and 1754.

Visitors may walk through the Council Chamber, where the king and his ministers meet several times a year. The **State Apartments,** with magnificent baroque ceilings and fine tapestries; the **Bernadotte Apartment;** and the **Guest Apartment** are on view. They're beautifully furnished in Swedish rococo, Louis XVI, and Empire style.

The **Skattkammaren,** or Treasury, in the cellar, is worth a visit. It exhibits one of the most celebrated collections of crown jewels in Europe. You'll see a dozen crowns, scepters, and orbs, along with antique jewelry. Be sure to see the **Royal Armory,** Slottsbacken 3, also in the cellar. Kings used to ride in these elegant gilded coaches. You'll also see coronation costumes from the 16th century, weapons, and armor.

Gustav III's collection of sculpture from the days of the Roman Empire can be viewed in the **Antikmuseum (Museum of Antiquities).**

Changing of the Royal Guard: In summer you can watch the parade of the military guard daily. In winter it takes place on Wednesday and Sunday; on the other days there's no parade, but you can see the changing of the guard. The parade route on Monday through Saturday begins at Sergels Torg and proceeds along Hamngatan, Kungsträdgårdsgatan, Strömgatan, Gustav Adolfs Torg, Norrbro, Skeppsbron, and Slottsbacken. On Sunday the guard departs from the Army Museum, going along Riddargatan, Artillerigatan, Strandvägen, Hamngatan, Kungsträdgårdsgatan, Strömgatan, Gustav Adolfs Torg, Norrbro, Skeppsbron, and Slottsbacken. For information on the time of the march, ask at the Tourist Center in Sweden House. The changing of the guard takes place at 12:15pm Monday to Saturday and at 1:15pm on Sunday in front of the Royal Palace.

Kungliga Husgerådskammaren. © **08/402-61-30** for Royal Apartments and Treasury, 08/402-61-34 for the Skattkammaren, 08/10-24-88 for Royal Armory, or 08/402-61-30 for Museum of Antiquities. Entry to the Royal Apartments, Royal Armory, Museum of Antiquities, and Treasury is 70SEK ($9.10) adults, 35SEK ($4.55) seniors and students, free for children under 7. A combination ticket to all parts of palace is 110SEK ($14) adults, 65SEK ($8.45) students and children. Apartments and Treasury Sept–June Tues–Sun noon–3pm (closed in Jan), July–Aug daily 10am–5pm; closed during government receptions. Royal Armory daily 10am–5pm. Museum of Antiquities mid-Aug daily 10am–4pm. T-bana: Gamla Stan. Bus: 43, 46, 59, or 76.

ON NORRMALM
Moderna Museet (Museum of Modern Art) ★   The museum focuses on contemporary works, including kinetic sculpture, by Swedish and international artists. Highlights include a small but good collection of cubist art by Picasso, Braque, and Léger; Matisse's *Apollo* découpage; the famous *Enigma of William Tell* by Salvador Dalí; and works by Brancusi, Max Ernst, Giacometti, and Arp, among others. There's also a collection of pop art—Robert Rauschenberg *(Monogram),* Claes Oldenburg, and Andy Warhol. Among 1960s works by prominent New York artists are Oldenburg's 12-foot-high *Geometric Mouse; Fox Trot,* an early Warhol; and *Total Totality All,* a large sculpture by Louise Nevelson.

Stockholm Attractions

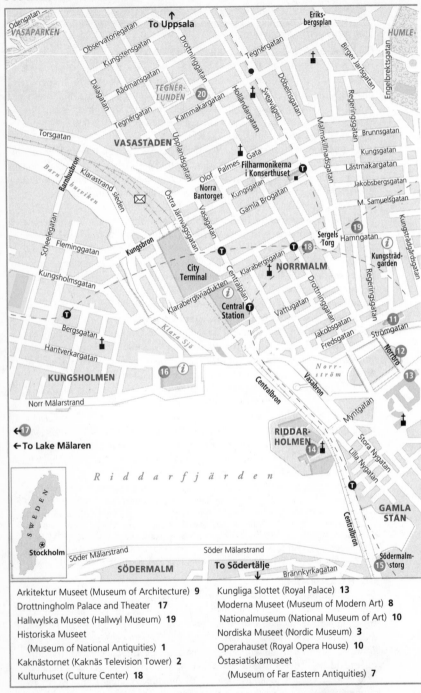

Arkitektur Museet (Museum of Architecture) **9**

Drottningholm Palace and Theater **17**

Hallwylska Museet (Hallwyl Museum) **19**

Historiska Museet
   (Museum of National Antiquities) **1**

Kaknästornet (Kaknäs Television Tower) **2**

Kulturhuset (Culture Center) **18**

Kungliga Slottet (Royal Palace) **13**

Moderna Museet (Museum of Modern Art) **8**

Nationalmuseum (National Museum of Art) **10**

Nordiska Museet (Nordic Museum) **3**

Operahauset (Royal Opera House) **10**

Östasiatiskamuseet
   (Museum of Far Eastern Antiquities) **7**

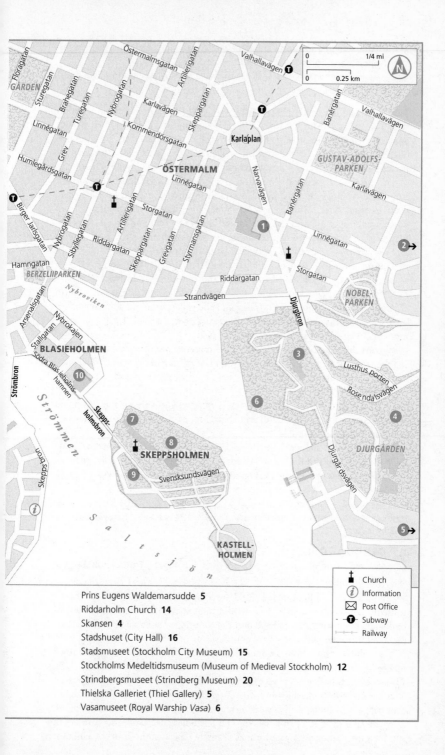

Prins Eugens Waldemarsudde **5**

Riddarholm Church **14**

Skansen **4**

Stadshuset (City Hall) **16**

Stadsmuseet (Stockholm City Museum) **15**

Stockholms Medeltidsmuseum (Museum of Medieval Stockholm) **12**

Strindbergsmuseet (Strindberg Museum) **20**

Thielska Galleriet (Thiel Gallery) **5**

Vasamuseet (Royal Warship *Vasa*) **6**

Museum activities include a children's workshop, concerts, films, discussions, and theater. There's also a cafe and pub.

Skeppsholmen. ℭ 08/519-55-200. Free admission. Tues–Wed 10am–8pm; Thurs–Sun 10am–6pm. T-bana: Kungsträdgården. Bus: 65.

Nationalmuseum (National Museum of Art) ★★ At the tip of a peninsula, a short walk from the Royal Opera House and the Grand Hotel, is Sweden's state treasure house of paintings and sculpture. Founded in 1792, it's one of the oldest museums in the world. Its collections include a wide assortment of masterpieces by such artists as Rembrandt and Rubens *(Sacrifices to Venus)*.

The first floor focuses on applied arts (silverware, handicrafts, porcelain, Empire furnishings, and the like). First-time visitors, if pressed for time, may want to head directly to the second floor. Here, among the paintings from northern Europe, is Lucas Cranach's most amusing *Venus and Cupid.* Also displayed is a rare collection of Russian icons, most of them—such as *St. George and the Dragon*—from the Moscow School of the mid–16th century.

The museum shows an exceptional number of excellent paintings by such masters as Perugino *(St. Sebastian),* Ribera (his oft-rendered *Martyrdom of Bartolomé*), El Greco *(Peter and Paul),* Giovanni Bellini *(Portrait of Christ),* Lotto *(Portrait of a Man),* and Poussin *(Bacchus).* The gallery contains some outstanding Flemish works, notably Rubens's *Bacchanal at Andros* and *Worship of Venus,* and Jan Brueghel's *Jesus Preaching from the Boat.*

Perhaps the most important room in the museum has one whole wall featuring the works of Rembrandt—*Portrait of an Old Man, Portrait of an Old Woman,* and *Kitchen Maid* (one of the most famous works in Stockholm). Here also is *The Oath of the Batavians.*

In yet another room is Watteau's *Lesson in Love,* and another room is noted for its Venetian works by Guardi and Canaletto, as well as English portraits by Gainsborough and Reynolds.

Modern works include Manet's *Parisienne;* Degas's dancers; Rodin's nude male *(Copper Age)* and his bust of Victor Hugo; van Gogh's *Light Movements in Green;* landscapes by Cézanne, Gauguin, and Pissarro; and paintings by Renoir, notably *La Grenouillère.*

Södra Blasieholmshamnen. ℭ 08/519-54-300. Admission 75SEK ($9.75) adults, 60SEK ($7.80) seniors and students, free for children under 16. Tues 11am–8pm; Wed–Sun 11am–5pm. T-bana: Kungsträdgården. Bus: 2, 62, 65, or 76.

AT DJURGÅRDEN

The forested island of Djurgården (Deer Park) lies about 3km (1¾ miles) to the east of Gamla Stan (Old Town).

Skansen ★★★ Often called "Old Sweden in a Nutshell," this open-air museum contains more than 150 dwellings on some 30 hectares (74 acres) of parkland. They originally stood all over the country, from Lapland to Skåne, and most are from the 18th and 19th centuries.

The exhibits range from a windmill to a manor house, to a complete town quarter. Browsers can explore the old workshops and see where book publishers, silversmiths, and druggists plied their trades. Many handicrafts for which Swedes later became noted (glassblowing, for example) are demonstrated, along with traditional peasant crafts, such as weaving and churning. For a tour of the buildings, arrive no later than 4pm. Folk dancing and open-air concerts are also featured. In summer, international stars perform at Skansen. Check at the Tourist Center for

Frommer's Favorite Stockholm Experiences

Experiencing Skansen. Butter churning or folk dancing, there's always something to intrigue people of all ages here. Wander at leisure through the world's oldest open-air museum (which covers about 30 hectares/74 acres of parkland), getting a glimpse of Swedish life in the long-ago countryside.

Strolling Through Gamla Stan at Night. To walk the narrow cobblestone alleys of the Old Town on foot at night is like going back in time. It takes little imagination to envision what everyday life must have been like in this "city between the bridges."

Taking the Baths. Swedes are fond of roasting themselves on wooden platforms like chickens on a grill, then plunging into a shower of Arctic-chilled water. After this experience, bathers emerge lighthearted and lightheaded into the fresh northern air, fortified for an evening of revelry.

Watching the Summer Dawn. In midsummer at 3am, you can get out of bed, as many Swedes do, and sit on a balcony to watch the eerie blue sky—pure, crystal, exquisite. Gradually it's bathed in peach as the early dawn of a summer day approaches. Swedes don't like to miss a minute of their summer, even if they have to get up early to enjoy it.

information on special events. There's much to do on summer nights (see "Stockholm After Dark," later in this chapter), and many places to eat.

Djurgården 49–51. ℰ **08/442-80-00.** Admission 30SEK–80SEK ($3.90–$10) adults, depending on time of day, day of the week, and season; 20SEK–30SEK ($2.60–$3.90) children 6–15; free for children 5 and under. Historic buildings Oct–Apr daily 10am–4pm; May daily 10am–8pm; June–Aug daily 10am–10pm; Sept daily 10am–5pm. Bus: 47 from central Stockholm. Ferry from Slussen.

Vasamuseet (Royal Warship Vasa) ✦✦✦   This 17th-century man-of-war is the top attraction in Scandinavia—and for good reason. Housed near Skansen in a museum specially constructed for it, the *Vasa* is the world's oldest complete and identified ship.

On its maiden voyage in 1628, in front of thousands of onlookers, the Royal Warship *Vasa* capsized and sank almost instantly to the bottom of Stockholm harbor. Its salvage in 1961 was an engineering triumph. On board were more than 4,000 coins, carpenters' tools, sailors' pants (in a color known as Lübeck gray), fish bones, and other items of archaeological interest. Best of all, 97% of the ship's 700 original decorative sculptures were found. Carefully restored and impregnated with preservatives, they are now back aboard the stunning ship. It once again carries grotesque faces, lion masks, fish-shape bodies, and other carvings, some still covered with the original paint and gilt.

A full-scale model of half of the *Vasa's* upper gun deck has been built, together with the admiral's cabin and the steering compartment. Several carved wooden figures represent the crew. By walking through the "gun deck" and the exhibit of original objects (including medical equipment, preserved clothes, and a backgammon board), you can get an idea of life aboard the ship.

Another exhibit tells the story of naval warfare in the *Vasa's* brief heyday. A diorama shows a battle fought by the Swedish and Polish navies in 1627. The ships, sculpted in copper, are positioned on a large cupola. Inside the cupola, a film illustrates the horrors of war at sea.

Galärvarvsvägen 14, Djurgården. ℂ 08/5195-4800. Admission 70SEK ($9.10) adults (Wed 5–8pm 50SEK/$6.50), 40SEK ($5.20) seniors and students, 10SEK ($1.30) children 7–15, free for children under 7. June 10–Aug 20 daily 9:30am–7pm; Aug 21–June 9 Wed 10am–8pm, Thurs–Tues 10am–5pm. Closed Jan 1, May 1, Dec 23–25, and Dec 31. Bus: 47 or 69. Ferry from Slussen year-round, from Nybroplan in summer only.

ON KUNGSHOLMEN

Stadshuset (Stockholm City Hall) ★★

Built in the "National Romantic Style," the Stockholm City Hall (Stadhuset), on the island of Kungsholmen, is one of the finest examples of modern architecture in Europe. Designed by Ragnar Ostberg, it was completed in 1923. A lofty square tower rising 100m (328 ft.) high dominates the red brick structure. It bears three gilt crowns, the symbol of Sweden, and the national coat-of-arms. There are two courts: the open civic court and the interior covered court. The Blue Hall is used for banquets and other festive occasions, including the Nobel Prize banquet. About 18 million pieces of gold and colored-glass mosaics cover the walls, and the southern gallery contains murals by Prince Eugen, the painter prince. The 101 City Council members meet in the council chamber.

Hantverksgatan 1. ℂ 08/508-290-59. Admission 60SEK ($7.80) adults, free for children under 12. Tower additional 20SEK ($2.60). May–Sept daily 9am–4:30pm. City Hall tours (subject to change) June–Sept daily at 10am, 11am, noon, 2pm, and 3pm; Oct–May daily at 10am and noon. T-bana: Centralen or Rådhuset. Bus: 3 or 62.

NEAR STOCKHOLM

Drottningholm Palace and Theater ★★★

Conceived as the centerpiece of Sweden's royal court, this regal complex of stately buildings sits on an island in Lake Mälaren. Dubbed the "Versailles of Sweden," Drottningholm (Queen's Island) lies about 11km (6¾ miles) west of Stockholm. The palace, loaded with courtly art and furnishings, sits amid fountains and parks, and still functions as one of the royal family's official residences.

On the grounds is one of the most perfectly preserved 18th-century theaters in the world, **Drottningholm Court Theater** (ℂ **08/759-04-06**). Between June and July, 30 performances are staged. Devoted almost exclusively to 18th-century opera, it seats only 450 for one of the most unusual entertainment experiences in Sweden. Many performances sell out far in advance to season-ticket holders. The theater can be visited only as part of a guided tour, which focuses on the original sets and stage mechanisms.

For tickets to the evening performances, which cost 165SEK to 610SEK ($21–$79), call ℂ **08/660-82-25.**

Ekerö, Drottningholm. ℂ 08/402-62-80. Palace 60SEK ($7.80) adults, 30SEK ($3.90) students and persons under 26; theater guided tour 60SEK ($7.80) adults, 30SEK ($3.90) students and persons under 26; Chinese Pavilion 50SEK ($6.50) adults, 25SEK ($3.25) students. All free for children under 7. Palace Oct–Apr Sat–Sun noon–3:30pm; May–Aug daily 10am–4:30pm; Sept daily noon–3:30pm. Theater guided tours in English May weekends 11am, noon, 1pm, 3pm; June–Aug daily 11am, noon, 1pm, 3pm; Sept daily noon, 2pm. Chinese Pavilion Apr and Oct daily 1–3:30pm; May daily noon, 2pm; June-Aug daily 11am, noon, 2pm, 3pm; Sept daily 2pm. T-bana: Brommaplan, then bus no. 301 or 323 to Drottningholm. Ferry from the dock near City Hall.

Millesgården ★★

On the island of Lingingö, northeast of Stockholm, is the former villa and sculpture garden of Carl Milles (1875–1955), the country's foremost sculptor. Although it takes time to reach the villa from the center of Stockholm, it is worth the trip. Some of the artist's most important works are found here, including his monumental and much-reproduced sculpture *Hands of God*. Sculptures sit atop columns on terraces in this garden of almost magical proportions set high above the harbor and the city landscape. These are copies of his most famous works; the originals are found all over Sweden and also in the United States. In his early works you can see how much he was influenced by the French sculptor Auguste Rodin (1840–1917), and also by Art Nouveau. But his later works took on a more simplified quality that was both dramatic and expressive. As you wander about, you are immediately overcome by how strongly Milles relied on mythological themes. The site also includes his personal collection of works by other leading sculptors. The villa displays a unique collection of art from both the Middle Ages and the Renaissance, plus rare artifacts excavated in the ruins of ancient Rome and Greece.

Carl Milles Väg 2, Lidingö. ℭ **08/446-75-90.** Admission 75SEK ($9.75) adults, 60SEK ($7.80) seniors and students, 20SEK ($2.60) children 7–16, free for children under 7. May–Sept daily 10am–5pm; Oct–Apr Tues–Fri noon–4pm, Sat–Sun 11am–5pm. T-bana: Ropsten, then bus to Torsviks Torg or train to Norsvik. Bus: 207.

MORE TO EXPLORE
GAMLA STAN & NEIGHBORING ISLANDS

Östasiatiskamuseet (Museum of Far Eastern Antiquities) *Finds*   The permanent collection at this small, intimate museum consists of archaeological objects, fine arts, and handicrafts from China, Japan, Korea, and India. The collection is one of the finest and most important of its kind outside Asia. Among the outstanding displays are Chinese Neolithic painted pottery, bronze ritual vessels, archaic jades, wood carvings, ivory, lacquerwork, and enamelware. You might see Chinese glass, Buddhist sculpture, Chinese painting and calligraphy, T'ang tomb pottery figurines, Sung classical stoneware (such as *celadon* and *temmoku*), Ming blue-and-white wares, and Ch'ing porcelain made for the Chinese and European markets. The building was erected from 1699 to 1700 as stables for Charles (Karl) XII's bodyguard.

Skeppsholmen. ℭ **08/519-55-750.** Admission 50SEK ($6.50) adults, free for children under 16. Tues noon–8pm; Wed–Sun noon–5pm. T-bana: Kungsträdgården. Bus: 65 to Karl XII Torg; 7-min. walk.

Riddarholm Church ✰   The second-oldest church in Stockholm is located on the tiny island of Riddarholmen, next to Gamla Stan. It was founded in the 13th century as a Franciscan monastery. Almost all the royal heads of state are entombed here, except Christina, who is buried in Rome.

There are three principal royal chapels, including one, the Bernadotte wing, that belongs to the present ruling family. Karl XIV Johan, the first king of the Bernadotte dynasty, is buried here in a large marble sarcophagus.

Riddarholmen. ℭ **08/402-61-30.** Admission 20SEK ($2.60) adults, 10SEK ($1.30) students and children. May 15–Aug 31 daily 10am–4pm; Sept Sat–Sun noon–3pm. Closed Nov–May 14. T-bana: Gamla Stan.

Stockholms Medeltidsmuseum (Museum of Medieval Stockholm)   Built around archaeological excavations, this museum traces the city's founding and development during the Middle Ages. Exhibits include parts of the old city wall that date to 1530, which were discovered from 1978 to 1980. In essence, the museum opens a window on the Middle Ages. Objects tell you about children's games, women's work, monastic life, and other activities. The museum also houses the *Riddarsholm* ship (from around 1520), which was excavated in 1930, with some of its leather goods, ceramics, and nautical artifacts well preserved.

Strömparterren, Norrbro. © **08/508-31-790.** Admission 60SEK ($7.80) adults, 40SEK ($5.20) students and seniors, free for children 18 and younger. July–Aug daily 11am–4pm; Sept–June Tues and Thurs–Sun 11am–4pm, Wed 11am–6pm. Bus: 43.

ON NORRMALM

Hallwylska Museet (Hallwyl Museum) *Finds* Sweden has never seen a collector to compare with Countess Wilhelmina von Hallwyl. She spent nearly three-quarters of a century collecting "things," most of them rare and valuable. She carefully cataloged them and left them to the state upon her death. Today the most eccentric of Stockholm's museums is in a turn-of-the-20th-century residence of great splendor. The house is a fine example of the skilled craftsmanship of its day.

The catalog of this passionate collector came to 78 volumes, so you can imagine the amount of decorative art on display. Open to the public since 1938, the collection includes priceless paintings, rare tapestries, silver, armor, weapons, antique musical instruments, glassware, even umbrellas and buttons (but only the finest ones). The aristocratic Hallwyl family occupied this town house from 1898 to 1930. One of the three daughters became a sculptor and studied with the great Carl Milles. On the tour, you learn historical tidbits. This house had a modern bathroom even before the royal palace. Ask about summer evening concerts presented in the central courtyard.

Hamngatan 4. © **08/519-55-599.** Guided tours 65SEK ($8.45) adults, 30SEK ($3.90) students and children 7-18, free for children under 7. Guided tours in Swedish: Tues–Fri noon, 1, 2, and 3pm; Sat–Sun noon, 1, and 3pm; extra tour Wed 6pm. Only 1 tour in English: Sun 1pm. T-bana: Kungsträdgården.

Historiska Museet (Museum of National Antiquities) ★★ This is the nation's finest repository of Swedish—especially Viking-era—relics; many were unearthed from ancient burial sites. The collection of artifacts dates from prehistoric to medieval times and includes Viking stone inscriptions and coins minted in the 10th century. In 1994, in the presence of King Carl XVI Gustaf and Queen Silvia, a Gold Room was inaugurated. It features Viking silver and gold jewelry, large ornate charms, elaborate bracelet designs found nowhere else in the world, and a unique neck collar from Färjestaden. The valuable treasury is underground, along long corridors and behind solid security doors.

Narvavägen 13–17. © **08/519-556-00.** Admission 60SEK ($7.80) adults, 50SEK ($6.50) seniors, 30SEK ($3.90) students, free for children under 15, 140SEK ($18) family. Sept–May Tues–Wed and Fri–Sun 11am–5pm, Thurs 11am–8pm; June–Aug daily 11am–5pm. T-bana: Karlaplan or Östermalmstorg. Bus: 47 or 69.

Kaknästornet (Kaknäs Television Tower) *Moments* In the northern district of Djurgården stands the tallest man-made structure in Scandinavia—a 152m (499-ft.) radio and television tower. Two elevators run to an observation platform, where you can see everything from the cobblestoned streets of Gamla Stan (Old Town) to the city's modern concrete-and-glass structures and the archipelago beyond. A moderately priced restaurant that serves classic Swedish cuisine is at the top of the tower.

Mörkakroken. © **08/789-24-35** or 08/667-2105. Admission 30SEK ($3.90) adults, 15SEK ($1.95) children 7–15, free for children under 7. May–Aug daily 9am–10pm; Sept–Apr daily 10am–9pm. Closed Dec 24–25. Bus: 69.

AT DJURGÅRDEN

Nordiska Museet ★★ This museum houses an impressive collection of Swedish implements, costumes, and furnishings from the 1500s to the present. The most outstanding museum of national life in Scandinavia, it contains more than a million objects. Highlights include dining tables and period costumes ranging from matching garters and ties for men to purple flowerpot hats from the 1890s. In the basement is an extensive exhibit of the tools of the Swedish fishing trade, plus relics from nomadic Lapps.

Djurgårdsvägen 6–16, Djurgården. © 08/5195-6000. Admission 75SEK ($9.75) adults, 50SEK ($6.50) seniors, 40SEK ($5.20) students, free for children under 18. Free for all Mon. Daily 10am–5pm. Bus: 44, 47, or 69.

Prins Eugens Waldemarsudde ★★ This one-time residence of the "painting prince" functions as an art gallery and a memorial to one of the most famous royal artists in recent history, Prince Eugen (1865–1947). The youngest of Oscar II's four children, he was credited with making innovative contributions to the techniques of Swedish landscape painting. He specialized in depictions of his favorite regions in central Sweden. Among his most publicly visible works are the murals on the inner walls of the City Hall.

Built between 1903 and 1904, and set directly on the water, the house is surrounded by a flower and sculpture garden. Eugen's private collection of paintings, which includes works by Edvard Munch, Carl Larsson, and Anders Zorn, is one of the most rewarding aspects of the residence. The house and its contents were willed to the Swedish government after the prince's death and opened to the public in 1948.

The house and art gallery are furnished as the prince left them. While at Waldemarsudde, see the **Old Mill,** built in the 1780s.

Prins Eugens Väg 6. © 08/545-837-00. Admission 75SEK ($9.75) adults, 55SEK ($7.15) seniors and students, free for children under 19. Tues–Wed and Fri–Sun 11am–5pm; Thurs 11am–8pm. Bus: 47 to the end of the line.

Thielska Galleriet (Thiel Gallery) ★★ At the tip of Djurgården, this gallery houses one of Sweden's major art collections. Many feel it surpasses the Prins Eugens Waldemarsudde collection. The sculpture and canvases here were acquired by Ernst Thiel, a financier and banker who eventually went bankrupt. The Swedish government acquired the collection in 1924.

Some big names in Scandinavian art are here, including Norway's Edvard Munch and Sweden's Anders Zorn (see his nude *In Dreams*). Gustav Fjaestad's furniture is also displayed. You'll also see a portrait of Nietzsche, whom Thiel greatly admired. Works by Manet, Rodin, and Toulouse-Lautrec, among others, round out the collection. Thiel is buried on the grounds beneath Rodin's statue *Shadow.*

Sjötullsbacken 6–8, Djurgården. © 08/662-58-84. Admission 50SEK ($6.50) adults, 30SEK ($3.90) seniors and students, free for children under 16. Mon–Sat noon–4pm; Sun 1–4pm. Bus: 69.

ON SÖDERMALM

Stadsmuseet (Stockholm City Museum) Housed in a building dating from 1684, the Stadsmuseet depicts the history of Stockholm and its citizens. Exhibits portray life in the industrial city throughout the past few centuries. Daily at 1pm, a 30-minute slide show in English describes Stockholm from the 16th century to the present.

Ryssgården, Slussen. © 08/508-31-600. Admission 50SEK ($6.50) adults, 40SEK ($5.20) seniors, free for children under 7. Tues–Wed and Fri–Sun 11am–5pm; Thurs 11am–9pm. T-bana: Slussen. Bus: 43 or 46.

ESPECIALLY FOR KIDS

The open-air park Skansen (see earlier in this chapter), on Djurgården, offers **Lill-Skansen,** the children's own "Little Skansen." There's a petting zoo with lots of child-friendly animals, including pigs, goats, and horses. Lill-Skansen offers a break from the dizzying (and often tantrum-inducing) excitement frequently generated by a commercial amusement park. A miniature train ride through the park is about as wild as it gets. Lill-Skansen is open daily in summer from 10:30am to 4pm.

Kids can spend a day or several at Skansen and not get bored. Before going to Skansen, stop off at the *Vasa* **Museum,** which many youngsters find an epic adventure. The evening can be capped by a visit to **Gröna Lunds Tivoli** (see "Stockholm After Dark," later in this chapter), which also is on Djurgården.

A LITERARY LANDMARK

Strindbergsmuseet (Strindberg Museum)   This building, popularly known as "The Blue Tower," is where August Strindberg, the dramatist and novelist, spent his last 4 years (1908–12). It contains a library, three rooms with his furnishings, and books, articles, and letters representing the last 20 years of his life. The library is a typical working author's library, with fiction and nonfiction works, including encyclopedias in Swedish, German, English, and French. Many of the volumes are full of pen and pencil markings—comments on the contents, heavily marked deletions of points he did not approve of, and underlines indicating his diligent research into matters that concerned him.

Of special interest to those familiar with Strindberg's plays is that he furnished his rooms like stage sets from his plays, with color schemes as he visualized them. The dining room contains sculpture, casts of busts, and masks evoking people and events that were important to him.

Drottninggatan 85. (C) 08/411-53-54. Admission 40SEK ($5.20) adults, 25SEK ($3.25) students and seniors, free for children. Tues–Sun noon–4pm. T-bana: Rådmansgatan.

ARCHITECTURAL HIGHLIGHTS

In Stockholm, architects or architecture buffs are often captivated by such grand buildings as Drottningholm Palace and Riddarholm Church. But many of the expanding suburban "cities" of Stockholm also are worth seeing for their urban planning and architecture, which in Sweden is among the most advanced in the world.

One of these model developments is **Farsta,** completed in 1960, although much altered since then. It lies 10km (6¼ miles) from the heart of Stockholm and can be reached by the Farsta train departing from the Central Station, or by taking bus no. 18 to the end of the line. With its traffic-free shopping mall, bright and airy modern apartment houses, and contemporary stores and restaurants, this makes a pleasant afternoon tour.

Arkitektur Museet (Museum of Architecture)   Founded in 1962 in a building designed by the Spanish architect Rafael Moneo, this museum illustrates the art of architecture combined with social planning. It displays copies of rooms, buildings, places, and cities from different eras, covering 1,000 years of Swedish architecture. The history of the buildings is presented in chronological sections. The collection consists of some two million sketches, drawings, and documents, plus a half-million photographs and about 1,000 architectural models. The library alone has some 25,000 volumes, most donated by Swedish architects. The library is dedicated to the memory of the Swedish diplomat Raoul Wallenberg, known for his humanitarian efforts in Hungary in 1944 and 1945. Less well known is that Wallenberg was a trained architect. His few existing drawings, mainly from his student days in the United States, are in the museum's archives.

Skeppsholmen. (C) 08/587-27-000. Free admission. Tues–Wed 10am–8pm; Thurs–Sun 10am–6pm. Bus: 65.

WALKING TOUR 1 GAMLA STAN (OLD TOWN)

Start:	Gustav Adolfs Torg.
Finish:	Slussplan.
Time:	3 hours.
Best Times:	Any day it's not raining.
Worst Times:	Rush hours (Mon–Fri 8–9:30am and 5:30–7pm).

Begin at:

① Gustav Adolfs Torg

In the Royal Palace facing the square, Gustavus III, patron of the arts, was assassinated here at a masked ball in 1792.

Walk across Norrbro (North Bridge) heading toward the Royal Palace, passing on your right the:

② Swedish Parliament

The Parliament building at Helgeandsholmen dates from 1897, when its foundation stone was laid. It can be visited only on guided tours.

Along the bridge on your left are stairs leading to the:

③ Medeltidsmuseet (Museum of Medieval Stockholm)

This museum on Strömparterren contains objects and settings from medieval Stockholm, including the Riddarholmship and parts of the old city wall.

TAKE A BREAK
One of the hidden cafes of Stockholm, **Café Strömparterren**, Helgeandsholmen (② 08/21-95-45), also is one of the most centrally located—just next door to the Medeltidsmuseet. Many Stockholmers come here for a morning cup of coffee and a stunning view of the waterfront. In summer, tables are placed outside; the interior of the cafe is built into the walls under Norrbro.

After leaving the museum, turn to the right and walk back to the bridge until you come to Slottskajen. Here, directly in front of the Royal Palace, make a right turn and head to Mynttorget, site of the Kanslihuset, a

government office building erected in the 1930s. The neoclassical, columned facade remains from the Royal Mint of 1790.

Continue straight along Myntgatan until you reach Riddarhustorget. On your right is the:

④ Riddarhuset

The Swedish aristocracy met in this 17th-century House of Nobles during the Parliament of the Four Estates (1665–68).

Continue straight across Riddarholmsbron (bridge) until you come to the little island of:

⑤ Riddarholmen

Called "the island of the knights," Riddarholmen is closely linked to the Old Town. You'll immediately see its chief landmark, the **Riddarholmskyrkan (church)** with its cast-iron spire. Founded as an abbey in the 13th century, it has been the burial place of Swedish kings for 4 centuries.

Walk along the right side of the church until you reach Birger Jarls Torg. From there, take the 1-block-long Wrangelska Backen to the water. Then go left and walk along Södra Riddarholmshamnen.

Veer left by the railroad tracks, climb some steps, and go along Hebbes Trappor until you return to Riddarholmskyrkan. From here, cross over Riddarholmsbron and return to Riddarhustorget.

Cross Stora Nygatan and take the next right onto Storkyrkobrinken, passing the landmark Cattelin Restaurant on your right. Continue along this street, past the Lady Hamilton Hotel, turning right onto Trångsund, which leads to:

⑥ Stortorget (Great Square)

Take a seat on one of the park benches—you've earned the rest. This plaza was the site of the Stockholm

Blood Bath of 1520 when Christian II of Denmark beheaded 80 Swedish noblemen and displayed a "pyramid" of their heads in the square. The Börsen on this square is the Swedish Stock Exchange, a building dating from 1776. This is where the Swedish Academy meets every year to choose the Nobel Prize winners in literature.

At the northeast corner of the square, take Källargränd north to view the entrance, opening onto Slottsbacken, of the:

7 Royal Palace

The present palace dates mainly from 1760 after a previous one was destroyed by fire. The changing of the guard takes place on this square.

On your right is the site of the:

8 Storkyrkan

This church was founded in the mid-1200s but has been rebuilt many times since. It's the site of coronations and royal weddings; kings are also christened here. The most celebrated sculpture here is *St. George and the Dragon*, a huge work dating from 1489. The royal pews have been used for 3 centuries, and the altar, mainly in ebony and silver, dates from 1652. This is still a functioning church, so it's best to visit when services are not in progress. It's open Monday through Saturday from 9am to 7pm, and Sunday from 9am to 5:30pm; admission is free.

Continue right along Slottsbacken, either visiting the palace now or saving it for later. Go right as you reach Bollhusgränd, a cobblestone street of old houses leading to:

9 Köpmantorget

One of the most charming squares of the Old Town, Köpmantorget contains a famous copy of the *St. George and the Dragon* statue.

From the square, take Köpmanbrinken, which runs for 1 block before turning into:

10 Österlånggatan

Now the site of many restaurants and antiques shops, Österlånggatan was once Old Town's harbor street.

Continue along Österlånggatan, but take the first left under an arch, leading into:

11 Stora Hoparegränd

Some buildings along this dank street, one of the darkest and narrowest in Gamla Stan, date from the mid-1600s.

Walk down the alley toward the water, emerging at Skeppsbron (bridge). Turn right and walk for 2 blocks until you reach Ferkens Gränd. Go right again up Ferkens Gränd until you return to Österlånggatan. Go left on Österlånggatan until you come to Tullgränd. Take the street on your right:

12 Prästgatan

This street was named after the priests who used to live here. As you climb the street, look to your left to Mårten Trotzigs Gränd, a street of steps that's the narrowest in Gamla Stan.

Continue along Prästgatan, passing a playground on your right. Turn right onto Tyska Brinken until you see on your right:

13 Tyska Kyrkan

Since the beginning of the 17th century, this has been the German church of Stockholm. The church has a baroque interior and is exquisitely decorated.

After you leave the church, the street in front of you will be Skomakargatan. Head up this street until you come to Stortorget once again. From Stortorget, take Kåkbrinken, at the southwest corner of the square. Follow this little street until turning left at:

14 Västerlånggatan

This pedestrian street is the main shopping artery of Gamla Stan and the best place to purchase gifts and souvenirs of Sweden.

Follow Västerlånggatan to:

15 Järntorget

This street used to be known as Korntorget when it was the center of the copper and iron trade in the 16th and 17th centuries. At times in its long history, Järntorget has been the place of punishment for "wrongdoers." The most unusual statue in Stockholm stands here—a **statue of Evert Taube,**

Walking Tour 1: Gamla Stan (Old Town)

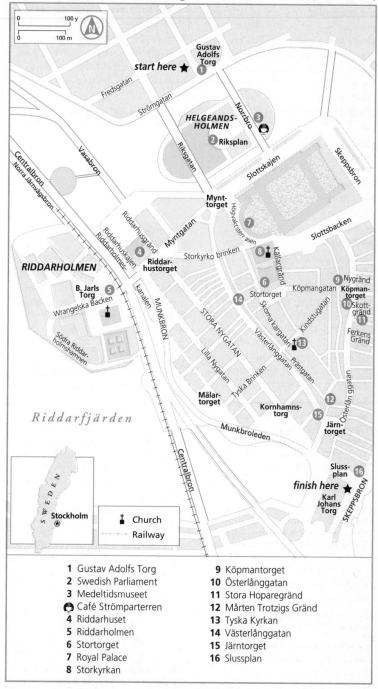

0   100 y
0   100 m

Gustav Adolfs Torg

start here ★ **①**

Fredsgatan

Strömgatan

Norrbro

HELGEANDS-HOLMEN **③**

Riksgatan

② Riksplan

Vasabron

Slottskajen

Skeppsbron

Myntgatan

Mynt-torget

Slottsbacken

Riddarhusgränd

Riddarhuskajen

Riddarholms-

Centralbron

Nora Järnvägsbron

Högvaktsterrasen

⑦

Källargränd

④

RIDDARHOLMEN

Riddar-hustorget

Storkyrko brinken

⑧

Nygränd

⑨

B. Jarls Torg **⑤**

Wrangelska Backen

Kanalen

MUNKBRON

STORA NY GATAN

⑥ Stortorget

Köpmangatan

Köpman-torget

⑩ Skott-gränd

⑭

Skomakargatan

Kindstugatan

⑪

Södra Riddar-holmshamnen

Lilla Nygatan

Västerlånggatan

Prästgatan

⑬

Ferkens Gränd

Tyska Brinken

Riddarfjärden

Mälar-torget

Kornhamns-torg

⑫

Österlånggatan

Munkbroleden

⑮

Järn-torget

Centralbron

Sluss-plan **⑯**

finish here ★

Karl Johans Torg

SKEPPSBRON

SWEDEN

Stockholm

✝ Church

Railway

1 Gustav Adolfs Torg	**9** Köpmantorget
2 Swedish Parliament	**10** Österlånggatan
3 Medeltidsmuseet	**11** Stora Hoparegränd
Café Strömparterren	**12** Mårten Trotzigs Gränd
4 Riddarhuset	**13** Tyska Kyrkan
5 Riddarholmen	**14** Västerlånggatan
6 Stortorget	**15** Järntorget
7 Royal Palace	**16** Slussplan
8 Storkyrkan	

the troubadour and Swedish national poet of the early 1900s. He's carrying a newspaper under his arm, his coat draped nonchalantly, his sunglasses pushed up high on his forehead.

From the square, take Järntorgsgatan to:

⑯ **Slussplan**

Here you can catch a bus to return to the central city, or you can board a ferry to Djurgården and its many museums.

WALKING TOUR 2 **ALONG THE HARBOR**

Start:	Stadshuset.
Finish:	Museum of Architecture.
Time:	3 hours.
Best Times:	Any day it's not raining.
Worst Times:	Rush hours (Mon–Fri 8–9:30am and 5:30–7pm).

Start at Hantverkargatan 1, on Kungsholmen:

❶ **Stadshuset (Stockholm City Hall)**

This island has some of the loveliest and most varied waterfront walks in the city. It took 12 years, 8 million bricks, and 19 million gilded mosaic tiles to erect this city hall, which can be visited on a guided tour. Go inside the courtyard on your own and admire the architecture.

When exiting the building, turn right and walk across Stadshusbron (City Hall Bridge) to Norrmalm. You'll see the Sheraton Hotel on your left, and on your right the Stadshus-cafeet, where sightseeing boats depart on canal cruises in summer. Walk past the boats and go under an underpass (watch out for fast-riding bicyclists).

Continue along the canal until you reach Tegelbacken, a waterfront square. At the entrance to the Vasabron (bridge), cross the street and continue along Fredsgatan. Veer right at the intersection, hugging the canal. This will take you to Rosenbad, a little triangular park.

At the canal-bordering Strömgatan, look at the building on your right:

❷ **Swedish Parliament**

You can visit this building on a guided tour.

Continue on to:

❸ **Gustav Adolfs Torg**

From here you have a panoramic view of the Royal Palace across the canal and of the Royal Opera straight ahead. This is one of the most famous landmark squares of Stockholm, and the most scenically located.

Strömgatan resumes at the corner of the Opera House, site of the Operakällaren, for many years the finest restaurant in Stockholm. Continue along until you reach the southern tier of the:

❹ **Kungsträdgården**

These royal gardens, the summer living room of Stockholm, reach from Hamngatan on the north side down to the water. Established in the 1500s as a pleasure garden for the court, they are now open to all, with cafes, open-air restaurants, and refreshment kiosks.

TAKE A BREAK
Since the late 1800s, the **Café Victoria**, Kungsträd-gården (℡ **08/10-10-85**), in the center of Stockholm, has attracted crowds. It's an ideal spot for a refreshing drink or snack at any time during the day or evening. It's open Monday through Saturday from 11:30am to 10pm and Sunday from noon to 7pm. (See "Stockholm After Dark," later in this chapter, for more information.)

Walking Tour 2: Along the Harbor

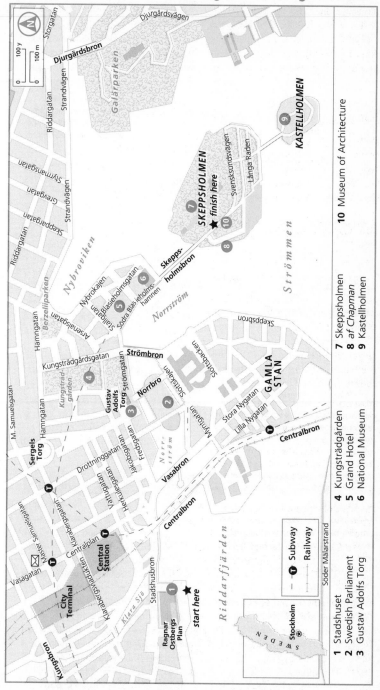

4 Kungsträdgården
5 Grand Hotel
6 National Museum

7 Skeppsholmen
8 af Chapman
9 Kastellholmen

10 Museum of Architecture

1 Stadshuset
2 Swedish Parliament
3 Gustav Adolfs Torg

--- Subway
······ Railway

107

Continue along the waterfront, past Ström-
bron, a bridge leading to Gamla Stan, and
emerge onto Södra Blasieholmshamnen. At
no. 8 is the:

⑤ Grand Hotel

For decades this has been the prestige
address of Stockholm, attracting
Nobel Prize winners as well as most
visiting dignitaries and movie stars.
On your right, any number of sightseeing boats depart in summer for
tours of the Stockholm archipelago.
From this vantage point, you'll have a
good view of the Royal Palace and
Gamla Stan.

Continue along Södra Blasieholmshamnen
until you reach (on your right) the:

⑥ National Museum

Here you find a repository of the
state's art treasures—everything from
Renoir to Rembrandt.

Cross the Skeppsholmsbron (bridge) leading
to the little island of:

⑦ Skeppsholmen

The island holds a number of attractions (see "Gamla Stan & Neighboring
Islands," under "The Top Attractions,"
earlier in this chapter).

After crossing the bridge, turn right along
Västra Brobänken. On your right you'll
pass the:

⑧ af Chapman

This "tall ship" with fully rigged masts
once sailed the seas under three different flags before being permanently
anchored in 1949 as a youth hostel.

Turn left onto Flaggmansvägen. Continue
along Holmamiralens Torg, passing the
Nordiska Institute on your right. Cut right
toward the water at Södra Brobänken. Take
a right turn and cross the bridge leading to:

⑨ Kastellholmen

This is one of the most charming, but
least visited, islands in Stockholm.
Head right along the water, going
around Kastellholmskajen. Circle
around and turn left at the end
of Kastelleton. Walk back along
Örlogsvägen, which runs through the
center of the small island.

Cross the Kastellholmsbron (bridge) and
return to the larger island of Skeppsholmen.
This time go straight along Amiralsvägen,
turning left onto Långa Raden. Cut right and
continue to walk along Långa Raden. The
first building on your left is the:

⑩ Museum of Architecture

The collection contains slides and
thousands of architectural drawings
and sketches from the last 100 years.

From this point at the end of
the walking tour, you can catch bus
no. 65 to take you back to the heart of
Stockholm.

2 Organized Tours

CITY TOURS The quickest and most convenient way to see the highlights
of Stockholm is to take one of the bus tours that leave from the Square of Gustaf
Adolff, near the Kungsträdgården.

Stockholm Sightseeing, Skeppsbron 22 (© 08/587-140-20), offers a variety of tours, mostly in summer. Tours depart from Gustaf Adolfs Torg in front
of the Dansmuseet. For "Panoramic Stockholm," a 1½-hour tour, costing
200SEK ($26), purports to show you Stockholm in record time. At least you'll
see the landmarks and several waterscape views. Departures are year-round. For
"Stockholm in a Nutshell," you can take a 2½-hour tour, costing 305SEK ($40),
with departures from April 8 to December 19. This tour shows you the highlights of Stockholm, including a sail around the royal park at Djurgården. A
more comprehensive tour, the "Grand Tour" lasts 3½ hours and costs 395SEK
($51). This tour is by both boat and bus. "Stockholm Then and Now" departs
June 28 to August 29, lasts 2½ hours, and costs 280SEK ($36). This bus and
walking tour has as its highlight a guided walking tour through Old Town with

its narrow alleys and tiny courtyards. Finally, from June 28 to August 22, you can go on a 45-minute "Horse and Carriage Tour," costing 90SEK ($12), and departing from Mynttorget by the Royal Palace.

OLD TOWN STROLLS Authorized guides lead 1-hour walking tours of the medieval lanes of Stockholm's Old Town. These walks are conducted daily from mid-June until late August, departing from the Royal Opera House at Gustav Adolfs Torg. The cost is 80SEK ($10). Tickets and times of departure are available from **Stockholm Sightseeing,** Skeppsbron 22 (© **08/587-140-20**).

CANAL CRUISES **Stockholm Sightseeing** (© **08/587-140-20**) offers the "Royal Canal Tour," April to mid-December daily, every half-hour on the hour. Tours cost 110SEK ($14) for adults and 65SEK ($8.45) for children. Visitors are ferried around the canals of Djurgården.

3 Spectator Sports

Soccer and **ice hockey** are the two most popular spectator sports in Sweden, and Stockholm is the home of world-class teams in both. The most important venue for any spectator sport in the capital, the **Stockholm Globe Arena (Globen),** lies less than 6.5km (4 miles) south of central Stockholm. Built in 1989, it's believed to be the biggest round building in the world, with a seating capacity of 16,000. It offers everything from political rallies, motorcycle competitions, and sales conventions to basketball and ice hockey games, tennis matches, and rock concerts. Its ticket office (© **08/600-34-00**) also sells tickets Monday through Friday from 9am to 4pm for most of Stockholm's soccer games, which are played in an open-air stadium nearby. The Globen complex lies in the suburb of Johnneshov (T-bana: Globen).

Another popular pastime is watching and betting on **trotting races.** These races usually take place on Wednesday at 6:30pm and on an occasional Saturday at 12:30pm in both summer and winter. (In winter an attempt is made to clear snow and ice from the racecourse; slippery conditions sometimes lead to unpredictable results.) Admission to **Solvalla Stadium** (© **08/635-90-00**), which lies about 6.5km (4 miles) north of the city center, is 40SEK ($5.20). From Stockholm, take the bus marked SOLVALLA.

For schedules and ticket information, inquire at your hotel or the city's tourist office, or buy a copy of *Stockholm This Week* from a newspaper kiosk.

4 Active Pursuits

GOLF For those who want to play golf at the "top of Europe," there is the **Bromma Golf Course,** Kvarnbacksvägen 28, 16874 Bromma (© **08/564-888-30**), lying 5km (3 miles) west of the center of Stockholm. It's a 9-hole golf course with well-maintained greens. Greens fees are 140SEK ($18), and golf clubs can be rented.

HORSEBACK RIDING (VIKING STYLE) Iceland horses—gentle and small—can be ridden at the **Haniwnge Iceland Horse Center** at Hemfosa, 37km (23 miles) south of Stockholm (© **08/500-481-81**). For 400SEK ($52), you can ride for 2½ hours; the price includes a picnic lunch. Aside from walking, galloping, trotting, and cantering, the horses have another gait, the *tölt,* a kind of equine speed walk that has no English translation.

SAUNA & SWIMMING A combination sauna, outdoor heated pool, and children's paddling pool, **Vilda Vanadis** is at Vanadislunden (© **08/30-12-11**), near the northern terminus of Sveavägen, within easy walking distance of the Oden Hotel and the city center. This really is an adventure park, with a variety of attractions, as well as a sauna and a restaurant. The entrance fee is 55SEK ($7.15), but once you're inside, the attractions are free. It's open daily from early May until the end of August, from 10am to 6pm.

TENNIS, SQUASH & WEIGHTLIFTING Aside from tennis at the **Royal Tennishall,** Lidingövägen 75 (© **08/459-15-00** for reservations), you can lift weights and enjoy a sauna and solarium. The center has 16 indoor courts, 5 outdoor clay courts, and 8 squash courts. Tennis courts cost 265SEK ($34) per hour; squash courts, 85SEK to 210SEK ($11–$27) for a 30-minute session; the weight room entrance fee is 45SEK ($5.85). The center is open Monday to Thursday from 7am to 11pm, Friday from 7am to 9pm, and Saturday and Sunday 8am to 9pm.

5 Shopping

THE SHOPPING SCENE

Stockholm is filled with shop after shop of dazzling merchandise—often at dazzlingly steep prices that reflect the high esteem in which Swedish craftspeople are held.

Bargain shoppers should proceed with caution. Some good buys do exist, but it takes a lot of searching. If you're a casual shopper, you may want to confine your purchases to handsome souvenirs and gifts.

Swedish glass, of course, is world-famous. Swedish wooden items are outstanding, and many people love Swedish functional furniture in blond pine or birch. Other items to look for include playsuits for children, silver necklaces, reindeer gloves, stainless-steel utensils, hand-woven neckties and skirts, sweaters and mittens in Nordic patterns, Swedish clogs, and colorful handicrafts from the provinces. The most famous souvenir to buy is the Dala horse from Dalarna.

SHOPPING STREETS & DISTRICTS Everybody's favorite shopping area in Stockholm is **Gamla Stan (Old Town).** Site of the Royal Palace, it even attracts such shoppers as the queen. The main street for browsing is **Västerlånggatan.** Many antiques stores are found here, but don't expect low prices.

In summer, **Skansen** is an interesting area to explore because many craftspeople display their goods here. There are gift shops (some selling "Skansen glass") as well as individuals who offer their handmade goods on temporary stands.

In the **Sergels Torg** area, the main shopping street is **Hamngatan,** site of the famous shopping center Gallerian, at the corner of Hamngatan and Sergels Torg, and crossing the northern rim of Kungsträdgården at Sweden House. Big department stores, such as NK and Åhléns, are located nearby.

The **Kungsgatan** area is another major district for shopping, stretching from Hötorget to the intersection of Kungsgatan and Vasagatan. **Drottninggatan** is one long pedestrian mall, flanked with shops. Many side streets branching off from it also are filled with shops. Hötorget, home to the PUB department store, is another major shopping district.

SHOPPING HOURS Stockholm shops are open Monday through Friday from 10am to 6pm, and Saturday from 10am to somewhere between 1 and 4pm. Once a week, usually on Monday or Friday, some of the larger stores are open from 9:30am to 7pm (July–Aug to 6pm).

> **Tips Avoiding Mr. Taxman**
>
> The value-added tax in Sweden, called MOMS, is imposed on all products
> and services, but you can avoid MOMS if you spend a total of at least
> 1,000SEK ($130). Just give the store your name, address, and passport
> number and ask for a tax-free check. Don't unwrap your purchase until
> after you've left Sweden. The customs official will want to see both the
> tax-free check and your purchase; you'll be given a cash refund, minus
> a small commission, on the spot. If you're departing by plane, hold on
> to your luggage until after you've received your refund, and then you
> can pack your purchase in your bag and check it (or carry the purchase
> with you, if it's not too big). At the **Tourist Center,** Hamngatan 27
> (✆ **08/789-24-95**), you can pick up a pamphlet about tax-free shopping
> in Sweden. (For more information, see "Taxes," under "Fast Facts: Sweden,"
> in chapter 2.)

AUCTIONS

Stockholms Auktionsverket (Stockholm Auction Chambers)   The oldest auction company in the world—it dates from 1674—holds auctions 2 days
a week from noon to "whenever." You can view the merchandise Monday to Friday from 11am to 2pm. An estimated 150,000 lots are auctioned each year—
everything from ceramics to Picassos. Nyvbrogatan 32. ✆ **08/453-67-00.** T-bana:
Östermalmstorg.

BOOKS & MAPS

Akademibokhandeln   The biggest bookstore in Sweden carries more than
100,000 titles. A wide range of fiction and nonfiction is available in English.
Many travel-related materials, such as maps, are also sold. Mäster Samuelsgatan 28.
✆ **08/613-61-00.** T-bana: Hötorget.

Sverige Bokhandeln (Sweden Bookshop)   Whatever's available in English
about Sweden can be found at this bookstore above the Tourist Center. The store
sells many rare items, including recordings of Swedish music. Slottsbacken 10.
✆ **08/453-7800.** T-bana: Gamla Stan.

CERAMICS

Blås & Knåda *Finds*   This store sells the best products made by members of a
cooperative of 50 Swedish ceramic artists and glassmakers. Prices begin at
200SEK ($26) for a single teacup and rise to as much as 25,000SEK ($3,250)
for museum-quality pieces. Hornsgatan 26. ✆ **08/642-77-67.** T-bana: Slussen.

Keramiskt Centrum Gustavsberg   Bone china, stoneware dinner services,
and other fine table and decorative ware are made at the Gustavsberg Ceramics
Center. A museum at the center displays historic pieces such as *parian* (a type of
unglazed porcelain) statues based on the work of the famous Danish sculptor
Torvaldsen and other artists. You'll also see hand-painted vases, Toby jugs,
majolica, and willowware, examples of Pyro (the first ovenware), royal dinner
services, and sculpture by modern artists.

Visitors can watch potters at work and see artists hand-painting designs. You
can even decorate a mug or plate yourself. A shop at the center sells Gustavs-
berg-ware, including seconds. Värmdö Island (21km/13 miles east of Stockholm). ✆ **08/
570-356-58.** Bus: 422 or 440.

DEPARTMENT STORES

Åhléns City   In the center of Stockholm, the largest department store in Sweden has a gift shop, a restaurant, and a famous food department. Also seek out the fine collection of home textiles, and Orrefors and Kosta Boda crystal ware. The pewter with genuine Swedish ornaments makes a fine gift item. Klarabergsgatan 50. ℂ **08/676-60-00.** T-bana: Centralen.

Nordiska Kompaniet (NK)   A high-quality department store since 1902, NK displays most of the big names in Swedish glass, including Orrefors (see the Nordic Light collection) and Kosta. Thousands of handcrafted Swedish items can be found in the basement. Stainless steel, also a good buy in Sweden, is profusely displayed. It's open Monday to Friday from 10am to 7pm, Saturday 10am to 6pm, Sunday noon to 5pm. Hamngatan 18–20. ℂ **08/762-80-00.** T-bana: Kungsträdgården.

PUB   Greta Garbo worked in the millinery department here from 1920 to 1922. It's one of the most popular department stores in Stockholm; the boutiques and departments generally sell midrange clothing and good-quality housewares, but not the international designer names of the more prestigious (and more expensive) NK. Massive and bustling, with an emphasis on traditional and conservative Swedish clothing, it offers just about anything you'd need to stock a Scandinavian home. There's also a restaurant. Hötorget 13. ℂ **08/782-1930.** T-bana: Hötorget.

FASHION

Fillipa K   One of the leading clothiers of Stockholm operates what they define as a large-scale boutique firmly entrenched in the middle-bracket cost category—the kind of place where a mother might take her young daughter for her first cotillion dress. Expect a wide array of casual dresses, cocktail dresses, and formal evening wear, along with the business uniforms that are so favored by Scandinavian office workers. There's also a collection of clothing for men—suits, blazers, and casual wear—that's a bit less extensive than for the women, but with the added advantage of a small-scale collection of fur coats—perfect for that chilly late autumn sojourn in the football bleachers of your old alma mater. Grev Turegatan 18. ℂ **08/545-888-88.** T-bana: Östermalmstorj.

NK   In the realm of menswear, this is Stockholm's answer to Harrod's in London. From Armani, Prada, and Gucci suits and shoes to the latest fashions in Levis and casual wear—it's all here. The largest of a chain of menswear stores scattered throughout Sweden, this has been around for more than a hundred years. From stocking outdoor gear and swimsuits, this store also maintains a boutique-within-the-boutique, the Swedish label TIGER (ℂ **08/762-8772**), which sells fine suits, shoes, and casual wear that's specifically tailored to Swedish tastes and builds. Hamngatan 18–20. ℂ **08/762-8000.** T-bana: Kungsträdgården.

FLEA MARKET

Loppmarknaden i Skärholmen (Skärholmen Shopping Center)   At the biggest flea market in northern Europe, you might find a pleasing item from an attic in Värmland. You might indeed find *anything.* Try to go on Saturday or Sunday (the earlier the better), when the market is at its peak. Admission is 10SEK ($1.30) for adults (15SEK/$1.95 on Sun), free for children. Skärholmen. ℂ **08/710-00-60.** Bus: 13 or 23 to Skärholmen (20 min.).

GEMS & MINERALS

Geocity *Finds*   Geocity offers exotic mineral crystals, jewelry, Scandinavian gems, Baltic amber, and lapidary equipment. The staff includes two certified gemologists who will cut and set any gem you select and do appraisals. The inventory holds stones from Scandinavia and around the world, including Greenland, Madagascar, Siberia, and South America. Kungsgaten 57. (✆) **08/411-11-40**. T-bana: Hötorget.

GIFTS & SOUVENIRS

Slottsbodarna (Royal Gift Shop)   This unusual outlet sells products related to or copied from the collections in the Royal Palace. Items are re-created in silver, gold, brass, pewter, textiles, and glass. Every item is made in Sweden. Royal Palace south wing, Slottsbacken. (✆) **08/402-61-48**. T-bana: Gamla Stan.

GLASS & CRYSTAL

Nordiska Kristall   Since 1918 this company has been in the vanguard of Swedish glassmakers. The pick of Swedish glass is on sale here. The company often stages pioneering exhibitions, showcasing its more innovative and daring designs. At this outlet you get both traditional experience in the classics in glass as well as bold new experiments. Kungsgatan 9. (✆) **08/10-43-72**. T-bana: Hörtorget.

Orrefors Kosta Boda   A fabled name in Swedish glass operates this "crystal palace" in the center of Stockholm. Two famous companies combined to form one outlet, with Orrefors focusing on clear vases and stemware, whereas Kosta Boda boasts more colorful and artistic pieces of glass. One of the best-selling items is the "Intermezzo Glass" with a drop of sapphire glass in its stem. 15 Birger Jarlsgatan. (✆) **08/545-040-8**. T-bana: Östermalmstorg.

Svenskt Glas   Royal families patronize this establishment, which features Swedish-made glass at every price level. You'll see Orrefors and Kosta Boda stemware, candlesticks, flower-shape bowls in full lead crystal, bar sets, vases, wineglasses, pitchers, and perfume bottles. Worldwide shipping is available. Karlavägen 61. (✆) **08/768-4024**. T-bana: Östermalmstorg.

HANDICRAFTS & GIFTS

Brinken Konsthantverk   On the lower floor of a building near the Royal Palace in the Old Town, this elegant purveyor of gift items will ship handcrafted brass, pewter, wrought iron, or crystal anywhere in the world. About 95% of the articles are made in Scandinavia. Storkyrkobrinken 1. (✆) **08/411-59-54**. T-bana: Gamla Stan.

DesignTorget   In 1994, the government-owned Kulturhuset (Swedish Culture House) reacted to declining attendance by inviting one of Stockholm's most influential designers and decorators, Jerry Hellström, to organize an avant-garde art gallery. Swedes modestly refer to it as a "shop." In a large room in the cellar, you'll find a display of handicrafts created by 150 to 200 mostly Swedish craftspeople. The work must be approved by a jury of connoisseurs before being offered for sale. The merchandise includes some of the best pottery, furniture, textiles, clothing, pewter, and crystal in Sweden, for 25SEK to 20,000SEK ($3.25–$2,600) per object. The most expensive object in the gallery, at the time of this writing, was a magnificently proportioned bathtub assembled from glued and laminated strips of wood. Almost as impressive were a series of ergonomically designed computer workstations. The organization maintains a branch in southern Stockholm, **DesignTorget Mode,** Götgatan 31 ((✆) **08/462-35-20**). It stocks clothing for men, women, and children, and furniture, with less emphasis on ceramics and handicrafts. In the Kulturhuset, Sergels Torg 3. ℭ 08/508-31-520. T-bana: Centralen.

Duka A large selection of crystal, porcelain, and gifts is available in this shop near the Konserthuset (Concert Hall). It offers tax-free shopping and shipping. Kungsgatan 41. ℭ 08/20-60-41. T-bana: Hötorget.

Gunnarssons Träfigurer (Finds This is one of the city's most interesting collections of Swedish carved wooden figures. All are by Urban Gunnarsson, a second-generation master carver. They include figures from World War II, such as Winston Churchill, and U.S. presidents from Franklin D. Roosevelt to Bill Clinton. There's also a host of mythical and historical European personalities. Prices range from 400SEK to 1,000SEK ($52–$130); larger pieces cost up to 2,000SEK ($260). The carvings are usually made from linden or basswood. Drottninggatan 77. ℭ 08/21-67-17. T-bana: Rådmansgatan.

Konsthantverkarna This store has an unusual selection of some of the best Swedish handicrafts, created by a group of artisans. All pieces must pass scrutiny by a strict jury before they're offered for sale. Choose from glass, sculpture, ceramics, wall textiles, clothes, jewelry, silver, brass, and wood and leather work. Each item is handmade and original. Ask about the tax-free service. Mäster Samuelsgatan 2. ℭ 08/611-03-70. T-bana: Östermalmstorg.

Svensk Hemslojd (Society for Swedish Handicrafts) Svensk Hemslojd offers a wide selection of glass, pottery, gifts, and wooden and metal handicrafts by some of Sweden's best artisans. There's a display of hand-woven carpets, upholstery fabrics, hand-painted materials, tapestries, lace, and embroidered items. You'll also find beautiful yarns for weaving and embroidery. Sveavägen 44. ℭ 08/23-21-15. T-bana: Hötorget.

HOME FURNISHINGS

Nordiska Galleriet This store features the finest in European furniture design, including the best from Scandinavia. Two floors hold the latest contemporary furniture. The store can arrange shipment. Nybrogatan 11. ℭ 08/442-83-60. T-bana: Östermalmstorg.

Svenskt Tenn Along "embassy row," Swedish Pewter (its English name) has been Sweden's most prominent store for home furnishings since 1924. Pewter is no longer king, and the shop now sells Scandinavia's best selection of furniture, printed textiles, lamps, glassware, china, and gifts. The inventory is stylish, and although there aren't a lot of bargains, it's an excellent place to see the newest trends in Scandinavian design. It carries an exclusive collection of Josef Frank's hand-printed designs on linen and cotton. It will pack, insure, and ship your purchases anywhere in the world. Strandvägen 5. ℭ 08/670-16-00. T-bana: Östermalmstorg.

LINENS

Solgården For the dwindling few who really care about luxury linens and elegant home-ware, such as lace and embroidery, this shop is the finest of its kind in Scandinavia. It was conceived by owner Marianne von Kantzow Ridderstad as a tribute to Gustav III, the king who is said to have launched the neoclassical style in Sweden. Ridderstad designed her shop like a country house with rough-hewn wood and whimsical furnishings. Each of her linens is virtually a work of art. The tablecloths are heirloom pieces. You'll cherish the work for its originality and loveliness. Karlavägen 58. ℭ 08/663-9360. T-bana: Rådmansgatan.

MARKETS

Östermalms Saluhall   One of the most colorful indoor markets in Scandinavia features cheese, meat, vegetable, and fish merchants who supply food for much of the area. You may want to have a snack or a meal at one of the restaurants. Nybrogatan 31. No central phone. T-bana: Östermalmstorg.

SHOPPING MALLS

Gallerian   A short walk from Sweden House at Kunådgården, this modern two-story shopping complex is, to many, the best shopping destination in Sweden. Merchandise in most of the individually managed stores is designed to appeal to local shoppers, not the tourist market—although in summer that changes a bit as more souvenir and gift items appear. Hamngatan 37. No phone. T-bana: Kungsträdgården.

Sturegallerian   In the center of Stockholm, this mall has a dazzling array of foreign and domestic merchandise, in some 50 specialty shops. Summer brings out more displays of Swedish souvenirs and gift items. There are also restaurants and cafes. Sturegallerian opened in 1989 and a year later was named "Shopping Center of the Year in Europe" by the International Council of Shopping Centers. Stureplan. ℂ 08/611-46-06. T-bana: Östermalmstorg.

TEXTILES

Handarbetets Vänner   This is one of the oldest and most prestigious textile houses in Stockholm. It also sells art weaving and embroidery items. Djurgårdsslatten 82–84. ℂ 08/545-68650. Bus: 47.

JOBS   Hand-painted fabrics from the JOBS family workshops in Dalarna are prized for their quality and the beauty of their design. Patterns are inspired by the all-too-short Swedish summer and by rural traditions. If you plan to be in Dalarna, you might enjoy visiting the **JOBS factory,** Västanvik 201, Leksand (℃ **0247/144-85**). Other items include tablecloths, handbags, and children's clothing. Stora Nygatan 19. ℃ **08/20-98-16.** T-bana: Gamla Stan.

TOYS

Bulleribock (Toys)   Since it opened in the 1960s, this store has carried only traditional, noncomputerized toys made of wood, metal, or paper. You won't find any plastic toys here. There are no war-games that many parents find objectionable. Many of these charming playthings are suitable for children up to age 10. As many as possible are made in Sweden, with wood from Swedish forests. Sveavägen 104. ℃ **08/673-61-21.** T-bana: Rådmansgatan.

6 Stockholm After Dark

Djurgården remains the favorite spot for both indoor and outdoor events on a summer evening. Although the more sophisticated may find it corny, this is your best early evening bet. Afterward, you can make the rounds of jazz venues and nightclubs, some of which stay open until 3 or 4 in the morning.

Pick up a copy of *Stockholm This Week,* distributed at the Tourist Center at Sweden House (see section 1 in chapter 3) to see what's going on.

THE PERFORMING ARTS

All the major opera, theater, and concert seasons begin in the fall, except for special summer festival performances. Fortunately, most of the major opera and theatrical performances are funded by the state, which keeps ticket prices reasonable.

CONCERT HALLS

Berwaldhallen (Berwald Concert Hall)   This hexagonal concert hall is Swedish Radio's big music studio. The Radio Symphonic Orchestra performs here, and other musical programs include lieder and chamber music recitals. The hall has excellent acoustics. The box office is open Monday to Friday from noon to 6pm and 2 hours before every concert. Dag Hammarskjölds Väg 3. **08/784-18-00.** Tickets 50SEK–400SEK ($6.50–$52). T-bana: Karaplan.

Filharmonikerna i Konserthuset (Concert Hall)   Home of the Stockholm Philharmonic Orchestra, this is the principal place to hear classical music in Sweden. The Nobel Prizes are awarded here. Constructed in 1920, the building houses two concert halls. One seats 1,600 and is better suited to major orchestras; the other, seating 450, is suitable for chamber music groups. Besides local orchestras, the hall features visiting ensembles, such as the Chicago Symphony Orchestra. Some series sell out in advance to subscription-ticket holders; for others, visitors can readily get tickets. Sales begin 2 weeks before a concert and continue until the performance begins. Concerts usually start at 7:30pm, with occasional lunchtime (noon) or "happy hour" (5:30pm) concerts. Most performances are broadcast on Stockholm's main classical music station, 107.5 FM. The box office is open Monday through Friday from 10am to 6pm, Saturday from 10am to 1pm. The concert hall is closed in July and early August. Hötorget 8. **08/10-21-10.** Tickets 120SEK–500SEK ($16–$65). T-bana: Hötorget.

OPERA & BALLET

Drottningholm Court Theater   Founded by Gustavus III in 1766, this unique theater is on an island in Lake Mälaren, 11km (6¾ miles) from Stockholm. It stages operas and ballets with full 18th-century regalia, period costumes, and wigs. Its machinery and 30 or more complete theater sets are intact and in use. The theater, a short walk from the royal residence, seats only 450, which makes it difficult to get tickets. Eighteenth-century music performed on antique instruments is a perennial favorite. The season is from May to September. Most performances begin at 8pm and last 2½ to 4 hours. You can order tickets in advance by phone with an American Express card. Drottningholm. **08/660-82-25.** Tickets 165SEK–510SEK ($21–$66). T-bana: Brommaplan, then bus no. 301 or 323. Boat from the City Hall in Stockholm.

Operahauset (Royal Opera House)   Founded in 1773 by Gustavus III (who was later assassinated here at a masked ball), the Opera House is the home of the Royal Swedish Opera and the Royal Swedish Ballet. The building dates from 1898. Performances are usually Monday through Saturday at 7:30pm (closed mid-June to Aug). The box office is open Monday through Friday from noon to 6pm (until 7:30pm on performance nights), Saturday from noon to 3pm. Gustav Adolfs Torg. **08/24-82-40.** Tickets 90SEK–510SEK ($12–$66); 10%–30% senior and student discounts. T-bana: Kungsträdgården.

THEATER

The theater season begins in mid-August and lasts until mid-June.

Kungliga Dramatiska Teatern (Royal Dramatic Theater)   Greta Garbo got her start in acting here, and Ingmar Bergman stages two productions a year. The theater presents the latest experimental plays and the classics—in Swedish only. The theater is open year-round (with a slight slowdown in July), and performances are scheduled Tuesday through Saturday at 7pm and Sunday at 4pm. The box office is open Monday through Saturday from 10am to 6pm. Nybroplan.

© **08/667-06-80.** Tickets 100SEK–400SEK ($13–$52); student discount available. T-bana: Östermalmstorg.

Oscars Teatern Oscars is the flagship of Stockholm's musical entertainment world. It's been the home of classic operetta and musical theater since the turn of the 20th century. Known for its extravagant staging of traditional operettas, it was also one of the first theaters in Europe to produce such hits as *Cats* in Swedish. The box office is open Monday through Saturday from 11am to 6pm. Kungsgatan 63. © **08/20-50-00.** Tickets 240SEK–375SEK ($31–$49). T-bana: Hötorget.

Regina Theater This is the only permanent English-language theater in Sweden, although its yearly repertoire is not always in English—you'll have to check to see what's playing at the time of your visit. Originally built in 1911 as a cinema, the building was converted for drama in 1960. The Regina Theater Company, established in 1980, presents everything from Victorian thrillers to Dickensian Christmas musicals. Its London-style theater pub is unique in Sweden. Open Tuesday through Saturday from noon to 8pm. American Express cardholders can reserve by phone. Drottninggatan 71A. © **081/411-63-20.** Tickets 170SEK–460SEK ($22–$60). T-bana: Hötorget.

LOCAL CULTURE & ENTERTAINMENT

Skansen Skansen arranges traditional seasonal festivities, special events, autumn market days, and a Christmas Fair. In summer, concerts, sing-alongs, and guest performances delight visitors and locals alike. Folk-dancing performances are staged from June to August Monday through Saturday at 7pm and Sunday at 2:30 and 4pm. From June to August, outdoor dancing is presented with live music Monday to Friday from 10 to 11:30pm. Djurgården 49–51. © **08/442-80-00.** Admission 70SEK ($9.10) adults, 25SEK ($3.25) children 6–15, free for children 5 and under. Bus: 44 or 47. Ferry from Slussen.

AN AMUSEMENT PARK

Gröna Lunds Tivoli Unlike its Copenhagen namesake, this is an amusement park, not a fantasyland. For those who like Coney Island–type amusements, it can be a nighttime adventure. One of the big thrills is to go up to the revolving tower for an after-dark view. The park is open daily from the end of April to September, usually from noon to 11pm or midnight. Call for exact hours. Djurgården. © **08/587-501-00.** Admission 60SEK ($7.80), 30SEK ($3.90) children 4-13, free for children under 4. Bus: 44 or 47. Ferry from Nybroplan.

THE CLUB & MUSIC SCENE
A HISTORIC NIGHTCLUB

Café Opera By day a bistro, brasserie, and tearoom, Café Opera becomes one of the most crowded nightclubs in Stockholm in the evening. Visitors have the best chance of getting in around noon during lunch. A stairway near the entrance leads to one of the Opera House's most beautiful corners, the clublike Operabaren (Opera Bar). It's likely to be as crowded as the cafe. The bar is a monumental but historically charming place to have a drink; beer costs 61SEK ($7.95). After 10pm, there is less emphasis on food and more on disco activities. Open daily from 5pm to 3am. At night, long lines form outside. Don't confuse this establishment with the opera's main (and far more expensive) dining room, the Operakällaren. Operahauset, Kungsträdgården. © **08/676-58-07.** Cover 100SEK ($13) after 11pm. T-bana: Kungsträdgården.

The Capital of Gay Scandinavia

Copenhagen thrived for many years as a refreshingly raunchy city with few inhibitions and fewer restrictions on alternative sexuality. Beginning in the mid-1990s, Stockholm witnessed an eruption of new gay bars, discos, and roaming nightclubs. Copenhagen's more imperial and, in many ways, more staid competition made the Danes' legendary permissiveness look a bit weak. Today, thanks partly to the huge influence of London's gay subcultures, no other city in Scandinavia offers gay-friendly nightlife options as broad and diverse as Stockholm's. Some of the new gay bars and clubs maintain fixed hours and addresses. Others, configured as roving parties, constantly change addresses. The acknowledged king of the gay underground is Swedish-born entrepreneur Ulrik Bermsio, who has been compared to the legendary Steve Rubell of Studio 54 fame. Listings for his entertainment venues—and those promoted by his less visible competitors—appear regularly in *QX*, a gay magazine published in Swedish and English. It's available at news kiosks throughout Stockholm. You can also check out the magazine's website (www.qx.se). And don't overlook the comprehensive website (www.rfsl. se) maintained by RSFL, a Swedish organization devoted to equal rights for gays.

Looking for a nonconfrontational bar peopled with regular guys who happen to be gay? Consider a round or two at **Sidetrack**, Wollmar Yxkullsgatan 7 (© **08/641-1688**; T-bana: Mariatorget). Small, and committed to shunning trendiness, it's named after the founder's favorite gay bar in Chicago. It's open Tuesday to Saturday from 6pm to 1am. Tuesday seems to be something of a gay Stockholm institution. Other nights are fine, too—something like a Swedish version of a bar and lounge at the local bowling alley, where everyone happens to be into same-sex encounters.

To find a Viking, or Viking wannabe, in leather, head for **SLM** (Scandinavian Leather Men), Wollmar Yxkullsgatan 18 (© **08/643-3100**; T-bana: Mariatorget). Technically, this is a private club. If you look hot, wear just a hint (or even a lot) of cowhide or rawhide, or happen to have spent the past 6 months felling timber in Montana, you stand a good chance of getting in. Wednesday, Friday, and Saturday from 10pm to 2am, the place functions as Stockholm's premier leather bar. You'll find lots of masculine-looking men on the street level and a handful of

DANCE CLUBS & DISCOS

The Daily News   One of the capital's most enduring entertainment emporiums, this place has flourished through dozens of changes over the years and was last renovated in 2004. Currently, there's a dance club and a pub in the cellar, a somewhat smaller dance floor and a bar on the street level, and a street-level restaurant that serves platters of Swedish and international food. On weekends, there's sometimes a line. Platters begin at around 78SEK ($10), full dinners at around 225SEK ($29). The place is open every night from 11pm to between 4 and 5am. In Sweden House (Sverigehuset), at Kungsträdgården. © **08/21-56-55**. Cover 65SEK–95SEK ($8.45–$12). T-bana: Kungsträdgården.

toys and restrictive accouterments in the cellar-level dungeon. On Saturday from 10pm to 2am, a DJ spins highly danceable music. It's closed on other nights.

If you need a caffeine fix and a slice of chocolate cake before all that leather and latex, you might want to drop into Stockholm's most appealing, best-managed gay cafe, **Chokladkoppen,** Stortorget 18-20 (© 08/203170; T-bana: Gamla Stan). Open daily from 9am to 11pm, it specializes in sandwiches, gorgeous pastries, and all manner of chocolate confections that appeal even to straight people. The staff is charming, and the clientele more gay than not.

Our remaining selections involve venues that cater to a gay crowd only on specific nights of the week. They're subject to change according to the outrageous whims of fashion and scheduling concerns. Examples include **Patricia,** Stadsgårdskajen 152 (© 08/743-0570; T-bana: Slussen). It's straight most of the week, and avowedly gay every Sunday between 7pm and 5am. Sprawling and labyrinthine, with three bars and a good sound system, it attracts gay folk from all walks of life and income levels. It's most crowded on Sunday during the summer, much less so in the winter. There's a restaurant on the premises.

Many gays and lesbians gather at **Torget,** Mälartorget 13 (© 08/20-55-60; T-bana: Gamla Stan), a cozy, Victorian-era cafe and bar in the Old City (Gamla Stan) that's open every afternoon for food and (more important) drinks around 5pm till around midnight. A gay place with a greater emphasis on its food, but with a busy and crowded bar area, and a particularly helpful and informative staff, is **Babs Köks n Bar,** Birger Jarlsgatan 37 (© 08/23-61-01; T-bana: Östermalmstorg). It's open Monday to Tuesday 5pm to midnight, Wednesday to Saturday 5pm to 1am, Sunday 4 to 10pm. A well-recommended disco that attracts a fun-loving, hard-dancing clientele that's both gay and straight is **Tip-Top,** Sveavagen 57 (© 08/32-98-00; T-bana: Rådmansgatan). It's open Monday to Saturday from around 7pm till between midnight and 3am, depending on business and the night of the week.

Finally, for a cozy little bar and restaurant in Gamla Stan or Old Town, head for **Mandus Bar Kök,** Österlångg 7 (© 08/206-60-55; T-bana: Gamla Stan), and the night is yours. The convivial crowd sits talking and drinking wine or beer late into the night.

Göta Källare Stockholm's largest and most successful supper-club-style dance hall has a reputation for successful matchmaking. Large, echoing, and paneled with lots of wood in *faux-Español* style, it has a terrace that surrounds an enormous tree. The restaurant serves platters of food priced at 95SEK to 200SEK ($12–$26). Menu items include tournedos, fish, chicken, and veal. Expect a middle-aged crowd. The live orchestra (which performs *Strangers in the Night* a bit too frequently) plays every night. The hall opens nightly at 8:30pm. In the Medborgplatsen subway station, Södermalm. © 08/642-08-28. Cover 80SEK ($10) after 11pm. T-bana: Medborgplatsen.

ROCK & JAZZ CLUBS

Fasching   This club attracts some of Sweden's best-known jazz musicians. Small and cozy, and well known among jazz aficionados throughout Scandinavia, it is cramped but fun. The venue varies according to the night of the week and the availability of the artists performing. At the end of the live acts, there's likely to be dancing to salsa, soul, and perhaps R&B. The club is open nightly from 7pm to 1am. Kungsgatan 63. ℂ 08/534-829-64. Cover 100SEK–250SEK ($13–$33). T-bana: Centralen.

Hard Rock Cafe   The Swedish branch of this chain is fun and gregarious. Sometimes an American, British, or Scandinavian rock band presents a live concert; otherwise, rock blasts from the sound system. Club sandwiches, hamburgers, T-bone steaks, and barbecued spareribs are available. Burgers cost 130SEK ($17), steaks are 200SEK to 250SEK ($26–$33), and a beer goes for 46SEK ($6). It's open Sunday to Thursday from 11:30am to 1am, Friday and Saturday from 11:30am to 3am. Sveavägen 75. ℂ 08/545-494-00. T-bana: Rådmansgaten.

Mondo   This is a mammoth complex on three stages, with five bars and four different dance floors. On increasingly fashionable Södermalm in southern Stockholm, it reigns supreme in the night, giving off "love and music," as it says. Hip-hop, reggae, and live rock dominate the night. The minimum age is 20. Medborgarplatsen 8. ℂ 08/673-10-32. Cover 40SEK ($5.20) after 10pm. T-bana: Mariatorget.

Pub Engelen/Nightclub Kolingen   The Engelen Pub, the Restaurant Engelen, and the Nightclub Kolingen (in the 15th-c. cellar) share a single address. The restaurant, which serves some of the best steaks in town, is open daily 5pm to midnight. Live performances, usually soul, funk, and rock by Swedish groups, take over the pub daily from 8:30pm to midnight. The pub is open Tuesday to Thursday 4pm to 1am, Friday and Saturday 4pm to 3am, Sunday 5pm to 3am. Beer begins at 42SEK ($5.45), and items on the bar menu cost 39SEK to 80SEK ($5.05–$10). The Nightclub Kolingen is a dance club nightly from 10pm to about 3am. It charges the same food and drink prices as the pub, and you must be at least 23 to enter. Kornhamnstorg 59B. ℂ 08/20-10-92. Cover 40SEK– 60SEK ($5.20–$7.80) after 8pm. T-bana: Gamla Stan.

Stampen   This pub attracts crowds of jazz lovers in their 30s and 40s. Guests crowd in to enjoy live Dixieland, New Orleans, and mainstream jazz, and swing music from the 1920s, 1930s, and 1940s. On Tuesday, it's rock 'n' roll from the 1950s and 1960s. A menagerie of stuffed animals and lots of old, whimsical antiques are suspended from the high ceiling. It's open Monday to Wednesday 8pm to 1am, Friday to Saturday 8pm to 2am. In summer, an outdoor veranda is open when the weather permits. The club has two stages, and there's dancing downstairs almost every night. Stora Nygatan 5. ℂ 08/20-57-93. Cover 100SEK–120SEK ($13–$16). T-bana: Gamla Stan.

A CASINO

Casino Cosmopol   At last Stockholm has a world-class casino and it's installed in the Palladium, a grand old movie house dating from 1918. Housing two restaurants and four bars, the casino is spread across four floors. Guests, who must be at least 20 years old, can play such classic games as American roulette, blackjack, Punto Banco, and seven-card stud. Open daily 1pm to 4am. Kungsgatan 56. ℂ 08/799-7557. Cover 30SEK ($3.90). T-bana Hötorget.

Travel Tip: He who finds the best hotel deal has more to spend on facials involving knobbly vegetables.

Hello, the Roaming Gnome here. I've been nabbed from the garden and taken round the world. The people who took me are so terribly clever. They find the best offerings on Travelocity. For very little cha-ching. And that means I get to be pampered and exfoliated till I'm pink as a bunny's doodah.

✳
✳ travelocity®

1-888-TRAVELOCITY / travelocity.com / America Online Keyword: Travel

THE BAR SCENE

Blue Moon Bar   Attracting a bevy of supermodels and TV actors, this is both a street-level bar and a basement bar, drawing a chic crowd to its modern decor. Although calling itself a bar, it is also a restaurant and a night club, or *nattklubb*, as the Swedes say. Recorded music is played. Open nightly from 7pm to 5am. Kungsgatan 18. ✆ 08/244700. Cover 70SEK–80SEK ($9.10–$10). T-bana: Östermalmstorg.

Cadier Bar   From the bar of this deluxe hotel—one of the most famous in Europe—you'll have a view of the harbor and the Royal Palace. It's one of the most sophisticated places in Stockholm. Light meals—open-face sandwiches and smoked salmon—are served all day in the extension overlooking the waterfront. Drinks run 107SEK to 117SEK ($14–$15); imported beer is 52SEK ($6.75). The bar is named for the hotel's builder. It's open Monday to Saturday from 11am to 2am, Sunday from 11am to 1am; a piano player performs Wednesday through Saturday from 9:30pm to 1:30am. In the Grand Hotel, Södra Blasieholmshamnen 8. ✆ 08/679-35-00. T-bana: Kungsträdgården.

Café Victoria   The most central cafe in Stockholm becomes crowded after 9pm in winter (7pm in summer). It attracts a varied crowd. Many patrons come just to drink, but you can have lunch or dinner in an interior section beyond the lively bar area. Light snacks cost 16SEK to 109SEK ($2.10–$14); main dishes are 139SEK to 198SEK ($18–$26). A bottle of beer will set you back 42SEK ($5.45). It's open Monday to Saturday 11:30am to 3am, Sunday 11:30am to 11pm. Kungsträdgården. ✆ 08/10-10-85. Cover 100SEK ($13) Mon–Fri. T-bana: Kungsträdgården.

Gondolen   You might find Gondolen's architecture as impressive as the view. Part of the structure is suspended beneath a pedestrian footbridge that soars above the narrow channel separating the island of Gamla Stan from the island of Södermalm. The engineering triumph was executed in 1935. The elevator hauls customers (without charge) up the equivalent of 11 stories to the '40s-style restaurant. The view encompasses Lake Malar, the open sea, and huge areas of downtown Stockholm. You'll pay 86SEK ($11) for a whiskey with soda. It is open Monday through Friday from 11:30am to 1am, Saturday from 1pm to 1am. Stadsgården 6. ✆ 08/641-70-90. T-bana: Slussen.

Icebar   Located in the Nordic Sea Hotel, this is known as Stockholm's "coolest" bar. The world's first permanent ice bar opened in 2001 in the heart of Stockholm. Amazingly, the interior is kept at temperatures of 27°F (–5°C) all year. The decor and all the interior fittings, right down to the cocktail glasses themselves, are made of pure, clear ice shipped down from the Torne River in Sweden's Arctic north. If you own one of those fabulous Swedish fur coats, the Icebar would be the place to wear it. Dress as you would for a dogsled ride in Alaska. In the bar you can order any drink from a Bahama Mama to an Alabama Slammer, although you may have to order liquor-laced coffee to keep warm. Vasaplan 4–7. ✆ 08/217177. T-bana: Centralen.

Sturehof   Since 1897, this pub and restaurant has been one of Stockholm's major drinking and dining venues. In the exact center of the city, it is now surrounded by urban sprawl and is attached to an arcade with other restaurants and shops. It remains a pleasant refuge from the city's congestion and is popular as both an after-work bar and a restaurant. It's open Monday to Friday from 11am to 2am. Beer costs 53SEK ($6.90). Stureplan 2. ✆ 08/440-57-30. T-bana: Östermalmstorg.

T.G.I. Friday's   This chain has invaded Stockholm and is today one of the most popular places for drinks or casual dining. Drawing homesick Americans as well as a fun-loving crowd of young Stockholmers, T.G.I. Friday's lies near the Stureplan at the heart of the city. On weekends, the place is a favorite with local families, drawing more of a singles crowd during the week. A big place with large windows, the restaurant decorates its walls with maps of various U.S. states. All the familiar T.G.I. food items are here, including smoked chicken quesadilla, potato skins, and Buffalo chicken strips, along with pastas, sandwiches, steaks, and ribs. Open Sunday to Thursday noon to 1am, Friday and Saturday noon to 3am. Birger Jarlsgatan 16. ℂ **08/611-31-31.** T-bana: Östermalmstorg.

7 Side Trips from Stockholm

Some of Sweden's best-known attractions are clustered around Lake Mälaren— centuries-old villages and castles (Uppsala and Gripsholm) that revive the pomp and glory of the 16th-century Vasa dynasty. You can spend a very busy day exploring Sigtuna, Skokloster Castle, Uppsala, and Gamla Uppsala, and stay overnight in Sigtuna or Uppsala, where there are good hotels. Another easy day trip is to Gripsholm Castle in Mariefred or Tullgarn Palace.

The boat trip from Klara Mälarstrand in Stockholm is popular. It leaves at 9:45am, goes along the beautiful waterway of Mälaren and the Fyris River to Sigtuna—where it stops for 2 hours—and arrives at Uppsala at 5pm. Here you can visit the cathedral and other interesting sights, dine, and then take the 45-minute train trip back to Stockholm. Trains run every hour until 11pm.

SIGTUNA ⽊

Founded at the beginning of the 11th century, Sigtuna, on the shores of Lake Mälaren, northwest of Stockholm, is Sweden's oldest town. **High Street (Stora Gatan),** with its low timbered buildings, is believed to be the oldest street in Sweden that still follows its original route. Traces of Sigtuna's Viking and early Christian heritage can be seen throughout the town.

Sigtuna has many church ruins, mostly from the 12th century. Chief among them is **St. Per's,** Sweden's first cathedral. The 13th-century **Monastery of St. Maria** is open to the public daily. The well-preserved **Town Hall** dates from the 18th century.

Wander the narrow streets, and if you have time, visit the **Sigtuna Museum,** Storogatan 55 (ℂ **08/597-838-70**), an archaeological museum that features early medieval artifacts found in the surrounding area. You'll see gold rings, runic inscriptions, and coins, as well as exclusive objects from Russia and Byzantium. Admission is 30SEK ($3.90) adults, 20SEK ($2.60) students and seniors; admission is free for children 15 and under. Hours are June through August daily from noon to 4pm; September through May Tuesday through Sunday from noon to 4pm.

One of the reasons for Sigtuna's resurgence is the **Sigtuna Foundation,** a Lutheran retreat and cultural center founded near the turn of the 20th century and often frequented by writers. It's open to the public daily from 1 to 3pm.

Daily buses and trains connect Stockholm to Sigtuna and Uppsala. From Stockholm, take a train to Märsta, then a bus for the 10-minute ride to Sigtuna.

WHERE TO STAY & DINE

Sigtuna Foundation ⽊ *Finds*   A stay at this massive building might provide one of your most memorable stopovers in Sweden. Intended as a center where sociological and philosophical viewpoints can be aired, the 1917 structure is

more a way of life than a hotel. Over the years, guest lecturers have included the Dalai Lama, various Indian gurus, and many of postwar Europe's leading theologians. The establishment functions as both a conference center and a guesthouse. There's no proselytizing, although there might be opportunities to share experiences. There are secluded courtyards, lush rose and herb gardens, and fountains. Recently all the guest rooms were refurbished in bland modern style, and modern bathrooms with tub/showers were added. To guarantee a room, be sure to make arrangements in advance. The foundation is less than 1.5km (1 mile) from the town center.

Manfred Björkquists Allé 2–4, S-193 31 Sigtuna. ✆ 08/592-589-00. Fax 08/592-589-99. www.sigtuna stiftelsen.se. 62 units. 600SEK–1,260SEK ($78–$164) double. Rates include breakfast. AE, DC, MC, V. Free parking. Bus: 570 or 575. **Amenities:** Restaurant; lounge; rooms for those w/limited mobility. *In room:* No phone.

Sigtuna Stadshotell ⭐ This Victorian-style hotel in the town center has been a popular choice for many years, with the most comfortable accommodations in town. The old-fashioned rooms are well kept, clean, and inviting. All units are nonsmoking and have neatly kept bathrooms with tub/showers. Full meals are served daily, with a la carte dinners going for 255SEK to 295SEK ($33–$38). These might include Gorgonzola-flavored cream of morel soup, scallop-of-salmon with vermouth sauce, medallions of reindeer with juniper berries, and braised snow grouse in cream sauce with apples and Calvados. For dessert, there's warm cloudberry jam with strawberry ice cream. In winter the restaurant is open daily 11:30am to 3pm and 6 to 11pm.

Stora Nygatan 3, S-193 00 Sigtuna. © **08/592-501-00**. Fax 08/592-515-87. www.sigtunastadshotell.se. 26 units. Mon–Thurs 2,190SEK–2,300SEK ($285–$299) double; 3,975SEK ($517) suite; Fri–Sun 1,690SEK– 1,890SEK ($220–$246) double, 2,650SEK ($345) suite. Rates include breakfast. AE, DC, MC, V. Free parking. Bus: 570 or 575. **Amenities:** Restaurant; bar; sauna; limited room service. *In room:* TV, dataport, minibar, hair dryer.

Skokloster Castle ★★   This splendid 17th-century castle is one of the most interesting baroque museums in Europe. It's next to Lake Mälaren, 65km (40 miles) from Stockholm and 50km (31 miles) from Uppsala. With original interiors, the castle is noted for its extensive collections of paintings, furniture, applied art, tapestries, arms, and books.

S-746 96 Sklokloster. © **018/38-60-77**. Admission 65SEK ($8.45) adults, 50SEK ($6.50) seniors and students, 20SEK ($2.60) children 7–18. Guided tours in English are offered May–Aug daily on the hour 11am–4pm; Sept Mon–Fri 1pm, Sat–Sun 1, 2, and 3pm. Closed Oct–Apr. From Stockholm, take the train to Bålsta, then bus 894.

Skokloster Motor Museum   On the palace grounds, this museum houses the largest collection of vintage automobiles and motorcycles in the country. One of the most notable cars is a 1905 eight-horsepower De Dion Bouton. The museum is open year-round.

S-746 96 Sklokloster. © **018/38-61-06**. Admission 50SEK ($6.50) adults, 25SEK ($3.25) children 7–14, free for children under 7. May–Sept daily noon–4pm. From Stockholm, take the train to Bålsta, then bus 894.

UPPSALA ★★★
68km (42 miles) NW of Stockholm

Sweden's major university city, Uppsala is the most popular destination of day-trippers from Stockholm—and for good reason. It has a great university and a celebrated 15th-century cathedral. Even in the Viking period, Uppsala was a religious center, and the scene of animal and human sacrifices in honor of the Norse gods. It's a former center of royalty as well. Queen Christina occasionally held court here. The church is still the seat of the archbishop, and the first Swedish university was founded here in 1477.

The best time to visit Uppsala is on April 30, Walpurgis Eve, when the academic community celebrates the rebirth of spring with a torchlight parade. The festivities last until dawn throughout the 13 student "nations" (residential halls).

ESSENTIALS
GETTING THERE   The **train** from Stockholm's Central Station takes about 45 minutes. Trains leave about every hour during peak hours. Some visitors spend the day in Uppsala and return to Stockholm on the commuter train in the late afternoon. Eurailpass holders ride free. **Boats** between Uppsala and Skokloster depart Uppsala daily at 11am and 7:30pm, returning to Uppsala at 5:45 and 11:30pm. Round-trip passage costs 150SEK ($20). For details, check with the tourist office in any of the towns.

VISITOR INFORMATION   The **Tourist Information Office** is at Fyris Torg 8 (© **018/727-4800**). It's open Monday to Friday 10am to 6pm, Saturday 10am to 3pm, and Sunday noon to 4pm (July to mid-Aug).

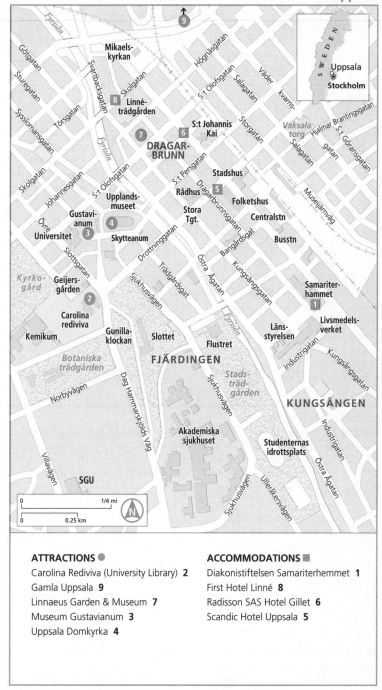

ATTRACTIONS ●

Carolina Rediviva (University Library) **2**
Gamla Uppsala **9**
Linnaeus Garden & Museum **7**
Museum Gustavianum **3**
Uppsala Domkyrka **4**

ACCOMMODATIONS ■

Diakonistiftelsen Samariterhemmet **1**
First Hotel Linné **8**
Radisson SAS Hotel Gillet **6**
Scandic Hotel Uppsala **5**

GETTING AROUND   Buses come in from the surrounding suburbs to the center of Uppsala and arrive at the Central Station, where the trains also arrive. Once you arrive in the center of Uppsala, all the major attractions are within easy walking distance. However, if you're going to explore Gamla Uppsala (see the box below), you need to take bus no. 2 or 54, departing from the Central Station.

SEEING THE SIGHTS

Carolina Rediviva (University Library)   At the end of Drottninggatan is the Carolina Rediviva, with more than 5 million volumes and 40,000 manuscripts, including many rare works from the Middle Ages. The most interesting manuscript is the *Codex Argenteus* (Silver Bible). Displayed in the exhibit room, it was translated into Gothic in the middle of the 3rd century and copied in about A.D. 525. It's the only book extant in old Gothic script. Also worth seeing is *Carta Marina,* the earliest map (1539) of Sweden and its neighboring countries.

Drottninggatan. ✆ **018/471-39-00.** Admission 20SEK ($2.60) adults, free for children under 12. Exhibit room June 14–Aug 15 Mon–Fri 9am–5pm, Sat 10am–5pm, Sun 11am–4pm; Aug 16–June 13 Sun 10am–5pm. Bus: 6, 7, or 22.

Linnaeus Garden & Museum ⚑   Swedish botanist Carl von Linné, known as Carolus Linnaeus, developed a classification system for the world's plants and flowers. His garden and former home are on the spot where Uppsala University's botanical garden was restored by Linnaeus in the style of a miniature baroque garden. Linnaeus, who arranged the plants according to his "sexual classification system," left detailed sketches and descriptions of the garden, which have been faithfully followed.

Linnaeus was a professor of theoretical medicine, including botany, pharmacology, and zoology, at Uppsala University. You can visit his house, which has been restored to its original design, and an art gallery that exhibits the works of contemporary local artists.

Svartbäcksgatan 27. ✆ **018/13-65-40** for the museum, or 018/10-94-90 for the garden. Museum 25SEK ($3.25) adults, free for children. Gardens 20SEK ($2.60), free for children under 15. Museum June–Sept 15 Tues–Sun noon–4pm. Closed Sept 16–May. Gardens May–July daily 9am–9pm; Aug and Sept daily 9am–7pm. Closed Oct–Apr. Walk straight from the train station to Kungsgatan, turn right, and walk about 10 min.

Uppsala Domkyrka ⚑⚑   The largest cathedral in Scandinavia, this twin-spired Gothic structure stands nearly 120m (394 ft.) tall. Founded in the 13th century, it was severely damaged in 1702 in a disastrous fire and was then restored near the turn of the 20th century. Among the regal figures buried in the crypt is Gustavus Vasa. The remains of St. Erik, patron saint of Sweden, are entombed in a silver shrine. The botanist Linnaeus and the philosopher-theologian Swedenborg are also buried here. A small museum displays ecclesiastical relics.

Domkyrkoplan 2. ✆ **018/18-72-01.** Free admission to cathedral. Museum 30SEK ($3.90) adults, free for children under 16. Cathedral daily 8am–6pm. Museum Apr–Aug daily 10am–5pm; Sept–Mar daily noon-3pm. Bus: 1.

Museum Gustavianum *(Finds)*   Gustavianum is Uppsala University's oldest preserved building. Here you can see a number of attractions, including an Anatomical Theatre, the Augsburg Art Cabinet, and an exhibition about the history of the university itself. The museum also includes archaeological exhibitions, from Swedish prehistory to the Middle Ages. Some of the rarer pieces are from the Mediterranean and the Nile Valley, including the sarcophagus

Gamla Uppsala

About 15 centuries ago, "Old Uppsala" ⚔ was the capital of the Svea kingdom. In its midst was a grove set aside for human and animal sacrifices. Viking burial mounds dating from the 6th century are believed to contain the pyres of three kings.

Nearby, on the site of the old pagan temple, is a 12th-century **parish church,** once badly damaged by fire and never properly restored. Indeed, some people describe it as a stave church that turned to stone. Before Uppsala Cathedral was built, Swedish kings were crowned here.

Across from the church is the **Stiftelsen Upplandsmuseet,** Sankt Eriksgränd 6 (✆ **018/16-91-00).** The open-air museum with reassembled buildings depicts peasant life in Uppland. It's open from mid-May to August Tuesday through Sunday from noon to 5pm. Admission is 30SEK ($3.90) adults, 15SEK ($1.95) seniors, free for children under 18.

Gamla Uppsala, about 5km (3 miles) north of the commercial heart of Uppsala, is easily accessible by bus no. 2 or 24, both of which leave frequently from the Central Station.

Khonsumes, a priest from the 21st dynasty. In the historical exhibition on the ground floor you can see everything from student lecture notes from the first term in 1477—the year the university was founded—to the development of the institution over the years as a seat of learning through photographs and historical artifacts.

Akademigatan 3. ✆ **018/471-75-71.** Admission 40SEK ($5.20) adults, 30SEK ($3.90) students and seniors, free for children under 12. Mid-May to mid-Sept Tues–Sun 11am–5pm; off season Tues–Sun 11am–4pm. Bus: 1, 2, 51, or 53.

WHERE TO STAY

Diakonistiftelsen Samariterhemmet *Value*   One of the best bargains in town, this large guesthouse, run by a Christian charity, has spotless rooms with comfortable beds. Some units have neatly kept bathrooms with shower units. You can use the kitchenette with a refrigerator, and there's a TV lounge. Most of the units evoke an Ivy League dormitory. Smoking is not permitted.

Samaritergränd 2, S-753 19 Uppsala. ✆ **018/10-34-00.** Fax 018/10-83-75. 25 units, 12 w/bathroom. 620SEK ($81) double without bathroom; 820SEK ($107) double w/bathroom. Rates include breakfast. MC, V. **Amenities:** Breakfast room; lounge. *In room:* No phone.

First Hotel Linné ⚔   At the edge of Linnaeus Garden, this is one of the best-managed hotels in town. You'll probably be able to see Linnaeus's lovely garden from your window. The rooms feature modern furniture and plumbing, and each unit has a neatly kept bathroom with a tub/shower. One drawback is that the less expensive doubles are a bit cramped.

Skolgatan 45, S-75332 Uppsala. ✆ **018/10-20-00.** Fax 018/13-75-97. www.firsthotels.com. 116 units. Sun–Thurs 1,454SEK–1,654SEK ($189–$215) double, from 1,854SEK ($241) suite; Fri–Sat 854SEK ($111) double, from 954SEK ($124) suite. Rates include breakfast. AE, DC, MC, V. Parking 30SEK ($3.90). **Amenities:** Restaurant; bar; sauna; limited room service; laundry service; dry cleaning; nonsmoking rooms; rooms for those w/limited mobility. *In room:* TV, minibar, hair dryer, safe.

Radisson SAS Hotel Gillet ⚔   This attractively designed first-class hotel, built in 1972, offers well-furnished, medium-size rooms with good beds, modern furnishings, and beautifully kept bathrooms with tub/showers. With its two restaurants, the hotel is also one of Uppsala's major dining venues. The East West Bistro serves dinner Monday to Saturday; the more upscale Gillet Restaurant offers lunch and dinner Monday to Saturday. The restaurants are closed in July.

Dragarbrunnsgatan 23, S-75320 Uppsala. © 018/15-53-60. Fax 018/68-18-18. www.radissonsas.com. 160 units. 990SEK–1,740SEK ($129–$226) double; 1,500SEK–3,500SEK ($195–$455) suite. Rates include breakfast. AE, DC, MC, V. Parking 170SEK ($22). Bus: 801. **Amenities:** 2 restaurants; bar; indoor pool; sauna; limited room service; laundry service; dry cleaning; nonsmoking rooms; rooms for those w/limited mobility. *In room:* A/C, TV, dataport, minibar (in some), hair dryer.

Scandic Hotel Uplandia ★★ Located next to the bus terminal, this is the best hotel in town. It was constructed in two stages, in the 1960s and early 1980s. During the final enlargement, all rooms in the older section were brought up to modern standards. The hotel offers comfortably furnished rooms with newly renovated bathrooms equipped with tub/showers.

Dragarbrunnsgatan 32, S-751 40 Uppsala. © 800/633-6548 in the U.S., or 018/495-26-00. Fax 018/ 495-26-11. www.scandic-hotels.com. 133 units. 890SEK–1,935SEK ($116–$252) double. Rates include breakfast. AE, DC, MC, V. **Amenities:** Restaurant; bar; sauna; limited room service; laundry service; dry cleaning; nonsmoking rooms; rooms for those w/limited mobility. *In room:* A/C (in some), TV, dataport (in some), hair dryer.

WHERE TO DINE

Domtrappkällaren ★★ SWEDISH No other restaurant in Uppsala can compete with this one for charm and atmosphere. It was built in the town center on the ruins of 12th-century cathedral buildings. The vaulted ceilings and copies of Jacobean paintings in the main dining room complement the low-ceilinged, sun-flooded intimacy of the upper floors. On request, you can dine in a narrow room where unruly students were imprisoned in the Middle Ages, or in one that served as a classroom in the 17th century. The restaurant serves delectable salmon and reindeer and specializes in game. Salads are often exotic— one includes breast of pigeon with roasted nuts.

Sankt Eriksgränd 15. © 018/13-09-55. Reservations recommended. Main courses 175SEK–290SEK ($23–$38). AE, DC, MC, V. Mon–Sat 11:30am–2:30pm and 5:30-10pm. Closed Dec 24–26. Bus: 2.

Restaurant Flustret FRENCH In a riverside setting near the castle, this pavilion is an exact replica of its predecessor, a demolished Victorian building. Its spacious ground-floor dining room serves tasty meals, which might include lobster soup, salmon "boathouse style," veal steak Oscar, pheasant Véronique, and bananas flambé. A dance club on the second floor is open Saturday from 9pm to 4am. Admission is free before 9pm, 80SEK ($10) after 9pm.

Svandammen. © 018/100444. Reservations recommended. Main courses 60SEK–250SEK ($7.80–$33). AE, DC, MC, V. Mon–Fri 11am–2pm and 5–9pm; Sat–Sun 11am–midnight. Bus: 24.

Restaurant Odinsborg ★ (Value) SWEDISH In a century-old former private house, this restaurant serves strictly old-fashioned Swedish food. The culinary highlight in the Viking-theme dining room is the smorgasbord. A traditional roster of foods you might expect at a Swedish family celebration is laboriously prepared and laid out. Menu items include traditional preparations of fried herring, marinated salmon, smoked eel, and whitefish with a dill-flavored butter sauce. You might also try roasted lamb, chicken filets, or steak. Street addresses aren't used in Gamla Uppsala, but the restaurant is easy to spot.

Near the burial grounds, Gamla Uppsala. © 018/323-525. Daily smorgasbord 150SEK ($20). AE, DC, MC, V. Daily noon–6pm.

GRIPSHOLM CASTLE ★★

On an island in Lake Mälaren, **Gripsholm Castle** (℃ **0159/101-94**) is one of the best-preserved castles in Sweden. The fortress, built by Gustavus Vasa in the late 1530s, is near Mariefred, an idyllic small town known for its vintage narrow-gauge railroad.

During the reign of the 18th-century actor-king Gustavus III, a theater was built at Gripsholm, but the castle's outstanding feature is its large collection of portrait paintings.

Gripsholm Castle is 68km (42 miles) southwest of Stockholm. By **car,** follow E20 south; you can drive right to the castle parking lot. The Eskilstuna **bus** runs to the center of Mariefred (60SEK/$7.80 round-trip), as do the boats. **Boats** leave from mid-May to September at 10am from Klara Mälarstrand Pier (180SEK/$23 round-trip). The castle is a 10-minute walk from the center of Mariefred.

Even though Gripsholm was last occupied by royalty (Charles XV) in 1864, it's still a royal castle. It's open May 15 to September 15 daily 10am to 4pm; September 16 to May 14 Saturday and Sunday from noon to 3pm. Closed December 21 to January 1. Admission is 60SEK ($7.80) for adults, 30SEK ($3.90) ages 7 to 15, free for ages 6 and under.

WHERE TO STAY

Gripsholms Värdshus & Hotel ★★   Built as an inn in 1609 (it's one of the oldest in Sweden), this building was restored and reopened in 1989. It's now the most stylish and charming hotel in the region. It's a few steps from the village church, in the center of Mariefred, a 10-minute walk from the castle. Each guest room is individually decorated and furnished with a mixture of antiques and contemporary pieces. Bathrooms come equipped with tub/showers, heated floors, and towel racks. All rooms are nonsmoking.

The hotel has the best restaurant in the region (see "Where to Dine," below).

Kyrkogatan 1, S-647 23 Mariefred. ℃ **0159/34750.** Fax 0159/34777. www.gripsholms-vardshus.se. 45 units. 1,250SEK–2,190SEK ($163–$285) double; 500SEK–2,500SEK ($65–$325) supplement for suite, depending on the unit and the season. Rates include breakfast. AE, DC, MC, V. **Amenities:** Restaurant; bar; sauna; 24-hr. room service; laundry service; dry cleaning; 1 room for those w/limited mobility. *In room:* A/C, TV, dataport, minibar, hair dryer, safe.

WHERE TO DINE

Gripsholms Värdshus Restaurant ★ SWEDISH/INTERNATIONAL This elegantly appointed restaurant serves traditional Swedish food, local game dishes, and international cuisine. The main dining room has a veranda that opens onto Gripsholm Bay. The menu changes every season but is likely to include baked saddle of venison with herbs and mushroom pastry, grilled halibut accompanied by red paprika cream and basil ratatouille, or lamb cutlets smothered in Dijon mustard and shallots. For dessert, try the raspberry mousse parfait. Tastings in the wine cellar can be arranged.

Kyrkogatan 1. ℃ **0159/34750.** Reservations recommended. Main courses 115SEK–230SEK ($15–$30). AE, DC, MC, V. Midsummer daily noon–10pm; rest of year Mon–Fri 11:30am–2pm, Sat 12:30–4pm, Mon–Sat 6–10pm, Sun 12:30–4pm.

TULLGARN PALACE ★

The royal palace of Tullgarn, in Vagnhärad (℃ **08/551-720-11**), occupies a panoramic setting on a bay of the Baltic Sea. It was the favorite of Gustavus V (1858–1950), the great-grandfather of Sweden's present king. Construction began in 1719, and the well-kept interiors date from the late 18th century.

The palace is 60km (37 miles) south of Stockholm. By **car,** take E4 south about 60km (37 miles) and turn right at the sign that directs you to Tullgarns Slott, near Vagnhärad. It's another half kilometer (½ mile) to the palace. Getting here by public transportation is extremely inconvenient and not worth the trouble. You first have to take a train to Södertälje Södra (about 20 min.), and then wait for a bus to Trosa, which lies 7km (4¼ miles) south of the castle. From Trosa, you have to take a taxi the rest of the way. You could spend all morning just trying to get to the castle, so we recommend skipping it unless you have private transportation or endless amounts of time.

Admission is 50SEK ($6.50) for adults, 25SEK ($3.25) for students and children. The palace is open to the public on weekends from early May to early September. Guided tours leave the main entrance every hour from 11am to 4pm.

WHERE TO STAY

Romantik Stadtshotell Trosa ★   The most charming and historically evocative hotel in the region lies in the heart of Trosa, a quiet hamlet 7km (4¼ miles) south of Tullgarns Castle. Built in 1867 of yellow-tinged bricks and set in the center of the town, it was enlarged and modernized in the early 1990s. Today it provides cozy, clean rooms with a hint of the aesthetics of yesteryear: wooden floors and a scattering of antique accessories, always coupled with color schemes of yellow and green. Bathrooms with shower units are modern and up-to-date, in most cases added (or upgraded) in the mid-1980s. There's a restaurant on the premises that's open every day, year-round, for lunch and dinner.

Västra Langgatan 19, S-61921 Trosa. ℂ **0156/17070.** Fax 0156/16696. www.trosastadshotell.se. 44 units. Mid-June to mid-Aug and Fri–Sat year-round 1,400SEK ($182) double; rest of year 1,760SEK ($229) double. Rates include breakfast. AE, DC, MC, V. **Amenities:** Restaurant; bar; spa; Jacuzzi; sauna; nonsmoking rooms; rooms for those w/limited mobility. *In room:* TV, hair dryer.

WHERE TO DINE

Tullgarns Värdshus SWEDISH/FRENCH   This inn, in a wing of Tullgarn Palace, offers three-course lunches or dinners. You can sample such dishes as salted salmon with creamed potatoes (an old Swedish specialty), or perhaps pâté of wild boar. You can also order breast of wild duck with chicken liver mousse, or poached filet of salmon with chive-flavored butter sauce.

Or you can order a picnic lunch and eat in the royal park. Picnics of cold chicken or roast beef, with beer or coffee (in a take-out container), or a cup of coffee with a sandwich, can be ordered at the inn daily from 11am to 5pm.

In Tullgarn Palace, Vagnhärad. ℂ **08/551-720-26.** Main courses 139SEK–239SEK ($18–$31). MC, V. May 15–Aug 29 Mon–Fri noon–2:30pm and 5–7pm, Sat–Sun noon–7pm. Closed Aug 30-May 14.

SANDHAMN, VAXHOLM & THE ARCHIPELAGO OF STOCKHOLM ★★★

Stockholm is in what the Swedes call a "garden of skerries," an archipelago with more than 24,000 islands, islets, and rocks merely jutting out of the water. The islands nearest the city have become part of the suburbs, thickly populated and connected to the mainland by car ferries or bridges. Many others are wild and largely deserted, attracting boaters for picnics and swimming. Summer homes dot some of the islands. July is the peak vacation month, when yachts crowd the waters.

You can see the islands by taking a boat trip from Stockholm harbor. If you'd like to stop at a resort island, consider **Sandhamn,** where you'll find shops and restaurants. It takes about an hour to explore the entire island on foot. The beaches at the eastern tip are the best in the archipelago. **Vaxholm,** a bathing resort known as "the gateway to the northern archipelago," also makes a pleasant stop. Artists and writers have traditionally been drawn to Vaxholm, and some hold exhibits during the summer, when the tourist influx quadruples the population. The west harbor and the main sea route to the north are filled with pleasure craft.

ESSENTIALS
GETTING THERE Throughout the year (but more often in the summer), boats operated by several companies depart from in front of the Grand Hotel at Södra Blasieholmshamnen. Most of them are marked VAXHOLM and usually continue to Sandhamn after a stop in Vaxholm. Be sure to ask before boarding.

The trip from Stockholm through the archipelago to Sandhamn takes 3½ hours each way and costs 120SEK to 135SEK ($16–$18) one-way. The ferry trip to Vaxholm from Stockholm takes less than 40 minutes and costs 65SEK ($6.90) one-way. There are no car ferries. If you plan lots of travel around the archipelago, consider buying an **Inter-Skerries Card** for 490SEK ($64). The card allows 16 days of unlimited travel anywhere within the Stockholm archipelago for much less than the cost of individual tickets.

Vaxholm-bound boats depart every hour during the summer (about five times a day in winter) from the Strömkagen, the piers outside the Grand Hotel. For information, call the steamship company **Vaxholmes Belaget** (✆ **08/679-5830**).

Buses to Vaxholm (no. 670) often—but not always—go on to Sandhamn. They depart from the Central Station daily (unless inclement weather prevents it) every 30 minutes beginning at 6am. The last bus from Vaxholm leaves at 1am. A round-trip fare is 160SEK ($21), one-way 85SEK ($11). The trip takes 1 hour.

ORGANIZED TOURS
Strömma Kanal Steamship (✆ **08/587-14000**) offers a guided cruise in English through the canals and bays to Sandhamn. Tours depart from June to August at 10am and last 8 hours. The "Canal Cruise to Sandhamn" begins at 190SEK ($25); it's free for children under 12. The company also offers the "Thousand Island Cruise" through the Stockholm archipelago. The 11-hour guided tour includes lunch, dinner, and stopovers on four islands. Tours are available in July and August.

WHERE TO STAY
Vaxholm Hotel Built in 1902, this stone hotel, painted bright yellow, is at the pier where the ferries from Stockholm dock. It offers modern but rather bland guest rooms, all of which are nonsmoking. Each unit has a well-kept bathroom with a shower unit. Its dance club is open in the summer Friday and Saturday from noon to 2am. The cover charge is 80SEK ($10). An informal pub, Kabyssen, is at street level. One floor above is the Vaxholm Hotel Restaurant (see "Where to Dine," below).

Hamngatan 2, S-185 21 Vaxholm. ✆ **08/541-301-50.** Fax 08/541-313-76. info@vaxholmhotel.se. 42 units. 1,195SEK–1,600SEK ($155–$208) double; 2,700SEK ($351) suite. Rates include breakfast. AE, DC, MC, V. Closed Dec 24–Jan 1. Free parking. **Amenities:** 2 restaurants; bar; sauna; babysitting; laundry service; dry cleaning . In room: TV, hair dryer.

WHERE TO DINE
In Vaxholm
Vaxholm Hotel Restaurant ✦ SEAFOOD   This is the best place to dine in Vaxholm. It overlooks the water from the second floor of the hotel. The chef says

his specialties are "fish, fish, fish." The uncompromising house specialty—and the best buy—is a platter of pan-fried Swedish herring served with mashed potatoes. You can also order a number of other dishes, notably smoked reindeer with horseradish, tender tournedos stuffed with herbs and served with a mustard sauce, or poached filet of sole with white wine sauce. Summer desserts, including rhubarb pie, elderberry sorbet, and lingonberries (often with almond flan), are prepared from locally grown berries and fruits.

Hamngatan 2. ℂ 08/541-301-50. Reservations required in summer. Main courses 119SEK–270SEK ($15–$35). AE, DC, MC, V. Summer daily noon–10:30pm; off season daily noon–9pm. Closed Dec 24–Jan 1.

In Sandhamn

Sandhamns Värdshus SWEDISH   The islanders' favorite restaurant was established in 1672. It offers a view of the moored boats at the harbor. You can always get a good and reasonably priced meal here by selecting a fish dish or the local choice—steak with red onions.

Harbourfront. ℂ 08/571-53-051. Reservations required Sat–Sun. Main courses 95SEK–247SEK ($12–$32). AE, DC, MC, V. Mon–Thurs noon–2:30pm and 5–10pm; Fri noon–2:30pm and 5–10:30pm; Sat noon–2:30pm and Sun noon–9pm.

VÄSTERÅS

To the west of Stockholm, at a distance of 100km (62 miles), is the old city of Västerås, the capital of the province of Västmanlands. With its population of 125,000 inhabitants, Västerås is the sixth-largest city of Sweden. First mentioned in 1120, the town became the seat of a diocese. Although a thriving industrial city today, Västerås no longer plays such an important role in Swedish society. Visitors come to see the cathedral, one of the most magnificent in Sweden, and to explore the Old Town and other attractions.

The location is beautifully situated on Lake Mälaren. Many visitors not interested in the charms of Västerås itself come here to enjoy the lake and its thousands of boat trips in all directions.

For centuries, the town has been strategically situated on the old "King's Road" that linked Oslo in Norway to St. Petersburg in Russia. Founded at an estuary of the Svartån River, Västerås grew and prospered as the major harbor for exporting copper and iron from the mines at nearby Bergslagen. When silver was discovered in the Sala mines in the 1500s, the mineral was also shipped from Västerås, ushering in a period of great prosperity that continued with the industrial revolution of the 19th century.

Västerås grew so rapidly in the post–World War II era that workers from the south of Europe were transported here to work in the local factories. That accounts in part for the large foreign population in Västerås today.

The town has also played a large role in Swedish history. In 1527 King Gustav Vasa summoned the *Riksdag* (Swedish Parliament) to meet at Västerås. This became the first Reformation Parliament. Vasa won approval to curtail the powers of the Catholic church and to redistribute its riches. This was the first major break with Rome and was followed up with another Riksdag meeting a year later at the Council of Örebro when Lutheranism was adopted as the state religion of Sweden.

The major change in recent years to the cityscape was the erection of the 25-floor **Skrapan,** which Swedes call "the scraper." The building dominates the town with its glass facade, housing shops, offices, and a hotel. The scraper is linked to the mall, **Gallerian,** the major shopping mall of the city; the **Punkt** (its "parking house"); and the new **Congress Center.** Despite ancient roots, Västerås is a very modern city.

ESSENTIALS

GETTING THERE   Frequent trains run between Stockholm and Västerås during the day, with the trip taking less than an hour. Alternatively, you can take bus no. 846, run by **Swebuf** (© **0200/21-82-18**), which has frequent connections between the two cities. From Stockholm, motorists can take the E18 going immediately west via Enköping into Västerås.

VISITOR INFORMATION   Head for **Tourist information** at Storegatan 40 (© **021/10-38-30**). Summer hours are Monday to Friday from 10am to 7pm, Saturday from 10am to 3pm, and Sunday from 10am to 2pm. Off-season hours are Monday to Friday from 10am to 6pm, and Saturday from 10am to 3pm.

SEEING THE SIGHTS

Sightseeing begins at the **Domkyrkoplatsen,** the cathedral square, in the center of town lying to the immediate east of the River Svartån. A statue of the 17th-century bishop of Västerås, Johannes Rudbeckius (1581–1646), dominates the square. The statue is by Carl Milles, Sweden's most famous sculptor. Sweden's first school was founded on this square in 1623.

The main attraction here is the **Domkyrkan** ✦✦✦, Vestre Kyrkogatan 3 (© **021/814-611;** open daily 9am–5pm; free admission), the town's 13th-century cathedral that, in spite of subsequent changes and additions, remains one of the grandest in Sweden. Brick built with a double-sloped roof, the Dom is adorned with zigzags and lancets. In the 1500s and 1600s, the building was vastly expanded to include five aisles, the outer two enveloping the original chapels. The famous Swedish architect Nicodemus Tessin the Younger added the spire in 1693.

Impressive ecclesiastical art fills the cathedral's interior. The free-standing **baptismal chapel** ✦ is a 10-sided enclosure that was created in Lübeck, Germany, in 1622 and shipped north to Västerås. Made of oak, the chapel is a stunning piece with caryatids on its slender pillars and figures carved in niches on the panels underneath. Beyond and to the right is the baptismal chapel proper, with an **altarpiece** ✦ from the 1500s carved in Antwerp, Belgium. The work depicts the Virgin as "Queen of Heaven."

The oak and gilded **main altarpiece** ✦✦, which portrays the Passion and the Resurrection, was also made in Antwerp. To its right lies the **tomb** ✦ of Erik XIV, who died in 1577. This black Carrara marble monument on a base of red Öland sandstone is stunning funereal art. You can view the tomb on the south side of the ambulatory. Copies of the royal regalia surmount the top of the tomb.

The **chapel of the Apostles** ✦, directly west of the north door, contains another impressive altarpiece. This, too, came from Belgium in the 16th century, a design of Jan Borman. The paintings on the base of the altarpiece are by Jan van Coninxloo of Brussels. The cathedral also has a **museum** housing precious silver, vestments, rare books, and other ecclesiastical objects.

The open space around the church and the nearby streets comprise the **Gamla Stan** ✦, or Old Town, the most popular area for sightseers. Many of its well-preserved buildings date from the 18th century and currently house artists. The area, also known as Kyrkbackan, is full of steep cobbled lanes, so wear sturdy shoes.

To the west of Kyrkbackan and to the northwest of the cathedral lie two gardens, **Wallinska Kyrkogården** and **Bjorlingska Kyrkogården,** which offer you a chance to take a break. The latter garden borders the Svartån River.

The other major attractions lie on the southern tier of the city south of Storagaten. We recommend that after visiting the Old Town, you return to the riverbank and walk south, enjoying the view.

The first attraction you'll come upon is the **Fiskartorget,** site of the old fish market (long gone). In its place stands the modern Rådhuset, or town hall, which was constructed here in 1953 on the site of an old Dominican priory. Builders during excavations discovered 2,000 skeletons on the site, probably the victims of a 1521 massacre by Gustav Vasa's forces. *The Golden Bull,* by sculptor Allan Runefeldt, stands high on a pillar to the left of the town hall. In front of the entrance to the Rådhuset stands *The Cave of the Winds,* by Eric Grate. Locals irreverently refer to this sculpture as "the municipal deaf ear." Designed by Sven Ahlbom, the Town Hall contains the biggest carillon of Sweden, measuring 65m (213 ft.) high. Its ringing can be heard all over the historic core of the city. To the south of the Town Hall you can enjoy a "green lung," or Vasa Park.

The Old Town Hall from 1857 stands across Fiskatorget and is today the **Konstmuseum (Arts Museum),** Fiskartorget 2 (© 021/39-13-00), open in summer Tuesday through Sunday from 11am to 4pm. In winter, hours are Tuesday through Friday from 10am to 5pm, and Saturday and Sunday from 11am to 5pm. Admission is free. The museum stages a number of temporary exhibitions throughout the year, of both Swedish and modern Scandinavian painters. A permanent exhibition mainly of 20th-century Swedish art is also on display.

From the Fiskartorget you can cross a bridge over the river leading to Skepparbacken and the site of **Västeras Slott** on Slottsgatan. This castle was constructed at the mouth of the river in the 13th century. The building has been greatly altered over time, including major changes in 1737 when it was turned into the county governor's private residence. The *Riksdag,* or Parliament, in the 16th century convened at this castle.

Today you find a museum here. Entered from the courtyard, **Västmanlands Iäns Museum** is devoted to the history of the province, including some Iron Age artifacts found locally. Coins, medals, and ancient textiles form part of the exhibit. This museum is only of minor interest; spend less than an hour here. On the third floor is the beamed *Rikssalen,* or Hall of State, where Parliament once met. Before going to this museum, check with the tourist office (see "Visitor Information," earlier in this chapter) to see if this museum has reopened in 2005 following a major restoration.

Northwest of town, you can visit the **Vallby Friluftsmuseum** ⭐, an open-air museum at Vallbymotet (© 021/398-071). This museum is one of the largest of its type in Sweden. Old buildings were moved here from all over the province. You find an open-air theater with summer entertainment in the evening, as well as a cafe in the Village Square. Plenty of shops selling gifts and souvenirs are here, and you can visit various workshops, including a silversmith, a brushmaker, a potter, and a textile artist. The latest exhibit is the re-creation of a Viking farm.

WHERE TO STAY

Elite Stadshotellet ⭐   Although the second choice in town after the Radisson SAS, this is the most traditional place to stay and for years was the leading hotel of Västerås. Constructed in 1907 in the Art Nouveau style, the hotel was vastly renovated in 2001. Bedrooms are immaculately maintained, most often with twin beds and a little love seat. Many of the rooms are carpeted, others have hardwood floors. A newer section of the hotel contains more modern bedrooms, but these have less character than those in the original building. The interior of the hotel is decorated to match the classical facade. All the neatly kept bathrooms contain showers.

Stora Torget, S-721 03. Box 19 Västerås. © **800/528-1234** in the U.S., or 21-10-28-00. Fax 21-10-28-10. www.elite.se. 137 units. 795SEK–1,595SEK ($103–$207) double; 1,195SEK–2,495SEK ($155–$324) suite. Rates include continental breakfast. AE, DC, MC, V. Free parking. **Amenities:** Restaurant; bar; fitness center; sauna; 24-hr. room service; laundry service; dry cleaning. *In room:* TV, dataport, minibar (in some), hair dryer, iron/ironing board, safe.

Radisson SAS Plaza Hotel ★★ You can see this big, green glass building from miles around; it's the city's major modern landmark. The hotel opened in 1990 on the first 12 floors of a 25-story skyscraper. (The upper floors are reserved for office space as well as a restaurant and bar.) The hotel offers typical Radisson SAS efficiency and style. Rooms come in various configurations, but nearly all of them are spacious—some with carpets, others opening onto hardwood floors. Almost all of the well-maintained and tiled bathrooms have tub/showers. The hotel offers its own drinking and dining facilities, but it's built beside the city's largest shopping mall, with a choice of many other restaurants along with an array of shops.

Karlsgatan 9, S-721 09 Västerås. © **800/333-3333** in the U.S., or 21-10-10-10. Fax 21-10-10-91. www. radissonsas.com. 203 units. 639SEK–1,400SEK ($83–$182) double; 1,800SEK–2,600SEK ($234–$338) suite. Closed Dec 22–Jan 2. AE, DC, MC, V. **Amenities:** Restaurant; bar; sauna; limited room service; laundry service; dry cleaning; nonsmoking rooms; rooms for those w/limited mobility. *In room:* TV, dataport, minibar, coffeemaker, hair dryer, iron.

WHERE TO DINE

Limone Kok & Bar ITALIAN This semicasual dining and drinking choice is housed in an 1850s Officer's House formerly used by the military. At night the restaurant takes on a romantic glow. The food is among the best in town. You may recall a kitchen in sunny Italy as you dig into the selection of antipasti, such as Parma ham and mozzarella. The chef's special is *saltimbocca* (literally, "jump in your mouth") *al limone* tender veal cooked with Parma ham and fresh sage, and flavored with a white-wine sauce and lemon. It's also served with a Parmesan potato cake. You might also opt for an excellent grilled swordfish with fresh spinach and herb-marinated potatoes.

Storag. 4. © **21-83-09-45.** Reservations required. Main courses 150SEK–190SEK ($20–$25). AE, DC, MC, V. Mon–Sat 5:30–10pm; Mon-Fri 11am-1:30pm.

Tabazco Bar & Restaurang SWEDISH/INTERNATIONAL The cuisine is not at all as hot as the name of the restaurant suggests. In fact, it's quite soothing. About 80 diners, frequently young professionals from the area, fill this modern restaurant nightly. The food is rather uncomplicated, but the ingredients are first rate. If featured, there's nothing better than the lobster soup with fresh, fat prawns. You might also opt for an appetizer of fresh avocado stuffed with those same prawns. The chefs also prepare an excellent bruschetta, slices of country bread toasted over a wooden fire, rubbed with a clove of garlic, and soaked in extra-virgin olive oil. The specialties are beef and chicken, both of which are grilled to perfection, then served with a choice of six different homemade sauces. For the vegetarian, the menu includes a plate of tagliatelle with vegetables. You might also opt for the seafood platter for two, with the delectable salmon, shrimp, and assorted shellfish resting on the plate. For dessert, nothing beats the pecan ice cream, although the pastry chef will prepare various flambés.

Sturag. 20A. © **21-12-91-90.** Reservations recommended. Main courses 100SEK–299SEK ($13–$39). AE, MC, V. Mon–Tues 5–10:30pm; Wed–Thurs 11am–2pm and 5–11pm; Fri–Sat 11am–11pm.

5

Gothenburg & Beyond

Called the "gateway to northern Europe," Gothenburg (Göteborg in Swedish) is the country's chief port and second-largest city. Swedes often say that Gothenburg is a more welcoming town than Stockholm, and, in fact, a recent opinion poll showed that half the Swedish population would be happy to move to Gothenburg because of its friendly atmosphere. Canals, parks, and flower gardens enhance its appeal, as do a large number of museums (featuring everything from the world's only stuffed blue whale to modern art) and the largest amusement park in northern Europe. Gothenburg also is a convenient center for excursions to the fishing villages and lovely vacation resorts north of the city.

Gothenburg received its city charter from Gustavus Adolphus II in 1621. The port contains a shipyard, City-varvet, and a manufacturer of platforms for oil rigs, Götaverken/Arendal. The city also is the home of Volvo, the car manufacturer (whose plant is about a 15-min. drive from the city center), and of the Hasselblad space camera. Despite this heavy industry, Gothenburg's environmental programs have made it a European leader in developing new products and procedures for dealing with waste.

A walk down Kungsportsavenyn, known as *Avenyn* (the Avenue) is a Gothenburg tradition, even in winter, when the street is heated by underground pipes so that the snow melts away quickly. There are many outdoor cafes from which to watch the passing action on this wide, pedestrian thoroughfare.

1 Orientation

ARRIVING

BY PLANE   SAS (℃ **800/221-2350** in the U.S.; www.scandanavian.net) operates 5 to 10 daily flights from Copenhagen to Gothenburg (most of them nonstop) between 7:30am and 11:05pm. (Many Swedes who live on the west coast of Sweden consider Copenhagen a more convenient airport than the one in Stockholm.) SAS also operates 4 to 15 daily flights between Stockholm and Gothenburg, beginning about 7am and continuing until early evening.

Planes arrive at **Landvetter Airport** (℃ **031/94-10-00**), 26km (16 miles) east of Gothenburg. A *Flygbuss* (airport bus) departs every 30 minutes for the 30-minute ride to the central bus terminal, just behind Gothenburg's main railway station. Buses run daily between 5:15am and 12:15am. A one-way trip costs 70SEK ($9.10).

BY TRAIN   The Oslo-Copenhagen express train runs through Gothenburg and Helsingborg. Trains run frequently on a north-south route between Gothenburg and Helsingborg/Malmö in the south. The most traveled rail route is between Gothenburg and Stockholm, with trains leaving hourly in both directions; the trip takes 3 to 4½ hours.

Trains arrive at the **Central Station,** on one side of Drottningtorget. Inside the station is a currency exchange bureau and an office of the Swedish National Railroad Authority (SJ), which sells rail and bus tickets for connections to nearby areas. For information, call ℭ **771/75-75-75.**

BY BUS   There are several buses from Gothenburg to Helsingborg/Malmö (and vice versa) daily. Trip time from Gothenburg to Helsingborg is 3 hours, Gothenburg to Malmö, 3 to 4 hours. Several buses connect Stockholm and Gothenburg daily. The trip takes 6 to 7 hours. Gothenburg's bus station, at Nils Ericson Gate, is located behind the railway station. For information in Gothenburg, call **Swebus,** Sweden's largest bus company (ℭ **036/290-8000).**

BY FERRY   The **Stena Line** (ℭ **031/704-00-00**) has six crossings per day in summer from North Jutland (a 3-hr. trip); call for information on specific departure times, which vary seasonally. The vessels have excellent dining rooms.

From June to mid-August, there's service from Newcastle-upon-Tyne (England) to Gothenburg twice a week, taking 24 hours. This service is operated by **Scandinavian Seaways** (ℭ **031/65-06-50** for information). There's no rail-pass discount on the England-Sweden crossings.

BY CAR   From either Malmö or Helsingborg, the two major "gateways" to Sweden on the west coast, take E6 north. Gothenburg is 280km (174 miles) north of Malmö and 226km (140 miles) north of Helsingborg. From Stockholm, take E4 west to Jönköping and continue west the rest of the way through Borås to Gothenburg, a distance of 470km (291 miles).

VISITOR INFORMATION

Gothenburg Tourist Office is at Kungsportsplatsen 2 (ℭ **031/61-25-00;** www.goteborg.com), open June 3 to July 23 daily 9am to 6pm; September through May Monday through Friday 9am to 5pm, and Saturday from 10am to 2pm.

CITY LAYOUT

The layout of Gothenburg, with its network of streets separated by canals, is reminiscent of Amsterdam—not surprisingly, as it was designed by Dutch architects in the 17th century. Its wealth of parks and open spaces has given it a reputation as Sweden's greenest city.

Some of the old canals have been filled in, but you can explore the major remaining waterway and the busy harbor by taking one of the city's famous **Paddan sightseeing boats** (ℭ **031/60-96-70**). *Paddan* is the Swedish word for "toad," and the allusion is to the squat shape of the boats that enables them to navigate under the many low bridges. A Paddan service takes you from the point of embarkation, Kungsportsplatsen (near the Central Station), direct to the Liseberg amusement park. The park is the most popular visitor attraction in the area, attracting some three million visitors annually.

The best place to start sightseeing on foot is **Kungsportsavenyn (the Avenyn),** a wide, tree-lined boulevard with many sidewalk cafes. (Take a look at the "Gothenburg Attractions" map later in this chapter.) *Avenyn* leads to **Götaplatsen,** a square that's the city's artistic and historic center. Its centerpiece is a huge bronze fountain with a statue of the sea god Poseidon, sculpted by Carl Milles.

Fun Fact **High Bridge**

Spanning the Göta River, Älvsborg Bridge (the longest suspension bridge in Sweden) is almost 900m (2,952 ft.) long and built high enough to allow ocean liners to pass underneath.

Gothenburg's old commercial section lies on either side of the central canal. At the central canal is **Gustav Adolfs Torg,** dominated by a statue of Gustav himself. Facing the canal is the **Börshuset (Stock Exchange building).** On the western side is the **Rådhuset (Town Hall),** originally constructed in 1672. Around the corner, moving toward the river, is the **Kronhuset** (off Kronhusgatan), a 17th-century Dutch-designed building—the oldest in Gothenburg.

Gothenburg is dominated by its **harbor,** which is best viewed from one of the Padden boats. The major attraction here is the **Maritime Center** (see "Seeing the Sights," later in this chapter). The shipyards, whose spidery forms look as if they were made from an Erector Set, are dominated by the IBM building. Part of the harbor is connected by an overhead walkway to the shopping mall of **Nordstan.**

2 Getting Around

Visitors usually find that the cheapest way to explore Gothenburg (except on foot) is to buy a **Göteborgskortet (Gothenburg Card).** Available at hotels, newspaper kiosks, and the city's tourist office, it entitles you to unlimited travel on local trams, buses, and ferryboats; certain sightseeing tours; either free or discounted admission to the city's major museums and sightseeing attractions; discounts at certain shops; free parking in certain centrally located parking lots; and several other extras that usually make the card worthwhile. A ticket valid for 24 hours costs 175SEK ($23) for adults and 135SEK ($18) for children up to 17 years old; a 48-hour ticket is 295SEK ($38) for adults and 190SEK ($25) for children.

BY PUBLIC TRANSPORTATION (TRAM) A single tram ticket costs 20SEK ($2.60); a 24-hour travel pass goes for 50SEK ($6.50). If you don't have an advance ticket, board the first car of the tram—the driver will sell you a ticket and stamp one-way tickets. Previously purchased tickets must be stamped in the automatic machine as soon as you board the tram.

BY TAXI Taxis are not as plentiful as you might like. However, you can always find one by going to the Central Station. **To call a taxi,** dial ✆ **031/27-27-27.** A taxi traveling within the city limits now costs 155SEK to 320SEK ($20–$42). With the Gothenburg Card, you get a 10% reduction.

BY CAR Because of parking problems, a car is not a practical vehicle for touring Gothenburg. You may need a car to tour the surrounding area, but there is good public transportation within the city, as well as to many sights. **Avis** (✆ **031/80-57-80**) has a rental office at the Central Station and another at the airport (✆ **031/94-60-30**). **Hertz** also has an office at the center of town at the Central Station (✆ **031/80-37-30**) and one at the airport (✆ **031/94-60-20**). Compare rates and make sure you understand the insurance coverage before you sign a contract.

FAST FACTS: Gothenburg

Area Code The international country code for Sweden is **46;** the city code for Gothenburg is **031** (if you're calling Gothenburg from abroad, drop the 0; within Gothenburg, drop the 031).

Bookstores The biggest and most central is **Akademi Bokhandeln,** Norra Hamngatan 26 (✆ **031/61-70-31**).

Business Hours Generally, **shops** are open Monday through Friday from 10am to 6pm and Saturday from 10am to 4pm; **banks,** Monday through Friday from 9:30am to 3pm; and **offices,** Monday through Friday from 9am to 5pm.

Currency Exchange Currency can be exchanged at **Forex,** in the Central Station (✆ **031/15-65-16**), daily 7am to 9pm. There's also a currency exchange desk at Landvetter Airport, open daily 5:15am to 10:45pm.

Dentists Call the referral agency, Stampgatan (✆ **031/80-78-00**), Monday to Friday 8am to 8pm.

Doctors If it's not an emergency, your hotel can call a local doctor and arrange an appointment. If it's an emergency, go to **City Akuten,** Drottninggatan 45 (✆ **031/10-10-10**).

Drugstores A good pharmacy is **Apoteket Vasen,** Götgatan 12, Nordstan (✆ **0771/450-450**), open daily 8am to 10pm.

Embassies & Consulates There is no U.S. consulate in Gothenburg; Americans and citizens of Australia, Ireland, and New Zealand must contact their embassies in Stockholm. The **British Consulate** is at Götgatan 15 (✆ **031/339-33-00**), open Monday to Friday 9am to 1pm and 2 to 4pm.

Emergencies The number to call for nearly all emergencies (fire, police, medical) is ✆ **112.**

Eyeglasses Go to **Wasa Optik,** Vasaplatsen 7 (✆ **031/711-05-35**). It's open Monday to Friday 9am to 6pm.

Hairdressers & Barbers A good one is **Salong Noblesse,** Södra Larmgatan 6 (✆ **031/711-71-30**), open Monday to Friday 9am to 7pm and Saturday 9am to 3pm.

Internet The city library, **Stadsbibliotek,** Götaplatsen (✆ **031/61-65-00**), has free Internet access. Open Monday to Friday 10am to 8pm, and Saturday and Sunday 11am to 5pm (closed on Sun May–Aug).

Laundry & Dry Cleaning Laundries are hard to find. There's a centrally located one at Wasatvätten, Victoriagatan 22 (✆ **031/71-10-911**). For dry cleaning, go to **Express Kem,** Sriggattan 25 (✆ **031/15-84-83**).

Liquor Laws You must be 18 to consume alcohol in a restaurant, but 20 to purchase alcohol in liquor stores. No alcohol can be served before noon. Most pubs stop serving liquor at 3am, except special nightclubs with a license to stay open later. Liquor can be purchased at state-owned liquor shops known as *Systembolag,* but only Monday to Friday 9am to 6pm.

Lost Property Go to the police station (see "Police," below).

Luggage Storage & Lockers You can store luggage and rent lockers at the Central Station for 20SEK to 60SEK ($2.60–$7.80), depending on the size of the luggage.

Photographic Supplies An excellent store is **Expert,** Arkaden 9 (© 031/ 80-20-70), open Monday to Friday 10am to 6pm and Saturday 10am to 2pm.

Police The main police station is Polismyndigheten, Ernst Fortells Platz (© 031/739-20-00).

Post Office The main post office is at Nordstan (© 031/62-39-63), next to the Central Station. It's open Monday to Saturday 10am to 3pm.

Radio & TV Gothenburg has Swedish-language TV broadcasts on TV1, TV2, TV3, and TV4, and receives such British channels as Super Sky and BBC. National radio stations include P1, P2, P3, and P4; Radio Gothenburg broadcasts on 101.9 MHz (FM).

Shoe Repair Try **Mister Minit,** Nordstan (© 031/152-127). Repairs are made while you wait.

Taxes Gothenburg imposes no special city taxes other than the value-added tax (MOMS), which applies nationwide.

Transit Information For tram and bus information, call © 0771/41-43-00.

3 Where to Stay

Reservations are important, but if you need a place to stay on the spur of the moment, try the **Gothenburg Tourist Office,** at Kungsportsplatsen 2 (© 031/ 61-25-00; www.goteborg.com). It lists the city's hotels and boardinghouses, and reserves rooms in private homes. Reservations can be made in advance, by letter, or by phone. The tourist office charges a booking fee of 60SEK ($7.80). Double rooms in private homes start at around 200SEK ($26) per person. Breakfast is always extra.

The hotels listed in the following section as "expensive" actually become "moderate" in price on Friday and Saturday and during midsummer.

EXPENSIVE

Elite Plaza ★★   Equaled in Gothenburg only by the Radisson SAS Scandinavia, this late-19th-century insurance company was stunningly converted into a superior first-class hotel. All the major architectural features of this palatial 1889 structure were preserved, including the stucco ceilings and mosaic floors. The public lounges are adorned with modern art, and all the rooms and plumbing have been updated to give the building a new lease on life. Lying in the center of town, the hotel is within a short walk of the Central Station and the Opera House. Bedrooms are midsize to spacious, each with a new private bathroom with a tub/shower. Its drinking and dining facilities—with friendly bartenders and smooth service—are another reason to stay here.

Vastra Hamngatan 3, S-404 22 Göteborg. © 031/720-40-00. Fax 031/720-40-10. www.elite.se. 139 units. Sun–Thurs 1,995SEK–2,600SEK ($259–$338) double, 3,600SEK–4,800SEK ($468–$624) suite; Fri–Sat 1,200SEK–1,500SEK ($156–$195) double, 4,800SEK ($624) suite. Rates include breakfast. AE, DC, MC, V. Tram: 1, 6, 9, or 11. **Amenities:** Restaurant; bar; 24-hr. room service; babysitting; laundry service; dry cleaning; nonsmoking rooms. *In room:* TV, dataport, minibar, hair dryer, safe, trouser press (in some).

Hotel Gothia Towers ★★   This well-respected government-rated four-star hotel, which rises 18 mirror-plated stories above Sweden's largest convention center, was the tallest building in Gothenburg until it was surpassed in the late 1990s by a competitor. A total of 410 rooms are in its Gothia West Tower,

Gothenburg

ATTRACTIONS ●

Botaniska Trädgården
  (Botanical Garden) **12**
Drotting Kristinas Jaktslott
  (Queen Christina's
  Hunting Lodge) **7**
East India House
  (Museum of Gothenburg) **5**
Feskekörka (Fish Church) **8**
Göteborg
  Maritima Centrum **2**
Göteborgs
  Konstmuseum **14**
Göteborgsoperan
  (Gothenburg
  Opera House) **3**
Guldhedens Våtterntorn
  (Water Tower) **13**
Kronhusbodarna **4**
Liseberg Park **20**
Röhsska Konstsöjdmuseet **18**
Slottsskogen **11**
Stadsbibliotek (Library) **16**
Stadsteatern (Theater) **15**
Trägårdsföreningen **25**

ACCOMMODATIONS ■

Elite Plaza **6**
Hotel Best Western
  Eggers **28**
Hotel Gothia Towers **21**
Hotell Royal **26**
Hotel Onyxen **22**
Hotel Opera **29**
Hotel Örgryte **24**
Hotel Winn **1**
Novotel Göteborg **10**
Quality Panorama
  Hotel **19**
Quality Hotel 11 **9**
Radisson SAS
  Park Ave Hotel **23**
Radisson SAS
  Scandinavia **17**
Scandi Hotel Europa **27**
Tidblom's Hotel **9**

renovated in 2001; the others in its Gothia East Tower were extensively renovated in 2003. The brisk, friendly format places it among Scandinavia's best
business-oriented hotels. Rooms are comfortable, contemporary, and tasteful.
Touches of wood, particularly the hardwood floors, take the edge off any sense
of cookie-cutter standardization. Bathrooms are spacious, with tub/showers.
Rooms on the top three floors are more plush and feature enhanced amenities
and services. A covered passageway runs directly to the convention center.

Mässans Gata 24, S-402 26 Göteborg. ℂ 031/75-08-800. Fax 031/750-88-82. www.hotel-gothia.se. 704
units. Mon–Thurs 2,090SEK–2,590SEK ($272–$337) double; Fri–Sun 990SEK–1,490SEK ($129–$194) double;
2,500SEK–7,000SEK ($325–$910) suite. AE, DC, MC, V. Tram: 4 or 5. **Amenities:** 2 restaurants; 3 bars; fitness
center; sauna; limited room service; laundry service; dry cleaning; nonsmoking rooms; rooms for those w/
limited mobility. *In room:* TV, dataport, minibar, coffeemaker, hair dryer, iron, safe, trouser press.

Quality Hotel 11 ★ *Finds* This harborfront inn is a real discovery, lying west
of the center at Eriksberg. This three-story brick-and-glass waterfront building
could have been a warehouse back in the 19th century. A contemporary choice,
it is characterized by its multilevel terraces. If you don't mind the slightly inconvenient location across the harbor from the center of town, it is a winning
choice, with vistas of the water from every room. To reach it, you can take a bus
or else follow the signs to Norra Älvstranden if you're driving.

Bedrooms are spacious, for the most part, with attractive Scandinavian modern furnishings on wooden floors with pastel fabrics. Each room comes with a
tiled bathroom with a tub/shower. Because of its location, it is relatively undiscovered but worth the effort to get here. The staff is extremely helpful and cour-
teous. All rooms are nonsmoking.

Maskingatan 11. ℂ 031/779-11-11. Fax 031/779-11-10. www.hotel11.se. 184 units. Sun–Thurs
1,800SEK–1,910SEK ($234–$248) double, from 2,245SEK ($292) suite; summer and Fri–Sat 990SEK ($129)
double, from 1,485SEK ($193) suite. Rates include breakfast buffet. AE, DC, MC, V. Parking 95SEK ($12). Bus:
16. **Amenities:** Restaurant; bar; 24-hr. room service; laundry service; dry cleaning; rooms for those w/limited
mobility. *In room:* A/C, TV, dataport, minibar, safe (at additional charge).

Radisson SAS Park Avenue Hotel ★★ Constructed in 1950 and renovated
in the '90s, this Radisson property stands on Gothenburg's major boulevard.
Everyone from Henry Kissinger to the Beatles, and David Rockefeller to the
Rolling Stones, has stayed here. The hotel has 10 floors, with attractively
designed bedrooms. Upper-floor units enjoy excellent views of the city. Bathrooms are a bit tiny but are equipped with tub/showers, and overall the rooms
are well maintained.

The hotel's gourmet dining room, Belle Avenue, is one of the best known
in Gothenburg. It specializes in game and fresh fish from the Atlantic. The
hotel's famous nightclub, Madison Nightclub, is recommended separately (see
"Gothenburg After Dark," later in this chapter).

Kungsportsavenyn 36–38, S-400 16 Göteborg. ℂ 800/333-3333 in the U.S., or 031/758-40-00. Fax 031/
758-40-01. www.radissonsas.com. 318 units. June 19–Aug 16 1,410SEK–1,485SEK ($183–$193) double,
2,600SEK ($338) suite; Aug 17–June 18 1,895SEK ($246) double, 2,600SEK ($338) suite. Rates include break-
fast. AE, DC, MC, V. Parking 245SEK ($32). Tram: 1, 4, 5, or 6. Bus: 40. **Amenities:** Restaurant; bar; fitness cen-
ter; sauna; 24-hr. room service; babysitting; laundry service; dry cleaning; nonsmoking rooms; rooms for those
w/limited mobility. *In room:* TV, dataport, minibar, coffeemaker, hair dryer, safe, trouser press.

Radisson SAS Scandinavia Hotel ★★★ This unusual deluxe hotel surrounds a large atrium, which seems like a tree-lined city square indoors. It stands
opposite the railroad station, and it's one of the best-run and best-equipped
hotels in Sweden. Opened in 1986, the hotel offers the finest rooms in town;
they're large, with good beds, and luxuriously appointed. Bathrooms are first

class, with tub/showers. The fifth floor of the hotel contains the exclusive concierge rooms with extended service and speedier check-ins. These upgraded accommodations are most often booked by the business community.

Södra Hamngatan 59–65, S-401 24 Göteborg. © 800/333-3333 in the U.S., or 031/758-50-50. Fax 031/ 758-50-01. www.radissonsas.com. 349 units. 1,390SEK ($181) double; 2,450SEK–3,000SEK ($319–$390) suite. AE, DC, MC, V. Parking 245SEK ($32). Tram: 1, 2, 3, 4, 5, or 7. Bus: 40. **Amenities:** Restaurant; bar; indoor pool; fitness center; sauna; 24-hr. room service; babysitting; laundry service; dry cleaning; nonsmoking rooms; rooms for those w/limited mobility. *In room:* TV, dataport, minibar, hair dryer, safe.

Scandi Hotel Europa ★★ This is one of the largest hotels in Scandinavia; a big, bustling blockbuster of a building that rises eight bulky stories across from Gothenburg's railway station. Built in 1972 of concrete and glass, the hotel underwent a massive renovation that ended in 1994, which added thousands of slabs of russet-colored marble. Today it's a member of one of Scandinavia's most upscale chains, Proverbis, and the well-trained staff includes dozens of young graduates from hotel training schools. Bedrooms are outfitted in monochromatic tones of either autumn-inspired browns or pale Nordic tones of blue, and have conservative, modern furniture as well as up-to-date bathrooms equipped with tub/showers. The largest, most plush, and most recently renovated rooms lie on the hotel's sixth floor.

Köpmansgatan 38, P.O. Box 11444, S-404 29 Göteborg. © 031/751-65-00. Fax 031/751-65-11. 450 units. Sun–Thurs 1,995SEK ($259) double, 2,295SEK ($298) suite; Fri–Sat 950SEK ($124) double, 1,300SEK ($169) suite. Rates include breakfast. AE, DC, MC, V. Parking 150SEK ($20). Tram: 1 or 5. **Amenities:** Restaurant; 2 bars; indoor pool; sauna; limited room service; laundry service; dry cleaning; nonsmoking rooms; rooms for those w/limited mobility. *In room:* A/C, TV, dataport, minibar, hair dryer.

MODERATE

Hotel Best Western Eggers ★ *Finds* The second-oldest hotel in Gothenburg was built in 1859, predating the Swedish use of the word to describe a building with rooms for travelers. Many emigrants to the New World spent their last night in the old country at the Hotel Eggers, and during World War II, the Germans and the Allies met here for secret negotiations. Today it's just as good as or better than ever, with stained-glass windows, ornate staircases, and wood paneling. Rooms vary in size, but they are all individually furnished and beautifully appointed, with large bathrooms equipped with tub/showers. In the hotel dining room, gilt leather tapestry and polished mahogany evoke the 19th century.

Drottningtorget, SE 40125 Göteborg. © 800/528-1234 in the U.S. and Canada, or 031/333-44-40. Fax 031/333-44-49. www.bestwestern.com. 67 units. June 24–Aug 8 and Fri–Sat year-round 1,040SEK–1,430SEK ($135–$186) double; rest of year 1,750SEK–2,130SEK ($228–$277) double. Rates include breakfast. AE, DC, MC, V. Parking 90SEK ($12), valet parking 195SEK ($25). Tram: 1, 2, 3, 4, 5, 6, 7, 8, or 9. Bus: 40. **Amenities:** Restaurant; bar; limited room service; laundry service; dry cleaning; nonsmoking rooms. *In room:* TV, dataport, hair dryer.

Hotel Onyxen *Value* Clean, well run, and family managed, this hotel was originally built around 1900 as a many-balconied apartment house. In the 1980s, its interior was extensively reconfigured into a streamlined and efficiently decorated hotel. Bedrooms have high ceilings, with comfortable beds, and, in most cases, a color scheme of white and pale blue. Bathrooms come with shower units and are small but well maintained. There's a residents' pub and cocktail lounge near the lobby, but the only meal served is breakfast.

Sten Sturegatan 23, S-412 52 Göteborg. © 031/81-08-45. Fax 031/16-56-72. www.hotelonyxen.com. 34 units. July–Aug and Fri–Sat year-round 1,090SEK ($142) double; rest of year 1,490SEK–1,590SEK ($194–$207) double; extra bed 200SEK ($26). Children an additional 100SEK ($13). Rates include breakfast. AE, DC, MC, V. Tram: 4 or 5. **Amenities:** Breakfast room; bar; laundry service; dry cleaning; nonsmoking rooms. *In room:* TV, dataport, hair dryer, iron, trouser press.

Hotel Opera   In 1994, the Hotel Ekoxen joined forces (and facilities) with another hotel to become the Hotel Opera. It's an up-to-date, well-run hotel that often attracts business travelers, although summer visitors gravitate to it as well. Both buildings date from the late 19th century but were upgraded in the 1990s. All rooms are individually designed and tastefully furnished, with neatly kept bathrooms equipped with tub/showers.

Norra Hamngatan 38, SE-41106 Göteborg. ✆ 031/80-50-80. Fax 031/80-58-17. www.hotelopera.se. 145 units. June 26–Aug 17 and Fri–Sat year-round 695SEK–895SEK ($90–$116) double; rest of year 1,295SEK–1,450SEK ($168–$189) double. Rates include breakfast. AE, DC, MC, V. Parking 100SEK ($13). Tram: 1, 4, 5, 6, 7, 8, or 9. **Amenities:** Restaurant; bar; Jacuzzi; sauna; laundry service; dry cleaning. *In room:* TV, dataport (in some), hair dryer.

Novotel Göteborg ⭐   This converted harbor-front brewery 4km (2½ miles) west of the center is a stylish hotel run by the French hotel conglomerate Accor. Each plushly carpeted room offers panoramic views of the industrial landscape. The room style is Swedish modern, with many built-in pieces, good-size closets, and firm sofa beds. Bathrooms tend to be small but they do have tub/showers. When it was completed in the 1980s, it was one of the most successful restorations of a 19th-century building in Sweden. There's a well-accessorized sauna, and laundry facilities are available.

Klippan 1, S-414 51 Göteborg. ✆ 800/221-4542 in the U.S., or 031/14-90-00. Fax 031/42-22-99. www.novotel.se. 148 units. June 26–Aug 10 and Fri–Sat year-round 890SEK–950SEK ($116–$124) double, 1,330SEK–1,530SEK ($173–$199) suite; rest of year 1,430SEK–1,590SEK ($186–$207) double, 1,690SEK–1,840SEK ($220–$239) suite. Rates include breakfast. AE, DC, MC, V. Free parking. From Gothenburg, follow the signs on E20 to Frederikshavn, then the signs to Kiel; exit at Klippan, where signs direct you to the hotel. Tram: 3 or 9. Bus: 91 or 92. **Amenities:** Restaurant; bar; room service; laundry service; dry cleaning; nonsmoking rooms; rooms for those w/limited mobility. *In room:* TV, dataport, minibar (in some), hair dryer, safe.

Quality Panorama Hotel ⭐ *Finds*   Spacious and dramatic, this 13-story hotel is a 10-minute walk west of the center of town. One of the tallest buildings in Gothenburg, the Panorama is a major hotel that gets surprisingly little publicity. The plant-filled lobby has a skylight, piano bar, and balcony-level restaurant. The bedrooms have stylish furnishings and soft lighting. Extras include wood floors and double-glazed windows. Bathrooms tend to be small. The finest accommodations are found on floors 7 through 13.

Eklandagatan 51–53, S-400 22 Göteborg. ✆ 031/767-70-00. Fax 031/767-70-73. www.panorama.se. 338 units (some with shower only). June 20–Aug 10 and Fri–Sat year-round 890SEK ($116) double, 1,330SEK ($173) suite; rest of year 1,650SEK ($215) double, 2,100SEK ($273) suite. Rates include breakfast. AE, DC, MC, V. Parking 35SEK ($4.55). Closed Dec 21–Jan 7. Tram: 4 or 5. Bus: 40 or 51. **Amenities:** Restaurant; bar; Jacuzzi; sauna; limited room service; laundry service; dry cleaning; nonsmoking rooms; rooms for those w/ limited mobility. *In room:* TV, dataport, minibar, hair dryer.

INEXPENSIVE

Hotell Royal   Founded in 1852, the oldest hotel in Gothenburg still in use is about .5km (½ mile) from the railroad station. All major bus and tram lines pass close by. It's decorated in a typical 19th-century style, with wrought-iron banisters and heavy cast-bronze lamps at the stairs. In the reception area is a unique hand-painted glass ceiling. The rooms are individually designed and modernized, with ample bathrooms equipped with shower units.

Drottninggatan 67, S-411 07 Göteborg. ✆ 031/700-11-70. Fax 031/700-11-79. www.hotel-royal.com. 82 units. June 22–Aug 14 and Fri–Sat year-round 890SEK–990SEK ($116–$129) double; rest of year 1,295SEK–1,395SEK ($168–$181) double. Rates include buffet breakfast. AE, DC, MC, V. Parking 130SEK ($17), depending on the size of the car (located across the street). Tram: 1, 2, 3, 4, 5, or 6. Bus: 60. **Amenities:** Breakfast room; lounge; nonsmoking rooms. *In room:* TV, hair dryer.

Hotel Örgryte Named after the leafy residential district of Örgryte, this family-owned hotel lies 1.5km (about 1 mile) east of the commercial core of Gothenburg. It was originally built around 1960 and renovated many times since, most recently in the mid-1990s. Rooms were upgraded and outfitted with pastel-colored upholstery and streamlined, uncomplicated furniture that makes use of birch-veneer woods. Rooms are medium-size, often big enough to contain a sitting area; bathrooms are rather cramped but do contain tub/showers. Both the exterior and the public areas are clean but not particularly inspired in their design, but overall, the place provides decent, safe accommodations at a relatively reasonable price.

Danska Vägen 68–70, SE-41659 Göteborg. ℂ 031/707-89-00. Fax 031/707-89-99. www.hotelorgryte.se. 70 units. Sun–Thurs 1,445SEK ($188) double; Fri–Sat 890SEK ($116) double; 1,665SEK–2,025SEK ($216–$263) suite. Rates include breakfast. AE, DC, MC, V. Parking 100SEK ($13). Bus: 60 or 62. **Amenities:** Restaurant; bar; sauna; laundry service; dry cleaning; nonsmoking rooms. *In room:* TV, dataport, hair dryer.

Hotel Winn This no-nonsense but comfortable and affordable four-story hotel is about 3km (1¾ miles) north of Gothenburg's ferryboat terminal. Functional and modern, its bedrooms are more comfortable than you might imagine from the uninspired exterior. Each is outfitted in pastel shades, with well-kept bathrooms equipped with tub/showers.

Gamla Tingstadsgatan 1, S-402 76 Göteborg. ℂ 031/750-1900. Fax 031/750-19-50. www.winnhotel.com. 121 units. June 15–Aug 15 and Fri–Sat year-round 995SEK ($129) double; rest of year 1,395SEK ($181) double. Rates include breakfast. AE, DC, MC, V. Free parking. Bus: 40, 45, 48, or 49. **Amenities:** Restaurant; bar; indoor pool; sauna; laundry service; dry cleaning; nonsmoking rooms; rooms for those w/limited mobility. *In room:* TV, dataport, minibar, hair dryer.

Tidblom's Hotel ★ *Finds* Set 3km (1¾ miles) east of Gothenburg's center, in a residential neighborhood filled with other Victorian buildings, this hotel was built in 1897 as a dormitory for Scottish craftsmen imported to work at the nearby lumber mill. Despite its functional purpose, its builders graced it with a conical tower, fancy brickwork, and other architectural adornments that remain in place today. After stints as a warehouse, a delicatessen, and a low-rent hotel, the building was upgraded in 1987 into a cozy, charming, and well-accessorized hotel. Guest rooms have good, firm beds; ample bathrooms with tub/showers; and wooden floors—and have more flair and character than you'll find at many larger, more anonymous hotels in Gothenburg's center. A restaurant recommended in the "Where to Dine," later in this chapter is located on the premises.

Olskroksgatan 23, S-416 66 Göteborg. ℂ 031/707-50-00. Fax 031/707-50-99. www.tidbloms.com. 42 units. June 28–Aug 8 Sun–Thurs 1,500SEK ($195) double; Fri–Sat 940SEK ($122) double. Rates include breakfast. AE, DC, MC, V. Free parking. Tram: 1, 3, or 6. **Amenities:** Restaurant; bar; sauna; 24-hr. room service; laundry service; dry cleaning; nonsmoking rooms; rooms for those w/limited mobility. *In room:* TV, dataport, minibar, hair dryer, safe.

4 Where to Dine

EXPENSIVE

Fiskekrogen ★★ SEAFOOD One of the most appealing seafood restaurants in Gothenburg occupies a building across the canal from the Stadtsmuseum, in a handsome, internationally modern setting whose sea-green and dark-blue color scheme reflects the shades of the ocean. Fiskekrogen prides itself on a medley of fresh seafood that's artfully displayed and prepared with a zest that earns many loyal customers throughout the city. One of the most appealing aspects of the place is a display of seafood on ice—succulent oysters, fresh lobster, fat crayfish, clams, and mussels. After viewing this spread, you can tell the waiter what you prefer for dinner. More conventional seafood dishes include poached tournedos of cod with beetroot marmalade and a horseradish-butter sauce; and grilled halibut with a ragout of baby scallops, bacon, onions, mushrooms, and Zinfandel.

Lilla Torget 1. © **031/10-10-05.** Reservations recommended. Main courses 250SEK–350SEK ($33–$46); small menu 595SEK ($77); big menu 795SEK ($103). AE, DC, MC, V. Mon–Fri 11:30am–2pm and 5:30–11pm; Sat 1–11pm. Tram: 6, 9, or 11. Bus: 16.

Fond ★★ SCANDINAVIAN/CONTINENTAL   An address patronized by the town's discerning gourmets, this is the domain of Stefan Karlsson, a media darling and winner of several culinary citations. He has chosen an attractive modern backdrop for his restaurant, lying in the Lorensberg sector of town. Light Scandinavian wood furnishings, wall panels, and Italian chairs form a backdrop for the cooking, which seems to show more finesse than most rival establishments and reflects the personality and style of the chef. In other words, he puts his personal stamp on every dish, each one prepared with market-fresh ingredients.

Select a table, if available, with a panoramic view over the Avenue and watch the world go by as you partake of one delectable course after another. Memorable dishes worth ordering include a choice loin of Swedish lamb with wine gravy and a side of sugar-glazed cabbage. Cabbage appears again in a mousse with scallops. The hearts at our table were won by the deep-fried crayfish with a black pepper glaze and baby carrots with an orange sauce. A classic is the boiled crayfish so beloved in Sweden, served with fresh dill. Desserts are made fresh daily and are meticulously crafted and full of flavor.

Götaplatsen. © **031/81-25-80.** Reservations required. Main courses 105SEK–335SEK ($14–$44). AE, DC, MC, V. Mon–Fri 11:30am–2:30pm; Mon–Sat 5pm–midnight.

Le Village ★ *Finds* FRENCH   An exclusive and popular place with Gothenburgers for years, this is a winning choice if someone doesn't purchase the table and chairs from you during the course of a meal. Yes, everything—all the furnishings and paintings—are for sale, as Le Village is connected to an antiques store. It is traditionally Swedish in decor, with light wooden furnishings and tasteful art.

The chefs know their recipes well, and they don't launch daring new culinary experiments on you. Their cooking technique is sharp, precise, and carefully based on an ability to bring out the natural flavors in fine foodstuffs. A recent and stellar example of their prowess is Swedish cabbage with veal loin flavored with French mustard. Their seasonal meat dishes are also reinforced by tasty concoctions of chicken, the recipes varying from night to night. The chefs also turn out an excellent appetizer of fish soup, often made with mushrooms. Each dessert is made fresh daily—try, for example, the chocolate tofu.

Tredje Långgatan 13, Linnéstaden. © **031/242-00-31.** Reservations recommended. Main courses 160SEK–189SEK ($21–$25). AE, DC, MC, V. Mon–Fri 11:30am–2pm and 6–11pm. Closed Sat–Sun. Tram: Lies near Järntorget tram stop.

Restaurang Räkan/Yellow Submarine ★ SEAFOOD   This is one of Gothenburg's best seafood restaurants. Not surprisingly, it has a nautical decor with buoy lamps, wooden-plank tables typical of the Swedish west coast, and a shallow-bottomed re-creation of a Swedish lake. Your seafood platter arrives on a battery-powered boat with you directing the controls. You can order various combinations of crayfish (in season), along with prawns, poached sole, mussels, lobster, filet of gray sole, and fresh crabs. If you don't want fish, a choice of

Picnic Fare

Go to **Saluhallen,** Kungstorget, for the makings of an elegant picnic. This colorful indoor market was built in 1888 and sells meat, fruit, vegetables, delicatessen products, and everything in between. You can find quail, moose, and reindeer; fruits and vegetables from all over the world; and bread, coffee, olives, pâtés, and more. Much of the food is already cooked and will be packaged for you to take out. If you don't feel like venturing outside, there are four restaurants and a coffee bar in the building. The hall is open Monday to Thursday 8:30am to 6pm, Friday 8am to 6pm, and Saturday 8am to 1pm. Take tram no. 1, 4, 5, or 6 to Kungsportsplatsen.

Once you've packed your picnic basket with goodies, go to any of Gothenburg's major parks (see "Parks & Gardens," in "Seeing the Sights," later in this chapter). Especially recommended is **Trädgårdsföreningen,** across from the Central Station, although there's a 15SEK ($1.95) entrance fee.

---

chicken and beef dishes is available. Attached to the restaurant is a popular pub, Yellow Submarine, named for the Beatles song.

Lorensbergsgatan 16. ℂ **031/16-98-39.** Reservations recommended. Main courses 169SEK–220SEK ($22–$29). AE, DC, MC, V. Mon–Sat 5–11pm; Sun 3–10pm. Tram: 1, 3, 4, 5, or 6. Bus: 40.

Restaurant 28+ ★★★ INTERNATIONAL/FRENCH   Cozy, intimate, and reeking of Old World charm, this is a chic and stylish restaurant whose trio of dining rooms are lit with flickering candles and capped with soaring masonry ceiling vaults. It's the city's hippest culinary venue, featuring main courses that include cooked crayfish with a fennel-flavored *nage* (an aromatic broth), smoked filet of char in a red wine and butter sauce, grilled breast of pigeon, and saddle of reindeer with Jerusalem artichokes and blackberry vinaigrette. We have consistently found that the finest—and most imaginative—cuisine in Gothenburg is served here. The items taste fabulously fresh, and the food is handled faultlessly in the kitchen and delicately seasoned. The service is the city's best, and the sommelier will offer expert guidance—although you might think the tax on wine is so high that you're putting someone's kid through college. The most demanding palates in Gothenburg leave here satisfied.

Götabergsgatan 28. ℂ **031/20-21-61.** Reservations recommended. Fixed-price menus 795SEK–895SEK ($103–$116); main courses 295SEK–445SEK ($38–$58). AE, DC, MC, V. Mon–Sat 6–11pm. Bus: 40. Tram: 1, 4, 5, or 6.

Sjömagasinet ★★★ SEAFOOD   By far the most elegant and atmospheric restaurant in town, Sjömagasinet is located near the Novotel in the western suburb of Klippan, about 4km (2½ miles) from the center. The building, erected in 1775, was originally a warehouse. It contains a bar in cozy English colonial style, and another bar in the aerie.

Very fresh seafood is served here, evidenced in the shrimp-stuffed crepes with dill, shellfish with curry sauce, baked filet of beef and lobster, poached filet of sole with crayfish, and turbot béarnaise. Two very special dishes are the pot-au-feu of fish and shellfish, served with a chive-flavored crème fraîche, and poached filet of halibut with warm cabbage salad and potato salad.

Klippans Kulturreservat. ☎ **031/775-59-20.** Reservations recommended. Main courses 320SEK–450SEK ($42–$59); 3-course fixed-price lunch 400SEK ($52). AE, DC, MC, V. Mon–Fri 11:30am–2pm and 6–10pm; Sat 5–10pm; Sun 2–8pm in summer. Tram: 3 or 9. From the town center, head west on E3, following the signs to Frederikshavn, and then to Kiel; exit at Klippan and then follow the signs for the Novotel.

MODERATE

A Hereford Beefstouw ⭐ *Value* STEAK   This is the best and most appealing steakhouse in Gothenburg, with a reputation for expertly prepared Brazilian beef, and a salad bar that's the most varied and copious in town. One of the three separate dining rooms is smoke-free, and all have thick-topped wooden tables, lots of varnished pine, and touches of African oak. The only sauces available to accompany your beef are béarnaise-butter sauce, parsley butter sauce, and garlic butter sauce: the management believes in allowing the flavor of the meat to come through, unmasked by more elaborate seasonings. The largest platter is a 500-gram (17½-oz.) T-bone steak, a portion so large that we advise you to finish it at your own risk. Other platters, such as filet steaks, veal sirloins, and tenderloins, are more reasonably sized. A full list of wines and beers is available.

Linnégatan 5. ☎ **031/775-04-41.** Reservations recommended. Main courses 110SEK–350SEK ($14–$46); salad bar as a main course 125SEK ($16). AE, DC, MC, V. Mon–Fri 11:30am–2pm and 5–10pm; Sat 4–11pm; Sun 3–9pm. Tram: 2, 3, 6, 9, or 11.

Brasserie Lipp SWEDISH/FRENCH   Located on Gothenburg's busiest avenue, this brasserie was established in 1987, inspired by the legendary Left Bank bistro in Paris, with palate adjustments for Swedish tastes. Its good food is a combination of French and Swedish—for example, escargots in garlic-butter sauce, Lipp's Skagen toast (piled high with shrimp), Swedish entrecôte of beef with Dijon mustard sauce, grilled halibut with garlic-tomato sauce, carpaccio of beef, and Thai chicken. There's also *choucroute garnie* (sauerkraut with sausage and pork, the most famous dish served at its Paris namesake) and many different kinds of fish, most caught in the waters near Gothenburg.

Kungsportsavenyn 8. ☎ **031/711-50-58.** Reservations required. Main courses 170SEK–224SEK ($22–$29); daily platters 75SEK ($9.75). AE, DC, MC, V. Mon–Fri 11:30am–11:30pm; Sat–Sun 11:30am–midnight. Tram: 1, 4, 5, or 6. Bus: 40.

La Gondola ITALIAN   This lively restaurant evokes Venice with its striped poles, sidewalk awnings, and summer outdoor cafe. It makes the best pizzas in town, but there's also an elaborate menu with many classic Italian dishes. The spaghetti Gondola is very good, and the *saltimbocca* ("jump in your mouth") *alla romana,* a veal-and-ham dish, is tasty. You might also try one of the grilled specialties, including a tender, juicy steak. The minestrone is freshly made and filling, and a velvet-smooth ice cream is served. Every day there's a different lunch special and an a la carte dinner.

Kungsportsavenyn 4. ☎ **031/711-68-28.** Reservations recommended. Main courses 76SEK–236SEK ($9.90–$31); *dagens* (daily) lunch 72SEK–119SEK ($9.35–$15). AE, DC, MC, V. Daily 11:30am–11:30pm. Tram: 1, 4, 5, or 6. Bus: 38 or 75.

Lilla London SWEDISH/FRENCH   The quiet, publike atmosphere is a local favorite. The restaurant, down a flight of steps, is dark and attractively designed, with illuminated paintings of clipper ships and nautical accents. Full meals might include grilled chicken with morels, beef and lamb filet in a mustard-flavored cream sauce, filet mignon, or broiled salmon with fresh asparagus. This is merely good, standard fare, prepared with fresh ingredients and sold for a fair price. Less expensive light meals are also available. The pub sells about 10 different kinds of beer.

Avenyn/Vasagatan 41. ⓒ 031/18-40-62. Reservations recommended. Main courses 82SEK–210SEK ($11–$27). AE, DC, MC, V. Mon–Fri 5pm–1am; Sat 11am–3am; Sun 1pm–1am. Tram: 1, 4, 5, or 6. Bus: 40.

Restaurang Gillestugan SWEDISH/INTERNATIONAL   In the mid-1980s, local entrepreneurs put a new spin on one of Gothenburg's most nostalgic restaurants. They transformed the antique-looking establishment, which dates from 1918, into the city's busiest and most creative cabaret and supper club—though the street-level bar, the Tullen Pub, remains.

During the day the only entertainment is the good-natured, hard-working staff. But on Saturdays, Sundays, and Mondays from 9 to 11pm, musical, theatrical, or poetic events take over a small stage. Recent examples have included folk singers whose repertoire is in both Swedish and English, and an Elvis impersonator who is, local residents insist, better than the real thing. Some of the entertainment involves Swedish-language satire, so phone in advance to avoid any production that's too cryptic for foreigners.

The food is well prepared and served in generous portions, and there's no cover charge for the entertainment. Menu items include salmon *tartare* with horseradish sauce and fried onions, a mushroom and apple terrine with air-dried ham and spicy oil, filet of lamb with tomato and feta-cheese sauce, and baked, sliced, and fried potatoes.

Järntorget 6. ⓒ 031/24-00-50. Reservations recommended. Main courses 89SEK–208SEK ($12–$27); fixed-price menus 315SEK–330SEK ($41–$43). AE, DC, MC, V. Mon–Fri 11am–10:30pm; Sat–Sun noon–10:30pm. Bar Sun–Thurs 11am–1am; Fri–Sat 11am–3am. Entertainment 9–11pm. Tram: 1, 3, 4, or 9.

INEXPENSIVE

Froken Olssons Café SWEDISH   Less than 2 blocks from the *Avenyn*, this is a traditional favorite of Gothenburgers. It tends to be crowded and noisy at lunchtime. Even though there's a large interior, the crowd overflows onto an outdoor terrace in summer. At night, hot pies with a salad are featured, and you can also order baguette sandwiches filled with such ingredients as shrimp or ham and cheese. Light beer is served, but no wine or liquor. Basically, it's light cafe dining, with homemade soups and such main courses as entrecôte.

Östra Larmgatan 14. ⓒ 031/13-81-93. Coffee 22SEK ($2.85); *dagens* (daily) menu 50SEK–69SEK ($6.50–$8.95); hot pies with salad 55SEK ($7.15); sandwiches 25SEK–65SEK ($3.25–$8.45). MC, V. Mon–Fri 9am–10pm; Sat–Sun 10am–10pm. Tram: 1, 4, 5, or 6. Bus: 40.

Solrosen (Sunflower) VEGETARIAN   In the Haga district, a low-rise neighborhood of 18th- and early-19th-century buildings, this is the best vegetarian restaurant in Gothenburg. You serve yourself at the counter, with an all-you-can-eat salad bar that accompanies the main dishes. There's unlimited coffee and second helpings. Beer and wine are available.

Kaponjärgatan 4. ⓒ 031/711-66-97. Main courses 90SEK–180SEK ($12–$23). Daily menu 55SEK–70SEK ($7.15–$9.10). AE, DC, MC, V. Mon–Fri 11:30am–1am; Sat 2pm–1am. Tram: 1, 6, or 9.

Tidblom's Restaurang INTERNATIONAL   Set near the lobby of the recommended Tidbloms Hotel, this restaurant is particularly charming, thanks to the staff that works hard to keep things personalized. In the wood-paneled dining room, you can order well-seasoned dishes that include cream of chanterelle soup, seafood medley on toast, African-style beef in a piquant peanut sauce, salmon in a saffron-flavored cream sauce, and a combination of pork and beef prepared Provençal style with red wine and Lyonnaise potatoes.

Olskroksgatan 23. ⓒ 031/707-50-00. Main courses 85SEK–225SEK ($11–$29); fixed-price menus 225SEK–430SEK ($29–$56). AE, DC, MC, V. Mon–Fri 11:30am–1:30pm and 6–10pm; Sat 5–10pm; Sun 1–8pm. Tram: 1, 3, or 6.

5 Seeing the Sights

As with any new destination, often the problem is having too much to do. Following the itineraries below will help you plan your time so you can see as much as possible.

For a map of attractions, see p. 141.

SUGGESTED ITINERARIES

If You Have 1 Day

Enjoy a cup of coffee at one of the cafes along the *Avenyn* in the center of Gothenburg; then take the classic Padden boat ride, traveling through the moat and canal out to the harbor and the giant docks. Return for a stroll along the *Avenyn;* then take one of the summertime vintage trams to see part of the city ashore. Go to Liseberg amusement park in the evening.

If You Have 2 Days

For your first day, follow the suggestions above. On Day 2, take a boat trip to Elfsborg Fortress, leaving from the Stenpiren in the Gothenburg harbor and continuing under the Älvsborg Bridge to Elfsborg. In the afternoon, visit the Göteborgs Konstmuseum and the Botanical Garden.

If You Have 3 Days

For the first 2 days, follow the itinerary suggested above. On Day 3, get up early to visit the fish auction at the harbor (begins at 7am); then

go to the *Feskekörka* (Fish Church) nearby. Take tram no. 6 to Guldhedens Våttentorn (water tower) for a panoramic view of Gothenburg. Go to Götaplatsen to see the famed Poseiden fountain by Carl Milles. In the afternoon, visit the Röhsska Museum of Arts and Crafts and stroll through the rose-filled Trädgårdsföreningen across from the Central Station.

If You Have 4–5 Days

For Days 1 to 3, follow the itinerary suggested above. On Day 4, take an excursion to Marstrand, north of the city. On Day 5, visit Nordstan, the biggest shopping center in Scandinavia. Spend the remaining part of the day exploring the southern archipelago, which you can do free with your Gothenburg Card (see "Getting Around," earlier in this chapter). The MS *Styrsö* and the steamboat *Bohuslän* depart from Skeppsbron/Stenpiren for trips around the archipelago.

THE TOP ATTRACTIONS

For a quick overview orientation, visit the 120m-tall (394-ft.) **Guldhedens Vattentorn** (water tower), Syster Estrids Gata (© **031/82-00-09**); to get there, take tram no. 10 or bus no. 51 or 52 from the center of the city, about a 10-minute ride. The elevator ride up the tower is free, and there's a cafeteria/snack bar on top. The tower is open February to November (and sometimes in Dec) Saturday through Thursday from noon to 10pm.

Early risers can visit the daily **fish auction** at the harbor, the largest fishing port in Scandinavia. The amusing auction begins at 7am sharp. You also can visit the **Feskekörka (Fish Church),** on Rosenlundsgatan, which is in the fish market. It's open Tuesday through Friday from 9am to 5pm and Saturday from 9am to 1pm.

The traditional starting point for seeing Gothenburg is the cultural center, **Götaplatsen,** with its *Poseidon Fountain,* sculpted by Carl Milles. The trio of buildings here are the **Concert Hall,** the municipally owned **theater,** and the Göteborgs Konstmuseum.

East India House (Museum of Gothenburg) ★★   This museum focuses on the history—archaeological, cultural, technical, and medical—of Gothenburg and its environs. There is an array of interesting permanent exhibits, including displays from the Viking era and unique artifacts found in the area.

Norra Hamngatan 12. ℂ 031/61-27-70. Admission 40SEK ($5.20) adults, free for students and children under 20. June–Aug daily 10am–5pm; Sept–May Tues–Sun 10am–5pm. Tram: 1 or 9. Bus: 40, 58, or 60 to Brunnsparken.

Göteborg Maritima Centrum   Located on the harbor, this museum is partly aboard the destroyer *Småland,* equipped with guns and torpedoes. In authentic settings, you can see lightships, steamships, and tugboats, among other watercraft. There are cafes at the center and on the quay.

Packhujkajem 8. ℂ 031/10-59-50. www.gmtc.se. Admission 70SEK ($9.10) adults, 30SEK ($3.90) children 7–15, free for children under 7. July daily 10am–4pm; May–Aug daily 10am–6pm; Sept–Oct daily 10am–4pm; Nov Fri–Sun 10am–4pm. Closed Dec–Feb. Tram: 5 to Lilla Bommen.

Göteborgs Konstmuseum ★★★   Göteborgs Konstmuseum is the leading art museum of Gothenburg, with a good collection of modern art, notably French Impressionist. Bonnard, Cézanne, van Gogh, and Picasso are represented, along with sculpture by Milles and Rodin. The gallery is noted for its collection of the works of 19th- and 20th-century Scandinavian artists (Zorn and Larsson of Dalarna, and Edvard Munch and Christian Krohg of Norway). Old masters are also represented, including Rembrandt and Rubens. The modern section includes work by Francis Bacon and Henry Moore.

Götaplatsen. ℂ 031/61-29-80. Admission 40SEK ($5.20) adults, free for students and children under 20. Tues and Thurs–Fri 11am–6pm; Wed 11am–9pm; Sat–Sun 11am–5pm. Tram: 4, 5, 6 or 8. Bus: 40, 41, or 58.

Liseberg Park ★★   Scandinavia's largest amusement park is more than 75 years old, and in terms of numbers of visitors, this is the number one tourist attraction in Sweden. It's a bit corny and doesn't have the class and the style of Copenhagen's Tivoli; nonetheless, it is fun for the entire family. Some of Sweden's best performing artists entertain every summer at Stora Scenen, the park's main stage. The park's newest attraction is the Gasten Ghost Hotel, filled with things that go bump in the night. Other adventure rides include the Källerado rapid river, a simulated white-water trip through the wilds of northern Sweden, and the HangOver, the most harrowing roller coaster in northern Europe, traveling at a frightening speed with all the usual bends and loops. The rocket launcher fires you 60m (197 ft.) into the air; at the top you'll be weightless before you come screaming back down. For the younger set there's a children's playground with a circus, a kiddie roller coaster, and a rabbit house where the Liseberg rabbits live. Like Disneyland, there also is a Fairy Tale Castle where knights, fair damsels, and other period figures amuse children, who are then taken on a Dragon Boat ride, evoking Sweden's Viking era. Many Gothenburgers like to come here in summer to eat or dine, as there are 18 fast-food places and 10 restaurants, with food ranging from seafood in the harbor area to savory Italian pastas.

Korsvägen. ℂ 031/40-01-00, or 031/40-02-20 for daily programs and times. Admission 50SEK ($6.50) adults, free for children under 7. May Wed–Fri 3–10pm, Sat noon–11pm, Sun noon–10pm; June Sun–Thurs 3–10pm, Sat–Sun 3–11pm; July–Aug daily 11am–11pm; Sept Thurs–Fri 4–10pm, Sat 11am–10pm, Sun 11am–8pm. Tram: 4 or 5 from the city.

Röhsska Konstslöjdmuseet ★★   This museum houses a large collection of European furnishings, china, glass, pottery, and Asian artifacts plus permanent and temporary exhibits of modern handicrafts and industrial design. Among the exhibits are books, silver, and Chinese and Japanese art. The museum presents lecture series and guided tours.

Vasagatan 37–39. ⓒ 031/61-38-50. Admission 40SEK ($5.20) adults, free for students and those under 20. May–Aug Mon–Fri noon–4pm, Sat–Sun noon–5pm; Sept–Apr Tues noon–9pm, Wed–Sun noon–5pm. Closed Aug 15–Sept 21. Tram: 3, 4, 5, 7, or 10. Bus: 40, 41, or 58.

Stadsbibliotek   Toward the end of the *Avenyn* is the public library, on the left at Götaplatsen. This is the main library of Gothenburg, the home of some 450,000 volumes in 50 languages, and a cafe. The library also has a listening room with recorded music, as well as a reading room with more than 100 foreign daily newspapers. One hall features continuously changing exhibits.

Götaplatsen. ⓒ 031/61-65-00. Free admission. Mon–Fri 10am–8pm; Sat–Sun 11am–5pm (closed on Sun May–Aug). Tram: 3, 4, or 5. Bus: 40.

PARKS & GARDENS

Botaniska Trädgården (Botanical Garden) ★★   This park is Gothenburg's oasis of beauty and is, in fact, the most dramatic, cultivated bit of nature in western Sweden. The botanical gardens were first opened to the public in 1923 and have been improved considerably over the years with better landscaping and more stunning plantings. Winding paths stretching for a few kilometers have been cut through the gardens and you can stroll along at leisure, absorbing the beauty of nature at every turn. There are plants and landscape scenes from around the world: You can wander into a bamboo grove evoking Southeast Asia, or explore a Japanese dale. In spring, the blooming rhododendron valley is one of the most stunning sights of Gothenburg. The splendid rock garden alone is worth the journey and features ponds, rugged rocks, cliffs, rivulets, and a cascade.

Carl Skottsbergsgata 22A. ⓒ 031/741-11-00. Free admission to garden; greenhouses 20SEK ($2.60), free for children under 17. Garden daily 9am–sunset. Greenhouses May–Aug daily 10am–5pm; Sept–Apr daily 10am–4pm. Tram: 1, 7, or 8.

Slottsskogen ★★   With 110 hectares (272 acres), this is the largest park in Gothenburg. First laid out in 1874 in a naturally wooded area, today it has beautiful walks, animal enclosures, a saltwater pool, bird ponds, and an aviary, as well as a children's zoo (open May–Aug). A variety of events and entertainment take place here in summer. There's an outdoor cafe at the zoo, plus restaurants at Villa Bel Park and Björngårdsvillan.

Near Linnéplatsen. ⓒ 031/365-37-00. Free admission. Daily 24 hr. Tram: 1 to Linnéplatsen.

Trädgårdsföreningen ★★   Located across the canal from the Central Station, this park boasts a large rosarium that flourishes with about 10,000 rose bushes of 4,000 different species. The park's centerpieces are the palm house, a greenhouse maintained at subtropical temperatures even in the depths of winter, and a butterfly house containing beautiful butterflies that flutter through a simulation of a natural habitat. The city of Gothenburg sometimes hosts exhibits, concerts (sometimes during the lunch hour), and children's theater pieces in the park.

Entrances on Slussgatan (across from the Central Station) and Södra Vägen. ⓒ 031/365-58-58. Park 15SEK ($1.95) adults, free for children 17 and under, free for everyone Sept–Apr. Palm House 20SEK ($2.60) adults, free for children up to age 17. Daily 10am–5pm. Butterfly House is only open for private art exhibitions.

ARCHITECTURAL HIGHLIGHTS

Drottning Kristinas Jaktslott (Queen Christina's Hunting Lodge)   The rounded walls of this stone house—the oldest in Gothenburg—originally were conceived in the 1600s as part of an outpouring of civic pride (or civic savvy) when it was designated as a hideaway for Queen Christina during her occasional visits from Stockholm. Although the queen didn't use it very frequently, its stone and wood interior still evokes the austere majesty of this deeply religious, deeply troubled 17th-century monarch. Go to admire the architecture and don't expect a lot of exhibits (except for some Swedish antiques). In 1971, it was saved from demolition by the Ötterhallen Historical Preservation Society and the administration of the Gothenburg Historical Museum. There's a cafe that specializes in light snacks (try the piping-hot waffles) that begin at around 30SEK ($3.90).

Ötterhallegatan 16. ⓒ 031/13-34-26. Free admission. Daily 11am–4pm. Tram: 2, 3, 4, or 7 to Lilla Torget.

Kronhusbodarna   One of the architectural showpieces of Gothenburg, Kronhusbodarna originally was built in the 1650s; it's the oldest nonecclesiastical building in town. In the 1660s, it was pressed into service as the meeting place for the Swedish Parliament, which convened here hastily to welcome a visit from Charles X Gustav during his wars with Denmark. For many years, the building functioned as a warehouse and repair center for the Swedish military, stockpiling sailcloth and armaments. Today its echoing interior accommodates a number of small-scale and rather sleepy artisans' studios. See "Shopping," below.

Kronhusgatan 1D. No phone. Tram: 1 or 7 to Brunnsparken.

ESPECIALLY FOR KIDS

At **Liseberg Park** (see "The Top Attractions," above), every day is children's day. The Liseberg Cirkus is a fun fair, and there are always comic characters to play with children. The pony merry-go-round, children's boats, and a fun-on-wheels merry-go-round all are free for tots.

Your children may want to stay at the amusement park's hotel, in the city center, a short walk from the park. **Hotel Liseberg Heden,** Sten Sturegatan S-411 38 Göteborg (ⓒ **031/750-69-109;** fax 031/750-69-30; www.liseberg.se), offers discounted summer rates. They include breakfast and coupons for free admission to the amusement park and many of its rides and shows. Between May and September, the discounted rate for double rooms is 930SEK ($121). From October to April, doubles cost 930SEK ($121) Friday and Saturday, and 1,275SEK ($166) Sunday to Thursday. The hotel accepts major credit cards (Amex, Diners Club, MasterCard, and Visa). It was built in the 1930s as an army barracks and later functioned as a youth hostel. Today, after tons of improvements, it's a very comfortable first-class hotel. To reach the 172-room hotel, take tram no. 4 or 5 to Berzeliegaten.

Naturhistoriska Museet I Göteborg, Slottsskogen (ⓒ 031/775-24-00), displays stuffed and mounted animals from all over the world, including Sweden's only stuffed blue whale. It's open June to August daily 11am to 5pm; September to May Tuesday to Friday 9am to 4pm, and Saturday and Sunday 11am to 5pm. Admission is 60SEK ($7.80) for adults, free for children up to 19 years old. Tram: 1, 2, or 6. Bus: 51 or 54 to Linnéplatsen.

There's also a **children's zoo** at Slottsskogen from May to August (see "Parks & Gardens," above).

A restaurant that kids find especially intriguing is **Restaurang Räkan/Yellow Submarine** (see "Where to Dine," earlier in this chapter), where seafood platters arrive at your table in battery-powered boats.

ORGANIZED TOURS

A sightseeing boat trip along the canals and out into the harbor will show you the old parts of central Gothenburg and take you under 20 bridges and out into the harbor. **Paddan Sightseeing Boats** ✈ (© 031/60-96-70) offers 55-minute tours from May to September 15 daily from 10am to 5pm, from September 12 to October 6 daily from noon to 3pm. They leave from the terminal at Kungsportsplatsen in the city center. The fare is 85SEK ($11) for adults, 50SEK ($6.50) for children 6 to 12, and free for kids under 4. A family ticket (two adults and two children) costs 216SEK ($28).

Nya Elfsborg (© 031/60-96-70) is docked in the 17th-century fortress at the harbor's mouth. This boat takes you on a 90-minute tour from Lilla Bommen through the harbor, to and around Elfsborg Fortress, built in the 17th century to protect the Göta Älv estuary and the western entrance to Sweden. It still bears traces of hard-fought sea battles against the Danes. Carvings on the prison walls tell tales of the threats to and hopes of the 19th-century prisoners-for-life. A guide will be waiting for you at the cafeteria, museum, and souvenir shop. There are five departures per day from mid-May to the end of August. The fare is 95SEK ($12) for adults, 60SEK ($7.80) for children to 12 years old.

MS *Poseidon* is available for an evening cruise of the archipelago. For information about available tours, check with the tourist office (see "Orientation," earlier in this chapter), or **Bohus Line** (© 031/13-30-37), which provides excursion packages, brochures, tickets, and timetables. The tour costs 375SEK ($49) for adults and 180SEK ($23) for children 6 to 12. The 4-hour trip departs at 7pm Tuesday to Saturday.

For a guided 1-hour **bus tour** of Gothenburg, go to the tourist office or call © 031/60-96-70 (see "Visitor Information," earlier in this chapter) for details. City tours are offered five times daily June to August. From September to May, the tour runs only on Saturday twice a day. The fare is 80SEK ($10) for adults, 50SEK ($6.50) for children and students.

6 Shopping

THE SHOPPING SCENE

Many residents of Copenhagen and Helsingør come to Gothenburg just for the day to buy Swedish merchandise. You can, too, but you should shop at stores bearing the yellow-and-blue TAX-FREE SHOPPING sign. These stores are scattered throughout Gothenburg (see "Fast Facts: Sweden," in chapter 2, for more information).

MAJOR SHOPPING DISTRICTS   Nordstan, with its 150 shops and stores, restaurants, hotels, patisseries, coffee shops, banks, travel agencies, and the post office, is the largest shopping mall in Scandinavia. Here you can find almost anything, from exclusive clothing boutiques to outlets for the major confectionery chains, to bookshops. There's also a tourist information center. Most shops here are open Monday through Friday 10am to 7pm and Saturday from 10am to 4pm.

Kungsgatan/Fredsgatan is Sweden's longest pedestrian mall (3km/1¾ miles in length). The selection of shops is big and varied. Near these two streets you'll also find a number of smaller shopping centers, including Arkaden, Citypassagen, and Kompassen.

At **Grönsakstorget/Kungstorget,** little carts are put up daily with flowers, fruits, handicrafts, and jewelry, among other items. It's right in the city center, a throwback perhaps to the Middle Ages.

The often-mentioned *Avenyn,* with its many restaurants and cafes, also has a number of stores selling merchandise of interest to visitors.

Kronhusbodarna, Kronhusgatan 1D (℃ **031/711-08-32;** see "Architectural Highlights," above), houses a number of small-scale and rather sleepy studios for glassblowers, watchmakers, potters, and coppersmiths, some of whom sell their goods to passersby. They can be visited, if the artisans happen to show up (call ahead to make arrangements). Take tram no. 1 or 7 to Brunnsparken.

SHOPPING A TO Z
DEPARTMENT STORES

Bohusslöjds   This store has one of the best collections of Swedish handicrafts in Gothenburg. Amid a light-grained birch decor, you'll find wrought-iron chandeliers, unusual wallpaper, fabric by the yard, and other items such as hand-woven rugs, pine and birch-wood bowls, and assorted knickknacks, ideal as gifts or souvenirs. Kungsportsavenyn 25. ℃ **031/16-00-72.** Bus: 5B or 40.

C. J. Josephssons Glas & Porslin   This store has been selling Swedish glass since 1866 and has established an enviable reputation. The selection of Orrefors crystal and porcelain is stunning. There are signed original pieces by such well-known designers as Bertil Vallien and Goran Warff. There's a tourist tax-free shopping service plus full shipping service. Korsgatan 12 and Kyrkogatan 34. ℃ **031/17-56-15.** Tram: 6, 9, 11, or 41. Bus: 16 or 60.

Nordiska Kompaniet (NK)   Because this is a leading department store, shoppers are likely to come here first (also recommended in Stockholm; see section 5 in chapter 4). The store's packing specialists will take care in shipping your purchases home for you. Typical Swedish and Scandinavian articles are offered here—more than 200,000 items, ranging from Kosta Boda "sculpture" crystal, Orrefors crystal in all types and shapes, Rorstrand high-fired earthenware and fine porcelain, stainless steel, pewter items, dolls in national costumes, leather purses, Dalarna horses, Finnish carpeting, books about Sweden, Swedish records, and much, much more. Östra Hamngatan 42. ℃ **08/762-87-55** or 762-80-00. Bus: 40.

FASHION

Gillblad's   This fashion outlet is known for its high-quality, well-made clothing for men and women. The inventory is tasteful, not flashy, and just the way its long-standing clients like it. It's especially noted for its collection of men's and women's suits for the office. Kyrkøgaten 19. ℃ **031/10-88-46.** Tram: 3.

Hennes & Mauritz   Established in the 1940s, this is a well-established clothing store for women that keeps an eye on what's happening in cutting-edge fashion around the world. The spirit here is trendy, with an emphasis on what makes a woman look chic and youthful for nights out on the town. Despite its undeniable sense of flair, garments are less expensive than you might suppose, with lots of low-markup bargains for cost-conscious shoppers. Kungsgatan 55–57. ℃ **031/711-00-11.** Tram: 1, 4, or 5.

Ströms   This is the most visible emporium for clothing for men in Gothenburg, with a history at this location that goes back to 1886. Scattered over two floors of retail space, you'll find garments that range from the very formal to the very casual, and boutique-inspired subdivisions that contain ready-to-wear garments from the leading fashion houses of Europe. Despite the fact that most of its fame and reputation derives from its appeal to men, to a lesser extent it also sells garments for women and children. Kungsgatan 27–29. ℃ **031/17-71-00.** Tram: 1, 2, or 3.

HANDCRAFTS

Lerverk   This is a permanent exhibit center for 30 potters and glass-making craftspeople. Västra Hamngatan 24–26. ✆ 031/13-13-49. Tram: 1, 2, 3, 4, or 7 to Grönsakstorget.

7 Gothenburg After Dark

To the Gothenburger, there's nothing more exciting than sitting outdoors at a cafe along the *Avenyn* enjoying the short-lived summer season. Residents also like to take the whole family to the Liseberg amusement park (see "Seeing the Sights," earlier in this chapter). Although clubs are open in the summer, they're not well patronized until the cool weather sets in.

For a listing of entertainment events scheduled at the time of your visit, check the newspapers (*Götenborgs Posten* is best) or inquire at the tourist office. If Swedish dinner theater interests you, see Restaurang Gillestugan under "Where to Dine," earlier in this chapter.

THE PERFORMING ARTS
THEATER
The Gothenburg Card (see "Getting Around," earlier in this chapter) allows you to buy two tickets for the price of one. Call the particular theater or the tourist office for program information. Performances also are announced in the newspapers.

Folkteatern   This theater stages productions of Swedish plays or foreign plays translated into Swedish. The season is from September to May, and performances are Tuesday through Friday at 7pm and Saturday at 6pm. Olof Palmes Plats (by Järntorget). ✆ 031/20-38-20. Tickets 120SEK–200SEK ($16–$26). Tram: 1, 3, or 4.

Stadsteatern   This is one of the major theaters in Gothenburg, but invariably the plays are performed in Swedish. Ibsen in Swedish may be too much of a challenge without knowledge of the language, but a musical may still be enjoyed. The season runs from September to May. Performances usually are Tuesday through Friday at 7pm, Saturday at 6pm, and Sunday at 3pm. Götaplatsen. ✆ 031/61-50-50. Tickets 190SEK–220SEK ($25–$29). Bus: 40.

OPERA & BALLET
Göteborgsoperan (Gothenburg Opera House)   This elegant new opera house was opened by the Swedish king in 1994 and features theater, opera, operettas, musicals, and ballet performances. It's situated right on a dock with views overlooking the water, and there are five bars and a cafe in the lobby. The main entrance (on Östra Hamngatan) leads to a foyer with a view of the harbor; here you'll find the box office and cloakroom. Big productions can be staged here on a full scale. You'll have to check to see what performances are scheduled at the time of your visit. Packhuskajen. ✆ 031/10-80-00, or 031/13-13-00 for ticket information. Ticket prices depend on the event. Tram 5.

CLASSICAL MUSIC
Konserthuset   In the very center of Gothenburg, this is the major performance hall for classical music. In season (Sept–June), world-class performers appear. Götaplatsen. ✆ 031/726-53-00. Tickets 270SEK–440SEK ($35–$57), but could range lower or higher depending on the performance. Bus: 40. Tram: 3 or 5.

THE CLUB & MUSIC SCENE
NIGHTCLUBS
Bubbles   In stark contrast to the sprawling size of the Trädgår'n (see below), this nightclub and cocktail lounge is small-scale and intimate. Outfitted in pale

colors and attracting a clientele over 30, it's the most popular late-night venue in Gothenburg, sometimes attracting workers from restaurants around town who relax and chitchat here after a hard night's work. There's a small dance floor, but most visitors ignore it in favor of mingling at the bar. Open daily from 8pm to 5am. Avenyn 8. ✆ **031/10-58-20.** Tram: 1, 4, 5, or 6.

Madison Nightclub In this leading nightclub along Sweden's west coast, the dinner-dance room sometimes features international stars. Past celebrities have included Marlene Dietrich and Eartha Kitt. The dance floor is usually packed. The international menu consists of light supper platters such as crab salad or toasted sandwiches. Beer begins at 50SEK ($6.50). Open Tuesday through Saturday from 11:30pm to 3am. In the Radisson SAS Park Avenue Hotel, Kungsportsavenyn 36–38. ✆ **031/20-60-58.** Cover 80SEK–100SEK ($10–$13); hotel guests enter free. Tram: 1, 4, 5, or 6. Bus: 40.

Oakley's Country Club Set within a former fire station, and with a scarlet facade that stands out from its neighbors, the restaurant portion of this club opened in 1998 as a tongue-in-cheek parody of what you might find in the old Wild West.

Beginning at 9pm, things get lively with singers reminiscent of Dale Evans, can-can dancers who belt out excerpts from *Annie Get Your Gun,* and a scantily clad trapeze artist who advises men in the audience how to lasso a bedmate or a bride. Expect a sense of camp and an interpretation of the American vernacular style that you might never, ever have expected east of the Atlantic. Menu items include sophisticated interpretations of New American cuisine, including chile-roasted crayfish, Mississippi alligator ribs, Caesar salads studded with crayfish, "Annie's Blackened Salmon," "Buffalo Bill's Rib-eye Steak," and the restaurant's own version of spare ribs. There is a particularly elegant room offering cigars and brandies. Main courses cost 154SEK to 235SEK ($20–$31), and the club is open Monday to Friday from 11am to 2pm, and Tuesday to Saturday 6 to 11pm. Tredje Långgatan 16. ✆ **031/42-60-80.** Reservations recommended. Tram: 1, 3, 4, or 9.

Trädgoårn This is the largest and most comprehensive nightspot in Gothenburg, with a cavernous two-story interior that echoes on weekends with the simultaneous sounds of a restaurant and a dance club. No one under 25 is admitted to this cosmopolitan and urbane venue. Cover charge for the disco is 100SEK ($13). Main courses in the restaurant are 170SEK to 270SEK ($22–$35). The restaurant is open Monday to Friday 11:30am to 2pm and Wednesday to Saturday 6 to 10:30pm. The disco is open Friday to Saturday 11pm to 5am. Allegaten 8. ✆ **031/10-20-80.** Tram: 1, 3, or 5.

A CASINO

Casino Cosmopol In a building constructed in 1865, this is a palace of amusement, offering games, food, drink, entertainment, and, of course, casino games such as blackjack, poker, Punto Banco, and American roulette. Naturally, there are slot machines—204 in all. The best restaurant is Casanova on the second floor, offering panoramic views of the harbor. The stage next to the Jackpot Bar Bistro, located just beside the games, features occasional entertainment. Guests must be 20 years of age and carry some form of official photo ID. Entrance fee is 30SEK ($3.90) for a day pass. Open daily 1pm to 4am. Packhusplatsen 7. ✆ **031/333-55-00.** Tram: 1 or 2.

A DANCE CLUB

Valand This combination restaurant and dance club, one floor above street level in the center of town, is the biggest and best known in Gothenburg. As you enter there's a restaurant on your left and a large bar and dance floor on your right. There's also a small-stakes casino with blackjack and roulette. The minimum age for entry is 25. The club is open Thursday through Saturday from 8pm to 3am. For some memorable food, head for Lilla London, one floor below (see "Where to Dine," earlier in this chapter). Vasagatan 41. ✆ 031/18-30-93. Cover 80SEK–100SEK ($10–$13) for disco after 10pm. Tram: 1, 4, 5, or 6. Bus: 40.

GAY GOTHENBURG

Greta   Named in honor of Greta Garbo, whose memorabilia adorns the walls, this is the leading gay bar and restaurant in Gothenburg, with a clientele that includes all ages and all types of gay men and lesbians. Two animated bars rock and roll in ways that are completely independent from the on-site restaurant. Decor is a mixture of the kitschy old-fashioned and new wave, juxtapositioned in ways that are almost as interesting as the clientele. Menu items change at least every season but might include fish and lime soup, lamb filet with mushrooms in a red-wine sauce, breast of duck with potato croquettes, or a creamy chicken stew baked in phyllo pastry. Every Friday and Saturday night from 10pm till 3am, the place is transformed into a disco. Tuesday to Thursday 5pm to 1am; Friday to Saturday 5pm to 3am. The cover charge is 50SEK ($6.50). Drottningsgaten 35. ✆ 031/13-69-49. Reservations recommended Fri–Sat. Main courses 95SEK–195SEK ($12–$25). AE, MC, V. Tram: 1, 2, or 3.

8 Easy Excursions to the Bohuslän Coast & Halland

From Gothenburg's center, you can head north to explore the Bohuslän Coast or go south to visit Halland, the Swedish Riviera. These trips are best from June to early September, as they are far more enjoyable in fair weather than when winter winds are blowing.

THE BOHUSLÄN COAST 🎇🎇

North of Gothenburg, the scenery of Bohuslän is dominated by the sea. Out in the archipelago, the waterways wind their way past myriad islands, sunken rocks, sounds, inlets, and waterside communities. Away from the coast, the countryside is varied, with wilderness areas, forests, mountains, and lakes offering wonderful opportunities for outdoor activities. You can cycle along carefully laid-out tracks, hike the Bohusleden Trail (tourist offices have maps), go fishing, play golf, or take out a canoe.

Many Swedes have summer cottages in this chain of islands, which are linked by bridges or short ferry crossings. Train service is possible from Gothenburg through to Uddevalla (which is industrial) and on to Strömstad. Buses also cover the coast, but service is infrequent. It's best to take a **driving tour** of the coast, following the E6 motorway north from Gothenburg to one of the following destinations.

KUNGÄLV

If you're pressed for time, at least see Kungälv, 17km (11 miles) north of Gothenburg and reached by bus no. 301, 302, 303, or 330 from the Central Station. For information, contact **Kungälv Turistbyrå,** Fästningsholmen, S-442 81 Kungälv (✆ 0303/23-92-00), usually open June to August Monday to Saturday 9:30am to 6pm and Sunday noon to 4pm, off season Monday to Friday 9am to 6pm. The office also handles information for Marstrand (see below).

The 1,000-year-old town of Kungälv, known by the Vikings as Kongahälla, has a panoramic position by the river of Nordre Älv. The well-preserved old

The Bohuslän Coast & Halland

✈ Airport
⛴ Ferry

E6
Åmål
Strömstad
165
Ed
Bengtsfors
Tanumshede
172
Mellerud
Fjällbacka
Högsäter
45
Vänern
Smögen
Uddevalla
Lysekil
Vänersborg
Orust
Trollhättan
Vara
42
E6
Tjörn
Göta River
E20
Vårgårda
Marstrand
Kungälv
Alingsås
Gothenburg
Borås
Ferry to
Frederikshavn,
England, and
Germany
40
Landvetter
27
Kungsbacka
Kinna
Viskan
41
Tjolöholm
E6
E20
Åtran
153
Ullared
Varberg
Ferry to Grenå
Kammarebo
Kattegat
Falkenberg
Nissan
Getinge
Oskarström
Tylösand
Halmstad
Ferry to Grenå
and Oslo
Laholsbukten
E6
E20
Torekov
Båstad
Mölle
Hallands-
åsen
Ängelholm
E4
Helsingør
Helsingborg
DENMARK

SWEDEN
Stockholm

0 ___ 30 mi
0 ___ 30 km

town consists of **Gamla torget (the old square),** a church, and the cobbled streets of **Östra gatan** and **Vastra gatan,** where you'll find old wooden houses built centuries ago. An island in the river, **Fästningsholmen,** is an idyllic spot for a picnic.

On the E6 highway lie the ruins of the 14th-century **Bohus Fästning,** Fästningsholmen (℗ **0303/156-62**). This bastion played a leading role in the battles among Sweden, Norway, and Denmark to establish supremacy. Bohus Fästning (Bohus Castle and Fortress) was built by order of Norway's King Haakon V on Norwegian territory. After being ceded to Sweden in 1658, it was used as a prison. Climb the **tower** known as *Fars Hatt* ("Father's Hat") for a panoramic view. Hours of operation are from May 1 to August 31 daily 10am to 7pm; from September 1 to September 30 daily 11am to 5pm; closed off season. Admission is 25SEK ($3.25) for adults; 10SEK ($1.30) for children 7 to 16, students, and seniors; and free for ages 6 and under.

WHERE TO STAY & DINE

Hotel Fars Hatt ⊛   Established in the 17th century in the town center, close to the river, this site was used to refresh travelers with fish, game, and ale. Today the tradition continues, albeit in a four-story building from the 1960s. The restaurant menu offers a wide selection of Swedish and international dishes, and nonguests are welcome. The bedrooms are well furnished, each modern and recently renovated, with good beds and ample bathrooms equipped with tub/showers.

Torget S-442 31 Kungälv. ℗ **0303/109-70.** Fax 0303/196-37. www.farshatt.se. 120 units. Mon–Thurs 1,090SEK ($142) double; Fri–Sun 830SEK ($108) double; 1,200SEK–1,500SEK ($156–$195) suite. Rates include breakfast. AE, DC, MC, V. Free parking. **Amenities:** Restaurant; bar; lounge; outdoor pool; sauna; laundry service; dry cleaning; nonsmoking rooms; rooms for those w/limited mobility. *In room:* TV, dataport, hair dryer (in some).

MARSTRAND ⊛⊛

This once-royal resort, frequented by the former Swedish king, Oscar II, is on a secluded island. Its little shops, art galleries, and pleasant places to walk are reminiscent of Nantucket, Massachusetts. Part of the fun of Marstrand is the ferry journey here; it lies 25km (16 miles) west of Kungälv.

To reach the island, drive north along E6 from Gothenburg, exiting at the signs pointing to Marstrand. These lead you to the village of Koön, where you'll park your car. From the wharf at Koön, ferryboats depart every 20 minutes for Marstrand. No cars are allowed on either the ferryboats or the island. The round-trip costs 15SEK ($1.95).

Another alternative is the no. 312 bus, which departs from Gothenburg's Central Station. Buses leave every hour year-round; no reservations are necessary. For 100SEK ($13), you can purchase a combined bus and ferry ticket to the island. The bus stops first in the hamlet of Tjuvkil and then continues on to the wharf at Koön.

Young people from Gothenburg and its environs flock to Marstrand on weekends, filling up the clapboard-sided hotels. The resort, quiet all week, comes alive with the sounds of folk singers and the twang of guitars. The big event on Marstrand's calendar is the annual **international regatta,** which usually takes place July 5 to July 11.

The 17th-century **Carlsten Fortress** (℗ **0303/602-65**) towers over the island. After you climb up the hill, visit the chapel and then walk through the secret tunnel to the fortress, which dates from 1658 when Charles X Gustav decided that it should be built to protect the Swedish west-coast fleet. The bastions around the lower castle courtyard were constructed from 1689 to 1705, and then completed during the first half of the 19th century. Admission is 60SEK ($7.80) for adults, 20SEK ($2.60) for children 7 to 15, free for children 6 and under. It's open June through August daily from noon to 4pm. Tours are conducted at 2pm and 5pm.

WHERE TO STAY

Batellet   In the town center, this former bathing house has been converted into a youth hostel with four or five beds per room. All rooms and bathrooms are unisex. It attracts an international crowd. June through August are the busiest months. You can prepare your own breakfast in the communal kitchen. Guests make their own beds.

Batellet S-440 30 Marstrand. ℂ **0303/600-10.** Fax 0303/60-607. 100 4-bed units, none with bathroom. 235SEK ($31) per person. MC, V. **Amenities:** No phone.

Grand Hotel Marstrand   This landmark building operates as a conventional hotel throughout the summer months but turns into a convention center when the cold winds begin to blow. Built at the close of the 19th century and frequently renovated and altered since, it was called "the grand old lady of Marstrand," back in the days when people tended to speak in such politically incorrect terms. Although today's clients are not as elegant as those who arrived with steamer trunks long ago, the Grand still holds its own. Renovations preserved the original architectural charm while adding modern conveniences. Bedrooms are well furnished and spacious, opening onto views of Paradise Park and the boat-filled harbor. Bathrooms are winners here: Decorated in classic white with brass fittings, all include showers and those old-fashioned bathtubs that grandpa and grandma used to bathe in. All rooms here are nonsmoking. Even if you're not a guest, consider patronizing the hotel's restaurant on the ground floor.

Radhusgatan 3, S-440 30 Marstrand. ℂ **0303/603-22.** Fax 0303/600-53. www.grandmarstrand.se. 22 units. 1,695SEK ($220) double; 1,895SEK ($246) suite. AE, DC, MC, V. **Amenities:** Restaurant; bar; sauna; limited room service; babysitting; laundry service; dry cleaning . *In room:* TV, minibar, hair dryer.

WHERE TO DINE

Restaurant Tenan INTERNATIONAL   The most sophisticated restaurant in town lies on the street level of the Grand Hotel, within a trio of rooms that combines memorabilia and photos of the America's Cup Race with dark colors and respectful references to Sweden's royal family. During July and August you can dine on a spacious outdoor terrace. Recommended items include platters of smoked fish with dill sauce, terrines of foie gras with warm brioches and fresh butter, seafood soups and piquant shellfish stews, anglerfish in a garlic-flavored saffron sauce, North Atlantic lobster with drawn butter and parsley, trout with almonds, and frilled filets of beef with pepper and mushroom sauce.

In the Grand Hotel, Paradisparken. ℂ **0303/603-22.** Reservations recommended. Main courses 270SEK–295SEK ($35–$38). AE, DC, MC, V. Daily noon–3pm and 6–11pm.

LYSEKIL ✸✸

This 200-year-old town, with its wooden houses and narrow alleyways, is a good base for exploring the coast. Today it also contains a number of workshops for artisans, artists, and craftspeople who find the area a perfect retreat from the world.

Lysekil lies directly on the seashore, set against a backdrop of pink granite rocks. Fishing areas, as well as some of the best waters for diving in northern

Europe, are found here. In summer there are occasional seal-watching trips, as well as sailing trips. Ask at the **tourist office** at Sodra Hamngatan 6 (© **0523/ 130-50**), open Monday to Saturday 9am to 7pm, Sunday 11am to 3pm.

If you're driving, take Route E6 north from Gothenburg to Uddevalla, then head west along Route 161. An express bus from Gothenburg (no. 840 or 848) runs every 2 hours during the day.

The best sight in town is **Havets Hus,** Rosvikstorg (© **0523/165-30**), a sea aquarium with a collection of animal and plant life from the Gullmaren and North Sea. The main attraction here is a tunnel aquarium showing a variety of different species such as cod, ray, halibut, lobster, shark, and much more. At this tunnel, massive fish swim over and around you. At a special pool, children can feel spiky starfish and slimy algae. Wave machines make some biotopes especially realistic. From February 9 to June 13 and August 23 to October 31, it is open daily 10am to 4pm. From June 14 to August 22, hours are daily 10am to 6pm. Admission is 70SEK ($9.10) for adults, 35SEK ($4.55) for children 5 to 15 years old. The aquarium is a 5-minute walk from the tourist office, heading down toward the water.

The entire shoreline around Lysekil is a nature reserve, with some 275 varieties of plant life. Guided "marine walks" and botanical tours are at times offered in the summer (ask at the tourist office; see above).

On the way north to Tanumshede (see below), we always continue north along the E6, but cut west near Rabbalshede to follow Route 163 to **Fjällbacka,** which, in our view, is one of the most perfect, picture-postcard little fishing villages of Sweden. Houses are painted in bright shades with a wealth of gingerbread. Swedes call this *snickargladje,* although Americans are more familiar with the term "Carpenter's Gothic."

It was here that we traveled once to interview screen legend Ingrid Bergman, star of the classic *Casablanca* and other films. She'd invited us for lunch, which consisted of a loaf of freshly baked bread and a great big red beet. A lunch such as this isn't at all uncommon in Sweden in the summertime. Ms. Bergman's summer house was on one of the islands off the coast. In town, Swedes remember her fondly, and the main square is called Ingrid Bergman Square, with a statue of the screen goddess looking out over the water to her former home. Her ashes were scattered over the sea nearby.

You're likely to fall in love with the town, so you should consider an overnight stay at the 23-room **Stora Hotellet** (© **0525/310-03;** fax 0525/310-03). Each room is decorated to depict a faraway place and costs 1,450SEK to 1,540SEK ($189–$200) double.

WHERE TO STAY & DINE

Hotel Lysekil   Built with brown bricks and copper, in a traditional, gable-roofed design, this is one of the most prominent hotels in town—a focal point for most of the town's business meetings, conventions, and corporate rendezvous. Bedrooms are smaller than one may hope and are conservatively decorated with angular furniture and comfortable beds. Bathrooms also are small but come with shower units.

Rosvikstorg 1, S-453 30 Lysekil. © **0523/66-55-30**. Fax 0523/155-20. www.hotel-lysekil.net. 50 units. 1,190SEK–1,290SEK ($155–$168) double. Rates include breakfast. AE, DC, MC, V. **Amenities:** Restaurant; bar; nightclub; laundry service; dry cleaning; nonsmoking rooms. *In room:* TV.

Lysekil Havshotell ★ *(Finds)*   Less than a kilometer (¾ mile) west of the town center, this hotel began its existence in 1900 as an upscale private home. Set behind a turn-of-the-20th-century scarlet-and-white facade, within its own gardens, it has polite, well-rehearsed service, public rooms that evoke a bygone age, and comfortable bedrooms that were upgraded and renovated in 1993. Each unit has a neatly kept bathroom with a tub/shower. The staff here will prepare you a simple platter of food on request—virtually whenever you want it—but other than breakfast, meals are not served on a regular basis. Access from the center of Lysekil is particularly pleasant, as you can follow the seafront quays most of the way.

Turistgatan 13, S-453 30 Lysekil. © 0523/797-50. Fax 0523/142-04. www.strandflickorna.se. 15 units. 995SEK–1,195SEK ($129–$155) double; 1,395SEK–1,595SEK ($181–$207) suite. Rates include breakfast. AE, DC, MC, V. Free parking. **Amenities:** Breakfast room; bar; laundry service; dry cleaning; nonsmoking rooms. *In room:* TV, minibar (not in summer), dataport.

TANUMSHEDE ★★★

The next destination of interest is Tanumshede, known for the greatest concentration of Bronze Age rock carvings in Scandinavia. If you're not driving, you can take an express bus to Tanumshede; they travel from Gothenburg five times each day, and the trip takes 2 hours.

As you enter town, you can pay a visit first to the **Tourist Office,** Bygdegårdsplan (© **0525/183-80**), the local tourist bureau. Information regarding the best ways to visit the Bronze Age carvings is available here. The office is open from June to mid-August Monday to Thursday 8am to noon and 1 to 4:30pm, Friday 8am to noon and 1 to 3pm. Off-season hours are Monday to Friday 8am to noon and 1 to 4:30pm.

In 1994, the rock carvings of Tanum were included in the UNESCO World Heritage List. Just to the east of Tanumshede, you can visit the **Vitlycke Museum** (© **0525/209-50**), which is open April to September daily 10am to 6pm, off season Tuesday to Sunday 11am to 5pm. The museum charges 50SEK ($6.50) for adults and 40SEK ($5.20) students and seniors, free for ages up to 20 years old. The museum documents the history of rock carvings and offers excursions— sometimes by moonlight—to the actual attraction. You also can obtain a map, "The Rock Carving Tour," which guides you easily among the carvings of northern Bohuslän, showing the way to Bohuslän's 10 most interesting rock-carving faces. Four are in Tanum and constitute the World Heritage area. Close to the museum, a Bronze Age farm is a full-scale reconstruction of a dwelling and farm from the era of the rock carvings. At a restaurant in the museum, the cuisine is inspired by Bronze Age raw materials such as meat and venison, fish and shellfish, parsley root, sorrel, and chickweed. Gooseberry ice cream rounds off this repast.

WHERE TO STAY & DINE

Tanums Gestgifveri ★★   This hotel, one of the oldest continuously operating inns in the district, was established in 1613 in a forest about 10km (6¼ miles) inland from the sea. From the outside, it looks like a prosperous Swedish farmhouse, with rambling porches painted in tones of pale ochre. Bedrooms are old-fashioned, cozy, and, in most cases, accented to some degree with varnished paneling. Within a separate building, also constructed in the early 1600s but with many additions and improvements during the early 20th century, there's a well-managed restaurant that's classified as a Relais & Châteaux. Most residents of the hotel opt to dine here as well, but if you're just passing through, you should know that gastronomes go out of their way to visit this spot. Specialties include a succulent version of fish stew served with rice and braised fresh vegetables, freshwater catfish with wine sauce, and sautéed anglerfish with garlic sauce.

Apoteksvägen 7, SS-45731 Tanumshede. © **0525/290-10.** Fax 0525/295-71. www.tanumsgestgifveri.com. 30 units. 980SEK–1,480SEK ($127–$192) double; 1,990SEK–2,290SEK ($259–$298) suite. Rates include breakfast and dinner. AE, DC, MC, V. Closed Dec 24–Jan 30. **Amenities:** Restaurant; pool; sauna; limited room service; laundry service; dry cleaning; nonsmoking rooms; rooms for those w/limited mobility. *In room:* TV, minibar.

STRÖMSTAD

Thirty-two kilometers (20 miles) north of Tanumshede, Strömstad knew greater glory in the 18th century when it was one of the most fashionable spas in Sweden. The town makes an excellent stopover for those heading farther north into the wilds of Sweden. Many Norwegians also pass through here because of ferry links to Sandefjord, Fredrikstad, and Halden in Norway. Strömstad also is the jumping-off point for those wishing to explore the Koster Islands, Sweden's most westerly inhabited islands.

Fun Fact **Sunspot**

Strömstad claims to have more hours of sunshine than anywhere else in Sweden.

Until 1658, Strömstad was part of Norway. Today it is a fishing harbor and, in summer, a lively tourist center. Lying on the salty Skaggerrak on the borderline between Sweden and Norway, it's a place of rolling waves, cliffs warmed by the sun, and sandy beaches. A fish market is still held here at 7am Tuesday through Friday.

For information, head first for the tourist office, **Strömstad Tourist,** Torget. It's open June to August daily 9am to 6pm, off season Monday to Friday 9am to 5pm, Saturday 10am to 2pm. For more information, call © **0526/62330.**

Strömstad is linked by rail to Gothenburg, a 3-hour journey. The E6 Express Bus between Gothenburg and Oslo also stops off here. Motorists should follow Route 176 off the E6 for a distance of 12km (7½ miles).

Many visitors use Strömstad merely as a refueling stop for trips over to the **Koster Islands**. If you have time for only one island, make it **Nordkoster (North Koster),** which is a large nature reserve. You can explore the whole island on foot in about 2 hours; cars are prohibited. **Sydkoster (South Koster)** is three times the size of North Koster and can be toured by bike. Before heading there, ask at the Strömstad tourist office how to arrange rentals. The waters around both islands are the warmest in Sweden for summer swimming. You can also go bird- or seal-watching on this island. The islands abound in wildflowers. In Strömstad, ferries leave from Laholmen and cost 110SEK ($14) round-trip. The tourist office keeps a list of ferry schedules, which are subject to change because of weather conditions.

WHERE TO STAY & DINE

Hotel Laholmen This is the larger and better-accessorized of Strömstad's two hotels, with a policy of remaining open year-round. Built in 1994, it parallels the shoreline of a small peninsula that jutts seaward from the center of town. Low and sprawling, and flanked on one side by a busy marina, the hotel has a streamlined, modern decor and comfortable bedrooms that, although monochromatic, are well maintained and cozy, with well-kept little bathrooms equipped with tub/showers. Public areas have big windows, touches of varnished paneling, and a sense of spaciousness. There's no pool or health club on the premises, although the staff will direct you to nearby facilities. There is, however, a big dining room serving good regional food (lots of fish), a disco, and an indoor-outdoor restaurant that operates only between June and early September.

S-452 30 Strömstad. ℂ **0526/197-00.** Fax 0525/100-36. www.laholmen.se. 152 units. Mon–Thurs 1,490SEK–1,740SEK ($194–$226) double, Fri–Sat 1,350SEK–1,600SEK ($176–$208) double; 2,700SEK ($351) suite (breakfast included year-round). AE, DC, MC, V. Parking 75SEK ($9.75). **Amenities:** Restaurant; 2 bars; sauna; limited room service; laundry service; dry cleaning. *In room:* TV, minibar (in some), hair dryer, safe.

HALLAND: THE SWEDISH RIVIERA ⭐

Halland lies south of Gothenburg and, because of its white sandy beaches, is the fastest-growing tourist district in the country. During the summer months, the population of the region doubles.

Windsurfing is the major regional sport here, and Halland has produced many champions. Consistent, steady winds and shallow shoreline waters provide ideal conditions. Mellbystrand, Tylösand, Ringenäs, and Skrea are the beaches most favored by windsurfers.

In addition to the beaches, Halland's network of rivers and lakes gives the region its life and character. There are more than 900 bodies of water in the province and many of these inland lakes and rivers are ideal for canoeing and camping. Many places have public access areas with docks, swimming

> ⸜ *Fun Fact*   **Good Living**
>
> Halland locals like pointing out that its inhabitants live longer and take less sick-leave than other Swedes.

areas, and barbecues. Some lakes boast blossoming water lilies and flowering meadows that extend down to the water's edge. Many salmon waters have been restored in recent years, and both salmon and trout make their way over the Atlantic to Halland's rivers. A number of lakes offer good perch and pike fishing.

Halland's mild winters and early springs help make it Sweden's most golf-intensive region. In all, there are 30 golf courses in the province. Try either the **Båstad Golf Club** at Boarp (ℂ **0431/783-70**), or the **Bjäre Golf Club** at Solomonhög (ℂ **0431/36-10-53**), both located right outside the center of Båstad.

Our favorite places (as either bases or stopovers) include the following resorts:

KUNGSBACKA & TJOLÖHOLM

Once an important town in its own right, today **Kungsbacka** is merely a southern suburb of Gothenburg. However, it makes a good base for exploring one of the major attractions along the west coast of Sweden—the "English" castle of Tjolöholm, lying 12km (7½ miles) south of Kungsbacka. In summer you can ask for information at the little **tourist office** (ℂ **0300/834-595**), in the town center.

Tjolöholm Slott ⭐ at Fjärås (ℂ **0300/544-200**) lies on a beautiful peninsula in Kungsbackafjorden. It was built by a Scottish merchant, J. F. Dickson, at the turn of the 20th century in a mock English style. Pronounced *chewla*-home, Tjolöholm came about through a design contest in the 1890s. In his late 20s, Lars Israel Wahman won the competition and created this stunning, stately home.

Dickson was an avid horse breeder, but today the huge stables and indoor riding track have been converted into a cafe. A carriage museum on the site contains carriages but also a unique horse-drawn vacuum cleaner.

You can explore the manor house, with its walls of Flanders marble and a regal oak-paneled study by Liberty's of London. The bathrooms and boudoirs are fabulous, and the children's nursery was inspired by the designs of Charles Rennie Mackintosh. It's also fun to explore the grounds, which slope down to a sandy beach. The house is open April to June 14 Saturday and Sunday 11am to 4pm, June 15 to August 31 daily 11am to 4pm, September Saturday and Sunday 11am to 4pm. The entrance fee is 60SEK ($7.80) adults, 15SEK ($1.95) children.

A Cutting Tale

Regrettably, Dickson never saw the completion of his castle, Tjolöholm Slott. He cut himself as he opened a champagne bottle and fatally poisoned himself when he wrapped the lead cap around his wound.

Nearby you can explore the **Fjärås Bracka Open Air Museum** (no phone), in Äskhult, a tiny village that still reflects its 17th- and 18th-century heritage. In the 19th century, 35 people lived here; the last inhabitant died in 1964. Four buildings remain on the sites where they originally were constructed. The oldest house dates from the 17th century. The houses have never been painted, and their gray timber walls give the place a special character. The site is open year-round daily 10am to 6pm, September only on Saturday and Sunday from 10am to 6pm. Admission is free.

If you're not driving, you can reach Tjolöholm by public transportation. A local train takes 20 minutes to go from Gothenburg's Central Station to Kungsbacka. Once at Kungsbacka, a bus runs to the house, departing Kungsbacka daily at 11am and returning in the afternoon. In July and August, a special SJ bus runs directly to Tjolöholm from Nils Ericsonplatsen in Gothenburg. For further information, call the tourist office at (℃ **0300/834-595.**

VARBERG

Forty-five kilometers (28 miles) south of Kungsbacka is the atmospheric old town of Varberg, which enjoyed fame in the 19th century as a bathing resort. Today Varberg is one of Sweden's most popular coastal resorts, known for its nude beaches. Within walking distance of the town center, you'll also find Apelviken Bay, where surfers flock from all over Europe to enjoy the waves.

Stop in at the **Varberg Tourist Office,** Brunnsparken (℃ **0340/887-70**), for complete information about the town. From mid-June to mid-August, it's open Monday to Saturday 9:30am to 7pm, Sunday 1 to 6pm. In August its hours are Monday to Friday 9:30am to 6pm, Saturday 10am to 2pm.

From Gothenburg, regular trains run down the coast with frequent service to Varberg. Motorists can head south along E6 from Gothenburg.

Stena Line (℃ **0340/690-900**) also offers ferry service year-round to Grenå in Denmark; a one-way ticket costs 140SEK to 150SEK ($18–$20) weekdays, 170SEK to 200SEK ($22–$26) Saturday and Sunday, and the sea journey takes 3 hours and 45 minutes.

All the **attractions of Varberg** ⚓ can easily be explored on foot, as most of them lie along the seafront. The major attraction is the 13th-century fortress, complete with moat, **Varbergs Fästning** (℃ **0340/185-20**), set on a rocky promontory in the sea. It was home to the Swedish king Magnus Erikkson. Important peace treaties with Denmark were signed here in 1343, but the fortress is best known for a suit of medieval clothing belonging to the **Bocksten Man,** a 600-year-old murder victim. The man was garroted, drowned, impaled, and then buried in a local bog until discovered by a Swedish farmer in 1936. His suit of ordinary clothing is the only known medieval clothing still in existence and consists of a cloak, a hood, shoes, and stockings. Thick, red ringlets cascade around his skull. Three stakes were thrust through his body. The idea, supposedly, was to ensure that his spirit never escaped to pursue his murderers.

The fortress also contains a **prison** from 1850; it was the first Swedish prison to be built with individual cells. Lifers were held here, with the last one "departing" in

1931. The museum is open daily 10am to 6pm. Admission is 50SEK ($6.50) adults, 10SEK ($1.30) children 6 to 17. Much of the museum isn't worth seeing, as it features things like fishing exhibits. There are, however, paintings by the Varberg School. The most famous artists of this 19th-century movement included Nils Kreuger, Karl Nordström, and Richard Bergh.

If you walk down **Strandpromenaden** for about 5 minutes, you'll reach some well-known nude beaches. **Kärringhålan** and **Skarpe** are reserved for women, whereas men bathe nude at **Goda Hopp.** This segregation of the sexes on a nude beach is rather unusual in Sweden, where "mixed" nudity is more commonplace.

Where to Stay

Varbergs Stadthotell ✦ This hotel, the grandest and most imposing building in town, was built in 1902 as a Belle Epoque replica of a French château; it accepted socially prominent and well-heeled guests for overnight stays. Set on the main square of town, it's hard to miss—which is good because it also houses the town's best restaurant. (See "Where to Dine," below.) In 1997, all of its bedrooms were radically upgraded and renovated, generally with a contemporary look that's a lot more modern than the building's ornate exterior. One wing, however, retains a greater emphasis on old-time grandeur, with some of the original antiques, higher ceilings, larger proportions, and better views over the town's main square. All the bedrooms, which vary widely in size, are well maintained, with good beds and ample bathrooms with shower units. The staff is polite and hard-working.

Kungsgatan 24–26, S-432 41 Varberg. ℂ 800/528-1234 in the U.S., or 0340/161-00. Fax 0340/69-01-01. www.bestwestern.com. 122 units. Late June to early Aug and Fri–Sat year-round 1,095SEK–1,245SEK ($142–$162) double; rest of year 1,495SEK ($194) double. AE, DC, MC, V. Bus: 1 or 3. **Amenities:** Restaurant; bar; indoor pool; spa; sauna; 24-hr. room service; laundry service; dry cleaning; nonsmoking rooms; rooms for those w/limited mobility. *In room:* TV, dataport, minibar, hair dryer.

Where to Dine

Café & Krog Stadt ✦ SWEDISH/CONTINENTAL Everything about this space evokes the grand age of dining. Built as part of a self-consciously upscale palace hotel in 1902, it has a high ceiling, a scattering of antiques, crystal chandeliers, formal service, and a pastel-and-gold color scheme that is very soothing. Menu items include smoked chicken breast with tomato-and-basil sauce, shellfish with "vineyard" (white wine) sauce, cream of crayfish soup with sherry, sliced Serrano ham with wild mushrooms and lingonberry sauce, poached halibut with bouillabaisse sauce and fried potatoes, and filets of reindeer with juniper berry sauce. The cooking is first rate, and the ingredients used are the finest in the area.

In the Varbergs Stadthotell, Kungsgatan 24–26. ℂ 0340/161-00. Reservations recommended. Main courses 150SEK–300SEK ($20–$39). AE, DC, MC, V. Daily noon–2pm and 7–10pm. Bus: 1 or 3.

FALKENBERG

Known for its sandy beaches and salmon fishing, Falkenberg is the most attractive resort along the Swedish Riviera. It lies 29km (18 miles) south of Varberg, 26km (16 miles) north of Hamstad, and 93km (58 miles) south of Gothenburg. Sleepy all winter, the town comes alive in summer, as visitors flock here to enjoy some 9.5km (6 miles) of sandy beaches, the best of which include Skrea Strand, Ugglarp, Långasand, Boberg, and Rinsegård. Regardless of the beach you choose, you'll find the Kattegatt to be the best bathing water in Sweden.

In the center of the long west coast of Sweden, Falkenberg is easily reached; it enjoys frequent bus and train service from Gothenburg, as it lies on the Gothenburg/Malmö rail line. Motorists leaving Varberg can continue southeast along E6 into Falkenberg.

Before exploring the area, you might head for the **Falkenbergs Turistbyrå,** Holgersgaten 11 (© **0346/886-100**). The office is open from mid-June to August Monday to Saturday 9:30am to 6pm, Sunday 2 to 6pm. From September to mid-June, it is open Monday to Friday 10am to 5pm.

Named after the falcons that once were hunted here, Falkenberg is a well-preserved medieval town. Walk through its old town, lying to the west of the river, and you'll discover a warren of wooden cottages and narrow lanes paved with cobblestones. By the bridge over the Ätran River lie the ruins of a medieval fortress destroyed by an army of peasants in the 15th century. Close to the bridge stands **St. Laurentii Kyrka** ★★, a church surrounded by cobblestone streets. The interior contains wall and ceiling paintings from the 1600s and 1700s. This church dates from the 12th century and was saved from demolition because it was put to secular use—as a shooting range, a movie house, and even a gym. In the 1920s, it was reconsecrated.

The major attraction is **Falkenbergs Museum,** Söderbron (© **0346/886-125**), which is housed in a four-story grain warehouse near the bridge. The museum displays artifacts removed from excavations in the area and, surprisingly, a re-creation of life in the 1950s. There are mementos of dance bands of the era along with a stylized cafe, even a shoe-repair shop of the time. It is open June to August daily noon to 4pm. Off-season hours are Tuesday to Friday and Sunday noon to 4pm. Admission is free.

The River Ätran runs through central Falkenberg and offers some of Sweden's best salmon fishing, although the waters today are overfished and catches are not what they used to be. The inventor of the mining safety lamp, Sir Humphrey Davy, came here in the 1820s to go fly-fishing. He popularized the glories of salmon fishing on the river and in time was followed by a parade of rich British sportsmen. If you'd like to try your luck, you can pick up a fishing license from the tourist bureau (see earlier in this section), which entitles you to catch three fish per day; the license costs 100SEK ($13).

Where to Stay & Dine

Grand Hotel Falkenberg   This grand, imposing hotel was originally built in 1931 in the center of town, adjacent to the lake. At the time, bedrooms occupied only the first and third floors, with the second floor devoted to a reception space for parties and municipal functions; today bedrooms are also found on the second floor. Each of these units is outfitted in pale colors, with internationally modern furniture, good beds, and modern bathrooms with tub/showers.

The white-walled in-house restaurant, set near the lobby on the hotel's ground floor, is open daily for lunch and dinner.

Hotellgatan 1, Box 224, S-311 23 Falkenberg. © 0346/14-450. Fax 0346/144-59. www.grandhotelfalkenberg.se. 70 units. Sun–Thurs 1,250SEK ($163) double; Fri–Sat 970SEK ($126) double. AE, DC, MC, V. Rates include breakfast. Free parking. **Amenities:** Restaurant; bar; fitness center; sauna; limited room service; laundry service; dry cleaning; nonsmoking rooms; rooms for those w/limited mobility. *In room:* TV, dataport, minibar, hair dryer.

Finds **A Note for Shoppers**

The oldest pottery still operating in Scandinavia, **Törngren's,** Nygatan 34 (© **0346/169-20**), dates from 1789. It may, in fact, be the oldest pottery in the north of Europe. The pottery is still on the original site and continues to be run by the same family after seven generations. Open Monday to Friday 10am to 6pm, Saturday 10am to 2pm.

Hotel Strandbaden   This hotel was built in the early 1990s on a low, rocky bluff directly above a sandy beach, overlooking a sea dotted with weathered rocky islets. Its three floors contain cozy, well-appointed, and modern public rooms. While devoid of flair, the conservatively decorated bedrooms are clean, well maintained, and comfortable, with ample bathrooms equipped with shower units. There's a restaurant and bar that's open daily for lunch and dinner. During the summer, most guests spend their days at the beach; the rest of the year, they swim free in the *Klitterbad.* Set only 9.1m (30 ft.) from the hotel itself, it's the largest indoor saltwater pool in Sweden, with an echoing interior space that's worthy of an Olympic competition.

Havsbadsallén, S-311 42 Falkenberg. (℃ **0346/714-900.** Fax 0346/161-11. www.strandbaden.se. 135 units. Sun–Thurs (and summer) 1,095SEK–1,295SEK ($142–$168) double, 1,450SEK–1,550SEK ($189–$202) suite; Fri–Sat 850SEK–1,050SEK ($111–$137) double, 1,150SEK–1,250SEK ($150–$163) suite. Rates include breakfast. AE, DC, MC, V. Free parking. Bus: 555 from Halmstad. **Amenities:** 2 restaurants; 2 bars; indoor pool; fitness center; sauna; limited room service; laundry service; dry cleaning; nonsmoking rooms; rooms for those w/limited mobility. *In room:* TV, minibar, hair dryer.

HALMSTAD ✪
Once a grand walled town and a major stronghold of Danish power, Halmstad lies 145km (90 miles) south of Gothenburg and 40km (25 miles) south of Falkenberg, and is the golf capital of Sweden. Aside from the fabled Tylösand course, there are six courses in town. In summer, Swedes and Danes (in the main) flock to Halmstad's fabled strip of wide, white, sandy beach called Tylösand. Along with the adjacent Ringenäs and Frösakull beaches, this is one of the longest beaches in Scandinavia.

Long a Swedish resort, Halmstad today is one of the fastest-growing towns in the country. Halmstad is forever linked to the memory of Christian IV, king of Denmark (1588–1648), who left his mark on the town. He spent a lot of time here and built Halmstad Castle, where in 1619 he entertained the Swedish king Gustav Adolf II with 7 solid days of festivities.

Shortly after that meeting, a fire destroyed most of the town but spared the castle. After the fire, Christian created a Renaissance town with a high street, *Storgatan,* and a grid of straight streets unlike the narrow, crooked ones of old. If you walk along *Storgatan,* you'll see many Renaissance-style merchants' houses from that rebuilding period. The Danes were driven out in 1645 and Halmstad returned to Sweden. Because the town had lost its military significance, the walls were torn down. All that remains is *Norre Port,* one of the great gateways.

Motorists can follow E6 southeast from Falkenburg. Halmstad lies on the major rail lines between Malmö and Gothenburg, so there is frequent service throughout the day.

Halmstads Turistbyrå, Österskans, just by the Österbro Bridge (℃ **035/ 13-23-20**), is open June to August Monday to Friday 9am to 6pm, Saturday 10am to 1pm, and Sunday 11am to 6pm. Off-season hours are Monday to Friday 9am to 5pm.

Seeing the Sights
In the town center, **Stora Torg,** the market square, contains Europa and the Bull, a fountain group ✪ designed by Carl Milles with mermen twisted around it. Flanking one side of the plaza is the **St. Nikolai kykra,** Kyrkogatan (℃ **035/ 15-19-43**), a 14th-century church. It and the castle were the only major structures to survive from the era of Christian IV. The church contains some of the finest **stained-glass windows** ✪✪✪ in Sweden. The tall windows were created by Einar

Forseth (1892–1988), who designed the golden mosaics in Stockholm's Stadhuset and the mosaic paving for England's Coventry Cathedral. Erik Olson (1901–86), part of the fabled Halmstad Group, Sweden's first Surrealists, conceived the two smaller circular windows. The church is open daily 8:30am to 6pm and charges no admission.

The town's major landmark is **Halmstad Slott** ⚑, which King Christian IV commissioned Hans van Steenwinckel, a Dutchman, to build in 1620 as part of Halmstad's defense system. Currently, it is the residence of the county governor and is not open to the public, although you can see it from the outside and walk through the surrounding gardens 24 hours a day for free.

Along the river stands **Museet i Halmstad** ⚑, Tollsgatan (© **035/16-23-00**), which contains exhibits from local archaeological digs of only minor interest. The chief treasure of the museum is its **painted wall hangings** ⚑⚑, known in Swedish as *bonader,* on the second floor. This collection of naïve folk paintings are stunning and very typical of this part of western Sweden, most often depicting scenes from the Bible. Curiously, the costumes and the settings are not from ancient days at all but evoke the 18th and 19th centuries in which they were painted. In the upper-floor rooms are home interiors from the 1600s through the 1800s. Here you'll find an array of artifacts that includes everything from Gustavian harps to 1780s square pianos. On the top floor are paintings by the Halmstad Group, the fabled Surrealists of Sweden. The museum is open Wednesday from noon to 8pm, and Thursday to Tuesday 10am to 4pm. Admission is 40SEK ($5.20) adults and 20SEK ($2.60) for children ages 7 to 15. Three kilometers (1¾ miles) north of the town center, **Mjsellby Konstgård,** Mjallby (© **035/316-19**), also displays the art of the Halmstad Group. This group was composed of six artists, including the brothers Axel and Erik Olson and their cousin Waldemar Lorentzon, along with Esaias Thorén, Stellan Mörner, and Sven Jonson. They were post-Cubists who first worked here in 1929. In time, they developed a Nordic form of Surrealism that was deeply rooted in the landscapes of Halland. Many members of the group continued to produce until the 1980s. Set in the beautiful Halland countryside, the art center here was established by the daughter of Erik Olson. Along with permanent exhibitions from the Halmstad Group, the site is host to temporary exhibitions, often by great masters such as Le Corbusier. To reach the center if you're not driving, take bus nos. 350 to 351 and ask to be let off at the nearest stop. (*Be warned:* The museum is still nearly a kilometer, or ¾ mile, away.) The hours are Tuesday to Sunday 1 to 5pm. Admission is 40SEK ($5.20).

Where to Stay & Dine

Best Western Grand Hotel ⚑   Originally built in 1905, this hotel sports a mock-medieval block-tower jutting skyward from its exposed corner. Set within a short walk from the railway station, traditionally it has attracted artists and business travelers to its well-upholstered, well-heeled interior. Accommodations were recently renovated and upgraded. Look for solid comfort and a no-nonsense approach to the business of inn-keeping, as reflected by the spick-and-span bathrooms with shower units.

Stationsgatan 44, S-302 45 Halmstad. © 035/280-81-00. Fax 035/280-81-10. www.grandhotel.no. 108 units. July to mid-Aug and Fri–Mon year-round 860SEK–960SEK ($112–$125) double; rest of year 1,250SEK ($163) double; 1,650SEK ($215) junior suite. Rates include breakfast. AE, DC, MC, V. Parking 27SEK ($3.50). Bus: 1. **Amenities:** Restaurant; bar; fitness center; sauna; 24-hr. room service; laundry service; dry cleaning; nonsmoking rooms; rooms for those w/limited mobility. *In room:* TV, dataport, hair dryer.

Hotel Tylösand ★★ (Kids)   One of the most dramatically modern resorts in the region, this hotel occupies a parcel of rock-and-scrub-covered seafront land on a south-facing peninsula about 9km (5½ miles) west of Halmstad. In summer, the place is filled with families on holiday enjoying the nearby beaches and wide-open landscapes. The rest of the year, management works hard to fill the place with corporate conventions and theme weekends during which guests partici-pate in wine tastings and spa treatments, and recuperate from the stresses of everyday life. Bedrooms are airy, well furnished, and stylish, each decorated with light touches and pale colors, plus adequate-size bathrooms equipped with tub/showers. Throughout the premises, in both bedrooms and public areas, views extend over an eerie, sometimes surreal landscape that can be soothing, invigorating, isolated, and wild.

The hotel contains a trio of restaurants ranging from an informal bistro to a formal modern area with light that floods in from a Nordic interpretation of a greenhouse. One of them features live dance music that's presented whenever there are enough guests in residence to justify the expense.

Tylöshusvägen P.O. Box 643, S-301 16 Halmstad. © **035/305-00.** Fax 035/324-39. www.tylosand.se. 230 units. Sun–Thurs 1,500SEK ($195) double; Fri–Sat 1,395SEK ($181) double. AE, DC, MC, V. Free parking. **Amenities:** 3 restaurants; 4 bars; 2 pools (1 indoor); health spa; sauna; 24-hr. room service; babysitting; laun-dry service; dry cleaning; nonsmoking rooms; rooms for those w/limited mobility. *In room:* A/C (in some), TV, dataport, minibar, hair dryer, safe.

BÅSTAD ★★★

Jutting out on a peninsula surrounded by hills and a beautiful landscape, Båstad is the most fashionable international seaside resort in Sweden, and lies 179km (111 miles) south of Gothenburg and 105km (65 miles) north of Malmö.

All the famous international tennis stars have played on the courts at Båstad. Contemporary Swedish players—inspired by the feats of Björn Borg—receive much of their training here. There are more than 50 courts in the district, in addi-tion to the renowned Drivan Sports Centre. Tennis was played here as early as the 1880s and became firmly established in the 1920s. King Gustaf V took part in these championships for 15 years from 1930 onward under the pseudonym of "Mr. G," and Ludvig Nobel guaranteed financial backing for international tournaments.

Golf has established itself almost as much as tennis, and the Bjäre peninsula offers a choice of five courses. In 1929, Nobel purchased land at Boarp for Bås-tad's first golf course. The bay provides opportunities for regattas and different kinds of boating. Windsurfing is popular, as is skin diving. In summer, sea bathing also is popular along the coast.

The Bjäre peninsula, a traditional farming area, is known for its early pota-toes, which are served with pickled herring all over Sweden.

By car, head west on Route 115 from Båstad. If you're not driving, you'll find speedy trains running frequently throughout the day between Gothenburg and Malmö. Six buses a day also arrive from Helsingborg; the trip takes 1 hour. For tourist information, **Båstad Turism,** Kyrkgatan 1 at Stortorget (© **0431/750-45**), is open from June 20 to August 7 Sunday to Friday 10am to 6pm and Saturday 10am to 4pm, off season Monday to Saturday 10am to 4pm. You can book hos-tel rooms here from 170SEK ($22) per person or rent bikes for 50SEK to 80SEK ($6.50–$10) per day. They also will provide information about booking tennis courts, renting sports equipment, or reserving a tee time for a round of golf.

Exploring the Area

The most interesting sights are not in Båstad itself but on the Bjäre peninsula (see below). However, before leaving the resort, you may want to call or visit **Mariakyrkan (Saint Mary's),** Köpmansgatan (✆ **0431/78700**). Open daily from 9am to 4pm, it's one of the landmark churches of Skåne. Saint Mary's was built between 1450 and 1500. Its tower was restored as recently as 1986, and the entire interior renewed in 1967. Inside are many treasures, including a sculpture of Saint Mary and Christ from about 1460 (found in the sanctuary). The altarpiece is from 1775, but the crucifix is medieval. The angel with trumpet above the altar is from about the same time. The pulpit is from 1836, its hourglass from 1791. In the northern nave is a church clock from 1802 and various fresco paintings.

Båstad is noted for one of the principal attractions of southern Sweden, the **Norrvikens Trädgårdar (Norrviken Gardens)** ★★★, Kattvik (✆ **0431/723-70**), 2.5km (1½ miles) west of the resort's center. Founded in 1906 by Rudolf Abelin, these gardens have been expanded and maintained according to his plans, embracing a number of styles. One is Italian baroque, with a pond framed with pyramid-shape boxwood hedges and tall cypresses. A Renaissance garden's boxwood patterns are reminiscent of the tapestry art of 15th-century Italy; in the flower garden, bulbs compete with annuals. There also are a Japanese garden, an Oriental terrace, a rhododendron dell, a romantic garden, and a water garden.

At Villa Abelin, designed by the garden's founder, wisteria climbs the walls and blooms twice a year. The villa houses shops, exhibits, and information facilities. There are also a restaurant and a cafeteria on the grounds.

The gardens can be viewed from May 1 to September 6 daily 10am to 8pm. Admission is 90SEK ($12) for adults, 45SEK ($5.85) for children under 12.

With the time you have remaining after exploring the gardens, you may want to turn your attention to the **Bjäre Peninsula** ★★, the highlight of the entire region, where the widely varied scenery ranges from farm fields to cliff formations. Before exploring in depth, it's best to pick up a detailed map from the Båstad tourist office (see above).

The peninsula is devoted to sports, including windsurfing, tennis, golf, hiking trails, and mountain biking. It has white, sandy beaches reaching down to the sea. Riding paths and cycle roads also are set aside for these activities. You can play golf at five different 18-hole courses from early spring. The Båstad tourist office can provide more information.

If you don't have a car, public transport is provided by bus no. 525, leaving Båstad every hour Monday through Saturday. It traverses the center of the peninsula.

The Skaneleden walking trail runs the entire perimeter of the island and is also great for cycling. However, the terrain is quite hilly in places, so you need to be in fabulous shape.

On the peninsula's western coast is the sleepy village of **Torekov,** a short drive from Kattvik. Here you'll find a bathing beach and pier where early-morning bathers can be seen walking down to the sea in bathing gowns and sandals.

From Torekov, you can take a boat to explore **Hallands Väderö,** an island off the west coast of Sweden. Old wooden fishing boats make the 15-minute crossing on the hour from June to August. From September to May, departures are every 2 hours. The cost is 73SEK ($9.50) round-trip, with the last departure at 4pm daily. For more information, call **Bokningstelefon Halmstad** (✆ **0431/36-30-20**).

One of Sweden's few remaining seal colonies exists on Hallands Väderö. "Seal safaris" come here to view, but not disturb, these animals. In addition to seals, the island is noted for its rich bird life, including guillemots, cormorants, eiders, and gulls.

Outdoor Activities

GOLF   The region around Båstad is home to five separate golf courses. Two of them accept nonmembers who want to use the course during short-term visits to the region. They include the **Båstad Golf Club,** Boarp, S-269 21 Båstad (© **0431/783-70;** to reach it, follow the signs to Boarp and drive 4km/2½ miles south of town), and the **Bjåre Golf Club** ✿, Solomonhög 3086, S-269 93 Båstad (© **0431/36-10-53;** follow the signs to Förslöv, driving 10km/6¼ miles east of Båstad). Both charge greens fees of 235SEK to 500SEK ($31–$65) for 18 holes, depending on the season, and both have pro shops that will rent you clubs. Advance reservations for tee times are essential.

TENNIS   Båstad is irrevocably linked to the game of tennis, which it celebrates with fervor, thanks to its role as the longtime home of the **Swedish Open.** If you want to improve your game, consider renting one of the 14 outdoor courts (available Apr–Sept) or one of the six indoor courts (available year-round) at the **Drivan Tennis Center,** Drivangårdens Vandrarhem (© **0431/685-00**). Set about a kilometer (¾ mile) north of Båstad's town center, it's the site of a corps of tennis professionals and teachers, who give lessons for 250SEK ($33) per hour. Both indoor and outdoor courts rent for 100SEK ($13) per hour. And if you really want to immerse yourself in the spirit of the game, consider renting a bunk bed within the establishment's youth hostel, priced at 125SEK to 200SEK ($16–$26) per person. Functional-looking barrack-style bedrooms within the compound are designed for two to four occupants, and often are the temporary home of members of tennis teams from throughout Scandinavia. Originally established in 1929, this club built most of the tennis courts you see today around 1980.

Where to Stay

Hotel-Pension Enehall   On a slope of Hallandsåsen Mountain, only a few minutes' walk from the sea, this cozy, intimate place caters mainly to Swedish families and the occasional Dane or German. There are many personal touches here, and the rooms, although small, are adequately equipped with good beds and tiny bathrooms with shower units. All rooms are nonsmoking. The food is tasty, and the service polite and efficient.

Stationsterrassen 10, S-26900 Båstad. © 0431/750-15. Fax 0431/750-14. www.enehall.se. 40 units. 795SEK ($103) double. Half-board 595SEK ($77) per person. Rates include breakfast. AE, DC, MC, V. Free parking. Bus: 513. **Amenities:** Restaurant; bar; sauna; 1 room for those w/limited mobility. *In room:* TV.

Hotel Riviera   Often a favorite venue for conferences, this is one of the better hotels in the area, and takes on a somewhat festive air in summer. Located by the sea, about a kilometer (¾ mile) from the railroad station and about 3km (1¾ miles) east of the town center, it offers views from many of its modern bedrooms, as well as its 300-seat restaurant. Both bedrooms and bathrooms are small, but the comfortably furnished bathrooms have tub/showers. Nonsmoking rooms and excellent housekeeping result in impeccably clean accommodations. Guests can relax by sitting out in the gardens or on the terrace. The kitchen serves a superb combination of Scandinavian and international food; in season there often is dancing to a live band.

Rivieravägen 33, S-269-39 Båstad. © **0431/369-050.** Fax 0431/761-00. www.hotelriviera.nu. 50 units. 820SEK ($107) double. Rates include breakfast. AE, DC, MC, V. Closed Sept–Apr. Free parking. **Amenities:** Restaurant; bar . *In room:* TV.

Hotel Skansen ★★ Although it isn't as expensive as some of those within the chain, this hotel is associated with some of the most opulent and prestigious hotels in Sweden, including the Grand Hotel in Stockholm. It's also the most visible tennis venue in Sweden, surrounded with eight tennis courts that are the home every year to the Swedish Open. As such, it has housed, usually more than once, the most famous tennis stars in Sweden, including Björn Borg, Anders Järryd, and Henrik Holm. A few minutes' walk from the marina and 5m (16 ft.) from the beach, it was originally built as a warehouse for grain in 1877. Today it incorporates its original building (which today is listed as a national monument) with four more recent structures that surround eight tennis courts, some of which are equipped with stadiums for the above-mentioned tennis competitions. The interior has a beamed roof, pillars, and views of the sea. Renovated in 1997, bedrooms are airy, elegant, and traditionally outfitted with conservative furniture, including good beds with ample private bathrooms containing shower units.

The in-house restaurant is open daily year-round but is closed on Sunday in the winter. Set within the oldest of the five buildings comprising the hotel, it serves Swedish and international cuisine. The rest of the year, meals are served only to hotel guests, and only by special arrangement. A cafe operates year-round and offers seating in the courtyard during warm weather.

Kyrkogatan 2, S-269 21 Båstad. © **0431/55-81-00.** Fax 0431/55-81-10. www.hotelskansen.se. 136 units. 990SEK–1,560SEK ($129–$203) double; 2,800SEK ($364) suite. Rates include breakfast. AE, DC, MC, V. Free parking. Bus: 513; 5-min. walk. **Amenities:** Restaurant; bar; indoor pool; 8 tennis courts; fitness center; sauna; babysitting; nonsmoking rooms; rooms for those w/limited mobility. *In room:* A/C (in some), TV, dataport, minibar, hair dryer, safe.

Where to Dine

The preceding hotels all have good restaurants, although you should call in advance for a reservation. But if you're just passing through, consider dropping in at the **Solbackens Café & Wåffelbruk,** Italienska vägen (© **0431/70-200**). If the weather is fair, opt for a table on the terrace overlooking the water. This cafe is locally famous, known since 1907 for serving Swedish waffles and other delights.

Centrecourten SWEDISH/INTERNATIONAL In a town as obsessed with tennis as Båstad, you'd expect at least one restaurant to be outfitted in a tennis-lovers' theme. In this case, it consists of a cozy and small-scale dining room with photos of such stars as Björn Borg, a scattering of trophies, old-fashioned tennis memorabilia, and tennis racquets. Menu items include fresh fish, such as mussels, lemon sole, and cod; breast of duck with a bacon-flavored purée of potatoes; and brisket of beef with chanterelles and shallots. The food is merely good, but the ingredients are fresh and the flavors often enticing, especially in the seafood selections.

Köpmansgatan 70b. © **0431/75275.** Reservations recommended. Pizza 55SEK–75SEK ($7.15–$9.75); main courses 100SEK–150SEK ($13–$20). AE, MC, V. Daily noon–11pm.

Båstad After Dark

One good option is **Pepe's Bodega,** Warmbadhuset Hamnen (© **0431/369169**), where spicy food and festive cocktails evoke southern Spain, northern Mexico, or some undefined hideaway in a forgotten corner of South America. It's open

Wednesday through Sunday for both food and an active bar life, from 5 till 11pm for food, and until 1am for drinks.

ÄNGELHOLM

This is the major beach area for the city of Helsingborg. Its nearly 6.5km (4 miles) of golden sand attract a thriving summer business, as Helsingborg lies only 30 minutes away by train.

For information about the area, contact the **Ängelholms Turistbyrå,** Stortorget (© **0431/821-30**). It is open June to August Monday to Friday 9am to 6pm, Saturday 9am to 4pm, and in July only Sunday 11am to 3pm. Off-season times are Monday to Friday 9am to 4pm.

Frequent trains throughout the day link Båstad or Helsingborg with Ängelholm in less than 30 minutes. Buses also arrive frequently from Båstad. Motorists from Helsingborg in the south or Båstad in the north can travel the express highway, E6.

Seeing the Sights

The great botanist Carolus Linnaeus claimed, "Nowhere in Europe surpasses the place in charm, beauty, climate, and prosperity." A bit of an exaggeration, but Ängelholm and its surrounding area certainly are blessed with a varied and scenic landscape of coast and plain. The **Rönneå,** one of Sweden's loveliest rivers, begins in Lake Ringsjön and runs into the sea at Skälderviken Bay. The tourist office (see above) can provide details in summer about how to go for a canoe ride on this river.

Because of Ängelholm's position on this river, it was the cause of many bitter battles between Danes and Swedes. In 1658, following the peace of Roskilde, Ängelholm and the province of Skåne itself became firmly Swedish. The town was virtually destroyed by fierce fires in 1745 and 1802. The clay cuckoo—a ceramic pot—is the symbol of Ängelholm, which is very much a pottery town; potters have worked here since the 17th century. The pot is sold at dozens of stores throughout the town and is the best souvenir of a visit here.

Hantverksmuseum or the **Ängelholm Craft Museum,** Tingstorget (© **0431/ 875-03**), is housed in Sweden's oldest prison, which dates from 1780. It depicts the history of ceramics in the area and has exhibits of the work of well-known local artists. It is open May to August Tuesday to Friday 11am to 4pm and Saturday 10am to 2pm. In September it is open Saturday and Sunday 11am to 4pm. Admission is free.

Where to Stay & Dine

Hotell Erikslund ★ *Finds*   Set within rolling farmland, 7km (4¼ miles) south of Ängelholm, this hotel attracts lots of vacationing motorists (especially Germans) in summer during their explorations of the Swedish Riviera. It was built in 1991 in a vaguely Iberian style that includes sprawling, white-sided wings and a central tower that's capped with a gently sloping terra-cotta roof. Grounds surrounding the property are lavishly planted with roses and perennials, encouraging walks in the natural grandeur of the surrounding region. Bedrooms are artfully simple, with glowing hardwood floors and simple but tasteful furnishings, usually made from varnished birch and upholstery in such Nordic colors as pale and midnight blue, and stark white walls. The bathrooms are rather small but are equipped with tub/showers. On the premises is a warm and cozy restaurant, Joel's, where twin dining rooms (one apple green, one white) serve Swedish and international cuisine. Although there's no golf course on the premises, about

---

Fun Fact   **Inter-Galactic Tourist Stop**

Ängelholm is big with UFO buffs. In 1946, Gösta Carlsson, a railway worker, claimed to have encountered tiny aliens from across the galaxy. Apparently, Carlsson was rather convincing; ever since, European UFO conferences have been held here. The tourist board often runs tours to the site of the alleged landing from outer space.

---

a dozen of them lie within a radius of about 32km (20 miles). The staff at this hotel is familiar with the best of them and can direct interested players.

Erikslund, S-262 96 Ängelholm. ② **0431/415-700**. Fax 0431/415-710. www.hotellerikslund.se. 140 units. Mid-June to late Aug and Fri–Sat year-round 795SEK ($103) double; rest of year Sun–Thurs 1,095SEK–1,390SEK ($142–$181) double. AE, DC, MC, V. Free parking. Bus: 506 from Ängelholm. **Amenities:** 2 restaurants; bar; solarium; health spa; sauna; nonsmoking rooms; rooms for those w/limited mobility. *In room:* A/C, TV.

6

Skåne (Including Helsingborg & Malmö)

In Sweden's southernmost corner, the province of Skåne offers varied scenery, large forests, and many waterways. The sea, with its ample, uncrowded beaches, is always within reach. And many of the larger towns have a Continental aura because of their proximity to other European countries.

Denmark and the rest of Europe are easier to reach than ever before. In 2000, the Øresund Fixed Link between Denmark and Sweden was completed and opened to the public. A new artificial island was constructed halfway across the Øresund to connect 3km (1¾ miles) of immersed railway and motorway tunnels and a 7.7km (4¾-mile) bridge. This link between Copenhagen and Malmö benefits culture, education, and research in both countries, as well as business and transportation. With three million people living within a 49km (30-mile) radius of the link, the region has the largest population concentration in Scandinavia. Skåne's major urban cities are **Malmö, Helsingborg,** and the university and cathedral city of **Lund,** but many visit the little villages and undiscovered coastal towns in the summer months.

Skåne may not have fjords and snow-capped mountains, but it has just about everything else: sandy beaches, sea resorts, and ports; medieval churches and ancient cities and towns; the finest castles (often surrounded by beautiful grounds and moats); some of the country's most stately cathedrals; and fertile plains, virgin forests, rolling hills, and thriving farms. Many poets, authors, and painters have found inspiration here.

The first settlers were deer hunters and fishers who moved from the south of Europe as the ice melted. Over thousands of years, their ancestors left many traces, from the Stone Age to the Viking Age and the early beginnings of Christianity. Once Skåne belonged to Denmark, but since 1658 it has been a firm part of the Swedish kingdom. There are no fewer than 300 small medieval parish churches in the province—all still in use. Castles and mansions, many founded 400 or 500 years ago, dot the landscape.

Many beaches for swimming and sunbathing run along Skåne's coast. Like Halland (see chapter 5), it is known as the Swedish Riviera.

Skåne is easy to reach. You have a wide choice of flights, either to Malmö's Sturup Airport or to the Copenhagen airport, from which there are frequent hovercraft connections directly to the center of Malmö. Hovercraft also run between downtown Copenhagen and Malmö, and every 15 or 20 minutes, day or night, connections are possible by car ferry from Helsingør, Denmark, to Helsingborg, Sweden. If you're traveling by car, there are ferry routes from Denmark, Germany, and Poland.

Skåne

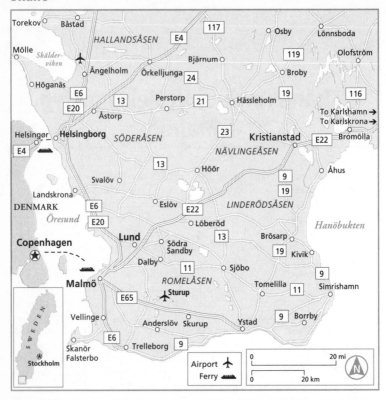

Torekov Båstad
HALLANDSÅSEN E4 117 Osby Lönnsboda
Mölle Skälder-viken 119 Olofström
Ängelholm Bjärnum Broby
Örkelljunga 24
Höganäs E6 Perstorp 21 Hässleholm 19 116
E20 13 Åstorp
Helsingør Helsingborg SÖDERÅSEN 23 Kristianstad E22 Bromölla
E4 NÄVLINGEÅSEN To Karlshamn → To Karlskrona →
13 Höör 9 Åhus
Svalöv 19
Landskrona E6 Eslöv E22 LINDERÖDSÅSEN
DENMARK Öresund E20 Löberöd Hanöbukten
Copenhagen Lund Södra Sandby 13 Brösarp
Dalby 19 Kivik
11 Sjöbo
Malmö ROMELÅSEN Tomelilla 11 9
E65 Sturup Simrishamn
Vellinge 9 Borrby
Anderslöv Skurup Ystad
E6 Trelleborg 9
Skanör Falsterbo
Stockholm SWEDEN
Airport ✈ 0   20 mi
Ferry ⚓ 0   20 km

1 Helsingborg

230km (143 miles) S of Gothenburg, 560km (347 miles) SW of Stockholm, 63km (39 miles) N of Malmö

At the narrowest point of the Øresund (Öresund in Swedish), 5km (3 miles) across the water that separates Sweden and Denmark, sits this industrial city and major port. Many people from Copenhagen take the 25-minute ferry ride (leaving every 20 min.) across the sound for a look at Sweden.

Of course, what they see isn't "Sweden," but a modern city with an ancient history. In the Middle Ages, Helsingborg and Helsingør together controlled shipping along the sound. Helsingborg is mentioned in the 10th-century *Njal's Saga* (an ancient Viking document), and other documents also indicate that there was a town here in 1085. The city now has more than 100,000 inhabitants and the second-busiest harbor in the country. This is the city that introduced pedestrian streets to Sweden, and it has long promenades along the shore of the sound.

Helsingborg (Hålsingborg) recently rebuilt large, vacant-looking sections of its inner city into one of the most innovative urban centers in Sweden. The centerpiece of these restorations lies beside the harbor and includes an all-glass building, the **Knutpunkten,** on Järnvägsgatan. Contained within are the railroad, bus, and ferryboat terminals; an array of shops similar to a North American mall; and a heliport. Many visitors say the sunlight-flooded railroad station is the cleanest, brightest, and most memorable they've ever seen. In addition, many dozens of

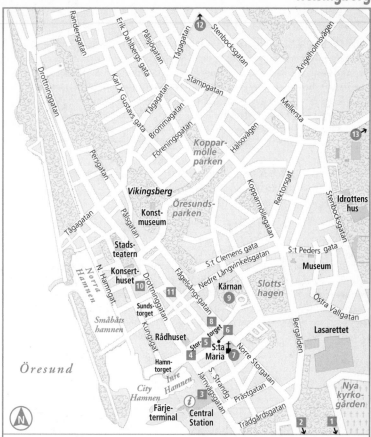

ATTRACTIONS ●

Fredriksdal Open-Air Museum
and Botanical Garden **13**
Kärnan (The Keep) **9**
Mairakyrkan (Church of St. Mary) **7**
Sofiero Slott **12**

ACCOMMODATIONS ■

Comfort Hotel Nouveau **2**
Elite Hotel Mollberg **4**
Elite Marina Plaza **10**
Hotel Helsingborg **6**
Hotel Högvakten **8**
Hotell Linnéa **3**
Hotell Viking **11**
Radisson/SAS Grand Hotel
Helsingborg **5**
Scandic Horisont **1**

† Church
ⓘ Information
┈ Railway

Fun Fact **The Goose of Honor**

The tip of the Scandinavian peninsula was where Selma Lagerlöf's *The Wonderful Adventures of Nils* began. The story of the hero, who travels on the back of a wild goose, has been translated into all major languages. In reality, however, the web-footed, flat-billed, large-bodied geese of Skåne are tame and never travel far from home. No doubt they regret this on November 10 when Scanians celebrate this almost sacred bird with a gargantuan dinner—one enjoyed by everyone but the geese.

---

trees and shrubs have transformed the center city into something like a verdant park, with trees between the lanes of traffic.

ESSENTIALS

GETTING THERE   By Ferry   Ferries from Helsingør, Denmark, leave the Danish harbor every 20 minutes day or night (trip time: 25 min.). For information about ferryboats in Helsingborg, call © **042/18-61-00;** for information on the Danish side, call © **33-15-15-15.** The cost of the ferryboat for pedestrians is 23SEK ($3) each way or 40SEK ($5.20) round-trip. The regular round-trip cost of the ferryboat for a car with up to five passengers is 560SEK ($73). There's a reduction for drivers planning to return to Sweden the same day; in that event, the round-trip fare is 295SEK ($38) for passage.

By Plane   The Ångelholm/Helsingborg airport lies 30 minutes from the center of the city, with regular connections to Stockholm's Arlanda airport. There are between two and four flights per day (flying time: 1 hr.). For SAS reservations, call © **0770/72-77-27.**

By Train   Trains run hourly during the day between Helsingborg and Malmö, taking 50 minutes. Trains arrive four times per day on the 5-hour trip from Stockholm, and they also leave Helsingborg twice per day for Stockholm. Trains between Gothenburg and Helsingborg depart and arrive twice a day (trip time: 2½ hr.). Call © **042/10-43-50** for information.

By Bus   Three buses per day link Malmö and Helsingborg. Two leave in the morning and one in the afternoon, the trip taking 1 hour and 10 minutes. Buses leave twice per day from Gothenburg and arrive in Helsingborg in 3¼ hours. Buses to and from Stockholm leave once per day (trip time: 9 hr.). Call © **0200/21818** for more information.

By Car   From Malmö, head north on E6 for 1 hour; from Gothenburg, drive south on E6 for 2½ hours; from Stockholm, take E4 south for 7½ hours until you reach Helsingborg.

VISITOR INFORMATION   The tourist office, **Helsingborg Turistbyrå,** Rådhuset (© **042/10-43-50;** www.helsingborg.se), is open from May to September 15 Monday to Friday 9am to 8pm, and Saturday and Sunday 9am to 5pm; September 16 to April Monday to Friday 9am to 6pm and Saturday 10am to 2pm.

GETTING AROUND   Most of Helsingborg's sights are within walking distance; however, if your legs are tired and the weather less than perfect, you can always take a city bus, numbered 1 to 7. Most buses on their way north pass the Town Hall; those heading south go by Knutpunkten. You can buy tickets on board the buses for 16SEK ($2.10). Tickets are valid for transfer to another city bus line as long as you transfer within 1 hour from the time the ticket was stamped. For information, call © **042/10-43-50.**

SEEING THE SIGHTS

Built in 1897, the **Town Hall (Rådhuset),** Drottninggatan 1 (© **042/10-50-00**), has handsome stained-glass windows depicting scenes from the town's history. Two memorial stones outside were presented by the Danes and the Norwegians to the Swedes for their assistance during World War II. There is also a sculpture relief representing the arrival of Danish refugees.

In the main town square, the **Stortorget** is a monument commemorating General Stenbock's victory at the Battle of Helsingborg in 1710 between Sweden and Denmark.

Fredriksdal Open-Air Museum and Botanical Garden ★★   This is among the largest and most complete open-air museums in Sweden, covering some 28 hectares (69 acres) of rolling land within a 20-minute walk east of the town center. The park was built around a manor house constructed in 1787. After going through the main entrance, you can explore the rose garden, which has about 450 different types of roses, all part of one of Sweden's most remarkable botanical gardens. An open-air theater was built in 1927. You also can wander through the French Park and the English Park.

Gisela Trapps Vag 1. © 042/104-540. Admission 50SEK ($6.50), free for children 16 and under. Park June–Aug daily 10am–7:30pm; Sept–May daily 11am–5pm. Manor June–Sept daily 11am–5pm; Oct–May daily 10am–3pm. Bus: 2, 3, 7, or 254.

Kärnan (The Keep) ★   One of the most important medieval monuments in Sweden, and the symbol of Helsingborg, Kärnan rises from the crest of a rocky ridge in the city center. The origins of this 30m-tall (100-ft.) square tower—built in the 11th century—are mysterious; it adopted its present form in the 1300s. Its name translates as "the keep," a moniker related to its original position as the most central tower (and prison) of the once-mighty Helsingborg Castle. The thickness of its walls (about 4m/13 ft.) make it the most solidly constructed building in the region. An object of bloody fighting between the Swedes and the Danes for generations, the castle and its fortifications were demolished in 1679. Of the once-mighty fortress, only Kärnan (which was restored and rebuilt in 1894) remains.

The easiest way to reach Kärnan is to board the elevator, which departs from the *terrasen* (terrace) of the town's main street, the *Stortorget.* For 5SEK (65¢) per person, you'll be carried up the rocky hillside to the base of the tower. However, many visitors avoid the elevator, preferring instead to climb a winding set of flower-flanked steps as part of their exploration of the city. Once inside the tower, an additional 147 steps remain before you're rewarded with one of the most sweeping views in the district.

Kärngränden (off the Stortorget). © 042/105-991. Admission 20SEK ($2.60) adults, 10SEK ($1.30) children 8–16. Apr–May Tues–Fri 9am–4pm, Sat–Sun 11am–4pm; June–Aug daily 11am–7pm. Bus: 1 or 6.

Mariakyrkan (Church of St. Mary)   A short walk east from the harbor, this church was constructed in the 13th century but substantially rebuilt in the 15th century in a Danish Gothic style that evokes a basilica. Although the facade is plain, the interior is striking. Particularly noteworthy are the medieval altarpiece and its intricately carved Renaissance pulpit. If the sun is shining, the modern stained-glass windows are jewel-like.

Södra Storgatan. © 042/37-28-30. Free admission. June–Aug Mon–Sat 8am–6pm, Sun 9am–6pm; Sept–May Mon–Sat 8am–4pm, Sun 9am–4pm. Bus: 1 or 6.

Sofiero Slott ✦✦   One of the most famous buildings in southern Sweden, lying 5km (3 miles) north of Helsingborg, this castle was constructed in 1864 and 1865 to be the summer residence of King Oscar II and his wife, Sofia. In 1905 it was bequeathed to their grandson, Gustav Adolph, and his wife, Margareta, who enlarged the site and created some of the most memorable gardens in the country. Their interests supposedly sparked a nationwide interest in landscape architecture, which continues stronger than ever throughout Sweden today. After his coronation, Gustav Adolph spent his last days here, eventually bequeathing Sofiero as a gift to the city of Helsingborg in 1973. In 1993, many of the original gardens were re-created in memory of their designer, Queen Margareta. Today the most visited sites include the 1865 castle, which contains a cafe and restaurant; the rose garden; and the Rhododendron Ravine, with an estimated 10,000 rhododendrons, which are in their full glory in early June.

Sofierovägen. ⓒ 042/137-400. Admission 60SEK ($7.80) adults, free for children. Daily 11am–5pm. Closed Oct to mid-Apr. Bus: 219 or 221.

SHOPPING

In the center of Helsingborg you'll find a number of shopping possibilities, including **Väla Centrum,** which is one of the largest shopping centers in all of Scandinavia. To reach it, follow Hälsovågen and Ångelholmsvägen north about 6km (3¾ miles; it's signposted), or take bus no. 202 from Knutpunkten. Seemingly everything is here under one roof, including 2 large department stores and 42 specialty shops, selling everything from shoes to tropical fish.

The best bookstore in town is **Bengt Bökman,** Bredgattan 22 (ⓒ **042/10-71-00**), with many English-language editions. The best place to buy glass is **Duka Carl Anders,** Kullag 17 (ⓒ **042/24-30-20**), which carries the works of such prestigious manufacturers as Kosta Boda and Orrefors.

POTTERY

Northwest Scania is known as the pottery district of Sweden. The first Scanian pottery factory was founded in 1748 in Bosarp, 15km (9¼ miles) east of Helsingborg. The city of Helsingborg got its first factory in 1768 and another began manufacturing in 1832. Since then, the tradition has been redeveloped and revitalized, making the area famous far beyond the borders of Sweden.

At a point 7km (4¼ miles) south of Helsingborg, you can visit **Raus Stenkarlsfabrik,** less than a kilometer (½ mile) east of Råå (look for signs along Landskronavagen). It is open May to August Monday to Friday 10am to 6pm, Saturday 10am to 4pm; in the off season, you must call and make an appointment. Call ⓒ **042/26-01-30** for more information.

In Gantofta, 10km (6¼ miles) southeast of Helsingborg, lies **Jie-Keramik** (ⓒ **042/990-31**), one of Scandinavia's leading manufacturers of hand-painted decorative ceramics, wall reliefs, wall clocks, figures, and other such items. You can visit a factory shop or patronize a cafe on-site. From Helsingborg, drive south to Råå, then follow the signs to Gantofta. You also can take bus no. 209 from Knutpunkten in the center of Helsingborg. The outlet is open June to August daily noon to 6pm. Off-season hours are daily noon to 4pm.

If you drive 20km (12 miles) north of Helsingborg to Höganäs, you'll find two famous stoneware factories. **Höganäs Saltglaserat** (ⓒ **042/33-83-33**) has been manufacturing salt-glazed stoneware since 1835. Today the classic, salt-glazed Höganäs jars with their anchor symbol are still in production. Everything is made by hand and fired in coal-burning circular kilns from the turn of the 20th century. The shop here is within the factory, so you can see the throwers in action and go inside the old kilns. Open year-round Monday to Friday 9am to 4pm and Saturdays in June, July, August, and September 10am to 1pm. The other outlet, **Höganäs Keramik** (© **042/35-11-31**), is Scandinavia's largest stoneware manufacturer. In the Factory Shop, inaugurated in 1994, flawed goods from both Höganäs Keramik and Boda Nova are on sale at bargain prices. This outlet is open from May to August Monday through Friday from 9am to 6pm, Saturday and Sunday 10am to 5pm. Off-season hours are Monday to Friday 10am to 6pm, Saturday 10am to 4pm, and Sunday 11am to 4pm.

WHERE TO STAY
EXPENSIVE
Radisson SAS Grand Hotel Helsingborg ★★★   Helsingborg's grandest hotel, an imposing brick monument built in 1926, underwent a radical upgrade in 2003. It's one of the most visible Swedish hotels in the Radisson SAS chain, and one of the most appealing hotels in southern Sweden. It combines high-ceilinged, richly paneled public areas and spacious, well-accessorized guest rooms with elaborate ceiling moldings, old-world decorative touches, and lots of modern comforts and conveniences. The renovated rooms have ample bathrooms.

Stortorget 8–12, Box 1104, S-251 11 Helsingborg. © 800/333-3333 in the U.S., or 042/38-04-00. Fax 042/38-04-04. www.radissonsas.com. 117 units. Mid-June to Aug and Fri–Sun year-round 890SEK–1,140SEK ($116–$148) double, 1,490SEK–1,990SEK ($194–$259) double; rest of year 1,600SEK ($208) double, 1,950SEK–2,450SEK ($254–$319) suite. Rates include breakfast. AE, DC, MC, V. Parking 125SEK ($16). Bus: 7B or 1A. **Amenities:** Restaurant; bar; sauna; 24-hr. room service; laundry service; dry cleaning; nonsmoking rooms; rooms for those w/limited mobility. *In room:* TV, dataport, minibar, hair dryer.

MODERATE
Comfort Hotel Nouveau ★ *Finds*   Once a somewhat nondescript and out-moded hotel from the 1960s, the Hotel Nouveau was radically reconfigured and upgraded in 1996. The result is a tastefully decorated building built of ocher brick and touches of marble. The decor throughout draws on upscale models from England and France, and includes chintz curtains, varnished mahogany, often with wood inlays, and warm colors inspired by autumn. Rooms are nice and cozy—not particularly large, but well maintained, with tasteful fabrics, frequently renewed linen, and small but adequate bathrooms equipped with shower units. As a thoughtful touch, a fresh flower is often placed on your pillow at night.

Gasverksgatan 11. S-250 02 Helsingborg. © 042/37-19-50. Fax 042/37-19-59. www.choicehotelseurope.com. 95 units. Mid-June to mid-Aug and Fri–Sat year-round 890SEK ($116) double; rest of year 1,495SEK ($194) double; 1,195SEK–1,695SEK ($155–$220) suite. AE, DC, MC, V. Free parking. Bus: 7A or 1A. **Amenities:** Restaurant; bar; indoor pool; sauna; laundry service; dry cleaning; nonsmoking rooms; rooms for those w/limited mobility. *In room:* TV, dataport, minibar, hair dryer.

Elite Hotel Mollberg   This is arguably Sweden's oldest continuously operated hotel and restaurant. Although a tavern has stood on this site since the 14th century, most of the building was constructed in 1802. Its elaborate wedding-cake exterior and high-ceilinged interior have long been its hallmarks. A major renovation was carried out in 1986, with several minor restorations throughout the 1990s. Its first-class rooms are equipped with beautifully maintained bathrooms.

Stortorget 18, S-251 14 Helsingborg. © 042/37-37-00. Fax 042/37-37-37. www.elite.se. 104 units. 1,390SEK–1,590SEK ($181–$207) double; 2,200SEK ($286) suite. Rates include breakfast. AE, DC, MC, V. Parking 90SEK ($12). Bus: 7A, 7B, 1A, or 1B. **Amenities:** Restaurant; bar; sauna; limited room service; laundry service; dry cleaning; nonsmoking rooms; solarium. *In room:* TV, dataport, minibar, hair dryer.

Elite Marina Plaza ⭐⭐   This is Helsingborg's most innovative and most talked-about hotel, opening onto panoramic views of the Öresund. It's adjacent to the city's transportation hub, the Knutpunkten. The atrium-style lobby overflows with trees, rock gardens, and fountains. Guest rooms line the inner walls of the hotel's atrium and have a color scheme of marine blue with nautical accessories. The adequate bathrooms are equipped with tub/showers.

Kungstorget 6, S-251 10 Helsingborg. (©) 042/19-21-00. Fax 042/14-96-16. www.marinaplaza.elite.se. 190 units. 860SEK–1,520SEK ($112–$198) double; 1,490SEK–2,900SEK ($194–$377) suite. Midsummer discounts available. AE, DC, MC, V. Parking 120SEK ($16). Bus: 41, 42, 43, or 44. **Amenities:** Restaurant; bar; sauna; limited room service; laundry service; dry cleaning; nonsmoking rooms; rooms for those w/limited mobility. *In room:* TV, dataport, minibar, hair dryer, safe.

Hotel Helsingborg ⭐   Of the three hotels that lie along this grand avenue, this one is closest to the city's medieval tourist attraction, the Kärnan. It has a heroic neoclassical frieze and three copper-sheathed towers, and occupies four floors of what used to be a bank headquarters, dating from 1901. The high-ceilinged rooms are pleasantly modernized and flooded with sunlight. They retain a certain *Jugendstil* (Art Nouveau) look, with strong colors and many decorative touches. All rooms were upgraded and renovated in the early 1990s, with good beds and perfectly functional bathrooms equipped with tub/showers.

Stortorget 20, Box 1171, S-252 23 Helsingborg. (©) 042/37-18-00. Fax 042/37-18-50. www.hkchotels.se. 56 units. 795SEK–1,495SEK ($103–$194) double; 1,100SEK–1,600SEK ($143–$208) suite. Rates include breakfast. AE, DC, MC, V. Parking 90SEK ($12). Bus: 7A, 7B, 1A, or 1B. **Amenities:** Breakfast room; bar; sauna; laundry service; dry cleaning; nonsmoking rooms; rooms for those w/limited mobility. *In room:* TV, dataport, hair dryer.

Scandic Horisont   Near a park at the edge of the town's commercial center, this hotel with its futuristic facade was built in 1985. Guest rooms are comfortably conservative, with plush upholstery, soundproof windows, and comfortable mattresses. Bathrooms are well maintained and have tub/showers. The hotel is about a kilometer (½ mile) south of the ferryboat terminal.

Gustav Adolfs Gate 47, S-250 02 Helsingborg. (©) 800/780-7234 in U.S. and Canada, or 042/49-52-100. Fax 042/49-52-111. www.scandic-hotels.com. 164 units. 890SEK–1,590SEK ($116–$207) double; 2,330SEK ($303) suite. Rates include breakfast. AE, DC, MC, V. Free parking. Bus: 7B, 1B, or 2. **Amenities:** Restaurant; bar; Jacuzzi; sauna; laundry service; dry cleaning; nonsmoking rooms; rooms for those w/limited mobility. *In room:* TV, dataport, hair dryer.

INEXPENSIVE

Hotel Högvakten ⭐ *Value*   A 5-minute walk from the ferryboat terminal for boats headed across the straits to Denmark, this Best Western hotel was built as a private town house in 1914. Its well-designed interior underwent a radical renovation in 1996. The recently refurbished rooms are bright and fresh, and generally quite spacious. State-of-the-art bathrooms come with tub/showers and are extremely well maintained. Only breakfast is served, but a member of the polite, attentive staff can direct you to restaurants—many within easy walking distance from the hotel.

Stortorget 14, PO Box 1074, SE-251 10 Helsingborg. (©) 800/780-7234 in U.S. and Canada, or 042/38-04-90. Fax 042/38-04-99. www.hotelhogvakten.com or www.bestwestern.com. 40 units. Mid-June to mid-Aug and Fri–Sun year-round 810SEK–910SEK ($105–$118) double; rest of year 1,250SEK–1,350SEK ($163–$176) double. Rates include breakfast. AE, DC, MC, V. Parking 100SEK ($13). Bus: 7A, 7B, 1A, or 1B. **Amenities:** Breakfast room; sauna; limited room service; laundry service; dry cleaning; nonsmoking rooms. *In room:* TV, dataport, hair dryer.

Hotell Linnéa ⭐ *Finds*   Conveniently located a few yards from where ferries from Denmark pull in, this is a pleasant, small-scale hotel that occupies a pink Italianate house, built in 1897. The scale and detailing might remind you of something in a historic neighborhood of New Orleans. Guest rooms are appealingly outfitted, with comfortable beds and high-quality furnishings that include tasteful reproductions of 19th-century antiques. Bathrooms are small but adequate and come mostly with tub/showers. Only breakfast is served, but many reliable dining choices are close by.

Prästgatan 4, S-252 24 Helsingborg. (C) 042/37-24-00. Fax 042/37-24-29. www.hotell-linnea.se. 30 units. July–Aug and Fri–Sat year-round 795SEK–995SEK ($103–$129) double; rest of year 1,030SEK–1,250SEK ($134–$163) double, 1,350SEK–1,600SEK ($176–$208) suite. Rates include breakfast. AE, DC, MC, V. Parking 110SEK ($14). Bus: 7A or 7B. **Amenities:** Breakfast room; bar; laundry service; dry cleaning. *In room:* TV.

Hotell Viking   In the center of town, less than 2 blocks north of the Drottninggatan, this hotel looks more historic, more cozy, and a bit more artfully cluttered than many of its more formal and streamlined competitors. It was built during the late 19th century as a row of shops where the owners usually lived upstairs from their businesses. Today, after a radical remodeling in the mid-1990s, you'll find a carefully preserved sense of history; a pale color scheme of grays, beiges, and ochers; and a hands-on management style by the resident owners. Guest rooms are cozy, neat, and functional. Bathrooms are a bit small, but adequately outfitted with tub/showers.

Fågelsångsgatan 1, S-252 20 Helsingborg. (C) 042/14-44-20. Fax 042/18-43-20. www.hotellviking.se. 40 units. Mid-June to July and Fri–Sun year-round 765SEK–865SEK ($99–$112) double; rest of year 1,345SEK ($175) double. Rates include breakfast. AE, DC, MC, V. Free parking. Bus: 7A, 7B, 1A, or 1B. **Amenities:** Breakfast room; bar; laundry service; dry cleaning; nonsmoking rooms; rooms for those w/limited mobility. *In room:* TV, minibar, hair dryer.

WHERE TO DINE

Anna Kock ★★ SWEDISH   Decorated with the kind of antique knickknacks you might find in a Swedish farmstead, and modern Swedish watercolors, this cozy restaurant contains only 11 well-tended tables. Opened in 1989, it was named after "Anna the Cook," a locally famous chef to the region's early-20th-century bourgeoisie and aunt of the present owners, Claes and Sussan Andren. Menu items reflect the best of both modern and old-fashioned culinary techniques. Your meal might include Anna's pickled herring served with a Dutch bleu cheese sauce, filet of reindeer on a bed of morels and lingonberry sauce, breast of wild duck with kumquat sauce and rhubarb chutney, fried filet of lemon sole with vermouth sauce and whitebait roe, or sautéed eggplant on a bed of mushrooms with pasta and tomato sauce. Lunches are simpler and less expensive than the carefully executed dinners that are the norm here.

Järnvägsgatan 23. (C) 042/18-13-00. Reservations recommended at dinner. Main courses 125SEK–195SEK ($16–$25); lunch platters 65SEK ($8.45); 2-course fixed-price dinner 195SEK ($25). AE, DC, MC, V. Tues–Fri 11am–2pm and 5:30–10pm; Sat noon–10:30pm. Bus: 3, 5, 7, 9, or 12.

Elinor ★ SWEDISH/CONTINENTAL   One of the best restaurants in town, Elinor is in a modest 1920s house on a pleasant walkway in the town center. There's a small bar for aperitifs and a well-upholstered dining room outfitted in soft pastels. The menu depends on seasonal changes. Though less influenced by nouvelle cuisine than it was in the past years, the restaurant offers well-prepared and often tantalizing dishes, such as marinated herring with Swedish caviar and an onion and sour-cream sauce, filet of reindeer with fresh morels, a ragout of shrimp with chanterelles, and unusual preparations, based on the seasons, of crayfish, lobster, turbot, salmon, trout, pheasant, duck, and partridge. Desserts often showcase such semiwild fruits as lingonberries, cloudberries, and blueberries. Plans are in the works for a less expensive wine bar annex.

Kullagatan 53. ⓒ **042/12-23-30.** Reservations required. Main courses 150SEK–280SEK ($20–$36); fixed-price lunch 85SEK–145SEK ($11–$19); fixed-price dinner 380SEK–565SEK ($49–$73). AE, DC, MC, V. Mon–Sat 11:30am–2:30pm and 6–10:30pm. Closed July and lunch in early Aug. Bus: 1 or 6.

Gastro ★★ CONTINENTAL/FRENCH   Set within a modern, big-windowed building of yellow brick overlooking the city's historic core, this is one of the best restaurants in Helsingborg. Within a room decorated with birchwood veneer, pale tones of monochromatic gray, and a medley of riveting modern paintings, you can enjoy specialties based on Swedish ingredients, prepared using Mediterranean culinary techniques. Menu items vary with the season, but our favorites are pan-fried scallops with sun-dried and marinated tomatoes, served with a terrine of green peas, or a superb fried breast of duckling with onions, carrots, and *prosciutto*. Expect lots of fresh fish from the straits of Helsingborg and the Baltic, and lots of savoir-faire from the well-versed, attentive staff.

Södra Storg 11–13. ⓒ **042/24-34-70.** Reservations recommended. Main courses 80SEK–280SEK ($10–$36). AE, DC, MC, V. Mon–Sat 7–10pm. Closed July. Bus: 11.

Pälsjö Krog SWEDISH   Set within a 10-minute drive north of the center of Helsingborg, this brightly painted yellow wood-sided building was originally constructed around 1900 as a bathhouse beside the beach. As such, it was filled at the time with cubicles for seabathers to change clothes. In the late 1990s, it was transformed into a cozy Swedish restaurant, the kind of place where local families—often with grandmothers in tow—come to enjoy recipes that haven't changed very much since the end of World War II. Within a large dining room painted in tones of pale yellow and decorated with hints of Art Deco, you'll get food items that include grilled pepper steak, sirloin with béarnaise sauce, poached Swedish salmon with dill sauce, and aromatic local mussels steamed with herbs in white wine. Drinkers and smokers appreciate the cozy aperitif bar near the entrance, where cigars are welcomed and where the staff can propose a wide assortment of after-dinner cognacs.

Drottinggatan 151. ⓒ **042/14-97-30.** Reservations not necessary. Main courses 129SEK–219SEK ($17–$28). AE, DC, MC, V. Daily 11:30am–2:30pm and 6–10pm.

Restaurang La Petite *Value* FRENCH/MEDITERRANEAN   In a charming old house that evokes provincial France, this bistro has been going strong ever since it opened its doors in 1975. Still relatively undiscovered by the foreign visitor, it serves classics based on time-tested French recipes. We're talking about those longtime favorites that for decades have characterized French bistro fare: onion soup, savory frog legs, and steaming kettles of mussels in a wine-laced sauce studded with garlic. Basically, it's an uncomplicated, good-tasting cuisine of the type the French might call comfort food. You're welcomed at this pleasant little spot, the waitstaff inviting you to enjoy their tasty dishes in which they seem to take a justified pride.

Bruksgatan 19. ⓒ **042/21-97-27.** Reservations required on weekends only. Main courses 155SEK–239SEK ($20–$31). AE, DC, MC, V. Mon–Sat 11:30am–2pm; Mon–Thurs 5:30–10pm; Fri–Sat 5:30–11pm.

SS Swea SEAFOOD/SWEDISH   This is a restaurant ship at Kungstorget that is furnished like luxury cruisers that used to cross the Atlantic. It offers market-fresh food deftly handled by skilled chefs and served in a cozy ambience by a thoughtful waitstaff. Some of the best and most freshly caught seafood at the port is presented here in a wide-ranging menu guaranteed to appeal to most tastes. Appetizers might range from everything from iced gazpacho to a Greek salad studded with feta cheese. However, most diners prefer one of the fish starters, especially the smoked salmon. Fish platters, which depend on the catch of the day, also dominate the main course agenda. Our recently served flounder, served with bacon-flavored mushrooms, was superb in every way. The meat eater will find comfort in a classic pepper steak with *pommes frites,* among other offerings. You might also try the filet mignon, laced with Black and White scotch.

Kungstorget. © 042/13-15-16. Reservations required. Main courses 170SEK–245SEK ($22–$32); fixed-price 3-course menu 245SEK ($32). Mon–Thurs 6–10pm; Fri 6–11pm; Sat 1–11pm; Sun 1–8pm.

HELSINGBORG AFTER DARK

Helsingborg has had its own city symphony orchestra since 1912. In 1932, its **Concert Hall,** or *Konserthuset,* opened at Drottninggatan 19 (© 042/10-42-70). One of the finest examples of 1930s Swedish functionalism, today the hall is still the venue for performances by the 50-piece orchestra. The season opens in the middle of August with a 10-day *Festspel,* a festival with a different theme every year. Tickets are available at the **Helsingborg Stadsteater City Theater,** Karl Johans Gata (© 042/10-68-00 or 042/10-68-10), which dates from 1817. Today's city theater is one of the most modern in Europe; of course, performances are in Swedish.

With a decor that includes crystal chandeliers and lots of original paintings (which often are rotated with works by various artists), **Marina Nightclub,** Kungstorget 6 (© 042/19-21-00), is set within the Hotel Marina Plaza. It admits only clients 24 or older. It's open Friday and Saturday 11pm till around 5am.

An English-inspired pub that draws a busy and sometimes convivial crowd is **Telegrafen,** Norra Storgatan 14 (© 042/18-14-50), where live music, especially jazz, is presented on either of two levels devoted to maintaining a cozy environment for drinking, chatting, and flirting. Live-music enthusiasts should also consider an evening at one of the largest jazz venues in Sweden, **Jazzklubben,** Nedre Långvinkelsgatan 22 (© 042/18-49-00). Keynote nights include Wednesday, Friday, and Saturday, when live Dixieland, blues, Celtic ballads, and progressive jazz are featured beginning around 8:30pm. Most other nights, based on a schedule that varies with the season and the whims of the staff, the place functions as a conventional bar.

2 Malmö ★ ★

285km (177 miles) S of Gothenburg, 618km (383 miles) SW of Stockholm

Sweden's third-largest city, a busy port across the Øresund sound—now linked by the Øresund Bridge from Copenhagen—is the capital of Skåne and a good base for exploring the ancient castles and nearby manor. It's an old city, dating from the 13th century.

From early days, Malmö (pronounced mahl-*mer*) prospered because of its location on a sheltered bay. In the 16th century, when it was the second-largest city in Denmark, it vied with Copenhagen for economic and cultural leadership. Reminders of that age are **Malmöhus Castle** (see below), the **Town Hall,** and the **Stortorget,** plus several homes of rich burghers. Malmö has been a Swedish city since the end of a bloody war in 1658, when the Treaty of Roskilde incorporated the province of Skåne into Sweden.

ESSENTIALS

GETTING THERE   By Plane   Malmö's airport (© 040/613-11-00) is at Sturup, 30km (19 miles) southeast of the city. It receives international flights from London, plus flights from cities within Sweden, including Gothenburg

Malmö

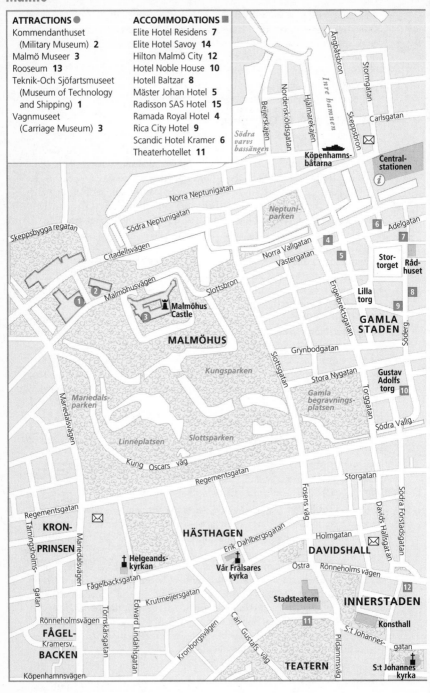

ATTRACTIONS ●

Kommendanthuset
(Military Museum) **2**
Malmö Museer **3**
Rooseum **13**
Teknik-Och Sjöfartsmuseet
(Museum of Technology
and Shipping) **1**
Vagnmuseet
(Carriage Museum) **3**

ACCOMMODATIONS ■

Elite Hotel Residens **7**
Elite Hotel Savoy **14**
Hilton Malmö City **12**
Hotel Noble House **10**
Hotell Baltzar **8**
Mäster Johan Hotel **5**
Radisson SAS Hotel **15**
Ramada Royal Hotel **4**
Rica City Hotel **9**
Scandic Hotel Kramer **6**
Theaterhotellet **11**

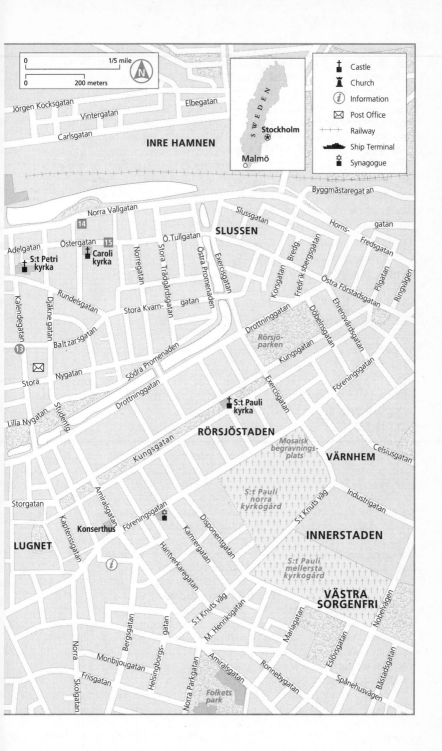

Legend:
- Castle
- Church
- Information
- Post Office
- Railway
- Ship Terminal
- Synagogue

Jörgen Kocksgatan
Vintergatan
Carlsgatan
Elbegatan

INRE HAMNEN

SWEDEN
Stockholm
Malmö

Byggmästaregatan

Norra Vallgatan

Slussgatan
Horns-
gatan
Fredsgatan

SLUSSEN

14
Östergatan **15**
Adelgatan
† **S:t Petri kyrka**
† **Caroli kyrka**
Ö.Tullgatan
Norregatan
Stora Trädgårdsgatan
Östra Promenaden
Exercisgatan
Bredg.
Korsgatan
Fredrik sbergsgatan
Östra Förstadsgatan
Pilgatan
Ringvägen

Rundelsgatan
Stora Kvarn- gatan
Kalendegatan
Djäkne gatan
Baltzarsgatan
13
Nygatan
Drottninggatan
Rörsjö-parken
Kungsgatan
Döbelnsgatan
Ehrensvärdsgatan
Föreningsgatan

Stora
Södra Promenaden
Drottninggatan
Exercisgatan

Lilla Nygatan
Studentg.

† **S:t Pauli kyrka**

RÖRSJÖSTADEN

Mosaisk begravnings-plats

VÄRNHEM
Celsiusgatan

Kungsgatan

Amiralsgatan
Storgatan
Kaptensgatan
Konserthus
Föreningsgatan
† **S:t Pauli norra kyrkogård**
S:t Knuts väg
Industrigatan

LUGNET

Disponentgatan
Kamrergatan
Hantverkaregatan
INNERSTADEN

S:t Pauli mellersta kyrkogård

VÄSTRA SORGENFRI
Nobelvägen

Bergsgatan
Norra
Uatö6
S:t Knuts väg
M. Henriksgatan
Mariagatan
Esbjörsgatan
Båstadsgatan
Monbijougatan
Helsingborgs-
Norra Parkgatan
Amiralsgatan
Ronnebygatan
Spånehusvägen
Friisgatan
Skolgatan
Folkets park

(trip time: 50 min.) and Stockholm (trip time: 1 hr.). Two airlines that serve the airport are **Malmö Aviation** (℃ **040/660-29-00**) and **SAS** (℃ **770/727-727**). The city's major international link to the world is Copenhagen Airport at Copenhagen, to which Malmö is connected by hovercraft service.

By Train   The Stockholm-Copenhagen express train has a branch service through to Malmö (℃ **040/202-000**). Service is frequent between Gothenburg and Malmö (trip time: 3½-hr.). From Helsingborg to Malmö (trip time: 45 min.), trains leave hourly. From Stockholm, travel is 4½ hours aboard the high-speed X-2000 train, 6 to 7 hours aboard slower trains. There also is train service between Copenhagen and Malmö. Trains depart from the central railway stations of both cities at 20-minute intervals. The cost each way is 88SEK ($11).

By Bus   Two buses daily make the 4½-hour run from Gothenburg to Malmö. For bus information, call **Travelshop** (℃ **040/33-05-70**).

By Car   From Helsingborg, motorists can head southeast along Route 110 directly into the center of Malmö.

VISITOR INFORMATION   The **Malmö Tourist Office,** Central Station Skeppsbron 2 (℃ **040/34-12-00;** www.malmo.se), is open Monday to Friday 9am to 7pm, and Saturday and Sunday 10am to 5pm.

GETTING AROUND   It's easy to walk around the city center, although you may need to rely on public transport if you're branching out to sights on the periphery. An individual bus ticket costs 15SEK ($1.95) and is valid for 1 hour. You also can purchase a 200SEK ($26) magnetic card, which offers a slight reduction on the fare and can be used by several passengers at the same time. Both types of tickets are sold on the bus. (You must have exact change.)

SEEING THE SIGHTS

The **Malmö Card,** which is available from the Malmö Tourist Office, entitles visitors to free admission to most of the city's museums during the period of its validity. It also grants free parking, free bus travel within the city limits, and discounts in selected shops and restaurants. A card that's valid for 1 day costs 130SEK ($17); one that's valid for 2 days goes for 160SEK ($21); one that's valid for 3 days is 190SEK ($25). An adult who has a Malmö card can be accompanied, with no additional charge, by two children up to 16 years old.

The Renaissance-era square surrounding the **fountain** on Stortorget is important architecturally, but the fountain itself is one of the most imaginative in Scandinavia and includes a nightingale, the symbol of Malmö. Built in 1964, it commemorates the most important events in the city's history—for example, when the Swedes took the city back from the Danes in 1710.

Dominating Stortorget is the town hall, or **Rådhuset,** which still retains its look of Renaissance splendor. It dates from 1546 but was restored by Helgo Zetterwall in the 1860s. It borders the east side of the square. It is especially impressive when illuminated at night. In the center of the square stands an equestrian statue of Carl X Gustav commemorating the return of Skåne to Sweden from Denmark in 1658. There are occasional tours of the interior; check with the tourist office (see above).

Nearby lies **Lilla Torg** ★★, Malmö's most charming square, an attractive cobbled square with many fine half-timbered buildings dating from the 16th to the 18th centuries—it looks like a film set. In addition to its fountains and cafes, many handicraft shops are found here. For many centuries this was the bustling open-air marketplace of Malmö, however, in the 20th century, a covered market replaced the open-air booths and stalls. Today a modern market building also houses a number of restaurants. In summer, there are a lot of jewelry stalls.

Four major attractions are under the direction of Malmö Museer (© 040/341-000). Heading the list is **Malmöhus Castle,** on Malmöhusvägen, founded in the 15th century by Eric of Pomerania and rebuilt by Christian III in the 16th century. Once a prison (the earl of Bothwell, third husband of Mary Queen of Scots, was incarcerated here in 1568–73), the castle now houses the **City Museum,** the **Natural History Museum,** the **Aquarium** and **Tropicarium,** and the **Konstmuseet** ✿✿. The last contains a collection of old Scandinavian masters, especially those from southern Sweden, such as Carl Fredrik Hill (1849–1911), one of Sweden's best landscape painters and a forerunner of European modernism. Most interesting is the collection of Russian oil paintings from around 1900—the largest collection outside Russia. It also houses some modern art and good samples of Swedish furniture and textiles. The lyrical sketches in the foyer are by Carl Larsson, one of Sweden's best-known artists. West of Stortorget, the castle can be easily reached on foot.

Also in the group, across the street from the castle, is **Kommendanthuset,** Malmöhusvägen, a military museum and a piece of history in its own right, displaying military artifacts and equipment. **Teknik-Och Sjöfartsmuseet (Museum of Technology),** on Malmöhusvägen, is near the Kommendanthuset. Ancient means of communication are exhibited, as well as the submarine *U-3.* Technical history from the steam engine to the jet can be traced. The children's department even has a pirate ship, and in summer an old-fashioned tramway is in operation. The **Vagnmusset (Carriage Museum),** housed in the former military horse stable at Drottningtorget, displays carriages from the 18th century, coaches, and cycles.

We recommend buying a ticket, costing 40SEK ($5.20) for adults, 10SEK ($1.30) for children 7 to 15 years old, which admits you to all sites mentioned above if visited on the same day. The museums are open September to May noon to 4pm, June to August 10am to 4pm.

Malmö's **St. Petri (St. Peter's Church)** ✿, on Göran Olsgatan (© 040/35-90-43), lies a block east of the Rådhus. Dark and a bit foreboding on the exterior, it is light and airy within. This Gothic church originated in the 14th century, when Malmö was under the control of the Hanseatic League, and was modeled on Marienkirche, a famous church in Lübeck, Germany. Other than the slender pillars and supporting ogive vaulting, the church's most stunning feature is its **Krämarkapellet,** or tradesmen's chapel, from the 1400s. Amazingly, the original artwork remains. At the Reformation, the artwork here was viewed as "redundant," and the chapel was sealed off, which, in effect, protected its paintings from the overzealous "restoration" of the reformers. Look for the impressive New Testament figures surrounded by decorative foliage on the vaulted ceiling. Also notice the tall retable from 1611 and an exquisitely carved black limestone and sandstone pulpit from 1599. The octagonal baptismal font from 1601, as well as the pulpit, were the work of master craftsman Daniel Tommisen. The church is open Monday to Friday 10am to 4pm, Saturday 10am to 6pm, and Sunday from 10am to 6pm. Admission is free.

A final attraction, **Rooseum** ✿✿, Gasverksgatan 22 (© 040/121-716), is one of the country's most outstanding art museums, installed in what had been an electricity-generating station at the turn of the 20th century. In 1988 it was converted into this elegant museum, the brainchild of Fredrik Ross (1951–91), an art collector whose stated desire was to showcase modern art movements through a series of thematic exhibitions and shows. Although strongest in Nordic art, the exhibitions are international in scope. Hours are Wednesday to Friday 2pm to 8pm, Saturday and Sunday noon to 6pm, and the cost is 40SEK ($5.20).

A NEARBY MUSEUM

Svaneholm, between Malmö and Ystad, was founded in 1530 as a fortress and later was partially converted into an Italian-style palace. Today it houses a museum of paintings, furnishings, and tools dating primarily from the 18th and 19th centuries. The establishment is owned by the Svaneholm Castle Cooperative Society Ltd. For information, write Svaneholm Museum, S-274 00 Skurup (© 0411/400-12).

Admission to the castle is 25SEK ($3.25) for adults and 5SEK (65¢) for children 6 to 14 years old. It's open May, June, and August Tuesday to Sunday 10am to 5pm; July daily 10am to 5pm; September Wednesday to Sunday 11am to 4pm. The castle is open other times upon request. An on-site restaurant (© 0411/450-40) serves regional specialties. Reaching Svaneholm is difficult by public transportation; a train from Malmö stops at Skurup, but it's a walk of about 3km (1¾ miles) from there. Therefore, many visitors opt to go by taxi the rest of the way. During the summer, the castle offers free transportation from Skurup, but you must call 1 hour in advance.

SHOPPING

Malmö's main pedestrian shopping street is **Södergatan,** which leads south of Stortorget toward the canal. Alternatively, if you haven't found what you are looking for in the specialty shops below, try **Hansa Companiet,** Stora Nygatan 50 (© 040/77-000), Malmö's Continental mart, a shopping complex with more than 40 shops, cafes, and restaurants. The latest fashions and items for the home are among the many specialties featured here. However, most foreign visitors come by to check out its selection of Swedish souvenirs and handicrafts.

BOOKS

Åkards Antikvariat   This is one of the largest secondhand bookstores in Scandinavia. Some of its volumes—very rare indeed and superexpensive—are said to date from the dawn of the printing press. Books of all shapes, sizes, and subjects can be found, even the latest John Grisham thriller. Hundreds of the titles are in English. Klostergata. © 046/211-24-99.

COINS

Lunds Mynthandel   Arguably the best coin shop in Scandinavia is this outlet, which also sells books on numismatics. Its rarest coins—virtually museum pieces—date from 600 B.C., making them among the most ancient in Europe. Klostergata 5. © 046/144-36.

CRYSTAL & GLASSWARE

Juvelerare Hugo Nilsson   This shop, established in 1927, features some of the most famous names in Danish jewelry-making, including Georg Jensen, Rauff, and Ole Lynggaard. Jewelry by Finnish designers such as Lapponia also is sold. Södra Tullgatan 2. © 040/12-65-92.

FASHION

Mattssons Päls   This is one of Sweden's leading furriers. Saga mink coats and jackets are the most luxurious buys, but Mattssons has a full range of fine furs at prices lower than in the United States. In the boutique are fur-lined poplins and accessories, all tax-free for tourists. The store lies a 5-minute walk from the Central Station and the Copenhagen boats. Norra Vallgatan 98. ℂ 040/12-55-33.

HANDICRAFTS

Ålgamark *(Finds)* An unusual collection of Nordic arts and crafts is sold at Ålgamark, where you'll find Viking jewelry (replicas in pewter, bronze, silver, and gold), along with handicrafts from Swedish Lapland. Traditional pendants, bracelets, and knives are also sold. Östra Rönneholmsvägen 4. ℂ 040/97-49-60.

Form Design Centre Nearby, at 16th-century Lilla Torg, you can visit this museum-like exhibition space with boutiques selling upscale handicrafts, including Swedish textiles by the yard, woodcarvings, and all manner of other crafts. Lilla Torg 9. ℂ 040/664-51-50.

WHERE TO STAY
EXPENSIVE

Hilton Malmö City ✰✰ Malmö's most visible international luxury hotel rises 20 stories from a position in the commercial heart of town. Built in 1989, it boasts sweeping views of the Öresund region from almost all its bedrooms. The top three floors contain only suites and a well-engineered health club. Many of the guests are business travelers, often attending one of the dozens of conventions that attract participants from throughout Europe. The spacious rooms are tastefully and comfortably appointed, with light colors, and many electronic amenities. The bathrooms are luxurious and equipped with tub/showers. Suites are among the best in town, with kitchenettes and large sitting areas. Some of the suites have their own Jacuzzi.

Triangeln 2, S-200 10 Malmö. ℂ 040/693-47-00. Fax 040/693-47-11. www.hilton.com. 214 units. June 24–Aug 7 and Fri–Sat year-round 1,090SEK ($142) double; rest of year 1,220SEK–1,990SEK ($159–$259) double; 4,530SEK ($589) suite. Rates include breakfast. AE, DC, MC, V. Parking 90SEK ($12). Bus: 14 or 17. **Amenities:** 2 restaurants; bar; fitness center; sauna; business services; 24-hr. room service; babysitting; laundry service; dry cleaning; nonsmoking rooms; rooms for those w/limited mobility. *In room:* A/C, TV, dataport, minibar, hair dryer, iron/ironing board.

Hotel Noble House ✰✰ One of the most modern and up-to-date hotels in town—and certainly the most glamorous—is named after the best-selling novel by James Clavell (the former owner was a great devotee of the writings of Clavell). The comfortable pastel-colored rooms are decorated with copies of early-20th-century Swedish paintings. Because of the four-story hotel's convenient location in the town center, its quietest rooms face the interior courtyard. Each room has a standard hotel-size bathroom with a tub/shower.

Gustav Adolfs Torg 47, S-211 39 Malmö. ℂ 040/664-30-00. Fax 040/664-30-50. www.hkchotels.se. 130 units. June 24–Aug 15 and Fri–Sat year-round 950SEK ($124) double, 1,450SEK ($189) suite; rest of year 1,545SEK ($201) double, 2,145SEK ($279) suite. Rates include breakfast. AE, DC, MC, V. Parking 145SEK ($19). Bus: 10, 11, 17, or 20. **Amenities:** Breakfast room; bar; sauna; laundry service; dry cleaning; nonsmoking rooms; rooms for those w/limited mobility. *In room:* TV, dataport, minibar, hair dryer (in some), safe.

Mäster Johan Hotel ✰ A very personalized choice for a chain hotel, this well-run and comfortable selection lies in the heart of Malmö, close to shopping, entertainment, and transportation, including trains, ferries, and airport buses. Built in 1990 and remodeled at the millennium, it is a restored 19th-century building that has been completely brought up to 21st-century standards with its modern amenities. Bedrooms are midsize, each beautifully maintained and coming with a tiled bathroom with a tub/shower. Grace notes are the wooden oak floors, the Asian carpets, and the cherrywood pieces in French provincial.

Mäster Johanstan 13, S-211 21. © 040/664-64-00. Fax 040/664-64-01. www.masterjohan.se. 69 units. Fri–Sat 1,300SEK–1,500SEK ($169–$195) double; Sun–Thurs 2,045SEK ($266) double; 3,150SEK ($410) junior suite. AE, DC, MC, V. Bus: 14 or 176. **Amenities:** Bar; gym; sauna; 24-hr. room service; laundry service; dry cleaning; nonsmoking rooms; rooms for those w/limited mobility. *In room:* TV, dataport, kitchenette in suites, coffeemaker (in some), hair dryer, iron/ironing board, safe.

Radisson SAS Hotel ⭐ The Radisson SAS contains tastefully decorated rooms, with elegant bathrooms equipped with tub/showers. Built in 1988, the seven-story hotel lies only a 5-minute walk from the train station, which provides transportation to Copenhagen in only 40 minutes. As an added convenience, the hotel bus stops nearby. If you don't want to go out at night, try the hotel's excellent Thott Restaurant, serving both Swedish traditional dishes and international specialties.

Östergatan 10, S-211 Malmö. © 800/333-3333 or 040/698-40-00. Fax 040/698-40-01. www.radissonsas.com. 229 units. June 5–Aug 5 1,211SEK–1,390SEK ($157–$181) double; Aug 6–June 4 Mon–Thurs 2,000SEK–2,200SEK ($260–$286) double; year-round Fri–Sun 1,090SEK–1,390SEK ($142–$181) double; from 3,000SEK ($390) suite. Rates include breakfast. AE, DC, MC, V. Parking 160SEK ($21). Bus: 14 or 17. **Amenities:** Restaurant; bar; sauna; 24-hr. room service; babysitting; laundry service; dry cleaning; nonsmoking rooms; rooms for those w/limited mobility. *In room:* TV, minibar, hair dryer.

MODERATE

Elite Hotel Savoy ⭐ This hotel has figured prominently in Malmö history, as its origins date back to the 14th century. Famous guests have included Dag Hammarskjöld, actress Liv Ullmann, actor Alan Alda, and Johnny ("Tarzan") Weissmuller. It boasts some of the most plushly decorated accommodations in Sweden. Rooms contain champagne-colored upholstery, cabriole-legged or Chippendale-style furniture, excellent beds, and all the extras of a deluxe hotel. Well-maintained bathrooms come in a wide variety of sizes, with tub/showers. In the hotel restaurant, you can order from an international menu, perhaps stopping for a before-dinner beer in the British-style pub, the Bishop's Arms.

Norra Vallgatan 62, S-201 80 Malmö. © 040/66-44-800. Fax 040/66-44-850. www.savoy.elite.se. 109 units. June 19–Aug 9 and Fri–Sat year-round 790SEK–1,050SEK ($103–$137) double; rest of year 1,650SEK–1,850SEK ($215–$241) double; 2,050SEK ($267) suite. Rates include breakfast. AE, DC, MC, V. Parking 145SEK ($19). Bus: 14 or 17. **Amenities:** Restaurant; bar; fitness center; sauna; limited room service; laundry service; dry cleaning; nonsmoking rooms. *In room:* TV, dataport, minibar, hair dryer, safe.

Hotell Baltzar ⭐⭐ *Finds* Around 1900, an entrepreneur who had made a fortune selling chocolate moved into a private home whose turrets, towers, and fanciful ornamentation resembled a stone-carved confection. Several decades later, when it became an elegant and prestigious hotel, it expanded into one of the neighboring buildings. Today you'll find a hotel with many charming corners and cubbyholes. Grace notes include frescoed ceilings, substantial-looking antiques, and elaborate draperies in some of the public areas. The comfortable, high-ceilinged guest rooms have been upgraded, with furnishings (including good beds) and parquet floors that would suit a prosperous private home. The medium-size bathrooms are impeccably maintained and equipped with tub/showers. The location on an all-pedestrian street keeps things relatively quiet inside. Breakfast is the only meal served.

Södergatan 20, S-211 24 Malmö. © 040/665-5700. Fax 040/665-5710. www.baltzarhotel.se. 40 units. Mon–Thurs 1,300SEK–1,700SEK ($169–$221) double; Fri–Sun 850SEK–950SEK ($111–$124) double. Rates include breakfast. AE, DC, MC, V. Free parking. Bus: 10. **Amenities:** Breakfast room; 24-hr. room service; laundry service; dry cleaning; nonsmoking rooms. *In room:* TV, minibar, hair dryer, safe.

Rica City Hotel Built in 1912, the hotel lies on Malmö's main square, facing the Town Hall, a short walk from the railway station and the ferryboat terminals for Copenhagen-bound ships. In 1992 the guest rooms were rebuilt in a taste-ful modern format. The hotel is owned by the Salvation Army, which strictly forbids the consumption of alcohol on the premises. It's also part of a hotel chain (City Hotels) that operates four other Swedish hotels. The rooms are larger than you might expect, and the mattresses are good. Bathrooms tend to be cramped but are well maintained with tub/showers.

Stortorget 15 S-211 22 Malmö. © **040/660-95-50.** Fax 040/660-95-59. www.rica.se. 82 units. Mon–Thurs 1,445SEK–1,545SEK ($188–$201) double; Fri–Sun 950SEK–1,050SEK ($124–$137) double. Rates include breakfast. AE, DC, MC, V. Parking 130SEK ($17). Bus: 17. **Amenities:** Breakfast room; lounge; sauna; laundry service; dry cleaning; nonsmoking rooms. *In room:* TV, minibar, hair dryer.

Scandic Hotel Kramer ⚜ At the side of the town's main square, this château-style twin-towered building is one of Malmö's landmark hotels. Built in 1875, it was renovated at the height of the Art Deco era. Between 1992 and 1994, the rooms were redecorated again with an old-fashioned sense of nostal-gia, vaguely reminiscent of staterooms on a pre–World War II ocean liner. Each has a marble bathroom with a tub/shower, dark paneling, curved walls, and kitschy 1930s-style accessories.

Stortorget 7, S-201 21 Malmö. © **040/693-54-00.** Fax 040/693-54-11. www.scandic-hotels.com. 113 units. 1,995SEK ($259) double; 3,700SEK ($481) suite. Rates include breakfast. AE, DC, MC, V. Parking 185SEK ($24). Bus: 14, 17, or 20. **Amenities:** Restaurant; bar; sauna; limited room service; laundry service; dry cleaning; nonsmoking rooms. *In room:* TV, minibar, hair dryer, Internet.

Theaterhotellet The only negative aspect of this hotel is its banal-looking 1960s-era facade; it's no uglier than hundreds of other contemporaneous Scan-dinavian buildings, but it isn't particularly inviting or pleasing. Inside, however, you'll find a cozy, tasteful, and colorful establishment that attracts many repeat clients. Appealing touches include tawny-colored marble floors, lots of elegant hardwood paneling, lacquered walls in tones of amber and beige, and spots of vibrant colors in the guest rooms (especially jewel tones of red and green) that perk up even the grayest of Swedish winter days. Rooms were renovated in 1996 with new furniture and mattresses, plus new bathrooms with showers and tubs. Less than a kilometer (about ½ mile) south of the railway station, the hotel is near a verdant park and the Stadstsheater. Only breakfast is served, but you can usually get someone to bring you a sandwich and coffee.

Rönngatan 3, S-211 47 Malmö. © **040/665-58-00.** Fax 040/665-58-10. www.teaterhotellet.se. 44 units. Sun–Thurs 1,200SEK–5,500SEK ($156–$715) double; Fri–Sat 750SEK ($98) double; 1,400SEK–1,550SEK ($182–$202) suite. Rates include breakfast. AE, DC, MC, V. Parking 125SEK ($16). Bus: 11. **Amenities:** Break-fast room; bar; limited room service; laundry service; dry cleaning; nonsmoking rooms. *In room:* TV, dataport (in some), minibar (in some), hair dryer.

INEXPENSIVE

Elite Hotel Residens ⚜ *Value* In 1987, a team of local investors enlarged the white-sided premises of a historic 1517 inn with the addition of a new brick-and-stone structure. The interconnected structures provide solid, comfortable, and upscale lodgings near the railroad station. Except for certain corners where an effort was made to duplicate a woodsy-looking men's club in London, many of the public areas are outfitted in a glossy, modern setup with lots of mirrors, touches of chrome, and polished marble floors. Guest rooms are more traditionally outfitted and larger than you might expect. They have hardwood floors or wall-to-wall carpeting, good beds, well-upholstered furnishings, and, in some cases, Oriental carpets. The medium-size bathrooms are equipped with tub/showers. Windows are large and double-insulated against noise from the urban landscape outside.

Adelgatan 7, S-211 22 Malmö. ✆ **040/664-48-90.** Fax 040/664-48-95. www.elite.se. 69 units. June to mid-Aug and Fri–Sat year-round 850SEK ($111) double; rest of year 1,595SEK ($207) double. Rates include breakfast. AE, DC, MC, V. Parking 145SEK ($19). Bus: 14 or 17. **Amenities:** Breakfast room; 24-hr. room service; laundry service; dry cleaning; nonsmoking rooms. *In room:* TV, dataport (in some), minibar, hair dryer.

Ramada Royal Hotel   This hotel, adjacent to a canal in the historic core of Malmö, is composed of three antique buildings. The most visible is a stately early-20th-century neoclassical town house; the oldest dates from the 1500s. Bedrooms are rather small but inviting. Bathrooms are a bit cramped but do contain tub/showers. The owners, the hard-working Kilström brothers, maintain a small conference center and work hard to keep their hotel ship-shape.

Norra Vallgatan 94, S-211 22 Malmö. ✆ **040/664-2500.** Fax 040/12-77-12. www.ramadainternational.com. 38 units. July and Fri–Sat year-round 795SEK–1,495SEK ($103–$194) double, 1,495SEK ($194) suite; rest of year 1,29SEK5–1,495SEK ($168–$194) double, 1,695SEK–1,895SEK ($220–$246) suite. AE, DC, MC, V. Free parking on street 8pm–9am; otherwise, 15SEK ($1.95) per hour 9am–6pm. Bus: 14 or 17. **Amenities:** Breakfast room; bar; laundry service; dry cleaning; nonsmoking rooms. *In room:* TV, dataport, minibar, hair dryer.

WHERE TO DINE
EXPENSIVE
Årstiderna I Kockska Huset ★★ SWEDISH/INTERNATIONAL   One of the most prestigious restaurants in Malmö lies on a "perpetually shadowed" medieval street. It was built in the 1480s as the home and political headquarters of the Danish-appointed governor of Malmö, Jürgen Kock. In its own richly Gothic way, it's the most unusual restaurant setting in town, with vaulted brick ceilings, severe-looking medieval detailing, and a deliberate lack of other kinds of adornment. Owners Marie and Wilhelm Pieplow have created an environment where the prime ministers of Sweden and Finland, as well as dozens of politicians, artists, and actors, have dined on exceedingly good food. Menu items change with the seasons; the establishment's name, *Årstiderna,* translates from the Swedish as "The Four Seasons." Likely to be featured are fried monkfish with parsley butter, salmon roe, and Norwegian lobster; orange-glazed wild duck with flap mushrooms and honey-rosemary sauce; filet of venison in an herb crust with chanterelle mushrooms and juniper-berry sauce; Swedish beefsteak with red wine and potato gratin; and a chocolate terrine with cloudberry sorbet and a compote of blackberries.

Frans Suellsgatan 3. ✆ **040/23-09-10.** Reservations recommended. Main courses 190SEK–355SEK ($25–$46); fixed-price lunch 85SEK–185SEK ($11–$24); fixed-price dinner 330SEK–500SEK ($43–$65). AE, DC, MC, V. Mon–Fri 12:30–11pm; Sat 5–11pm. Bus: 14 or 17.

Hipp ★★ SWEDISH/FRENCH   Set beneath one of the most ornate and stately looking gilded ceilings in Malmö, this restaurant—noted for its superb and often very complex food—has welcomed some of the town's most prestigious visitors. These have included prime ministers, ambassadors, and the Hollywood actor who played the role of Freddy Kruger in the blood-fest *Nightmare on Elm Street.* This spot began life in 1897 as a cabaret theater; and many of its original Belle Epoque embellishments and soaring crystal chandeliers are still in place. Menu items are lavish, French-inspired, and served with panache; they might include a superb breast of duckling with chanterelles, garlic puree, sweetbreads, and Szechuan-style pepper sauce; and roasted lamb with sauerkraut, braised salsify, and truffles. Every Friday and Saturday, the place is transformed into a dance club of the same name.

Kalendegatan 12. ✆ **040/97-40-30.** Reservations recommended. Main courses 170SEK–210SEK ($22–$27); set menu 590SEK ($77). AE, MC, V. Tues–Sat 5–10pm. Closed 2 weeks in July. Bus: 14 or 17.

Johan P ★ (Finds) FISH/SEAFOOD   Some of the most appealing seafood in Malmö is prepared and served in this artfully simple, mostly white dining room. The result is an almost pristine setting where the freshness of the seafood is the main draw. Menu items are prepared fresh every day, based on whatever is available at the nearby *Saluhallen* (marketplace). Examples include an award-winning fish soup that's inspired by the traditions of Provence; a leek-and-potato vichyssoise served with fresh mussels and a timbale of pike; baked monkfish with mustard-flavored spaetzle, served with dried ham and braised cabbage in a tomato-flavored broth; and an old-fashioned version of chicken dumplings with mushroom risotto and sweet-and-sour tomato sauce. Dessert might include a mousse made with bitter white chocolate, served with dark-chocolate madeleines and coffee sauce.

Saluhallen, Landbygatan 3. ⒸⒸ 040/97-18-18. Reservations recommended. Main courses 82SEK–300SEK ($11–$39); 2-course fixed-price menu 285SEK ($37); 3-course fixed-price menu 295SEK ($38). AE, MC, V. Mon–Fri 11:30am–10pm; Sat 11:30am–midnight. Bus: 14 or 17.

Restaurant Kramer Gastronomie ★ CONTINENTAL/FRENCH Accessed through the lobby of the also-recommended hotel, this restaurant serves the best food of any hotel dining room in Malmö. There's an upscale, woodsy-looking bar that's separated from the brown and off-white dining room with a leaded glass divider, and an attention to cuisine that brings a conservative, not particularly flashy clientele back again and again. The composition of the fixed-price menus changes every week, and it's relatively common for a group of business partners to spend 3 hours at table sampling the seven-course *menu dégustation.* The food is faultlessly fresh and handled beautifully by the kitchen staff that believes in delicate seasonings and perfectly cooked dishes. The chef is dedicated to his job, personally shopping for market-fresh ingredients to inspire his imagination. Menu items include shots of shellfish bouillon served with Parmesan chips and coriander salsa; scallops with grilled tuna and bacon; blackened filet of beef with pecorino cheese, lemon wedges, arugula, and a sauce made with a reduction of *court bouillon* and red wine; and chargrilled halibut with glazed turnips, truffle butter, and dill oil. Pastas here are upscale and esoteric, including a version with spinach, crayfish, fried filet of sole, and dill sauce.

In the Scandic Hotel Kramer, Stortorget 7. ⒸⒸ 040/693-54-00. Reservations recommended. Main courses 200SEK–350SEK ($26–$46); 3-course fixed-price menu 310SEK ($40). AE, DC, MC, V. Mon–Fri 5–11pm; Sat 6–11pm. Bar open till 1am. Bus: 10.

MODERATE

Centiliter & Gram ★ CONTINENTAL   This is one of Malmö's hottest restaurants, with a hipster clientele that includes lots of well-known painters and football (soccer) stars, as well as dozens of media and PR people. It occupies an artfully minimalist gray-and-mauve-colored space whose focal point is a centrally placed bar. Guests often stay to flirt long after their dishes have been cleared away. Menu items change with the seasons and with whatever food fad happens to be in vogue in London, Stockholm, or Paris at the time. Stellar examples include a parcel of Italian goat cheese baked in phyllo pastry with a tomato and basil sauce; black mussels with white wine and cream sauce served with a tomato *bruschetta;* deliberately undercooked (that is, "pink") duck breast with teriyaki sauce and an orange and mango-flavored chutney; and grilled halibut and scallops with a spicy Thai red curry, coconut milk, and jasmine-flavored rice. The establishment's name, incidentally, derives from wine (which is measured in centiliters) and food (which is measured in grams).

Stortorget 17. ⓒ **40/12-18-12.** Reservations recommended. Main courses 110SEK–225SEK ($14–$29). AE, DC, MC, V. Wed–Thurs 5:30pm–1am; Fri–Sat 5pm–3am. Bus: 10.

Lemongrass ASIAN   Lemongrass is set in one large, spartan room that's devoid of the artsy clutter of many Asian restaurants. Instead, on pale gray walls, you'll find clusters of exotic-looking orchids, as well as tufted bunches of the lemon grass for which it was named. There's a bar where you can wait for your table, if you have to, and a menu that contains food items from Japan (including sushi), China, and Thailand. A staff member will help you coordinate a meal from disparate culinary styles in ways that you might have expected only in Los Angeles, London, or New York.

Grunbodgatan 9. ⓒ **40/30-69-79.** Reservations recommended. Main courses 115SEK–197SEK ($15–$26); 7-course fixed-price menu 325SEK ($42). AE, MC, V. Mon–Thurs 6pm–midnight; Fri–Sat 6pm–1am. Bus: 6 or 10.

Rådhuskällern *Value* SWEDISH   This is the most atmospheric place in Malmö, located in the cellar of the Town Hall. Even if you don't eat here, at least drop in for a drink in the pub or lounge. The severe exterior and labyrinth of underground vaults were built in 1546; the dark-vaulted dining room was used for centuries to store gold, wine, furniture, and food. Menu staples include halibut with lobster sauce, plank steak, filet of veal, pepper steak, and roast duck; and there's always an array of daily specials. Although the fare is first-rate here, it never overexcites the palate.

Kyrkogatan 5. ⓒ **040/790-20.** Reservations recommended. Main courses 185SEK–190SEK ($24–$25); 1-course lunch 75SEK ($9.75). AE, DC, MC, V. Mon–Fri 11:30am–2pm and 6–11pm; Sat 6–11pm. Bus: 14 or 17.

Salt & brygga ⭐ *Finds* SWEDISH/MEDITERRANEAN   Opening onto a large patio with a panoramic view of the Öresund, this post-millennium restaurant was immediately hailed as restaurant of the year the moment it opened. It is an organic dining room, serving healthful food from the province of Skåne cooked with the influences of the Mediterranean kitchen. There is a large selection of organic wine, cider, and beer. Built along the quayside, it is an atmospheric place at which to dine and is unique in this part of Sweden. Guests dine in relative simplicity, enjoying freshly prepared dishes that are especially noteworthy in the offerings of shellfish-studded casseroles. The smoked coalfish (*saithe* on the menu) makes a fine and tasty appetizer. We are also especially fond of their different versions of risotto. Vegetarians gravitate to the savory vegetable lasagna, which somehow doesn't taste bland. Desserts are prepared fresh daily and don't overly rely on sugar for their appeal.

Sundspromenade 7. ⓒ **040/611-59-40.** Reservations recommended. Main courses 150SEK–245SEK ($20–$32); fixed-price lunch 89SEK ($12). AE, DC, MC, V. Mon–Fri 11:30am–3pm and 6–10pm.

Wallman's Salonger CONTINENTAL   Large enough for 400 diners at a time, and painted a heady shade of bordeaux red, this is the most entertaining restaurant in Malmö—with a most entertaining staff. At one end of the restaurant is a stage upon which members of the staff—each a candidate for a job in the theater—will sing, dance, and wonderfully amuse you. Meals consist of an assortment of steaks, soups, salads, seafood, veal, or pork dishes; they are flavorful, although not particularly spectacular, but since most clients are gyrating on the dance floor before 11pm anyway, no one especially cares.

Generalsgatan 1. ⓒ **040/74945.** Reservations recommended. 3-course fixed-price menus 380SEK–495SEK ($49–$64). AE, DC, MC, V. Wed–Sat 7:30pm–3am. Kitchen closes at 11pm. Closed May to mid-Aug.

~SENTIALS

~TTING THERE **By Train** Trains run hourly from Malmö (see earlier in ~ chapter), only a 15-minute ride. Call ✆ **0771/77-77-77.**

~Bus Buses also arrive hourly from Malmö, but they take 30 minutes. Call **0771/77-77-77.**

~Car From Gothenburg, head south along E6; Malmö and Lund are linked ~ an express highway, only a 20-minute drive.

~SITOR INFORMATION The tourist information office, **Lunds Turist-~rå,** at Kykogatan 11 (✆ **046/35-50-40**), is open June to August Monday to Fri-~y 10am to 6pm, and Saturday and Sunday 10am to 2pm; September to May ~onday to Friday 10am to 5pm.

~EEING THE SIGHTS

~otaniska Trädgården (Botanical Gardens) A block east of the cathedral, ~ese gardens contain some 7,500 specimens of plants gathered from all over the ~orld. On a hot summer day, this is the most pleasant place to be in Lund. Clus-~ers of students congregate here, stretching out beneath the trees, and families ~ften use the grounds to enjoy a picnic lunch. Serious horticulturists should visit ~hen the greenhouses are open.

~östra Vallgatan 20. ✆ 046/222-73-20. Free admission. Gardens daily 6am–8pm; greenhouses daily ~noon–3pm. Bus: 1, 2, 3, 4, 5, 6, or 7.

Domkyrkan (Cathedral of Lund) ★★★ With this ancient cathedral, Romanesque architecture in Scandinavia reached its height; the **eastern exterior** ★★ of the church is one of the finest expressions of Romanesque architecture in northern Europe. The sandstone interior has sculptural details similar in quality and character to those in Lombardy and other parts of Italy. There also is a **crypt** ★★★ with a high altar dedicated in 1123, and intricately carved **choir stalls** ★★★ from about 1375.

A partly reconstructed 14th-century **astronomical clock** not only tells the time and the date, but stages a splashy Middle Ages–style tournament—complete with clashing knights and the blare of trumpets. And that's not all: The three wise men come out to pay homage to the Virgin and child. To see all this, time your visit to the cathedral for when the clock strikes noon (1pm on Sun) or ~3pm.

~Kyrkogatan. ✆ 046/35-87-00. Free admission. Mon–Fri 8am–6pm; Sat 9am–5pm; Sun 9am–6pm. Bus: 1, 2, ~, 4, 5, 6, or 7.

~istoriska Museet Founded in 1805, this is the second-largest museum of ~archaeology in Sweden. Collections trace the development of the people of ~kåne from antiquity to the Middle Ages. One of the skeletons displayed here is ~at of a young man dating from around 7000 B.C.—one of the oldest human ~keletons found in northern Europe. Most collections from the Bronze Age ~me from tombs. During excavations in eastern Skåne, a large grave field was ~nearthed; the jewelry and weapons found are on display. The medieval exhibi-~n is dominated by church art.

~oftstorg 1. ✆ 046/222-79-44. Admission 30SEK ($3.90) adults, 15SEK ($1.95) children 12–18, free for ~dren under 11. Tues–Fri 11am–4pm; Sun noon–4pm. Closed Mon and Sat. Bus: 1, 2, 3, 4, 5, 6, or 7.

~lturen (Museum of Cultural History) ★★ After leaving the cathedral, ~lk across the university grounds to *Adelgatan*, which the local citizens consider ~ir most charming street. Here you'll find Kulturen, another of Sweden's open-air

INEXPENSIVE

Anno 1900 ★ *Finds* SWEDISH The name of this place gives a hint about its decor, which includes lots of antique woodwork and accessories from the heyday of the Industrial Revolution. There's a garden in back that's open during warm weather, if you want a break from turn-of-the-20th-century fussiness. Menu items derive from tried-and-true classics: old-fashioned versions of cauliflower soup, halibut with horseradish sauce, chicken dumplings with noodles, roasted beef, steaks, *frikadeller* (meatballs), and fried herring. If you have a Swedish grandmother, bring her here—she'll feel right at home.

Norra Bultoftavagen 7. ✆ 040/18-47-47. Reservations recommended. Main courses 100SEK–225SEK ($13–$29); fixed-price lunch 110SEK ($14). AE, DC, MC, V. Mon–Fri 11:15am–2pm; Tues–Thurs 6–11pm. Bus: 14 or 17.

Casa Mia ITALIAN Venetian gondola moorings ornament the front terrace of this Nordic version of a neighborhood trattoria. Troubadours stroll from table to crowded table singing Neapolitan ballads, and your waiter is likely to address you in Italian. You might begin with a steaming bowl of *stracciatella alla romana* (egg-and-chicken soup) or the fish soup of the house, then move on to penne with shrimp, basil, cream, and tomatoes, or spaghetti with seafood. Later you can dig into *saltimbocca alla romana* (veal with ham), a portion of grilled scampi, escalope of veal stuffed with goose liver, or an array of grilled meats with aromatic herbs. There are more than 15 types of pizza on the menu, and pastries are offered for dessert. Okay, it's not as good as the food served in a typical trattoria in northern Italy, but the cuisine is a refreshing change of pace.

Södergatan 12. ✆ 040/23-05-00. Reservations recommended. Pastas and pizzas 87SEK–135SEK ($11–$18); 1-course *dagens* (daily) menu 98SEK ($13). AE, DC, MC, V. Mon–Sat noon–midnight; Sun noon–11pm. Bus: 14 or 17.

Restaurant B & B (Butik och Bar) SWEDISH/INTERNATIONAL This well-managed, relatively inexpensive bistro is in a corner of the *Saluhallen* (food market), which provides the fresh ingredients that go into each menu item. In a simple, old-fashioned setting, with glowing hardwood floors, pristine white walls, and a scattering of antiques that evokes the Sweden of long ago, you'll find flavorful, unpretentious food. It's international cuisine, with occasional emphasis on Swedish staples known to every grandmother, including creamy fish soup in the Swedish style. Most of the other dishes are more exotic, including New Orleans versions of jambalaya, Cajun-inspired tagliatelle with blackened chicken and fiery sauces, teriyaki pork, roasted chicken with tiger prawns, and pasta with a salmon-flavored vodka sauce.

Saluhallen, Landbygatan 52. ✆ 040/12-71-20. Reservations recommended. Main courses 80SEK–130SEK ($10–$17); fixed-price lunch 65SEK ($8.45). AE, DC, MC, V. Mon–Sat noon–10pm. Bus: 14 or 17.

MALMÖ AFTER DARK

For serious after-dark pursuits, many locals, especially young people, head for nearby Copenhagen. However, there are several local amusements, as well, the best of which are previewed below.

From May to September, locals head for **Folkets Park (People's Park),** Amiralsgatan 35 (✆ **040/709-90**), where sprawling amusement grounds and pleasure gardens, dancing pavilions, vaudeville performances, and open-air concerts all draw big crowds. Children will enjoy the playhouse, small zoo, reptile center, and puppet theater. Restaurants also dot the grounds. Hours are daily from 3pm to midnight in summer, noon to 6pm in winter. Admission is free; however, some performances require an admission price of 50SEK to 110SEK ($6.50–$14). Take bus no. 11, 13, or 17 from the Gustav Adolfs Torg.

Dancing is the rage at the creatively designed **Nightclub Etage,** Stortorget 6 (© **040/23-20-60**). Initially conceived as an upscale bar and restaurant in the late 1980s, this nightspot lowered its prices and began marketing to a mass audience in the early 1990s. Despite its lowered expectations, the bar has not seemed to suffer as a result. It's reached by climbing a circular staircase from an enclosed courtyard in the town's main square. Satellite bars open and close regularly on every floor. The complex is open Monday and Thursday through Saturday from 11pm to at least 4am, depending on the crowd. Cover for the dance club ranges from 60SEK to 80SEK ($7.80–$10).

Many love affairs, some of which have segued into marriages, have gotten a boost at **Swing Inn,** Hamburgsgatan 3 (© **040/12-22-21**), where romantic dancing is the norm. Attendees tend to be over 35 and the recorded music is reminiscent of a '60s variety show. There's a restaurant on the premises serving platters of traditional Swedish food Thursday to Saturday between 10 and 11:30pm. Main courses cost from 120SEK to 175SEK ($16–$23). Music and bar activities are scheduled on Thursday 10pm to 1am, Friday from 10pm to 3am, and Saturday from 10pm to 4am. The cover charge is 80SEK ($10) after 11pm.

The largest nightclub in Malmö, **Club Privée,** Malmborgsgatan 7 (© **040/97-46-66**), contains five floors and tends to attract a slightly younger (20–25) clientele on Friday than it does on Saturday (20–30). Set near the Gustav Adolfs Torg, in the center of town, it has a decor that replicates an English pub—there are, for example, lots of Chesterfield sofas. There's a bar, and different music is played on each of the establishment's five floors. It's open only on Friday and Saturday nights from 11pm to 5am. The cover ranges from 80SEK to 100SEK ($10–$13), and a large beer costs 45SEK ($5.85).

Nostalgic for Britain? The best replica of a British pub is the **Bishop's Arms,** Norra Vallgatan 62 (© **040/664-48-88**), at the Savoy Hotel. Some of the best and coldest beer in town is served here, and there's always a congenial crowd.

Those seeking cultural activities after dark should get tickets to the Malmö Symphony Orchestra, which is renowned across Europe. It performs at the **Konserthus,** Föreningsgatan 35 (© **040/630-45-06**). The tourist office distributes programs of other cultural events.

3 Lund ✶✶

18km (11 miles) NE of Malmö, 302km (187 miles) S of Gothenburg, 602km (373 miles) SW of Stockholm

Lund was probably founded in 1020 by Canute the Great, ruler of the United Kingdom of England and Denmark, when this part of Sweden was a Danish possession. However, the city's 1,000-year anniversary was celebrated in 1990 because archaeological excavations show that a stave church was built here in 990. The city really made its mark when its cathedral was consecrated in 1145, after which Lund quickly became a center of religion, politics, culture, and commerce for all of Scandinavia.

The town has winding passageways, centuries-old buildings, and the richness of a university town. Lund University, founded in 1666, continues to play an active role in town life.

The most exciting time to be in Lund, as in Uppsala, is on Walpurgis Eve, April 30, when student revelries signal the advent of spring, but a visit to Lund at any time is a pleasure.

ACCOMMODATIONS ■
Best Western Hotel Djingis Khan **1**
Grand Hotel **3**
Hotel Concordia **4**
Hotel Lundia **2**
Scandic Star **9**

ATTRACTIONS ●
Botaniska Trädgården (Botanical Gardens) **8**
Domkyrkan (Cathedral of Lund) **5**
Historiska Museet **7**
Kulturen (Museum of Cultural History) **6**

museums. This one contains reassembled sod-roofed farms and manor houses, a carriage museum, ceramics, peasant costumes, Viking artifacts, old handicrafts, and even a wooden church moved to this site from the glassworks district.

Tegnérsplatsen. (©) **046/35-04-00.** Admission 50SEK ($6.50) adults, free for children. Apr 15–Sept daily 11am–5pm; Oct–Apr 14 Tues–Sun noon–4pm. Bus: 1, 2, 3, 4, 5, 6, or 7.

WHERE TO STAY

The tourist office (see above) can help you obtain housing in **private homes** for as little as 225SEK ($29) per person per night.

Best Western Hotel Djingis Khan ★ *Finds*   Within a 15-minute walk north of the town center, this hotel was originally built in the 1970s as employee housing for a local hospital. It became a pleasant, well-managed hotel in the early 1990s. Two of its wings still contain private apartments, but it's mostly made up of attractively modern guest rooms outfitted in a conservatively comfortable style. They have good beds and small but adequate bathrooms with shower stalls. Public areas contain lots of English-inspired dark paneling, Chesterfield sofas, and an ambience that might remind you of a private men's club in London.

The hotel's name, incidentally, comes from the most famous satirical comedy *(Ghenghis Khan)* ever produced in Lund. It was written in the 1950s by Hasse Alfredsson, and this hotel was named in its honor.

Margarethevägen 7, S 222 40 Lund. (©) **800/780-7234** in the U.S. and Canada, or 046/33-36-10. Fax 046/46-33-36-10. www.djingiskhan.se or www.bestwestern.com. 55 units. Sun–Thurs 1,595SEK ($207) double; Fri–Sat 800SEK ($104) double. Rates include breakfast. AE, DC, MC, V. Closed July. Free parking. Bus: 3 or 93. **Amenities:** Restaurant; bar; indoor pool; fitness center; sauna; 24-hr. room service; laundry service; dry cleaning; nonsmoking rooms; rooms for those w/limited mobility. *In room:* TV, dataport, minibar, hair dryer.

Grand Hotel ★★   This château-style hotel, the most prestigious in town, overlooks the fountains and flowers of a city park. The marble lobby is grand. Rooms in the hotel's conical corner tower are the most desirable. All the guest rooms are decorated in old-fashioned style. The bathrooms are moderate in size, with tub/showers.

Bantorget 1, S-221 04 Lund. (©) **046/28-06-100.** Fax 046/28-06-150. www.grandilund.se. 84 units. June 7–Aug 8 and Fri–Sat year-round 995SEK–1,590SEK ($129–$207) double, 2,900SEK ($377) suite; Aug 9–June 6 1,795SEK–2,275SEK ($233–$296) double, 4,200SEK ($546) suite. Rates include breakfast. AE, DC, MC, V. Parking 100SEK ($13). Bus: 1, 2, 3, 4, 5, 6, or 7. **Amenities:** Restaurant; bar; fitness center; sauna; limited room service; laundry service; dry cleaning; nonsmoking rooms. *In room:* TV, dataport, minibar, hair dryer.

Hotel Concordia ★   Next door to the brick house where August Strindberg lived in 1897, this charming, ornate building was constructed in 1882 as a private home. It served as a student hotel for some time and was then upgraded to serve a broader clientele. The modernized rooms are moderate in size and sedate, with good beds. The bathrooms are a bit small, but equipped with neatly kept showers. Housekeeping here is among the finest in town. The hotel is a 5-minute walk south of the railroad station.

Stålbrogatan 1, S-222-24 Lund. (©) **046/13-50-50.** Fax 046/13-74-22. www.concordia.se. 65 units. Sun–Thurs 1,520SEK ($198) double; Fri–Sat 950SEK ($124) double; 1,800SEK ($234) suite. Rates include breakfast. AE, DC, MC, V. Parking 50SEK ($6.50). Bus: 1, 2, 3, 4, 5, 6, or 7. **Amenities:** Breakfast room; lounge; fitness center; sauna; laundry service; dry cleaning; nonsmoking rooms. *In room:* TV, dataport, minibar, hair dryer, iron.

Hotel Lundia   Under the same management as the Grand Hotel (see above), this is the most pleasantly situated and one of the most modern hotels in town, lying in the vicinity of the train station. The interior has winding staircases, white marble sheathing, and big windows. Guest rooms have adequately sized tile bathrooms with tub/showers and are designed with Scandinavian fabrics and unusual lithographs. Most units are moderate in size; singles are a bit cramped.

Knut den Stores Gata 2, S-221 04. © **046/280-65-00.** Fax 046/280-65-10. www.lundia.se. 97 units. Late June to early Aug and Fri–Sat year-round 995SEK ($129) double; rest of year 1,995SEK ($259) double; 2,100SEK–4,100SEK ($273–$533) suite. Rates include breakfast. AE, DC, MC, V. Parking 100SEK ($13). Bus: 1, 2, 3, 4, 5, 6, or 7. **Amenities:** Restaurant; bar; limited room service; laundry service; dry cleaning; non-smoking rooms; rooms for those w/limited mobility. *In room:* TV, dataport, minibar, hair dryer, safe.

Scandic Star 🞯 This hotel, a 20-minute walk from the town center, is the most comfortable in Lund. Built in 1991, it attracts lots of business conventions, as well as rock stars and movie actors known throughout Sweden. Each of the hotel's double rooms is configured as a minisuite, with a separate sitting area and traditional, conservative furnishings that would fit into a well-appointed upper-middle-class Swedish home. The public areas are more international and contemporary than the bedrooms and have lots of potted or hanging plants, wicker furniture, and well-maintained bathrooms with tub/showers.

Glimmervägen 5, PO Box 11026, SE-220 11 Lund. © **046/285-25-00.** Fax 046/285-25-11. www.scandic-hotels. com. 196 units. Mid-June to mid-Aug and Fri–Sat year-round 880SEK ($114) double; rest of year 1,590SEK ($207) double; 1,600SEK–3,900SEK ($208–$507) suite. AE, DC, MC, V. Free parking. Bus: 3 or 7. **Amenities:** Restaurant; bar; indoor pool; fitness center; sauna; limited room service; laundry service; dry cleaning; non-smoking rooms; rooms for those w/limited mobility. *In room:* TV, minibar, hair dryer, iron, safe.

WHERE TO DINE

Barntorget 9 🞯 SWEDISH/CONTINENTAL Charming and traditional, this restaurant occupies a white-painted, wood-sided structure that, at the time of its construction in the 1860s, contained three separate residences and that later functioned as a bakery, a motorcycle repair shop, and a clothing store. Today, in a much-gentrified form, amid frescoed ceilings, flower pots, and holders for the candles (up to 120 per night) that illuminate this place, you'll enjoy a sophisticated medley of ingredients cooked in Swedish, and sometimes vaguely French, ways. The best examples include marinated mussels and snails in garlic sauce, traditional Swedish meatballs and duck breast with orange sauce, and minced veal with cream-based gravy and mashed potatoes. Other excellent choices include roast lamb, tournedos of veal, braised pike-perch, and pan-fried lemon sole. It lies within a very short walk of Lund's railway station.

Barntorget 7–9. © **046/32-02-00.** Reservations recommended. Main courses 165SEK–215SEK ($21–$28). AE, DC, MC, V. Mon–Thurs 6–10pm; Fri–Sat 6–11pm. Bus: 2 or 4.

Brasserie Lundia SWEDISH This brasserie is the only restaurant in Lund with its own in-house bakery. At lunch, when it's one of the most popular cafeterias in town, it serves crisp salads, open-faced sandwiches, and hot dishes as part of the full cafeteria meals. At night, it's an a la carte restaurant with waitress service, serving steak tartare, fettuccine with salmon, tagliatelle bolognese, grilled filet mignon, grilled pork cutlet with pepper sauce, deep-fried Camembert, and seven kinds of alcohol-rich after-dinner coffees. Although no one ever accused the kitchen staff of being overly experimental here, what you get isn't bad. Everything is well prepared, and there's good, relaxed service. It has an inviting decor with wood and russet-colored marble tables.

In the Hotel Lundia, Knut den Stores Gata 2. © **046/280-65-00.** Reservations required Fri–Sat. Main courses 125SEK–180SEK ($16–$23). AE, DC, MC, V. Mon–Fri 11:30am–11:30pm; Sat 1–10pm; Sun 1–11pm. Bus: 1, 2, 3, 4, 5, 6, or 7.

Dalby Gästgifveri 🞯 *Finds* SWEDISH If you really want to flatter the pride of the local residents of this hamlet (pop. 2,000), you'll acknowledge that the village inn, Dalby Gästgifveri, is the oldest of its kind in Skåne. That isn't completely true, however, as the house that contains it has burned to the ground (and been rebuilt) at least twice since 1870. But during excavations conducted on the village church next door, evidence was unearthed that supports the belief that a tavern and inn associated with the church was serving food and drink to passersby in the 12th century. So come to this tavern knowing that there has been a tradition of innkeeping here for a long, long time. The wood-sided structure is painted in the colors of the Skanish flag (ocher and oxblood red). Within a pair of street-level dining rooms loaded with rustic antiques, from a church-side location in the heart of the village, you'll enjoy menu items that local homes have served in Skåne for many decades. Fine examples include smoked eel with lemon sauce, yellow-tomato soup, a Skanish omelet laced with pork and served with lingonberries, roasted lamb with rosemary, entrecote with garlic butter sauce, and an all-vegetarian main course, corn schnitzels (a form of fritter). The restaurant is a 15-minute drive east of Lund.

Tengsgatan 6, in Lund's suburban hamlet of Dalby. © 046/20-00-06. Reservations recommended. Main courses 80SEK–190SEK ($10–$25); fixed-price lunch (available Mon–Fri only) 75SEK ($9.75). AE, DC, MC, V. Mon–Fri 11:30am–8pm; Sat 1–8pm; Sun 1–5pm. Bus: 160 from Lund.

Gloria's Bar and Restaurant AMERICAN   The success of this American-inspired sports and western bar would gladden the heart of any U.S.-born ideologue. On two floors of an old-fashioned building in the historic center of town, it has a crowded and likable bar in the cellar and an even larger bar upstairs. Scattered throughout the premises are photographs and posters of American sports heroes, baseball and football memorabilia, and Wild West artifacts. Draft beer costs 49SEK ($6.35) for a foamy mug. The restaurant serves copious portions of such rib-stickers as hamburgers and steaks, and an array of Cajun-inspired dishes. The staff wears jeans, cowboy boots, and shirts emblazoned with Gloria's logo. Various styles of live music are performed between 9:30 and 11:30pm each Thursday. Friday and Saturday feature a disc jockey spinning rock.

St. Petri Kyrkogata 9. © 046/15-19-85. Reservations recommended. Main courses 99SEK–249SEK ($13–$32). AE, MC, V. Mon–Fri 11:30am–10:30pm; Sat 12:30–11pm; Sun 1–11pm. Bus: 1, 2, 3, 4, 5, 6, or 7.

Ø Bar ★ *(Finds* INTERNATIONAL   One of the most interesting restaurants in Lund defines itself as a "laboratory for chefs" because of the experimental nature of a menu that changes virtually every week. The venue looks like it might have been designed by a Milanese post-modernist, with blue and ash-white walls and a strictly minimalist kind of angularity. It's usually mobbed every night both with diners and with clients of the convivial bar area. Here you're likely to meet students from the university *and* their professors, all animated in dialogue. Menu items include filet of elk with thyme sauce, served with apple and potato muffins; grilled halibut served with lemon oil, horseradish, and house-made pasta; and lime-flavored clam chowder with Vietnamese spring rolls.

Mårtenstorget 9. © 046/211-22-88. Reservations recommended. Main courses 95SEK–195SEK ($12–$25). AE, DC, MC, V. Daily 11:30am–midnight; bar until 1 or 2am. Bus: 1 or 2.

Staket *(Value* SWEDISH/CONTINENTAL   An old tavern that serves good food in an unspoiled atmosphere, this establishment occupies the cellar and street level of a 15th-century building. The step-gabled brick facade is a historic landmark. Menu items include crabmeat cocktail, lobster or goulash soup, white filet of pork, tournedos of beef, a mixed grill, marinated salmon, pickled herring, baked potatoes with black curry, and whitefish toast. Although both dining rooms are equally appealing, fondues (a ritual in which skewers of meat are cooked at your table in pots of heated oil) are served only in the cellar.

Stora Södergatan 6. © **046/211-93-67**. Reservations recommended. Main courses 155SEK–190SEK ($20–$25). AE, DC, MC, V. Mon–Thurs noon–10:30pm; Fri–Sat noon–11:30pm; Sun noon–10pm. Bus: 1, 2, 3, 4, 5, 6, or 7.

LUND AFTER DARK

Most dance clubs in Lund tend to operate only on weekends, when the clientele includes many students from the nearby university. Examples include **Tegner's Restaurant,** Sandgatan 2 (© **046/131-333**), which has a dance floor in the basement of the already-recommended **Gloria's Restaurant,** every Friday and Saturday beginning at 10:30pm. Entrance is free. Another dance choice, also open only Friday and Saturday, is the **Palladium,** Stora Södergatan 13 (© **046/ 211-66-60**), a beer pub with a college-age clientele. Admission is free.

With its small dance floor, **Basilika,** Stora Södergatan 13 (© **046/211-66-60**), occasionally hosts live bands from England or Europe. The big nights here are Friday and Saturday, when a 50SEK ($6.50) cover charge is imposed. A final hot spot is **Stortorget,** Stortorget 1 (© **046/139-290**), which has a DJ at night and a surprising age requirement (for a university town). You must be over 22 to enter.

SIDE TRIPS FROM LUND

From Lund, you may want to make a side trip to **Dalby Church** ⭐, 5-240 12 Dalby (no phone), in Dalby, 13km (8 miles) east of Lund. This starkly beautiful, well-preserved 11th-century former bishop's church built of stone is the oldest church in Scandinavia; be sure to visit its crypt. Open daily from 9am to 4pm. Several buses a day (nos. 158 and 161) run between Lund center and Dalby.

About a 30-minute drive northeast of Lund (off Rte. 23) is the **Castle of Bosjökloster** ⭐⭐, Höör (© **0413/250-48**). Once a Benedictine convent founded around 1080, it was closed during the Reformation in the 16th century. The great courtyard is spectacular, with thousands of flowers and exotic shrubs, terraces, and a park with animals and birds. Indoors is the vaulted refectory and the stone hall where native arts and crafts, jewelry, and other Swedish goods are displayed. You can picnic on the grounds or enjoy lunch at a simple restaurant in the garden for 100SEK ($13).

The entire complex is open daily from May 1 to September 30 from 8am to 8pm; the museum and exhibition hall inside the castle, daily from 10am to 6pm. Admission is 60SEK ($7.80) for adults, seniors, and students; free for children up to age 16. In the park stands a 1,000-year-old oak tree. The castle lies 45km (28 miles) from Malmö and 29km (18 miles) from Lund. From Lund, there's a train link to Höör. Once at Höör, take the "ring bus" marked Bösjokloster which travels 5km (3 miles) south on Route 23 to the castle.

4 Ystad ⭐

55km (34 miles) E of Malmö, 46km (29 miles) W of Simrishamn

Ystad makes a good base for exploring the castles and manors of Skåne. An important port during the Middle Ages, Ystad retains its ancient look, with about 300 half-timbered houses, mazes of narrow lanes—even a watchman who sounds the hours of the night in the tower of St. Mary's Church.

Devotees of the silent screen know of Ystad as the birthplace of Valentino's "beautiful blond Viking" Anna Q. Nilsson, who was born here in 1890 and whose fame at one time was greater than that of Greta Garbo, a fellow Swede. Some of Nilsson's greatest films were *In the Heart of a Fool* (1921); *Ponjola*

(1923), in which she played a boy; and *Midnight Lovers,* finished in 1925, the year of a horseback-riding accident that ended her career. Today she is remembered mainly for appearing in a cameo role as one of the "waxworks" in the 1950 Gloria Swanson classic *Sunset Boulevard.*

ESSENTIALS

GETTING THERE   By Train   There are good rail connections between Malmö and Ystad. From Monday to Saturday trains run roughly on the hour between Malmö and Ystad, taking 1 hour. On Sunday, there are only six daily trains from Malmö. For more information, call **0771/777-77-77.**

By Bus   There are three daily buses Monday to Saturday from Malmö to Ystad, taking 1 hour. On Sunday, there is only one bus.

By Car   From Malmö, head east on Route 65. For more information, call ℂ **0200/21818.**

VISITOR INFORMATION   The tourist bureau, **Ystads Turistbyrå,** St. Knuts Torg, (ℂ **0411/577681;** www.ystad.se), is at the bus station in the same building as the art museum *(Konstmuseum).* It's open from November to May Monday to Friday 9am to 5pm; June to August Monday to Friday 9am to 8pm, Saturday 10am to 7pm, Sunday 11am to 6pm; September to October Monday to Friday 9am to 6pm, Saturday 11am to 2pm.

SEEING THE SIGHTS

St. Maria Kyrka   The focal point of the town is this church dating from the early 1200s. Every century that followed brought new additions and changes. Regrettably, many of its richest decorative features were removed in the 1880s because of changing tastes. However, some of the more interesting ones were brought back in a restoration program occurring 4 decades later. The chancel with the ambulatory is late Gothic, and the church spire dates from 1688. Inside, look for the baptismal chapel with a richly carved German altar from the 15th century. The font came from Lübeck, Germany, in 1617, and the iron candelabra is a very early one from the 1300s. The early-17th-century baroque pulpit also is worth a look.

Stortorget. ℂ **0411/69-20-0.** Free admission. June to mid-Sept daily 10am–6pm.

Museum of Modern Art (Ystads Konstmuseum)   Permanent exhibits feature mainly Scandinavian and Danish art from the last 100 years, and there also is a small military museum. The Ystad Tourist Office is in the same building as the museum.

St. Knuts Torg. ℂ **0411/57-72-85.** Admission 30SEK ($3.90). Tues–Fri noon–5pm; Sat–Sun noon–4pm.

City Museum (in the Grey Friars Monastery) (Stadsmuséet i Gråbrödraklostret)   This is the only museum in Sweden residing in a medieval monastic house. Constructed in 1267, the building is a monument from the Danish era in the town of Ystad. Various antiquities in the museum trace the history of the area.

St. Petri Kykoplan. ℂ **0411/577-286.** Admission 30SEK ($3.90). Mon–Fri 10am–5pm; Sat–Sun noon–4pm.

WHERE TO STAY

Hotell Continental ✸✸   Although it has modern appointments, this is one of Skåne's oldest hotels, dating from 1829. The rooms are furnished in tasteful Italian-inspired decor and have a number of modern extras. The bathrooms are well proportioned and equipped with tub/showers. A restoration added marble sheathing to the lobby and gleaming crystal chandeliers. The hotel owners take a personal interest in the welfare of their guests. It's opposite the train station and close to the ferry terminal.

Hamngatan 13, S-271 00 Ystad. © **0411/137-00.** Fax 0411/125-70. www.hotelcontinental-ystad.se. 52 units. June 21–Aug 4 and Fri–Sat year-round 940SEK–1,090SEK ($122–$142) double; rest of year 1,090SEK–1,300SEK ($142–$169) double. AE, DC, MC, V. Parking 20SEK ($2.60). **Amenities:** Restaurant; bar; limited room service; babysitting; laundry service; nonsmoking rooms; rooms for those w/limited mobility. *In room:* TV, dataport, hair dryer.

Hotel Tornväktaren *(Value)*   Much of the charm of this simple bed-and-breakfast hotel derives from its hard-working owner, Mr. Roy Saifert. His home is a turn-of-the-20th-century stone-built, red-trimmed structure with a garden, 10 minutes on foot from the railway station. Rooms are outfitted in pale pastels with lots of homey touches that include frilly curtains, wall-to-wall carpeting, and lace doilies covering painted wooden furniture. Units with bathrooms have neatly kept showers. All rooms are nonsmoking. Other than a filling morning breakfast, no meals are served.

St. Östergatan 33, S-271-34 Ystad. © **0411/784-80.** Fax 0411/729-27. 9 units, 5 with bathroom. 790SEK ($103) double with bathroom; 690SEK ($90) double without bathroom. Rates include breakfast. AE, MC, V. Free parking. **Amenities:** Breakfast room; lounge. *In room:* TV.

Ystads Saltsjöbad *(Finds)*   Beautifully situated on 4 hectares (10 acres) of forested land beside the sea, this hotel is close to Sweden's southernmost tip. It was built in 1897 by one of the most famous opera stars of his day, Swedish-born Solomon Smith. Designed as a haven for the Gilded Age aristocracy of northern Europe, it consists of three connected four-story buildings with big-windowed corridors, set close to the sands of an expansive beach. The guest rooms are comfortably furnished in turn-of-the-20th-century style. Each unit has a neatly kept bathroom with a tub/shower. All rooms are nonsmoking. About half of them were refurbished in the mid-1990s.

The clientele changes throughout the year. In the summer, the hotel caters to beachgoers; in the winter, it's often filled with corporate conventions. The neighborhood provides good opportunities for healthful pastimes such as tennis and golf.

Saltsjöbadsgatan 6, S-271 39 Ystad. © **0411/136-30.** Fax 0411/55-58-35. www.ystadssaltsjobad.se. 108 units. June 19–Aug 26 1,080SEK–1,140SEK ($140–$148) double; Sept–June 18 1,110SEK–1,190SEK ($144–$155) double; year-round Mon–Thurs 3,390SEK ($441) suite; year-round Fri–Sun 2,050SEK ($267) suite. AE, DC, MC, V. Closed Dec 23–Jan 6. Free parking. **Amenities:** Restaurant; bar; cafe; 2 pools (1 indoor); spa; sauna; limited room service; laundry service; dry cleaning. *In room:* A/C, TV, dataport (in some), hair dryer.

WHERE TO DINE

Lottas Restaurang INTERNATIONAL   Fans praise it as one of the most popular and bustling restaurants in town; its detractors avoid it because of slow service by a small staff that sometimes seems impossibly overworked. Everyone awards high marks, however, for the well-prepared cuisine. Meals are served in a brick dining room within a century-old building that once functioned as a private home. The menu runs to conservative, old-timey Swedish cuisine, which might include fried and creamed filet of cod with dill-flavored boiled potatoes, pork schnitzels with asparagus and béarnaise sauce, tenderloin of pork with mushrooms in cream sauce, and marinated breast of chicken with roasted potatoes. For dessert, try warm chocolate cake with ice cream.

Stortorget 11. © **0411/788-00.** Reservations recommended. Main courses 152SEK–182SEK ($20–$24). AE, DC, MC, V. Mon–Sat 5–10pm.

Restaurant Bruggeriet ★ SWEDISH/INTERNATIONAL This novel restaurant was originally built in 1749 as a warehouse for malt. In 1996, a team of local entrepreneurs installed a series of large copper vats and transformed the site into a pleasant, cozy restaurant and brewery. Today they specialize in two "tastes" of beer—a lager and a dark—that are marketed under the brand name *Ysta Färsköl*. Depending on their size, they sell for 27SEK to 48SEK ($3.50–$6.25) per mug. Food items served here seem carefully calibrated to taste best when consumed with either of the two beers. Examples include fried herring marinated in mustard and sour cream and served with mashed potatoes, grilled salmon with red-wine sauce, marinated and baked Swedish lamb with garlic and herbs, tenderloin steak with brandy sauce, and a succulent version of barbecued ribs you might have expected in New Orleans.

Långgatan 20. ☎ 0411/69-9999. Reservations recommended. Main courses 138SEK–215SEK ($18–$28). AE, DC, MC, V. Mon–Fri 11:30am–10pm; Sat-Sun noon-midnight.

Sandskogens Vardshus *(Finds* SWEDISH Set about 1.5km (1 mile) east of Ystad's center, this structure was originally built in 1899 as a summer home for the town's mayor. It was converted to a restaurant in the 1930s, and ever since, it has provided local diners with well-prepared Swedish specialties that include marinated mussels; toast with whitebait roe, sour cream, and onions; fried brill with caramelized butter sauce; turbot with shrimp and Swedish caviar; gratin of lobster with lemon sole; and lingonberry or cloudberry parfait (in season).

Saltsjøvagen, Sandskogen. ☎ 0411/147-60. Reservations recommended. Main courses 110SEK–205SEK ($14–$27); fixed-price lunch 125SEK ($16); fixed-price dinner 225SEK ($29). AE, DC, MC, V. Daily 11:30am–10pm. Closed Jan–Feb.

Store Thor SWEDISH/FRENCH One of the most reliable lunchtime restaurants in Ystad occupies a series of vaulted cellars that were built as part of a monastery in the 1500s. Several hundred years later, the Rådhus (Town Hall) was reconstructed after a disastrous fire above the monastery's cellars. Today, amid small tables and romantic candlelight, you can enjoy such tasty dishes as shellfish soup with saffron, beef filet stuffed with lobster, marinated and grilled tenderloin steak, grilled angler-fish with basil-cream sauce, saddle of lamb with fresh herbs, and roast reindeer with mushrooms and game sauce.

Stortorget 1. ☎ 0411/185-10. Main courses 98SEK–195SEK ($13–$25). AE, DC, MC, V. Mon–Sat 11:30am–4pm and 5-10pm; Sun 4–9pm.

5 Simrishamn

630km (391 miles) S of Stockholm, 95km (59 miles) E of Malmö, 40km (25 miles) E of Ystad

One of the most idyllic towns along the Skåne coastline, Simrishamn features old half-timbered buildings, courtyards, and gardens. This seaport is the jumping-off point to the Danish island of Bornholm.

ESSENTIALS

GETTING THERE **By Train** Ten trains a day (eight on Sat and Sun) make the 45-minute run between Malmö and Simrishamn. For information, call ☎ 0771/77-77-77.

By Bus Nine buses per day arrive from Kristianstad (four a day on Sat–Sun), and 10 buses per day arrive from Ystad (three on Sat–Sun). From Lund, there are eight daily buses. Tickets can be purchased onboard these buses. Call ☎ 0771/77-77-77.

By Car   From Ystad, our last stopover, continue east along Route 10.

VISITOR INFORMATION   For information about hotels, boardinghouses, summer cottages, and apartments, check with the tourist bureau. **Simrishamns Kommun Turistbyrå,** Tullhusgatan 2 (© **0414/160-60**), is open June to August Monday to Friday 9am to 8pm, Saturday 10am to 8pm, and Sunday 11am to 8pm; September to May Monday to Friday 9am to 5pm.

SEEING THE SIGHTS

Other than the charming little town itself, there isn't much to see after you've walked through the historic core. (The major attractions are in the environs; see the following.) The Old Town is a maze of fondant-colored tiny cottages that in some ways evoke a movie set. The chief attraction is **St. Nicolai Kirke,** Storgatan (© **0414/41-24-80**). It's open June to September Monday to Saturday 10am to 6:30pm, Sunday noon to 6:30pm; October to May Monday to Friday 10am to 3pm, Saturday 10am to 1pm.

Originally constructed as a fisherman's chapel in the 12th century, the church literally dominates the town. It's built of chunky sandstone blocks, with a brick porch and step gables. Over the years there have been many additions. A nave was added in the 1300s, although the vault dates from the 1400s. Inside look for the flamboyantly painted pulpit from the 1620s. The pews and votive ships on display were installed much later, in the 1800s. Outside you'll see two sculptures, both by Carl Milles, called *The Sisters* and *Angel with Trumpet.*

NEARBY ATTRACTIONS

Backakra   Located off the coastal road between Ystad and Simrishamn is the farm that Dag Hammarskjöld, the late United Nations secretary-general, purchased in 1957 and intended to make his home. Although he died in a plane crash before he could live there, the old farm has been restored according to his instructions. The rooms are filled with gifts to Mr. Hammarskjöld—everything from a Nepalese dagger to a lithograph by Picasso.

The site is 31km (19 miles) southwest of Simrishamn and can be reached by the bus from Simrishamn marked YSTAD. Likewise, a bus from Ystad, marked SIMRISHAMN, goes by the site. Scheduling your return might be difficult because of infrequent service—check in advance.

Other than the caretakers, the site is unoccupied most of the year, with the exception of 18 members of the Swedish Academy, who are allowed to use the house for meditation and writing whenever they want.

S-270 20 Loderup. © **0411/52-66-11.** Admission 30SEK ($3.90) adults, free for children. June 8–Aug 16 daily noon–5pm; May 16–June 7 and Aug 17–Sept 20 Sat–Sun noon–5pm. Closed Sept 21–May 15.

Glimmingehus   Located 10km (6¼ miles) southwest of Simrishamn, this bleak castle was built between 1499 and 1505. It's the best-preserved medieval keep in Scandinavia, but the somewhat Gothic, step-gabled building is unfurnished. Visitors can order snacks or afternoon tea at a cafe on the premises. June through August, a guided tour in English leaves at 2pm every day. Lots of events take place in summer, including theatrical presentations, lectures, medieval meals with entertainment, and even a medieval festival in August.

Hammenhög 276 56. © **0414/186-20.** Admission 50SEK ($6.50) adults, 30SEK ($3.90) children 7–18 years old. Daily 10am–6pm. Closed Nov–Mar. From Simrishamn follow Rte. 10 southwest for 10km (6¼ miles) to the village of Hammenhög and then follow the signs.

Kivik Tomb   Discovered in 1748, this remarkable find, Sweden's most amazing Bronze Age relic, is north of Simrishamn along the coast of Kivik. In a 1931 excavation, tomb furniture, bronze fragments, and some grave carvings were uncovered. Eight floodlit runic slabs depict pictures of horses, a sleigh, and what appears to be a fun-loving troupe of dancing seals. You can reach the site by car.

Bredaror. No phone. Admission 10SEK ($1.30). Daily 10am–6pm. Closed Sept–Apr. From Simrishamn follow Rte. 10 northwest to the village of Kivik, at which point the tomb is signposted.

WHERE TO STAY

Hotel Kockska Gården (✔alue)   An unspoiled black-and-white half-timbered coaching inn, this hotel is built around a large medieval courtyard in the town center. Its lounge combines the old and new, with a stone fireplace contrasted with balloon lamps. The guest rooms have been modernized, and the furnishings are up-to-date with tastefully coordinated colors and good beds. Bathrooms tend to be small but do contain neatly kept shower units. The only meal served is breakfast.

Storgatan 25, S-272 31 Simrishamn. ℂ **0414/41-17-55.** Fax 0414/41-19-78. 18 units. 790SEK–990SEK ($103–$129) double. Rates include breakfast. AE, MC, V. Free parking. **Amenities:** Breakfast room; lounge; nonsmoking rooms. *In room:* TV.

Ramada Hotel Svea ⚐   Painted pale yellow, with a red-tile roof like those of older buildings nearby, this is the best-recommended hotel in town and the site of a fine restaurant (**Restaurant Svea,** see below). Although much of what you'll see today was rebuilt and radically renovated in 1986, the origins of this waterfront hotel in the town center date from around 1900. Many of its well-appointed, conservatively comfortable rooms overlook the harbor; all rooms have good beds and medium-size bathrooms equipped with tub/showers. The hotel's only suite, the Prince Eugen, is named after a member of the royal family of Sweden who stayed here shortly after the hotel was built.

Strandvägen 3, S-272 31 Simrishamn. ℂ **800/854-7854** in U.S. and Canada, or 0414/41-17-20. Fax 0414/143-41. www.ramadainternational.com. 59 units. 1,090SEK–1,590SEK ($142–$207) double. AE, DC, MC, V. Free parking. **Amenities:** Restaurant; bar; sauna; laundry service; dry cleaning; nonsmoking rooms; rooms for those w/limited mobility. *In room:* TV, dataport, hair dryer, safe.

WHERE TO DINE

Restaurant Svea ⚐ SWEDISH/INTERNATIONAL   The best restaurant in town lies within the pale yellow walls of the recommended Hotel Svea. Within a modern, mostly beige room whose windows overlook the harbor, the kitchen focuses on very fresh fish pulled from local waters. However, the kitchen also turns out beef, pork, chicken, and some exotic meats, such as grilled filet of ostrich (the chef added it to the menu mainly as a conversational oddity). Other menu items include strips of smoked duck breast in lemon sauce, a platter of artfully arranged herring that can be prepared at least three different ways, filet of fried sole with white-wine or tartar sauce, fish of the day prepared au gratin with shrimp and lobster sauce, medallions of pork with béarnaise sauce, and a succulent filet of beef with salsa-style tomato sauce.

In the Hotel Svea. Strandvägen 3. ℂ **0414/41-17-20.** Reservations recommended. Main courses 135SEK–210SEK ($18–$27); 3-course menu 195SEK ($25). AE, DC, MC, V. Daily 4–10pm. Closed Dec 21–Jan 8.

6 Kristianstad ⚐

73km (45 miles) N of Simrishamn, 95km (59 miles) NE of Malmö, 126km (78 miles) SE of Vaxjö

Called the "most Danish of Sweden's towns," Kristianstad actually was a part of Denmark—for 44 years. But its founder, Christian IV of Denmark, still makes his presence felt in many ways. In fact, the town, originally known as Christianstat, was issuing banknotes with a Danish king imprinted on them as late as 1898.

The city was founded in 1614 to defend the Danish kingdom against Swedish attacks. The fort laid out by Christian IV was northern Europe's most modern. The fortification period ended in 1847, and once the ramparts were leveled, Kristianstad expanded, building Parisian-style boulevards that earned for it the name "Little Paris." The only parts of the fortification still left are portions of the northernmost system surrounding what now is the residential district of Utanverken. After a century and a half without the restricting fortifications, Kristianstad has expanded to become the largest town in the county, just as Christian IV had hoped.

ESSENTIALS

GETTING THERE **By Train** There is frequent rail service throughout the day from Malmö; the trip takes 1 hour and 15 minutes. Call ✆ **0771/757-575.**

By Bus Local buses arrive several times a day from Ystad (trip time: 1 hr., 30 min.) and also from Simrishamn (same trip time). Call ✆ **0711/77-77-77.**

By Car From Simrishamn, our last stopover, head northwest along Route 10 until you come to the junction with Route 118, at which point you go north into Kristianstad.

VISITOR INFORMATION The **Kristianstads Turistbyrå** is at Stora Torg 291 80 (✆ **044/135-335;** www.kristianstad.se). It is open in summer Monday to Friday 9am to 7pm, Saturday 9am to 3pm, and Sunday 2 to 6pm. Off-season hours are Monday to Friday 10am to 5pm, and the last Saturday of each month 10am to 2pm.

SEEING THE SIGHTS

A Renaissance town created in 1614 by Christian IV, the "builder king" of Denmark, Kristianstad is eastern Skåne's most historic center. Thanks to a grid plan laid out by this long-ago king, it is still easy to find your way around.

Those arriving at the train station are greeted by one of the city's major landmarks, **Trefaldighertskyrkan,** or the Holy Trinity Church, Västra Storgatan (✆ **044/20-64-00**). It's open daily from 9am to 4pm year-round. Built between 1617 and 1628, it is the most beautiful Renaissance church in Scandinavia. The grandiose exterior contains seven splendid spiraled gables; the high windows allow the light to flood inside. Inside, the vaulted design and slender granite pillars create an unusually beautiful architectural setting. Most of the church appointments date from the time of Christian IV, including the carved oak benches, the altarpiece, and the marble and alabaster pulpit, as well as the magnificent organ facade built in 1630.

Directly across from the church lies *Storatorg,* the major town square, and the setting for the 19th-century **Rådhus** or Town Hall, located on Västra Storgatan. In a niche under the hands of the Town Hall clock stands a statue of Christian IV, a zinc copy of Bertel Thorvaldsen's bronze original that is in Christian IV's sepulcher in Denmark's Roskilde Cathedral. The current town hall replaced an older building in 1891 and is built in Christian IV's Renaissance-style like structures in Copenhagen. Step through the arms-emblazoned portal and you'll be greeted by a bronze bust of Christian IV sculpted with exceptional skill by François Dieussart in 1643. The original stands in Rosenborg Palace in Copenhagen.

North of *Storatorg* is the **Regionmuseet,** Östra Boulevarden (✆ **044/13-52-45**), sheltered in a structure that was originally intended as a royal palace for Christian

IV in 1616. In time, however, it became an arsenal for Danish partisans during the bloody conflicts with Sweden. The building acquired its present look in the 1780s, becoming a regional museum in 1959. The art and handicraft collections here are worth seeing, especially the treasure trove of silver. The works of local artists also are displayed, and there is an array of interesting textiles. The museum is open June to August daily 11am to 5pm. Off-season hours are Tuesday to Sunday noon to 5pm (first Wed of every month open until 9pm). Admission is free.

A short walk east of Storatorg will take you to the **Filmmuseet (Film Museum),** at Östra Storgatan 53 (*©* **044/13-57-29**). It's open Tuesday to Friday and Sunday from 1 to 4pm, and closed on Monday and Saturday. Admission is free. Kristianstad was the cradle of the Swedish film industry. This unique museum is housed in the oldest film studio (1909) still standing in Sweden. Outside the door you're greeted by an early movie camera. On videotape inside you can view the flickering works of Sweden's first film directors.

When you tire of museums, head for **Tivoli Park,** which can be reached from the Film Museum by wandering down any of the roads to its right. Stroll beneath the avenues of horse chestnut trees and enjoy a drink at the **Fornstugan Café.** In the park is a theater built in the Art Nouveau style in 1906 by Axel Anderberg, who designed the Stockholm Opera. At the north end of the park is Barbacka Cultural Center, a lively home for the town's art gallery. There's also a cafeteria.

Some residents claim that the best way to admire the topography around Kristianstad involves taking a boat ride on the nearby lakes and rivers. From early May to mid-September, a **sightseeing steamer** ⚓ departs from Kristianstad for 2-hour tours of lakes Araslövs and Hammar, with time spent on the River Helge å as well. Departures usually are daily at 11am, 2pm, and 6pm, and the cost is 80SEK ($10) adults, 45SEK ($5.85) children 4 to 14 years old. There's a cafeteria on board, and lots of deck space to enjoy the midsummer sunlight. For information and reservations, contact the tourist office (see above).

A NEARBY PALACE

Bäckaskog ⚓ Fifteen kilometers (9¼ miles) north of Kristianstad, this country palace of King Charles XV stands in a 16-hectare (40-acre) park managed by the Swedish Forest Service. The castle, a National Trust building, was a monastery founded in the early 13th century. The chapel dates from 1230, but its tower is from 1640. At Bäckaskog, you'll find a biblical garden featuring trees, bushes, and herbs mentioned in the Bible or having some other religious connection.

There is a restaurant, plus 15 hotel rooms and 4 suites (all in a contemporary style) that are open to guests all year. A double goes for 1,200SEK to 1,400SEK ($156–$182); suites range from 1,400SEK to 1,600SEK ($182–$208).

Exhibitions and sales of art and country furniture can be attended even when the castle is not open to visitors. The palace can be reached by taxi from Kristianstad; call **Taxi Allians** at *©* **044/246246.** If you're driving from Kristianstad, go 15km (9¼ miles) north along E66 until you reach the turnoff for Fjälkinge, at which point Bäckaskog is signposted.

S-290 34 Fjälkinge. *©* **044/530-20.** Free admission. Apr–Sept daily 8am–6pm; Oct–May daily 10am–5pm.

WHERE TO STAY

Hotell Turisten ⚓ *Finds* Near the heart of town, this hotel was originally built in the 1700s as the private home of the local judge. Today it boasts some of the most elaborate brickwork in town, especially on its second floor where windows are gracefully arched and mullioned. Bedrooms are outfitted with more style and taste than you might have guessed from the hotel's relatively inexpensive rates. None is particularly large, but in view of their coziness and carefully chosen decorations, guests usually find that the rooms—particularly the beds—are very comfortable. Bathrooms equipped with shower units tend to be very small. Be aware that many staff members here don't speak English. All rooms are nonsmoking.

Vestre Storgatan 17, S-291-32 Kristianstad. © 044/12-61-50 or 044/10-30-99. www.turisten.se. 31 units. June to mid-Aug and weekends 750SEK–995SEK ($98–$129) double; mid-Aug to May 995SEK–1,195SEK ($129–$155) double; 1,195SEK ($155) suite. Rates include breakfast. AE, DC, MC. V. Parking 64SEK ($8.30). **Amenities:** Breakfast room; bar; sauna; laundry service; dry cleaning. *In room:* TV, dataport.

Quality Hotel Grand ⚑   The largest and most centrally located hotel in Kristianstad occupies a position near the railway station; it was built in the early 1960s and features a conservative brick facade. In 1985, its size was doubled with a new four-story wing, and the interior was radically modernized; it is now one of the best in town. Today you'll find a series of busy conference rooms and bedrooms that are conservatively outfitted in a style that's just a bit banal but very comfortable, with ample bathrooms equipped with tub/showers.

An in-house restaurant serves lunch and dinner daily. The bar is a two-story space named Grands. A separate restaurant, open only on Saturday nights, features a live orchestra that offers contemporary and supper-club dance music for cheek-to-cheek dancing. Computers are available for use by guests.

Storgatan 15, Box 45, SE-291 21 Kristianstad. © 044/28-48-00. Fax 044/28-48-10. www.choicehotels.se. 148 units. Mid-June to mid-Aug and Fri–Sun year-round 790SEK ($103) double; rest of year 1,520SEK ($198) double. Rates include breakfast. AE, DC, MC, V. Free parking. Bus: 11. **Amenities:** Restaurant; bar; sauna; limited room service; laundry service; dry cleaning; nonsmoking rooms; rooms for those w/limited mobility. *In room:* TV, dataport (in some), minibar, hair dryer.

WHERE TO DINE

Den Lilla Tavernan GREEK   This is Kristianstad's only Greek restaurant. In part because it reminds so many locals of their holidays in the Mediterranean, it attracts repeat business. The decor evokes a simple taverna on one of the Greek islands, with solid wooden furniture, a low-key and decidedly unpretentious decor, and a blue-and-white color scheme that reflects the colors of the Greek flag. Menu items include all the Greek standards: stuffed grape leaves, moussaka, many different preparations of lamb (including well-seasoned kabobs), and fish. A honey-drenched portion of baklava makes a worthy dessert. A few of these dishes lose a little something in their transmigration to frigid Sweden, but it's at least a change of pace from standard Swedish fare.

Nya Boulevarden 6B. © 044/21-63-04. Reservations recommended on weekends. Main courses 50SEK–120SEK ($6.50–$16). AE, DC, MC, V. Daily 4–11pm.

7 Karlshamn

508km (315 miles) S of Stockholm.

Long a rival of Karlskrona (see later in this chapter), this old port city and naval port has often been a battleground between the Danes and the Swedes. On the border of Skåne, Karlshamn is actually in Sweden's smallest province of Blekinge and makes a good stopover for those traveling from Kristianstad in the west to Kalmar in the north on the road to Stockholm.

From its lowly beginnings as a small fishing village, Karlshamn developed because of its location in a deep, well-sheltered bay at the mouth of the Mieån River, where it flows into the Baltic. In 1666 the Swedish king, Karl X Gustav, a cousin of his predecessor, Queen Christina, granted the town a charter.

The town's original name of Bodekull was changed to Karlshamn in honor of the king who came to the throne when Christina abdicated. The king often battled the Danes during his short reign. Defeating the forces of Fredrik III of Denmark, Karl entered into the Peace of Roskilde, which on February 26, 1658, granted Sweden control of the province of Skåne as well as Blekinge.

Karl X Gustav decided to found a naval port here in 1658. The great city architect Erik Dahlberg drew up plans to defend the city from attack. In time the port proved difficult to defend, and the big naval plans envisioned for it were abandoned. The last garrison at Frisholmen came to an end in 1864.

The golden era for Karlshamn, as evoked in its museums and galleries, was in the 19th century, when it became world famous for its manufacture of brandy and punch and for the processing of tobacco—notably snuff.

ESSENTIALS

GETTING THERE   About six trains a day depart from Stockholm year-round, with a travel time of 5¼ hours. Transit requires a transfer in the town of Hessleholm, a 90-minute ride from Karlshamn. There are four buses per week from Stockholm, traveling with many stops en route, but without a change of bus required, from Stockholm. They depart Monday, Thursday, Friday, and Sunday at 9am; arrive in Karlshamn at 6pm; and are very slow. For more information, call the local bus company, © 771/75-75-75.

VISITOR INFORMATION   For information about Karlshamn and the area, go to the **Karlshamn Tourist Office** at Ronnebygatan 1 (© 454/81203). From mid-June to mid-August, it's open Monday to Friday 9am to 7pm, Saturday 10am to 6pm, and Sunday noon to 6pm. The rest of the year, it's open Monday to Friday 9am to 5pm.

SPECIAL EVENTS   One of the most fun events occurs for a few days in July (dates vary) every summer: the **Karlshamn Baltic Festival.** Visitors from all over Sweden, and even Copenhagen, flock here for the festivities. Music and live entertainment fill the town, mixed with the smell of fish frying to feed the hordes. Herring sandwiches are a big favorite. Music seems to come from every corner. Samba orchestras provide exotic rhythms, dance, and naked flesh; brass bands march up and down the streets. On one street corner you might find someone playing a barrel organ, on the next corner classical music will fill the air, and farther on, you can listen to African tones or else American rock from the 1970s. The revelry and good times continue into the wee hours in the pubs. Music, clowns, amazing floats, and exotic costumes mark the event. The tourist office (see above) will have dates and more details of events to be staged.

SEEING THE SIGHTS

The chief attraction in town is the **Karlshamns Kulturkvarter** ✸✸, at the corner of Vinkelgatan and Drottninggatan. Here one finds the town's most historic buildings, some of which have been turned into small galleries and museums.

Entered at Vinkelgatan, the **Karlshamns Museum** (© 454/14-868) is the chief attraction of the Culture Quarter. This is a treasure trove of relics from the "attic" of the little province of Blekinge. There's a little bit of everything, ranging from intriguing folk art and costumes, relics left from former industries, to nautical and maritime glories, to the lost Swedish art of painted ceilings. One room even commemorates Alice Tegnér (1864–1943), a name still known to all Swedish school children because of the songs she wrote for them.

After a visit, you can go into the courtyard and see some other galleries, including the **Stenhuset,** with its exhibitions of elaborate wrought-iron work,

18th- and 19th-century wall decorations, and antique organ fronts. The quaint **Holländarhuset,** the seat of Dutch merchants who once had a lucrative trade with Karlshamn, has been converted into a workshop, which you can visit. One gallery, **Tobaksladen** ★★, is now a tobacco museum, with artifacts of the days when the processing of tobacco and snuff was the major industry in Karlshamn. This industry flourished in the 17th and 18th centuries.

On the far side of the Vinkelgatan, you can drop in to visit an art gallery, **Konsthall,** installed in an old tobacco warehouse. The museum features displays of modern Swedish art and has some beautiful samples of Swedish mural paintings and painted ceilings, which were originally in the old town hall.

The final attraction is the **Punschmuseet.** This museum relives the grand heyday when "Karlshamns Flagg" was the punch of choice in many a home in Western Europe. Flavored with arrak, this was a sweet, spirits-based drink. One type was distilled from the juice of the coconut palm, the other from molasses and rice. You can still see some of the equipment used in the original 19th-century distillery. The punch was launched by J. N. von Bergen, who became celebrated in Sweden as a great entrepreneur in the 19th century. He was also the largest producer of playing cards in Sweden, but was mainly known for his "Punsch" liqueur, and aquavit. The factory setting is authentic, with equipment, machinery, bottles, wooden barrels, and other relics. One admission charge of 20SEK ($2.60) for adults, free for children under 17, grants admission to the museum's main core and, between mid-June and mid-August, the other components that comprise this museum compound. From mid-June to mid-August, the museum's main core and all of the museum's "satellites" (Holländerhuset, Tobakladen, the art gallery, and the Punschmuseet) are open Tuesday to Sunday noon to 5pm. The rest of the year (mid-Aug to mid-June), only the museum's main core is open, Monday to Friday 1 to 4pm. Admission is the same, regardless of the time of year you visit.

Thanks to the town's prosperity and industries, many wealthy merchants built lavish homes here. Several are gone today, but some still stand. You can visit the best of these, **Skottsbergska Gården,** at Vinkelsgata 6 (© **454/14-868**), near the Karlshamns Museum. This is an impressive example of an 18th-century merchant town house, and it's still filled with antiques and wall paintings specially commissioned by local artists. It's open only between mid-June and mid-August every Tuesday to Sunday noon to 5 pm. Admission for adults, children, and students costs 10SEK ($1.30).

At the harbor and *Hamnparken* **(harbor park),** you can see one of the most famous statues in Sweden, erected here in 1959. Axel Olsson created a **monument** ★★—much reproduced—to honor the Swedes who emigrated to America from southern Sweden. The characters represented, Kristina and

---

Finds **A Cafe with a View**

We like to spend an hour or two in summer sitting at the **Café Utsikten,** Vägga (© **454/10-325**), set about 1.2km (¾ mile) south of the town center. It was originally built as a private villa in the 17th century. It's open only from early June to September. Right on the sea, the cafe offers the best view of the Firth of Karlshamn and the 17th-century citadel on the island of Frisholmen. On a summer day we also like to walk along the seafront promenade to another tiny harbor where fishmongers hawk smoked eel, mackerel, and fresh salmon.

Moments Sailing the Turbulent Baltic

A midsummer diversion that's available in Karlshamn is an ocean cruise, operated by **Hauglund Shipping Company,** Gästhaum (the harbor front; ℂ **414/14-958**). Boats depart twice a day between mid-June and mid-August. It costs 180SEK ($23) per person, lasts for 2½ hours, and goes along the scenic harbor front and along the jagged coastline. Call ahead to verify prices.

Karl-Oskar, are those depicted in Vilhelm Moberg's monumental work *The Emigrants,* which was made into a film starring Liv Ullman and Max von Sydow. The book detailed the hardships and tribulations that drove Swedes to leave their homeland for the promise of America. The farmer looks out to the sea, whereas his wife turns her head back to the land she is leaving. An exact duplicate of this statue graces the center of a town in America's Midwest, in Lindstrom, Minnesota. The relief in Olsson's work is one of the emigrant ship, *Charlotta.*

In a beautiful little rose garden to the west stands another statue, that of a barefooted girl named *Maja,* a character created by Alice Tegnér, the famous writer of children's songs.

In summer, boats leave from the quay, taking you over to the **Kastellet (castle),** the old fortress built on the island of Frisholmen to protect Karlshamn from the Danes or other invaders from the Baltic nations. In 1676 the Danes overpowered the fortifications here, but the Swedish forces retook the castle the following year. The Danes returned victoriously in 1710 and took the fortress once more. But after the Swedes paid a huge ransom, the Danes sailed back to Copenhagen within the year. That wasn't the end of Karlshamn's troubles. About half the members of the garrison, as well as half the inhabitants of Karlshamn, were afflicted with the plague in 1711. The fortifications date from 1675. At its peak the garrison had a force of 400 soldiers. However, all of them pulled out at the end of 1864, and Kastellet is no longer used for military purposes. Once on the island, you can visit the fortifications, including the wall, casemates, powder, and gun emplacements, each well preserved. You're also allowed to visit the dungeon and look at a "poisoned well."

Today Kastellet is merely a ruin, without barriers, and open to view by anyone who wants to wander among the battlements. The ferryboat ride takes 10 minutes each way, departs every hour between early June and late August, and costs 50SEK ($6.50) per person round-trip. (There are no discounts for children, but children under 5 ride free if they're with guardians.) For more information, contact the **Hauglung Shipping Company,** Gästhamn (the harbor front), Karlshamn (ℂ **414/14-958**). Call ahead to verify prices.

Some visitors carry a picnic from the mainland. Others visit the **Kastellet Cafeteria** (ℂ **454/12-527**), which is positioned at the point where the ferryboats land. Congenial owner Rolf Bildström serves pastries, coffee, and sandwiches, and displays the works of local artists for sale. The cafe maintains completely erratic summer-only hours, opening only during the operation of the ferryboat that connects this island to the Swedish mainland.

Motorists can also drive 10km (6¼ miles) along E22 to reach **Eriksberg Natureservat,** a beautiful park and nature reserve where some 800 animals roam freely. The collection of animals is particularly rich in red and fallow deer along with European bison. You can drive through a luxuriant deciduous woodland, following tracts of coniferous forests until you come to a little lake that is known as a setting for the increasingly rare red water lily, best seen in late spring and early summer. On-site is a children's zoo and a cafeteria.

From E22 take exit Åryd east of Karlshamn and follow the signposts. **Eriksbergs Nature Park** (📞 454/600-58) is open only as follows: June and August daily noon to 8pm, July daily noon to 9pm. Once inside, you'll drive your car in a 13.5km (8¼-mile) circle, getting out only at clearly designated "safety points" en route. The danger from wild animals is a cause for concern. Admission costs 80SEK ($10) per adult, 40SEK ($5.20) for children 8 to 12, free for children under 7; family ticket 200SEK ($26).

WHERE TO STAY

First Hotel Carlshamn   One of the most reliable stopovers along the Swedish coast is found at this hotel erected in 1987. It offers first-class comfort, although the decor is a bit bland. Nonetheless, you get solid comfort in one of the mid-size bedrooms with twins or a queen-size bed. The floors are wooden, and the walls on each floor are in different colors. All accommodations have small, tiled bathrooms with showers (five with bathtubs as well). There are Jacuzzis and small living rooms in the suites. The on-site restaurant, Arrak, isn't run by the hotel, but the staff will gladly make reservations for you.

Varvsgatan 1, S-374 35 Karlshamn. 📞 454/89-000. Fax 454/89-150. www.firsthotels.com. 99 units. 690SEK–1,389SEK ($90–$181) double; 1,909SEK ($248) suite. Rates include continental breakfast. Children under 15 stay free in parent's room. AE, DC, MC, V. Closed Dec 20–Jan 2. **Amenities:** Restaurant; bar; sauna; laundry service; dry cleaning; nonsmoking rooms; rooms for those w/limited mobility. *In room:* TV, dataport, hair dryer.

Scandi Karlsamn   Typical of the rather modern and impersonal hotels erected along the Baltic in the late 1960s, this is a well-run and comfortable choice. The interior of this three-story, white-brick building is much more inviting on its interior than its exterior suggests. The staff is helpful, and the furnishings are kept up-to-date. The rooms are decorated in bright pastels such as lemon yellow to chase away the gloom of a gray day. All the small bathrooms are nicely kept and contain showers; 20 units have a tub/shower.

Jannebergsvagen 2, S-374 32 Karlshamn. 📞 454/58-87-00. Fax: 454/58-87-11. 101 units. 850SEK–1,490SEK ($111–$194) double. Children under 13 stay free in parent's room. Rates include continental breakfast. AE, DC, MC, V. **Amenities:** Restaurant; bar; indoor pool; fitness center; sauna; nonsmoking rooms. *In room:* TV, hair dryer, Internet.

WHERE TO DINE

Kopmanngarden ITALIAN   The cuisine is modern, but the building itself dates from the 1600s and there's a certain nostalgia about the setting. In casual, relaxing surroundings, this family-run place is one of the warmest and most inviting in town. In summer diners can request a table in the garden. Many pizza joints lie in the area, but the best pies are served here. Recipes are time-tested and familiar, including spaghetti Bolognese and a tender and well-flavored chateaubriand. Yes, they serve an old-fashioned banana split, evocative of America in the 1950s, for dessert.

Drottninggatan 88. 📞 454/157-40. Reservations recommended. Main courses 75SEK–160SEK ($9.75–$21). AE, DC, MC, V. Mon and Wed–Thurs 4–10pm; Fri 4–11pm; Sat 12:30–11pm; Sun 12:30–10pm.

Restaurant Terrassen ★ SWEDISH/ITALIAN   This is one of the best restaurants in town, an intimate and candlelit place that can comfortably handle 80 discerning patrons every night. Ingredients of the highest quality are skillfully handled by the well-trained kitchen staff. Lots of fresh fish, depending on the catch of the day, is featured on the menu, and the salmon, trout, and sole are particularly delectable. The chef's real specialty, however, is 30 different types of steak, especially a succulent cut of chateaubriand. Although primarily a Swedish restaurant, the chefs prepare a number of Italian dishes as well. For dessert? Dare you try the fried Camembert with a special orange marmalade? There is also a moderately priced and well-chosen wine list.

Ronnebygatan 12. (℃) **454/17-263.** Reservations recommended. Main courses 125SEK–205SEK ($16–$27). AE, DC, MC, V. Mon–Fri 11:30am–11pm; Sat noon–1am; Sun noon–9pm.

KARLSHAMN AFTER DARK

Many nightclubbing locals gravitate over to the **Loch Ness Pub and Restaurang,** Ronnebygatan 22 (℃ **454/12-600**). Living up to its namesake, the club is decorated with "memories of Scotland," including tartans. On some nights they have live rock-'n'-roll bands but don't charge a cover. Many Scotch whiskeys from Talisker to Glen Livet are sold, as well as beer on tap. Open daily from 5pm to 1am.

8 Karlskrona

111km (69 miles) E of Kristianstad, 201km (125 miles) NE of Malmö, 107km (66 miles) SE of Växjö, 500km (310 miles) SW of Stockholm

This port city is a major bastion for the Swedish Navy on the country's southern flank. The city makes an idyllic stopover for visitors en route between Kristianstad and Kalmar to the north. By royal command of King Karl XI in 1680, the port for the navy base was founded here. Today it's one of the few remaining naval ports in the world that is almost fully intact. In 1998 UNESCO declared Karlskrona a Heritage Site.

The city opens onto an archipelago of more than 30 islands (depending on how many islets you want to count), but many of these are off-limits and under the control of the Swedish military. In the heyday of the Cold War in 1981, a Soviet submarine spying on Swedish military installations ran aground here, and Karlskrona made world headlines. Today, in a more peaceful era, Karlskrona is likely to make the papers only as host port for the International Cutty Sark Tall Ships' race.

Immediately east of Skåne, Karlskrona is the capital of the old province of Blekinge, which coincides with the modern county of the same name. Blekinge is the smallest province in Sweden and, like Skåne itself, once belonged to Denmark until Sweden reclaimed it in 1658.

ESSENTIALS

GETTING THERE   Karlskrona lies on the main rail link between Stockholm and southern Sweden and points west. There are frequent **trains** throughout the day. **Svenda Bus** services the area from Stockholm (take no. 31). **Motorists** can follow E66 north from Kristianstad or the same motorway southwest from the port of Kalmar (also the same route from Stockholm farther north).

VISITOR INFORMATION   For information about the town and the area, go to the **Karlskrona Tourist Office,** Stortorget 2 (℃ **0455/30-34-90**). In summer, hours are Monday to Friday 10am to 5pm, Saturday and Sunday 9am to 4pm. Off-season hours are Monday to Friday 10am to 5pm, Saturday 10am to 1pm. Boat trips of the archipelago are often available in summer; ask at the tourist office for details.

SEEING THE SIGHTS

Stortorget ✦✦, or the main square of town, is one of the biggest and most beautiful in northern Europe. In the middle of the square is a statue of Karl XI, who founded the town.

Two baroque churches designed by Nicodemus Tessin the Younger dominate the square. Both of these escaped the great fire of 1790. Started by a laundry maid, the fire swept over the town, which was later rebuilt, its baroque style giving way to a more neoclassical motif.

In the middle of the square, the church, **Fredrikskyrkan,** is from 1744 and named after King Fredrik (1720–51). If something looks unfinished, it is. Tessin planned for the church to have spires on its squat towers. A series of Ionic pilasters grace the interior, and the three dozen bells in the south tower are rung daily, the "music" resounding throughout the historic core. Standing opposite the church is the neoclassical **Rådhus,** or town hall, from 1795.

The other church, **Trefaldighetskyrka,** is circular in shape and is referred to as "the German church," even though that community stopped worshipping here in 1846. The church was completed in 1750, and Tessin based his design on the Pantheon in Rome. The roof burned in the great fire, and the present wooden roof is painted with *trompe l'oeil* coffering. The oldest artifact in the church is a red Öland limestone font from 1685. The church shelters the tomb of one of Sweden's greatest naval heroes, Admiral Hans Wachmeister, who in July 1700 sailed from the harbor with 38 ships and 8 frigates. With his ship *Kung Karl* loaded with 1,000 men and 108 guns, he defeated the Danish fleet at Öresund.

A celebration, **Lövmarknad,** on the day before Midsummer's Eve, is one of the liveliest and most attended events on the southern coast of Sweden and takes place on this square. During the celebration, Swedes decorate their houses, churches, and other structures with flowers, and raise a maypole. All members of the community dance around the maypole until late in the evening. The dancing is accompanied by traditional music and the wearing of folkloric costumes. Dancing, drinking, and dining highlight the festivities, including the eating of the first potatoes of the year, which accompany platters of pickled herring and sour cream.

Marinmuseum (Naval Museum) ⊛, at Admiralitetsslatten (© **0455/53-902**), dates from 1752 and is one of the oldest naval museums in Sweden. Lying on the island of Stumholmen, the museum traces the country's naval heritage through various exhibits, including a marvelous collection of **figureheads** ⊛ and ship models from the 18th to the 19th centuries. Old maps, maritime charts, plans for ship designs, navigating equipment, artifacts pulled up from the sea (including parts of actual ships), weapons, uniforms, and shipyard handicrafts are on parade. You can also see a full-scale replica of the *Hiorten,* a post ship from 1692. You find the museum along a long pier. Moored along the quays are the minesweeper *Bremon,* the *Spica* torpedo boat, and a fully rigged training ship, *Jarramas.* Open June to August daily 10am to 6pm, September to May Tuesday to Sunday 11am to 5pm. Admission is 50SEK ($6.50).

The oldest wooden church in Sweden, the red-painted **Admiraliteskyrkan (Admiralty Church;** © **0455/10-356**), lies on Bastiongatan on the naval island, a few minutes from Stortorget. Built in 1685, the church was supposed to be temporary, but its stone replacement was never built. Named Ulrica Pia after Queen Ulrica Eleonora, wife of Karl XI, the church may have been designed by Erik Dahlberg, the original town planner. (Dahlberg gave Karlskrona its broad streets, monumental buildings, and large squares.) The church contains a number of treasures, including a pulpit hourglass from 1693 and an altarpiece that's a copy of *Thrust of the Lance,* by Rubens. Crowning the altar is a cross given to a Swedish sea captain by the Patriarch of Constantinople in 1744. The church is open from June to August daily from 9am to 5pm. In the off season, you have to make an appointment with the tourist office to see it. Admission is free.

In front of the Admiraliteskyrkan is Karlskrona's most beloved **statue.** It depicts ex-constable Matts Rosenbom, who froze to death on New Year's Eve in 1717. He was found in the morning with his hand outstretched, his hat pulled over his ears, and a beggar's bundle on his back. Since then, the wooden statue of Rosenbom has tipped its hat to all who give alms to the poor.

To reach the oldest part of Karlskrona, take Hantverkaregatan to **Björkholmen,** a hilly island settled by shipbuilders with many 18th-century houses still standing. The occupants of these little wooden houses with their small gardens lived in exceedingly cramped conditions. The streets in the area are named after types of boats and Swedish admirals.

After a visit, you can head back to the north quay and the *Fisktorget,* the site of an antique covered market, with fishing boats tied up along the pier. This is the landing stage for any boats touring the archipelago.

You can also visit the **Blekinge Lans Museum** ★, Fisktorget 2 (© **0455/ 30-49-60**), which opened in 1899. The museum consists of a row of old houses that includes the **Blekinge County Museum** ★, with exhibitions and artifacts of this small maritime province. The main building, Greevagården, dating from 1705, was the mansion of Admiral Hans Wachtmeister. Inside you'll find rooms filled with antiques and paintings, all evocative of the rich life enjoyed by some in the 18th century. The mansion adjoins a lovely garden. It is open mid-June to mid-August daily 10am to 6pm. During other months, hours are Tuesday to Sunday 11am to 5pm and Wednesday 11am to 7pm. Admission is 20SEK ($2.60), free for ages 17 and under.

Leonardo da Vinci Ideale ★, Drottninggatan 28 (© **0455/25-573**) is a museum created from the private Kulenovic collection. Its chief treasure is *The Youngest Madonna,* by Leonardo da Vinci. Although this is the painting that gets all the press, we have a lot of other favorites here, including *A Stolen Kiss,* by Jea Honoré Fragonard; *Stilleben,* or still life, by Georges Braque; another *Stilleben* by Henri Matisse; plus a startling *Medical Care,* by Peter Bruegel. Two paintings are by Vincent van Gogh: *Portrait* and *Sheep.* Other exhibits include a drawing by Da Vinci, rare porcelain from the Topkapi Palace in Istanbul, a stunning gem-studded goldpiece from South Asia (ca. 1900), and a cabinet by the French architect André Charles Boulle (1642–1732). The museum can be visited May to August Wednesday to Sunday 11am to 6pm. Admission is 20SEK ($2.60).

Still partly a military base, **Kungsholm Fort,** on the island of Kungshomen, can be visited in summer. You must go with a guide since some of the area is restricted. This impressive fortress was contructed in 1680 to protect Karlskrona from frequent Danish intrusions. Denmark wasn't Karlskrona's only enemy, as the port was blockaded by the Russians in the 1780s and faced British attempts at domination in the 19th century. Architecturally, the curiosity of the fortress is a circular harbor contructed into the Kungsholm itself, with only a narrow passage leading out into the Baltic. Excursions can be arranged through the tourist office (see above) from June to August at 10am and 3pm on Tuesday, Thursday, and Saturday. Tours cost 140SEK ($18) for adults and 70SEK ($9.10) for children ages 12 to 16 (free for children 11 and under). For bookings and information, call © **0455/30-34-90.**

In summer you can also take boat tours of the archipelago, seeing dozens of small islands—really "islets"—in the impressive harbor. Some boats visit the islands, and many visitors often take along a picnic lunch to enjoy. Many of the islands also have small trails for hiking. **Affärs Verken Bättrafik,** at Fisktorget (© **0455/78-330**), offers the best cruises, lasting half a day and costing 110SEK to 125SEK ($14–$16) for adults or 50SEK to 60SEK ($6.50–$7.80) for children 7 to 16 years old. Departures are daily June through August at 8am and 11am, with a final tour at 3:45pm.

OUTDOOR PURSUITS

Many Swedes visit Karlskrona in summer for its 30 beaches, 7 of which lie in the center. The most central, **Stumholmen Beach** is also one of the best. This sandy beach, ideal for kids, has a bridge and diving tower along with a restaurant. Next to the beach is the famous naval museum (see above).

Drägsö Beach is another favorite in the archipelago, lying only 5 minutes from the historic core and linked to the main island with a bridge. You'll find beaches and towering cliffs along with activities like canoeing, water-skiing, and fishing.

Karlskrona also opens onto great waters for both saltwater and freshwater fishing. To become part of a fishing trip, call **Senoren's Sportfishing Tours** (© 0455/44-010), which takes fishermen to the far reaches of the archipelago. **Hasslö Island Touring & Fishing Service** (© 0455/332-124) also offers great fishing in freshwater streams or in the Baltic.

WHERE TO STAY

First Hotel Statt ⭐   This turn-of-the-20th-century property in the center of the port is the hotel of choice in Karlskrona. After getting a little tattered, it was completely refurbished in 1999. Guests enjoy such architectural grace notes as candelabras and grand stairwells throughout. Every room is decorated individually. Some are carpeted and others contain hardwood floors. Each room comes with a private bathroom with shower (20 also have tub/showers). For locals, the hotel is a dining and entertainment center.

Ronnebygatan, S-371 33 Karlskrona. © 45-51-92-50. Fax 45-51-69-09. www.firsthotels.com. 107 units. 808SEK–1,509SEK ($105–$196) double; 2,053SEK ($267) minisuite. Children under 12 stay free in parent's room. Rates include continental breakfast. AE, DC, MC, V. **Amenities:** Restaurant; bar; pub; nightclub; sauna; laundry service; dry cleaning; nonsmoking rooms. *In room:* TV, dataport, hair dryer, iron.

Hotel Conrad   This hotel consists of two buildings: one a modern structure, the other—called the Culture House—dating back to the 16th century. The entire hotel was renovated in 1999. The hotel's main portion offers simply furnished but comfortable bedrooms. The six minisuites in the Culture House are more luxurious, and since they cost the same as the regular doubles, you should opt for one of them. Blue and yellow were used extensively throughout. All the units have their own bathrooms with showers (about 25% with tub/showers).

Västra Kopmansgatan 12, S-371 34, Karlskrona. © 0455/36-32-00. Fax 0455/36-32-05. www.hotelconrad.se. 48 units. Mon–Thurs 1,095SEK ($142) double, 1,145SEK ($149) suite; Fri–Sun and summer 745SEK ($97) double, 845SEK ($110) suite. Children under 6 stay free in parent's room. Rates include continental breakfast. AE, DC, MC, V. **Amenities:** Breakfast lounge; sauna; laundry service; dry cleaning; nonsmoking rooms. *In room:* TV, minibar, hair dryer, iron.

WHERE TO DINE

If you're just passing through for the day, or if you're sticking around for dinner, your best bet is the dining room at the First Hotel Statt Karlskrona.

KARLSKRONA AFTER DARK

The leading after-dark diversion is at **Kino's Nightclub,** Borgmästaregatan 17 (© 0455/31-11-00), a bar, nightclub, and restaurant that rocks to a DJ all night long. Expect a cover charge ranging from 40SEK to 80SEK ($5.20–$10).

Kalmar & the Southeast

Much of southeast Sweden falls into the province of Småland, which includes the historic city of Kalmar and also the "Kingdom of Crystal" centered in Växjö. Many visitors make day trips down from Stockholm just to visit famous glassworks such as Orrefors, but the province has so much more to offer than that. The province also is associated with elk, large forests, flowering meadows, and long stretches of *gädesgårdar* (the timber fences typical of this region). There also are some 5,000 lakes teeming with fish.

Olaus Magnus wrote back in the 16th century, "The forces of nature work in a more secretive and wonderful way on Lake Vättern than they do anywhere else." The city of Jönköping lies on the southern shores of Lake Vättern (not to be confused with the even larger lake of Vänern). The towns along this lake are just as appealing to tourists as Kalmar and the glassworks. The best centers are Granna, Vadstena, and Motala.

The area formed by Vättern actually touches four provinces, not just Småland. Land of myth and legend, the lake is one of the oldest cultural areas in the north of Europe. The water here is so pure that some 400,000 people use it as their drinking water supply. Despite the clarity of its water, the lake is notorious for its unpredictability; many a ship now lies at the bottom.

Finally, and if time remains, you can visit Örebro, beyond Motala and 60km (37 miles) north of Lake Vättern. Örebro is Sweden's sixth-most populous city, lying on the shores of Lake Hjalmaren, the country's fourth-largest lake.

1 Kalmar ⟨⋆⟩

292km (181 miles) NE of Malmö, 110km (68 miles) E of Växjö, 409km (254 miles) S of Stockholm, 340km (211 miles) E of Gothenburg

A coastal town opposite the Baltic island of Öland, historic Kalmar contains Sweden's best-preserved Renaissance castle (see below). Today a thriving commercial center, Kalmar still retains many 17th-century buildings and sea captains' houses, many clustered around the *Stortoget* (main square) in the center of town. The first large-scale Swedish emigration to America, more than 3 centuries ago, originated in Kalmar (and ended up in Wilmington, Delaware).

Historically, the town is forever linked to the Kalmar Union, the treaty that three northern crowns signed here in 1397 linking Denmark, Norway, and Sweden into an ill-fated but united kingdom. Queen Margrethe of Denmark headed the union, which was dissolved in 1523.

ESSENTIALS

GETTING THERE **By Plane** **Kalmar Airport** (⟨©⟩ **0480/758810**) receives two to four daily flights from Stockholm, taking 50 minutes. The airport is 5km (3 miles) west of the town center.

Kalmar

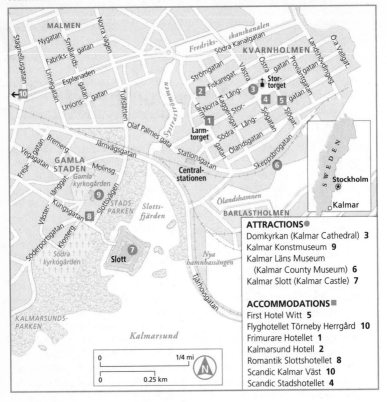

By Train   Seven trains a day make the 6½-hour run between Stockholm and Kalmar. Eight daily trains arrive from Malmö, taking 3 hours and 20 minutes. Call ℂ **771/75-75-75.**

By Bus   Three to seven buses a day make the 7-hour trip from Stockholm. From Gothenburg, there is one bus on both Friday and Saturday, taking 6 hours. For information, call ℂ **0200/21818** (within Sweden only).

By Car   From Stockholm, take E66 south.

VISITOR INFORMATION   The Kalmar Tourist Office, **Turism I Kalmarbygåden,** is located at Olandkagen 9 (ℂ **0480/153-50;** www.kalmar.se/turism), near the railway station right in the town center. The office is open June 1 to July 27 and August 16 to August 31 Monday to Friday 9am to 7pm, and Saturday and Sunday 10am to 4pm; July 28 to August 15 Monday to Friday 9am to 9pm, and Saturday and Sunday 10am to 5pm; September to May Monday to Friday 9am to 5pm.

CASTLES, CATHEDRALS & MORE
Still surrounded by parts of its old fortified walls, the 17th-century New Town is a warren of cobblestone streets and market squares. This town was created in 1647 after a devastating fire that caused the townspeople to move away from the old town to create this newer town on Kvarnholmen.

Domkyrkan (Kalmar Cathedral)   From the marketplace, you can wander over to *Stortorget* to visit the town's 17th-century cathedral. **Kalmar Cathedral** is the only one in Sweden without a bishop, but it still is an impressive building. It was designed in 1660 by Nicodemus Tessin the Elder in the Italian Renaissance style. Tessin visited Rome and found inspiration there. The bright, massive space of the interior is a reminder that the cathedral was built when Sweden was one of the great European powers. The altar was designed by Tessin the Younger, and it shimmers with gold. It's surrounded by a series of sculptures called *Faith* and *Mercy*.

Stortorget. ✆ 0480/123-00. Free admission. Mon–Fri 7am–8pm; Sat–Sun 9am–8pm. Bus: 1, 2, 7, or 9.

Kalmar Konstmuseum   The Kalmar Museum of Art contains works by Swedish painters Anders Zorn and Carl Larsson, along with other masterpieces from the 19th century up to the present day. Special and thematic exhibitions are also held in the gallery. Sketches and finished works by important Swedish designers are displayed in the design gallery.

Slottsvägen 1D. ✆ 0480/42-62-82. Admission 40SEK ($5.20) adults, free for 20 years old and younger. Fri–Tues 11am–5pm; Thurs 11am–8pm. Bus: 1, 2, 7, or 9.

Kalmar Läns Museum (Kalmar County Museum)   The county museum's exhibits are in an old mill along the harbor. One of its most interesting exhibits is of the royal ship **Kronan,** which sank in the Baltic Sea off the island of Öland during a battle against the Danes and the Dutch in 1676. Only 42 of the 840 men aboard survived. The museum is responsible for excavation at the wreck site. Objects found by the marine archaeologists—glass bottles, tin plates, nautical instruments, a seaman's chest, and many old coins—are on display. In another exhibit, the museum re-creates the world of Jenny Nyström (1854–1946), a native of Kalmar who went to Paris and became a famous artist. Models, reproductions, and original paintings evoke her world and art. Outside the exhibits is a cafe.

Skeppsbrogatan 51. ✆ 0480/45-13-00. Admission 50SEK ($6.50) adults, 25SEK ($3.25) seniors and students, free for children 18 and under. June 15–Aug 15 daily 10am–4pm; off season Tues–Fri 10am–4pm. Bus: 1, 2, 7, or 9.

Kalmar Slott (Kalmar Castle) ★★★   Founded in the 12th century, this strategically situated castle once was called the key to Sweden, and it's the principal sight in town. It was here that the Danish Queen Margrethe of Denmark launched the Kalmar Union, uniting the crowns of Denmark, Norway, and Sweden. In the 16th century, under order of King Gustavus Vasa and two of his sons, Erik XIV and Johan III, this medieval fortress with a moat was transformed into a Renaissance palace. Be sure to see the restored castle chapel as well as the prison for women, which was in use in the 18th and 19th centuries. English-language tours are conducted from mid-June to mid-August daily at 11am and 3pm. To get here from the train station, turn left on Tullbron.

Kungsgatan 1. ✆ 0480/451-490. Admission 75SEK ($9.75) adults, 20SEK ($2.60) children 7–16, free for children 6 and under. Apr–Oct 10am–6pm; winter opens only on the 2nd weekend of each month 10am–4pm. Bus: 1, 2, 7, or 9.

SHOPPING

If you're searching for antiques, head for **Anderssons Antik,** Esplanaden 6 (✆ **0480/47-41-62**), or **Caboms Antik,** Esplanaden 17 (✆ **0480/209-01**). For one of the best selections of ceramics and glassware, try **Noshörningen,** Olof Palmes gata 1 (✆ **0480/151-25**). Another good selection is found at **Mats Nordell,** Milingsgatan 7 (✆ **0480/41-11-01**). The town's best art gallery is **Arch Galleri,** Västra Sgögatan 8 (✆ **0480/42-05-80**).

WHERE TO STAY

Kalmar offers an adequate range of accommodations, although many choose to stay on the island of Öland (see chapter 8).

The Kalmar Tourist Office (see above) can help you rent rooms in **private homes** for 250SEK ($33) for a single and from 350SEK ($46) for a double. Some of the private homes charge an additional 40SEK ($5.20) for sheets.

EXPENSIVE

Romantik Slottshotellet 🏰   In the center of Kalmar, close to the castle, this hotel wins as a traditional, nostalgic favorite. A gracious old house on a tranquil street, facing a waterfront park, it lies an easy walk from the train station. Each of the bedrooms has a different style of decoration and furnishing, with touches such as wallpaper, wooden floors, old-fashioned chandeliers, and brass or wood headboards reminiscent of a country house in England. Rooms vary widely in shape and style, but all are equipped with average-size bathrooms with showers. Everything is kept spotlessly clean. The hotel consists of both a main building from 1864 and three annexes. Even the annexes have charming rooms. Breakfast is served in the pavilion, and on winter evenings tea and coffee are offered in the lounge. The hotel also offers facilities for those who want to cook their own meals. In summer, full restaurant service is offered on the terrace; otherwise, only breakfast is served. There also is access to a sauna and solarium.

Slottsvägen 7, S-392 33 Kalmar. ☎ **0480/882-60.** Fax 0480/882-66. www.romantikhotels.com/kalmar. 36 units. 1,150SEK–1,650SEK ($150–$215) double; 1,650SEK–1,930SEK ($215–$251) suite. Often weekend reductions. Rates include breakfast. AE, DC, MC, V. Free parking. Bus: 1, 2, 7, or 9. **Amenities:** Restaurant; bar; sauna; limited room service; laundry service; dry cleaning; nonsmoking rooms; solarium. *In room:* TV, dataport, minibar.

MODERATE

First Hotel Witt 🏰 *Kids*   Although the foundations and some of the inner walls of this hotel date from the 1600s, most of what you'll see, both inside and out, dates from the 1970s, when what remained of the decrepit original was rebuilt and reconfigured. In 1997, bedrooms were renovated and furnished with conservatively dignified and very appealing furniture, new paint jobs, hardwood floors, and, in some cases, good copies of Oriental carpets. In addition to appealing to the average traveler—often couples or businesspeople—the hotel designer planned some units especially for female travelers, families, persons with disabilities, and those with allergies. Rooms are generous in size, with attractive styling and excellent bathrooms containing tub/showers. Views usually extend out over Kalmar Sound, and the hotel's position in the heart of the old town is extremely convenient to virtually everything in the center.

Södra Långgatan 42. S-392 31 Kalmar. ☎ **0480/15250.** Fax 0480/15265. www.firsthotels.com. 112 units. Mid-June to Aug and Fri–Sun year-round 850SEK–950SEK ($111–$124) double, 1,408SEK ($183) suite; rest of year 1,149SEK–1,545SEK ($149–$201) double, 1,653SEK ($215) suite. Rates include breakfast. AE, DC, MC, V. Free on-street parking, 95SEK ($12) in hotel garage. Bus: 1, 2, or 3. **Amenities:** Restaurant; bar; indoor pool; gym; sauna; limited room service; laundry service; dry cleaning; nonsmoking rooms; rooms for those w/limited mobility. *In room:* TV, dataport, hair dryer, iron.

Kalmarsund Hotell   Set in the heart of Kalmar, near the railway station, this hotel originated in 1982 when a 40-year-old complex of shops and offices was transformed into the well-maintained, well-managed hotel you see today. The staff here is responsible and motivated, and bedrooms are snug, modern, cozy, and nicely decorated with conservative modern furniture. Bathrooms are functional and usually tiled, each with a tub/shower. There's an attractive restaurant, Fiskarejatan Kroj.

Fiskaregatan 5, S-392 32 Kalmar. ⓒ **0480/181-00.** Fax 480/41-13-37. www.kalmarsundhotel.se. 85 units. Mon–Thurs 1,435SEK ($187) double, 1,950SEK ($254) suite; Fri–Sun 870SEK ($113) double, 1,250SEK ($163) suite. Rates include breakfast. AE, DC, MC, V. Parking 95SEK ($12). Bus: 3. **Amenities:** Restaurant; bar; sauna; limited room service; laundry service; dry cleaning; nonsmoking rooms; rooms for those w/limited mobility. *In room:* TV, dataport, minibar, hair dryer.

Scandic Kalmar Väst *(Value)* Comfortable, conservative, and well managed, this hotel is a low-rise two-story building erected in the 1970s and located about 2.5km (1½ miles) west of Kalmar's central core. The bedrooms are modern, clean, and outfitted with comfortable beds. Although small, bathrooms are equipped with adequate shelf space and tub/showers.

Dragonvagen 7, S-392 39 Kalmar. ⓒ **0480/469-300.** Fax 0480/469-311. www.scandi-hotels.com. 148 units. June 25–Aug 8 and Fri–Sat year-round 800SEK–890SEK ($104–$116) double; rest of year 1,490SEK ($194) double. Rates include breakfast. AE, DC, MC, V. Free parking. **Amenities:** Restaurant; bar; indoor pool; sauna; limited room service; nonsmoking rooms; rooms for those w/limited mobility; solarium. *In room:* TV, dataport, hair dryer, iron, safe.

Scandic Stadshotellet 🌟 Located on the main square in the heart of the city, the Stadshotellet was built in 1906. It still retains its romanticized architecture, with gables and a bell tower overlooking the cathedral, and is close to the train station. In 1999 a major renovation was completed, and the hotel now looks better than ever, with many of its original Art Nouveau touches still in place. Cut-glass chandeliers and even a library give the aura of a rich private home. Modular bathrooms with showers are adjoined by large bedrooms (among the most spacious in town) with bedside TV controls, feather pillows and duvets, hardwood floors, and distinctive built-in furniture. Half the accommodations contain dataports, and some are nonsmoking. There's also a nightclub that is open on weekends.

Stortorget 14, S-392 32 Kalmar. ⓒ **0480/496-900.** www.scandic-hotels.com. 126 units. June 6–Aug 2 and Fri–Sat year-round 950SEK–1,000SEK ($124–$130) double, 1,290SEK ($168) suite; rest of year 950SEK–1,590SEK ($124–$207) double, 1,590SEK ($207) suite. AE, DC, MC, V. Parking 95SEK ($12). Bus: 1, 2, 7, or 9. **Amenities:** Restaurant; bar; sauna; nonsmoking rooms. *In room:* TV, hair dryer.

INEXPENSIVE

Flyghotellet Törneby Herrgård 🌟 *(Finds)* This stately hotel lies on 1.2 hectares (3 acres) of verdant parkland, near clear springs and streams, 5km (3 miles) west of Kalmar, and a 1-minute drive from the airport. Although there has been an inn on this site since 1616, the elegantly symmetrical building you see today dates from the 1870s, when it was constructed as a manor house in a style similar to the classical ruins of Pompeii. Inside, Dagmar and Agneta Herlin have decorated their hotel and home with a roster of worthy antiques and color schemes that are almost universally pink-toned or salmon. Bedrooms are cozy, well maintained, and charming, each with a small bathroom with a shower.

Flottiljvägen 9, S-392 41 Kalmar. ⓒ **0480/200-24.** Fax 0480/202-24. 18 units. Sun–Thurs 1,295SEK ($168) double; Fri–Sat 895SEK ($116) double. Rates include breakfast. AE, DC, MC, V. Bus: 2. **Amenities:** Restaurant; bar; outdoor pool; sauna; limited room service; laundry service; dry cleaning; nonsmoking rooms. *In room:* TV, hair dryer.

Frimurare Hotellet One of the most visible and centrally located hotels in Kalmar, Frimurare Hotellet occupies a prominent site at the corner of the main square, in a richly detailed Italianate building that was constructed in 1875 as a headquarters for the local branch of the Freemasons. Today, after extensive renovations that were completed in the mid-1990s, the two lowest floors of the three-story building are devoted to a comfortable, cozy hotel; the stately top floor is still the domain of the Freemasons, one of Kalmar's most active social and charitable organizations. Bedrooms are well maintained and, in most cases, have high ceilings and appealingly formal furnishings, including well-maintained private bathrooms with tub/showers or just tubs. All rooms are non-smoking. There's a copious breakfast buffet included in the room price, and an in-house sauna.

Larmtorget 2. S-39232 Kalmar. © **0480/15230.** Fax 0480/85887. 34 units. Fri–Sat 735SEK–825SEK ($96–$107) double; Sun–Thurs 995SEK–1,160SEK ($129–$151) double. Rates include breakfast. AE, DC, MC, V. Bus: 2. **Amenities:** Breakfast lounge; solarium; sauna. *In room:* TV, dataport, hair dryer.

WHERE TO DINE

Byttan Restaurant ⭐ SWEDISH   In the city park near the base of the castle, a 10-minute walk south of the town center, is one of the best spots for dining in Kalmar. From a terraced pavilion overlooking the water, you can sample one of the many soups Byttan Restaurant specializes in; they, too, are some of the best in town. Examples include cream of lobster and cream of mushroom. Main courses range from omelets to filet of beef with red-wine sauce and forest mushrooms. Other dishes that might tantalize your palate include veal steak in a pepper-flavored cream sauce, sliced tenderloin of pork with red-wine and herb sauce, and our all-time favorite here, salmon with a Riesling sauce (you also can order it with butter sauce). Guests may dine in the pavilion or in the vine-covered courtyard. The food is good and attractively prepared, and even if you don't come for a meal, the restaurant is a good place to have afternoon tea.

In 1994, the restaurant was enlarged with the addition of a bistro-inspired annex known as Däcket. Outfitted with wood paneling and shades of pale green, in summer it serves the same menu, during the same hours, as the main dining area. In winter, however, it features a simpler menu costing about 15% less than in the main dining area.

Slottsvägen 1. © **0480/163-60.** Reservations recommended in summer. Fixed-price lunch 68SEK ($8.85); main courses 162SEK–185SEK ($21–$24). AE, DC, MC, V. June–Aug Mon–Sat 11am–2pm and 5–9pm, Sun 1–5pm; Dec–May daily 11am–2:30pm and 8–10pm. Closed Sept–Nov.

Kalmar Hamn Krog ⭐⭐ INTERNATIONAL   Established in 1988, this quickly became the most stylish and gastronomically sophisticated restaurant in Kalmar, and it remains so today. Traditionally, Kalmar Hamn Krog is the site of celebratory meals and anniversary parties—it's that special. The restaurant was built from scratch on an old pier where steamships used to deposit passengers from the neighboring island of Öland. Today the interior is all blue and white. The kitchen staff slaves away to maintain the restaurant's high-ranking position in Kalmar, and the products that go into the cuisine are the best in the city. Recommended dishes include pork filet with a port-wine sauce, or the grilled halibut with a dill and lemon-grass stew. We also are especially fond of the filet of pike-perch in a sweet-and-sour curry sauce. One unusual specialty is the grilled steak with piña colada sauce. The latter gives the meat a scent of coconut-flavored rum and a hint of the tropics—most unusual in these northern climes. The wines are from Austria, the United States, and France, among other countries.

Skeppsbrogatan 30. © **0480/411-020.** Reservations required. Main courses 182SEK–250SEK ($24–$33); fixed-price lunch 70SEK ($9.10); fixed-priced dinner 249SEK ($32). AE, MC, V. Mon–Fri 11:30am–2pm; Mon–Sat 5–10pm.

Salut ⭐ *Finds* SWEDISH/CONTINENTAL   This is our favorite middle-bracket bistro in Kalmar, with reasonable prices, enough variety to please any palate, and a refreshing lack of pretensions. It consists of two separate dining rooms, one brick-lined and designated for smokers and another with wallpaper and oil paintings that's reserved for nonsmokers. An attentive staff offers dishes that include at least a half-dozen kinds of pasta, including vegetarian pastas, seafood pastas, and one version with strips of grilled steak and Gorgonzola sauce. Also look for grilled salmon with saffron sauce, grilled steaks with your choice of at least four different sauces, filets of sole with white-wine sauce, and a dessert specialty of deep-fried Camembert with hot cloudberry preserves. Meals are prepared with fresh ingredients whenever available, and no sauce or spice overwhelms the natural flavor. The food is consistently generous and well prepared.

Storgatan 10. ℂ **0480/870-87.** Reservations recommended. Fixed-price lunch 62SEK ($8.05); main courses 84SEK–188SEK ($11–$24). AE, DC, MC, V. Daily 11am–11pm. Bus 4, 11, or 401.

Tommy's Italian-American Restaurant INTERNATIONAL   Set on the lobby level of the also-recommended hotel, this is a warm, cozy denlike room that celebrates the kind of Italian-American context that's celebrated on cheery American sitcoms. Expect painted depictions on the walls of both the Italian and the U.S. flag, red-and-white-checkered tablecloths, flickering candles, a long and hospitable bar area, and food that includes pasta, quesadillas, Caesar salads, baby back ribs, burgers, grilled fish—most caught within Swedish seas and lakes—and all kinds of juicy steaks.

In the Kalmarsund Hotell, Fiskaregatan 5. ℂ **0480/18100.** Reservations recommended. Main courses 109SEK–189SEK ($14–$25). AE, DC, MC, V. Mon–Sat 6–10pm.

KALMAR AFTER DARK
If a major cultural event is being staged, its likely venue is the local concert hall: **KalmarSalen,** Skeppsbrogatan 49 (ℂ **0480/42-10-00**). Otherwise, most of the nighttime activity centers on **Krogers,** Lärmtorget 7 (ℂ **0480/265-50**). It is merely a bar and offers no live entertainment.

2 Växjö

110km (68 miles) W of Kalmar, 443km (275 miles) S of Stockholm

Sweden's "Kingdom of Crystal" starts in Växjö, the central community for all of Småland. Some 16 factories here produce world-renowned Swedish crystal. The name Växjö comes from *Vägsjön,* or "lake where the roads meet." In addition to glassworks, this 14th-century city offers scenic lakes and forests, and traditional red-timbered cottages.

ESSENTIALS
GETTING THERE   By Plane   There are two daily flights between Stockholm and Växjö, arriving at the Växjö Airport, 9km (5½ miles) north of the center. For flight information, call ℂ **0470/759-210.**

By Train   There are train connections from Gothenburg, leaving at 7am daily and arriving in Växjö at noon; from Malmö, leaving at 6:14am and arriving in Växjö at 12:18pm.

Trains arrive hourly throughout the day from Kalmar. Call ℂ **771/75-75-75.**

By Bus   From Stockholm, buses leave on Monday to Saturday (take Express Bus) at 9am and 4pm; Sunday noon, 1:30pm, 3pm, and 5pm. Call ℂ **771/77-77-77.**

By Car   From Stockholm, take E4 south to Norrköping, then continue south along E66 to Kalmar. At Kalmar, head west on Route 25.

Växjö

ATTRACTIONS●
Småland Museum **3**
Svenska Emigrantinstitutet
    (House of Emigrants) **2**
Växjö Cathedral **1**

ACCOMMODATIONS■
First Hotel Cardinal **6**
Hotel Statt **4**
Hotel Värend **5**
Royal Corner Hotel **7**
Scandic Hotel Växjö **8**

VISITOR INFORMATION The **Växjö Tourist Information Office,** located at Stationen Kungsgatan 11 (© **0470/414-10**), is open mid-June to mid-August Monday to Friday 9:30am to 6pm, Saturday 10am to 2pm, and Sunday 10am to 2pm; off season, Monday to Friday 9:30am to 4:30pm.

SEEING THE SIGHTS

In summer, between mid-June and late August, tours on Lake Helgåsjön are conducted aboard the century-old steamer *S/S Angaren Thor,* which reigns as one of the oldest wood-fired steamships in Scandinavia today. Don't expect state-of-the-art hardware aboard this ship, as part of the allure derives from old-fashioned brass fittings and a maritime dowdiness that is rapidly on the way to achieving high camp. A 2½-hour tour costs 125SEK ($16); a 3½-hour tour, which usually includes some kind of food, goes for 400SEK ($52). Other tours to more distant parts of the lake are arbitrarily scheduled, and are canceled and reactivated according to the weather, prior bookings, and the whim of the owners. For information and reservations, inquire at the local tourist office.

Småland Museum   Established in 1792, this is the oldest provincial museum in Sweden. Since 1996, the museum—which is located near the train station—has been much improved and enlarged, with a new wing focusing on the history of Swedish glassmaking. You'll see tools and archives from the early days of the craft, with a special collection of more than 25,000 pieces. In a separate exhibit are displays of the finest artistic examples of **Swedish glass** ★★★ produced over the centuries. In other areas of the museum you can view one of Sweden's largest art exhibits, collections of coins, religious objects, weapons, and a special room housing an ethnological collection. Forestry and agricultural exhibits are also included.

Södra Järnvägsgatan 2. (✆) **0470/70-42-00.** Admission 40SEK ($5.20) adults, 20SEK ($2.60) students, free for those 19 and under. June–Aug Mon–Fri 10am–5pm, Sat–Sun 11am–5pm; Sept–May Tues–Fri 10am–5pm, Sat–Sun 11am–5pm. All buses.

Svenska Emigrantinstitutet (House of Emigrants) ★★   This institution, founded in 1968, documents the 1.3 million Swedish people who left their homeland during the "America fever" years—the 1850s to the 1920s—and moved to the United States. The house contains exhibits on emigrant history as well as archives and a research library. A permanent exhibition, the *Dream of America,* presents insights into the background and consequences of the emigration. Minnesota Day is a folk festival held the second Sunday in August each year, drawing thousands of Swedes and Swedish-Americans.

Museiparken. (✆) **0470/201-20.** Admission 40SEK ($5.20) adults, 5SEK (65¢) children 7-16 years old. June–Aug Mon–Fri 9am–5pm, Sat 11am–4pm, Sun 11am–4pm; Sept–May Mon–Fri 9am–4pm, Sat–Sun 11am–4pm. Bus: 4.

Växjö Cathedral   Legend has it that this cathedral stands on the spot where St. Sigfrid (Småland's missionary from York, England, in the 11th c.) erected his little wooden church. The cathedral has copper-clad towers and a bright interior, and its chimes are heard three times a day. Summer concerts are held in the cathedral Thursdays at 8pm.

Adjacent to the cathedral is **Linnéparken (LinnéPark),** named for Carl von Linné (Carolus Linnaeus), the Swedish botanist who developed the scientific categories of plants. In the park, an arboretum displays 24 categories of perennials. There also are other flower gardens throughout and a playground for children. The cathedral is in the town center, by **Linnéparken.**

Linnégatan. (✆) **0470/704-824.** Free admission. Daily 9am–5pm. Bus: 4.

SHOPPING IN THE KINGDOM OF CRYSTAL

Between Kalmar and Växhö, within an hour's drive, are several glassworks, including **Orrefors** and **Kosta Boda.** Kosta Glassworks and Boda Glassworks have been the leading names in Swedish crystal since the 19th century. However, they have pooled their resources to become "Kosta Boda" and now operate as one empire, although many of their original glassworks still maintain a separate identity. Not only can you go on Sweden's grandest shopping trip, but you can see master glassblowers—among the world's finest—at work.

Åfors Glasbruk ★★   At a point 29km (18 miles) west of Nybro and 50km (31 miles) south of Växjö, Åfors is a Kosta Boda glassworks, the domain of glass designers Bertil Vallien and his wife, Ulrica Hydman-Vallien, two of the most famous names in Swedish glass. It also is the showcase of Gunnel Sahlin, who often brings experiences of nature into the blowing room with her. She likes to combine contrasting elements—soft round forms and simple lines, and silky smooth surfaces and bright, brilliant color. Bertil Vallien is known for his stout Château Bohème glasses, rustic and masculine with a satisfying heft. His wife Ulrica's work is simple and clean, using strong colors. This place is especially popular with Christmas shoppers, as it is known for its ornaments. Rte. 25, Eriksmala. (C) **0471/41814.** Factory shop Mon–Fri 9am–6pm; Sat 10am–4pm; Sun 11am–5pm.

Boda Glasbruk ⭐   Although the Boda Glassworks (founded in 1864) long ago merged its administration with that of the Kosta Glassworks, this is the showroom for production of the Boda division of the conglomerate. Playful, even cheeky design is given free rein at Boda. Designers make wine glasses that dance, salad bowls that evoke the sweet smells of summer, and vases in which you can hear whispers of the jungle. The glass innovators here love to goad your senses and are never afraid to test the limits of their material. Sometimes glass might be combined with iron, while at other times decorated with feathers! Located in the village of Boda, about 19km (12 miles) west of Nybro, it offers a discounted collection of seconds. Their flaws are almost imperceptible, but their prices are substantially lower than normal retail for more perfect pieces. Storgatan (Hwy. 25). (C) **0481/42410.** Free admission. Mon–Fri 9am–6pm; Sat 10am–3pm; Sun 11am–4pm. Bus: 218 from Lessebo, which has rail links to Växjö.

Kosta Glasbruk   This main headquarters of the Kosta complex was founded in 1742 by two former generals, Anders Koskull and Georg Bogislaus Stael von Holstein, who at first brought in glass-blowing talent from Bohemia, which was then the reigning kingdom of crystal. Kosta pioneered the production of crystal, which must, by law, contain about one-fourth oxide. Here you can see the old Kosta Museum, with articles from the 18th and 19th centuries as well as exhibitions of contemporary glass. Despite Kosta's merger with the nearby Boda Glassworks, this entity retains much of its separate identity. The best buys here are on items that have been discontinued. Artists here tell us they get their inspiration from just about anything—the dew on a meadow, the morning mist on a lake, or a Swedish summer sky. Storavägen 96, Hwy. 28. (C) **0478/345-00.** Late June to early Aug Mon–Fri 9am–7pm, Sat 10am–5pm, Sun 11am–5pm; off season Mon–Fri 10am–5pm, Sat 10am–3pm, Sun 10am–3pm. Located between Eriksmala and the junction with Rte. 31, 19km (12 miles) east of Orrefors.

Målerås Glasbruk   Set within a 10-minute drive from Orrefors (see below), this factory belongs to one of the few independent glassmakers still left in the glass district, the Målerås company. Much of their production revolves around the engravings of master artisan Mats Jonasson, whose trademark involves vivid images that are a bit less formal than those produced by competing (larger) manufacturers. Vivid images such as a Dalmatian pup, his eyes glowing with mischief, are captured in the clearest of crystal, as well as images of flora and fauna. Especially intriguing here is the Black Magic collection, bowls in dramatic black glass with a sandblasted rim. The effect has been likened to one of Småland's deep forest ponds. After careful inspection of the seconds here, we could find no flaws, but the designer could—hence the reduced prices. Prices here are about half what you'd pay for similar purchases in Stockholm. Rte. 31, 15km (9¼ miles) NW of Orrefors. (C) **0481/31400.** Free admission. Mon–Fri 9am–6pm; Sat 10am–5pm; Sun 11am–5pm.

Orrefors Glasbruk ⭐⭐   Orrefors, between Nybro and Lenhovda, 40km (25 miles) west of Kalmar, is one of the most famous names in Swedish glass. Guided tours are conducted Monday to Friday from 9:30am to 2:30pm any time someone shows up. During most of the year a visit incorporates tours of

Buying Swedish Glass

The temperature inside the furnace is 2,066°F (1,130°C). The gatherer reaches into its flaming interior, gathers the glowing melt on the blowing iron, and hands it over to the blower. The caramel-soft material sizzles as it is shaped against wet newsprint in the hands of the gaffer. Only an expert's touch will do now—a touch schooled by years of experience. When it's time for the gaffer to put the handle on a pitcher, he has to "see" how hot the glass is. If it's too hot, the attachment will run off or go through the pitcher. If it's too cold, it will be impossible to attach. Hand-blown glass is a living craft, born in the hands of glass workers.

Shopping in the Kingdom of Crystal is one of Sweden's best tourism opportunities, especially if you keep the following points in mind: An average purchase can save you as much as 75% off stateside prices—and if you're willing to settle for seconds or glass with certain flaws, you can save still more. Even if it is flawed, the glassware sold in the area is much superior to what you are likely to find in your local shopping mall back home. However, before heading here it's always best to do some advance scouting of the glass outlets in Stockholm, so you'll be familiar with the prices when you arrive. Seek out the red tags in the Växjö outlets; they signal that the glass has been greatly reduced in price for quick clearance. You can always look for special promotional deals that might be offered at any time of the year, depending on an outlet's inventory.

Bumps, discoloration, nicks, and bubbles are the most common faults in "seconds," but sometimes they are virtually unnoticeable except to a trained eye. Ask a factory if it's selling any discontinued styles. These products are invariably marked down for quick clearance. If you're a collector, you no doubt already know that a signed piece of art glass has value whereas an unsigned piece does not. Before leaving the store, make absolutely certain that the piece of glass you purchased (obviously not art glass) can go into the dishwasher. If it can't, you'll have to wash the glass by hand. Detergents can cause glass to lose some of its luster.

If you're a light shopper, you can hand-carry your purchases back on the plane, providing they are carefully wrapped. You also can have the store ship your glass home for you. On certain items, assuming you're getting a bargain, the cost of glass purchased in the "kingdom" can still be about 50% cheaper in Sweden than in the United States, even when shipping costs are added. As a rule, shipping costs equal about 30% of the marked price on the item. If your glass arrives broken, take a picture of the damaged merchandise and send it with a letter along with a copy of your receipt to the factory at which you made the purchase. All breakage is replaced.

Finally, count on visiting no more than six to eight outlets per day. Pick up a map at the tourist office in Växjö and devise your attack plan from that.

divisions that include glassblowers, cutters, and engravers of fine glass. In July, the cutters and engravers are on vacation, although demonstrations of glass-blowing are still available. It's possible to purchase seconds (in most cases, hardly distinguishable from perfect pieces) and gift shipments can be arranged. Tax-free shopping can also be arranged in the factory's shop.

Although a handful of Orrefor subsidiaries (Sandvik and Strömbergshyttan) also offer tours of their factories, the most complete and comprehensive tours are presented by Orrefors. The best plan may be to tour Orrefors first and then inquire about specialized tours of the company's subsidiaries. Rte. 31, Orrefors. © 0481/341-995. Free admission. June–July Mon–Fri 10am–4pm, Sat 11am–4pm, Sun noon–4pm; Aug–May Mon–Fri 10am–6pm, Sat 10am–4pm, Sun noon–4pm.

Studioglas Strömbergshyttan   Lying 31km (19 miles) east of Växjö, along Route 25, is the domain of three master blowers: Håkan Gunnarsson, Leif Persson, and Mikael Axenbrandt. The trio started this studio in 1987 with a determination to experiment to the utmost limit. The three glassblowers give their own creativity free rein in front of the furnace, creating dishes, vases, and decorative pieces with an utterly free approach to the glowing melt. Colors are brilliant and freely combined. Look for Anna Örnberg's work, which has a youthful audacity and a warm sense of humor; her vases and small bowls seem to burst with joy. For example, Anna puts pouting lips on fruit-colored fish vases that balance on their tail fins. The best days to visit are Monday and Wednesday, when you can see more artisans at work. Hovmantorp. © 0478/310-75. Free admission. Mon–Fri 9am–6pm; Sat 10am–4pm; Sun noon–4pm.

THE WORLD'S OLDEST WORKING PAPER MILL

Lessebo Papermill *Finds*   In the heart of the glassworks district, the small town of Lessebo on Route 25, lying 35km (22 miles) west of Orrefors, has as its major attraction this paper mill, the world's oldest working producer of hand-made paper. In existence since 1693, the mill is open to the public, so you can watch as paper passes through the various stages of production, from cotton pulp to individual sheets that are pressed and hung to dry. There's a gift shop where you can purchase handmade products, and tours are available in English, costing 250SEK ($33) for anywhere from 10 to 22 persons. You should call in advance and make arrangements if you want a formal tour; however, most visitors just show up, collect the English-language pamphlets, stroll around the property, drop into the gift shop, and ask questions of the friendly, polite staff, most of whom speak English. Hwy. 25, Lessbro. © 0771/110000. Free admission. Mon–Fri 8am–6pm; Sat–Sun 10am–4pm.

WHERE TO STAY

First Hotel Cardinal ✪   This appealing, traditionally decorated four-story hotel on Storgatan (the main street of town) provides first-class service to a clientele that includes lots of business travelers. In the late 1980s, the owners of this hotel radically renovated a turn-of-the-20th-century apartment building and then restored the entire property in 1997. Bedrooms are well upholstered and decorated with more formality than you might expect—in some cases, with Oriental carpets and a scattering of exposed timbers and beams under the eaves. Beds are especially comfortable, often with hypoallergenic bed coverings. Bathrooms are medium-size and come equipped with shower. Bäckgatan 10, S-352 30 Växjö. © 0470/722800. Fax 0470/722808. www.firsthotels.com. 71 units. July–Aug and Fri–Sat year-round 824SEK ($107) double, 1,250SEK ($163) suite; rest of year 1,531SEK ($199) double, 1,930SEK ($251) suite. Rates include breakfast. AE, DC, MC, V. Parking 85SEK ($11). **Amenities:** Restaurant;

bar; gym; sauna; limited room service; laundry service; dry cleaning; nonsmoking rooms; rooms for those w/limited mobility. *In room:* TV, dataport, minibar, hair dryer.

Hotell Värend ★ *Finds*   Under the management of the hardworking Wadsworth family, this hotel emerged from the premises of what was originally built as a four-unit apartment house in the 1890s. Richly renovated and upgraded in 1996, but with very few of its original architectural adornments, the hotel lies just a 5-minute walk north of Växjö's main square, within a quiet residential neighborhood filled with private homes. Good-size bedrooms are clean, tasteful, simple, and well insulated against the harsh winters of central Sweden—safe havens for a cost-effective night or two. The beds are very comfortable and the bathrooms, though small, are beautifully maintained, and include tub/showers. All rooms are nonsmoking.

Kungsgatan 27, S-352 33 Växjö. © **0470/104-85.** Fax 0470/362-61. www.hotellvarend.se. 24 units. July and Fri–Sat year-round 650SEK ($85) double; rest of year 790SEK ($103) double. Rates include breakfast. AE, DC, MC, V. Free parking. **Amenities:** Restaurant (only breakfast); 1 room for those w/limited mobility. *In room:* TV, dataport.

Hotel Statt *Value*   This venerable old hostelry has, after several restorations, become a choice place to stay, successfully combining the old and the new. Bedrooms have a bit of style and flair—they often have hardwood floors and provide a homelike feeling with Oriental carpeting. Bathrooms are larger than average and often luxuriously appointed—some with a Jacuzzi, and all with a tub/shower. The hotel's restaurant is outfitted like a rustic Swedish tavern, with strong, dark colors and a traditional menu of *husmanskost* (country cooking). Windows can be opened for gusts of fresh air.

Kungsgatan 6, S-351 04 Växjö. © **0470/134-00.** Fax 0470/448-37. 134 units. June 19–Aug 9 and Fri–Sun year-round 795SEK ($103) double, 1,025SEK ($133) suite; rest of year 1,395SEK ($181) double, 1,795SEK ($233) suite. Rates include breakfast. AE, DC, MC, V. Free parking. Bus: 4. **Amenities:** Restaurant; bar; nightclub; 24-hr. room service; laundry service; dry cleaning; nonsmoking rooms; rooms for those w/limited mobility. *In room:* TV, dataport (in some), minibar (in some).

Royal Corner Hotell   In the town center, this first-class hotel rises six floors, taller than any other structure in town. The view from the upper floors offers panoramic vistas of Småland. Built in 1985 and since then well maintained, the hotel—with its standardized bedrooms outfitted with Nordic pieces and functional style—might remind you of a good American hotel. Rooms are only slightly larger than average, and bathrooms are small but beautifully maintained with shower stalls and tubs.

Liedbergsgatan 11, S-352 32 Växjö. © **800/780-7234** in the U.S., or 0470/701000. Fax 0470/701-010. www.royalcorner.se. 158 units. Sun–Thurs 1,495SEK ($194) double; Fri–Sat 790SEK ($103) double; 898SEK–1,795SEK ($117–$233) suite. AE, DC, MC V. Free parking. Bus: 4. **Amenities:** Restaurant; bar; indoor pool; fitness center; sauna; limited room service; laundry service; dry cleaning; nonsmoking rooms; rooms for those w/limited mobility. *In room:* A/C, TV, dataport, hair dryer.

Scandic Hotel Växjö *Value*   One of the best-value hotels in Växjö, built in 1979, the Scandic offers well-furnished bedrooms, including some large enough for families. Each room is fitted in bright shades of blue, green, or pink and yellow, with good beds and small but well-maintained bathrooms with tub/showers. The hotel lies 3km (1¾ miles) west of the center of town on the road going to the airport.

Hejaregatan 19, S-352 46 Växjö. © **0470/736-000.** Fax 0470/736011. www.scandic-hotels.com. 123 units. Sun–Thurs 1,451SEK ($189) double; Fri–Sat 750SEK ($98) double. Rates include breakfast. AE, DC, MC, V. Free parking. Bus: 4. **Amenities:** Restaurant; bar; indoor pool; sauna; nonsmoking rooms; 1 room for those w/limited mobility. *In room:* TV, dataport.

WHERE TO DINE

Throughout the environs of Växjö and Orrefors, you'll find lots of separate and independent restaurant options, but one of the most enduring dining traditions involves an age-old method of cooking fish, potatoes, and sausages in the cooling chambers of the glassworks. Inaugurated during an era when fuel was conserved with something approaching religious zeal, the tradition, known as *Hyttsill,* developed into a slow-cooking method that made simple, hearty food particularly succulent, especially to hungry factory workers toiling in the cold.

This antique presentation is duplicated today as part of randomly scheduled evening entertainment provided by three of the region's biggest glassmakers. After the day's closing of some of the factories, usually around 3pm, trestle tables and simple chairs are carried onto the factory floor as a means of duplicating the simple communal meals of long ago. During the summer months, the large glassworks usually rotate the days and hours of their presentations.

Advance reservations are necessary, and per-person fees average 325SEK ($42) for a full meal, with schnapps and beer an additional 30SEK to 40SEK ($3.90–$5.20) per glass. The meals invariably include such traditional glassmakers' dishes as herring with cream and onions, roasted or baked potatoes (traditionally these were baked in the hot ashes produced as a byproduct of the firing process), pork sausages, mustard, bread and butter, local cheeses, and cheesecake.

As part of the package, the organizers of these events usually include live musical entertainment and demonstrations of glassblowing. Be warned in advance that this is very much a movable feast. Even during the peak of midsummer, there's likely to be only about three of them scheduled during any week; during the winter, they might occur only once a month as a specially arranged group event that individuals can attend if they reserve a spot in advance. To be certain of getting a place, phone each of the glassworks individually, or phone any of the tourist offices within the area, for information and confirmations. For information and reservations for a meal served within the floor, call the **Kosta Glassworks** at © **0478/34529,** the **Bergdala Glassworks** at © **0478/31650,** or the **Orrefors Glassworks** at © **0481/34000.**

Orrefors Inn ⚘ SWEDISH   Set in the center of the cluster of glass factories that have always dominated the economy of Orrefors, this historic inn was established in 1898 within four dining rooms of a wood-sided building that remains very similar to the original. You might imagine yourself in a rustic farmhouse, dining on a menu that's unrelentingly Swedish and in many ways authentic to the cuisine that many locals remember from childhood. Menu items include grilled salmon or steak served on a wooden platter, Swedish meatballs with brown sauce and roasted potatoes, and local moose steak with forest mushrooms and boiled potatoes. Don't expect the grand or experimental cuisine you might look for in Stockholm; instead, you'll get rib-sticking fare that can perk you up for a round of glass shopping at any of the nearby gift shops.

Hwy. 22, Orrefors. © **0481/300-59.** Main courses 75SEK–155SEK ($9.75–$20); fixed-price menu 75SEK ($9.75). AE, DC, MC, V. Mid-Oct to mid-Mar Mon–Fri 9am–6pm, Sat 11am–4pm, Sun noon–5pm; mid-Mar to mid-Oct Mon–Fri 9am–2pm.

3 Jönköping

350km (217 miles) SW of Stockholm, 150km (93 miles) NE of Gothenburg, 200km (124 miles) NE of Helsingborg

At the southern rim of Lake Vättern, this is the lake's largest town. It once was famous for manufacturing matchsticks, and the original factory from the 1840s still stands, although it no longer makes this product. However, a fascinating cultural area has been built up around the match museum. It's called the *Tänd-sticksområdet,* or "matchstick area."

Pronounced *yun-shurp-ing,* Jönköping is one of the oldest trading centers in Sweden, left over from the Middle Ages when it was granted its town charter in 1284. In the 19th century, the town was virtually synonymous with the match-sticks used all over Europe and the local merchants became prosperous. However, in 1932, when demand had dwindled drastically, the local match tycoon, Ivar Kruger, shot himself rather than face bankruptcy. The end came to the industry shortly thereafter.

Today a thriving town of some 52,000 people, Jönköping is a good base for exploring some of the more interesting points along the southern tier of Lake Vättern.

ESSENTIALS

GETTING THERE   By Train   There's rail service from Stockholm every other hour throughout the day, with transfers required en route at the junction of Nässgö. Travel time from Stockholm by train, depending on transfers, takes about 3½ hours. From Kalmar, there usually are five trains per day to Jönköping, with two transfers required en route. Travel time ranges from 4 to 5 hours, depending on connections. For information and timetables, call © **771/75-75-75.**

By Bus   Bus transfers to Jönköping are preferable to train transfers, as they're more frequent and, in most cases, more direct. There's at least one bus an hour arriving from Stockholm throughout the day, with no changes required en route. The trip takes about 4½ hours. For bus information and timetables, call © **0200/21818** (within Sweden).

By Car   From Växjö, continue along Route 30 northwest, directly into Jönköping.

VISITOR INFORMATION   The **Jönköping Turistbyrån** is at Resecentrum (© **036/10-50-50;** www.jonkoping.se/turism). Open Monday to Friday 9am to 6pm, Saturday 9:30am to 2pm, Sunday 11am to 4pm. Otherwise, hours are Monday to Friday 11am to 4pm, closed on weekends.

MATCHES & MORE

Built in 1844, the town's largest match factory today is the home of **Tänd-sticksmuséet,** Västra Storgatan 18 (© **036/10-55-43**). The museum documents the industry that made Jönköping famous and displays everything from match-making machines to matchbox labels. Before Jönköping entered the industry, matches were extremely dangerous. Phosphorous was used on the striking head, which was both poisonous to the factory workers and dangerous in the box when the match heads were rubbed against each other. But in 1855, Johan Edvard Lundström of Jönköping invented the safety match, which used red amorphous phosphorus on the striking surface of the box itself. This invention revolutionized the industry. A video is shown documenting the town's former industry. From May to August, hours are Monday to Friday from 10am to 5pm, Saturday and Sunday 10am to 3pm. From September to April, it is open Tuesday to Saturday 11am to 3pm. Admission is 40SEK ($5.20) for adults, free for 18 and younger.

Another museum of note is **Jönköping Lans Museum,** Dag Hammarskjölds Plats 4 (© **036/30-18-00**), the county museum that traces the history of Små-land, often to archaeological digs. The history of the area is documented over the past 10,000 years. Exhibits extend into modern times, up to the invention of the sewing machine. There is also a collection of Swedish art, focusing mainly on the works of John Bauer, who became famous in Sweden for his Tolkienesque depictions of trolls and gnomes. Admission is 40SEK ($5.20), free for ages 18 and under. Open Tuesday to Saturday 11am to 5pm.

Finally, **Friluftsmuséet,** Stadsparken (© **036/301800**), is an open-air museum in the town park. Interesting from a historical point of view, it exhibits numerous old Småland buildings—notably a cottage from the 17th century. It's open June to August 11am to 5pm daily; closed the rest of the year.

WHERE TO STAY

Comfort Home Hotel Victoria ★   Set within the western sector of the town center, very close to the Västra Torget marketplace, this hotel evolved from the historic core of a once private stately home that was originally built in 1885. In 1991, it was radically renovated and enlarged into a modern-day member of a nationwide chain. Despite this role as a member of a formula-based chain, it has an intelligent staff and really conveys a sense of intimacy. Some of the public areas retain their original architectural details, elaborate cove moldings, and rich panels; bedrooms tend to be conservatively and appealingly decorated, usually with off-white walls and rich, dark upholstery. All of them have very good, sleep-friendly beds and ample-size bathrooms equipped with showers. The hotel's centerpiece is its inner courtyard, which, since 1991, has been sheltered from the elements with a greenhouse-style glass canopy.

F. E. Elmgrens Gata 5, Box 173, S-551 13 Jönköping. © **036/71-28-00.** Fax 035/71-50-50. www.victoriahome. com. 90 units. Sun–Thurs 1,295SEK–1,695SEK ($168–$220) double, 1,795SEK–1,995SEK ($233–$259) suite; Fri–Mon 750SEK–995SEK ($98–$129) double, 995SEK–1,195SEK ($129–$155) suite. Rates include breakfast. AE, DC, MC, V. Parking 85SEK ($11). **Amenities:** Restaurant; indoor pool; Jacuzzi; sauna; laundry service; dry cleaning; nonsmoking rooms; rooms for those w/limited mobility. *In room:* TV, dataport, minibar, hair dryer.

Elite Stora Hotellet ★★   This is one of the stateliest hotels in southeastern Sweden; its splendor emulates some of the architectural glory of a princely palace. Radically renovated in 1995, it's positioned in the heart of town, adjacent to an all-pedestrian street lined with shops, on the narrow isthmus that separates Lake Vättern from the smaller Lake Munksjön. Inside there is a curious blend of modern design that alternates with allegiance to the hotel's historic core. You'll find a modern-looking reception area that includes an ornate neoclassical banqueting room known as the Hall of Mirrors. The largish bedrooms are clean, well maintained, and evocative of an upscale private home—one that's faithful to elegantly rustic farmhouse models. Each has a hardwood floor and either flowered or checked upholstery that deliberately evokes old-fashioned Sweden. The ample-size bathrooms contain tub/showers and are well maintained.

Hotellplan, Box 23, S-551 12 Jönköping. © **800/843-3311** in the U.S., or 036/10-00-00. Fax 036/215-50-25. www.elite.se. 135 units. June–Aug and Fri–Sun year-round 745SEK ($97) double; rest of year 1,495SEK ($194) double; 2,095SEK ($272) suite. Rates include breakfast. AE, DC, MC, V. Parking 70SEK ($9.10). **Amenities:** Restaurant; 2 bars; sauna; limited room service; laundry service; dry cleaning; nonsmoking rooms; rooms for those w/limited mobility. *In room:* TV, dataport (in some), minibar, hair dryer.

John Bauer Hotel ★   One of the most famous and beloved artists to emerge from Jönköping was John Bauer (1882–1918), whose whimsical Art Nouveau–style illustrations for children's books are among the most famous in Sweden. This government-rated four-star hotel, which was built in the early 1980s, is named in his honor. In the center of town, its design is neither the most elegant, the most fashionable, nor necessarily the best decorated in Jönköping. But it is a homey, welcoming hotel, with a kind of kick-off-your-shoes-in-the-lobby-bar feeling. The bedrooms aren't particularly cutting edge in their decor but are cozy, clean, and warm, with ample bathrooms with tub/showers.

Södra Strandgatan 15, Box 2192, S-550 02 Jönköping. ℂ 800/633-6540 in the U.S., or 036/34-90-00. Fax 036/34-90-50. www.johnbauer.se. 100 units. June–Aug and Fri–Sat year-round 695SEK–950SEK ($90–$124) double, 1,350SEK ($176) suite; rest of year 875SEK–1,495SEK ($114–$194) double, 2,050SEK ($267) suite. Rates include breakfast. AE, DC, MC, V. Parking: 75SEK ($9.75). **Amenities:** Restaurant; bar; sauna; limited room service; laundry service; dry cleaning; nonsmoking rooms; rooms for those w/limited mobility. *In room:* TV, dataport (in some), minibar, hair dryer, iron (in some).

WHERE TO DINE

Entre Bar & Restaurant ★ *Finds* INTERNATIONAL   This restaurant made a splash when it opened, having ripped out the decor of an outmoded, old-fashioned predecessor and reinstalling an all-beige sleek-looking and minimalist replacement that's dotted with unusual modern art and still-life photographs of hunger-inducing food. Its position on the town's all-pedestrian main street guarantees a busy lunchtime crowd, and the creative interpretation of international food items keeps people coming back for more. Your meal might begin with a platter containing three different preparations of salmon (marinated, smoked, and a "surprise" version), carpaccio of veal, or an Iberian-inspired gazpacho. Main courses might feature a creative twist on a Provençal bouillabaisse made from fresh and saltwater Swedish fish, including halibut, roasted pork served with chanterelles, potato cakes, and a butter-and-lingonberry sauce. Other choices include saltwater char with citrus risotto, a citrus and fennel sauce, and a crispy pastrylike "square" made from fresh nectarines and apricots. Dessert, anyone? Consider a napoleon (puff pastry) stuffed with Bailey's liqueur and banana slices and drizzled with a pineapple salsa.

Borgmästaren Gränd. ℂ 036/16-14-40. Reservations recommended. Main courses 145SEK–235SEK ($19–$31); set-price lunch 65SEK ($8.45). AE, DC, MC, V. Mon–Sat 11:30am–3pm and 6–11pm.

Trôttoaren SWEDISH/INTERNATIONAL   In this previously recommended hotel, this 150-seat restaurant is located on the ground floor. It is one of the finest dining rooms in the area, patronized by locals and visitors alike. The fare is not particularly imaginative but is filling and hearty, even robust at times, and is prepared with first-rate ingredients. Our recent platter of Swedish lamb was perfectly baked and seasoned, emerging aromatically from the oven. The chef also uses various preparations for his chicken dishes, especially one delightful version in a sherry sauce. Of course, you can anticipate well-flavored and tender steaks as well. For international flavor, specialties such as fajitas also appear on the menu.

In the Elite Stora Hotellet, Hotellplan. ℂ 036/10-00-00. Reservations recommended. Main courses 138SEK–1,258SEK ($18–$164). Fixed-price menu 235SEK ($31). AE, DC, MC, V. Mon–Tues 6–11pm; Wed–Sat 6pm–midnight.

JÖNKÖPING AFTER DARK

In the previously recommended Elite Stora Hotellet, Hotellplan (ℂ 036/10-00-00), **The Bishop's Arms** is an authentic-looking British-style pub, boasting Jönköping's largest selection of beer and whiskeys. In all, 22 beers are on tap, plus 140 different types of whiskey. Its trappings imported directly from England, it is the most popular place for a relatively young crowd to meet and socialize at night. If you're hungry, there's also a limited menu offering pub grub such as fish and chips, even nachos. Hours are Sunday to Thursday 4 to 11pm, or else Friday to Saturday 4:15pm to 2am.

4 Along the Shores of Lake Vättern

Jönköping (see above) can serve as your gateway to Lake Vättern, especially if you're driving north from Småand. However, even more charming places can be found along the lake, especially the towns of Gränna and Vadstena, as well as Motala.

This is Sweden's second-largest lake (the similarly named Lake Vänern is much larger; see chapter 9).

Following the eastern shore, E4 is the most scenic route, providing panoramic vistas across the lake. The lake can be a sailor's nightmare at times, as it is known for its rough waters and often strong winds.

The sports-minded are attracted to the lake, especially for angling. The average depth of the lake is 38m (125 ft.) and the deepest measured depth, south of Visingsö, is 127m (417 ft.). There are 28 different fish species remaining in this freshwater inland lake, which once was a sea bay. Some of these species have lived here since the Ice Age, including the famous Vättern alpine char. There is also an array of pike, perch, and pike-perch, along with grayling, salmon, and brown trout.

As a place for swimming, Lake Vättern has both a good and a bad reputation. Good because there aren't many inland lakes that can offer such long, Riviera-like beaches with water that is virtually drinkable; bad because of its great depth, and a temperature that one day can be suitable for swimming and the next day icy cold.

GRÄNNA
To reach this lakeside town, head north from Jönköping along E4. After a distance of 40km (25 miles), you reach Gränna, which lies at a point 280km (174 miles) southwest of Stockholm and 230km (143 miles) east of Gothenburg. The town of Tranås lies 40km (25 miles) from Gränna and is on the main rail route between Stockholm and Malmö. From Tranås, several buses make the final run to Gränna.

You can head first for the **Gränna-Visingsö Turistbyrå,** Brahegatan 48 (© **0390/410-10** or 0390/401-93), open June to September daily 10am to 7pm. The rest of the year, hours are Monday to Friday 11am to 4pm.

Gränna was founded in 1652 by Count Per Brahe, one of the first Swedish counts to be governor of Finland. Nowadays it is mainly a summer town with boutiques, arts and crafts stalls, and a harbor area with camping, bathing, and restaurants. The town is known for its striped peppermint candy and for its devotion to hot-air ballooning. Per Brahe encouraged the planting of pear orchards in the environs, and pears from Gränna today are ranked as the finest in Scandinavia.

The **peppermint candy** industry is still going strong, and almost everyone who comes here picks up one or several as a souvenir. These red-and-white candy sticks, or *Polkargris,* were first made in 1859 by widow Amalia Eriksson. Today they come in a wide assortment of flavors, shapes, and colors, including sugar-free.

SEEING THE SIGHTS
Grännaberger, or Gränna Mountain, can be reached either by car from the road between Gränna and Tranås or by climbing the steps that begin in a couple of places in town. Here you find a splendid view and a fine area for walking, plus a few buildings from the 17th century. If you're energetic, you can walk along a

trail to **Skogstornet (Forest Tower),** from which the view of the area around
Lake Vättern is panoramic. The Gränna area is a rich repository of Iron Age
weapons, tools, *menhirs* (monoliths), and burial grounds, some 4,000 years old.

Gränna was the birthplace of the North Pole balloonist-explorer Salomon
August Andrée, who made an ill-fated attempt in 1897 to cross the pole in the
balloon *Ornen* (Eagle). The remains of the expedition were found in 1930 and
can be seen in the **Andrée Museum,** Brahegatan 48 (© **0390/410-15**). With
funding by Alfred Nobel and King Oscar, the flight north toward the pole lasted
only 3 days. The balloon was forced to make a landing on ice. After 6 weeks of
trekking, Andrée and his men died, either from the cold or trichinosis, con-
tracted when they ate raw meat from a polar bear they'd speared. Their frozen
but well-preserved bodies and their equipment were discovered by a Norwegian
sailing ship, and the artifacts of that trip are on display at this museum.
Museigården, a part of the museum, houses exhibits illustrating the history of
the area. The museum is open from mid-May to mid-September daily 10am to

7pm, from mid-September to mid-May daily 11am to 4pm. Admission is 50SEK ($6.50) for adults and 20SEK ($2.60) for children.

NEARBY VISINGÖ ISLAND

A 20-minute ferry trip will take you from Gränna to the island of Visingsö, 6.5km (4 miles) across the water, for 40SEK ($5.20) adults, 20SEK ($2.60) children round-trip. Ferryboats leave every 20 minutes during the day in summer and eight times per day in winter. Boats depart from the central harbor at Gränna; for information, call ℂ 0390/410-25. There's a tourist office (summer information) near the point where the ferryboat docks.

The island can be traversed by car in 5 minutes, as it's long but very narrow. There are no road names or street numbers. In summer, some of the island residents meet arriving ferries with horse-drawn carriages for an excursion past the architectural highlights of the island (see below). The cost is 75SEK ($9.75) per adult, 40SEK ($5.20) for children 6 to 16, for a 90-minute tour. There is no phone to call for information—it's all very casual.

This has been an important site since humans first set foot here some 6,000 years ago and large, Viking-era graves indicate how busy the area once was. On the southern part of the island are the remains of Sweden's oldest secular building, **Nås Castle,** built around 1150. According to the Icelandic sagas, it had a large treasury and was an important target in the fighting between the eastern and western parts of southern Sweden in the Middle Ages. The castle burned down in 1319.

The remains of another castle, **Visingsborg,** are by the harbor. This was the seat of the Brahe family. The most illustrious member of the clan was Per Brahe (1520-1590), Count of Visingsö. Brahe was one of Gustavus Vasa's Privy Councillors. The Brahe family also built the island's **parish church** in the 1680s, using the walls of the Stroja medieval church as the foundations. The tower and the door of the sacristy are from the old church; the door has old runic writing signifying that it was made in the 11th century. The church is baroque, unusual by Swedish standards. Also to be seen on Visingsö is Count Brahe's reconstructed 17th-century garden.

Kumlaby Church, whose oldest parts date from the 12th century, has well-preserved 15th-century murals. Visitors can climb the tower to a small roof balcony where they have a panoramic view of the island. The church is open only June to August daily from 10:30am to 5pm, charging an admission of 10SEK ($1.30) adults, 5SEK (65¢) children 5 to 16 years old.

WHERE TO STAY & DINE

Hotel Gyllene Uttern   The "Golden Otter" is the honeymoon Shangri-la of Sweden, complete with a baroque wedding chapel in the basement. A step-gabled imitation castle built in 1937 overlooking Lake Vättern, 4km (2½ miles) south of Gränna on the highway (E4) to Stockholm, Gyllene Uttern offers the best in food and lodgings in the area. The main dining room is highlighted by gilt-framed paintings (copies of great masters), medieval suits of armor, deeply set windows with views of the lake, and a bas-relief fireplace. Food is served to both guests and nonguests, and regional specialties are featured.

Although the dining room and public rooms are in the main building, it contains only nine guest rooms; the rest of the rooms are spread across the grounds in the annexes that were constructed in the 1960s. Note that the seven rooms in the main (ca. 1930) building are the most nostalgic and old-fashioned—and they will remain that way. The rooms within the two more modern annexes are more contemporary in their furnishing and decor. All the rooms are equipped with fine bathrooms with tub/showers. Cabins, each crafted from wood in a rustic style, are available only in summer and contain only the most basic (hot-plate-style) cooking equipment.

On E4, S-563 92 Gränna. © **0390/108-00.** Fax 0390/418-80. www.gylleneuttern.se. 52 units, 6 cabins. Sun–Thurs 1,395SEK–1,695SEK ($181–$220) double, 2,150SEK ($280) suite; Fri–Sat 1,150SEK–1,695SEK ($150–$220) double, 2,150SEK ($280) suite; 571SEK–800SEK ($74–$104) cabin (available in summer). AE, DC, MC, V. Free parking. **Amenities:** Restaurant; bar; sauna; limited room service; laundry service; dry cleaning; nonsmoking rooms; rooms for those w/limited mobility. *In room:* TV, hair dryer.

Hotell Västanå Slott ⭐ *Finds* Although there are dozens of stately manors scattered throughout Sweden, this is one of the few that is open to the public. Formal and rigidly symmetrical, with a neoclassical design and a red-tile roof, it originally was built in 1590 and by 1641 was the power base for what eventually became the Vasa family dynasty. Ironically, the building was rendered smaller (not larger) during two subsequent renovations. In 1770, parts of its original roof were demolished and rebuilt, and in 1928, the entire third floor was pulled down and the castle got the design and look one sees today. If you overnight here, realize in advance that to some extent you are invading the much-treasured precincts of what some still consider a private home. Smoking is not permitted in any room. Bedrooms are high-ceilinged and spacious reminders of another era, with antiques, good carpets, and dramatic, sometimes allegorical paintings. Public rooms include suits of armor, frescoed ceilings, and historic mementos. No meals are served other than breakfast, but a nearby 18-hole golf course, where greens fees cost 280SEK to 330SEK ($36–$43), maintains a clubhouse where robust platters of food are served at both lunch and dinner every day. There's a tennis court within a short walk of the historic castle.

S-563-92 Gränna. © **0390/107-00.** Fax 0390/418-75. www.vastanaslott.se. 20 units. 750SEK–1,200SEK ($98–$156) double. MC, V. Closed Jan–Apr. Free parking. **Amenities:** Restaurant; laundry service; dry cleaning; rooms for those w/limited mobility. *In room:* Dataport.

VADSTENA ⭐

The most important stopover on the Göta Canal trip is this medieval town on the eastern shores of Lake Vättern; it's full of narrow streets and old frame buildings. The Middle Ages were Vadstena's great age of glory. The convent and church of St. Birgitta were known far and wide, and pilgrims thronged to see the saint's relics. King Gustav Vasa was a regular visitor in the 16th century and built the famous Vadstena castle. In fact, there was a royal palace in Vadstena as early as the 13th century, when Birgitta was a lady-in-waiting before she went on to found the convent. Today there are still Sisters of St. Birgitta at Vadstena Convent. Vadstena is also known all over Sweden for its handmade lace—to see samples of this delicate product, walk along *Stora Gatan,* the main street.

Vadstena lies 256km (159 miles) southwest of Stockholm, 260km (161 miles) northeast of Gothenburg, and 60km (37 miles) north of Gränna. From the last stopover at Gränna, continue north along E4 until you reach the junction with Route 50, at which point you veer off the main highway and continue along 50 until you reach Vadstena. Bus no. 840 runs daily from Jönköping, and bus no. 855 departs from the Central Station in Stockholm, but only on Friday and Sunday. If you're driving here from Stockholm, take E4 southwest; at the junction of Route 206, head northwest.

The tourist bureau, **Vadstena Turistbyrå,** is located at Rådhustorget, S-592 80 Vadstena (© **0143/315-70;** www.vadstena.se). It's open June daily 10am to 6pm; July daily 10am to 7pm; August 1 to August 13 daily 10am to 6pm; August 14 to August 31 daily 10am to 5pm; September 1 to September 12 Monday to Friday 10am to 4pm, and Saturday and Sunday 11am to 3pm; September 13 to April 29 Monday to Friday 11am to 2pm; and May daily 11am to 4pm.

SEEING THE SIGHTS

Vadstena Abbey ★★★   Built between the mid–14th and 15th centuries to specifications outlined by its founder, St. Birgitta (Bridget) of Sweden, this Gothic church is rich in medieval art. Parts of the abbey date from 1250. The abbey housed the nuns of St. Birgitta's order until their expulsion in 1595.

The New Monastery and Church, built in 1973, show the same traditional simplicity of style St. Birgitta prescribed for her order. The view to the huge windows is the only decoration in this otherwise stark church. The nuns, who returned to Sweden in 1963, will show the church and their guesthouse to interested visitors at times convenient to their own schedule. It's a 3-minute walk from Stora Torget.

Grasgatan 31. ✆ 0143/29850. Free admission. May and Sept daily 9am–5pm; June and Aug daily 9am–7pm; July daily 9am–8pm; Oct–Apr Mon–Sat 9am–3pm, Sun 11am–1pm.

Vadstena Castle   Founded in 1545 by Gustavus Vasa, king of Sweden, but not completed until 1620, this is one of the most splendid Renaissance Vasa castles, erected during a period of national expansion. It dominates the town from its position on the lake, just behind the old courthouse in the southern part of town. Vadstena was last inhabited by royalty in 1715 and was restored in the 19th century. Since 1899, the greater part of the castle has been used for provincial archives. In 1998, the Swedish federal government began, at vast expense, a massive renovation of the castle. The castle will remain open throughout the renovations.

Slottsvägen. ✆ 0143/31570. Admission 50SEK ($6.50) adults, 10SEK ($1.30) children 7–15, free for children 6 and under. June daily 11am–7pm; July daily 10:30am–6pm; Aug daily 11am–5pm; Sept–May Mon–Fri 11am–4pm.

WHERE TO STAY

Starby Kungsgård   As an estate, this place dates from the 1200s, when it was known for the fertility of its soil and its feudal prestige. In 1520, Swedish king Gustav Vasa added it to his roster of houses and castles, thereby beginning a fashion for members of the royal family and members of their entourage (including the legendary courtesan Hedwig Eleanora) to drop in for rest and relaxation. The building as you see it today, which lies less than a kilometer (about ½ mile) south of the town center, dates mostly from the late 1800s, except for wings built in 1984 that contain most of the establishment's bedrooms. Each of these is furnished with modern furniture, pastel colors, and sleek, functional styling with small bathrooms. Regrettably, the experience you'll have here will be a bit more staid and conservative than the building's racy origins would suppose. Some of the big attractions are the indoor swimming pool, the health club, and the Valven restaurant, which is recommended separately below.

Ödeshögsvägen, S-592 30 Vadstena. ✆ 0143/751-00. Fax 0143/751-70. www.edbergs.com. 61 units. July and Fri–Sat year-round 995SEK ($129) double; rest of year 1,295SEK ($168) double. Rates include breakfast. AE, DC, MC, V. Free parking. **Amenities:** Restaurant; bar; indoor pool; spa; sauna; nonsmoking rooms; rooms for those w/limited mobility. *In room:* TV, dataport.

Vadstena Klosterhotellet ★ *Finds*   What once was the premier religious stronghold in Sweden has been transformed into a hotel and conference center that welcomes individuals (and occasional church and civil groups) into its sprawling and echoing medieval premises. Set adjacent to the abbey church, about 640m (700 yards) from Vadstena Castle, it's contained within one wing of an L-shape building that was constructed in the 12th century as a convent. The remainder of the building—which includes 59 nuns' cells and the longest triple-barrel vault (57m/187 ft. long) in northern Sweden—can be explored without hindrance. As such, you'll get the feeling of living in a compact and discreetly modernized subdivision of a vast and once-mighty compound that included lodgings for monks, nuns, and various church hierarchies.

Accommodations are severely dignified and deliberately spartan-looking, with dark-stained copies of furniture inspired by medieval models, stark white walls, and a vague and anything-but-plush sense of their original function as lodgings for penitents. They are nonetheless comfortable, with high ceilings and simple, small, but adequate bathrooms with showers. Rooms that overlook the lake are at the high end of the price spectrum; units fronting the town and forest are at the low end.

Klosterområdet, S-592 00 Vadstena. ℂ 0143/315-30. Fax 0143/136-48. www.klosterhotel.se. 70 units. 895SEK–1,450SEK ($116–$189) double; 2,000SEK–2,500SEK ($260–$325) suite. Rates include breakfast. AE, DC, MC, V. Free parking. **Amenities:** 2 restaurants; bar; sauna; laundry service; dry cleaning; nonsmoking rooms; rooms for those w/limited mobility. *In room:* TV, dataport.

WHERE TO DINE

Rådhuskällaren SWEDISH   A meal here affords the opportunity to visit the interior of the oldest courthouse and town hall in Sweden, as the restaurant lies within an early-14th-century cellar, beneath vaulted ceilings, above medieval flagstone floors. Menu items are rib-sticking, substantial fare designed to ward off the cold of a Swedish winter. Examples include such staples as roasted beef with horseradish sauce, fried filets of codfish with dill sauce and boiled potatoes, tenderloin of pork with mushrooms in cream and béarnaise sauce, poached filet of lemon sole with an asparagus and leek ragout, and halibut steak with horseradish sauce. Dessert might be a slice of warm chocolate cake with elder flower ice cream.

Rådhustorget. ℂ 0143/121-70. Reservations recommended. Main courses 68SEK–178SEK ($8.85–$23). AE, DC, MC, V. Mid-May to Aug daily noon–10pm; Sept to mid-May Fri–Sat 3pm–2am.

Valven ⭐ SWEDISH/INTERNATIONAL   Set beside Vadstena's busiest commercial thoroughfare, this restaurant occupies a series of vaulted stone rooms that originally were built in the 15th century by the local church. Today the place is warmly illuminated, partially by candlelight, and maintained as the showcase restaurant by the also-recommended **Starby Kungsgård Hotel**, which lies within a 5-minute walk to the south. Regardless of where you sit within this place, a staff member will hand you two different menus, the simpler of which contains dishes such as cheese platters, steaks, salads, and sandwiches, and grilled chicken with herb sauce. The more elaborate menu offers a more upscale and finely honed cuisine, including grilled turbot with saffron sauce, tournedos with pepper sauce, smoked filet of reindeer, and bouillabaisse. Dessert might include a gratin of chocolate with forest berries and house-made ice cream.

Storgatan 18. ℂ 0143/123-40. Reservations recommended. Main courses on bistro menu 98SEK–163SEK ($13–$21); main courses on "restaurant menu" 189SEK–208SEK ($25–$27). Mon–Sat 11:30am–3pm and 6–10pm; Sun 11:30am–8pm. AE, DC, MC, V.

MOTALA

On the eastern shore of Lake Vättern, a stone's throw from the Göta Canal, Motala is called the "bicycle town," as it contains 50km (31 miles) of designated bicycle paths, which many local residents use year-round. Every June sees the running of the world's largest bicycle exercise race around Lake Vättern. The town lies 210km (130 miles) southwest of Stockholm, 472km (293 miles) northeast of Helsingborg, and 263km (163 miles) northeast of Gothenburg.

From Vadstena, continue north along Route 8, with Lake Vättern on your right, and you'll come to Motala after a drive of 13km (8 miles). If you're not driving, you can take bus no. 16, which runs along the eastern side of Lake Vättern.

Before reaching Stockholm, Göta Canal cruises go to Motala. And before reaching the canal, waters of the lake go to a flight of five locks, a dramatic sight that makes Motala one of the highlights of the Göta Canal cruises. Motala was designed by Baltzar von Platen, one of the waterway's creators, and he remains a popular local hero. His grave and statue lie side by side on the canal sidewalk.

For information about Motala and the surrounding area, call at the **Motala Turistbyrå,** Hamnen (© **0141/22-52-54;** www.motala.se), open June to August Monday to Friday 9am to 7pm, Saturday and Sunday 9am to 5pm. Off-season hours are Monday to Friday 9am to 5pm.

SEEING THE SIGHTS

The fan-shape layout of Motala was the creation of Baltzar von Platen. The town is rather bland but makes an excellent center for exploring nearby attractions. A pleasant way to enjoy the canal and its surroundings is to go cycling along the old towpath. Bikes can be rented at the tourist office kiosk down by the harbor from June to mid-August daily from 9am to noon and 4 to 8pm, for 100SEK ($13) per day.

Also intriguing is the boat trip along the canal to Borensburg, 20km (12 miles) east of Motala. In summer, these 5-hour boat trips leave Motala at 10:30am and cost 250SEK ($33) round-trip, 180SEK ($23) one-way.

Varamon Beach lies just 3km (1¾ miles) east of town. The beach offers a kilometer (½ mile) of golden sand, making it one of Scandinavia's largest inland bathing beaches. It has the warmest waters in Lake Vättern (which isn't saying much), and the sand is often thick with milk-white bodies soaking up the summer sun. It's also a venue for windsurfing. Locals like to call Varamon their "Riviera of Lake Vättern."

Motala has some museums, but all are of only minor interest. The best is the **Motala Motor Museum** (© **0141/588-88**), lying at the edge of the harbor. Cars of various eras are intriguingly exhibited—for example, parked outside an Esso Station. Music of the car's era blares from radio sets. All the vintage cars displayed in the showrooms are kept in shiny mint condition. Admission is 50SEK ($6.50) adults, 40SEK ($5.20) students, 30SEK ($3.90) children 7 to 15. Hours are May to September daily 10am to 8pm; from October to April Monday to Friday 8am to 4pm, Saturday and Sunday 11am to 5pm.

WHERE TO STAY

First Hotel Statt ⊛   The most highly recommended and most prestigious hotel in town was originally built in 1880 in a location adjacent to *Stora Torget* (the town's main square) and enlarged in 1923. Rising four floors, with access to a pleasant garden that's centered on a circular reflecting pool, it offers a traditional, consciously upscale decor that includes dozens of yards of fabric sewn into the most elaborate draperies in town, and a mostly Chippendale or Queen Anne decor in the public areas. Throughout, there's a sense of plush, well-heeled bourgeoisie taste, and such architectural adornments as ceiling friezes showing cherubs cavorting across vineyards, surrounded by formal, usually neoclassical moldings. Bedrooms have high ceilings, formal furnishings, plush carpets, and small but very clean bathrooms with showers.

Stora Torget, Box 19, S-591 21 Motala. © **0141/21-64-00.** Fax 0141/21-46-05. www.firsthotels.se or www. motalastadshotell.com. 64 units. Mid-June to mid-Aug and Fri–Sat year-round 953SEK–1,053SEK ($124–$137) double, 2,995SEK ($389) suite; rest of year 1,363SEK–1,500SEK ($177–$195) double, 2,995SEK ($389) suite. Rates include breakfast. AE, DC, MC, V. Parking 6SEK (80¢) per hour 9am–6pm; otherwise free. **Amenities:** Restaurant; bar; sauna; 24-hr. room service; laundry service; dry cleaning; nonsmoking rooms; rooms for those w/limited mobility; solarium. *In room:* TV, dataport (in some), minibar, safe.

Ramada Palace Hotel   Set within the heart of Motala and favored by business travelers from Germany, France, the United Kingdom, and the United States, this three-story hotel is a pleasant, well-managed place that was originally built in 1964. Throughout, you'll find a bland but comfortable kind of international modernity, especially within the bedrooms. Here, amid wall-to-wall carpets, sometimes-frilly curtains, well-padded beds, and a writing table, you'll find a place where even older members of your management team would feel comfortable. The more expensive rooms are labeled business class and are larger and more comfortable. Each room comes with a well-maintained private bathroom with a tub/shower.

Kungsgatan 1, S-591 30 Motala. © **0141/21-66-60.** Fax 0141/572-21. www.ramadapalace.se. 55 units. Mid-June to Aug and Fri–Sat year-round 950SEK ($124) double; rest of year 1,350SEK ($176) double; 1,640SEK ($213) suite with Jacuzzi. Rates include breakfast. AE, DC, MC, V. Free parking. **Amenities:** Bar; sauna; laundry service; dry cleaning; nonsmoking rooms; rooms for those w/limited mobility. *In room:* TV, dataport, hair dryer, iron.

WHERE TO DINE

Restaurant First Hotel Statt ★ SWEDISH/CONTINENTAL   This is the most formal, most intricate, and most elaborate restaurant in Motala, with an antique setting within the oldest (ca. 1880) section of the town's most formal hotel. Beneath high ceilings and elaborate cove moldings, in a Queen Anne–style setting, you'll find well-prepared food that's often based on local ingredients. These include venison, pheasant, and grouse (in season); and a year-round local delicacy consisting of freshwater char from nearby lakes, poached with herbs and served with boiled potatoes and hollandaise sauce. The menu changes frequently but includes whitefish roe with chopped onions, sour cream, and chopped egg yolks; smoked salmon with horseradish sauce and shrimp, and tournedos of beef with tomato-garlic sauce. Expect lots of wedding and anniversary parties conducted within the private function rooms of this restaurant, and a sense of local municipal politics within the nerve center of this very small town.

Stora Torget. © **0141/216-400.** Reservations recommended. Fixed-price lunch 69SEK ($8.95); main courses 80SEK–210SEK ($10–$27). AE, DC, MC, V. Daily 11:30am–1:30pm and 4–11pm.

ÖREBRO

Our final destination, Örebro, lies 60km (38 miles) north of Lake Vättern and is strategically located on the main route from southwest Sweden to the capital city of Stockholm. Sweden's sixth-most-populous city, it borders the shores of Lake Hjälmaren, the fourth-largest lake in the country.

Its castle (see below) is one of the most famous in Sweden, and it also lies at the River Svartån, which is studded with water lilies in summer. To the immediate west of the center is Lake Tysslingen, which is best reached by a leisurely bike ride. Many birders come here to view the lake in the spring when thousands upon thousands of whooper swans temporarily settle on the way to Finland from their winter retreats.

Motorists departing our last stopover at Motala can continue north along Route 50 until they reach the junction with E3, an express highway that will carry them north into the center of Örebro.

You can also visit Örebro directly on a main east-west train from Stockholm (trip time: 2 hr.). For information about the town, contact **Destination Öre-bro,** Slottet (in the castle; © 019/21-21-21). It is open June to August Monday to Friday 10am to 6pm, Saturday and Sunday 10am to 4pm. Off-season hours are Monday to Friday 10am to 6pm, Saturday and Sunday from 10am to 2pm.

EXPLORING THE AREA

We suggest you take a bike ride out to **Lake Tysslingen;** you can rent a bike at **Servicecentralen,** Hamnplan (© 019/21-19-09), for 50SEK ($6.50) per day, 250SEK ($33) weekly. The tourist office (see above) can provide information about boat tours of **Lake Hjälmaren** on either M/S *Linna* or M/S *Gustav Lagerfbjelke.* A 3-hour boat cruise costs 220SEK ($29) round-trip.

The town's major attraction is **Örebro Slott** (© 019/21-21-21), a castle that for more than 700 years has kept a watchful eye on everyone crossing the bridge over the River Svartån. The oldest part of the castle, a defensive tower, was erected in the latter half of the 13th century. The tower was expanded in the 14th century to make an even larger stronghold. Toward the end of the 16th century, one of the most impressive Renaissance castles in Sweden was con-structed here. The castle lies on an island in the Svartån and dominates the town. Over the years, the castle has been restored, and restored again. Today it has a grand, romantic exterior, although not much remains inside. There is no original furniture, and much of the interior is used for county offices. Never-theless, tour guides valiantly struggle to re-create the romance and lore of the *slott.* The beamed *Rikssalen,* or Parliament Hall, remodeled in 1927, has several portraits, notably that of Karl XI and his family. Surprisingly, they have bulging eyes because of the arsenic used to whiten their faces. The newly organized *Slottsmuseet* functions as a county museum, displaying the saga of the county since the days of the Stone Age. From May to September only, guided tours in English are conducted daily at 2pm, costing 50SEK ($6.50) per person.

Beautifully situated on the banks of the Svartån in the center of Örebro is the little, wooden, open-air village of **Wadköping.** The village consists of a collec-tion of ancient buildings from Örebro and the surrounding countryside. Opened in 1965, it contains 18th-century timbered structures in the traditional barn red, and lovely, bright 19th-century wooden houses that have all been moved to this site in the city park, *Stadsparfken.* Nowadays, Wadköping is thriv-ing with a cafe, craftspeople at work, shops, some minor museums, exhibitions, a theater, and puppet shows. The entire area can be visited May to August Tues-day to Sunday from 11am to 5pm, September to April Tuesday to Sunday from 11am to 4pm. Admission is free.

The major church of town is **St. Nicolai Kyrka,** Stortorget (© 019/ 12-40-25), dating from 1260 and standing on the main square of Örebro. It was extensively restored in the 1860s, so little of its former medieval character remains. The church is a frequent venue for temporary art exhibitions. It was here in 1810 that Jean Baptiste Bernadotte, Napoleon's marshal, was elected suc-cessor to the Swedish throne.

SHOPPING

If you're interested in Swedish handicrafts, the finest outlet along Lake Vättern is **Konsthantverkarna,** Järntorgsgatan 2 (© 019/10-79-05), a shop in central Örebro run by professional craft workers. No junk is allowed here, and the crafts are not only well made, but charming; they are ideal for gifts and souvenirs.

WHERE TO STAY & DINE

Ritz City Hotel   Set in the town center, behind an angular, brick-and-stucco facade, this six-story hotel was built in 1985 and has done a thriving trade with business travelers ever since. A member of a well-respected nationwide chain, it offers cozy, pastel-colored bedrooms with flowery prints and a cheerful, cooperative staff. All bedrooms are equipped with modern bathrooms with tub/showers.

Kungsgatan 24, S-702 24 Örebro. ℂ **019/601-4200.** Fax 019/601-4209. www.simplehotels.com. 83 units. July to mid-Aug and Fri–Sat year-round 790SEK ($103) double, 1,210SEK ($157) suite; rest of year 1,245SEK ($162) double, 1,345SEK ($175) suite. Rates include breakfast. AE, DC, MC, V. Parking 50SEK ($6.50) per day in nearby public garage. **Amenities:** Sauna; laundry service; dry cleaning; nonsmoking rooms; rooms for those w/limited mobility. *In room:* TV, minibar.

Scandic Grand Hotel ⭐   A seven-story structure erected in the mid-1980s in the center of town, this hotel provides clean, well-maintained accommodations and a thoroughly international and modern style that's widespread across the world. Despite an upscale decor that includes lots of hardwood panels, marble floors, and a dramatic modern staircase within the lobby, there are touches that will remind you of the charming aspects of Sweden, the most visible of which is a well-trained staff. Bedrooms contain aspects that evoke a living room in a comfortably contemporary modern home, partly because of the occasional sofa and, in some cases, reproductions of Turkish or Persian carpets. Each unit comes with an excellent bathroom with a tub or shower.

Fabriksgatan 21–23, Box 8112, S-700 23 Örebro. ℂ **019/767-4300.** Fax 0191/767-4311. www.scandic-hotels. com/grandhotel. 221 units. Mid-June to mid-Aug and Fri–Sat year-round 710SEK ($92) double; rest of year 1,700SEK ($221) double; 2,590SEK ($337) suite. Rates include breakfast. AE, DC, MC, V. Parking 125SEK ($16). **Amenities:** Restaurant; bar; Jacuzzi; sauna; limited room service; laundry service; dry cleaning; nonsmoking rooms; rooms for those w/limited mobility. *In room:* TV, dataport, hair dryer, iron.

8

The Baltic Islands:
Öland & Gotland

Two of the most rewarding destinations in all of Scandinavia lie in the Baltic Sea: the islands of Öland and Gotland, each with a long history and each popular in summer when the Swedes themselves flock here for sunshine and beaches. And flock they do; although some 60,000 people live on Gotland year-round, in summer that number can reach almost a million.

Called the "island of sun and winds," Öland is known for its luxuriant vegetation. There are plants here from Iberia, the Alps, and eastern Europe that survived the Ice Age and the warmer postglacial period. Many are found in no other Scandinavian country, and there is a profusion of orchids, some 30 species in all. Öland also is a land from prehistoric times. Remains from 4,000-year-old burial chambers can be seen here, as well as many runic stones from the Viking era.

Today the inhabitants of Öland make their living mainly from agriculture, fishing, food production, industry, and tourism. This flat, rural Baltic island is covered in windmills and connected to southern Sweden by one of the longest bridges in Europe. Its best center is Borgholm, the capital, a small resort with a recreational harbor on the west coast of the island. Shallow, crystal-clear waters make Öland's beaches as family-friendly as the weather: This is Sweden's sunniest province.

Two hundred years ago, a British visitor called Ölanders "the Italians of the north," suggesting a more extroverted streak than mainland Swedes.

After a visit, you can decide that for yourself.

As fascinating as Öland is, we recommend Gotland, particularly its ancient capital of Visby, if you have time to visit only one island.

Because the climate is milder on Gotland than in the rest of Sweden, the scenery here offers a wide variety of flora and fauna. Vast, white beaches and midsummer waters much warmer than you might expect are the big lure in summer, although many visitors, especially foreigners, come to take in its unique landscape of statuesque limestone formations, cliffs, forests, heaths, and meadows.

In Gotland, some 1,000 farms dating from the Viking era—and medieval times in general—are still in use today. Off the coast of Gotland lie several other islands, each unique. Farthest to the north is Gotska Sandön, a place of myths and legends and the stronghold of Sweden's last pirates. Just a stone's throw off the north coast lies Fårö, familiar to many as a once-favorite retreat of Olof Palme, Ingmar Bergman, and other political and cultural personalities. To the west, the twin Lilla and Stora Karlsö islands are famed for their huge colonies of guillemots and other sea birds.

If you don't have time to absorb the island itself, try at least for a look at Visby, which in 1995 was put on UNESCO's World Heritage list. Visby is the capital of Gotland and is surrounded by well-preserved medieval walls. Some 2,000 citizens live within these walls today. Once a Viking trading station, Visby, in the 12th century, developed into a leading commercial center for trade across the Baltic Sea. In time it became one of the most important cities of the Hanseatic League. The city grew and prospered as 13 ruined churches, two monasteries, a cathedral, and 200 buildings resting on medieval foundations attest today. Within the walls are several shops, restaurants, pubs, and clubs, many of which are open year-round.

1 Öland ⓕ★

40km (25 miles) E of Kalmar, 470km (291 miles) S of Stockholm

More Swedes emigrated from Öland to the United States during the 19th century than from any other province in Sweden. Ultimately, the Baltic island would lose a quarter of its population. Many émigrés, however, returned here to retire. Little wonder, considering how beautiful it is, with its sandy beaches, its treeless steppe *(Alvaret)* covered with wildflowers, its bird life, and its profusion of windmills silhouetted against the summer sky.

One of Europe's longest bridges, nearly 6.5km (4 miles) long, connects Kalmar with Öland. At 140km (87 miles) long and 16km (10 miles) wide, this is Sweden's second-largest island but its smallest province. Beaches run along both coasts, and there is only one town, Borgholm, a summer retreat. The royal summer residence is at Solliden. To rent a summer house on the beach, get in touch with the tourist office (see below).

ESSENTIALS

GETTING THERE   By Bus   Buses run from the Kalmar terminal to Borgholm on Öland in less than an hour; take no. 101 or 106. Call ⓒ **0200/21818** (only within Sweden).

By Car   From Kalmar, take the bridge over the sound, then turn left onto Route 136 to reach Borgholm.

VISITOR INFORMATION   Go to the **Ölands Tourist AB,** Färjestaden (ⓒ **0485/560-600;** www.olandsturist.se), at the Öland end of the famous 6.5km (4-mile) bridge. It's open May to July 4 and August 9 to August 31 Monday to Friday 9am to 6pm, Saturday 9am to 4pm, and Sunday 10am to 3pm; July 5 to August 8 and September to April Monday to Friday 9am to 5pm.

OUTDOOR ACTIVITIES

BIKING   Öland is great cycling country. Although there are those who bike the entire 129km (80-mile) stretch of the island, others are less ambitious. Whatever your cycling plans, you'll find seemingly endless cycle tracks along flat roads.

Bike rentals are available near the point where the ferryboat will deposit you from the Swedish mainland, at **Färjestaden Cykelaffär,** Storegatan 67 (ⓒ **0485/ 300-74**), for 100SEK ($13) per day.

GOLFING   Ekerum Golf Course, Ekerum, S-387-92 Borgholm (ⓒ **0485/ 800-00**), is 16km (10 miles) south of Borgholm, surrounded by the rolling lushness of an isolated region near the island's center. This course was created in 1991 as part of the Sunwing Ekerem Hotel. It's open April to November. Driving ranges lie between verdant forests and rolling fields. It charges greens fees of between 250SEK and 400SEK ($33–$52) per day, depending on the season. You can choose from an 18-hole course and a 9-hole course that lies immediately adjacent.

Öland

Långe Erik

Byxelkrok

Ferry to Oskarshamn

Böda Sand

Böda
Crown
Park

Böda

136

Löttorp

Högby

Källa

Föra

Kårehamn

Köpingsvik

Borgholm

Räpplinge

Gårdslösa

Långlöt

136

Runsten

Ölandsbron
(bridge to Kalmar)

Norra
Möckleby

Färjestaden

Gårdby

Vickleby

Stenåsa

Mörbylånga

Hulterstad

STORA

ALVARET

Degerhamn

136

Gräsgård

Ferry
Lighthouse
Airport

Grönhögen

Näsby

Långe Jan

s u n d

B a l t i c   S e a

K a l m a r -

Stockholm

Kalmar

ÖLAND

0   10 mi

0   10 km

SEEING THE SIGHTS
A PREHISTORIC VILLAGE
Eketorp Ring-Fort ★★★   Öland's most interesting attraction is this prehistoric fortified village that has been excavated and reconstructed so that visitors
can see how people lived in this area centuries ago. This site, built inside of a
ring-shape enclosure for defensive purposes, is unique in Scandinavia, as it represents the only prehistoric fort to be rebuilt. It's on the island's extreme southern tip, 35km (22 miles) south of Mörbylånga, rising starkly from a treeless
landscape of steppelike tundra.

Eketorp is one of 15 known prehistoric forts on the island. Excavations have
shown three phases of settlement here from A.D. 300 to 1300. Today a large
selection of the massive wall that encircled this ring-fort has been reconstructed,
along with Iron Age houses within the walls. You can see dwellings, cattle byres,
and storehouses reconstructed using ancient crafts and materials, as well as
species of livestock. Objects found in the excavations include simple tools, skillfully crafted jewelry, and weapons. The best of these finds are exhibited in a
museum inside the fort wall.

Degerhamn. ℂ **0485/66-20-00.** Admission 50SEK–60SEK ($6.50–$7.80) adults, 20SEK–30SEK ($2.60–$3.90)
for children 7–14. May 1–June 19 daily 10am–5pm; June 20–Aug 8 daily 10am–6pm; Aug 9–Sept 15 daily
10am–5pm. Unless you have a car, getting here is tricky, although 5 buses a day (no. 103) come here from the
Mörbylånga bus station. 2 buses make the run on Sat and only 1 on Sun. Check with the tourist office (see
above) for bus timetables.

IN BORGHOLM
The actual capital, **Borgholm,** merits a passing visit. It is extremely overcrowded
during the month of July, when tourists, mainly the Swedes themselves, overrun
its bars, cafes, and pizzerias. At that time it takes on a carnival atmosphere, later
settling down for a long winter's nap.

Just to the north of the town center of Borgholm you can visit the ruins of
Blårör, the island's largest Bronze Age cairn, although there isn't much to see
here today. When it was discovered in 1849, the tomb in its center had already
been plundered by grave robbers. In 1920, four more tombs were discovered,
but they, too, had been plundered. What remains are a few sunken granite
stones. This site is mainly for serious archaeologists.

Borgholms Slott ★   This attraction, one of Sweden's most important historical monuments, lies just to the southwest of the center of Borgholm at the top of
the sheer, steep face of the Landborg Cliffs. In the Middle Ages, this was one of
the major royal castles of Sweden and was a center of intrigue and endless battles.
Subject to frequent attacks, it guarded the sound and was Sweden's southernmost
outpost against Denmark. The castle was partially destroyed during the Kalmar
War (1611–13). King Karl X Gustav ordered that the castle be restored and
turned into a baroque palace, but building was interrupted in 1709 because of a
cash shortage. In 1806, fire reduced the palace to its present ruins. Remains of
the original fortified circular tower can still be seen in the northwest corner of the
inner courtyard.

Lying only a short walk south is the royal family's Italian-style villa, which
they often use as their residence in summer. This white palace was built between
1903 and 1906 by Queen Victoria of Sweden, and used as a summer retreat.
Their home is off limits, but you can wander to Solliden Park (see below), the
gardens of the villa.

The Blue Maiden

Off the west coast of Öland lies one of the most remote and "forgotten" islands of the Baltic, **Blå Jungfrun,** whose name translates as "the Blue Maiden." It rises high above the Kalmar Straits, 127m (417 ft.) above the sea bed and 450m (1,476 ft.) above sea level. Inhabited only by colonies of birds and wildlife, it's noteworthy for its bare, windswept cliffs; slabs of red granite; and thousands of rocky outcroppings. More of a rock spur than an island, it measures less than 1.5km (1 mile) long, and less than a kilometer (½ mile) wide, covering an area of about 65 hectares (161 acres). Designated as a national park, the island has two separate harbors, both of which lie near the northern tip: Lervik to the east and Sikhamn to the west. The direction and intensity of the wind at the time of your arrival will determine which of the two the crew of your ferryboat will use for a landing. Seas surrounding the island are tricky: Even a light wind can make it difficult to approach the island's rocky coastline.

Olaus Magnus, a famous Swedish bishop, mentioned Blå Jungfrun as long ago as 1555. Carl von Linné (Linnaeus) was the first to describe the island in detail, having visited it in 1745 during his "Journey to Öland and Gothland."

Later the forest and plant life suffered the impact of drought and the foolish mistake of introducing rabbits, which caused much damage to vegetation. Quarrying in 1904 brought more ecological disasters, especially when the largest of the great caves on the island were blown up. After World War I forces mobilized to save the island; industrialist Torsten Kreuger donated enough money for the island to be purchased and turned over to Sweden as a national park.

Once on the island, you can observe how the granite dome was covered by sediment some 500 million years ago and how the island took

---

Borgholm (℗ 0485/10232. Admission 60SEK ($7.80) adults, 20SEK ($2.60) ages 12–17, free for children 11 and under. May–Aug daily 10am–6pm. To get there, you can walk to a nature reserve signposted from the center of Borgholm. By car, take the first exit south of Rte. 136.

Solliden Park   Queen Victoria also commissioned the landscaping of Solliden's extensive gardens and parkland, which many devotees rate as some of the loveliest in Sweden. Exhibitions about Swedish royalty are housed in a new pavilion, which also contains a gift shop. On-site is a *creperie* selling ice cream, crepes, and drinks. Borgholm. (℗ 0485/153-56. Admission 55SEK ($7.15) adults, free for children under 7. May 15–Sept 15 daily 11am–6pm.

IN CENTRAL ÖLAND

To explore Central Öland, you can travel east from Borgholm (bus no. 102 runs here) following signs to Räpplinge. This brings you to Storlinge Kvarna, a row of seven windmills. Less than .5km (⅓ mile) south, you arrive at **Gärdslösa,** the island's best-preserved medieval church. Inside is a pulpit made in 1666 along with paintings from the 1200s.

Your major stopover will be about 2km (a mile or two) south in the village of **Himmelsberga** ★★, which is preserved as an open-air museum with farms built shape about 1 million years ago during the Quaternary Ice Age. The larger boulder fields in the south of the island always draw much interest, as do the lichens and bird life. You're sure to see the island's black guillemot, as well as rare birds such as the water pipit and the velvet scoter. Even the white-tailed sea eagle can often be viewed.

The "labyrinth," the only ancient monument on the island, was first mentioned by von Linné, who called it "Trojeborg." An intricate maze of paths, it lies on a level area of rock on the southern slope of the island.

The best way to view the attractions of the Blue Maiden involves signing up for one of the summer (June–Aug only) tours of the island conducted by local fishermen. Check with the tourist office to hook up with such an excursion.

An alternative method of reaching the Blue Maiden involves departures from Oskarshamn, on the Swedish mainland. From the harbor at Oskarshamn, the M.S. *Soltust* departs every day of the week except Monday at 9:30am, with a return scheduled for 4:30pm. Transit takes about 90 minutes each way, allowing about 3 hours to explore, on foot, the hiking trails that crisscross the island. A kiosk on the island dispenses maps and local information about how best to appreciate this sparsely inhabited island's charms. Round-trip transit costs 160SEK to 170SEK ($21–$22) adults, 80SEK ($10) children 6 to 15 years old. For information and reservations, call the tourist office of Iskarshamn at © **0491/88188**. To contact the local branch (in Kalmar) of the Swedish National Park Service, the organization that oversees the hiking trails on the Blue Maiden, call © **0480/82195**.

along both sides of the narrow village road. The heart of the museum consists of three large farms with buildings dating from the 18th and 19th centuries. You can see furnishings, farm equipment, carriages, and sleighs common to that period in Öland's history. In the Cottage Café, you can order freshly baked cakes to be consumed under the shade of walnut and maple trees in a garden. The gallery offers a constantly changing array of art and handicraft shows. The site is open from May 15 to September 15 (closed in off season) daily 10am to 6pm (last entrance at 5:30pm). During the summer, activities ranging from open-air theater productions to concerts with jazz and folk music captivate visitors. For more information, call © **0485/56-10-22**.

IN SOUTH ÖLAND

Stora Alvaret, a giant limestone plain, dominates the southern part of the island. This great plateau is almost entirely devoid of trees, covering an area 37km (23 miles) long and 15km (9 miles) wide. The thin soil in places gives way to bare limestone outcrops, creating the impression of a barren landscape. Yet the area is teeming with life and is, in fact, the last refuge for a number of unique plant and animal species. You'll see everything from colorful orchids to soaring skylarks in the spring, from rockroses to golden plovers in summer, and from rose hips to cranes in the autumn. **Vickleby** is the most attractive village stopover.

Capellagården Vickleby is the site of a craft college founded in the late 1950s by Carl Malmsten. Today the college is a training school for cabinet making, woodworking, ceramics, textiles, design, and horticulture. It also has one of Sweden's largest herb gardens, containing a wide variety of unusual plants. During the summer, the college stages exhibitions and sales in the old Vickleby school.

Vickleby. ✆ **0485/361-93.** Admission 10SEK ($1.30) adults, free for children under 16. June 1–Aug 22 daily 10am–5pm, but call first. Reached on Rte. 136 between Fårjestaden to the north and Mörbylånga to the south.

Ottenby Naturum ✿ At the southern tip of Öland sits this exhibition of nature and culture, one of the best bird-watching sites anywhere in Sweden. An ornithological station here conducts research. The surrounding area was an ancient park and the hunting ground of kings. In the 16th century, King Johan III stocked the park with fallow deer, and the strain still thrives here today. The park also is the breeding ground for the rare golden oriole. At Ottenby you can also see the coast-to-coast wall built by King Karl X Gustaf in 1650 to fence off the deer and to improve hunting.

Otenby Nature Reserve. ✆ **0485/66-12-00.** Admission 50SEK ($6.50). Apr 8–Apr 12 daily 11am–3pm; May daily 11am–4pm; June 1–July 4 daily 11am–5pm; July 5–Aug 8 daily 10am–8pm; Sept and Oct Sat–Sun only 11am–3pm. From Borgholm follow Rte. 136 all the way south to the southern tip of the island, where you'll see Ottenby Naturum signposted with hiking trails leading you into the reserve.

IN NORTH ÖLAND

From Borgholm head north on Route 136 to find a more varied landscape than in the south. At Föra, a village 20km (12 miles) to the north, stands **Die Kirche von Föra,** with its well-preserved defensive tower. In the Middle Ages, churches often doubled as fortresses. If it's open, look inside the interior, which still has a medieval aura, with a cross dating from the 15th century.

North of the village of Sodvik, you come to **Lilla Horns Iovangar (Little Horn Forest Meadows),** which are abundantly flowering meadows best viewed in the late spring.

Before you reach the village of Källa, you'll spot **Källa Kyrka,** which stands lonely and deserted today after its last parishioners departed in 1888. In a setting of flowery meadows, this church from the Middle Ages has drystone walls; however, its furnishings are long gone. On-site are ancient burial tombs. The church was last "modernized" in the 14th century, and it was frequently attacked during Baltic wars.

Continuing north, you arrive at the village of Högby, site of **Högby Kyrka och Kyrkstallare,** a religious shrine from the Middle Ages, now in ruins.

After leaving Högby, your last major village will be Böda before you reach the island's largest greenbelt, the stunningly beautiful **Böda Kronopark.** Before going all the way to the northern tip of the *kronopark,* you can make a slight 9.5km (6-mile) detour west from Böda on Route 136 to see the Skäftekarr Museum.

One of Öland's newest attractions, the **Skäftekarr Museum,** Lottorp (✆ **0485/ 22-111**), opened in 1998 on the site of the archaeological excavations of an Iron Age village. On the premises is an exhibition showing what farm life was like in the 6th century A.D., and a reconstruction of several of the village's gravesites. The site also contains nearly a dozen well-preserved foundations of stone buildings, each attributed to five separate farms established between A.D. 300 and 700. You should know in advance that this location is still in the process of being excavated and enlarged. On-site is an unusual botanical garden planted by a local gardener during the mid–19th century. It boasts 100 or so different trees and bushes and is ideal for country rambles. Midsummer festivities, including musical events and lectures, are staged at this park. Adjacent to the park is a 2.5km (1½-mile) path that's splendid for walks. The path follows a "cultural route," passing the ancient settlements from the Iron Age. You can order a complete meal or light refreshments at the cafe built in 1860. The site is open year-round Wednesday to Sunday 10am to 4pm. From May 1 to August 8, hours are daily 10am to 6pm; August 9 to August 22, daily 11am to 4pm; August 23 to October 3, Friday to Sunday 11am to 4pm. Admission costs 60SEK ($7.80) for adults and 30SEK ($3.90) for children 6 to 15. Children under 6 enter free.

This northern "crown" over Öland is shaped like a bird's head, the beak facing east. The island's best beaches are here, lying for the most part on the eastern coastline. The beaches start at Böda Sand. The best and most frequented stretch runs for 1.5km (1 mile) north of Kyckesand. One section is signposted and reserved for nudists.

Finally, you reach the island's most scenic part, **Trollskogen**, or "Trolls Forest." This storm-swept forest with ivy-covered trunks is at the very northeastern tip of Öland. Part of Böda Crown Park, it is like a setting from a child's fairy tale—you almost expect to see a wicked witch emerge at any time from the gnarled trunks of the ancient oaks. This forest offers some of the island's most dramatic walks.

SHOPPING ON ÖLAND

The items you haul back from Öland will probably involve either durable clothing suitable for nature walks in the rugged outdoors, or examples of local handicrafts and pottery made by arts-oriented refugees from urban life. One of the most appealing outlets for ceramics and pottery is **Lotta & Mary,** Hamnen, very close to the piers of Färjestaden (© **0485/318-81**), where the idiosyncratic and painstakingly crafted ceramics of a team of local artisans are displayed and sold. Nearby, at **Atelje Ölandssnipan,** Hamnplanen, Färjestaden (© **0485/319-95**), some of the most artfully crafted miniature ship models in Sweden are displayed, each authentic to one or another of the many vessels that have sought shelter in Öland's harbor.

An interesting collection of antiques is stockpiled and sold at **Antikgården,** Salomonstorp, in the hamlet of Köpingsvik (© **0485/727-83**). And if you happen to be driving near the northern tip of the island, consider a visit to yet another ceramics studio, **Glömminge Krukmarkeri** (© **0485/372-26**), which lies in the heart of the hamlet of Glömminge, 9.5km (6 miles) north of the point where the bridge from the Swedish mainland first deposits you on Öland.

WHERE TO STAY

Ekerum Golf & Resort ☆ Set 15km (9¼ miles) south of Borgholm, this hotel was built in 1991 at the same time as the adjacent Ekerum golf courses, the best on the island. The hotel is designed as an avant-garde complex of buildings, the older of which have red roofs, ocher-colored walls, and shades of their former use as farmhouses. The newer buildings are white-sided postmodern structures, the largest of which is a three-story gabled building with prominent bay windows and a design that seems inspired by early-20th-century stylings. Accommodations are clean, conservative, and tasteful, each with a shower-only bathroom, wood-burning stove, and comfortable, not-frilly furniture where a golf enthusiast might feel at home after time on the links. A restaurant and a bar are on the premises.

Ekerum, S-387-92 Borgholm. ℂ **0485/80000.** Fax 0485/80010. www.ekerum.com. 72 2–bedroom apts with kitchens (sleep 4); 1,395SEK ($181) for 4 beds. AE, DC, MC, V. Free parking. Closed Nov–Apr. Bus: 101. **Amenities:** Restaurant; bar; indoor pool; gym; sauna; nonsmoking rooms; rooms for those w/limited mobility. *In room:* A/C, TV, hair dryer, iron.

Guntorps Herrgård *Value* Set less than a kilometer (½ mile) southeast of Borgholm's center, the premises of this hotel were built in 1918 as the family home of the merchants and politicians who controlled the island's commerce around the turn of the 20th century. New wings were added to the stately building in 1986; shortly thereafter, a restaurant, open only for dinner, was added as well. Today you'll find clean, well-maintained, and rather simple bedrooms with neatly kept shower-only bathrooms.

Guntorpsgatan, 387-36 Borgholm. ℂ **0485/13-000.** Fax 0485/13-319. www.guntorp.oland.com. 32 units. 995SEK ($129) double (sleeps 4). Rates include breakfast. AE, DC, MC. Free parking. **Amenities:** Restaurant; bar; indoor pool; sauna; limited room service; laundry service; dry cleaning; rooms for those w/limited mobility. *In room:* TV, dataport, minibar, hair dryer, iron.

Halltorps Gästgiveri ★★ Set near the geographic center of the island, 9.5km (6 miles) south of Borgholm, this tasteful and reliable hotel occupies one of the oldest manor houses of Öland, a yellow-sided complex of steep-roofed buildings dating from the 17th century. Launched as a hotel in 1975, and renovated and massively enlarged in 1991, it has a tranquil, farmland setting, with a view across the Kalmarsund and the Halltorp Forest. Once it was a royal farming estate, and between the end of World War I and the early 1970s, it functioned as a home for the elderly before its limestone walls were reinforced and it was transformed into an inn. Bedrooms are cozy and intimate, often with beamed ceilings, and each is outfitted with an artfully old-fashioned allure that's the result of serious effort on the part of a team of decorators. About two-thirds are within a newly built annex; the remaining dozen or so are within the original manor house. Each is named after a region of Sweden, with a decor that's inspired by traditional models from that region. Unlike many other hotels on the island, this one remains open all year. All units have a tidy, tiled bathroom with a tub/shower.

Högstrum, S-387 92 Borgholm. ℂ **0485/850-00.** Fax 0485/850-01. www.halltorpsgastgiveri.se. 36 units. 1,390SEK ($181) double; 1,900SEK ($247) suite. Prices include breakfast. AE, DC, MC, V. Free parking. From Borgholm, take bus 101 or 106. **Amenities:** Restaurant; bar; 2 saunas; limited room service; laundry service; dry cleaning; nonsmoking rooms; solarium. *In room:* TV, dataport, hair dryer.

Hotell Borgholm This establishment, restored after a 2004 fire, has been in the restaurant business far longer (since 1850) than it has been a hotel. But in the 1950s, the site was enlarged with a pleasant and airy set of bedrooms that have been renovated several times since then. The hotel is convenient to everything in Borgholm—it's only about 5m (16 ft.) from the *Storegatan,* the town's main street—and remains open throughout the winter for the many Swedish and European business travelers who make it their home during their time in Borgholm. Bedrooms have high ceilings and are tastefully decorated in a monochromatic style, with a heavy emphasis on bordeaux-red with white trim and conservative furnishings. Each unit comes with a neatly tiled bathroom with shower.

Trädgårdsgatan 15, S-387 31 Borgholm. ℂ **0485/770-60.** Fax 0485/124-66. www.hotellborgholm.com. 29 units. 1,000SEK ($130) double; 1,700SEK ($221) suite. Rates include breakfast. AE, DC, MC, V. Free parking. Closed Jan–Feb. **Amenities:** Restaurant; bar. *In room:* TV, iron.

Hotel Skansen   Positioned among trees, forests, and fields, 34km (21 miles) south of Borgholm, this hotel is targeted by ecologists, nature lovers, and anyone who's interested in getting away from the pressures of urban life. It's composed of three separate buildings, each with an old-fashioned ocher-colored exterior that might remind you of an antique inn, and a tile roof. The oldest of the buildings dates from 1811; the entire compound was tastefully renovated in 1991. Public areas combine modern furnishings, some of them upholstered in black leather, Persian carpets, and hardwood floors. Bedrooms are simple but comfortable, and outfitted with angular modern furniture with emphasis on white walls and varnished hardwoods. Each room comes with a compact private bathroom with shower.

S-386 21 Färjestaden. (?) **0485/30530.** Fax 0485/34804. www.hotelskansen.com. 31 units. Selected weekends July to mid-Aug and Sun–Thurs year-round 790SEK–990SEK ($103–$129) double; Fri–Sat 650SEK ($85) double; 1,980SEK ($257) suite. Rates include breakfast. AE, DC, MC, V. Free parking. Bus: 101. **Amenities:** Restaurant; bar; outdoor pool; Jacuzzi; sauna; limited room service; laundry service; dry cleaning. *In room:* TV, dataport (in some), hair dryer, iron.

Strand Hotell ★★   This is the largest, splashiest, and most glittery hotel on Öland, the closest thing there to a seafront resort in Atlantic City, New Jersey. Built in 1952 and massively enlarged in 1973, it was renovated in 1991 into a venue that's much, much better accessorized. Most accommodations are within a four-story building whose sides taper into a lopsided pyramid as they rise, a design that creates large, sun-flooded terraces for many of the rooms inside. Each is outfitted with pale colors and modern furniture usually made from blond laminated woods such as birch. Many of them overlook an upscale marina, part of which is owned by the hotel, and which once won an award as the best privately owned yacht harbor in Sweden. About 16 of the units with kitchens are privately owned and used as vacation homes by urbanites. These are rented out by the week (selected weeks only) during some periods when the owners are out of town. All accommodations come with neatly tiled private bathrooms with tub or shower.

Villagatan 4, S-387 88 Borgholm. (?) **0485/888-88.** Fax 0485/88899. www.strand.borgholm.se. 1,190SEK–1,890SEK ($155–$246) double; 1,990SEK ($259) suite; apts with kitchen available only on selected weeks in summer for 7,090SEK–11,090SEK ($922–$1,442) per week double occupancy. Rates include breakfast. AE, DC, MC, V. Free parking. Bus: 101. **Amenities:** 2 restaurants; 6 bars; indoor pool; sauna; 24-hr. room service; laundry service; dry cleaning; nonsmoking rooms; rooms for those w/limited mobility. *In room:* TV, minibar, hair dryer, safe.

WHERE TO DINE

Halltorps Gästgiveri ★   SWEDISH   Set within the previously recommended inn (see "Where to Stay," above), this is the most nostalgic and appealing restaurant in Öland. The dining rooms evoke old-fashioned Sweden, but in a way that's charming and with none of the drawbacks of that less mechanized, less convenient age. Menu items are usually seasoned with herbs and vegetables from nearby suppliers, which arrive ultrafresh at frequent intervals. Two particularly appealing specialties include filets of cod brought in by local fishers, fried and served with parsley-flavored butter, and filets of island lamb with thyme sauce and au gratin potatoes. Unlike many competing restaurants on the island, this one is open year-round.

In the Halltorps Gästgiveri Hotel, Borgholm. (?) **0485/850-00.** Reservations recommended. Main courses 235SEK–295SEK ($31–$38); fixed-price menu 375SEK–510SEK ($49–$66). Vegetarian menu 285SEK ($37). AE, DC, MC, V. Daily noon–10pm; winter daily noon–8pm. From Borgholm, take bus 101 or 106.

Restaurant Bakfickan ★ *Finds* INTERNATIONAL   The dining room of the Hotel Borgholm—restored after a fire—doesn't look particularly fancy or glamorous. In fact, it's a modern, somewhat nondescript room with pastel walls and tables that are just a bit overcrowded. But according to local gastronomes, this is the best restaurant on Öland, with food that's at the top of the A-list for its international flair, subtle flavors, and panache. The culinary force behind its excellence is German-born Karin Fransson, an entrepreneur who is widely recognized as the most sophisticated chef and culinary mentor on the island. Marvelous things are done here to local lamb and fish (especially codfish). A typical meal might include garlic-fried mussels from local waters; smoked and baked salmon served cold with a compote of tomatoes, a timbale of avocados, and a lime-basil sauce; or roasted Öland lamb wrapped in bacon and served with a potato and parsnip strudel and marinated peppers.

In the Hotel Borgholm, Trädgårdsgatan 15. ✆ 0485/77060. Reservations recommended. Main courses 245SEK–290SEK ($32–$38). Fixed-price 2-course menu 350SEK ($46); 3-course menu 410SEK ($53); 4-course menu 510SEK ($66). AE, DC, MC, V. June–Aug daily 6–10pm; Sept–May Tues–Sat 6–10pm.

ÖLAND AFTER DARK

The island's most popular pub lies in Borgholm and attracts clients from throughout the island. The local favorite is **Pubben,** Storgatan 18 (✆ **0485/124-15**). Open September to April nightly from 4pm to 1am, and May to August noon to 1am daily, it stocks nearly 50 brands of whiskey—enough to make you feel you've wandered into a single-malt pub in Scotland.

2 Gotland ★★ & Visby ★★

219km (136 miles) S of Stockholm, 150km (93 miles) S of Nynäshamn, 89km (55 miles) E of the Swedish mainland

In the middle of the Baltic Sea sits the island of Gothland—the ancient home of the Goths—about 121km (75 miles) long and 56km (35 miles) wide. Swedes go to Gotland—Sweden's most popular tourist island—for sunny holidays by the sea, whereas North Americans tend to be more interested in the old walled city of Visby. An investment of a little extra time will reveal that Gotland, with its cliffs, unusual rock formations, bathing beaches, and rolling countryside, is rich territory. Buses traverse the island, as do organized tours out of Visby.

From the end of the 12th century and throughout the 13th, the walled city of Visby rose to the zenith of its power as the seat of the powerful Hanseatic merchants and the trade center of northern Europe. During its heyday, 17 churches were built, step-gabled stone houses were erected, and the townspeople lived in relative luxury. Visby eventually was ransacked by the Danes, however, and fell into decline. Sometime late in the 19th century, when Visby was recognized as a treasure house of medieval art, it became a major attraction and the number-one spot in Scandinavia for experiencing the charm of the Middle Ages.

ESSENTIALS

GETTING THERE   By Plane   Visitors can fly **SAS** to Gotland from Stockholm; there are three daily flights, which take about 30 minutes. For information and schedules, call ✆ **0770/72-77-27.** There is no bus service.

By Boat   Those who want to take the boat to Gotland must first go to Nynäshamn; by bus from Stockholm, it's about a 1-hour ride. The last car-ferry to Visby leaves at 11:30pm and takes about 3 hours and 15 minutes. In summer there also are five daily connections. You can make reservations through your

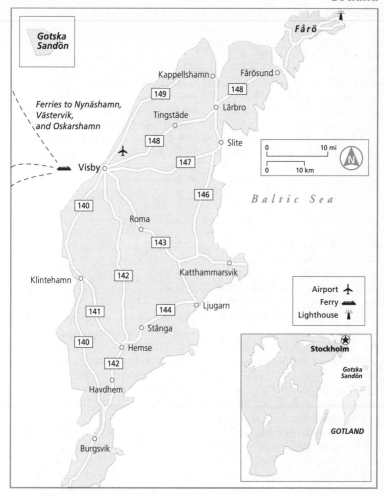

travel agent or directly with the ferry service, **Destination Gotland,** for cabin or car space. It's wise to book deck space if you plan to travel on a weekend. Call ℂ **0498/201-020** in Stockholm.

VISITOR INFORMATION   In Visby, contact the tourist bureau, **Gotlands Turist Service,** Österväg 1 (ℂ **0498/20-33-00**), open May to August Monday to Friday 8am to 7pm, Saturday and Sunday 7am to 6pm; September to April Monday to Friday 8am to 5pm, Saturday and Sunday 10am to 4pm.

A SPECIAL EVENT   During the annual **Medieval Week** ✮✮ in August, for 8 days Visby once again becomes a Hanseatic town. At the harbor, Strandgatan swarms with people in medieval dress, many of them tending market stalls. You meet the blacksmith, barber, cobbler, and trader. Musicians play the hurdy-gurdy, the fiddle, and the flute; jesters play the fool. Toward nightfall a kingly procession comes into the square. The program has more than 100 such events during the festival, along with medieval mystery plays, masses, choral and instrumental music, tournaments, and displays of horses, as well as archery competitions, fire-eaters, belly dancers, and walking tours of the medieval town.

EXPLORING GOTLAND BY CAR

From Visby, drive north on Route 149, heading toward the fishing port of **Lickershamn.** Look for a narrow trail along the cliffs. This path leads you to a rock that juts into the water. Known as the *Maiden,* this promontory offers some of the best views on Gotland.

From Lickershamn, continue along Route 149, passing to the towns of **Ire** and **Kappelshamn.** From Kappelshamn, follow Route 149 south to the junction with Route 148 in **Lärbro.** Here, go north on Route 148 to **Fårösund.** The village of Fårösund sits on the shores of the 1.5km (1-mile) wide Fårösund channel, which separates the small island of **Fårö** (sheep island) from the main island of Gotland. You can take a ferry to Fårö to visit some of the island's superb beaches.

From Fårösund, take Route 148 back to Lärbro. A few kilometers past Lärbro, take Route 146 southwest toward **Slite.** Follow it down the coast to **Aurungs.** Here, go west on a secondary road heading toward **Siggur.** In Siggur, follow signs south to the village of **Dalhem.** The most remarkable sight in Dalhem is the village church, situated just outside town. Its wall paintings and stained glass are the finest on Gotland. Train buffs may enjoy visiting the Railway Museum located in the old train station.

From Dalhem, continue south on the road that brought you to town. Head toward **Roma.** Look for the ruins of Roma Abbey, a Cistercian monastery destroyed during the Protestant Reformation.

Head west from Roma on a secondary road toward Route 140 that runs along Gotland's western coast. You'll pass to the villages of **Bander** and **Sojvide** before you reach Route 140. Follow it south to **Burgsvik,** a popular port and resort town. Just east of Burgsvik, visit the small hamlet of **Öja.** Its church boasts a triumphal cross dating from the 13th century.

After visiting Öja, return to Burgsvik. Here you head south, passing to the villages of **Bottarvegården** and **Vamlingbo.** At the southern tip of Gotland you'll find **Hoburgen,** with its towering lighthouse. Along with the lighthouse, you'll encounter cliffs, many with strange rock formations, and a series of caves.

Return to Burgsvik to connect with Route 140. Turn off after **Fidenäs,** following Route 142 toward **Hemse.** Outside Hemse, take Route 144 to **Ljugarn,** a small port and resort town on Gotland's east coast. You can visit the small customs museum. Just south of Ljugarn, on a secondary road, is a series of Bronze Age stone sculptures. The seven rock formations, depicting ancient ships, form the largest group of stone settings on the island.

Follow Route 143 northwest from Ljugarn and return to Visby.

SEEING THE SIGHTS
IN VISBY

Nothing on Gotland is more impressive than the **Ringmuren** ★★★, the town walls that stretch for 3.5km (2¼ miles) around Visby. They are riddled with medieval gates and towers. There is both a land wall and a sea wall, the latter 5.3m (17 ft.) tall. It was built as a fortification sometime in the late 1200s, incorporating an ancient gunpowder tower, the **Kruttornet** ★. The crenellated land wall is only 6m (20 ft.) high. Amazingly, a total of 27 of the original 29 towers are still standing.

Visby

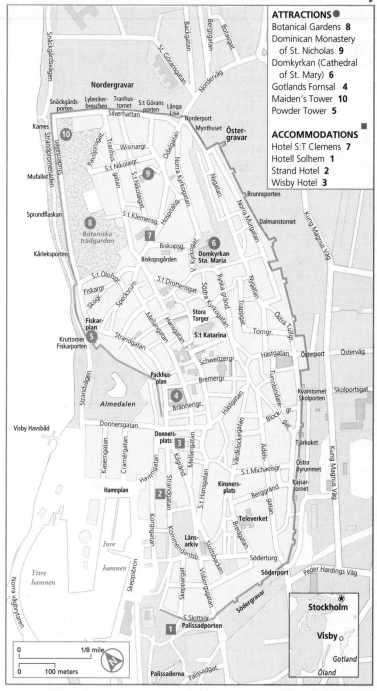

ATTRACTIONS ●
Botanical Gardens **8**
Dominican Monastery
  of St. Nicholas **9**
Domkyrkan (Cathedral
  of St. Mary) **6**
Gotlands Fornsal **4**
Maiden's Tower **10**
Powder Tower **5**

ACCOMMODATIONS ■
Hotel S:T Clemens **7**
Hotell Solhem **1**
Strand Hotel **2**
Wisby Hotel **3**

Snäckgårdsvägen
Backgatan
Bergsgatan
Botalgat.
S:t Göransgatan
Nordervåg

Nordergravar

Snäckgårds-porten
Lybecker-breschen
Tranhus-tornet
S:t Görans porten
Långa Lisa
Silverhattan
Norderport
Öster-gravar

Kames
Mynthuset
Strandpromenaden

Pavlljonsgat.
Wismargr.
Tranhus
S:t Nikolaig.
S:t Nikolaigat.
Odalgatan
Norra Kyrkogatan
Nygatan

Mufallet

Brunnsporten
Norra Murgatan
Kung Magnus Väg

Sprundflaskan
S:t Klemensg.
Hospitalsg.
Dalmanstornet

8 *Botaniska trädgarden*

7
Biskopsg.
6 **Domkyrkan Sta. Maria**

Kårleksporten
Biskopsgården
V. Kyrkogat.

S:t Olofsgr.
S:t Drottensgat.
Södra Kyrkogatan
Ryska gränd
Nygatan
Östra Tullgr.

Fiskargr.
Speckrum
Trappgat.
Skogr.

Fiskar-plan
Mellangatan
Stora Torger

5 Kruttornet Fiskarporten
Strandgatan
Hangatan
S:t Katarina
Torngr.

Strandvägen
Schweitzergr.
Hästgatan
Österport
Östervåg

Almedalen
Packhus-plan
Bremergr.
Lumbindare-gr.
Kvarntornet
Skolporten
Skolportsgat.

4 Brännerigr.
Hästgatan
Block-gat.

Visby Havsbåd
Donnersgatan
Vårdklockegatan
Tjärkoket

Kaserngatan
Cramérgatan
Donners-plats 3
Mellangatan
Adels-gatan
Östra Byrummet

Hamngatan
S:t Michaelsgr.
Kajsar-tornet

Hamnplan 2
Strandgatan
S:t Hansgatan
Kligård
Kinsners-plats
Berggränd

Inre
Korggatan
Televerket
Bredgatan

Yttre hamnen
hamnen
Läns-arkiv
Kommendantsb.
Slotsbacken
Södertorg

Norra vägbyrlaren
Skeppsbron
Skeppargatan
Visborgsgatan
Söderport
Peder Hardings Väg
Söderport

Stockholm ⊛

Visby ○

Gotland

S. Slottsgr.
1 **Palissadporten**

0   1/8 mile
0   100 meters

Palissaderna Palissadgat.
Öland

Visby is a good town for walkers, but you may want to take one of the organized tours that are offered in season. Because so many of the sights, particularly the ruins of the 13th- and 14th-century churches, are better appreciated with some background, we recommend the tours that take 2 hours each and cost 85SEK ($11) per participant. They're offered only in summer, between mid-June and mid-August. Between mid-June and mid-July, English-language tours are conducted every Wednesday and Saturday at 10am.

In town, you can walk about, observing houses from the Middle Ages, ruined fortifications, and churches. Notable among these is the **Burmeisterska Huset,** the home of the *burmeister,* or the leading German merchant, at Strandgatan 9.

You can walk down to the old **Hanseatic harbor** (not the same harbor in use today) and stroll to the **Botanical Gardens,** which have earned for Visby the title "City of Roses." You'll pass two of the most famous towers in the old wall—the **Maiden's Tower** (a peasant girl was buried alive here for helping a Danish king) and the **Powder Tower** (the oldest fortification in Visby).

In the heyday of its power and glory, little Visby boasted 17 churches. Only one today, **Domkyrkan (Cathedral of St. Mary)** ★★, is in use. Found at Kyrkberget, it was dedicated in 1225 and was built with funds collected by German merchant ships. Pope Clement VI in Avignon gave his permission to build the so-called Swertingska chapel in 1349. The church was damaged in four serious fires: 1400, 1586, 1610, and 1744. It attained its status as a cathedral in 1572. The only original fixture left is a sandstone font from the 1200s. The landmarks of Visby are the two towers of the church. The tower at the western front is square, whereas two slimmer ones appear on the east. In the interior, one of the curiosities is the fringe of grotesque angels' faces beneath the pulpit. Hours are daily 8am to 8pm. Free admission. For more information, call ✆ **0498/206-800.**

Also of interest are the ruins of the former **Dominican Monastery of St. Nicholas** just down the road from Domkyrkan. The church has a rose window cut from a single big stone—it's more than 3m (10 ft.) in diameter. Work began on the monastery in 1230, but it was destroyed by Lübeck forces in 1525. For more information, call ✆ **0498/206-800.**

Another sightseeing recommendation is the impressive **Gotlands Fornsal** ★★, the Historical Museum of Gotland, Strandgatan 14 (✆ **0498/29-27-00**), on a medieval street noted for its step-gabled houses. The museum contains some of the most interesting artifacts discovered on Gotland, including carved stones dating from A.D. 400, art from medieval and later periods, plus furniture and household items. It's open from May 15 to August daily 10am to 5pm, September to May 14 Tuesday to Sunday noon to 4pm. Admission is 60SEK ($7.80) for adults, free for children 16 and under.

ON THE ISLAND

At the **Turistbyrå,** Östervåg 1 (✆ **0498/20-33-00**), ask what island tours are scheduled during your visit; these daily tours (different every day) are the best way to get a quick overview of Gotland. The price can be as low as 70SEK ($9.10) for a brief walking tour or as high as 400SEK ($52) for a complete tour of the island by van.

One thing you can be sure of is that each tour will visit the **Lummelunda Grottan,** Lummelunds Bruk (✆ **0498/273050**), a karst cave formed of limestone bedrock by a subterranean stream. The explored part of the stream cave stretches for 4km (2½ miles) and contains stalactite and stalagmite formations, fossil remains, and subterranean waters. The part of the cave with some of the

Tips **Planning Ahead**

For all its attractions, Visby doesn't have enough hotels. Because accommodations are packed in summer, you need to reserve in advance. If at all possible, telephone for reservations from Stockholm or from home, before you leave.

biggest and most beautiful chambers is open to visitors. It's located 13km (8 miles) north of Visby along Route 149. A bus departs from Österport Visby from June 19 to August 14 daily at 2pm. The cave is open from May to June 25 daily 9am to 4pm, June 26 to August 14 daily 9am to 6pm, August 15 to September 14 daily 10am to 4pm (closed at other times). Visits on your own cost 70SEK ($9.10) for adults, 50SEK ($6.50) for children 5 to 15, free for children 4 and under.

One tour goes to **northern Gotland and Fårö.** A bus takes you to the ferry port of Fårösund, with a 7-minute ferry ride over the strait followed by an excursion around Fårö (Sheep Island) so that you can see dwarf forests and moors.

The tours take place in summer on Tuesday and Thursday from 8:30am to 5:30pm.

SHOPPING

The most memorable goods available for acquisition on Gotland are produced on the island, usually by individual craftspeople working in highly detailed, small-scale productions. One store at which you can find such products is **Yllet,** St. Hansgatan 19, Visby (© **0498/21-40-44**), where clothing made from wool produced by local sheep is sold in the form of sweaters, scarves, hats, gloves, coats, and winter wear for men, women, and children. Colors here tend to be natural and soft, usually deriving from the untinted, unbleached fibers originally produced by the sheep themselves. Also, don't overlook the gift shop that's showcased within the island's historical museum, **Gotlands Fornsal,** Strandgatan 14, Visby (© **0498/29-27-00**), where reproductions of some of the museum's art objects are for sale, as well as handicrafts and textiles made on the island.

Gotland is home to dozens of independent artists, who mostly work out of their own houses or studios manufacturing ceramics, textiles, woodcarvings, or examples of metalwork. Their merchandise tends to be marketed by cooperatives— loosely organized networks that publicize and display the works of artists. The artists' work is judged by a panel that decides whether their products are qualified to represent the local art and handicraft scene. Objects are displayed and can be purchased at two separate agencies: **Galerie & Butik Gotland Konsthantverkare,** Hästgatan (© **0498/21-03-49**), and **Galerie Kvinnfolki,** Donnersplats 4 (© **0498/21-00-51**). Kvinnfolki limits its merchandise to items crafted by women, which includes jam made from local berries, textiles, children's clothing, and a line of cosmetics made on the island from all-natural oils, emollients, and pigments.

WHERE TO STAY

If you should arrive without reservations, contact the **Gotland Resort** (© **0498/ 20-12-60**). The English-speaking staff will try to arrange for rooms in a hotel or private home in or near Visby. The average rate for accommodations in a private home is 220SEK ($29) per person, per night.

IN VISBY

Hotell Solhem One of the most recently renovated hotels in Visby was built in 1987 on a slope overlooking the harbor, a few blocks north of the center. In 1998, its size was doubled, thanks to a new addition designed to match the hotel's existing core with ocher-colored walls, prominent gables, a terra-cotta roof, and a vague sense of the seafaring life of the early 19th century. Bedrooms are comfortable, cozy, and warm, with simple but tasteful furniture and small bathrooms equipped with shower units.

Solhemsgatan 3, S-621 58 Visby. ℂ 0498/25-90-00. Fax 0498/25-90-11. www.hotelsolhem.se. 94 units. 790SEK–1,560SEK ($103–$203) double. Rates include breakfast. AE, DC, MC, V. Free parking. Closed Sat–Sun Jan–Feb. **Amenities:** Breakfast room; lounge; sauna; babysitting; laundry service; dry cleaning; nonsmoking rooms; rooms for those w/limited mobility. *In room:* TV, dataport, hair dryer.

Hotel S:t Clemens ★ *Value* This 18th-century building in the town center has been successfully transformed into a well-run little hotel. It's decorated tastefully in a modern style, with light pastels used effectively. It's open year-round, and the staff is helpful and efficient. In spite of the hotel's age, all of its bathrooms have modern shower and toilet facilities with adequate shelf space. All renovations were carried out with care, so as not to ruin the architecture. No two rooms are identical; your choices range from the smallest single in the shoemaker's old house with a view over church ruins, to a four-bed unit with a sloping ceiling and the greenery of the botanical gardens framing the window. Even the old stable offers rooms especially for guests with allergies. A comfortable, cozy atmosphere permeates the whole place, which is comprised of a series of five antique buildings connected by two pleasant gardens.

Smedjegatan 3, S-621 55 Visby. ℂ 0498/21-90-00. Fax 0498/27-94-43. www.clemenshotell.se. 30 units. 760SEK–1,440SEK ($99–$187) double; 1,650SEK–2,400SEK ($215–$312) suite; additional bed 250SEK ($33) extra. Rates include breakfast. AE, DC, MC, V. Free parking. **Amenities:** Breakfast room; lounge; sauna; nonsmoking rooms; rooms for those w/limited mobility. *In room:* TV, dataport, hair dryer.

Strand Hotel This popular four-story hotel—a Best Western—was built in 1982 on the waterfront a short walk from the harbor. Groups of people tend to congregate in the lobby, and the comfortable bedrooms are tastefully modern. The bathrooms are well maintained with up-to-date plumbing that includes shower stalls. Breakfast is the only meal served.

Strandgatan 34, S-621 56 Visby. ℂ 800/528-1234 in the U.S., or 0498/25-88-00. Fax 0498/25-88-11. www.strandhotel.net. 112 units. 790SEK–1,760SEK ($103–$229) double; 3,600SEK ($468) suite. Rates include breakfast. AE, DC, MC, V. Free parking. **Amenities:** Breakfast room; bar; indoor pool; sauna; limited room service; babysitting; laundry service; dry cleaning; nonsmoking rooms; rooms for those w/limited mobility. *In room:* TV, dataport, minibar, hair dryer.

Wisby Hotel ★★ When this hotel was radically restored and upgraded in the early 1990s, it became the best and most glamorous on the island. Set close to the harbor front in the town center, its historic core includes medieval foundations and the type of solid stonework you'll see elsewhere in Visby. Radiating outward from the core are newer additions that span several centuries. The best feature of the hotel, which makes it the finest place to stay off season, is a winter garden, a bold combination of steel, glass, and Gotland sandstone. You can relax in a leather armchair with a drink and admire the greenery and the changing Nordic light. The bedrooms are conservatively elegant, and some have reproductions of 18th-century furniture. The bathrooms are a bit small but are equipped with tub/showers.

Strandgatan 6, S-621 24 Visby. ℂ 0498/25-75-00. Fax 0498/25-75-50. www.wisbyhotell.se. 134 units. 1,280SEK–1,930SEK ($166–$251) double; 2,635SEK–4,800SEK ($343–$624) suite. Rates include breakfast.

AE, DC, MC, V. Free parking. **Amenities:** 2 restaurants; 2 bars; lounge; indoor pool; sauna; limited room service; laundry service; dry cleaning; nonsmoking rooms; rooms for those w/limited mobility. *In room:* TV, dataport, minibar, hair dryer.

NEARBY HOTELS

Toftagården Hotell & Restaurang   Set adjacent to the island's coast, 19km (12 miles) south of Visby, and separated from the beach only by a windbreak of trees, this cozy, family-managed hotel developed from a core that was established shortly after World War II. Much improved and enlarged since then, its most visible section was built in the 1980s as a gable-fronted replica of a large private house. Both the conventional bedrooms and the quintet of cottages are cozy, comfortably outfitted with simple furnishings. The variation in prices derives from the fact that a handful of them were renovated less recently than the more expensive units and have older, slightly more worn upholstery and furniture. All accommodations are nonsmoking and contain private bathrooms, with either tubs or showers.

Part of the allure of this place derives from its well-managed restaurant, which serves specialties from Gotland and the rest of Sweden every day from noon to 8pm (until 10pm July–Aug). Specialties include roasted Gotland lamb and different preparations of salmon.

Tofta. S-621 98 Visby. (**€) 0498/29-70-00.** Fax 0498/26-56-66. www.toftagarden.se. 70 units, plus 10 cottages. 550SEK–1,490SEK ($72–$194) double. Rates include breakfast. AE, DC, MC, V. Free parking. **Amenities:** Restaurant; bar; outdoor pool; sauna; laundry service; dry cleaning; rooms for those w/limited mobility; solarium. *In room:* TV, hair dryer, iron, safe.

Villa Alskog ★★   Our favorite nest on the island is this restored 1840 building close to the sandy beaches and a delight in every way, offering real old-fashioned Gotland hospitality. Stone fences, open spaces, and a tree-studded landscape create an atmosphere of long ago, although there's also an outdoor pool as a modern touch. The inn is currently enjoying an expansion, and more modern amenities will be in place for 2005. Their aim is to entice guests to relax and "use their minds instead of just watching TV." The decor is traditional Swedish, with bright colors and wooden floors. Bedrooms are midsize and beautifully maintained, with comfortable, tastefully furnished modern bathrooms with shower stalls. Full spa treatments, along with a Japanese hot tub, are available. In the lobby, you can avail yourself of a 24-hour buffet. The food is good, with lots of Swedish flavor. In a public area, guests can avail themselves of a phone, TV, and dataport connection.

Alskog, S-620 16 Ljugarn. (**€) 0498/49-11-88.** Fax 0498/49-11-20. www.villa-alskog.se. 30 units. 900SEK ($117) double. AE, DC, MC, V. **Amenities:** Restaurant; bar; pool; gym; spa; sauna; room service (7am–midnight); laundry service; nonsmoking rooms; rooms for those w/limited mobility. *In room:* No phone.

WHERE TO DINE

Burmeister ITALIAN/INTERNATIONAL   This large restaurant in the town center offers dining indoors or under shady fruit trees in the garden of a 16th-century house originally built for the wealthiest citizen of Visby. Diners can look out on the surrounding medieval buildings from many of the tables. The cuisine is rather standard international, never achieving any glory, but not disappointing, either. The place is incredibly popular in summer, and long lines form—so they must be doing something right. Pizza is the most popular menu choice. After 10pm in summer, the restaurant becomes a dance club; the cover charge ranges from 100SEK to 200SEK ($13–$26).

Strandgatan 6, Visby. 🕐 **0498/21-03-73.** Reservations required. Main courses 139SEK–229SEK ($18–$30); pizzas 95SEK–119SEK ($12–$15). AE, DC, MC, V. June 20–Aug 5 Mon–Sat noon–4pm and 6–11pm. Disco mid-June to Aug 5 Mon–Sat 10pm–2am.

Clematis SWEDISH   Imbued with a medieval atmosphere, this summer-only restaurant has been a tourist favorite since it opened in the late 1980s. Cookery inspired by recipes of the Middle Ages, accompanied by jesters, musicians, and fire-eaters, attempts to re-create Visby in an age gone by. Medieval feasts are a feature here, even arranged for special parties during December. As the costumed staff is bringing you your platter, they are likely to break into a medieval tune. Yes, it's all so very campy, but an enduring favorite.

The building itself is from the 13th century, and all the props are either real or copies from excavations on Gotland. You are given a flat slab of bread instead of a plate, accompanied by a jug of red wine or a cellar-cooled beer. The only eating utensil is a knife—no forks, please. Begin with such old-fashioned dishes as salt-pork dumplings or else smoked flounder, and follow with such favorites as a whole chicken stuffed with prunes and apples, or marinated and grilled pork on the bone with honey-fried carrots and turnips. For dessert, how about a pear toffee with lavender cream? Instead of ordering a la carte, you can also select a full medieval banquet that includes the likes of apples, nuts, candied rose petals, smoked leg of lamb, sausages, honey-fried cabbage, lamb chops, spare ribs, and dessert.

Strandgatan 20. 🕐 **0498/29-27-27.** Reservations not accepted. Main courses 95SEK–255SEK ($12–$33); medieval banquet 260SEK ($34). AE, DC, MC, V. June–Sept daily 6–11pm.

Donners Brunn ✹✹ FRENCH/SWEDISH   This is a real discovery and the finest restaurant on island. Its chef and owner is Bo Nilsson, the former chef of Operakällaren, arguably the finest restaurant in Stockholm. Branching out on his own, he has taken over this 17th-century building, constructed of orange-colored brick, on a small square in the heart of town and has established a showcase for his own refined cuisine. He makes great use of market-fresh produce and often produces dishes that are truly sublime. His menu is seasonally adjusted so that diners can enjoy the best of flavors and produce at any time of the year. Just a 2-minute walk from the harbor, diners relax comfortably, perusing an enticing menu of the chef's specialties, the signature dish being Gotland lamb with fresh asparagus served with a freshly made hollandaise. You might begin with a tempting platter of Baltic herring, or else a pot of mussels flavored with chorizo sausage. Always count on a fresh fish platter along with a selection of other main dishes that can range from the humble to the noble, depending on the night. Desserts are freshly made and frequently changing, but are always a delight.

Donners plats 3. 🕐 **0498/27-10-90.** Reservations required in summer. Main courses 200SEK–250SEK ($26–$33). AE, DC, MC, V. June–Sept daily 6pm–2am. Off season Mon–Sat 6pm–midnight.

Gutekällaren SWEDISH   This restaurant and bar in the town center originally was built as a tavern in the early 1600s on foundations that are much older. It was enlarged in 1789 and today is one of the oldest buildings (if not *the* oldest) in Visby. It offers fresh fish and meat dishes, including some vegetarian specialties. You might begin with a fish soup made with lobster and shrimp, then follow with filet of sole Waleska or roast lamb chops. The dessert specialty in summer is a parfait made of local berries. Cookery here is solid and reliable, with fresh ingredients. The ambience is sober for this fun-loving island of summer fun, but once the dining is out of the way, the place livens up considerably (see "Visby After Dark," below).

Stortorget 3, Visby. ℂ **0498/21-00-43**. Reservations recommended. Main courses 175SEK–235SEK ($23–$31). AE, DC, MC, V. Daily 6–11pm.

Munkkällaren ⭐ SWEDISH/INTERNATIONAL. This restaurant, although not the most expensive in town, is one of the best. You'll recognize it in the center of Visby by its brown wooden facade. The dining room, which is only a few steps from the street, is sheathed in white stone, parts of which date from 1100. In summer, the management opens the doors to two more pubs in the compound. The main pub, Munken, offers platters of good tasting and flavorful *husmanskost* (Swedish home cooking), including *frikadeller* (meatballs). In the restaurant you might begin with escargots in creamy garlic sauce, or toast with Swedish caviar. Specialties include shellfish stew, salmon-stuffed sole with spinach and a saffron sauce, and venison in port-wine sauce. Live music is often performed in the courtyard, beginning around 8pm. After the music stops, a dance club opens every night from 11pm to 2am. Admission to the club is 80SEK to 150SEK ($10–$20).

Lilla Torggränd 2, Visby. ℂ **0498/27-14-00**. Reservations required in summer. Main courses 90SEK–225SEK ($12–$29). AE, DC, MC, V. Restaurant daily 6–11pm; pubs daily 6pm–2am (June 1–Aug 7 noon–11pm).

VISBY AFTER DARK

There's a lot more energy expended on star-gazing, wave-watching, and ecology in Gotland than on bar-hopping and nocturnal flirting. But if you want to heat it up after dark, there's a limited offering nonetheless. The island's premier venue for folks over 40 who enjoy dancing "very tight" (ballroom style) occurs every Saturday night at the **Borgen Bar,** Hästgatan 24 (ℂ **0498/24-79-55**), which contains a restaurant, a dance floor, and recordings that get patrons dancing (the music ranges from the big band era to more modern, supper-club selections). A hipper alternative where dancers are less inclined to wrap themselves romantically in each other's arms is the **Munkkälleren,** which was recommended previously as a restaurant and derives at least some of its business from its role as a bar and late-night, weekend-only dance club. A similar atmosphere is found at **Gutekälleren,** another previously recommended restaurant, whose interior becomes a dance club either 2 or 4 nights a week, beginning around 10pm, for high-energy dancers mostly ages 35 and under. If you happen to be a bit older than 35, you'll still feel comfortable hanging out at the establishment's bar, soaking up aquavit and the local color.

SOUTHERN GOTLAND

As charming as Visby is, many savvy Swedes prefer to stay in southern Gotland in the hamlet of Burgsvik, 90km (56 miles) south of Visby. This is a popular port and resort town. If you have a car, you may want to check it out.

WHERE TO STAY

Pensionat Holmhällar *Value* The origins of this hotel date from 1940, when it was built as a barracks and administrative center by the Swedish army as they pondered the political role they should take vis-à-vis the growing menace of Nazi Germany. In 1949, it was enlarged and adapted into a resort hotel, and further enlarged throughout the course of the 1960s and 1970s. Today it incorporates three separate buildings and 16 simple cottages within an area of natural beauty, 20m (66 ft.) from one of the best beaches in the southern region of Gotland. Bedrooms are a step up from army barracks in comfort, but they are small. Bathrooms also are rather cramped, but each has a shower. The clientele tends to be interested in nature, ecology, and beach life, and comes to escape the distractions of the outside world. There's a restaurant on the premises that maintains impossibly early hours (dinner is served only from 5 to 7pm) and specializes in family-style set menus priced at 75SEK ($9.75) each.

Know in advance that this place is much more appealing in summer than in winter: Between October and March, services and access to most of this hotel are radically curtailed. All dining and drinking facilities are closed, and only a handful of the outlying cottages are available for rent. These cost 450SEK ($59) for a double without bathroom, and 600SEK ($78) for a double with bathroom. In addition, no linens or towels are provided off season, so you'll have to bring your own.

Vamlingbo, S-620-10 Burgsvik. ℂ **0498/49-80-30.** Fax 0498/49-80-56. 50 units. 500SEK ($65) double; 500SEK ($65) per person for apt. MC, V. Free parking. **Amenities:** Restaurant; sauna.

Värdshuset Björklunda ⭐ *Value*   Originating in the 1890s as an unpretentious farmhouse, this hotel developed during the 1970s into a well-respected inn that's directed today by charming and hardworking members of the Jacobson family. Set near a small beach, within a forest, and beside the main highway leading south into Burgsvik, the inn draws a loyal clientele to its restaurant between June and August.

Within a cozy, traditionally decorated dining room, you can order culinary specialties from Gotland and, to a lesser extent, from the rest of Sweden as well. Examples include smoked filets of lamb, barbecued lamb (a treat available only on Sat nights), and fresh salmon served with saffron sauce. Main courses run 60SEK to 160SEK ($7.80–$21). Menu service is curtailed and presented on an "as needed" basis the rest of the year, so if you arrive between October and April, it's likely that your meal will be served *en famille* with the Jacobsons, without the fanfare of a commercial restaurant, but with some of the warmth and conviviality of a private home. Bedrooms are simple and modern, a function of a radical renovation that was completed in 1995. Although fairly comfortable, rooms are extremely small. Bathrooms—each with a shower—also are a bit cramped. All rooms are nonsmoking.

S-620 10 Burgsvik. ℂ **0498/49-71-90.** Fax 0498/49-78-50. 22 units. 820SEK ($107) double. Rates include breakfast. AE, DC, MC, V. Free parking. **Amenities:** Rooms for those w/limited mobility. *In room:* TV, no phone.

9

The Göta Canal & Lake Vänern

Connecting Gothenburg and Stockholm with a direct inland water route, the Göta Canal makes for an unforgettable journey with 65 locks between the North Sea and the Baltic. The canal is called "Sweden's blue ribbon," and it runs to the province of Västergötland between Lake Vänern and Lake Vättern (often confused because of the similarity in their names).

The shifting scenery along the entire length of the canal makes it among the most beautiful panoramas in Europe. It's preferable to see it by water, but you can also drive or cycle along the canal.

The history of the canal dates from 1810, when the former naval officer Baltzar von Platen, assisted by some 60,000 soldiers, began what was to be a 22-year project. The first of the locks was built in Forsvik in 1813 and is still in use today.

Toward the end of the 19th century, the canal's importance as a transport artery began to diminish. Gradually, however, the idea of using it for leisure activities began to catch on, and today 4,000 boats a year use the canal, in addition to a significant number of passenger vessels and even canoes.

The towpaths are almost as busy as the canal itself. Where oxen once could be seen giving barges and sailing craft a much-needed tow, you now find walkers and cyclists making their way to the leafy countryside.

One of the highlights of any trip along the Göta Canal is to take in views of Lake Vänern, an inland sea that has existed since 6500 B.C., although back then it covered a much larger area than today. It is the largest lake in Sweden and the third-largest lake in Europe, encompassing 2,130 sq. km (831 sq. miles). It is 145km (90 miles) long and 80km (50 miles) wide at one point.

The present-day Lake Vänern took shape during the Iron Age around 300 B.C. Some 20 tributaries of varying size feed water into the lake, although that water is discharged to just one outflow, the River Göta. The amount of water being discharged is just over 500,000 liters (132,100 gal.) per second, which, in effect, means the water in the lake is changed every ninth year. The lake boasts about 20,000 small islands and rocks, forming the world's largest freshwater archipelago.

1 The Göta Canal ★★★

A fascinating summer boat trip and one of Sweden's major attractions is the 4-day **Göta Canal cruise** ★★, which covers 560km (347 miles) from Gothenburg (Göteborg) in the west to Stockholm in the east (or vice versa). The Göta Canal is composed of a series of artificial canals, lakes, and rivers connected by a series of 65 locks (the highest is more than 90m/295 ft. above sea level), and the 4-day cruise makes four or five stops along the way. Day trips and longer cruises also are offered.

The Göta Canal

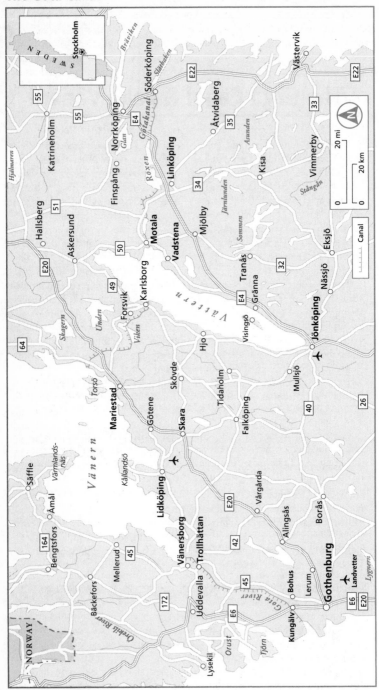

The canal was begun in the early 19th century for the purpose of transporting goods across Sweden, thereby avoiding expensive tolls levied by Denmark on ships entering and leaving the Baltic Sea. However, soon after the canal was completed, Denmark waived its shipping tolls, and the railway between Stockholm and Gothenburg was created, thereby allowing for the cheaper and faster shipment of goods across Sweden. Thus the canal became more of a tourist attraction than a means of transportation.

Boats depart Gothenburg heading east along the Göta älv River. About 30 minutes outside Gothenburg, you'll see the 14th-century **Bohus Fortress.** This bastion played a leading role in the battles among Sweden, Norway, and Denmark to establish supremacy. Bohus Castle and Fortress (Bohus Fästning) was built by order of Norway's Haakon V on Norwegian territory. After the territory was ceded to Sweden in 1658, Bohus Fortress was used as a prison. Climb the tower, **"Father's Hat,"** for a panoramic view. Farther down the river, the boat will pass the town of **Kungälv,** known by the Vikings as Konghälla, whose traditions are 1,000 years old.

As the boat proceeds eastward on the Göta's clear water, the landscape becomes wilder. About 5 hours into the journey, you reach the town of **Trollhättan,** home of one of Europe's largest power stations. The once-renowned Trollhättan Falls, now almost dry, can be seen at their full capacity only in July. Today most of the water is diverted to a series of underground channels to the power station.

After passing to a series of locks, boats enter **Lake Vänern,** Sweden's largest lake, with a surface area of more than 2,130 sq. km (831 sq. miles). The trip across Lake Vänern takes about 8 hours. Along the way you'll pass **Lidköping,** home of the famous Rörstrand porcelain. Lidköping received its charter in 1446. North of Lidköping, on the island of Kållandsö, stands **Läckö Slott,** a castle dating from 1298. Originally home of the bishops of Skara, the castle was given to King Gustavus Vasa in 1528 and later presented to Sweden's great hero, Gen. Magnus Gabriel de la Gardie.

Having crossed Lake Vänern, the boats once again enter the canal. A series of locks, including the canal's oldest at Forsvik, carry the steamers to Sweden's second-largest lake, **Lake Vättern** (see chapter 7). This lake is famous for its beauty and translucent water. At some points, visibility reaches a depth of 15m (49 ft.).

Along the eastern shore of Lake Vättern sits the medieval town of **Vadstena,** the most important stopover on the Göta Canal trip. Within the town are old narrow streets and frame buildings. It's known throughout Sweden for its delicate handmade lace, which you can see by walking along Stora Gatan, the main street. Also of interest is the **Klosterkyrkan (Abbey Church).** Built between the mid–14th and the 15th centuries to specifications outlined by its founder, St. Birgitta (Bridget) of Sweden, this Gothic church is rich in medieval art. Parts of the abbey date from 1250; the abbey sheltered the nuns of St. Birgitta's Order until they were expelled in 1595.

Another important sight is **Vadstena Castle.** Construction began under Gustavus Vasa, king of Sweden in 1545, but was not completed until 1620. This splendid Renaissance Vasa castle, erected during a period of national expansion, dominates the town from its moated position on the lake, just behind the old courthouse in the southern part of town. Royalty has not lived in the castle since 1715, but it was restored in the 19th century.

Boats bound for Stockholm depart Lake Vättern and pass to two small lakes, Boren and Roxen. Just south of Lake Roxen you'll find the university town of

Linköping, site of a battle between Roman Catholic King Sigismund of Poland and Duke Charles of Södermanland (later Charles IX). Charles won the battle and established Linköping as part of Sweden rather than a province of Rome. In the town's main square stands the Folkung Fountain, one of sculptor Carl Milles's most popular works. Northwest of the main square you'll find the cathedral, a not quite harmonious blend of Romanesque and Gothic architecture.

From Linköping, boats enter Lake Roxen and continue their journey northeast by canal to **Slätbaken,** a fjord that stretches to the sea. Steamers then continue along the coast to Stockholm.

The **Göta Canal Steamship Company** offers turn-of-the-20th-century steamers, including its 1874 *Juno,* which claims to be the world's oldest passenger vessel offering overnight accommodations. The line also operates the 1912 *Wilhelm Tham* and the newer—that is, 1931—*Diana.* Passengers can walk, jog, or bike along the canal path, and there are organized shore excursions at many stops along the way.

For bookings, contact **Scantours** (© 800/223-7226 or 310/636-4656). The 4-day cruises begin at 8,817SEK ($1,145) per person, double occupancy (extra bed 485SEK/$630); 6-day cruises from 13,552SEK ($1,760) per person (extra bed 485SEK/$630). Discounts are given for early reservations.

2 Trollhättan

70km (43 miles) N of Gothenburg, 437km (271 miles) SW of Stockholm

Once early inhabitants learned how to harness the power of the Göta River, they began to build sawmills along its banks. By the early 16th century, a small community had been established. The building of the Göta Canal in the 18th and 19th centuries gave Trollhättan its first major thrust toward the future. Hundreds of laborers moved in to build the canal and its locks, and houses sprang up on the islands and banks of the river as the community grew.

In time, cheap electricity obtained directly from the power stations at the falls attracted business companies that led to major industries (including Saab). Companies such as Saab helped put Trollhättan on the Nordic map, and they employ a good percentage of the town's 50,000 inhabitants.

ESSENTIALS

GETTING THERE   By Train   About 22 trains roll into Trollhättan every day from Gothenburg, each of them direct, and each taking about 1 hour. For information about train service into Trollhättan, call © 771/75-75-75.

By Bus   Likewise, about 15 buses arrive every day in Trollhättan from Gothenburg, taking 1½ hours. For schedules and information, call © 0200/21818.

By Car   From Gothenburg, head north on Route 45.

VISITOR INFORMATION   For facts on the area, go to the **Trollhättan Tourist Office,** Åkersjövägen 10 (© 0520/48-84-72; www.trollhattan.se). It is open June to August Monday to Saturday 10am to 6pm, and September to May Monday to Friday 10am to 4pm.

SEEING THE SIGHTS

In Trollhättan, the Göta River takes a mighty leap, a spectacular sight that has attracted visitors to the town for centuries. The best spots for viewing these waterfalls include Kopparklinten, Nyckelbergeet, and Spikön Island. Trollhättan's *Fallensdagar* (Fall Days) is the best-known event in town and occurs during

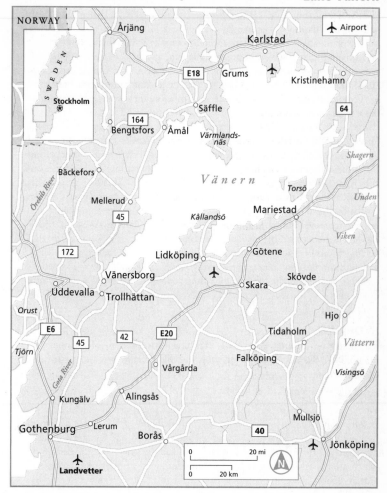

3 days in July (dates vary annually). The Göta River and the waterfalls are celebrated in this nearly 40-year-old festival. Outdoor stages are used for entertainment, and the town's pubs, restaurants, and clubs do a lively business.

The Göta River has the highest flow of any Swedish river and stretches for 90km (56 miles). The waterfalls at Trollhättan, with a drop of 31m (102 ft.), once were an obstacle difficult to overcome; however, they have since been harnessed. Today you can see the water flow into the gorge at a rate of 90,000m (295,200 ft.) per second—but only at certain times, such as Fall Days in July.

A nearby attraction, about 2km (1¼ miles) south of town, is **Kanalmuseet,** Slussområdet (© **0520/47-22-51**), which lies at the top of a 31m (104-ft.) "staircase" created by the locks. It tells the story of the Trollhättan Canal in pictures, models, and tools. An on-site cinema shows historic footage of the locks throughout their history. It is open between June and August 20 daily from 11am to 7pm, and off season from noon to 5pm Saturday and Sunday. Admission is 20SEK

($2.60) per person. To reach it from the center of town, follow the signposts pointing to SLUSSARNA ("The Locks").

One of the most exciting things to do is to take a walk along the falls. The promenade is called **Schleusenpromenade,** and a walk along this pathway will reveal ruins of the failed canals of the 18th century. In the Gamle Dal'n Park area, locks from the early and mid–19th century remain. Information boards tell of the huge obstacle the falls once presented before they were tamed, and how the unique industrial landscape you see today came about.

If you stroll south on the promenade, you reach the **Innovatum Kunskapen Hus** (© 0520/48-84-80), which answers your questions about energy and power in the area with slide shows, computers, energy cycles, water pumps, and many more hands-on exhibits. This 1910 building housing the institute contains 13 massive generators. The admission fee is 50SEK ($6.50) adults, 30SEK ($3.90) children 7 to 19; hours are Tuesday to Sunday 11am to 4pm.

If you cross the canal and head into Trollhättan's industrial hinterland, you'll come to the **Saab Bilmuseum,** Åkerssjövägen, Nohans Industriområde (© 0520/ 843-44), where you can experience more than 50 years of innovative car engineering. From two-stroke to turbo, the history of Saab is presented dramatically. The museum displays an example of every model of Saab ever built, and designs for those to come in the future. Open from June 8 to August 22 daily 10am to 6pm; otherwise, Tuesday to Friday 11am to 4pm. Admission is 50SEK ($6.50) adults, 30SEK ($3.90) children 6 to 16.

SHOPPING

The best place for arts and crafts is **Handkraft Trollhättan,** Magasinsgatan 1 (© 0520/42-92-42), a year-round shop with high-quality arts and crafts made by local artisans.

WHERE TO STAY

First Kung Oscar Hotel   Set in the center of town, near Trollhättan's community center, this five-story hotel originated in the 1950s as an apartment house. In the late 1980s, it was adapted and upgraded into a hotel that looks rather plush, at least from the inside. The strongest points are the bedrooms, which are appealingly and rather formally decorated in pleasing tones of soft gray and beige. Each unit comes with a tiled bathroom with shower.

Drottninggatan 17, S-461 32 Trollhättan. © 0520/47-04-70. Fax 0520/47-04-71. www.kungoscar.se. 76 units. Sun–Thurs 1,345SEK ($175) double, 1,503SEK ($195) suite; Fri–Sat 798SEK ($104) double, 898SEK ($117) suite. Rates include breakfast. AE, DC, MC, V. Free parking. Bus: 11. **Amenities:** Cafe (Mon–Thurs); bar; sauna; laundry service; dry cleaning; nonsmoking rooms; solarium. *In room:* TV, dataport, minibar, hair dryer, iron, trouser press.

Hotel Trollhättan   Near the town's main square (Drottningtorget), this hotel originated in the 1950s as a small guesthouse above the post office. Today, after a renovation and enlargement in the late 1980s, the hotel has two additional floors (although the town's main post office still occupies the establishment's ground floor). Inside you'll find an efficiently decorated, functional, and practical refuge that's favored by business travelers and out-of-town relatives of local homeowners during occasions such as weddings and anniversaries. Bedrooms have hardwood floors, big windows, small bathrooms with tub/showers, and relentlessly functional furnishings.

Polhemsgatan 6, S-461 30 Trollhättan. © 0520/125-65. Fax 0520/154-71. www.hoteltrollhattan.se. 54 units. Mid-June to Aug and Fri–Sun year-round 650SEK ($85) double; rest of year 965SEK ($125) double. Rates include breakfast. AE, DC, MC, V. Free parking. **Amenities:** Restaurant; bar; sauna; limited room service; laundry service; dry cleaning; nonsmoking rooms; rooms for those w/limited mobility. *In room:* TV, dataport, minibar, iron.

Scandic Swania ★★ The grandest, most attractive hotel in town is this red-brick monument, dating from 1916, that features an ornately detailed roof. Frequent renovations since then, most recently in 1998, have brought it up to modern-day standards while retaining the monumental staircases, high ceilings, and, in some cases, elaborate cove moldings of its original construction when it was built as the city hall. It sits directly beside the Göta Canal, in the heart of town, and as such often is the rendezvous point for various public service organizations and charities. Bedrooms are traditional, conservative, and comfortable, not at all experimental or prone to decorative risk-taking. However, they are among the most reliable and biggest in town, and certainly have the best beds. Bathrooms are well maintained and equipped with tub/showers.

Storgatan 47–49, S-461-26 Trollhättan. ℂ **0520/89-000.** Fax 0520/890-01. www.scandic-hotels.com. 196 units. Sun–Thurs 1,595SEK ($207) double, 2,220SEK ($289) minisuite for 2; Fri–Sat 850SEK ($111) double, 1,800SEK ($234) minisuite for 2. Rates include breakfast. AE, DC, MC, V. Free parking. **Amenities:** Restaurant; bar; disco; indoor pool; sauna; limited room service; laundry service; dry cleaning; nonsmoking rooms; rooms for those w/limited mobility. *In room:* A/C, TV, dataport, minibar, hair dryer.

3 Vänersborg 🏛

15km (9¼ miles) north of Trollhättan, 85km (53 miles) N of Gothenburg

The famed poet Birger Sjöberg may have exaggerated a bit in calling Vänersborg "Little Paris," but it is, nonetheless, one of the most idyllic stopovers along the Göta Canal.

Vänersborg grew from its roots in Brätte, a medieval trade center next to Vassbotten. The glory days of Brätte were the early 1600s. (In 1944 the region was excavated by archaeologists.) It took a great many workers in Brätte to unload the Vänern ships and reload the goods onto horse-drawn carriages. In time, it became difficult for ships to enter the bay, as the bottom was silting up. More land was needed for expansion, and Vänersborg grew up as a result of this. It was granted its town charter in 1644 and became the county seat in 1679.

When the Trollhättan Canal was built, shipping became a major source of income. Light industry, administration, and schools later would become part of Vänersborg's profile. In 1834, a fire leveled the town, turning it into a heap of smoking ash in just 14 hours. Only a handful of buildings survived. Afterward, the new city design included a wide firebreak street to avoid another catastrophe.

ESSENTIALS

GETTING THERE By Train Ten trains arrive from Stockholm every day; depending on the train, the trip takes between 3 and 5 hours. Most require you to change trains in Herrlgungå en route. About 10 nonstop trains arrive from Gothenburg daily and take about an hour. For information, call ℂ **771/75-75-75.**

By Bus At least two buses arrive from Stockholm every day, a travel time of 6 hours, as well as a handful of buses from Gothenburg (travel time: about 90 min.). For bus information affecting Vänersborg and the towns around it, call ℂ **0200/21818.**

By Car From Trollhättan, our last stopover, continue north along Route 45 into Vänersborg.

VISITOR INFORMATION The **tourist office** in Vänersborg is one of the few in Sweden that changes its address according to the season. Between June and August, it's at the railway station (© **0521/27-14-00;** www.vanersborg.se), where it operates Monday to Friday 8am to 7pm, Saturday and Sunday 10am to 4pm. The rest of the year, it operates Monday to Friday 8am to 5pm at Sundsgatan 6B. For written inquiries, address your correspondence to P.O. Box 77, S-462 40 Vänersborg, Sweden.

SEEING THE SIGHTS

Torget, laid out in 1860, became the town's market area. It is still the center of town and a good place from which to start exploring. The chief attraction in town is the **Vänersborg Museet,** Plantaget (© **0521/600-62**), which displays objects from around the world. The West African bird collection is its most famous exhibit. Its exhibits have hardly changed since the late 19th century, and it remains appropriately gloomy. A reconstruction of Birger Sjöberg's home can be seen. He, of course, was the city's great poet and troubadour, who called Vänersborg "Little Paris." It includes many of his personal belongings and authentic pieces from the turn of the 20th century. Other collections are devoted to natural history, agriculture, and a history of music. The museum is open June to August Tuesday to Thursday, Saturday, and Sunday noon to 4pm. Off-season hours are Tuesday to Thursday, Saturday, and Sunday noon to 4pm. Admission is 20SEK ($2.60).

Anyone who is interested in handicrafts, particularly doll making, may appreciate the exhibits within the **Vänersborg Doll Studio & Museum,** Residensgatan 2 (© **0521/615-71**). It's open June 15 to August 15 Tuesday to Friday 10am to 1pm and 2 to 6pm, and Saturday 10am to 1pm; rest of the year Tuesday to Friday 2:30 to 6pm, and Saturday 10am to 1pm. It's housed in the oldest wooden structure still standing in Vänersborg—the building was built in the 1790s—but the dolls go back only to the 1890s. You can view Birgitta Pererson's own prize-winning dolls, and her work is available for purchase in the on-site shop, along with a full range of doll-making materials. Entrance is 40SEK ($5.20) adults, 20SEK ($2.60) children 5 to 18.

East of town, you can visit the twin bluffs of **Halleberg** and **Hunneberg,** which are 500 million years old. Halleberg and Hunneberg have been used as hunting grounds since the 1500s. Traditionally, this was Swedish elk country, but disease has reduced the stock to around 120 animals. However, there is still a great deal of other wildlife, including deer, hare, and foxes. King Oscar II began the tradition of holding the royal elk hunt here, and hunting rights are still held by the Swedish king. Today the "elk safaris" hunt with cameras rather than guns. Ask at the tourist office in Vänersborg if you'd like to frame some Swedish elk.

You also can visit the **Naturskola Nature Center** at Hunneberg (© **0521/22-37-70**), a center that explores the history, flora, and fauna of the twin bluffs. It is open Monday to Friday 9am to 3pm, weekends by appointment. There's a cafe on-site and plenty of information available about the wildlife still living in the surrounding hills. The cafe is open daily 10am to 4pm.

SHOPPING

At **Konsthantverkarna i Vänersborg** ✦, Edsgatan 5 (© **0521/107-47**), more than 20 craftspeople and artisans present their work for sale under one roof. This is one of the best places to shop for handicrafts along Lake Vänern. It is open Monday through Saturday.

WHERE TO STAY

Park Inn Ronnums Herrgård ⭐ *Finds*   This much-renovated 18th-century manor house is a particularly charming, small-scale place to stay. Sheathed with yellow clapboards and a red roof, it lies within its own park, with window views that sweep out over the surrounding forest and the low hills nearby. Bedrooms are outfitted with pastel colors and furniture that's more contemporary than what you'll find within the main house. Each room comes with a tidily kept private bathroom with a tub/shower. There is a bar and a cozy restaurant where, amid 19th-century Swedish antiques, dinner specialties include platters of Swedish herring, Swedish caviar, venison with Swedish chanterelles, and a roster of dessert parfaits.

S-468 30 Vargön. ℂ 0521/223270. Fax 0521/26-00-09. www.softwarehotels.se/ronnum. 60 units. Mid-June to mid-Aug and Fri–Sat year-round 1,160SEK ($151) double, 1,650SEK ($215) suite; rest of year 1,385SEK ($180) double, 1,900SEK ($247) suite. AE, DC, MC, V. Free parking. From Vänersborg, drive south for 5km (3 miles), following the signs to Vargön. **Amenities:** Restaurant; bar; Jacuzzi; sauna; limited room service; laundry service; dry cleaning; nonsmoking rooms; rooms for those w/limited mobility. *In room:* TV, minibar, hair dryer, iron (in some).

Quality Hotel Vänersborg   Adjacent to the Göta Canal, 1.5km (1 mile) south of the center of Vänersborg, this four-story hotel was built in 1977 and renovated in the mid-1990s. Inside you'll find intensely colorful public areas. Bedrooms are angular and modern looking, with somewhat spartan lines that are softened by ample use of wood-veneered panels and spaces that seem a bit larger than they are, thanks to large mirrors. Bathrooms, though small, are spotless and contain tub/showers. This member of a chain benefits from a cooperative and well-trained staff.

Nabbensberg, S-462 40 Vänersborg. ℂ 0521/621-20. Fax 0521/609-23. www.choicehotels.se. 119 units. June 19–Aug 15 and Fri–Sat year-round 1,790SEK ($233) double; rest of year 1,285SEK ($167) double. Rates include breakfast. AE, DC, MC, V. Free parking. **Amenities:** Restaurant; bar; pool; gym; sauna; laundry service; dry cleaning; nonsmoking rooms; rooms for those w/limited mobility. *In room:* TV, dataport, hair dryer (in some), iron.

WHERE TO DINE

Motorists may consider driving outside of town to Park Inn Ronnums Herrgård for some of the most elegant dining in the area (see "Where to Stay," above).

Koppragrillen INTERNATIONAL   Set in a 1960s-era building in the center of town, within a dining room cozily outfitted in a conservative rustic style, this is one of the very few independent restaurants that remains open every day for both lunch and dinner. Menu specialties feature an array of well-seasoned dishes that include halibut with fresh tomatoes and banana-flavored butter sauce, boiled venison with horseradish sauce, filet of beef with Madeira sauce, and grilled veal or chateaubriand with béarnaise sauce.

Sundsgatan 11. ℂ 0521/181-51. Reservations recommended. Main courses 85SEK–168SEK ($11–$22). AE, DC, MC, V. Mon–Fri 11am–11pm; Sat–Sun noon–11pm.

4 Lidköping

140km (87 miles) NE of Gothenburg, 55km (34 miles) NE of Vänersborg

Lidköping really is two towns, divided by the River Lidan. During the Middle Ages, the Old Town (east bank) developed at the river's only fjord as a commercial center with busy river traffic. It received its town charter in 1446. Then, in the 1670s, the Earl of Läckö began systematic construction of a new town on the west bank of the river. The straight streets and rectangular blocks used in laying out the town have been mostly preserved to the present. Notably, the great square, still used as the marketplace for the town and surrounding countryside, was surprisingly modern for the period.

Since the Middle Ages, Lidköping's economy has been based on trade and handicrafts. Given its location between the old main road from Götaälvdalen (the Göta River valley) and the shipping lanes on Lake Vänern, it was inevitable that it would develop into a commercial center for the area.

ESSENTIALS

GETTING THERE   By Train   Trains arrive in Lidköping at frequent intervals from both Stockholm (between two and four times a day, depending on the day of the week), and Gothenburg (eight per day Mon–Fri and between two and three per day on weekends, depending on the season). Transits from Stockholm require a change of equipment in the town of Hallsberg, and a total travel time of 3 hours. Alternatively, you can travel by train from Stockholm to the town of Skövde, then continue by bus for an additional 45 minutes to Lidköping. Buses are more or less timed to coincide with the arrival of trains. Travel time from Gothenburg requires 2 hours and sometimes a change of equipment in the railway junction of Herrljunga en route. For rail information in Lidköping, call ⓒ 771/75-75-75.

By Bus   Bus travel to Lidköping from both Stockholm and Gothenburg is less convenient than the equivalent trip by train. There are two buses per day from Stockholm, each taking 4 hours for the trip, and about two per day from Gothenburg, requiring about 2 to 2½ hours. For information, call ⓒ 0200/21818.

By Car   From Vänersborg, continue northeast along Route 44 into Lidköping.

VISITOR INFORMATION   For information, go to the **Turistbyrån i Lidköping,** Bangatan 3 (ⓒ 0510/77-05-00; www.lidkoping.se). It's open from June to mid-August Monday to Saturday 10am to 8pm, Sunday 1 to 6pm. The rest of the year, hours are Monday to Friday 9am to 5pm, Saturday 9am to 1pm.

SEEING THE SIGHTS

The open-air markets that trace their origins from 1680 are still held in the market square in the new town, although in a somewhat modified condition from the early days. Trade goods today consist of such foodstuff as vegetables, cheese, fruit, baskets, clothing, pottery goods, and "necessary commodities." The market usually is held on Wednesday and Saturday, as well as on the 6 weekdays before Christmas Day. May to August hours are from 7am to 2pm, and from 8am to 2pm in other months.

Gamla Rådhuset (or **Town Hall**), located in the center of town at Nya Stadens Torg, now is synonymous with Lidköping. The building originally was the hunting lodge of the Earl of Läckö and was moved from Kålland to become

---

 Fun Fact   **A Time-Honored Tradition**

One market tradition has been maintained from the days when farm animals and fresh meat (now banned) were a part of the goods offered for sale or trade: On each market day, traders collect around the square and wait for the Town Hall clock to strike. The custom is that no one enters the square before the clock has chimed six or seven strokes.

---

the town hall here. Today it houses a cafe, a handicrafts-center, and the Tourist Bureau.

The town's claim to fame is the **Rörstrands Fabriksbod** ★★, Fabriksgatan 4 (© **0510/823-46**). Sweden's oldest and most prestigious ceramics works, founded in 1726, is known for its beautiful china and stoneware. It lies in the heart of a bleak industrial area near the lake. Far more interesting than the on-site Porslinsmuseum is the number of designs for sale. It is open Monday to Friday 10am to 6pm, Saturday 10am to 2pm, and Sunday noon to 4pm. Normally, you can visit on your own; however, in June and August, guided tours are offered for 15SEK ($1.95).

Among the museums, **Vänermuseet,** Frammnäsvägen 2 (© **0510/77-00-65**), is devoted to the Lake Vänern region. One project that has attracted much attention is the charting of wrecks on the bottom of Lake Vänern. Artifacts removed from the wrecks are on display. One of the high points of the exhibition here is glass artist Bertil Vallien's 3m-long (9¾-ft.) glass boat, which hovers like a compass needle pointing north to Lake Vänern, Sweden's largest lake and the third-largest in Europe. Other exhibitions focus on the countryside and cultural history of the lakeside region. There is room for children to play, too. Kids can take the helm of the cargo boat *Dahlia* in a full gale, or punt across the channel in the museum's own ferryboat. In 1998, a new exhibition of Sweden's oldest meteorite and ancient fossils opened. You also can purchase handicrafts in the museum shop or have lunch in the on-site Näcken restaurant. The museum is open Tuesday to Friday 10am to 5pm, Saturday and Sunday noon to 5pm; summer, open Monday, too, 10am to 5pm. Admission is 40SEK ($5.20) for adults, 20SEK ($2.60) children 7 to 18, free for children under 7.

A PALATIAL EXCURSION

Läckö Slott ★ Only the royal palace in Stockholm is larger than this 13th-century castle on an island in Lake Vänern. The castle was at the apex of its glory when Magnus Gabriel de la Gardie, a contemporary of Queen Christina, made it the cultural center of Västergötland province. In 1682, Karl XI confiscated the castle in hopes of curtailing the power of the nobility. By 1830, all of its furnishings had been auctioned off, but many of the original antiques have since been reclaimed and brought back to the Renaissance palace. A walk to the castle grounds is one of the highlights of a visit here. Off the courtyard in the old castle storeroom, an on-site restaurant has been established. Each year the castle stages a different exhibit; these can range from medieval jousting to contemporary art. During June, July, and August, visitors can either promenade to the place on their own or take a guided tour (loosely scheduled for whenever people show up) in Swedish and English that's included in the price of admission. From May to September, the site is open the same hours, but the departure times of the tours are more rigidly defined, and guests must participate in one of them.

© **0510/103-20.** Admission 70SEK ($9.10) adults, 20SEK ($2.60) children 7–15, free for children 6 and under. May–Sept daily 10am–6pm. Closed off season. From Lidköping, drive immediately north of the town along a small secondary road. There is no route number, so follow signs to Läckö. Go all the way to the end of the road (23km/14 miles).

WHERE TO STAY

Best Western Edward Hotel ★ *Finds* Rising from a position near the river in the heart of town, this three-story hotel was constructed in 1984 in a solidly built design that resists the fiercest storms and the most frigid Swedish winters. Public areas are floored with slabs of marble and have the kind of contemporary detail that you might associate with an airport check-in desk. Bedrooms are outfitted in tones of beige and autumn-inspired colors, with built-in headboards and a sense of modern, no-nonsense efficiency. One of the best aspects is the mechanized beds whose heads and feet can be raised or lowered according to a sleeper's wishes. Bathrooms are snug but adequate, with good shelf space and tub/showers.

Skaragatan 7, S-531 32 Lidköping. © 800/528-1234 in the U.S., or 0510/790000. Fax 0510/790099. www. edwardhotel.se. 59 units. July to mid-Aug and Fri–Sat year-round 840SEK ($109) double, 1,395SEK ($181) suite; rest of year 1,595SEK ($207) double, 1,995SEK ($259) suite. Rates include breakfast. AE, DC, MC V. Free parking. **Amenities:** Restaurant; bar; sauna; limited room service; laundry service; dry cleaning; nonsmoking rooms; rooms for those w/limited mobility. *In room:* TV, minibar, hair dryer, iron/ironing board (in some), safe (in some), trouser press.

Hotell Läckö This is one of the less sophisticated hotels of Lidköping, with a staff that doesn't speak a lot of English, and an old-fashioned setup that you'll either find charming or not, depending on your tastes and levels of indulgence. It's housed within a once-stately building that originally was built as a hotel around 1900 and that retains some, but not all, of its original architectural adornments. Each of the bedrooms is outfitted with a different, usually pastel, color scheme, and many retain some of the older furniture that was in place when the hotel originally opened. Although the hotel is old-fashioned, beds are modern, and all the doubles have small bathrooms with showers. Two singles are rented without a bathroom. You might appreciate the cozy and old-fashioned atmosphere, which is in direct contrast to glossier, newer, more internationally conscious hotels. All rooms are nonsmoking.

Gamla Stadens Torg 5, S-531 32 Lidköping. © 0510/230-00. Fax 0510/621-91. 19 units. Sun–Thurs 890SEK ($116) double; Fri–Sat 790SEK ($103) double. Rates include breakfast. AE, MC, V. Free parking. **Amenities:** Rooms for those w/limited mobility. *In room:* TV, hair dryer.

Hotel Stadt Lidköping Long a traditional favorite, this hotel has been considerably improved and upgraded over the years. Built in a classic town-house style, it is separated from the nearby riverbank by a row of linden trees. The hotel has been sedately modernized without losing its antique appeal. The medium-size bedrooms are well furnished, with good beds and ample-size bathrooms that are well maintained with tub/showers. We've found it to be the most active place in town. The lobby's registration desk is near an amusingly abstract statue of a baby elephant.

Gamla Stadens Torg 1, S-531 02 Lidköping. © 0510/220-85. Fax 0510/215-32. www.stadtlidkoping.se. 44 units. Sun–Thurs 1,260SEK ($164) double, 1,495SEK ($194) suite; Fri–Sat 760SEK ($99) double, 1,050SEK ($137) suite. AE, DC, MC, V. Free parking. **Amenities:** Restaurant; bar; nightclub; sauna; laundry service; dry cleaning; nonsmoking rooms; rooms for those w/limited mobility. *In room:* TV, dataport, hair dryer.

WHERE TO DINE

Eddie's Brasserie SWEDISH/INTERNATIONAL Set on the street level of the previously recommended hotel, within an angular and contemporary room outfitted with wood paneling and shades of pale green and yellow, this is one of the most animated and bustling restaurants in town. Menu items include a roster of traditional Swedish specialties, as well as more innovative and daring items from other parts of Europe and the world. Examples include shrimp and black roe in puff pastry; boiled chopped egg with anchovies and onions, served with Swedish brown bread; grilled salmon with garlic-braised prawns, lime-flavored yogurt, and chile oil; and a substantial-looking filet of beef with Provençal-style mushrooms.

In the Edward Hotel, Skaragatan 7. © 0510/790000. Reservations recommended. Main courses 110SEK–295SEK ($14–$38). AE, DC, MC, V. Mon–Fri 11:30am–2pm; Mon–Sat 6–11pm.

5 Skara ★

129km (80 miles) NE of Gothenburg, 350km (217 miles) SW of Stockholm, 25km (16 miles) SE of Lidköping

This highly recommended stopover lies between Karlstad and Gothenburg in the province of Västergötland, the ancient western country of the once-dreaded Goths. Skara, which is in the heart of the province, is reached by Highway 3 and makes a good center for exploring some of the district's major sights, such as Läckö Castle and Varnhem Abbey.

Both an educational center and a cathedral town, Skara was an ancient religious center even before Christianity came to Sweden. With its wooden buildings and green squares, it remains unspoiled.

ESSENTIALS

GETTING THERE   By Train   Lidköping doesn't have a railway junction of its own; consequently, rail passengers from everywhere, including the half-dozen trains arriving here from Gothenburg every day, disembark in the town of Skövde, 26km (16 miles) to the east of Skara. From there, they take a bus marked LIDKÖPING, at a cost of 40SEK ($5.20) each way to reach Skara. For information, call © 771/75-75-75.

By Bus   There also are about four express buses every day making the 2-hour trip from Gothenburg. Each deposits its passengers in the heart of town. For bus information, call © 0200/21818.

By Car   From Lidköping, follow Route 47 directly southeast into Skara.

VISITOR INFORMATION   For information about Skara and its surrounding area, head for the **Skara Turistbyrå,** Skolgatan 1 (© 0511/325-80; www.skara.se). Between early June and late August, it's open Monday to Friday 10am to 6pm, Saturday 10am to 2pm, and Sunday 1 to 5pm. The rest of the year, it's open Monday to Friday 10am to 1pm and 2 to 6pm.

SEEING THE SIGHTS

Skara Domkyrkan Sancta Maria   Classic in its purity of line, the twin-spired **Sancta Maria,** in the center of town, was founded in 1150 and then extensively restored in the 19th century. Inside look for the magnificent stained-glass windows by Bo Beskow. Excavations beneath the cathedral have revealed remains of Sweden's only known medieval crypt. One of the cathedral's treasures is a funeral chalice dating from 1065, the property of a bishop.

Järnvägatan. © 0511/20-179. Free admission. Summer daily 10am–7pm; rest of the year Sun–Wed and Fri–Sat 10am–4pm, Thurs 10am–7pm.

Lansbibliotek   North of the cathedral, next door to the diocesan library (Gamla Bibliotek) is a library from the 1850s combining the treasures of the diocese and the region. Some 300,000 books, among them 3,000 handwritten works, are contained in the library. Outstanding among them is the *Skara Missal,* the oldest preserved book written in Sweden, dating from 1150. The collections of the combined library facilities are used in connection with research of local history and genealogy. There also are books that can be borrowed and many magazines and newspapers for use by visitors, and free Internet access.

Prubbatorget. © 0511/320-60. Free admission. Mon–Thurs 11am–7pm; Fri 11am–6pm; Sat 10am–1pm.

Västergötland Museum ★ *Finds*   One of Sweden's most impressive provincial museums lies in Skara's town park; its collection is rich in artifacts, such as ecclesiastical woodcarvings and medieval stone art, from the surrounding district.

Angling Along Göta Älv

The southwestern parts of Lake Vänern and the valley of the River Göta have been called an angler's El Dorado. Fishers can troll for salmon and trout on Lake Vänern, or fly-fish on the River Göta. These are well-stocked trout waters in an area where spinning and fly-fishing are permitted for the price of a daily permit. The area also provides waters filled with pike, perch, and different members of the carp family.

Lake Vänern alone has some 30 different species of fish. The bay of Vänersborg offers the best variety of good fishing locations. During recent years about 35,000 young salmon and trout have been released annually into the lake to keep the stock plentiful. The ultimate goal is to make Lake Vänern the best angling lake in Europe.

Another good fishing spot is the plateau Hallsjön near Vargön and beautiful lake Hallsjön, which is well stocked with rainbow trout. The local district council of Vänersborg leases the lake from the crown. Between May and September they release 4 tons of rainbow trout into the lake. When available, char and brown trout are released. Both spinning and fly-fishing are allowed. With a bit of luck, you may encounter a Swedish elk on the shores of the lake while you're fishing. Fireplaces are provided along the lake for grilling food or simply enjoying a log fire, and there are wind shelters as well. The plateau of Hunneberg contains several lakes, notably Igelsjön and Kvarnsjön, which are restocked with rainbow trout every year. The other lakes contain good stocks of pike and perch.

Fishing licenses can be obtained at **Fiske-Shopen,** Sturgatan 29 (© **0520/361-15**), in Trollhättan, and also at the tourist office.

Near the main buildings of the museum is the **Old Village.** These wooden buildings from the 16th to the 19th centuries were torn down in the province and reassembled on this site. A megalithic grave known as a **stone cist** also has been brought here, as well as such workers' facilities as a smithy, a carpenter's workshop, and a windmill. Also nearby are the **Museum of Veterinary History** and the **Kråk Manor House,** a fully furnished 18th-century dwelling, where meals and refreshments are served in the old cellar. The **Agricultural Museum** is housed in a large cowshed from the village of Karleby, where the development of agriculture in Västergötland is shown from the first permanent farmers in the Neolithic period up to the present.

Stadträgården. © 0511/26000. Admission 40SEK ($5.20) adults, free for ages 18 and under. Mon–Fri 10am–5pm; Sat noon–5pm. Sept–May closed on Mon.

Skara Sommerland *(Kids* Scandinavia's largest leisure park for children offers a wealth of activities, including lots of swimming pools and water slides in Aqualand, gold panning, a water-ski lake, bumper boats, canoes, archery, trampolines, a minizoo, and pony riding, among other attractions—70 in all.

Skovde. © 0511/640-00. Admission 195SEK ($25) for anyone .9m (3 ft.) or more in height. Mid-May to late June daily 10am–5pm (Sat to 6pm); July–Aug daily 10am–7pm. Closed Sept to mid-May. Drive 8km (5 miles) east of town, following the signs to Skovde.

NEARBY ATTRACTIONS

Varnhem Kloster Kyrka   This former Cistercian monastery was completed in 1260 after the previous abbey burned. Angry Danes razed it again in the mid–16th century, but it was restored by Christina's friend, Count Magnus Gabriel de la Gardie, who is buried here. Designed as a cross-vaulted, three-aisled basilica, the medieval abbey also contains the grave of Birger Jarl, founder of Stockholm.

S-532 73 Varnhem. © **0511/265-59** or 0511/265-34. Admission 20SEK ($2.60) adults, 10SEK ($1.30) ages 7–15, free for children 6 and under. Apr and Sept daily 10am–4pm; May–Aug daily 9am–6pm. Drive east of Skara on Rte. 49 for 15km (9¼ miles).

Habo Kyrka   This church stands outside the village of Habo, 19km (12 miles) north of Jönköping, near Lake Vättern. (It's close enough to Varnhem to be visited on the same day.) Habo Kyrka is an old, barn-red frame church. From 1721 to 1723, it was enlarged to its present size. The sandstone altar was consecrated around 1347, and the baptismal font is from the 13th century.

Habo. © **036/496-01.** Free admission. Guided tours 10SEK ($1.30). May–Aug daily 8am–6pm; Oct–Mar daily 9am–4pm; Sept and Apr daily 9am–6pm. Situated 100km (62 miles) southeast of Skara on the southern edge of Lake Vättern. From Skara, follow signs to Falköping, then signs to Jönköping.

WHERE TO STAY

Hotel Stadskällaren   Of the three hotels in Skara, this is the oldest, most historic, and most charming. Constructed around 1900 as a hotel, it occupies a site in the city center, behind an old-fashioned gable-sided building with white walls and green shutters. Inside you'll find a blandly international contemporary decor, and bedrooms painted in soothing pastels. Each has a high ceiling, some original modern paintings, and a somewhat cramped arrangement that includes a writing table, a comfortable chair for reading, and a small-screen TV. The bathrooms, although small, are adequate for the job; they have tub/showers and are spotlessly maintained.

Skaraborgsgatan 15, S-532 22 Skara. © **051/11-34-10.** Fax 051/11-21-48. www.hotelliskara.nu. 32 units. Mon–Thurs 890SEK ($116) double; Fri–Sun 590SEK ($77) double. Rates include breakfast. AE, DC, MC, V. Free parking. **Amenities:** Restaurant; bar; sauna; limited room service; nonsmoking rooms. *In room:* TV, dataport, hair dryer, iron, safe.

Skara Stadshotell   In the heart of town, a block from the cathedral, this longtime favorite is built like a small French château. It is one of the best of the Stads hotels in the area, with a ballroom and dining room that often host social events. Its generally large bedrooms are impressive and decorated in a contemporary style with comfortable beds and good-size bathrooms with showers. The cuisine is among the town's finest, and in summer guests like to dine outside on the terrace.

Järnvägsgatan 5, S-532 31 Skara. © **0511/240-50.** Fax 0511/240-69. www.skarastadshotell.se. 75 units. Midsummer and Sat–Sun year-round 880SEK ($114) double; rest of year 1,300SEK ($169) double; 2,150SEK ($280) suite. AE, DC, MC, V. Free parking. **Amenities:** Restaurant; 3 bars; gym; sauna; laundry service; dry cleaning; nonsmoking rooms; rooms for those w/limited mobility. *In room:* TV, dataport, minibar (winter only), hair dryer.

WHERE TO DINE

Rosers Salonger   SWEDISH/INTERNATIONAL   In this previously recommended hotel, you get a true "taste of Sweden" in the well-prepared dishes that dazzle your palate here. Menus are thoughtfully prepared and served in generous portions. The 1875 hotel itself has a lot of tradition, and the dining room is also imbued with character. In summer dining overflows into an open-air

restaurant in the garden. High-quality raw materials go into the food preparation. The chef claims that "we want our patrons to receive a culinary experience
far beyond the ordinary," and in that he most often succeeds. We prefer to begin
with an appetizer of Swedish red caviar, or perhaps a platter of home-styled herring. For a main course, the most preferred and most authentic main dish is reindeer steak. Here it's laced with sherry and served in a white-mushroom sauce.

In the Skara Stadshotell, Järnvägsgatan 5. ℂ 0511/240-50. Reservations recommended. Main courses
190SEK–210SEK ($25–$27). AE, DC, MC, V. Mon–Sat 11am–2pm and 6–11pm.

6 Mariestad ⓒ

40km (25 miles) NE of Lidköping, 318km (197 miles) SW of Stockholm, 180km (112 miles) NE of Gothenburg

Called the "pearl of Lake Vänern," Mariestad is known for its many well-preserved old structures in its Gamla Stan (or Old Town). Despite several widespread town fires, many old structures still remain, including one building from
the 17th century. The town lies on the eastern shore of Lake Vänern and is one
of the best stopovers for those sailing the Göta Canal. It takes its name from
Maria von Pfaltz, the first wife of Duke Karl (later Karl IX).

This lakeside town is lovelier and less industrialized than Lidköping. Take
along a camera, as its medieval quarter and its harbor area have many scenic
views. The town contains a wide array of architectural styles, including Gustavian, Carolean, classical, and Art Nouveau. It's been called a "living museum" of
architecture.

ESSENTIALS
GETTING THERE   By Train   There's about one train per hour arriving in
Mariestad from Stockholm, usually with a change in Töreboda Skövde en route.
Depending on the train, transit takes from 2½ to 3 hours. There also are two or
three trains per day between Mariestad and Lidköping, a trip of about an hour,
on a not particularly busy rail line that runs perpendicular to the busier main
east-to-west rail routes. For information, call ℂ 771/75-75-75.

By Bus   Bus travel to Mariestad from Stockholm is less convenient than equivalent transit by train. There are two buses per day from Stockholm, each requiring between 3½ and 4 hours for the trip, and one or two from Lidköping, taking
less than an hour. For information, call ℂ 0200/21818.

By Car   From Lidköping (discussed earlier in this chapter), continue northeast
along Route 44 until you come to the junction with the express highway, E3,
which will carry you into Mariestad.

VISITOR INFORMATION   The **Mariestad Turistbyrå,** Hamnplan (ℂ 0501/
100-01; www.mariestad.se), is open June to August Monday to Friday 8:30am to
7pm, Saturday 8:30am to 1pm and 2 to 5pm, and Sunday 9:30am to 1pm and 2
to 5pm. From September to May, hours are Monday to Friday 8:30am to 4pm.

SEEING THE SIGHTS
If time is limited, head first for the Old Town, where you can walk medieval
streets and see some of the old buildings; the most interesting of these lie along
Kyrkogatan.

At Kyrkogatan 21 is the **first general hospital** in Mariestad, built in 1760,
the third such hospital in Sweden. At Kyrkogatan 31, you'll see a **timbered cottage** called Aron's House, a burger's house from the 17th century, which survived the fire of 1693.

The town's most important monument is **Mariestad Domkyrka** (cathedral), Kyrkogatan (no phone), open daily from June 15 to August from 7am to 9pm. The rest of the year it is open daily 7am to 4pm. This cathedral was built between 1593 and 1625 because of religious controversies between Duke Karl and his brother, King Johan III. In 1580 Värmland and the northern part of Västergötland were detached from the diocese of Skara and given a superintendent of their own, residing at Mariestad. The duke had the new cathedral built according to plans made by Dutchman Willelm Boy for the church of Santa Clara in Stockholm, thereby freely copying his brother's most important building in the Swedish capital. The nave gives a remarkable impression of unbroken unity following the traditions of the late Middle Ages. Vigorous vaults span a considerable width without supporting pillars. The present-day appearance of the cathedral was brought about by a restoration beginning in 1903 by the architect Folke Zetterval, who gave the spire its present height.

Other than the cathedral, the major attraction here is the **cruise** up to Lake Vänern to the start of the Göta Canal's main stretch at Sjotorp, 19km (12 miles) from Mariestad. Between Karlsborg and Sjotorp, boats pass through 21 locks. The most scenic section stretches up to Lyrestad, lying east of Sjotorp and 19km (12 miles) north of Mariestad on the motorway, E20. For information on lake and canal cruises for day trips, contact the tourist bureau (see above). Cruises cost 275SEK ($36), last 5 to 6 hours, and are conducted between June and late August only. Most of them begin at Sjotorp. For information, call © **0501/514-70.**

Other attractions in and around the town include the **Vadsbo Museum,** Marieholm (© **0501/632-14**), located in the wings of the county governor's residence in the town center. The building originally served as the governor's house in the 18th century. Exhibits include artifacts from the city history, a carriage collection, and temporary thematic and art exhibitions. In 1998, a small industry museum opened here as well. Admission is 20SEK ($2.60) adults, free for children. It is open June to August Tuesday to Sunday 1 to 4pm. Off-season hours are only Wednesday and Sunday 1 to 7pm.

The **Canal Museum (Kanalmuseet)** at Sjotorp, 19km (12 miles) from Mariestad, lies along the harbor at Hamn (© **0501/514-34**), and houses exhibitions showing the building of the Göta Canal and the operations of the Sjotorp shipyard. There also is a large collection of engine history, a ship and shipwreck exhibition, as well as various thematic shows. It is open daily June to August 9am to 6pm, charging 30SEK ($3.90) for adults, 10SEK ($1.30) for children. To reach Sjotorp, head north of Mariestad along Route 64. Closed off season.

Lugnås Rocks, on Lungnåsberget Hill, south of Mariestad (take E3 going south from Mariestad and look for signs at the hamlet of Lugnås), once was the site of a major milestone-manufacturing industry begun way back in the 12th century. One of the old caves is open for guided tours daily 11am to 5pm mid-June to August. The rest of the year, tours are conducted Monday to Friday 11am to 4pm, Saturday and Sunday 11am to 5pm. Admission is 40SEK ($5.20). For information about this attraction, inquire at the Mariestad tourist bureau (© **501/40686**).

WHERE TO STAY

Bergs Hotell ★ *Finds* Part of the allure of this 300-year-old hotel derives from its position in the oldest part of town, in a neighborhood composed only of equivalently antique houses. Set behind a one-story pink facade that from the back side reveals itself as a two-story structure, it's the domain of kindhearted landlady Elisabeth Åkerlind. No meals are served other than breakfast, but the cobble-covered courtyard in back, punctuated as it is with pear trees and flowers, is a charming place to read or write. Bedrooms are outfitted in a style similar to a Swedish beach house, with painted furniture; cozy, somewhat cramped dimensions; and very few grace notes other than a sense of antique Swedish charm and hints of the many generations who stayed here before you. All rooms are nonsmoking.

Kyrkogatan 18, S-542 30 Mariestad. © 0501/103-24. 5 units, none with bathroom. 630SEK ($82) double; 800SEK ($104) cottage; 200SEK ($26) extra bed. Rates include breakfast. AE, DC, MC, V. Free parking. **Amenities:** Breakfast lounge. *In room:* No phone.

Stadshotelleet ✦ The most substantial hotel in town appeals to overnight visitors with its nostalgia and antique charm, part of which derives from its construction more than a century ago. It was built in the 1880s, with salmon-colored stones rising three stories above the town's main square. Public rooms have high ceilings and retain some of their original detailing, and the dowdy bedrooms will appeal to anyone with an old-fashioned sense of virtue. Each comes with a small private bathroom with shower.

Nya Torget, S-54230 Mariestad. © 0501/138-00. Fax 0501/77640. 29 units. Sun–Thurs 1,190SEK ($155) double; Fri–Sat 850SEK ($111) double. AE, DC, MC, V. Free parking. **Amenities:** Breakfast room; bar; health club; sauna; nonsmoking rooms; rooms for those w/limited mobility. *In room:* TV, dataport, minibar, hair dryer.

WHERE TO DINE

St. Michel SWEDISH/INTERNATIONAL Although it's set within a separate premises, this restaurant is associated with the Stadshotelleet, which often steers its residents here. Cozy and well maintained, it serves good food that arrives in generous portions with a bit of culinary flair. Examples include filets "black and white" that mix pork cutlets with béarnaise sauce and beef filets with wine sauce on the same platter. Tournedos are served with your choice of three different sauces, and you also can order flambéed pepper steak or grilled filets of sole stuffed with lobster.

Kungsgatan 1. © 0501/199-00. Reservations recommended. Fixed-price lunch 70SEK ($9.10); main courses 125SEK–205SEK ($16–$27). AE, DC, MC, V. Daily 11am–2pm and 6:30–11pm.

10

Värmland & Dalarna

Two provinces in the heart of Sweden's southern region represent the soul of this Scandinavian nation. In the province of Dalarna lies Lake Siljan; Värmland, farther south, opens onto Lake Vänern, the third-largest inland sea in Europe.

In one of her most famous works, *The Saga of Gösta Berling,* Nobel Prize winner and native Swede Selma Lagerlöf lyrically described Värmland life in the early 19th century. Today parts of the province remain much as she saw it.

Karlstad, on the shores of Lake Vänern, makes an ideal stopover for exploring the province of Värmland. Among its chief waterways are the Göta River and the Göta Canal. A smaller body of water, Lake Vättern, lies to the east of Vänern.

Sometimes described as "Sweden in miniature," Värmland is a land of mountains, rolling hill country, islands, and rivers. Värmland is also a province of festivals, music, art, literature, and handicrafts. Visitors can enjoy boating, fishing, skiing, hiking, folklore, and historic sights.

Forests still cover a large part of Värmland, and the 274km-long (170-mile) Klarälven River carries logs to the industrial areas around Lake Vänern.

Dalarna is the most traditional of all the provinces, complete with maypole dancing, fiddlers' music, folk costumes, and handicrafts (including the Dala horse, Sweden's most popular souvenir). *Dalarna* means "valleys," and sometimes you'll see it referred to as Dalecarlia, the Anglicized form of the name.

Lake Siljan, perhaps the most beautiful lake in Europe, is ringed with resort villages and towns. Leksand, Tällberg, and Rättvik attract visitors during summer with sports, folklore, and a week of music. In winter, people come here for skiing.

Any time is good for a visit to Dalarna, but during midsummer, from June 23 to June 26, the Dalecarlians celebrate the custom of maypole dancing. At that time they race through the forest gathering birch bows and nosegays of wildflowers with which they cover the maypole. Then the pole is raised and, under the midsummer-lit sky, they dance around it until dawn, a good, respectable pagan custom.

The quickest and easiest way to reach these provinces is by train from the Central Station in Stockholm, a 4½-hour trip. All the following towns have good rail connections with each other. Motorists from Oslo can stop over in Dalarna before venturing on to the Swedish capital. Similarly, visitors to Gothenburg can head north to both Värmland and Dalarna before seeing Stockholm.

If you drive, however, you can see more of the scenery, including a spectacular section between Vadstena and Jönköping, where it winds along the eastern shore of Lake Vättern. If you want to see the area in a hurry and are dependent on public transportation, you can fly to Mora and use it as a center for exploring Dalarna, or fly from Stockholm to Karlstad and use that city as a base for exploring the Värmland

Värmland

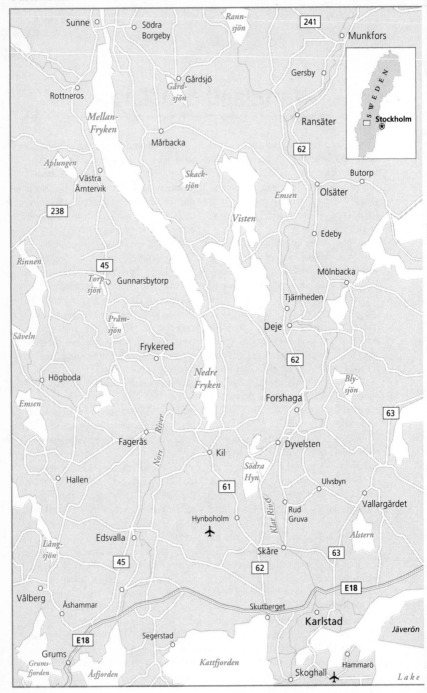

Sunne
Södra Borgeby
Rann- sjön
241
Munkfors
Gersby
Gårdsjö
Gård- sjön
Rottneros
Mellan- Fryken
Ransäter
62
Mårbacka
Aplungen
Skack- sjön
Butorp
Västra Ämtervik
Emsen
Olsäter
238
Visten
Edeby
Rinnen
45
Mölnbacka
Torp- sjön
Gunnarsbytorp
Tjärnheden
Präms- sjön
Deje
Säveln
Frykered
62
Nedre Fryken
Bly- sjön
Högboda
Forshaga
63
Emsen
Dyvelsten
Fagerås
Kil
Södra Hyn
Ulvsbyn
Hallen
61
Vallargärdet
Hynboholm
Rud Gruva
Alstern
Edsvalla
Skåre
63
Långs- sjön
45
62
E18
Vålberg
Åshammar
Skutberget
Karlstad
Jäverön
E18
Segerstad
Grums
Kattfjorden
Hammarö
Grums- fjorden
Åsfjorden
Skoghall
Lake

SWEDEN
Stockholm

290

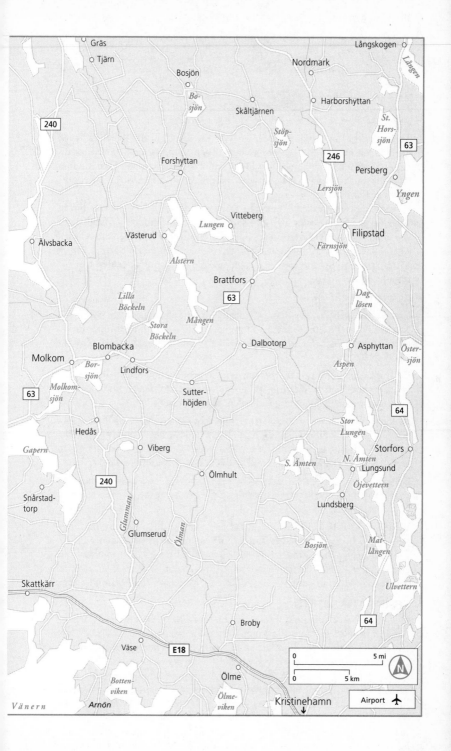

Gräs
Tjärn
Långskogen
Nordmark
Bosjön
Bo-sjön
Skåltjärnen
Harborshyttan
Lången
St. Hors-sjön
240
Stöp-sjön
246
63
Forshyttan
Persberg
Lersjön
Yngen
Vitteberg
Lungen
Västerud
Filipstad
Älvsbacka
Färnsjön
Alstern
Brattfors
Dag-lösen
Lilla Böckeln
63
Stora Böckeln
Mången
Dalbotorp
Asphyttan
Öster-sjön
Blombacka
Molkom
Bor-sjön
Lindfors
Aspen
63
Molkom-sjön
Sutter-höjden
64
Hedås
Stor Lungen
Storfors
Gapern
Viberg
S. Ämten
N. Ämten
Lungsund
240
Ölmhult
Öjevettern
Snårstad-torp
Lundsberg
Glumman
Bosjön
Mat-lången
Glumserud
Ölman
Skattkärr
Ulvettern
Broby
64
Väse
E18
0   5 mi
Ölme
0   5 km
N
Vänern
Botten-viken
Arnön
Ölme-viken
Kristinehamn
Airport ✈

291

district. Both Karlstad and Mora also have good rail connections from Stockholm. Many visitors see a "nutshell" version of central Sweden by taking the Göta Canal trip (see chapter 9).

1 Karlstad (⋆

248km (154 miles) NE of Gothenburg, 300km (186 miles) W of Stockholm

The capital of Värmland, this port city is at the mouth of the Klarälven River. Karlstad has many attractions for visitors, plus many moderately priced restaurants and comfortable hotels. Because of its location, it has long been a center for trade and transport, and is a good starting point for many of the tourist routes of Värmland.

A trading center called Thingwalla first stood on the site of the city, but in 1584 Duke Charles (later Sweden's King Charles IX) founded Karlstad. Here you can see Sweden's longest stone bridge, East Bridge, built in the 18th century. The oldest quarter, **Almen,** on Älvgatan, was saved from a disastrous fire in 1865. You can visit this area today and see the old grammar school and the Bishop's house.

ESSENTIALS

GETTING THERE   By Plane   Nine flights on SAS connect Stockholm and Karlstad daily, the "jump" taking 45 minutes. The airport lies less than 1.5km (1 mile) southwest of Karlstadt's center. For flight information, call (© **054/45-55-010.

By Train   Six trains per day run between Gothenburg and Karlstadt, 10 trains per day arrive from Stockholm, and three trains per day come from Oslo. Each takes about 3 hours. For rail information, call (© **711/75-75-75.**

By Bus   Three buses per day arrive from Gothenburg, taking 4 hours; four arrive weekly from Stockholm, taking 4½ hours; and two arrive weekly from Oslo, taking 4½ hours. Check locally for bus schedules, which change from month to month. For general information, call (© **0200/21818** (within Sweden).

By Car   From Stockholm, take E18 west all the way, and from Gothenburg head north along the E6 expressway, turning northeast at the junction of Route 45, which runs all the way to Karlstad.

VISITOR INFORMATION   Karlstad and most of the region around it are represented by the **Värmlands Tourist Office,** in the city's conference center, Dastratorggatan 26 (© **054/29-84-00**; www.varmland.org). It's open from June 16 to August 14 Monday to Friday 9am to 7pm, Saturday from 10am to 6pm, and Sunday 11am to 4pm; the rest of the year, Monday to Friday 9am to 5pm.

SEEING THE SIGHTS

One of the most appealing ways to get an overview of the geography around Karlstad involves taking a short-term cruise. The *Vestrag* is a small-scale lake cruiser with oversize windows and an on-board cafe. Its home port is Karlstad's **Imre Hamn (Inner Harbor),** where it embarks on between two and five cruises a day, depending on the schedule, between mid-June and late August. Tours average 1 hour in length and incorporate views of the city and the several islands situated near the entrance to its harbor. They cost 80SEK ($10) for adults and 50SEK ($6.50) for children ages 6 to 12 (free for 5 and under). Longer cruises that carry you farther away from the waters around Karlstad are scheduled at least twice a week aboard the *Polstjärnan,* the only steam-driven cruiser left in

Karlstad

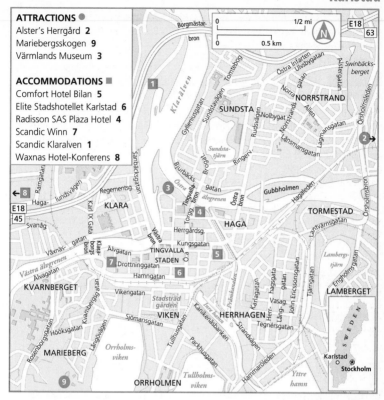

ATTRACTIONS ●
Alster's Herrgård **2**
Mariebergsskogen **9**
Värmlands Museum **3**

ACCOMMODATIONS ■
Comfort Hotel Bilan **5**
Elite Stadshotellet Karlstad **6**
Radisson SAS Plaza Hotel **4**
Scandic Winn **7**
Scandic Klaralven **1**
Waxnas Hotel-Konferens **8**

the waters of Lake Vänern. Specializing in the waters of the miniarchipelago near Karlstad, with a travel-time of 3 hours each, they cost 100SEK ($13) for adults and 50SEK ($6.50) kids 7 to 12; free for children under 6. Schedules vary from week to week and sometimes are canceled altogether because of inclement weather. For schedules and more information, contact Karlstad's tourist information office, or dial ℭ **054/29-84-00.**

Alster's Herrgård ⚘ *Finds* Lying 8km (5 miles) east of Karlstad on the Stockholm road, this manor is maintained in memory of Gustaf Fröding, one of Sweden's leading poets, who was born here in 1860. Squire Jan Fröding purchased the estate in 1837 and transformed its exterior. Gustaf was his grandchild. Today Alster's Manor is an affiliate of the Värmlands Museum and serves as a memorial to Gustaf. There is a Fröding exhibition here depicting the family and its possessions—one entire room is devoted to Gustaf's sisters. There also is a changing array of exhibitions devoted to the art, music, and culture of Värmland. A cafe is on the premises, and you can stroll through Fröding Grove.

Alsters Herrgårdsväg. ℭ **054/834-081.** Admission 30SEK ($3.90) adults self-guided tour, 30SEK ($3.90) adults conducted tour, free for anyone under 20. Daily 11am–6pm. Closed Sept–Apr. Bus: 14, 15, or 17.

Mariebergsskogen Mariebergsskogen is one of Sweden's top pleasure-parks, with a fair, dancing, a theater, and an open-air museum, as well as an animal park and a restaurant. The Tivoli-style section, the site of rides and small-scale amusements, is open only in summer. The Children's Petting Zoo is open year-round and contains a collection of tame animals (rabbits, goats, and lambs), which children can watch and sometimes touch. The park is on the southern outskirts, a 15-minute walk south of the town center.

Mariebergs Park. ℂ 054/29-69-90. Free admission. Park daily 7am–10pm.

Värmlands Museum After this museum outgrew its old quarters, a greatly expanded version reopened in summer 1998. The museum is the best repository of the history of Värmland; you can see how the province developed, from its early settlers and pilgrims to its mill towns and industries. Audiovisual programs give color and shape to the exhibits. Although changing exhibitions are staged here, there also is a permanent collection that includes the evolution of Värmland music from folk to modern. Other exhibits concern archaeology, textiles, Finnish immigration from the 16th to the 18th centuries, and the evolution of Karlstad with an emphasis on the 19th and 20th centuries.

Sandgrundsudden. ℂ 054/14-31-00. Admission 40SEK ($5.20) adults, free for ages 19 and under. June–Aug Fri–Wed 10am–5pm, Thurs 10am–9pm; Sept–May Tues–Sun 8:30am–5pm (closes at 9pm on Wed).

A NEARBY NOBEL ATTRACTION

Alfred Nobel's Björkborn Fifty-six kilometers (35 miles) east of Karlstad, near the hamlet of Karlskoga at the edge of Lake Möckeln, you'll find a white-sided manor house that was the home of the inventor, manufacturer, and philanthropist who established the Nobel Prize. It contains a library that's valued by scholars and that contains many of the philosophical and scientific tracts that were read by Alfred Nobel himself. You also can visit the laboratory where some of the armaments that later made Nobel's fortune, and which are said to have caused him an overwhelming sense of guilt, were developed. There's a cafe on-site and a staff that is proud of the site's role as the only Nobel-related museum in the world.

Karlskoga. ℂ 0586/833-11. Admission 60SEK ($6.35), free for children 9 and under. June–Aug daily 11am–5pm. Open in winter for groups by request. Take E18 56km (35 miles) east of Karlstad to the town of Karlskoga.

SHOPPING

Connoisseurs seek out Värmland antiques at **Blandorama,** Östra Kanalgatan 2 (ℂ 070/715-85-55). The best center for arts, crafts, and gifts is **Karin Lööf Keramik,** Sagerstagatan 8A (ℂ 054/57-25-14). Local jewelry is sold at **Isaksson Porfyr,** Zakridelslingen 6 (ℂ 054/15-19-00), and cut glass is offered by **Evys Presenter o. Alternativbokhandel,** Östra Torggatan 19 (ℂ 054/15-21-95).

WHERE TO STAY
EXPENSIVE

Comfort Hotel Bilan Back in the mid–19th century, this establishment was a prison, and there remains a prison museum in its basement. But today it's been successfully converted into a hotel where you won't feel imprisoned at all. The exterior is still a bit foreboding, but inside it warms considerably. The public rooms have been tastefully decorated, as have the rather small bedrooms, which are nonetheless comfortable and inviting, with private tiled bathrooms with shower units.

Karlsbergsgatan 3, S-652 24 Karlstad ℂ 054/10-03-00. Fax 054/21-92-14. www.hotelclub.net/hotel.reservations/Comfort_Hotel_Bilan_Karlstad.htm. 68 units. Sun–Thurs 1,550SEK ($202) double; Fri–Sat 940SEK ($122) double. AE, DC, MC, V. Rates include breakfast and evening buffet. **Amenities:** Dining room; pool for dips only; sauna; babysitting; laundry service; nonsmoking rooms; rooms for those w/limited mobility. *In room:* TV, dataport, minibar, hair dryer.

Elite Stadshotellet Karlstad ★ *Value*   This hotel, with a yellow-and-white imperial neobaroque facade, is one of the most impressive 19th-century hotels in all of Scandinavia. The bedrooms range from sedately modern to the more old-fashioned, but all are well maintained, with ample private bathrooms with tubs and showers. The hotel is a 5-minute walk north from the rail station.

Kungsgatan 22, S-651 08 Karlstad. ✆ 054/293-000. Fax 054/293-031. www.elite.com. 139 units. Sun–Thurs 1,395SEK–1,495SEK ($181–$194) double; Fri–Sat 795SEK–995SEK ($103–$129) double; 1,800SEK–2,700SEK ($234–$351) suite. Rates include breakfast. AE, DC, MC, V. Parking 90SEK ($12). **Amenities:** Restaurant; pub; indoor pool; sauna; limited room service; laundry service; dry cleaning; nonsmoking rooms; rooms for those w/limited mobility. *In room:* TV, dataport, hair dryer.

Radisson SAS Plaza Hotel ★★   This exclusive business and leisure hotel was awarded four stars by the Société Suisse des Hôteliers. Since it was built in 1984, the SAS has been considerably upgraded and improved. The rooms are elegantly decorated and generally spacious, with medium-size bathrooms equipped with tub/showers. The most expensive rooms are the business units, which have more work space, including a large desk. These units are equipped with minibars and provide robes.

The Plaza Garden, a popular brasserie, is located in the atrium and serves international cuisine. But the prestige restaurant is the **Plaza Vivaldi,** with its superb menu and well-stocked wine cellar in a gracious 19th-century setting (see "Where to Dine," below).

Västra Torggatan 2, SE-652 25 Karlstad. ✆ 054/100-200. Fax 054/100-224. www.radissonsas.com. 130 units. June–Aug 15 and Sat–Sun year-round 850SEK ($111) double; rest of year 1,439SEK ($187) double; 1,600SEK–2,600SEK ($208–$338) suite. AE, DC, MC, V. Parking 70SEK ($9.10). **Amenities:** Restaurant; bar; Jacuzzi; sauna; business center; room service; laundry service; dry cleaning; nonsmoking rooms; rooms for those w/limited mobility. *In room:* A/C, TV, minibar, hair dryer, iron/ironing board (in some).

Scandic Winn ★★   Although this establishment is part of a chain, it has charm and grace and is at the very top of Karlstad choices. It's also the most up-to-date in town. Built on the shores of the Klarälven River in the heart of Karlstad, it attracts both business travelers and vacationers. Most of the bedrooms are spacious, with ample-size bathrooms with tub/showers. Each has carpeting and traditional furnishings that are replaced when they start to show wear and tear. In 1998, the owners doubled the size of this hotel by buying the building next door and joining it to the hotel's existing core.

Café Artist is a well-frequented place known for its good food (see "Where to Dine," below). There's also a piano bar.

Norra Strandgatan 9–11, S-652 24 Karlstad. ✆ 054/77-64-700. Fax 054/77-64-711. www.scandic-hotels. com. 199 units. June 20–Aug 5 850SEK ($111) double; Aug 6–June 19 1,735SEK ($226) double; 1,435SEK–2,500SEK ($187–$325) suite. Rates include breakfast. AE, DC, MC, V. Parking 75SEK–130SEK ($9.75–$17). **Amenities:** Restaurant; bar; sauna; limited room service; laundry service; dry cleaning; nonsmoking rooms; rooms for those w/limited mobility. *In room:* TV, dataport, minibar, hair dryer.

MODERATE

Scandic Klarälven   Part of a chain, this comfortable, well-designed hotel is a well-recommended, middle-bracket place favored by business travelers from throughout Sweden. Set less than a kilometer (about ½ mile) north of Karlstad's commercial core, on a grassy strip of land midway between the Klarälven River and the E18 highway, this low-slung hotel was built around 1970 and renovated in the mid-1990s. Bedrooms contain unremarkable furniture with contemporary, international styling and monochromatic color schemes, plus spotless bathrooms equipped with tub/showers. The rooms at the cheaper end of the spectrum have only one double bed and are actually a bit too small to be considered comfortable. It's better to opt for one of the slightly more expensive rooms because they are a lot bigger and more comfortable.

Sandbäcksgatan 6, S-653 40 Karlstad. ℰ **054/77-645-00.** Fax 054/77-645-11. www.scandic-hotels.com. 143 units. June 30–Aug 22 and Fri–Sat year-round 710SEK–790SEK ($92–$103) double; rest of year 1,620SEK ($211) double. Rates include breakfast. AE, DC, MC, V. Free parking. **Amenities:** 2 restaurants; bar; indoor pool; sauna; laundry service; dry cleaning; nonsmoking rooms; rooms for those w/limited mobility. *In room:* TV, dataport, hair dryer.

INEXPENSIVE

Wåxnäs Hotel-Konferens   The best-known aspect of this well-managed hotel involves its restaurant, **Stek Huset,** which is one of the finest in the district (see "Where to Dine," below). The hotel itself was built almost as an afterthought to the restaurant in the 1970s, on a quiet triangle of land that abuts the E18 highway, less than 1.5km (about 1 mile) west of Karlstad's center. The two-story hotel offers clean, internationally modern bedrooms outfitted with angular, motel-style furniture that's comfortable but not particularly plush. The owners are a Swedish-Greek team headed by members of the Apostolidi family. Under separate management, there is a bowling alley on-site. The site of the hotel, incidentally, was famous throughout the 18th and 19th centuries as the biggest marketplace for horse trading in central Sweden.

Ventilgatan 1, S-654 45 Karlstad. ℰ **054/56-00-80.** Fax 054/56-88-19. www.stekhuset.com. 39 units. Mid-June to mid-Aug and Fri–Sat year-round 595SEK–695SEK ($77–$90) double; rest of year 795SEK–895SEK ($103–$116) double; 895SEK–995SEK ($116–$129) suite. Rates include breakfast. Free parking. Bus: 33 or 35. **Amenities:** Restaurant; bar; sauna; limited room service; babysitting; laundry service; dry cleaning; nonsmoking rooms; rooms for those w/limited mobility. *In room:* TV, dataport, minibar, hair dryer, safe.

WHERE TO DINE

Café Artist ✧ SWEDISH/FRENCH   Karlstad's best restaurant occupies the street level of the Scandic Winn (see "Where to Stay," above), although its culinary finesse is more obvious at nighttime than at lunch. The setting contains lots of 19th-century pinewood antiques and carefully finished paneling, which overall creates a cozy glow of old-fashioned well-being. The only option at lunchtime is a copious buffet attended by many of the town's office workers, who select from a generous medley of fish, meats, soups, salads, and vegetarian dishes. Evening meals are more elaborate, with well-choreographed service and menu items that include well-prepared olive-and-feta-stuffed chicken with herbs, garlic, and potato pie; and filet of lamb with sage and alpine char with a white-wine sauce. A dessert favorite is homemade vanilla ice cream with compote of warm cloudberries.

In the Scandic Winn, Norra Strandgatan 9–11. ℰ **054/77-64-700.** Reservations recommended for dinner on weekends. Lunch buffet 130SEK ($17) per person; dinner main courses 105SEK–220SEK ($14–$29). AE, DC, MC, V. Mon–Fri 11:30am–2:30pm and 5–11pm; Sat 5–11:30pm; Sun 6–10:30pm.

Plaza Vivaldi ✧ SWEDISH   One of the best restaurants in Karlstad is on the lobby level of the Radisson SAS Plaza (see "Where to Stay," above). Its decor combines modern with antique and traditional. Specialties of the chef are likely to include lime- and ginger-marinated salmon flavored with coriander, noisettes of reindeer with chanterelles, filet of veal in a creamy morel sauce, breast of pheasant with white-wine sauce and grapes, and filet of monkfish. The chefs are highly skilled and they've got imagination, but they never go too far. Their dishes are perfectly balanced and technically superb in every way.

In the Radisson Plaza Hotel, Vastra Torggatan 2. ℰ **054/10-02-00.** Reservations recommended. Main courses 100SEK–224SEK ($13–$29). AE, DC, MC, V. Mon–Sat 11:30am–11pm.

Stek Huset ★ INTERNATIONAL   Set on the lobby level of the Wåxnäs Hotel-Konferens (see "Where to Stay," above), this is one of the most famous and best-recommended restaurants in Karlstad, attracting diners from as far away as Jönköping. The setting is blue, dark red, and woodsy, with artfully illuminated tables and lots of drama associated with steaks and fish that frequently are flambéed at the table. The menu focuses on fish and on beefsteaks from both Sweden and Ireland. Two of the best-recommended dishes are a version of pepper steak that clients drive long distances to try, and a signature dish of deboned sole, grilled and served au gratin with creamed mushrooms and shrimp. A dessert that absolutely never fails to please clients is fresh raspberries with hot sabayon sauce and ice cream. A long list of wines from virtually everywhere is available to accompany your meal.

In the Wåxnäs Hotel-Konferens, Ventilgatan 1. ✆ **054/56-00-80.** Reservations recommended at lunch, required at dinner. Fixed-price lunches 65SEK–75SEK ($8.45–$9.75); main courses 77SEK–215SEK ($10–$28). AE, DC, MC, V. Mon–Fri 11am–10pm; Sat noon–10pm; Sun noon–8pm. Bus: 14 or 35.

KARLSTAD AFTER DARK
Restaurant Sandgrund, Sandgrundsudden (✆ **054/21-16-70**), is Värmland's best-known dance restaurant. Lots of people frequent this place, and it's easy to make new acquaintances. A pub and dance club on two floors, **Arena,** Kungsgatan 18 (✆ **054/21-95-95**), draws a lively, young crowd. One of the town's best pubs is **Bishops Arms,** in the Elite Stadshotellet Karlstadt, Kungsgatan 22 (✆ **054/ 29-30-00**). This is a classic pub opening on the Klarälven, and it offers a wide range of beer. Drawing even more business and enjoying greater popularity is **Wollpack Inn,** Järnsvägsgatan 1 (✆ **054/15-80-16**), a British-style pub.

2 Sunne

380km (236 miles) W of Stockholm, 61km (38 miles) NW of Karlstad, 288km (179 miles) NE of Gothenburg

Lying on Lake Fryken, Sunne is the center for tourism in Fryksdalen (Fryken Valley). The "land of legend," as Fryksdalen is known, is associated with the writings of Selma Lagerlöf. In fact, Sunne was the prototype for the village of Bro in *The Saga of Gösta Berling,* her most famous work. From Sunne, you can take boat trips on Lake Fryken or play golf on a 9-hole course.

In winter, Sunne often attracts skiers, as it has Värmland's highest lift capacity and the most modern cross-country stadium in Europe. Its slalom facility has a ski school, ski rentals, a ski shop, sports services, a restaurant, and a lodge. There are 10 descents that vary in difficulty; 4 of them are lit when twilight falls. Akka Stadium is the name of Sunne's ski stadium, and there are several cross-country trails starting from here. For information about skiing in the area, call **Ski Sunne** at ✆ **0565/602-80.**

ESSENTIALS
GETTING THERE   By Train   Four or five trains arrive daily on the 4½-hour trip from Stockholm, and from Gothenburg there are another four or five trains a day, which take 3⅔ hours. You always have to change trains in Kil, and sometimes in Hallsberg, depending on the train. From Oslo there are two trains per day, requiring a change in Kil; trip time is 3 to 4 hours. For more information, call ✆ **771/75-75-75.**

By Bus   If you're traveling from Stockholm, take the train. The bus trip is too complicated and has too many transfers. From Gothenburg, one bus a day arrives Monday through Friday on the 7¼-hour trip; transfer in Karlstad. Call ✆ **0200/21818** for schedules.

By Car   Drive north along routes 61 or 45 from Karlstad.

VISITOR INFORMATION   For information, the **Sunne Turistbyrå,** Kolsnasvagen 41 (℃ **0565/164-00**), is open from June 20 to August 5 daily 9am to 9:30pm; from August 6 to June 19, Monday to Friday 9am to 5pm.

SEEING THE SIGHTS

Sundsbergs Gård   In the center of Sunne, this museum presents various exhibits that illustrate domestic life over a 300-year period at a Värmland manor house. From the kitchen to the drawing room, exhibits are labeled to indicate what particular century or time period they represent. This summer-only museum is close to the landmark Hotel Selma Lagerlöf.

Ekebyvagen. ℃ **0565/103-63.** Admission 30SEK ($3.90). June 25–Aug 10 Wed–Sun noon–4pm. Closed Aug 11–June 24. Off season by appointment only.

NEARBY LITERARY ATTRACTIONS

Mårbacka Minnesgård ★★   On the other side of the water, 10km (6¼ miles) southeast of Sunne and 58km (36 miles) north of Karlstad, Mårbacka is the former home of Selma Lagerlöf (1858–1940), who won the Nobel Prize for literature. The pillared building is kept much as she left it at the time of her death. The estate is filled with her furnishings and mementos. It was disguised as Lövdala in her masterpiece *The Saga of Gösta Berling.*

Mårbackastiftelsen (Box 306). ℃ **0565/310-27.** Admission 65SEK ($8.45) adults, 30SEK ($3.90) children 5–15. May to mid-Sept daily 10am–4pm; off season Tues–Wed 11am–2pm.

Rottneros Herrgårde ★   This major attraction sits on the western shore of Lake Fryken and is one of the most famous fairyland-like settings in Sweden. Rotteros Manor, a site developed during the 13th century, provided the inspiration for the mythical manor house of Ekeby, which appears in Selma Lagerlöf's saga. Although the interior of the building is private, there's a manicured park and a world-class sculpture garden surrounding the building. Set amid verdant landscaping are more than 100 pieces of sculpture crafted by such artists as Carl Milles. The foremost sculptors of each of the neighboring Scandinavian countries are also represented: Kai Nielsen of Denmark, Gustav Vigeland of Norway, and Wäinö Aaltonen of Finland. On the grounds is a cafeteria and licensed restaurant.

Rottneros. ℃ **0565/602-95.** Admission 80SEK ($10). Mid-May to early June and late Aug Mon–Fri 10am–4pm, Sat–Sun 10am–6pm; mid-June to late June Mon–Fri 10am–5pm, Sat–Sun 10am–5pm; July to late Aug daily 10am–6pm. Take Rte. 45 4km (2½ miles) south from Sunne.

SHOPPING

Sunne is known for its long-standing tradition of arts and crafts. The landscape, nature, and translucent colors have "conspired" to spark creativity in local artisans, or so it is said. Visit the **Spa Shop** in the lobby of the Spa Hotel Selma Lagerlöf at Ekebyvägen (℃ **0565/166-00**) to purchase the bath salts, sea salts, dried kelp, mudpacks, and skin scrubbers that are used liberally within the spa facilities at this hotel. The array of skin scrubbers alone is guaranteed to keep you exfoliated and skin-toned; their modern designs, sometimes crafted from birch, will look good in your shower stall back home.

WHERE TO STAY & DINE

Hotel FrykenStrand (Value)   Set on well-kept lawns 3km (1¾ miles) north of the center of Sunne, a meter or so uphill from the waters of Lake Frykken, this is a three-story hotel whose two sections were built in the early 1960s and the early 1980s. During good weather, many of the hotel's social activities take place on masonry terraces that flank its edges. The sunny and very clean interior offers big-windowed views—especially from the hotel's dining room—of the surrounding lake and landscapes. Accommodations are comfortable; upholstered with plush, pastel-colored accessories; and outfitted like cozy nests—not overly large, but appealing and sleep-inducing. Each unit has a tidily kept bathroom equipped with a shower unit. The hotel restaurant is appealingly polite and friendly, with an emphasis on old-fashioned and traditional Swedish specialties.

By 80, S-686 93 Sunne. ✆ **0565/133-00**. Fax 0565/71-16-91. www.frykenstrand.se. 62 units. 910SEK–1,030SEK ($118–$134) double; 1,450SEK ($189) suite. Rates include breakfast. AE, DC, MC, V. Free parking. From Sunne, follow the signs to Torsby. **Amenities:** Restaurant; bar; 2 saunas; limited room service; all non-smoking rooms; rooms for those w/limited mobility. *In room:* TV, dataport, hair dryer.

Quality Hotel and Spa Selma Lagerlöf ★★   Completed in 1992, this is the only full-service spa in a Swedish hotel. Owned by a conglomerate of Danish and Swedish banks, it was launched in 1982 with the construction of a consciously old-fashioned core ("the hotel") designed like a stately Swedish manor house. Ten years later, a nine-story tower ("the spa") was built 274m (899 ft.) away, with modern bedrooms with balconies, convention facilities, and a full array of spa treatments. Most visitors check into the spa for a minimum of 3 days for a series of stress-reducing and health-promoting regimes. Sports enthusiasts appreciate the many opportunities in the surrounding region for skiing and hiking.

Bedrooms in both the spa and the hotel have ample bathrooms with tub/showers; they are the best and most up-to-date in Värmland. In the spa section, each of the 184 bedrooms is available only on a full-board basis. In the hotel, breakfast-only guests are accepted. Guests at the hotel must pay for extra activities, whereas spa guests get some activities, such as daily aerobics classes, free. However, all spa treatments require supplemental fees. Note that meals in the spa are diet-conscious and fat-free, whereas the hotel restaurant serves a sophisticated fare of Swedish regional specialties, some from Värmland, and top-rate international dishes—mainly continental—as well.

The hotel and spa lie at the edge of Lake Fryken, about a 5-minute drive south of the center of Sunne. Each of the separate buildings has its own reception staff, restaurant, and bars. The nightlife facilities in the older section usually are more animated and fun.

Ekebyvågen, S-686 28 Sunne. ✆ **0565/166-00**. Fax 0565/166-20. www.selmaspa.se. 156 units. Spa 1,695SEK ($220) per person double; mid-June to July 995SEK ($129) per person double. Rates include full board. Hotel 595SEK ($77) per person double; summer 495SEK ($64) per person. Rates include breakfast. All suites 500SEK ($65) per person supplement year-round. AE, DC, MC, V. Free parking. **Amenities:** 2 restaurants; 2 bars; 2 pools (1 indoor); health spa; sauna; laundry service; dry cleaning; nonsmoking rooms; rooms for those w/limited mobility. *In room:* A/C, TV, dataport, minibar, hair dryer, safe.

3 Filipstad

269km (167 miles) W of Stockholm, 309km (192 miles) NE of Gothenburg

The tourist center for the Bergslag (mining) area of Värmland, Filipstad was founded in 1611. It is almost certain that iron ore was mined in this region even before the black death of the 14th century, and documentary evidence establishes it as being a thriving business in 1413. The main mine products were iron and manganese ore, but silver, copper, lead, and zinc ore also were found. Even gold occasionally has been unearthed.

Today the Filipstad Bergslag smelting houses have vanished and only two mines remain in operation, but visitors can see the old open mine shafts, ruins

The Swede Who Helped Defeat the South

He may not have figured in *Gone With the Wind,* but John Ericsson, the famous Swedish inventor, helped the Union win the war against the Confederacy. Born near Filipstad on July 31, 1803, Ericsson joined the Swedish army in 1820. Eventually, he migrated to England, where he failed in a competition to create a new locomotive for the Liverpool and Manchester Railway when his "Novelty" developed engine trouble.

Disappointed, he moved to America, where he gained fame for his inventions, above all, the marine propeller. His fame was cemented when his warship, the Yankee *Monitor,* defeated the Confederate *Merrimac* on May 9, 1862. This victory saved the northern fleet and led to the Union naval forces quickly taking command of the sea, closing off Confederate ports by blockade.

Ericsson also invented the steam fire engine and the hot-air (or caloric) engine, and made several improvements in steam boilers. Even though this son of Filipstad lived abroad for much of his life, he placed his inventions at the disposal of the Swedish navy.

After a successful life as an inventor, John Ericsson died on March 8, 1889, in the United States. As he had requested to be buried at Filipstad on his native ground, his remains were transported to Sweden on the American armed cruiser *Baltimore.* He arrived back home with full honors and a magnificent hearse bearing his body. All the residents of Filipstad turned out to welcome home their now-famous native son.

On July 31, 1895, the John Ericsson Mausoleum was consecrated on the anniversary of Ericsson's birth. Once more, the town honored its great son, and the streets were decorated with flags, flowers, and several triumphal arches. The mausoleum lies at **Östra Kyrkogården (© 0590/ 187-50)** today and is often visited by Americans (at least, Yankees), among others. Every year since 1929, the John Ericsson Society places a wreath of flowers, in the shape of a propeller, at this mausoleum.

Every July 31, Filipstad stages a mock naval battle between the *Merrimac,* the armored vessel of the Confederates, and Ericsson's smaller, more easily maneuvered gunboat, the *Monitor.* The *Monitor* always wins, of course.

of ironworks, and grand manor houses where the ironmasters once lived. Other industries here include the making of Wasa Crispbread *(knäckebröd)* and tourism. Canoeing is a favorite summer activity, whereas downhill and cross-country skiing lure winter visitors.

Filipstad's main claim to fame (for Americans) is native son and inventor John Ericsson, who was born in nearby Långbanshyttan. (See box above.)

Ericsson's brother was Baron Nils Ericsson, a noted construction engineer in Sweden who is known for having planned and built Sweden's first main railway.

Another well-known Filipstad figure is poet Nils Ferlin, whose realistic statue sits on a park bench in the center of town.

ESSENTIALS

GETTING THERE   By Train   You can't take the train to Filipstad. The nearest station is at Kristinehamn or Karlstad, from which you can make bus connections to Filipstad. For rail information, call © **771/75-75-75.**

By Bus   Daily connections are possible from Karlstad. Call © **0200/21818** or 0563/532-34 for schedules. The bus ride from Karlstad to Filipstad, a distance of 60km (37 miles), takes about 40 minutes and costs about 40SEK ($5.20).

By Car   Follow Route 61 through Arvika to Kil. Drive through Forshaga to Route 63 to Molkom and Filipstad.

VISITOR INFORMATION   The **Filipstads Turistbyrå,** St. Torget 3D, S-682 27 Filipstad (© **0590/613-54;** www.filipstad.se), is open June to August Monday to Friday 9am to 6pm, and Saturday and Sunday 11am to 4pm; September to May Monday to Friday 10am to 4pm.

SEEING THE SIGHTS

A visit to Filipstad wouldn't be complete without an excursion to the little settlement of **Långbans Gruvby,** Hyttbacken (© **0590/221-81**), lying 19km (12 miles) northeast of the center. Mining on this site was carried out from the middle of the 16th century until 1972. The Långban mines were especially known in the 19th century for producing manganese, and during the last decades of their activity, they were primary sources of dolomite. More than 300 different kinds of minerals have been found here. Långban today is a well-preserved mining village with mine holes, shaft towers, a smelting house, workmen's houses, and a manor house. In 1803, the Swedish-American inventor John Ericsson was born in a wing of the old managing director's residence. The site is open Monday to Friday 10am to 4pm, and Saturday and Sunday noon to 4pm, charging 20SEK ($2.60), free for those up to 16 years old. For information call © **0590/222-15.**

Less than 1km (½ mile) from the town center, **Storbrohhyttan Hembygdsgården,** Munkeberg (© **0590/140-28**), is a restored blast furnace and ironworks that have been made into a mining museum with a wealth of artifacts. On-site is a crafts center, Tullhuset, that's open Monday to Friday year-round 10am to 5pm. An employee at Tullhuset shows newcomers the blast furnace lying a few steps away. The cost of the visit is 30SEK ($3.90).

The artisans of Filipstad sell and exhibit their handicrafts at **Kjortelgården,** Hantverksgatan 17 (© **0590/153-50**).

Lesjöfors Museum ★ *Finds*   This evocative museum illustrates 3 centuries of Värmland history. You'll find yourself transported to different epochs, feeling the spirit of Lesjöfors from the beginning of the 20th century. The museum not only presents the history of the steelworks that once were in the town, but also re-creates the society, organizations, sports, and housing of the workers who lived here. You'll see authentic environments, including the waiting room of the former factory. In the foundry hall you can view exhibits of some of the steel products once created here. (Artist Larseric Vänerlöf shaped an impressive sculpture from some of the different molds left behind when the factory shut down.) One section re-creates in minute detail a kitchen from the 1950s.

Lesjöfors. © **0590/31122.** Admission 40SEK ($5.20). June–Aug Mon–Fri 10am–4pm, Sat–Sun noon–4pm; Sept–May Thurs–Sat 2–5pm. Take Rte. 64 north of town 35km (22 miles).

WHERE TO STAY & DINE

Hennickehammars Herrgård ★★   Built in 1722 as the home of a wealthy landowner, this hotel, with its elegant detailing and symmetrical facade, is a comfortable country spot loaded with personality and charm. On lawns close to the edge of Lake Hemtjarn, 4km (2½ miles) south of Filipstad, rooms are either in one of several outbuildings or in the main manor house itself. Guests can swim in the lake, rent horses at a nearby riding school, play tennis, or enjoy golf at a course about 15km (9¼ miles) away. Each unit is stylishly comfortable, thanks to a renovation that improved the shower-only bathrooms.

The best dining in and around Filipstad is found at the hotel restaurant.

Lake Hemtjärn, Box 52, S-682 00 Filipstad. © 0590/608500. Fax 0590/608505. www.hennickehammar.se. 54 units. Fri–Sat 1,350SEK ($176) double; Sun–Thurs 1,550SEK ($202) double. AE, DC, MC, V. Free parking. **Amenities:** Restaurant; bar; pool; tennis court; fitness center; Jacuzzi; sauna; nonsmoking rooms; rooms for those w/limited mobility. *In room:* TV, hair dryer.

Hotel John   Set near the center of town, close to the junction of highways 64 and 65, this low-slung, two-story, white-walled hotel dates from 1974, when it was designed to cater to both roadside traffic and corporate conventions. Inside you'll find a tavern-style restaurant, wood-floored bedrooms with double-glazed windows, and decor typical of middle-bracket hotels throughout the Western Hemisphere. Bedrooms, although rather "motel-grade," are comfortable and fine for an overnight stopover. Bathrooms containing shower units are a bit tiny.

John Ericssonsgatan 8, S-68230 Filipstad. © 0590/125-30. Fax 0590/106-68. 47 units. Mid-June to mid-Aug and Fri–Sat year-round 730SEK ($95) double; rest of year 980SEK ($127) double. Rates include breakfast. AE, DC, MC, V. Free parking. **Amenities:** 2 restaurants; 2 bars; indoor pool; Jacuzzi; sauna; laundry service; dry cleaning; nonsmoking rooms; rooms for those w/limited mobility. *In room:* A/C, TV.

4 Falun ★

488km (303 miles) NE of Gothenburg, 229km (142 miles) NW of Stockholm

An exploration of the Dalarna region begins in Falun, the old capital of Dalarna; it lies on both sides of the Falu River. This town is noted for its copper mines; the income generated from copper has supported many Swedish kings. Just 10km (6¼ miles) to the northeast, you can visit the home of the famed Swedish painter Carl Larsson.

ESSENTIALS

GETTING THERE   By Train   There is frequent service during the day from Stockholm (trip time: 3 hr.) and from Gothenburg (trip time: 6 hr.). For schedules, call © 771/75-75-75.

By Bus   Buses operated by **Swebus** (© 0200/21-82-18) run between Stockholm and Falun either once or twice every Friday, Saturday, and Sunday, depending on the season. Coming from Gothenburg, although the distance is greater, buses arrive twice a day every day of the week, making frequent stops along the way.

By Car   If you're driving to Falun from Stockholm, take the E18 expressway northwest to the junction with Route 70. From here, continue to the junction with Route 60, where you head northwest. Falun is signposted.

VISITOR INFORMATION   The Falun Tourist Office, Trotzgatan 10–12 (© 023/830-50), is open from mid-August to mid-June every Monday to Friday 9am to 6pm, and Saturday 10am to 2pm. During summer, from mid-June to mid-August, it's open Monday to Friday 9am to 7pm, and Saturday and Sunday

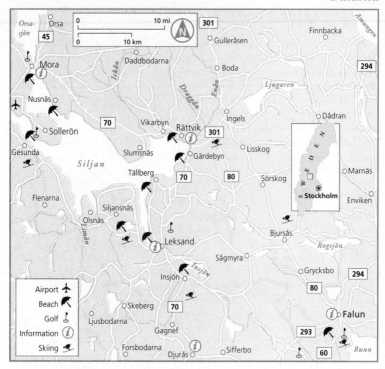

10am to 5pm. For more information on Falun, refer to the town's website at www.falun.se.

SEEING THE SIGHTS

Go first to the market square, *Stora Torget*, to see the **Kristine Church** (✆ 023/ 279-10), a copper-roofed structure dating from the mid–17th century (the tower itself dates from 1865). It's open daily 10am to 4pm, and admission is free. It closes at 6pm in summer.

Bjursås Ski Center This ski center has six mechanized ski lifts, 10 downhill slopes, and a restaurant or two. It does not, however, resemble a full-fledged ski resort like Gstaad or Chamonix. Don't expect much more than a big parking lot and lots of snow, ice, and midwinter darkness, with illuminated ski trails and a sense of family fun and Scandinavian thrift. Equipment can be rented.

S-790 21, Bjorsås. ✆ **023/774177.** Day pass 230SEK ($30) (Dec 13 to Easter only). Bjursberget is about 21km (13 miles) north of the center of Falun; follow the signs pointing to Råttuik.

Carl Larsson-gården ★★★ A 20-minute trip from Falun will take you to a small village, Sundborn, site of Lilla Hyttnas, Carl Larsson's home (now known as Carl Larsson-gården). Larsson became Sweden's most admired artist during his lifetime (1853–1919). Through Larsson's watercolor paintings of his own house, it has become known throughout Sweden. In the United States, reproductions of Larsson's watercolors, mainly of his wife, Karin, and their children, appear frequently on prints, calendars, and greeting cards. There are guided tours throughout the day, and English-language tours sometimes are available.

Falun

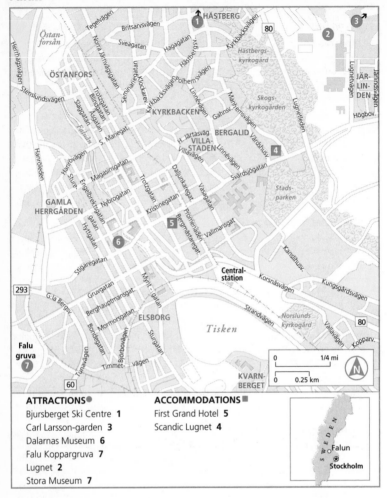

ATTRACTIONS ●

Bjursberget Ski Centre **1**
Carl Larsson-garden **3**
Dalarnas Museum **6**
Falu Koppargruva **7**
Lugnet **2**
Stora Museum **7**

ACCOMMODATIONS ■

First Grand Hotel **5**
Scandic Lugnet **4**

While at the home of the artist, you can also ask about viewing **Carl Larssons porträttsambling** ★★★ (a portrait collection donated by Larsson), displayed in the Congregation House next to the local church. The pictures, painted between 1905 and 1918, depict well-known local residents representing many different occupations. One of the best-known portraits is that of a carpenter, Hans Arnbon, of whom Larsson said: "Before the Devil can get his slippers on, Arnbon is standing there at his lathe or his bench." To reach the garden, take bus no. 64 from Falun to Sundborn, which is 5 minutes away from Carl Larsson-gården.

Carl Larssons Väg 12, Sundborn. ✆ 023/600-53. Admission 80SEK ($10) adults, 35SEK ($4.55) children 7–17, free for children 6 and under. May–Sept daily 10am–5pm; Oct–Apr by appointment only (call ✆ 023/60069 or 60053 for reservations). Bus: 64 from Falun.

Dalarnas Museum ★★★ This is Dalarna's most intriguing folk art museum. It's especially rich in genuine, old, colorful folk costumes and their accessories, and also exhibits the best collections of peasant wall paintings. The music section is especially interesting, and you can hear recordings of fiddlers and young

---

> (*Fun Fact* **Portrait of the Artist**
>
> Admired though Carl Larsson was during his lifetime, he could still hold a
> grudge. When his erstwhile friend, the playwright August Strindberg,
> published a vicious attack on Larsson, the artist took a knife and stalked
> Strindberg through the streets of Stockholm.

---

girls blowing the traditional small alp-horns. The Falun group of graphic artists
is well known in the Swedish art world, and the six artists who made up that
elite group in the early decades of the 20th century are displayed here. Of these,
Axel Fridell is the finest. A faithful reconstruction of Swedish writer Selma
Lagerlöf's study with its original furnishings has been installed in the museum.

Stirgaregatan 2–4. (C) **023/76-55-00.** Admission 40SEK ($5.20). Mon–Fri 10am–5pm; weekends noon–5pm.

Falu Koppargruva ★★★   This copper mine, around which the town developed, was the world's largest producer of copper during the 17th century; it supplied the raw material used for the roof of the Palace of Versailles. After a visit
to the mine in 1734, Carl von Linné called it "Sweden's greatest wonder, but as
terrible as Hell itself." Since 1970, when the mine was opened to the public,
more than one million visitors have taken the elevator 54m (177 ft.) below the
surface of the Earth and into the mine. Guides take you through old chambers
and winding passages dating from the Middle Ages. In one section of the mine
you'll see a shaft divided by a timber wall that's more than 195m (640 ft.) high;
this may be the world's tallest wooden structure. Today the only industrial product of the mine is pigment used for producing Sweden's signature red paint
(*Falu Rödfärg*), which is used not only on virtually all Swedish barns, but on
thousands upon thousands of private homes and even commercial and public
buildings. Buildings painted this shade of barn red have become virtual symbols
of Sweden.

Gruvplatsen. (C) **023/71-14-75.** Admission 90SEK ($12) adults, 45SEK ($5.85) children 7–18. May–Sept daily
10am–5pm; Oct–Apr Mon–Fri 11am–5pm. Tours must be booked in advance in winter.

Lugnet   This is one of Sweden's largest and most comprehensive sports com-
plexes. Its main fame derives from its selection in 1974 as the site for the cross-
country skiing World's Championship. Today it contains a large-scale hotel (the
below-recommended Scandic), a ski jump, an ice hockey rink, and a sports hall
that's the centerpiece for all the other facilities (including miles of cross-country
ski tracks and a campground), and the site of an indoor pool, a sauna, and a
steam bath.

S-79131 Falun. (C) **023/83500.** Admission 40SEK ($5.20) for a day's use of all the facilities (except massage).
Sports hall daily 8am–9pm.

Stora Museum ★★★   This museum is devoted to the technical and industrial past of the area, and depicts the history of its copper mountain. Most interesting here is a model room with Christopher Polhem's clever inventions.
Polhem (1661–1751) was the father of Swedish mechanics and loved using
devices such as mechanical alphabets. Entering this museum is like a step into
the 18th century; the tiled stoves, antiques, decorative molded plaster, and chandeliers all are of the era—either the genuine article or an exact replica. In the
coin cabinet, the entire history of minting copper coins is documented. Various
methods of producing iron are described in pictures and models.

Vid Falu Gruva. ☎ 023/71-14-75. Admission 40SEK ($5.20). May–Sept daily 10am–5pm; off season Mon–Fri 11am–5pm.

WHERE TO STAY & DINE

First Hotel Grand ⭐ This buff-colored hotel 90m (295 ft.) south of the landmark Falun Church was built in 1862, with a modern addition constructed in 1974. The complex was renovated in 2000, and the tastefully modern guest rooms are among the best decorated in town. All have good beds and ample-size bathrooms equipped with shower units.

Trotzgatan 9–11, S-791 71 Falun. ☎ 023/7948-80. Fax 023/14143. www.firsthotels.se. 151 units. Sun–Thurs 1,349SEK ($175) double; Fri–Sat 754SEK ($98) double; 2,495SEK ($324) suite. Rates include breakfast. AE, DC, MC, V. Parking 80SEK ($10). Bus: 701 or 704. **Amenities:** Restaurant; bar; indoor pool; fitness center; sauna; limited room service; laundry service; dry cleaning; nonsmoking rooms; rooms for those w/limited mobility. *In room:* TV, dataport.

Scandic Lugnet ⭐ Rising a dozen floors above a forested landscape, less than a 10-minute walk from the center of Falun, this hotel is one of the tallest buildings in town. As if that weren't enough, its pale green facade and futuristic detailing also make it one of the most unusual. Built in the early 1990s, with vertical rows of bay windows, it has well-crafted public areas outfitted in natural materials that include lots of stone and wood, and contemporary bedrooms. Although it has a chain hotel feel, the rooms are nonetheless well designed and furnished. The bathrooms are ample for the job, with shower units and a good supply of shelf space. The majority of the bedrooms are nonsmoking, and there also is an "environmental floor," where 97% of the waste of the room is recycled. Expect tour bus groups and a hardworking, sometimes slightly harassed staff (especially when hordes of newcomers check in collectively).

There's a bistro-style restaurant and a bar on the premises.

Svärdsjögatan 51, S-791 31 Falun. ☎ 023/669-2200. Fax 023/669-2211. www.scandic-hotels.com. 153 units. July–Aug and Fri–Sat year-round 790SEK ($103) double; rest of year 1,585SEK ($206) double; 990SEK–1,885SEK ($129–$245) minisuite. Rates include breakfast. AE, DC, MC, V. Free parking. **Amenities:** Restaurant; bar; indoor pool; sauna; laundry service; dry cleaning; nonsmoking rooms; rooms for those w/limited mobility; bowling alley. *In room:* TV, dataport, hair dryer.

5 Leksand ⭐⭐

48km (30 miles) W of Falun, 18km (11 miles) S of Rättvik, 267km (166 miles) NW of Stockholm

Leksands Noret is a doorway to Lake Siljan, and no less an authority than Hans Christian Andersen found the setting idyllic. Leksand in its present form dates from the early 1900s, when it was reconstructed following a fire that razed the community. However, some type of settlement has existed on this site since pagan times.

Many of the old traditions of the province still flourish here. Women occasionally don the traditional dress for church on Sunday, and in June and July the long "church boats" from Viking times may cross the lake carrying parishioners to church. These same boats compete in a church-boat race on the first Sunday in July. Since World War II, a miracle play, *The Road to Heaven,* has been presented here in open-air performances, providing an insight into the customs and folklore of Dalarna. The play runs for 10 days at the end of July.

ESSENTIALS

GETTING THERE   By Plane You can fly from Stockholm on **Skyways** (☎ 0771/959-500); the nearest airport is **Dala-Airport** (☎ 0243/645-00), in

> ## ⟨Moments⟩ Sweden's Best White-Water Rafting
>
> The best way to profit from the meltdown of Sweden's winter snows involves floating downstream atop the surging waters of the Klarälven River, a scenic stream that originates in the high altitudes of Norway and eventually flows through Värmland. Whitewater enthusiasts gravitate to its northern stretches; aficionados of calmer waters move to points near its southern terminus. One of the most respected outfitters for excursions along any length of this historic river is **Vildmark in Värmland,** P.O. Box 209, Torsby SE 68525 (✆ **0560/14040;** www.vildmark. se). Established in 1980 and known throughout the region for the quality of its guides, it offers canoe excursions along the northern lengths of the river between April and October, providing canoes, instruction, and all the equipment and excitement you'll need. More unusual than the white-water aspects of this place is what the company promotes along the calmer southern stretches, where as many as six million logs were floated downstream every year until the practice was halted for the most part in 1991. You'll be taught how to lash together a log raft, equivalent to what Huckleberry Finn might have built for treks on the Mississippi. On a raft lashed together with hemp rope, without metal fasteners or wire of any kind, you'll float downstream, past panoramic vistas, as part of treks that last between 1 and 7 days. Participants sleep either aboard their rafts, which consist of three layers of log stacked atop one another, or in tents along the shore. Rafts are suitable for between two and six passengers, and are eventually disassembled and sent to paper mills to be turned into pulp. A 4-day experience covering about 48 downstream kilometers (30 miles) costs 1,790SEK ($233) per adult; a 7-day jaunt covering twice that distance costs 2,130SEK ($277) per person.
>
> Less structured trips are offered by a competitor in Värmland, in a location 150km (93 miles) north of Karlstad. Here you can contact **Branäs Sport,** Branäs Fritidsanläggin, S-680 20 Sysslebäck (✆ **564/475-70**), an operation that devotes much of its time to the rental of cross-country skis, but also conducts white-water rafting on several nearby streams and rivers.

Borlänge, 50km (31 miles) south, from which there is frequent bus and train service to Leksand. Car rentals are available at the airport.

By Train   There's a direct train from Stockholm to Mora that stops in Leksand (travel time: 3½ hr.). For reservations and information, call ✆ **771/75-75-75.**

By Boat   Another way to reach Leksand is by boat, the *Gustaf Wasa* ✮; call ✆ **010/252-32-92** for information and reservations. Every Monday at 3pm it makes one long trip from Mora to Leksand (through Rättvik). The round-trip fare is 120SEK ($16) for adults, 60SEK ($7.80) for children. Tickets are sold on board.

By Car   From Falun, our last stopover, head north on Route 80 to Bjursås, then go west on a secondary road sign-posted as SÅGMYRA. Follow the signs into Leksand.

VISITOR INFORMATION   Contact the **Leksands Turistbyrå,** Norsgatan 23 (© **0247/79-61-30;** www.stab.se), open June 15 to August 10 Monday to Friday 10am to 8pm, Saturday 10am to 5pm, and Sunday 11am to 5pm; rest of the year, Monday to Friday 10am to 5pm, and Saturday 10am to 11pm.

A SPECIAL EVENT   Sweden's biggest music festival, **Music at Lake Siljan,** takes place during the first week of July. There are some 100 concerts covering a wide range of music at venues in both Leksand and Rättvik. Fiddle music predominates. For information, contact **Music at Lake Siljan,** Box 28, S-795 21 Rättvik (© **0248/102-90**).

ENJOYING THE OUTDOORS
A sports-oriented and health-conscious town, Leksand provides ample opportunity for outdoor sports. The town's tourist office can provide information on local swimming, cross-country skiing, curling, ice skating, tennis, and boat rides on Lake Siljan, all of which are available in or near the town center, depending on the season and weather conditions. There are downhill skiing facilities at **Granberget,** about 21km (13 miles) to the southwest. Granberget is neither the biggest nor the best ski facility in Sweden. On the premises are five mechanized lifts, one restaurant, and no hotels at all. A 1-day ski pass costs 180SEK ($23). For information, call or write **Ski Leksand Granberget,** S-79330 Leksand (© **0247/22330;** fax 0247/22306).

SEEING THE SIGHTS
Leksands Kyrka   Leksand's "Parish Church" was founded in the 13th century. It has retained its present form since 1715 and is still one of the largest rural churches in Sweden. During renovations in 1971, a burial site was found that dates from the period when the Vikings were being converted to Christianity.

Norsgatan, near the lake. © 0247/807-00. Free admission to the church; tour 200SEK ($26) per person. Mid-June to early Aug guided tours (in Swedish and English) Mon–Sat 10am–1pm and 2–5pm; Sun 1–5pm.

Hembygdsgårdar   This open-air summer museum is near the parish church. Situated in a cluster of 18th- and 19th-century buildings that are themselves part of the museum's collections, it features depictions by 18th- and 19th-century peasants of Christ and his Apostles in Dalarna dress.

Norsgatan. © 0247/802-45. Admission 20SEK ($2.60) adults, free for children. Mid-June to mid-Aug Mon–Fri noon–4pm; Sat–Sun noon–5pm.

WHERE TO STAY
During the summer, you may find it fun to rent a *stuga* (log cabin) with four beds for 1,900SEK to 4,500SEK ($247–$585) per week. You can use it as a base for exploring all of Dalarna. The **Leksands Turistbyrå,** Box 52, S-793 22 Leksand (© **0247/803-00**), will book you into one. You also can inquire about renting a room in a private home.

Masesgården ★★ *(Finds*   This is one of the most sports-and-fitness-conscious hotels in Sweden. It has a reputation for educating guests about new eating and exercise habits, and a philosophy of preventing disease and depression through proper diet and exercise. Most people spend a week, participating in supervised aerobic and sports regimes, not indulging in conventional spa-style pampering. Beside a sea inlet, with a view of Leksand across the fjord, it's a sprawling compound of low-slung buildings. Guest rooms are soothing and more plush than you might have imagined. Each comes with a well-maintained bathroom equipped with a shower unit.

The daily program includes lectures that stress the link between a healthy body and a healthy soul ("astrological reincarnation and modern lifestyles" is a favorite), and physical disciplines such as tai chi. Theme weeks concentrate on individual subjects, such as meditation and modern yoga, and Reiki healing through applied massage. Other activities include aerobics, sometimes in a swimming pool, and weight training. Classes are conducted in Swedish, but most staff members speak English. This is not a holiday for the faint-hearted. Be prepared to sweat and re-evaluate your lifestyle, in ways that might not always be completely comfortable.

Grytnäs 61, S-793 92 Leksand. © 0247/122-31. Fax 0247/122-51. www.masesgarden.se. 34 units, 23 with bathroom. 5,600SEK ($728) per person per week in double without bathroom; 6,200SEK–6,400SEK ($806–$832) per person per week in double with bathroom. Rates include all meals and 30 hours of supervised sports activities. AE, DC, MC, V. Free parking. **Amenities:** Restaurant; lounge; indoor pool; sauna; wellness programs. *In room:* No phone.

Moskogen Motel   The motel and red wooden huts at this "self-service holiday village" make a good base for excursions around the Lake Siljan area. The rooms are well furnished and comfortable, with good beds. Each unit has a tiny kitchen and a neatly kept bathroom with shower unit. A restaurant on the premises serves light lunches and dinners. The Moskogen is 1.5km (1 mile) west of the railway station.

Insjövägen 50, S-793 00 Leksand. © 0247/146-00. Fax 0247/144-30. 49 units. 930SEK ($121) double; 1,130SEK ($147) suite. Rates include breakfast. AE, DC, MC, V. Free parking. Bus: 58. **Amenities:** Breakfast room; bar; 2 pools (1 indoor); exercise room; Jacuzzi; sauna; laundry service; dry cleaning; nonsmoking rooms; rooms for those w/limited mobility. *In room:* TV, safe.

WHERE TO DINE

Bosporen SWEDISH   This restaurant, 360m (1,181 ft.) west of the railroad station, maintains longer, more reliable hours than any other place in town. Its Istanbul-derived name comes from the Turkish-born owners. The chefs are equally at home in the Swedish and Turkish kitchens. Shish kabobs and Turkish salads are featured, but you can also order fried Baltic herring, sautéed trout, fresh salmon, or plank steak. The cooking is fair and even a bit exotic in a town not renowned for its restaurants.

Torget 1. © 0247/132-80. Main courses 68SEK–225SEK ($8.85–$29). AE, DC, MC, V. Summer daily 11am–11pm; mid-Sept to May daily 3–10pm.

6 Tällberg ⭐

13km (8 miles) N of Leksand, 280km (174 miles) NW of Stockholm, 518km (321 miles) NE of Gothenburg

This lakeside village, charmingly in tune with the spirit and tradition of Dalarna, is our favorite spot in the whole province, and the area of choice for nature lovers in both summer and winter. Skiing, curling, skating, and sleigh riding are popular sports, and swimming and boating lure summer visitors. Tällberg's beauty was discovered after artists and other cultural celebrities built summer houses in the village.

ESSENTIALS

GETTING THERE   By Train   Trains from Gothenburg take about 7 hours, with a change in Börlange. There are direct trains daily from Stockholm, but with many stops, the trip time is about 3½ hours. Trains also make the 10-minute run between Leksand and Tällberg. Call © 771/75-75-75 for information.

By Bus   There is no direct bus service from Stockholm or Gothenburg. Bus passengers get off at either Leksand or Rättvik, where local bus connections can be made. Call © **0200/21818** for information.

By Car   Take the E18 expressway northwest from Stockholm, then turn onto Route 70 toward Börlange and drive all the way to Tällberg, a 3-hour drive.

VISITOR INFORMATION   For information, the Leksand Tourist Office handles queries (see above).

SEEING THE SIGHTS

For information on outdoor activities, ask the advice of the staff at any of the town's hotels. Of particular merit is the staff within the **Hotel Långbers**, S-79370 Tallberg (© **0247/50290**). Most indoor sports in Tällberg are guided by the staff at the **Feel House** (© **0247/89386**), which lies within a sports compound adjacent to the Hotel Dalecarlia (© **0247/89100**). Rebuilt in 1997, it contains an indoor pool, weight-lifting and exercise facilities, sauna and massage facilities, and a staff that knows virtually everything about sports within the Lake Siljan region.

One worthwhile attraction in the center of Tällberg is the **Holen Gustaf Ancarcronas,** Holen (© **0247/513-31**), a collection of nine wood-sided buildings that were restored and, in some cases, hauled into position from other parts of Dalarna under the guidance of collector and local resident Gustaf Ancarcronas between 1910 and 1911. Ancarcronas (1869–1933) amassed a considerable collection of folk artifacts during his lifetime, many of which are on display within the compound. It's open only for a limited part of each summer, from mid-June to early August daily from noon to 4pm. Admission and a guided tour costs 20SEK ($2.60).

Another attraction is **Fråsgården,** Ytterboda, a family farm estate dating from the 18th century, which today is configured as an open-air museum with a significant collection of Dalarna folk costumes. It maintains the same hours and same admission price as the above-mentioned Holen Gustaf Ancarcronas. During the seasons when both monuments are closed, you can get information about them by calling © **0247/802-45.** To reach Fråsgården from Tällberg, a distance of 5km (3 miles) to the south, follow the signs to Leksand, then the signs to Ytterboda.

WHERE TO STAY

Hotel Klockargården (see "Where to Dine," below), also rents bedrooms.

Akerblads i Tällberg ⭐ *Finds*   An old-fashioned family hotel since 1910, this establishment is 2km (1¼ miles) south of Tällberg station at the crossroads leading down to Lake Siljan. The core of the house is still the wooden storehouse in the courtyard, but there has been much rebuilding over the years, including an addition of minisuites. All rooms at the hotel are done in an attractive Dala-style (generally folkloric and typical of the 18th-c. farms in the area), with comfortable beds and small bathrooms equipped with tub/showers. During the winter, you can take advantage of a sleigh ride and then warm up with a log fire and hot mulled wine. For the less snowy weather, bicycles are available for 90SEK ($12) per day. The hotel restaurant is known for its home-style cooking, buffets, and homemade bread.

Sjögattu 2, S-793 70 Tällberg. © **0247/508-00.** Fax 0247/506-52. www.akerblads-tallberg.se. 69 units. 1,390SEK ($181) double; 1,790SEK ($233) minisuite. AE, DC, MC, V. Free parking. **Amenities:** Restaurant; bar; indoor pool; Jacuzzi; sauna; nonsmoking rooms; rooms for those w/limited mobility. *In room:* TV, minibar (in some), hair dryer.

Green Hotel ⭐ This hotel, whose wide array of rooms ranges from small to VIP size, is located on a lawn sloping down toward the lake less than a kilometer (½ mile) west of the railroad station. The staff wears regional costumes, and the lounge has a notable art collection. On the premises is a swimming pool whose surface is covered every Saturday night with a glass top and converted to a dance floor. Open year-round, the hotel offers an array of summer and winter sports. A few of the more luxurious bedrooms have their own fireplaces and private saunas. All units are nonsmoking and have well-kept bathrooms with tub/showers.

S-793 70 Tällberg. ⓒ **0247/502-50.** Fax 0247/501-30. www.greenhotel.se. 101 units. 900SEK–2,340SEK ($117–$304) double. Rates include breakfast. DC, MC, V. Free parking. **Amenities:** Restaurant; bar; 2 pools (1 indoor); Jacuzzi; sauna; limited room service; rooms for those w/limited mobility. *In room:* TV, hair dryer.

Hotel Dalecarlia ⭐⭐ This is the largest, most substantial, and most prestigious hotel in Tällberg, with a historic, woodsy-looking core that was built in 1910 and a state-of-the-art enlargement that was added in 1991. Set on sloping land near Lake Siljan, it evokes an alpine hotel in Switzerland, thanks to lots of varnished panels and a cozy, elegantly rustic public area that has plenty of comfy chairs for reading, gossiping, or hanging out. Bedrooms are outfitted in pastel tones, with medium-size tiled bathrooms containing shower units. Although much of its business derives from its appeal to the Scandinavian companies that hold conventions within its meeting rooms, it also offers many of the diversions and outdoor activities of a lakeside resort.

The hotel's dining room is a large, woodsy-looking affair with big windows overlooking the lake and attentive service from a uniformed staff.

S-793 70 Tällberg. ⓒ **0247/891-00.** Fax 0247/50240. www.dalecarlia.se. 80 units. 795SEK–1,890SEK ($103–$246) double. Rates include breakfast. AE, DC, MC, V. Free parking. **Amenities:** Restaurant; bar; indoor pool; health spa; sauna; nonsmoking rooms; rooms for those w/limited mobility. *In room:* TV, dataport, minibar, hair dryer.

Siljansgården *Kids* Originally built in 1915, this rustic, timber-sided hotel stands on 5 hectares (12 acres) on the shores of the lake 1.5km (1 mile) west of the railroad station. There's a private bathing beach on the grounds. The hotel bedrooms are simply furnished but comfortable. Each has a neatly kept bathroom with a shower unit. In addition, 12 rustic summer cottages are suitable for up to four occupants, making them a family favorite. As they're not heated, they are available only in summer. A restaurant in the main building is licensed for beer and wine only, and serves a one-course lunch and a three-course dinner. In spite of the winter snows, the hotel is open year-round. Cottage renters need to bring their own sleeping bags, but sheets can be rented.

Sjögattu 36, S-793 70 Tällberg. ⓒ **0247/500-40.** Fax 0247/500-13. www.siljansgarden.com. 31 units, plus 11 cottages. May–Aug 400SEK–850SEK ($52–$111) double; Sept–Apr 680SEK–880SEK ($88–$114) double; May–Sept 20 only 380SEK–680SEK ($49–$88) cottage. Rates include breakfast. DC, MC, V. Free parking. **Amenities:** Restaurant; lounge; sauna; laundry service; dry cleaning. *In room:* TV.

WHERE TO DINE

Restaurant at the Hotel Klockargården SWEDISH Some aspects of this place may remind you of a chalet in Switzerland, thanks to blackened wooden siding, steep roofs designed to shed snowfalls, and an artfully maintained rusticity. The hotel that contains it is composed of about a half-dozen 18th- and 19th-century wood-sided buildings, some of which were already here as part of a farmstead; others were hauled in from other parts of Dalarna. The compound, as you see it today, was rebuilt following old-fashioned aesthetics, in 1959.

Frankly, we value this place mostly for its restaurant, where local specialties include fried elk steak with juniper berry sauce, platters of fried whitefish with parsley-butter sauce, salmon from nearby Lake Siljan prepared in any of at least three different ways, and such conventional dishes as roasted chicken with dill, and fried steaks with garlic and wine sauce. The most appealing moment here is during the weekend smorgasbords, when the agrarian bounty of central Sweden makes itself visible on groaning buffet tables in a style that originated about a century ago.

The hotel also rents 40 well-maintained bedrooms, each of which is decorated with hand-woven textiles and woodcarvings created by local artisans. With breakfast included, doubles rent for 595SEK to 695SEK ($77–$90) per person; double-occupancy minisuites go for 895SEK to 1,500SEK ($116–$195) per person. Each has a TV and telephone.

Siljansvägen 6, S-793 70 Tällberg. © 0247/502-60. Fax 0247/502-16. Reservations recommended. Main courses 125SEK–165SEK ($16–$21); fixed-price menu 355SEK ($46). June 21–Sept 5 daily noon–2pm and 6–11pm; rest of year daily noon–2pm and 6–9pm.

7 Rättvik ★★

21km (13 miles) NE of Leksand, 275km (171 miles) NW of Stockholm

Rättvik, which has some of the best hotels in the district, is one of the most popular resorts bordering Lake Siljan. In summer, conducted tours begin here and go around Lake Siljan. Culture and tradition have long been associated with Rättvik; you'll find peasant costumes, folk dancing, Dalarna paintings, arts and crafts, fiddle music, and "church boats"—flamboyantly painted boats in which entire congregations floated for Sunday services. The old style of architecture is still prevalent, and you'll find many timber houses. Carpenters and painters from Rättvik are known for their craftsmanship.

ESSENTIALS

GETTING THERE   By Train   You can reach Rättvik by rail. The Stockholm train to Mora stops in Leksand, where you can catch another train for the short trip to Rättvik. Train information in Stockholm is available at the **Central Station** (© 771/75-75-75).

By Bus   Buses to Rättvik operate Friday to Sunday from Stockholm. There also is a bus connection between Leksand and Rättvik. For schedules, call © **0200/21818.**

By Car   From Leksand, head north on Route 70 into Rättvik.

VISITOR INFORMATION   The **Rättvik Tourist Office** is in the train station (© **0248/79-72-10;** www.stab.se). It's open from June 15 to August 10 daily 10am to 7pm, and Sunday 10am to 7pm; from August 11 to June 14 Monday to Friday 10am to 5pm.

SEEING THE SIGHTS

In central Sweden, the old saying "You can't see the forest for the trees" often holds true—literally! For an antidote to that, and a sweeping view that stretches for many kilometers, drive 5km (3 miles) east of town along the road leading to Falun. Here, soaring more than 24m (79 ft.) skyward, is a red-sided wooden tower, originally built in 1897, called the **Vidablick,** Hantverksbyn (© **0248/102-30**). Be warned in advance that there's no elevator and the stairs are steep. Admission is 20SEK ($2.60) for adults, 5SEK (65¢) for children 7 to 15. On the premises are a coffee shop and a souvenir stand. The complex is open only from May 1 to September 6 daily from 10am to 5pm.

Gammelgården ★★ (© **0248/514-45**) is an antique Dalarna farmstead whose pastures and architecture evoke the 19th century. The hours are erratic—basically, it's open whenever a farm resident is able to conduct a tour—so it's important to phone in advance. Upon prior notification, visits can be arranged throughout the year, but regular scheduling is most likely between mid-June and mid-August daily from noon to 5pm. Admission is 20SEK ($2.60). To reach Gammelgården from the center of Rättvik, 1.5km (1 mile) north of town along route 70, follow the signs pointing to Mora.

If you're interested in art, you can visit the artists' village (established by the Swedish artist Sören Erikson) at **Rättviks Hantverksby,** Gårdebyn (© **0248/ 302-50**).

WHERE TO STAY
EXPENSIVE
Hotel Lerdalshöjden ★ *Finds*   Near the top of a hill overlooking Rättvik, a 10-minute walk north of the lake, this building is a stylish renovation of a turn-of-the-20th-century hotel. The only remaining part of the original is the **Lerdalshöjden Restaurant** (see "Where to Dine," below). The guest rooms are well furnished and maintained. They have modern accessories and good-size bathrooms equipped with shower units. All rooms are nonsmoking.

S-795 22 Rättvik. © **0248/511-50.** Fax 0248/511-77. 95 units. 950SEK–1,050SEK ($124–$137) double; 1,700SEK ($221) suite. Rates include breakfast. DC, MC, V. Free parking. Bus: 58 or 70. **Amenities:** Restaurant; bar; fitness center; sauna; limited room service; laundry service; dry cleaning. *In room:* TV.

INEXPENSIVE
Hotel Gärdebygården *Value*   This hotel, off Storgaten in the town center, is a very good value. It opened in 1906 and was renovated in 1995. It lies within a short walk of the lake, and the hotel has expanded to include a trio of outlying buildings. The comfortable rooms are sedately outfitted, with conservative furniture and good firm beds, but the bathrooms with shower units are very small. Some units have a view of the lake. The big breakfast is almost like a Swedish smorgasbord. Some nights are devoted to communal sing-alongs. Cross-country ski trails and jogging paths are a short distance away.

S-795 36 Rättvik. © **0248/30250.** Fax 0248/30660. 87 units. 850SEK ($111) double. Rates include breakfast. MC, V. Free parking. Bus: 58 or 70. **Amenities:** Restaurant; bar; laundry service; dry cleaning. *In room:* TV, minibar, hair dryer.

WHERE TO DINE
Lerdalshöjden SWEDISH   This summer-only restaurant is the only original section remaining in the turn-of-the-20th-century hotel. It has long been a favorite with lake-district locals. They like its traditional, tasty Swedish home-style cooking, including fresh fish and beef dishes. Try steak tartare with bleak (a freshwater fish) roe, or fried ptarmigan with red-currant sauce.

If a hungry visitor arrives off season, he or she is often referred to the **Green Hotel** (© **0248/502-50**), signposted from the center of town and lying less than a kilometer (about ½ mile) away. This traditional hotel dates from the 1600s, when it first opened as an inn. Additional rooms were added in the 1960s. With breakfast and dinner included, charges year-round are around 1,000SEK ($130).

In the Lerdalshöjden Hotel. © **0248/511-50.** Reservations recommended. Fixed-price menu 295SEK ($31). DC, MC, V. Daily noon–2pm and 6–9pm. Closed Aug 16–June 14.

8 Mora (★★

45km (28 miles) W of Rättvik, 328km (204 miles) NW of Stockholm

In Upper Dalarna, between Lake Orsa and Lake Siljan, the provincial town of Mora is our final major stopover in the province. Summer travelers find this business and residential center a good base for exploring the district.

Mora was the village where Gustavus Vasa rallied the peasants in Sweden's 16th-century war against Danish rule. Every year in March, this event is commemorated by the 80km (50-mile) Vasa Race.

ESSENTIALS

GETTING THERE By Plane You can fly from Stockholm on **European Executive Express** (✆ 08/593-631-31); there are two flights per day Monday to Friday, and the flight time is 50 minutes. The airport (✆ 0250/301-75) is about 6.5km (4 miles) from the center; taxis meet arriving flights.

By Train There's direct rail service daily from Stockholm (trip time: 4 hr.). For information and schedules, call ✆ 771/75-75-75.

By Bus There are weekend buses leaving from Stockholm's Central Station for the 4¼-hour trip. Contact **Swebus Vasatrafik** at ✆ 0200/21818.

By Boat The *Gustaf Wasa* (see "Essentials," in the "Leksand" section, earlier in this chapter) travels between Mora and Leksand. The boat departs Leksand in the afternoon and leaves Mora at 3pm on Monday. The round-trip cost is 120SEK ($16) for adults and 60SEK ($7.80) for children. Call ✆ 010/252-32-92 for information and reservations.

By Car From Rättvik, continue around Lake Siljan on Route 70 to Mora.

VISITOR INFORMATION Contact the **Mora Turistbyrå,** Angbåtskajen (✆ 0250/59-20-20; www.siljan.se). It's open from June 15 to August 31 Monday through Friday 10am to 7pm, and Saturday and Sunday 10am to 5pm; September 1 to June 14, Monday to Friday 10am to 5pm.

SEEING THE SIGHTS

Mora is home to a **Santa complex** (✆ 0250/287-70), which features Santa's house and factory. Visitors can meet Santa and see his helpers making and wrapping presents for children all over the world, and children can enroll in Santa School and participate in troll and treasure hunts.

Mora also was the hometown of Anders Zorn (1860–1920), Sweden's most famous painter, and all of the town's top sights are associated with him. The first, **Lisselby,** is an area near the Zorn Museum made up of old houses that now are used as arts and crafts studios and boutiques.

Zornmuseet (Zorn Museum) ★★ This museum displays not only a wide array of the artist's own works (among them, *Midnight*), but paintings from his private collection—including works by Prince Eugen and Carl Larsson, also of Dalarna. Works by major foreign artists (sculptures by Kai Nielsen of Denmark and etchings by Rembrandt) also are exhibited, as well as rural art and handicrafts of Dalarna.

Vasagatan 36. ✆ 0250/592-310. Admission 40SEK ($5.20) adults, 2SEK (25¢) children 7–15. Mid-May to Aug Mon–Sat 9am–5pm, Sun 11am–5pm; Sept to mid-May Mon–Sat noon–5pm, Sun 1–5pm.

Zornsgården ★★ The artist's former home, adjoining the museum, has been left just as it was when Mrs. Zorn died in 1942. Its chief attraction, aside from the paintings displayed, is Zorn's personally designed Great Hall on the top floor.

Vasagatan 36. ⓒ **0250/592-310**. Admission 50SEK ($6.50) adults, 15SEK ($1.95) children 7–15. Mid-June to Aug Mon–Sat 10am–5pm, Sun 11am–5pm; Sept to mid-June Mon–Sat noon–5pm, Sun 1–5pm. Full tours of the house are conducted by guides at noon, 1, 2, and 3pm (in summer every 30 min.).

NEARBY SHOPPING IN NUSNÄS

In Nusnäs, about 9.5km (6 miles) southeast of Mora, you can watch the famous Dalarna horse *(dalahäst)* being made. You're free to walk around the workshops watching the craftspeople at work, and the finished products can be purchased at a shop on the premises. They also sell wooden shoes and other crafts items. **Nils Olsson Hemslöjd** (ⓒ **0250/372-00**) is open from June to mid-August Monday to Friday 8am to 6pm, and Saturday and Sunday 9am to 5pm; and from mid-August to May Monday to Friday 8am to 5pm, and Saturday 10am to 2pm. To find Nusnäs, take the signposted main road east from Mora, turning off to the right at Farnas. From Mora, bus no. 108 also runs to Nusnäs.

WHERE TO STAY

First Hotel Mora ⭐   The Mora is in the center of town across from the lakefront, a minute's walk from the tourist bureau. Renovations over the years have added sun terraces and glassed-in verandas. The interior is tastefully decorated with bright colors. All accommodations have comfortable furniture, including good beds and ample bathrooms equipped with shower units.

Strandgatan 12, S-792 00 Mora. ⓒ **800/528-1234** in the U.S. and Canada, or 0250/59-26-50. Fax 0250/ 189-81. www.firsthotels.com. 141 units. Sun–Thurs 1,345SEK ($175) double, 1,495SEK ($194) suite; Fri–Sat 896SEK ($116) double, 996SEK ($129) suite. Rates include breakfast. AE, DC, MC, V. Parking 70SEK ($9.10) in the garage, free outdoors. **Amenities:** Restaurant; bar; indoor pool; spa; sauna; limited room service; laundry service; dry cleaning; nonsmoking rooms; rooms for those w/limited mobility. *In room:* TV, dataport, safe.

Hotel Mora Parken ⭐ *Finds*   Although it lies within a 2-minute drive from the center of Mora, you'll get the impression that you're deep in the Swedish wilderness here, thanks to this hotel's location within a forested park, midway between a pond and the banks of the river Västerdal. Laid out in a low-slung, rustic design with a steeply peaked roof and lots of exposed wood, it was built in 1976 as a restaurant and expanded in 1982 into the sports-conscious establishment you see today. Accommodations are woodsy, simple, and uncomplicated, and although comfortable, far from being particularly plush. Each room has a neatly kept bathroom with a shower unit. This seems to suit the participants in the many conventions held here, who enjoy rowing boats and canoes and swimming in the nearby pond, hiking in the surrounding forest, and attending meals in the restaurants. The restaurant serves breakfast and lunch.

Pavkuagenl, S-792 25 Mora. ⓒ **0250/276-00**. Fax 0250/276-01. www.moraparken.se. 75 units. Mid-June to mid-Aug and Fri–Sun year-round 800SEK ($104) double; rest of year 1,050SEK ($137) double. Rates include breakfast. AE, DC, MC, V. Free parking. **Amenities:** Restaurant; bar; sauna; laundry service; dry cleaning; nonsmoking rooms; rooms for those w/limited mobility. *In room:* TV.

WHERE TO DINE

Terrassen ⭐ SWEDISH   One of the finest dining rooms in the area, this is a good bet for a meal even if you aren't staying at the hotel. Fresh produce is used whenever possible, and fresh fish and Swedish beef dishes are featured. You might begin with herring or a freshly made salad. Service is polite and efficient.

In the First Resort Mora, Strandgatan 12. ⓒ **0250/59-26-50**. Reservations recommended. Main courses 80SEK–191SEK ($10–$25). AE, DC, MC, V. Mon–Sat 6–9pm.

11

The Bothnian Coast

North of Stockholm, Sweden's east coast opens onto Bottenhavet, or the Gulf of Bothnia. Russia made many incursions here in the 18th century, devastating the land and often burning the towns. Many other towns were destroyed by natural fires, then quickly rebuilt with much broader streets to prevent the spread of fires in the future. However, many old wooden houses remain in such towns as Gävle and Hudiksvall.

Just south of the Arctic Circle, the geographical position of the area suggests a climate that can be daunting; the winters certainly are harsh, with temperatures often falling below freezing. However, the summer months, with their 24-hour-a-day sunshine, can be idyllic (if you disregard the mosquitoes). Most of the population here is concentrated in certain areas, such as in the two coastal cities of Umeå and Skellefteå. The activity of these cities contrasts with the utter tranquillity of the countryside west of the coastline, where there may be as few as four inhabitants per square kilometer. At times you'll feel you have the sparsely populated interior all to yourself.

The chief attraction of the Bothnian Coast is the stretch known as the High Coast or Höga Kusten, a 145km (90-mile) landmass of jagged coastline and rocky hills lying between Härnösand and Örnsköldsvik. The land is a combination of thousands of small lakes, wild rivers, and unspoiled coastlines, as well as vast forests of pine and spruce, high mountains, and low farmlands. In summertime, the islands and shallow sandy beaches are popular places for excursions, and many Swedes maintain summer homes in the area. The brand-new E4 expressway takes you right along the coast to all the towns recommended in this chapter.

1 Gävle

180km (112 miles) NW of Stockholm, 109km (68 miles) NW of Uppsala

The capital of the province of Gästrikland, Gävle has a population of 85,000 and is a major port for the shipment of ore and timber from the nearby mining regions. It can be your gateway to the Bothnian Coast.

Pronounced *Yerv*-le, it is the southernmost town of Norrland, a region making up two-thirds of the landmass of Sweden.

An old city, Gävle was granted its town charter in 1446, although you'd never know it today in this modern city of broad squares, wide avenues, and rather monumental buildings (at least by the standards of northern Sweden).

A fire swept across Gävle in 1869, virtually destroying the city. The place you see before you is the result of replanning in the wake of the disaster.

ESSENTIALS

GETTING THERE **By Train** Gävle is on a major rail line between Stockholm and the north (trip time is 2 hr.). For schedules, call © **0771/75-75-75.** Trains from Stockholm go through Uppsala, the university city.

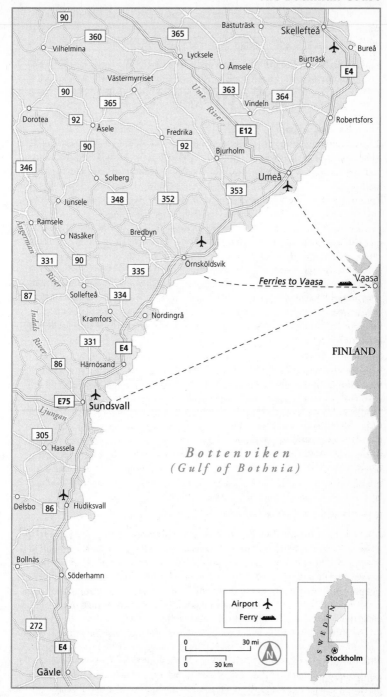

90
360
365
Bastuträsk ○
Skellefteå
○ Vilhelmina
240
Lycksele
Burträsk
○ Bureå
Västermyrriset
○ Åmsele
E4
90
363
Vindeln
364
365
○ Dorotea
92
○ Åsele
Fredrika
○ Robertsfors
90
92
Bjurholm
E12
346
○ Solberg
Umeå
348
352
353
○ Junsele
Ramsele
Bredbyn
331
90
Näsåker
335
Örnsköldsvik
Ferries to Vaasa
Vaasa
87
Sollefteå
334
Kramfors
○ Nordingrå
FINLAND
331
E4
86
Härnösand ○
E75
Sundsvall
305
○ Hassela
Bottenviken
(Gulf of Bothnia)
○ Delsbo
86
○ Hudiksvall
Bollnäs
○
○ Söderhamn
Airport ✈
Ferry ⛴
272
0   30 mi
0   30 km
E4
Gävle ○
S W E D E N
⊛ Stockholm

By Bus   There also is bus service between Uppsala and Gävle. For information, call © **0200/218218.**

By Car   From Uppsala, continue northwest into Gävle.

VISITOR INFORMATION   The **Gävle Tourist Office** is at Drottninggatan 37 (© **026/14-74-30**), open June to August Monday to Friday 9am to 6pm. Off-season hours are Monday to Friday 9am to 5pm. The tourist office is located close to the train station.

SEEING THE SIGHTS

If it's a summery, sunny day, consider a boat tour to the little island of **Limön** 🖈, which is part of an archipelago. For 40SEK ($3.20) per one-way ticket, the tourist office will book you on the tour. Limön has a nature trail and a mass grave and memorial to 19th-century sailors who went down at sea here. Boats depart from the quay at Södra Skeppsbron. Call © **026/14-74-30** for information and bookings.

The major attraction here is **Gamla Gefle,** a tiny section of old Gävle that escaped the disastrous fire in 1869 that destroyed most of the town. There really isn't a lot left of it, so you can imagine just how raging the fire must have been. You can still walk along some of the old cobblestone streets, especially Nedre Bergsgränd, Bergsgränd, and Övre Bergsgatan, which will give you some idea of what ancient Gävle must have looked like. In summer, these streets can be a delight, as homeowners fill their window boxes with flowers, especially geraniums. Most of the old wooden cottages are painted in pastels. Gamla Gefle lies south of the modern city.

Joe Hill Garden   This curiosity in Old Town was the birthplace of Johan Emanuel Hägglund in 1879. Changing his name to Joe Hill, he emigrated to the United States in 1902. In time, he became a working-class hero and a U.S. union organizer. His speeches became rallying cries to his comrades in the Industrial Workers of the World (Wobblies) and he even wrote folk songs that inspired underpaid laborers. However, in 1915, company bosses in Salt Lake City framed him for murder to remove him from the scene as an effective labor organizer. A jury found him guilty and he was executed. The scheme later was revealed, but the actual court process of exoneration never took place. The museum here is devoted to his legacy, including personal mementos. You can even see the telegram announcing his execution.

At Nedre Bergsgatan 28, Gamla Gefle. © 026/61-34-25. Free admission. June–Aug daily 9am–4pm.

Gävleborg County Museum 🖈 *Finds*   This very intriguing provincial museum is one of northern Sweden's best; its collection is a virtual textbook of Swedish art from the 17th century to the 1990s. Some of the country's best-known painters are represented: Alexander Roslin, Marcus Larsson, Ernst Josephsson, Carl Larsson, Sigrid Hjèrten, Peter Tillberg, Lena Cronqvist, Peter Dahl, Ernst Billgren, Ebba Matz, and Bianca Maria Barmen, among others. The collection is continually enlarged with new works.

The museum is rich in other exhibits as well, including some artifacts that date from the Stone Age and the Viking era. Some of the space is devoted to the 19th century, the glory days of Gävle when large ships sailed far up the river carrying cargo from all over the world. Exhibitions include pictures of the fire that destroyed Gävle, ships, and the re-creation of the interior of a middle-class family house.

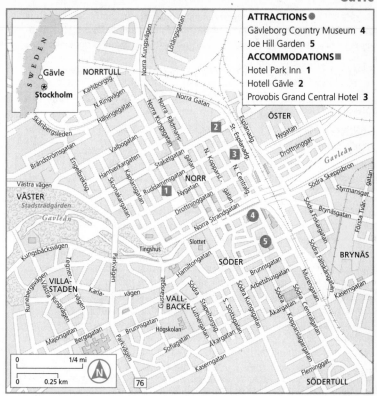

ATTRACTIONS ●
Gävleborg Country Museum **4**
Joe Hill Garden **5**
ACCOMMODATIONS ■
Hotel Park Inn **1**
Hotell Gävle **2**
Provobis Grand Central Hotel **3**

Gunnar Cyrén, the internationally known designer of glassware, lives in Gävle. The museum has the largest collection of objects by this craftsman. You can see sets of his glass, his art glassware, and even utility goods he designed in plastic and stainless steel. Look for the set of glass he designed especially for the 90th anniversary of the Nobel Prize awards in 1991.

Länsmuséet Gävleborg, Södra Strandgatan 20 (the other side of Gamla Gefle, on a canal). ℂ 026/65-56-00. Admission 40SEK ($5). June–Aug Mon–Fri 10am–4pm, Sat–Sun noon–4pm; Sept–May Tues and Thurs–Fri 10am–4pm, Wed 10am–9pm, Sat–Sun noon–4pm. Closed Dec 24, 25, and 31.

WHERE TO STAY

Hotell Gävle   One of the least pretentious hotels in town occupies a simple, brick-fronted building that's less than a 5-minute walk from the railway station. Inside you'll find a family-managed hotel that maintains lobby hours from 6am to 11pm Sunday to Thursday, Friday and Saturday 24 hours a day. (If you plan on arriving after the lobby is locked, someone will tell you the security code for the front door and make a key available to you if you phone in advance with details of your arrival time.) Bedrooms are artfully outfitted in tones of off-white and brown, accented with touches of mahogany and walnut, with small bathrooms with a tub or shower.

Staketgatan 44, S-803 11 Gävle. ℂ 026/-66-51-00. Fax 026/51-75-10. www.hotellgavle.se. 50 units. Mid-June to mid-Aug and Fri–Sat year-round 710SEK ($89) double; rest of year 1,175SEK ($147) double. Rates include breakfast. AE, DC, MC, V. Free parking. **Amenities:** Breakfast room; sauna. *In room:* TV, hair dryer.

Hotel Park Inn ⭐   This is one of the most modern and comfortable hotels in town, and it lies across the street from the main square. Designed with buff-colored brick and big windows, it's clean, well managed, and a popular choice for many of the region's business travelers. Inside, the lavish use of autumn tones warms and softens the glossy look of the marble and stone that sheathe many of the floors and walls of the public areas. Bedrooms are calm, quiet, comfortable, and soothing, and the small bathrooms come with a tub or shower. *Note:* This hotel is a member of Winn Hotels.

Norra Slottsgatan 9, P.O. Box 1417, S-801 38 Gävle. © 026/647000. Fax 026/64-70-09. www.software hotels.se. 200 units. Mid-June to mid-Aug and Fri–Sat year-round 870SEK ($109) double; rest of year 1,420SEK ($178) double; 2,750SEK ($344) suite. Rates include buffet breakfast. AE, DC, MC, V. Parking 100SEK ($13). **Amenities:** Restaurant; bar; indoor heated pool; sauna; room service (7am–10pm); laundry service; dry cleaning; nonsmoking rooms; rooms for those w/limited mobility. *In room:* TV, dataport (in some), minibar, hair dryer, trouser press.

Scandic Grand Central   This hotel was built in a smaller version in 1896, about the time that the railway tracks first connected Gävle with the rest of Europe. It was configured from the beginning as a site convenient to the railway station and was designed in a brassy, Belle Epoque motif reminiscent of a resort along the southern coast of England. In the 1960s it was massively expanded with new wings. Today, regardless of their position within the various wings of this hotel, rooms deliberately emulate the old-fashioned, nostalgic decor that was part of the establishment from the beginning. Expect modern comforts combined with heavy doses of turn-of-the-20th-century details in the forms of reproduction Victorian-era sofas, leather armchairs, busy patterns, and rich, dark colors. The bathrooms are small but perfectly efficient and have tub/showers.

Nygatan 45, P.O. Box 317, S-801 04 Gävle. © 026/49-58-400. Fax 026/49-58-411. www.scandic-hotels.com. 200 units. Mid-June to mid-Aug and Fri–Sat year-round 890SEK ($111) double, 1,190SEK ($149) suite; rest of year 1,450SEK ($181) double, 1,870SEK ($234) suite. Rates include buffet breakfast. AE, DC, MC, V. Parking 90SEK ($11). **Amenities:** Restaurant; bar; gym; sauna; room service (day service); laundry service; dry cleaning; nonsmoking rooms; 1 room for those w/limited mobility. *In room:* TV, dataport (in some) minibar, hair dryer, iron/ironing board, safe, trouser press.

WHERE TO DINE

Dionisios INTERNATIONAL/GREEK   This is a highly appealing restaurant whose maritime decor evokes the heady seafaring days of Gävle's supremacy as a trading center and seaport. The three founding partners, Zirre, Eva, and Tommy, named the place for their favorite Greek god. Surrounded by collections of old photographs and scaled-down model ships, you can order well-prepared platters whose portions are generous and flavorful. Worthy starters include a savory portion of grilled Cypriot cheese with Mediterranean herbs, a shrimp cocktail presented in a dish shaped like a boat, or a bowl of steaming lobster soup. Main courses might include halibut with snow peas and shrimp, marinated pork chops with chanterelles and gratin of potatoes, filet mignon with Madeira sauce, or salmon steak with spinach and lemon-flavored butter sauce.

Norra Kopmangatan 12B. © 026/10-60-65. Reservations recommended. Main courses 79SEK–229SEK ($9.90–$29). AE, MC, V. Daily 11am–11pm.

Matilda's ⭐ INTERNATIONAL   The most celebrated restaurant in Gävle occupies two small rooms of a 1950s-era building in the town center, each of which is outfitted in tones of green and white with touches of red. Meals are served only in the evening. Artfully positioned spotlights illuminate an open

> **Fun Fact   Coffee Country**
>
> Coffee is virtually the national drink of Sweden, in the same way a good cup of tea is the drink of England. As the home of the famous Gevalia coffee (the most northerly coffee-roasting plant in the world), Gävle is known to coffee drinkers everywhere.

kitchen whose activities seem more intense and more theatrical than at any other eatery in town. Menu items change with the season and the whim of the chef but are likely to include carpaccio of beef with olive oil, fresh basil, and grated Parmesan; a savory pie stuffed with Swedish cheddar and roe caviar; cream of shrimp soup with herbs; filet of beef with garlic-flavored cream sauce; veal filet saltimbocca; and filets of sea bass fried in butter and served with an herb-flavored cream sauce. Don't underestimate the desirability of snagging one of the 13 tables at this place: Reservations at Matilda's are more sought after than at any other restaurant in the region, so competition is intense—especially on weekends.

Timmermansgatan 23. © **026/62-53-49.** Reservations required. Main courses 109SEK–169SEK ($14–$21). AE, DC, MC, V. Mon–Thurs 5–11pm; Fri–Sat 5pm–midnight; Sun 2–9pm.

2 Söderhamn

250km (155 miles) NW of Stockholm, 71km (44 miles) NW of Gävle

An industrial port city of some 32,000 people, Söderhamn lies at the center of an archipelago of 500 islands. Storjungfrun is the largest island; the entire stretch of islands—from Furuvik in the south to Gnarpsbaden in the north—is called *Jungfrukusten,* or "Virgin Coast."

There used to be many fishing villages on these islands, but today only Skärså has an active fishing industry. The other islands now are devoted to leisure activities centered on summer cottages and pleasure boats. Depending heavily on the weather, the tourist boat M/S *Strömskär* provides trips through the islands of Söderhamn's archipelago. For information about these trips, call © **026/ 12-77-66.**

Söderhamn once was more important than it is today. Founded in 1620, it owed its early development to the achievements of Gustav II Adolf, who in 1617 won a long-standing war with the Russians. He established firm possession of a large portion of the Swedish coast. Söderhamn was ideal for development, as it stood in a safe place at the head of an 11km-long (6¾-mile) fjord.

Like Gävle, Söderhamn has suffered its share of fires. The most devastating, which destroyed virtually everything, came in 1876. After the debris was cleared, Söderhamn bounced back as a totally new town, with a grid pattern and ample parks.

ESSENTIALS

GETTING THERE   By Train   About five trains per day arrive from Stockholm. En route, each of the trains stops in both Uppsala and Gävle, picking up passengers for the continuation of the ride northward. The trip from Stockholm to Söderhamn takes 2 to 3 hours. From Uppsala it takes 1½ to 2 hours. For railway information, call © **0771/75-75-75.**

By Bus   Buses from Stockholm and Uppsala to Söderhamn are less convenient, less frequent, and slower than equivalent transits by train. Transit from Gävle takes about an hour. For bus schedule and information, call ✆ **0200/218218.**

By Car   From Gävle, continue along the coastal road, E4, into Söderhamn.

VISITOR INFORMATION   The **Söderhamn Tourist Office,** Resecentrum (✆ **0270/753-53**), is open from June to early August Monday to Friday 9am to 7pm, Saturday and Sunday noon to 5pm. At other times, it's open Monday to Friday 9am to 4pm.

SEEING THE SIGHTS

Söderhamn is a green oasis with extensive parks and flower gardens, making it a good city for long, refreshing walks. In all, some 100 plant species grow in various settings around town.

Oskarsborg Tower   For the best appreciation of the layout of the town, head for the Oskarsborg tower, which was inaugurated in 1895 by Gabriel Schöning and has become the symbol of Söderhamn. The tower is 22m (72 ft.) high and 63m (207 ft.) above sea level. From its top you can see one of the most panoramic views in the north of Sweden. In summer, a cafe is open here.

Östra Berget. Free admission. Mid-June to mid-Aug daily 9am–9pm. Follow the signs from the station along the rail tracks.

Söderhamn Museum   Söderhamn's major museum, which traces the regional history of the area, is housed in a former rifle-manufacturing workshop. You learn of Söderhamn's former role as a munitions center, when it manufactured weapons to help Sweden turn back the Russian tide and dominate northern Europe. You also can see, among other exhibits, relics from one of the town's earliest churches (no longer existing).

Oxtorgsgatan. ✆ 0270/157-91. Admission 30SEK ($3.75), free for children under 17. July to early Aug daily noon–5pm; winter months Sat–Sun noon–3pm.

OUTDOOR PURSUITS

Of course, you didn't come this far north to confine yourself to museum visits, with all the great outdoors awaiting you. The tourist office (see above) is particularly helpful in supplying information about what to see and do with Mother Nature.

The forests around Söderhamn stretch for miles and miles. Forest paths, nature reserves, and areas for rambling where you can find tranquillity abound. One good example is the **Mostigen Path,** which stretches for 17km (11 miles) east of the town center. Look for the signs adjacent to the tourist office.

Söderhamn Golf Course, Nygatan 5B (✆ **0270/281-300**), is beautifully situated on the coast, lying about 8km (5 miles) from the center of Söderhamn. It is an 18-hole, par-72 course in a particularly scenic woodland. There also is a driving range, golf shop, and clubhouse with changing rooms and a restaurant. Greens fees range from 150SEK to 300SEK ($19–$38) for 18 holes of golf, depending on the day of the week.

Fishing is popular at the mouth of the Ljusnan River, where there is a good chance of catching salmon, sea trout, and whitefish. Ten-kilo (22-lb.) "monsters" are not unheard of. The fishing waters extend over a stretch of about 8km (5 miles) between the Ljusne power station and the sea. The fishing season spans the entire year, but spring and autumn are the best periods. Fishing permits can be obtained from a vending machine at the clubhouse in Ljusne. You also can rent fishing cottages in the district. Call the above-mentioned tourist office for more information.

WHERE TO STAY

First Hotel Statt (★ *Finds*   This hotel represents one of the most unconventional pairings of new and old architecture we've seen in this part of Sweden. Its original core dates from 1880, when a dignified-looking two-story house was erected in a position about 450m (1,476 ft.) west of the Rådhus (town hall). In modern times, a series of enlargements and annexes were superimposed onto the hotel's original framework—not always with aesthetic success. The final result is a clean, respectable hotel with lots of exposed hardwood on the floors, dramatic draperies, and an overriding sense of well-maintained, no-nonsense modernity. Bedrooms are clean and warm and cozy, though somewhat banal in their decor and furnishings. Each has a private bathroom with shower.

Oxtorgsgatan 17, P.O. Box 64, SE-826 22 Söderhamn. © **0270/735-70.** Fax 0270/135-24. www.firsthotels.com. 78 units. Mid-June to mid-Aug and Fri–Sat year-round 793SEK ($99) double; rest of year 1,403SEK ($175) double; 1,603SEK ($200) suite. AE, DC, MC, V. Rates include buffet breakfast. Free parking. **Amenities:** Restaurant; bar; sauna; laundry service; dry cleaning; nonsmoking rooms; solarium; rooms for those w/limited mobility. *In room:* TV, dataport, hair dryer.

WHERE TO DINE

Stadtsrestaurang INTERNATIONAL   This restaurant is managed independently from the chain-member hotel that contains it and, as such, feels a bit more personal. The setting is proper and well laid out, with a decor that includes white linens, hardwood floors, and a sense of conservative well-being. Menu items include lots of fresh fish, usually grilled and served simply with lemon butter or hollandaise sauce; veal and chicken dishes; Swedish caviar spread on chunks of rough-textured rye bread; and chicken with a dill-flavored cream sauce. The cuisine, although flavorful, isn't very imaginative.

In the First Hotel Statt, Oxtorgsgatan 17. © **0270/414-10.** Reservations recommended. Fixed-price lunches 65SEK–100SEK ($8.15–$13); dinner main courses 150SEK–210SEK ($19–$26). AE, DC, MC, V. Mon–Sat 11am–2pm and 6–11pm.

3 Hudiksvall (★

300km (186 miles) NW of Stockholm, 52km (32 miles) NW of Söderhamn, 129km (80 miles) N of Gävle

With a population of 20,000, Hudiksvall is much smaller than Söderhamn, but many visitors find it more charming. It is the oldest town in Sweden north of Gävle, dating from 1582. Originally it grew up around Lillfjärden Bay at the mouth of the Hornån River, but in the early 1600s when the sea receded, Hudiksvall was forced to move closer to the water. Even today one is always conscious of the sea: The harbor is right in the town center, and locals have always survived by fishing and trade.

The town's heritage is visible in the typical fishermen's cottages along the Strömmingssundet Sound, the well-preserved wooden buildings of the Fiskarstan, and the area of town around Lilla Kyrkogatan.

Historically, Hudiksvall has been subject to attack, especially in the wars between Sweden and Russia. It came under particular assault in 1721 when virtually half the buildings here were razed to the ground.

Despite Hudiksvall's long history, the town also is very modern, with a lot of amenities and stores for such a small place. This is because it serves as the commercial center for the whole of northern Hälsingland, and people who live in remote wildernesses drive for miles and miles to come into town and shop.

In Sweden, Hudiksvall once was known as Glada Hudik, or "Lively Hudiksvall," a phrase coined in the mid–19th century, in the heyday of the pleasure-seeking timber barons of the district. Today its charming streets and beautiful old buildings are still lively in summer.

ESSENTIALS

GETTING THERE   By Train   Depending on the season and the route you take, there are between four and eight trains per day between Gävle and Hudiksval, and between six and seven per day from Stockholm and from Södermalm, both of which follow the same rail lines. Travel time from Södermalm is around 40 minutes, from Gävle between 60 and 75 minutes, and from Stockholm between 2½ and 3 hours. For rail schedules and fares, call ℂ **0771/75-75-75.**

By Bus   Bus travel from Stockholm and Gävle to Hudiksval is less convenient, and slower, than rail travel; but in some instances, especially on weekends, it's a bit cheaper. For bus schedules and fares from all points of Sweden into Hudiksval, call ℂ **0200/218218.**

By Car   From Söderhamn, our last stopover, follow E4 northwest.

VISITOR INFORMATION   The **Hudiksvalls Turistbyrå,** Storgatan 33 (ℂ **0650/191-00;** www.hudiksvall.se/turism), is open from mid-June to mid-August Monday to Friday 9am to 7pm, Saturday 10am to 6pm, and Sunday noon to 6pm. Otherwise, hours are Monday to Friday 9am to 4pm.

SEEING THE SIGHTS

An old town, Hudiksvall has a proud architectural heritage. As you're walking around town, examples worth seeking out include **Hantverksgården,** Störgutan 44, with its unique terraces overlooking Hudiksvallsfjärden Bay, and the **Hudiksvall Theater,** on Västra Tullgatan (ℂ **0650/19355**), formerly a spa.

Lillfjärden is an oasis in the heart of Hudiksvall. This former inlet from the sea was the site of the town's first harbor. Today it is a lake with a diverse bird life, an ideal place for a lovely walk.

The best place to go on a summer day is the small old harbor called Möljen, where locals head to soak up the precious (and fleeting) sunshine. Old fishermen's cottages and storefronts line this harbor. Here an assortment of shops, handicraft studios, and other retail outlets occupy what formerly were warehouses.

Bigger than Möljen, and also an interesting district to explore, **Fiskarstan** ✪, or Fishermen's Town, is reached by going down Storgatan behind the First Hotel Statt. Here you will find the best examples of late-18th- and 19th-century architecture—sometimes called "imperial architecture." Buildings here are wood paneled, and the cobblestone streets are narrow. Fishermen and their families lived here in little houses built close to each other, which helped break the bitter winds of winter. As you walk along the streets in summer, you'll see window boxes planted with brightly colored flowers.

If you'd like to learn something about the artistic and cultural history of the area, head for the **Halsingland Museum,** Storgatan 31 (ℂ **0650/196-00**). It's open Monday noon to 4pm, Tuesday to Friday 9am to 4pm (Wed until 8pm), and Saturday 11am to 3pm, charging no admission. Housed in a former bank, the museum displays finds from various archaeological digs in the area. Excavations uncovered an Iron Age burial site and a Malsta runic stone that was inscribed with upright strokes. Local medieval wood carving also is displayed, most of the work by Haaken Gulleson, who was the most distinguished artisan in this form. Boats, ship models, and fishing equipment reveal how the locals earned their livelihood. On the second floor is a display of peasant art collections including sledges, textiles, chests, and clocks, along with folkloric costumes. Middle-class interiors from the late 18th and 19th centuries are re-created. The paintings of John Sten hold particular interest. This local son dabbled in an extremely decorative and fanciful style.

EXPLORING THE ARCHIPELAGO

The **archipelago** ★★ around Hudiksvall is one of the most beautiful along the coast of northern Sweden. At the turn of the 20th century, more than 50 fishing villages and harbors thrived in the Hudiksvall archipelago. Today only a few full-time fishermen make their living here. Most of the old fishing villages now are filled in the summer with Swedes from other areas—often from Stockholm—who use fishers' cottages as summer homes.

In the northern part of the archipelago, the Hornslandet peninsula protrudes into the sea like a giant breakwater. Visitors will find two fishing villages on the peninsula—**Hölick** and **Kuggörarna.** You can bathe in the sea, fish in excellent waters, enjoy a variety of hikes, or visit an ancient cave. This is a naturalist's paradise, with many unique species of flora and fauna. Several areas now come under the protection of nature reserves.

The tourist office (see above) serves as a clearinghouse for all tours. Contact them for maps as well as the most up-to-date, thorough information available for regional excursions.

OUTDOOR PURSUITS

The area around Hudiksvall offers many excellent footpaths for **hiking.** A network of forest roads gives access to the paths at several points, so you can choose any length of walk you wish. You can camp along the way in the meager shelters provided (basically just sheds to protect you from heavy downpours). In theory, trails are open to winter hikers, although violent storms sometimes make hiking impossible. Maps and route descriptions are available at the tourist office (see above).

Sjuvallsleden Path ★ is a hilly path passing some of the highest peaks in Hälsingland (the province in which both Söderhamn and Hudiksvall lie). The path is 29km (18 miles) long and starts at the Ofärne activity center in Forsa, a small town lying immediately west of Hudiksvall. It takes you past seven traditional hill farms south of the Dellen lakes, finishing in Delsbo, a town northwest of Hudiksvall. Another path from Hudiksvall connects with it at Ofärne so you can walk all the way from Hudiksvall to the settlement at Delsbo, a distance of some 48km (30 miles).

The **Kolarstigen Path** is 32km (20 miles) long and fairly hilly; it takes you through the woods north of North Dellen lake, between Sörgimma and Hallboviken, passing six different hill routes. Finally, **Kajvallsleden Path** is 44km (27 miles) long, running between Delsbo and Ljusdal. It connects Sjuvallsleden and Ljusnanleden, which together constitute a footpath some 129km (80 miles) long, though undulating in places.

The majesty of the surrounding lakes and waterways makes them worthy places to go canoeing. Although other sites are closer to town, the best equipped of the lot is **Svågadalens,** Vildmarkscenter, Bjuråker (© **0653/310-22** or 070/687-79-56). Located in the isolated hamlet of Bjuråker, 65km (40 miles) northwest of Hudiksvall, they rent canoes during the summer months for 280SEK ($35) per day, plus the cost of any transportation for you and the canoe to the surrounding lakes and rivers. The staff there is well versed in recommending venues and itineraries that cover the surrounding lakes. For a fee of between 100SEK and 150SEK ($13–$19), they'll even meet you at prearranged times to transport you across land as a means of allowing you to explore more than one body of water during any given day or week. An equivalent rental outfit that's not as well rounded, but closer to Hudiksvall, is **Ankarmons Camping,** Iggesund (© **0650/20505**), which lies 9.5km (6 miles) south of Hudiksvall, and charges 100SEK to 150SEK ($13–$19) for a day's canoe rental.

Seven different **fishing** areas offer the keen fisherman a variety of waters, from lakes and rivers to stocked streams. You may fish freely in the sea without a permit, as long as you use a rod and line, rather than spear or net. Perch, pike, whitefish, salmon, grayling, Baltic herring, and sea trout are among your possible catches. You need a permit, however, to fish in local lakes and rivers. The tourist office has all the necessary information about fishing in the waters around Hudiksvall. Fishing permits also are on sale here; they range in price from 45SEK to 60SEK ($5.65–$7.50) each, depending on where you want to fish and what species are in season at the time.

SHOPPING

Many artists and craftspeople live and work in and around Hudiksvall, particularly on the shores of the beautiful Dellen lakes. Local crafts include woodcarving from the local pine and spruces, ceramics, leather items, and tinwork. The hotels recommended in this chapter each maintain small-scale kiosks providing a representative sampling of these goods. The tourist office (see above) will give you further details of galleries and exhibitions that may be open at the time of your visit.

WHERE TO STAY

First Hotel Statt ⚐ Set less than a kilometer (about ½ mile) north of the city's railway station, this is the grandest, most stately hotel in town. It was originally built in 1878 as a neoclassical villa, but in 1993, a team of entrepreneurs radically upgraded and enlarged its symmetrical, ocher-colored original core. Today, amid lawns and gardens, you'll find a gracefully integrated combination of new and old architecture, wherein the high ceilings and airiness of the original have been preserved, albeit with modern interior lines and lots of new marble floors and streamlined walls. Rooms in the establishment's original core are smaller, a bit less elegant, and cheaper than those in the newer sections. Each contains modern furniture that's well maintained, cozy, and appropriate to this hotel's role as a site for corporate conventions. Most rooms have views overlooking the sea. Bathrooms are rather small, containing showers or tubs.

Live orchestras sometimes play in the hotel's restaurant, attracting a crowd of dance enthusiasts, especially on Saturday nights. First Hotel Statt cuisine is a combination of international dishes and regional specialties using market-fresh ingredients.

Storgatan 36, P.O. Box 55, S-824 22 Hudiksvaal. © **0650/150-60.** Fax 0650/960-95. www.firsthotels.com. 106 units. Mid-June to mid-Aug and Fri–Sat year-round 854SEK ($107) double; rest of year 1,404SEK ($176) double; 1,695SEK ($212) suite. AE, DC, MC, V. Parking 75SEK ($9.40). **Amenities:** Restaurant; bar; indoor heated pool; exercise room; sauna; room service (7am–10pm); babysitting; laundry service; dry cleaning; nonsmoking rooms; solarium; rooms for those w/limited mobility. *In room:* TV, dataport, hair dryer, iron/ironing board.

Hotell Hudik ⭐ *(Finds)* The most appealing hotel in town wins approval with its personal service and thoughtful extras. Originally built of red brick around 1960, it was enlarged in 1980. Today, in its location in the town center near the hospital and the police station, it offers cozy bedrooms that are tastefully decorated and furnished, and spotlessly maintained. Rooms occasionally have themes, such as the Sailor's Room with a nautical decor. Bathrooms have tub/showers and adequate shelf space.

Norra Kyrkogatan 11, S-824 00 Hudiksvall. ℰ 0650/5410-00. Fax 0650/541-050. 53 units. Mid-June to early Aug and Fri–Sat year-round 795SEK ($99) double; rest of year 1,295SEK ($162) double. AE, DC, MC, V. Free parking. **Amenities:** Jacuzzi; sauna; laundry service; dry cleaning; nonsmoking rooms. *In room:* TV, minibar, hair dryer, safe.

WHERE TO DINE

Restaurant Cardinal ⭐ *(Finds)* INTERNATIONAL   On first glance, you may think you've entered an informal and sometimes boisterous Irish pub where the focus is exclusively on the bar trade. But don't be fooled because this place takes its food and service seriously—often to the point that hotel receptionists throughout Hudiksvall recommend it as the most appealing restaurant in town. Within a dark-green and dark-red decor inspired by the pubs of Ireland, you can order a medley of perfectly prepared fresh fish, chicken, steak, and pork dishes offered in combinations such as "black and white" filets (pork and filet steak served on the same platter with béarnaise, truffles, and mushroom sauce), smoked salmon stuffed with shrimp in a mayonnaise sauce, and filet Oscar (filets of pork with crabmeat, lemon, and béarnaise sauce).

Storgatan 24. ℰ 0650/10505. Reservations recommended. Fixed-price lunches (11am–2pm) 78SEK–99SEK ($9.75–$12); dinner main courses 109SEK–178SEK ($14–$22). AE, DC, MC, V. Daily 11am–10pm.

4 Sundsvall

390km (242 miles) NW of Stockholm, 243km (151 miles) NW of Oslo

A fire on Midsummer's Day in 1888 that ravaged old Sundsvall and left 9,000 residents homeless induced wealthy timber barons from the region's forests and sawmills to rebuild the town in stone to ensure that it would never again burn to the ground. Today this capital of the tiny province of Medelpad is known as "Stone City," and the buildings in the heart of Sundsvall appear just as they did at the end of the 19th century.

Thanks to a location between the great rivers Ljungan and Indalsälv, and through the rise of forestry in the 19th century, Sundsvall has long been a commercial center and one of the most important industrial areas in the north of Sweden. It has an enormous production of wood pulp, its chief commodity. It first received its town charter in 1624, a grant from Gustavus Adolphus, and its first major disaster occurred in 1721 when invading Russian troops burned it to the ground. Sundsvall then languished in obscurity until the 19th century, when timber barons moved in and launched it on the road to prosperity.

Just north of Sundsvall, Timrå is a coastal town known for its site at the river delta of Indalsälven. The delta was formed 200 years ago when an adventurous local legend, Wild Hussen, drained Ragundasjön lake and in the process altered the course of the river. The delta area offers a wide variety of flora, fish, and bird life. Timrå also is the site of the Sundsvall-Härnösand Airport-Milanda. A combined population of 115,000 makes the Sundsvall/Timrå region northern Sweden's most densely populated.

ESSENTIALS

GETTING THERE   By Plane   SAS (℗ **0770/727-727**) is the only carrier flying into Sundsvall; from Stockholm, there are nine nonstop flights a day, each taking about an hour. Planes land at the Sundsvall-Härnösand Airport-Midlanda. From the center of Sundsvall, at the bus station on Esplanaden, buses (each of which is marked FLYGPLATS) depart for the airport at intervals that coincide with the arrival and departure of flights.

By Train   There are about four trains a day from Gävle (trip time: 2½-hr.) and about seven trains a day from Stockholm (trip time: 5-hr.). For rail schedules, call ℗ **0771/75-75-75.**

By Bus   From both Gävle and Stockholm, there are four to five buses a day; their itineraries are a bit slower and less convenient than the trains'. For bus information, call ℗ **0200/218218.**

By Car   From Hudiksvall, continue northwest along E4.

VISITOR INFORMATION   Contact **Sundsvall Turism,** Stora Torget (℗ **060/ 61-04-50**), open from mid-June to mid-August, Monday to Friday 10am to 6pm, and Saturday 10am to 2pm. Off-season hours are Monday to Friday 11am to 5pm.

SEEING THE SIGHTS

You'll have plenty of space for walking around Sundsvall and seeing the stone structures. A broad major avenue, **Esplanaden,** cuts the grid of streets in two sections. Esplanaden itself is crossed by **Storgatan,** the broadest street in the city. The center square, **Storatorget,** is the most interesting part of the city. It's home to impromptu art exhibitions and is the site of a fresh fruit and vegetable market every Monday through Saturday, beginning at 9:30am.

At Storatorget, look at the **Gran Building** on the north site of the square. It is named for Peter Gran, a much-traveled apothecary. The entrance to the building is adorned with the town and county coats-of-arms. In the building, **Edvall's,** a jewelry shop, is the only fully intact shop interior in the town dating from the 1890s. Make sure to admire the magnificent hand-painted glass ceiling.

The town hall, or **Stadshuset,** stands on the south side of Storatorget. Built of stone in 1862, it only needed some repairs following the great fire that destroyed the town. The roof is ornamented by two groups of figures that symbolize the activities originally housed in the structure: police, jail, hotel, and rooms for celebrations. One of the groups depicts justice, blindfolded, with her scales and sword.

The town's best park, **Vängåvan,** lies northwest of Esplanaden. Its name, "gift from a friend," originated when two friends donated the land to the town in 1873. The park is dominated by a large fountain decorated with sculptures to represent the foundations of Sundsvall: commerce, shipping, industry, craftsmanship, knowledge, and wisdom. At the base of the fountain stand three bears holding the crests of Sundsvall, the county of Västernorrland, and Sweden.

Kultur Magasinet ★★ *Finds*   This "culture warehouse," which includes the museum below, is housed in a quartet of restored 19th-century warehouses. Once these warehouses were used to store flour, sugar, spices, coffee, dried fruit, and other products for the winter months when the townspeople were unable to

Sundsvall

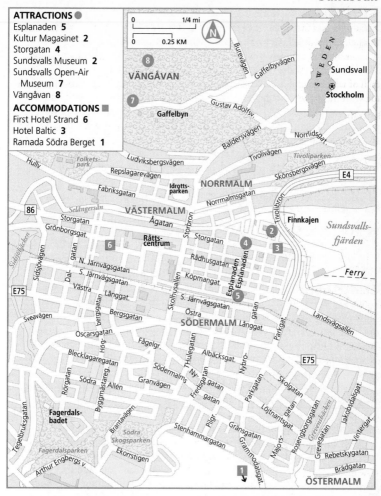

ATTRACTIONS ●
Esplanaden **5**
Kultur Magasinet **2**
Storgatan **4**
Sundsvalls Museum **2**
Sundsvalls Open-Air
  Museum **7**
Vängåvan **8**
ACCOMMODATIONS ■
First Hotel Strand **6**
Hotel Baltic **3**
Ramada Södra Berget **1**

0   1/4 mi
0   0.25 KM

VÄNGÅVAN

Gaffelbyn

SWEDEN
Sundsvall
Stockholm

Burevägen
Gaffelbyvägen
Gustav Adolfsv.
Baldersvägen
Norrlidsgat.
Tivolivägen
Tivoliparken
E4

Folkets park
Ludviksbergsvägen
Repslagarevägen
Skönsbergsvägen
Hull
Fabriksgatan
Idrotts-parken
NORRMALM
Norrmalmsgatan

86
Selångersån
VÄSTERMALM
Storgatan
Grönborgsgat.
Ågatan
Storbron
Storgatan
Tivolibron
Finnkajen
Sundsvalls-fjärden

Sidsjövägen
Dal-gatan
N. Järnvägsgatan
S. Järnvägsgatan
Västra
Långgat.
Bergsgatan
Råtts-centrum
Rådhusgatan
Köpmangat.
Skolhusallen
S. Järnvägsgatan
Östra
Esplanaden
Esplanaden
Ferry

Sidsjö-bäcken
Sveavägen
Östra bergsgatan
SÖDERMALM Långgat.
Parkgat.
Landsvägsallén

Oscarsgatan
Fågelgr.
Hög-
Blecklagaregatan
Södermalms
THulegatan
Albäcksgat.
Ny-
Nybro-
E75
Rörgatan
Södra
Allén
Granvägen
Byggmästareg.
Fredsgatan
Parkgat.
Skolgatan
gatan
Löjtnantsgat.
Rosenborgsgatan
Grevegatan
Jakobodalsgat.

Tegelbruksgatan
Fagerdals-badet
Brantavägen
Södra Skogsparken
Stenhammargatan
Pilgr.
Gränsgatan
Grammodalsgat.
Majors-
gatan
Grevenbäcken
Vintergat.
Rebetskygatan
Fagerdalsparken
Ekorrstigen
Arthur Engbergs v.
Brädgatan
1
ÖSTERMALM

E75

use the frozen waterways to buy these staples. Following its restoration, Kultur Magasinet became one of Sweden's most popular tourist attractions, drawing some 700,000 visitors annually.

The complex includes a children's cultural center, the town library, and the Café Skonerten, where you'll smell the aroma of newly baked buns and cakes. The center is also the venue for theater, lecture, debates, and speeches from writers and artists. Music—everything from folksingers to orchestras—dominates the agenda.

Parkersgatan 4, down by the harbor. © 060/19-18-00. Free admission. Mon–Thurs 10am–7pm; Fri 10am–6pm; Sat–Sun 11am–4pm.

Sundsvalls Museum   This widely varied major museum, with both permanent and temporary exhibits, is devoted to local history, handicrafts, and much more. Temporary shows tend to focus on art and photography. The museum's art collection includes works from Swedish artists of the 19th century, including Leander Engström, Arne Jones, Max Book, Birgitta Muhr, and Anders Boquist. In one section, "Sawmill Workers and Gentlemen," the Sundsvall's great timber era is re-created through models, portraits, and photographs. Another exhibit, "Sun Mountain Water," describes nature in Medelpad. "Högom Chieftain" is the name of an exhibit devoted to Norrland's richest burial site from the time of the great migrations around A.D. 500. "Town Which Transformed Itself" depicts the period between 1886 and 1891 when central Sundsvall emerged from a wooden town destroyed by fire to a European stone city with wide boulevards and richly decorated buildings. The museum also contains a reconstruction of Carl Frisendahl's Paris studio (he was a sculptor, drawer, and painter from Näsåker on the Ångerman River) and a large donation of his sculptures, sketches, and paintings.

Inside Kultur Magasinet (see above). (℃ 060/19-18-03. Admission 20SEK ($2.50) Jun–Aug; free otherwise. Mon–Thurs 10am–7pm; Fri 10am–6pm; Sat 11am–4pm.

IN NORRA & SÖDRA STADSBERGET

Sundsvall is situated in a valley between two hill towns, Norra and Södra Stadsberget. Norra is the lower of the two, 26m (85 ft.) above sea level. Here you'll find the **Sundsvall Open-Air Museum (Frilftsmuseum),** Norra Stadsberget (℃ **060/61-17-48**), which is open June to August Monday to Friday 9am to 6pm, Saturday noon to 4pm, and Sunday 11am to 4pm. Off-season hours are Monday to Friday 9am to 4pm. Admission is 20SEK ($2.50) adults, 10SEK ($1.25) children. The museum is housed in one of several old farm buildings gracing the hillside. For the children there is a farm zoo with domestic animals. More interesting for adults is the **Grankotten (Fir Cone) Restaurant,** with an outdoor summer terrace.

The hill to the south, **Södra Berget,** has developed into a center for **outdoor activities** in both summer and winter. An extensive system of trails, including Sweden's longest illuminated trail, stretches for 4km (2½ miles). The Tarzan and Bear Trails, with tunnels, lianas, and a rope bridge, offer fun for the whole family. The centerpiece of the mountain is a world-class slalom slope and a gigantic track system, the latter used by such international champions as Vladimir Smirnov. There also are numerous places to rest—cabins, cots, and cozy windbreaks in the middle of the woods. For more information, call the hotel **Södra Berget** (℃ **060/67-10-00**) or **Sidsjobacken** (℃ **060/61-09-26**), a site that helps administer the ski trails and rents ski equipment. A 1-day ski pass for unlimited use of these facilities costs 100SEK ($13).

A TRIP TO THE ISLAND OF ALNÖ

Alnö is a summer retreat with inviting beaches (and very cold waters!). Of these, **Tranviken,** on the southern tip, is the best and most popular. The island also is known for its geology; its bedrock is volcanic, with a rock type—nepheline syenite—that is found only here and in South Africa. Alnö is connected by bridge to the Swedish mainland and lies 7km (4¼ miles) east of Sundsval. Bus no. 1 makes hourly runs between Sundsval and the island's biggest hamlet, Wi, which is in the center.

Alnö Gamle Kyrka (℃ **060/55-36-50**) in Wi is by far the island's most interesting site, thanks to its origins in the 11th century. The church usually can be visited in summer daily from noon to 7pm. Other than that, the allure of Alnö derives from its rural charm and summer holiday ambience. In the winter it is drab and melancholy, and very isolated. The **Alnö Rural Community Center** is open June to August 10am to 6pm daily, presenting the Sawmill Era in its museum, along with a collection of rock samples. At the southern end of Alnö, not far from Tranviken, is the old fishing village of **Spikarna,** which has no charm beyond that of streets to wander. From Wi, catch the bus marked SPIKARNA.

SHOPPING

About a dozen craftspeople run **Myrstacken** at Nybrogatan 8 (© **060/61-06-74**), Sundsvall, selling their own work and that of others. Here you will find any number of handmade gifts, including stoneware and pottery, wooden trays and bowls, hand-woven carpets and tablecloths, and specially designed jewelry.

At **Skvaderboden,** on Norra Berget (© **060/61-17-48**), Sundsvall, you'll find, among other articles, handmade wooden replicas of that curious, imaginary beast, the *skvader.* This animal is said to be a cross between a hare and a wood-grouse cock.

Norrland's largest shopping center, and the focal point for thousands of shoppers who drive here from throughout the region, is the **IKEA-huset,** which lies in the hamlet of Birsta, 5km (3 miles) north of Sundsval. To reach it from Sundsval, drive north along Route E4, following the signs to Haparanda. The largest of more than 40 merchants within the complex is housewares and furniture giant **IKEA** (© **060/14-42-00**), whose warehouse-size premises function as Sweden's unofficial ambassador to designers, decorators, and average consumers around the world.

WHERE TO STAY

First Hotel Strand ⭐ Built of russet-colored bricks in the mid-1970s and set in the center of town within a pair of five- and six-story buildings, this hotel is a well-respected, well-planned member of a nationwide chain. Bedrooms are universally comfortable and well designed, and the bathrooms are well maintained. The best rooms are categorized as business-class rooms and are outfitted with hardwood floors and color schemes of dark blue and white. The less expensive rooms, although comfortable and well maintained, are less dramatic and have pastel-colored decor and more conventional-looking accessories.

The Primero Bar and Restaurant is one of the most appealing places to unwind in town, thanks to well-prepared food and stiff drinks.

Strandgatan 10, P.O. Box 459, S-851 06 Sundsvall. © 060/64-19-50. Fax 060/61-92-02. www.firsthotels.com. 203 units. Mid-June to mid-Aug and Fri–Sat year-round 808SEK ($101) double; rest of year 1,509SEK ($189) double, 1,659SEK ($207) junior suite; 1,859SEK ($232) with sauna year-round. AE, DC, MC, V. Free parking. **Amenities:** Restaurant; bar; indoor heated pool; fitness room; sauna; room service (7am–10pm); babysitting (on request); laundry service; dry cleaning; nonsmoking rooms; solarium; rooms for those w/limited mobility. *In room:* TV, minibar, hair dryer.

Ramada Hotel Baltic Despite many updates, enlargements, and renovations over the years, this turn-of-the-20th-century hotel still retains vague hints of its original detailing and architectural adornments. And although some aspects of the place may not particularly appeal to you (such as claustrophobically narrow upstairs hallways and an occasional sense of banal modernism), others (such as sections of the original masonry facade, and third-floor bedrooms where the ceilings slope inward like those in a romantic garret) are charming. Furnishings are comfortable and well maintained, albeit basic. You may feel a bit cramped in the small rooms, but the bathrooms are good and have showers.

Sjögatan 5, S-852 34 Sundsvall. © 060/14-04-40. Fax 060/12-45-60. www.baltichotell.com. 73 units. Mid-June to early Aug and Fri–Sat year-round 745SEK ($93) double; rest of year 1,150SEK ($144) double; 2,500SEK ($313) suite. AE, DC, MC, V. Rates include buffet breakfast. Parking 50SEK ($6.25). **Amenities:** Bar; sauna; room service (7am-1pm); laundry service; dry cleaning; nonsmoking rooms. *In room:* TV, dataport, minibar, hair dryer, iron/ironing board.

Södra Berget ⊕ *Finds* Named after the mountaintop on which it sits, this is one of the most modern hotels in town, and it certainly possesses the most panoramic views. Built in 1985 with four floors and renovated on a large scale in 2004, it's perched at a higher elevation than any other structure in town. Rooms are comfortable, with contemporary furniture and monochromatic color schemes of gray and blue; bathrooms come with showers. The suites come with individual saunas and are particularly recommended, especially since rates are not much higher than those of the conventional rooms. Much of the hotel's business derives from corporate conventioneers who come here for the most complete and comprehensive facilities along the Bothnian coast.

The more formal and appealing of the hotel's two restaurants is the Lille Mat-salan ("little dining room"), which serves lunch and dinner. Drinks are served in the sky bar on the hotel's uppermost (fourth) floor. The hotel has the most complete spa and massage facilities in town, with a battery of hydrotherapy and massage techniques. A network of hiking and jogging trails (25km/16 miles) begins and ends at the hotel.

P.O. Box 858, S-851 24 Sundsvall. © 800/528-1234 in the U.S., or 060/67-10-00. Fax 060/67-10-10. www.sodraberget.com. 182 units. Mid-June to mid-Aug and Fri–Sat year-round 930SEK ($116) double, 1,450SEK ($181) suite; rest of year 1,710SEK ($214) double, 1,930SEK ($241) suite. AE, DC, MC, V. Free parking. Follow the Nybrogatan and then the Gramn Ödalsgatan for 4km (2½ miles) south of the town center. **Amenities:** 2 restaurants; bar; 4 heated pools (2 indoor); gym; spa; Jacuzzi; sauna; room service (7am–10pm); massage; laundry service; dry cleaning; nonsmoking rooms. *In room:* A/C, TV, dataport, hair dryer.

WHERE TO DINE

Jops ⊕ *Finds* INTERNATIONAL This is the most fun, amusing restaurant in Sundsvall, with a clientele that swears by its sense of whimsy and a decor that looks like a shrine to pop art. Album covers decorate the ceiling; old-fashioned Swedish landscapes and framed cartoons cover the wood-paneled walls, and throughout you'll find the kind of kitsch that, if you have any sense of humor at all, will at least make you smile. The menu nicely combines Swedish cuisine with touches of the Orient and the New World. Examples include toast smeared with Swedish caviar, stir-fried prawns with ginger and garlic, potato skins stuffed with sirloin chunks and au gratin of cheese, and herb-laden kabobs with mushrooms and peppers. The burgers are the best in town.

Trädsgårdsgatan 35. © 060/12-19-66. Reservations recommended. Fixed-price lunch 65SEK ($8.15); dinner main courses 100SEK–208SEK ($13–$26). AE, DC, MC, V. Mon–Thurs 11am–11pm; Fri 11am–1am; Sat 5pm–3am.

SUNDSVALL AFTER DARK

Although the city seems to hibernate in the cold winter months, summer is a time to enjoy the outdoors. A lot of people still dance the fox trot, and bands have double-barreled names like Thor-Leifs or Sven-Ingvars. If you don't know the steps, you'll probably meet some Swedes who will be happy to teach you. From May to August only, there is dancing at **Sundsvall Folkets Park** (© **060/17-17-90**), or at **Oscar, Vängåvan** (© **060/12-98-11**).

5 Härnösand

550km (341 miles) NW of Stockholm, 50km (31 miles) N of Sundsvall

Founded in 1582, Härnösand is the oldest town in the administrative district of Västernorrland. A center of education, with some important industries, Härnösand lies in the province of Ångerman River. Like other towns along this coast, it's had its share of disasters, including two major fires, one in 1710 and another in 1714, plus a ransacking invasion by imperialistic Russians in 1721. It is the best base for exploring Ångermanland, the area of Sweden that most resembles Norway, with its jagged coastlines and long fjords stretching inland, and also the High Coast or Höga Kusten (see below).

Härnösand is built on islands connected by bridges. Lubbe Nordstrom, author of such books as *Lort Sverige* and *Petter Svenska,* called it "close to heaven as it is so beautiful." A bit of an exaggeration, but the setting is one of the most scenic in Sweden.

ESSENTIALS

GETTING THERE   By Train   About four trains a day run to Härnösand from Sundsvall, each taking between 45 and 60 minutes. Because of circuitous rail lines, however, it's faster and more convenient to take the bus. For railway information, call ℭ **0771/75-75-75.**

By Bus   There are 33 buses a day, each taking about 50 minutes, for the trip between Härnösand and Sundsvall. Because many folks who work in Sundsvall opt to live in Härnösand, they're usually filled with commuters just before and after the beginning of the workday. For bus information, call ℭ **0200/218218.**

By Car   Continue north from Sundsvall along E4.

VISITOR INFORMATION   The **Härnösand Tourist Office** is at Järnvägs- gatan 2 (ℭ **0611/881-40**), open June to August daily 8am to 6pm, September to May Monday to Friday 10am to 4pm.

SEEING THE SIGHTS

The town center is on the island of Härnön, and its main square, **Stora Torget,** is the most beautiful in the north of Sweden. The yellow residence of the gover- nor, an impressive bank building, and a beautiful art hall share this magnificent setting. In the middle of the square stands the sculpture *Evolution,* the work of Hagbard Sollös, a Norwegian artist.

From here you can stroll through the narrow lanes in **Östanbäcken,** the Old Town. Along the way, despite the fires that have swept through here, you can still see some 18th-century houses. Most of the shops and restaurants of Hörnosänd lie in and around Stora Torget.

Just a few kilometers from the center of Härnösand you'll find **Smitingens havsbad,** one of the best places for outdoor swimming in Norrland. The waters are icy cold, however, even in the middle of summer. The sandy beach is gener- ously long and suitable for children. In the area are some comfortable rocks warmed by the sun, which you can lie on (like a seal) to warm up. A cafe is here as well.

The chief attraction in the main part of town is the neoclassical **Domkyrkan,** Västra Kyrkogatan (ℭ **0611/24525**), the smallest cathedral in Sweden. An old stone church stood here in 1593 and remained intact through the fires of 1710 and 1714. When the Russians ransacked the town in 1721, however, it was badly damaged by fire. Using the walls that remained, rebuilding from 1842 to 1846 gave birth to the present-day cathedral. Today a dozen pillars support two side galleries. The baroque altar from 1728 was built by Jacob Saverberg. Above the entrance rises the powerful front of the organ, which the famous organ builder Johan Cahman built in 1731. In the vestry is a solid iron door from 1765, a leftover from the original church. Hours are daily from 10am to 4pm; admission is free.

From the center, signs direct you to the **Lansmuseet Murberget** (© 0611/ 88600), about 1.5km (1 mile) north of the town center, which incorporates two museums into one administrative whole. The larger and more appealing of the museums is the **Murberget Open-Air Museum,** the largest of its kind in Sweden outside of Stockholm's Skansen. If you don't have a car of your own, bus nos. 2 and 52 run here every hour in summer between May and August. More than 80 buildings have been moved from various country locations to the bucolic, peaceful grounds here. Examples include traditional Ångermanland farmhouses and an antique Murberg church, a building that's often the site of local weddings. The open-air museum is open June to August Tuesday to Sunday from 11am to 5pm. Entrance is free, but a guided tour of the premises, which departs virtually whenever you decide you want it, costs 600SEK ($75) per person.

The other of the two subdivisions is the **Lansmuseet Västernorrland** (© 0611/886-00), an indoor, year-round county museum devoted to the history of the area. Inaugurated in 1994, this museum contains, among other exhibitions, one of Sweden's largest collections of old weapons, including hunting, folk, and military weapons, some dating from the 17th century. Flintlock guns, spears, accessories, hunting traps, and tools—it's all here.

On-site local craftspeople also demonstrate traditional crafts, everything from embroidery to the forging of iron. Entrance is free. It maintains the same hours as the museum.

WHERE TO STAY

First Hotel Stadt 🖈   Few hotels along the Bothnian coast blend as gracefully as this one does with the surrounding houses. Part of this is because of its original construction many years ago as a compound of houses that share a communal rear courtyard. Even after a section of it was modernized in the 1960s, about a dozen of the rooms retained their high-ceilinged, big-windowed original configurations, and as such are a bit more charming and nostalgic than their more modern counterparts. (The old-fashioned rooms are those numbered 230–234 and those numbered 330–341.) Regardless of your room assignment, you'll find moderate size bedrooms with excellent bathrooms with a tub or shower. The hotel is the largest in town.

Skeppsbron 9, S-871 30 Härnösand. © **0611/55-44-40.** Fax 0611/55-44-47. 95 units. Mid-June to mid-Aug and Fri–Sat 853SEK ($107) double, 953SEK ($119) suite; rest of year 1,603SEK ($200) double, 1,903SEK ($238) suite. AE, DC, MC, V. Rates include buffet breakfast. Free parking. **Amenities:** Restaurant 300m (984 ft.) from the hotel; bar; fitness room; sauna; laundry service; dry cleaning; nonsmoking rooms; solarium; rooms for those w/limited mobility. *In room:* TV, dataport (in some), hair dryer.

WHERE TO DINE

The Highlander 🖈 *Value* SCOTTISH/INTERNATIONAL   Praised by virtually every hotel receptionist in town for the quality and large portions of its food, this pub and bistro celebrates the aesthetics and conviviality of Scotland. (Note the green-and-red, tartan-patterned carpeting and an array of at least 20 different brands of single-malt whiskeys.) The cuisine is consistently excellent and uses first-rate ingredients. Menu items include Highland steaks with a whiskey-flavored pepper sauce, fried salmon with a cream sauce and herbs, and savory hamburgers served with coleslaw, red onions, and English cheddar. What's the most popular single-malt scotch served within this paean to Scotland? Oban, a whiskey from the Western Highlands.

Nybrogatan 5. ℭ **0611/511170.** Main courses 79SEK–169SEK ($9.90–$21). MC, V. Mon–Fri 11am–2pm; Tues–Sat 6–11pm.

CONTINUING ALONG HÖGA KUSTEN (THE HIGH COAST) 🌟🌟

One of the most scenic and panoramic stretches of nature in all Sweden lies on the Bothnian coast between Härnösand and Örnsköldsvik. Along this stretch of Route 4, known as the High Coast, rolling mountains and luxuriant valleys seem to plunge into the gulf itself.

The coastline also is the setting for the Höga Kusten Bridge, the longest bridge in Sweden and the seventh-longest in the world. Built over the Ångermanälv River, it was inaugurated at Christmas in 1997. Its two towers, called pylons, are Sweden's tallest constructions, at 175m (574 ft.).

The coast presents a scenic panorama at every turn, from sheer cliffs rising above the turbulent waters to craggy outcroppings of rock. Occasionally you'll see a tranquil sandy cove. Dozens of islands, some hardly large enough to land on, lie off the coast. Many islands are much larger and provide a setting for pine forests. In summer, many Swedes like to walk the entire distance of the coast along **Höga Kusten leden,** which extends 129km (80 miles) from the new bridge just north of Härnösand to Varvsberget in Örnsköldsvik.

Depending on the time of the year of your visit, the tourist office (see "Visitor Information," above) will advise you on the best way of seeing the most scenic islands in the chain, using a combination of boat and bus. (These schedules are constantly being changed.) The loveliest islands in the archipelago include **Högbonden, Ulvön,** and **Trysunda.**

Just a 10-minute boat ride from the mainland, **Högbonden** has only nature to entertain you. Its sole building is a lighthouse at the highest point on the island, surveying a rocky plateau. The lighthouse has been turned into a youth hostel. To reach the island, go to Bönhamn, where the M/F *Högbonden* sails from mid-June to mid-August every 2 hours daily from 10am to 6pm. For information, call ℭ **0613/23005.** A return ticket costs 80SEK to 110SEK ($10–$14). In winter, you have to call to book a boat reservation.

Ulvön Island really is two islands: Norra Ulvön and uninhabited Södra Ulvön. Ulvön was once the site of a large fishing village, but over decades its settlers have mostly deserted it, leaving behind about 40 hearty souls. The main hamlet is Ulvöhamn, where you'll see many fishers' cottages and boat houses. Walk its narrow village street and duck in to look at the old fisherman's chapel before going to the **Café Måsen,** the major meeting place of town and the summer rendezvous point for boaters in the area. If you have time, take in the panoramic view from Lotsberget Hill. To reach the island, go to Docksta, from which the M/S *Kusttrafik* (ℭ **0613/105-50**) departs for Ulvön daily at 10:15am June through August, arriving in Ulvöhamn in about an hour. The cost of a return ticket is 150SEK ($19).

Boats departing from Ulvön also reach the island of **Trysunda** in about an hour, pulling into a narrow U-shape harbor, site of the island's tiny village. This is the best-preserved fishing village in Ångermanland, and it's nestled among the cliffs far out to sea. The village contains about 40 red-and-white fishermen's cottages right on the waterfront, along with a chapel from the 1600s. Many Swedes come here to bathe on the rocks in summer. The little island also is crisscrossed with many hiking trails. The M/F *Ulvön* sails from Ulvöhamn daily, costing 60SEK to 100SEK ($7.50–$13) one-way. For schedules, call ℂ **070/651-92-65.**

6 Umeå

700km (434 miles) N of Stockholm, 550km (341 miles) N of Gävle, 300km (186 miles) N of Sundsvall

With a population of 100,000 and an average age of 35, Umeå is a city of knowledge and culture with a multiethnic population. Some 50 native tongues, from Albanian to Wolof, are spoken here.

Norrland University's 20,000 students give the city a strong youthful presence. Wide, stylish boulevards and a fast-flowing river make for a dramatic cityscape.

It wasn't easy for Swedish kings to convert the Ume delta fishermen into city dwellers. The first town privileges (the town's charter) were granted in 1588, but few people settled there at first. It wasn't until 1622 that King Gustav II Adolf succeeded in getting people to live at Umeå and pursue trade.

The 18th century saw Umeå suffering from war and unrest, and plunder by Russian soldiers. In 1809, Umeå became the center for military operations when Sweden was drawn into the Napoleonic wars, during which it lost Finland and suffered greatly. It wasn't until the 1830s that business picked up as shipping, trade, and shipbuilding flourished. Timber barons moved in, and the mouth of the Ume River, Umeå became a major port. After Umeå was laid to waste by a devastating fire in 1888, a new city of well-ordered buildings and tree-lined avenues with fire breaks was built.

ESSENTIALS

GETTING THERE   By Plane   Access by air to Umeå is controlled by two airlines, the more visible of which is **SAS.** Less frequent service is offered by Norway-based **Braathens.** Between the two airlines, at least a dozen flights a day wing in from such places as Stockholm, Oslo, and Malmö. For information about flights on either airline, call ℂ **0770/727-727.**

By Train   A night train, whose compartments come with showers and breakfast, takes travelers from Stockholm to Umeå at least twice daily. Trip time is 9 hours. For schedules, call ℂ **0771/75-75-75.**

By Bus   Bus transit from Stockholm is faster and more efficient than equivalent transits by train because the roads heading north to Umeå are shorter than the somewhat more circuitous rail lines. Trip time is around 7½ to 8 hours, depending on road conditions. For schedules and information, call ℂ **0200/218218.**

By Car   From Härnösand, continue north along E4.

VISITOR INFORMATION   Umeå Turistbyrå, Renmarkstorget 15 (ℂ **090/ 16-16-16**), is open from mid-June to mid-August Monday to Friday 8am to 7pm, Saturday 10am to 4pm, and Sunday noon to 4pm. Off-season hours are Monday to Friday 10am to 5pm and Saturday 11am to 2pm.

SEEING THE SIGHTS

Umeå is called the "city of birch trees." Hundreds of these trees were planted along every boulevard following the fire of 1888 that destroyed the town. They are at their colorful best in autumn when university students return by the thousands, enlivening the city after a sleepy summer. Theater, opera, concerts, and other cultural attractions also return, bringing the city renewed vigor.

East of the tourist bureau, **Rådhuseplanaden (Town Hall Esplanade)** is a wide-open area with the city hall, constructed of red brick, lying to the south. Not many old wooden mansions are left, except in the district along and east of Östra Kyrkogatan, where you will find a rich concentration of antique houses. The redbrick neo-Gothic church on the Storgatan is from 1894. To the east of the church is **Döbelns Park,** named for Georg Carl von Döbeln, the commander who, on October 8, 1809, officially disbanded the Swedish/Finnish army when Finland fell to Russian control.

The town's major museum complex is called **Gammlia** (© 090/17-18-00) and can easily occupy the better part of your day. This sprawling area lies almost half a kilometer (½ mile) northeast of the town center and can be reached by driving or walking. Admission is free to all the museums. Hours are from June to August daily 10am to 5pm; off season Tuesday to Friday 10am to 4pm, and Saturday noon to 4pm.

The town's original museum, **Friluftsmuseet** ⚜, is still going strong. It consists of about 20 regional buildings in an open-air setting, with the oldest dating from the 1600s. Attractions include a grain-drying kiln, a windmill, a smokehouse for meats, an octagonal chapel still used for weddings, two threshing floors, a school, and a farmhouse. Guides dressed in folkloric clothing will show you around and answer questions. In an on-site bakery, the traditional unleavened bread of the north, *tunnbröd,* is prepared for you to sample. With its collection of barnyard animals, the place still has the feel of an active farm.

Most of the main museum collection is found in the **Västerbottens Museum** (© **090/17-18-00**), a repository of the history of the province. The exhibits go back to prehistoric times. A ski found here has been dated to 5200 B.C., making it the oldest in the world. Exhibits also trace the history of the region during the Industrial Revolution. Some exhibitions offer glimpses into reindeer breeding and Lapp or Sami culture. A scaled-down model, 3.8m (12 ft.) long, of Umeå's riverfront shows what a portion of the city looked like before the disastrous fire of 1888. The museum is open from June to mid-August Monday to Friday 10am to 5pm, Saturday and Sunday noon to 5pm. Off-season times are Tuesday to Friday 10am to 4pm, Saturday noon to 4pm, and Sunday noon to 5pm. There is no admission charge.

Linked to the Västerbottens Museum is the **Bilmuseum,** or **Picture Museum** (© **090-786-52-27**), which is run by the university. This is the venue for temporary exhibitions. Among its permanent collection, it houses the university art collection, including works by two of the most famous artists of Sweden, Carl Larsson and Anders Zorn. The museum is open from mid-June to mid-August daily noon to 5pm; off season Tuesday noon to 8pm, Wednesday to Saturday noon to 4pm, and Sunday noon to 5pm. Free admission.

WHERE TO STAY

First Stora Hotellet ⚜   Although its original premises have been massively improved and expanded over the years, most recently in 2002 when all its rooms were renovated, the origins of this hotel are almost 100 years old. At that time, it was the first stone-built public building in town, erected in the aftermath of the disastrous fire that had destroyed almost everything in Umeå. Since 1995, it has been a member of the nationwide First Hotel chain, which carefully preserves the bedrooms' original high-ceilinged configuration, despite well-planned overlays of modern carpeting and contemporary furnishings. Bathrooms are partially tiled, each with a shower.

Storgatan 46, S-903 26 Umeå. © **090/77-88-70.** Fax 090/13-30-55. www.firsthotels.com. 94 units. Mid-June to mid-Aug and Fri–Sat year-round 820SEK ($103) double, 1,160SEK ($145) suite; rest of year 1,453SEK ($182) double, 1,765SEK ($221) suite. Rates include breakfast. AE, DC, MC, V. Free parking. **Amenities:** Restaurant; bar; sauna; laundry service; dry cleaning; nonsmoking rooms; rooms for those w/limited mobility. *In room:* TV, hair dryer.

Scandic Hotel Plaza Umeå 🏆🏆   The most stylish and best-accessorized hotel in Umeå rises 14 white-and-pale-green floors from a position in the center of town. Built in 1992 with flair unmatched by any other hotel in the region, it offers well-maintained green-and-russet-colored rooms that are outfitted in an internationally inspired contemporary design. Each unit has well-upholstered furniture and a tiled bathroom with a tub/shower. The staff here is particularly well trained, with insights into many of the diversions and services available in the region.

The hotel contains Umeå's most appealing sauna, a compound of wood-sheathed rooms on the hotel's panoramic top floor; each super-heated cubicle provides a view out over the frigid landscapes of northern Sweden.

Storgatan 40, P.O. Box 3133, S-903 04 Umeå. © **090/20-56-300.** Fax 090/20-56-311. www.scandic-hotels.com. 196 units. Mid-June to Aug 9 and Fri–Sat year-round 940SEK ($118) double; rest of year 1,705SEK ($213) double; 2,995SEK ($374) suite. Rates include buffet breakfast. AE, DC, MC, V. Parking 85SEK ($11). **Amenities:** Restaurant; bar; gym; sauna; room service (7am–10pm); laundry service; dry cleaning; nonsmoking rooms. *In room:* A/C, TV, dataport (in some), minibar, hair dryer, iron/ironing board (in some), trouser press.

WHERE TO DINE

Brasserie Rop/Restaurant Whispers SWEDISH/INTERNATIONAL Which of these two restaurants you select may depend on whether you're in the mood for convivial, sometimes raucous, dialogue or for contemplative, hushed silence. Both lie near the lobby of Umeå's best hotel, but whereas Rop (Swedish for "speaking in a loud voice") offers just that, Whispers, as the name implies, is much quieter and more decorous. Rop contains close-spaced tables like a French brasserie's and serves sandwiches, burgers, pastas, pizzas, chicken fajitas, grilled fish, salads, and steaks. Whispers, part of whose space is within a glassed-in greenhouse with a view of the midwinter ice that clogs the nearby river, specializes in more elaborate, finely tuned cuisine. Much of this is based on local ingredients, including very fresh elk meat, moose, reindeer, salmon, and perch, often cooked with Arctic berries (including juniper berries, cloudberries, and whortleberries), herbs, and wine.

In the Provobis Umeå Plaza, Storgatan 40. © **090/20-56-300.** Reservations recommended evenings only. Rop Brasserie fixed-price lunch 65SEK ($8.15); main courses 70SEK–150SEK ($8.75–$19). Whispers main courses 150SEK–250SEK ($19–$31). AE, DC, MC, V. Rop Brasserie Mon–Thurs 5–11pm, Fri–Sat 5pm–midnight, Sun 5–9:30pm; Whispers Tues–Sat 6–10:30pm.

Lottas Krog INTERNATIONAL Purists might be amazed at the cross-cultural ease with which this kitchen turns out the national dishes of India, Mexico, and Sweden with equal insouciance, all within a street-level dining room whose hunting and fishing trophies and battered wood paneling evoke a sudsy pub in Ireland. Come here for a drink or two and a rib-sticking meal to help ward off the Lappish chill. It might include fajitas with chicken, beef, or vegetables; tandoori made from just about anything; grilled entrecôtes in garlic butter; and an all-Swedish version of marinated salmon in dill sauce. A daily special, depending on the season and the mood of the chef, might include freshwater trout and grilled reindeer filets, perhaps with juniper-berry sauce. You'll find it in the middle of town, close to Umeå's railway station. With 120 seats, it's usually easy to get a table.

Nygatan 22. ℂ 090/12-95-51. Reservations recommended. Main courses 105SEK–185SEK ($13–$23); set-price lunch 75SEK ($9.40). AE, DC, MC, V. Mon 5–10:30pm; Tues–Sat 11:30am–2:30pm and 3–10:30pm.

UMEÅ AFTER DARK

Don't think that just because you're in the far north of Sweden that folks here won't want to get down and party. If you have any nocturnal energy at all, you'll probably discover that the frigid air and long nights add an intensity to nightclubbing that simply doesn't exist in more clement climes to the south.

The town's most visible and largest nightlife compound is **Blå Kök o Bar (Blue Avenue),** Rådhusesplanaden 14 (ℂ 090/13-23-00). Within its multistory premises you'll find a dance club, two separate restaurants, a pub, and a stage for the presentation of live music. It's open every night from 5pm till 2am. Dinner service, where main courses cost from 89SEK to 120SEK ($11–$15), is a little earlier in the evening, with most of the musical pizzazz beginning around 9pm. There's a cover charge of between 20SEK and 80SEK ($2.50–$10) Saturday night between 9pm and midnight only. Although the venue caters to youthful enthusiasts most nights of the week, the slightly older crowd will feel more comfortable here on Thursdays, when live music stresses golden disco from the '70s and '80s, as opposed to the heavy metal and techno music that's the norm on other nights.

7 Skellefteå

818km (507 miles) N of Stockholm, 130km (81 miles) N of Umeå

This coastal town on the north coast of Sweden and between the banks of the Ume and Skellefte rivers is an industrial port. Its chief industry is the refining of metal ores from the nearby mining area of Boliden.

The town was founded after a religious edict issued in 1324 by King Magnus Eriksson, inviting all those "who believe in Christ or want to" to find a settlement here. Many Christians heeded the call, and by the end of the 1700s they had constructed the monumental **Skellefteå Church,** hailed as the largest and most beautiful building in the north of Sweden.

ESSENTIALS

GETTING THERE   By Train & Bus   Skellefteå does not have a railway station of its own; consequently, the trains rushing northward from southern Sweden pull into the station in the hamlet of Bastu Trask, 48km (30 miles) from the center of Skellefteå. And whereas that makes rail transit from Stockholm feasible (there's a day train and a night train, each taking 16 hr. to reach Bastu Trask from Stockholm), it makes rail transit from Umeå relatively inconvenient. Consequently, if you're looking for the easiest access to Skellefteå from Umeå, you'll find that any of the 23 **buses** (trip time: 2 hr. each way) are by far the faster and more convenient mode of access. For information about rail connections into Skellefteå, call ℂ 0771/75-75-75. For bus connections into Skellefteå, call ℂ 0950/23-900.

By Car   From Umeå, continue north along the E4 with the coast on your right.

VISITOR INFORMATION   The **tourist office** at Trädgårdsgatan 7 (ℂ 0910/73-60-20; http://turistinfo.skelleftea.se) is open from late June to early August Monday to Friday 10am to 5pm, Saturday and Sunday 10am to 2pm. Off-season times are Monday and Thursday from 8am to 5pm, Friday from 8am to 4pm.

SEEING THE SIGHTS

Finished in 1799 on a plan that corresponds to the shape of a Greek cross, **Skellefteå Kyrko (Skellefteå Church)** ☆, Kyrkogatan 5 (℡ **0910/78-78-00**), is open Monday to Friday throughout the year from 9am to 4pm. Noteworthy for its templelike porticoes and its cupola with a lantern, this building resides on the site of a church from the Middle Ages, of which only the 15th-century vestry is preserved. Its most valuable treasure is a collection of medieval **wood carvings** ☆. The six statues before the altar depict the Virgin and child, saints Erik and Katarina, St. Anne with Virgin and child, St. Michael, and St. Olof. The pulpit dates from 1648. Be sure to seek out the church's chief treasure, the **Virgin of Skellefteå** ☆, a walnut carving, probably German, that is 8 centuries old. It can be found near the altar and is one of the few remaining Romanesque images of the Virgin of Sweden.

The church, which is within an easy walk of the center, is part of the parish village of **Bonnstan**. These parish villages were commonplace in the provinces of Norbotten and Västerbotten in the north of Sweden. They consisted of a *kyrkstad,* as this one does, which is a series of simple wooden houses clustered around the church.

On Kyrkstand, you'll see five long rows of weather-beaten log houses with wooden shutters. These wooden houses are carefully preserved in their natural state by government authorities, and it's illegal to install electricity in them or modernize them in any way.

You can also visit **Nordanå** (℡ **0910/73-55-10**), an open-air museum reached by walking along Strandgatan. The largest building here houses the Skellefteå Museum in an old school. There's a cafe on-site, as well as a series of temporary exhibitions. The permanent collection includes displays of prehistoric relics, old coins, and a history of the industrial development of the area. The most intriguing exhibit is a collection of jewelry from the Bronze Age.

The open-air museum itself consists of about a dozen buildings—from a Lapp storage hut to shops selling handicrafts—moved to this site. One bakery demonstrates how bread was made the old-fashioned way, and the staff will sell you samples. Admission is free. The site is open year-round: Tuesday 9am to 9pm, Wednesday and Thursday 9am to 4pm, Friday to Monday noon to 4pm.

WHERE TO STAY

First Hotel Statt ☆   Built in 1995 adjacent to a river (the Skellefte Älv) that runs through the center of town, this is a well-managed, stylish, four-story hotel that's proud of its design by well-known architect Anders Tengbom. About 75% of the bedrooms were renovated within 2 years of its original construction, during a process that upgraded the rooms into versions more comfortable than they were originally. Decorated in warm, sunny colors to counterbalance the often dark days you'll find here, the rooms are quite spacious, with lovely wooden floors. Bathrooms, although small, are well equipped with either showers or tubs. The hotel's accommodations designed for women, called "First Lady" rooms, come with such extra touches as a peephole in the door, an iron, a tea maker, a full-length mirror, a make-up mirror, a beauty kit, and extra skirt hangers.

Stationsgatan 8, P.O. Box 1, S-931 21 Skellefteå. ℡ **0910/141-40.** Fax 0910/711-065. www.firsthotels.com. 91 units. Mid-June to mid-Aug and Fri–Sat year-round 804SEK ($101) double, 2,500SEK ($313) suite; rest of the year 654SEK ($85) double, 1,254SEK ($163) suite. Rates include breakfast. AE, DC, MC, V. Parking 65SEK ($8.15). **Amenities:** Restaurant; bar; gym; sauna; babysitting; laundry service; dry cleaning; nonsmoking rooms; solarium; rooms for those w/limited mobility. *In room:* A/C, TV, dataport, hair dryer.

Sweden's Parish Villages

After breaking with the Catholic Church in 1527, the Swedish clergy mandated that parishioners had to attend church to learn Lutheran fundamentals. Anyone residing within 9.5km (6 miles) of a church had to attend services every Sunday, those 9.5km to 19km (6–12 miles) from a church had to attend every other week; and those between 19km and 29km (12–18 miles) away had to attend every 3 weeks. Wooden houses were erected for anyone who lived farther away and could not get home by nightfall, particularly in the dark months of winter. They retired here after services and then returned home on Monday morning. Many people still live full-time in these old houses, especially in summer, and sometimes they are rented out to visitors.

Scandic Hotel ⭐ One of the largest and most modern hotels in town lies a 3-minute walk from the city's main square behind a modern, slope-roofed facade that looks capable of resisting the fiercest of Arctic blasts. Bedrooms are cozy, well upholstered, and contemporary looking, with a big-city stylishness that's a pleasant contrast to the masses of potted plants that fill up the atrium-style lobby. Rooms are a bit small, although each is provided with a generous working desk. The bathrooms are small but tidy, each with a shower.

Kanalgatan 75, S-931 78 Skellefteå. (℃ **0910/75-24-00.** Fax 0910/77-84-11. www.scandic-hotels.com. 131 units. Mid-June to mid-Aug and Fri–Sat (year-round) 790SEK ($99) double, 1,200SEK ($150) suite; mid-Aug to mid-June Sun–Thurs 1,570SEK ($196) double, 1,850SEK ($231) suite. AE, DC, MC, V. Free parking. **Amenities:** 2 restaurants; bar; indoor heated pool; gym; sauna; laundry service; dry cleaning; nonsmoking rooms; rooms for those w/limited mobility. *In room:* A/C, TV, hair dryer, iron/ironing board.

WHERE TO DINE

Restaurant Kriti ⭐ *(Finds* GREEK This restaurant is much acclaimed and celebrated in this part of Sweden, not only because its food is excellent, but because it's the only Greek restaurant in the entire northern tier of Sweden. As such, it does a busy trade with Nordics who arrive with fond memories of their past vacations along the Mediterranean, and who leave as ardent fans of the souvlaki, moussaka, calamari, lamb chops, and grilled salmon or whitefish that this place serves up with style. A selection of pizzas is available, and stuffed vine leaves and a roster of salads (including a tasty version with shrimp) work well as starters. Don't expect photographs of the Acropolis or any of the Greek aesthetic clichés. The establishment's most obvious concession to the Greek aesthetic derives from the music, which incorporates everything from *bouzouki* to popular Greek singers emulating Melina Mercouri.

Kanalgatan 51. (℃ **0910/77-95-35.** Reservations recommended. Pizzas 80SEK–100SEK ($10–$13); main courses 100SEK–225SEK ($13–$28). AE, DC, MC, V. Mon–Thurs 11am–2pm and 4:30–10pm; Fri 11am–2pm and 4:30–11pm; Sat 1–11pm; Sun 1–10pm.

12

Swedish Lapland

Swedish Lapland, or Norrland, as the Swedes call it, is Europe's last wilderness—9,400 sq. km (3,666 sq. miles) of more or less untouched nature. Norrland covers roughly half the area of Sweden, and one-quarter of the country lies north of the Arctic Circle. This wild, undisturbed domain of the midnight sun is a land of high mountains and plateaus; endless forests and vast swamplands; crystal-blue lakes and majestic mountains; and glaciers, waterfalls, rushing rivers, and forests.

Like the Grand Canyon and the Galapagos Islands, Lapland, whose natural wonders include a population of brown bear and alpine flora, is listed as a World Heritage Site. It has been occupied by the Samis since prehistoric times. Most still make their living from their reindeer herds.

The territory can be reached easily. Fast electric trains take you from Stockholm to Narvik in Norway, with stops at Kiruna and Abisko. The express train, *Nordpilen,* takes a day and a night to travel from Stockholm to far north of the Arctic Circle. Once here you'll find mail-coach buses connecting the other villages and settlements in the north.

It's much quicker to fly, of course, and there are airports at Umea, Lulea, and Kiruna. The last, for example, is reached by air in 4 hours from Stockholm. Those with more time may want to drive here. From Stockholm, just stay on E4, the longest road in Europe. From Stockholm to the Finnish border town of Haparanda, you'll ride along about 1,130km (701 miles) of good surface.

Various towns in Lapland can serve as a center from which to explore the Laponian area. Under these individual town listings we'll also preview national parks to visit in Laponia.

1 Enjoying the Great Outdoors

In the north of Sweden you'll find wilderness outside of every town, as well as forests, wild rivers, unspoiled coastlines, thousands of tranquil lakes, high mountains, and low farmlands. The town you stop over in may be dull, but getting to the town is part of the fun, as your trip will take you through pristine wilderness along roads that range from an express highway to the smallest logging road that winds its way deep into the forests.

Many visitors come north just to explore the national parks of Sweden. The most spectacular of the lot is **Muddus Nationalpark** (see "Gällivare," later in this chapter), some 49,000 hectares (121,030 acres) in all. Also from Gällivare, you can reach other national parks, including Stora Sjöfallet and Padjelanta. These parks combine to form Europe's largest national park, a landmass of 5,225 sq. km (2,038 sq. miles). Others come to explore the highest mountain in Sweden, **Kebnekaise,** at 2,090m (6,855 ft.)—see "Kiruna," later in this chapter.

Abisko is the best center for exploring **Abisko National Park,** where the mountains tower as high as 1,170m (3,838 ft.). Abisko also is one of the best

centers for watching the midnight sun, and it's the start of the longest marked hiking trail in Sweden, the **Kungsleden,** or "Royal Trail," which stretches from Abisko to Hemavan, a distance of 338km (210 miles).

As one of the last great wildernesses of Europe, Lapland offers a wide array of outdoor activities. You can play golf at the most northerly courses in the world, go on horseback riding trips, experience white-water rafting along rapids, or even go canoeing. In winter, dog and reindeer teams can take you on an adventure through the wilderness. Lapland has the best grayling fishing in Europe, and you can hunt for small game and elk.

Fishing trips, golfing jaunts, horseback riding, and especially dog and reindeer sledding should be arranged in advance through a tour group before you go to Sweden. It is usually not possible to just show up "on the doorstep" and book these activities. For general information and bookings once you are in Sweden, most questions can be answered by calling **Destination Kiruna,** at the **Ice Hotel,** Marknadsvägen 63, S-981 91 Jukkasjärvi, Sweden (© **0980/668-00;** fax 0980/668-90).

Tips **Bug Off!**

Mosquitoes arrive with the warm weather at the end of June and disappear at the end of August. The best way to protect yourself is to wear thick, preferably bright, clothing; avoid large stretches of water; and use mosquito repellent on exposed skin. Treat bites with Salubrin, Alsolsprit, or something similar.

Although Destination Kiruna can book you on last-minute sporting activities once you are in Sweden, it is better to book in advance. Contact **Lynx Ski Travel** (© **800/422-5969** in the U.S.).

GOLFING   If you want to set up some golfing adventure in north Sweden, this, too, should be arranged in advance. Of course, your chances of playing golf in Lapland will depend heavily on weather conditions, which may be dicey even in the summer. Summer is also the time when mosquitoes plague the golf courses, so be sure to slather on repellent before you hit the links. For information about a golf vacation, contact **Idrefjällen Golfklubb,** P.O. Box 32, S-790 91 Idre (© **0253/202-75**).

HIKING & CAMPING   Swedish Lapland is a paradise for hikers and campers (if you don't mind the mosquitoes in summer). Before you go, get in touch with the **Svenska Turistföreningen (Swedish Touring Club),** Stureplan 4c (Box 25), S-101 20 Stockholm (© **08/463-21-00**), which maintains mountain hotels and has built bridges, marked hiking routes, and even introduced regular boat service on some lakes.

Locals and visitors can enjoy hundreds of kilometers of marked hiking and skiing tracks (Mar–Apr and even May are recommended for skiing; hiking is best in the warm summer months). Some 90 mountain hotels or Lapp-type huts (called *fjällstugor* and *kåtor,* respectively) are available, with beds and bedding, cooking utensils, and firewood. Huts can be used for only 1 or 2 nights. The club also sponsors mountain stations (*fjällstationer*).

You must be in good physical condition and have suitable equipment before you set out because most of the area is uninhabited. Neophytes are advised to join one of the tours offered by the Swedish Touring Club (contact the club for more details).

SKIING   In spite of the bitter cold, many come here to ski in winter. At least snow is guaranteed here, unlike at some alpine resorts of Switzerland and Austria. Kiruna, Gällivare, and Arvidsjaur offer some of the best possible conditions for cross-country skiing. Local tourist offices will offer constantly changing advice about how to hook up with many of these activities, which naturally depend a great deal on weather conditions.

2 Luleå: The Gateway to Lapland

930km (577 miles) N of Stockholm

Our tour north begins in Luleå on the way to Lapland. This port city on Sweden's east coast at the northern end of the Gulf of Bothnia is 113km (70 miles) south of the Arctic Circle. Luleå is the largest town in Norrbotten; boats depart from its piers for some 300 offshore islets and skerries known for their flora and fauna.

Luleå

ATTRACTIONS●
Gammelstad **1**
Norrbottens Museum **2**

ACCOMMODATIONS■
Arctic Hotel **5**
Elite Stadshotellet **4**
Hotel Nordkalotten **6**
Quality Hotel Luleå **3**

Luleå has a surprisingly mild climate—its average annual temperature is only a few degrees lower than that of Malmö, on the southern tip of Sweden.

The town of Luleå is a port for shipping iron ore in summer. Its harbor remains frozen over until May. Fire destroyed most of the Old Town. The state-owned ironworks here have led to a dramatic growth in population.

Establishing a city this far north was laden with difficulties. Gustavus Adolphus may have founded the city in 1621, but it wasn't until 1940 that development really took hold. Today, as the seat of the University of Luleå, the town has a population of 70,000 and is liveliest when the students are here in winter, although most foreigners (except businesspeople) see it only in summer.

ESSENTIALS

GETTING THERE   By Plane   SAS runs 12 flights each weekday between Stockholm and Luleå (10 on Sat–Sun), which take 1¼ hours. There are 11 flights each weekday between Gothenburg and Luleå (seven on Sat–Sun), taking 2¼ hours. For information and schedules, call ℭ **0770/727-727.**

By Train   Six trains arrive daily from Stockholm (travel time: 15 hr.); an additional six come from Gothenburg (travel time: 19 hr.). Trains from Stockholm to Kiruna usually deposit passengers bound for Luleå at the railway junction at Boden, 9.5km (6 miles) northwest of Luleå. Here they board one of three

Moments   Northern Lights & the Midnight Sun

If you visit Lapland/Norrbotten (the remote northeastern province of Sweden) in the winter, you will see the **northern lights** ★★★, a sparkling display of colors that becomes visible at dusk.

The northern lights are shimmering lights with surging colors in the sky, a natural phenomenon that can amaze the observer just as much as the most lavish fireworks display. They often can be seen during the dark season, from early in the evening until midnight. The northern lights occur in the Arctic region and are seen more clearly and more frequently the farther north you travel.

The source of energy for the northern lights is the sun and the solar winds. Solar wind plasma is constantly emitted by the sun at a velocity of 400km (248 miles) per second. Some of the energy absorbed by the Earth's magnetic field accelerates the ions and electrons. The electrons are steered toward the polar regions, and, at a few hundred kilometers from the Earth, the electrons collide with atmospheric atoms and molecules. On collision, a small amount of the electrons' kinetic energy is transformed into visible light.

You also experience the **midnight sun** ★★★ above the Arctic Circle. By midnight sun, we mean that it is possible to see more than half of the sun when it is directly north. At midsummer, it can be seen south of the Arctic Circle, thanks to the refraction of light in the atmosphere. From a high hill with a good view to the north, the midnight sun can still be seen quite far to the south. The farther north you go, the longer this phenomenon lasts: In the far north, it's from the end of May to the end of July.

The light at night is milder and softer than the harsh, blinding sunshine of the day and creates an impression that time is somehow standing still. Many activities and events are connected with the midnight sun, including trips to the mountains, bike races, and fishing contests at night. Local tourist offices will have more information about these events.

connecting trains a day going between Boden and Luleå. Train traffic from Gothenburg to Luleå also necessitates a transfer in Boden. For more information, phone ☎ **0771/75-75-75.**

By Bus   A bus runs between Stockholm and Luleå on Friday and Sunday, taking 14 hours. For further information, call **Swebus** at ☎ **0200/218218.**

By Car   From Stockholm, take the E4 expressway north to Uppsala and continue northward along the coast until you reach Luleå.

VISITOR INFORMATION   Contact the **Luleå Tourist Office** at Storgatan 43B Luleå (☎ **0920/29-35-00; www.lulea.se**), open in summer Monday to Friday 9am to 7pm, and Saturday and Sunday 10am to 4pm; off season Monday to Friday 10am to 6pm and Saturday 10am to 2pm.

SEEING THE SIGHTS

Some of the most evocative and historic architecture in Luleå lies 9.5km (6 miles) north of the modern city in **Gammelstad (Old Town)** ⊙, the town's original medieval core, and a once-thriving trading center. Its demise as a viable commercial center began when the nearby harbor became clogged with silt and was rendered unnavigable. In 1649, a new city, modern-day Luleå, was established, and the Old Town—except the church described below—fell into decline and disrepair. Today it serves as a reminder of another era and is the site of the region's most famous church, **Gammelstads Kyrka,** also known as Neder Lulea Kyrka (no phone). Built in 1492, the church is surrounded by clusters of nearly identical red-sided huts, many of which date from the 18th and 19th centuries. The church rented these to families and citizens traveling to Luleå from the surrounding region as temporary homes during holy days. In 1996, UNESCO declared the church and the cluster of huts around it a World Heritage Site.

Gammelstad's other important site is the **Hägnan Museum** (also known as the Gammelstads Friluftsmuseum), 95400 Gammelstad (② **0920/293809**). Consisting of about a dozen historic buildings hauled in from throughout Norbotten, it's open between June 6 and August 15 daily from 11am to 5pm, depending on the season. Entrance is free. To reach Gammelstad from modern-day Luleå, take bus no. 8 or 9 from Luleå's center.

Adjacent to Gammelstad Bay you'll find some of the richest bird life in Sweden. Ornithologists have counted 285 different species of birds during the spring migrations. The best way to experience this cornucopia of avian life involves following a well-marked hiking trail for 7km (4.33 miles) south of Gammelstad. Signs will point from Gammelstad to the Gammelstads Vikens Naturreservat. For information about the trail, call the Luleå Tourist Office (see above). The trail, consisting of well-trod earth, gravel, and boardwalks, traverses marshy, usually forested terrain teeming with bird life. En route, you'll find barbecue pits for picnics and an unstaffed, unsupervised 9m (30-ft.) tower (Kömpmannholmen, no phone) that's useful for spying on bird nests in the upper branches of nearby trees. The trail ends in Luleå's suburb of Pörson, site of the local university, and site of a small-scale museum, **Teknykens Hus,** Pörson, 97187 Luleå (② **0920/ 492201**). Conceived as a tribute to the industries that bring employment and prosperity to Norbotten, it's open daily from 11am to 5pm in summer, and Tuesday to Friday 11am to 4pm in winter. Entrance fee is 50SEK ($6.50) for adults, 50SEK ($6.50) for children. From Pörson, after your visit to the museum, take bus no. 15 or 16 back to Luleå. Hiking along the above-mentioned trail is not recommended in winter, as heavy snowfalls obliterate the signs and the path, and it's unsafe for all but the most experienced and physically fit residents.

Norrbottens Museum   Close to the city center at Hermelin Park, Norrbottens Museum presents a comprehensive look at Norrbotten's history over the centuries, showing how people lived in these northern regions in bygone days. The museum possesses the world's most complete collection of Lapp artifacts.

Storgatan 2. ② 0920/24-35-00. Free admission. Tues–Fri 10am–4pm; Sat–Sun noon–4pm. Bus: 1, 2, 4, 5, 8, or 9.

WHERE TO STAY

Arctic Hotel ⊙   In the heart of town, this is a winning choice as both a hotel and a restaurant. With the best and most helpful staff in town, it is both functional and stylish, lying just a stone's throw from both the train station and the bus terminal. Airport buses also stop right at the entrance to the hotel. Unless it's a gray day, guest rooms are bright and fresh, each comfortably and attractively furnished in a modern style. The rather smallish bathrooms come equipped with shower, no tub. Thoughtful touches abound here, including coffee and crackers always available during the day in the lobby; on weekday evenings a light sandwich buffet with fresh fruit and vegetables is served. Guests can relax in the hotel's whirlpool bathrooms. Even if you're not a guest, consider patronizing the on-site Resaurang Eden. Its first-class cuisine includes such signature dishes as Arctic char with mushroom sauce, or even entrecôte of elk. The freshly caught Swedish salmon is another local dish to savor.

Sandviksgatan 80, S-972 34 Luleå. ℂ 0920/109-80. Fax 0920/60-787. www.arctichotel.se. 94 units. 799SEK–1,399SEK ($104–$182) double; 999SEK–1,699SEK ($130–$221) suite. AE, DC, MC, V. **Amenities:** Restaurant; bar; sauna; room service (6:30am–11pm); laundry service; nonsmoking rooms; rooms for those w/limited mobility. *In room:* TV, dataport, minibar (soft drinks only), coffeemaker (in some), hair dryer, iron/ironing board (in some).

Elite Stadshotellet ⚜ The stately, ornate, brick-and-stone building is the oldest (1900), grandest, and most traditional hotel in town. It's in the center of the city, next to the waterfront. The modernized public area has kept a few old-fashioned details from the original building. Guest rooms are comfortable and well furnished. Each unit has a well-maintained bathroom with a tub/shower.

Storgatan 15, S-971 81 Luleå. ℂ 0920/67-000. Fax 0920/670-92. www.elite.se. 135 units. Mon–Thurs 1,430SEK–1,640SEK ($186–$213) double, 2,500SEK ($325) suite; Fri–Sun 790SEK ($103) double, 2,500SEK ($325) suite. Rates include buffet breakfast. AE, DC, MC, V. Parking 100SEK ($13). Bus: 1, 2, 4, 5, 8, or 9. **Amenities:** Restaurant; bar; dance club; sauna; room service (7am–10pm); laundry service; dry cleaning; nonsmoking rooms; 1 room for those w/limited mobility. *In room:* TV, dataport (in some), minibar, hair dryer.

Hotel Nordkalotten ⚜ *Finds* Set 5km (3 miles) south of the town center, this is the most architecturally interesting hotel in the region, with some of the most charming grace notes. It originated in 1979, when the city of Luleå established a tourist information center on its premises. In 1984, the hotel was acquired by an independent entrepreneur who was lucky enough to secure thousands of first-growth pine logs (many between 600 and 1,000 years old) that had been culled from forests in Finland and Russia. To create the comfortable hotel you'll see today, he hired well-known Finnish architect Esko Lehmola to arrange the logs into the structural beams and walls of the hotel's reception area, sauna, and convention center. The result, which could never be duplicated today simply because the raw materials are no longer available, is a hotel where the growth rings of the wood reveal hundreds of years of forest life—direction of sunlight, climate changes, and rainfall—a source of endless fascination for foresters and botanists.

Most unusual of all is a dining and convention room set within what is shaped like an enormous tepee—also crafted from the ancient trees—that's flooded with sunlight from wraparound windows. Guest rooms are outfitted in soothing tones of beige and gray, with conservatively contemporary furnishings, tiled bathrooms with showers, and wall-to-wall carpeting. Double rooms have their own private saunas.

Lulviksvägen 1, S-972 54 Luleå. ℂ 0920/20-00-00. Fax 0920/199-09. www.nordkalotten.com. 172 units. Mid-June to mid-Aug 790SEK ($103) double and suite; Fri–Sat year-round 1,330SEK ($173) double and suite; Sun–Thurs year-round 1,813SEK ($236) double and suite. AE, DC, MC, V. Free parking. From Luleå's center, follow the signs to the airport. **Amenities:** Restaurant; bar; indoor heated pool; sauna; laundry service; dry cleaning; nonsmoking rooms; rooms for those w/limited mobility. *In room:* TV, dataport, minibar.

Quality Hotel Luleå ⊛ Built in 1979 and most recently renovated in 2003, this hotel has six stories, two of which are underground. It lies on Luleå's main street in the town center. Guest rooms are comfortable but blandly international in style and decor. Each unit has a neatly kept bathroom with a tub/shower.

Hotel Luleå's restaurant specializes in charcoal-grilled meats. A dance club in the cellar is open Thursday through Saturday from 9pm to 3am year-round. The admission is 80SEK ($10), but there is no charge for hotel guests.

Storgatan 17, S-971 28 Luleå. ✆ **800/221-2350** in the U.S., or 0920-20 10 00. Fax 0920/20-10-12. www. choicehotels.se. 210 units. Mon–Thurs 1,395SEK–1,595SEK ($181–$207) double; Fri–Sun 890SEK ($116) double; 2,995SEK ($389) suite. Rates include buffet breakfast. AE, DC, MC, V. Parking 125SEK ($16). Bus: 1, 2, 4, 5, 8, or 9. **Amenities:** Restaurant; bar; dance club; indoor heated pool; sauna; room service (6am–11pm); laundry service; dry cleaning; nonsmoking rooms; rooms for those w/limited mobility. *In room:* TV, dataport, minibar, hair dryer.

WHERE TO DINE

The Restaurants at the Hotel Nordkalotten ⊛ SWEDISH/LAPPISH Some clients come for a meal at this hotel just to see what hundreds of thousands of kronors' worth of exotic and very old timber can produce. (See the hotel review, above.) Once you get here, however, you'll also find well-prepared cuisine, a polite and friendly welcome, and flavors that are unique to Sweden's far north. Lunch is usually served in the tepee-shape building that's the hotel's trademark; dinner, traditionally, is in the *Renhagen* (Reindeer) Restaurant, where log walls, a flagstone-built fireplace, and flickering candles create a soothing but dramatic ambience. Menu items include the liberal use of elk, reindeer, salmon, forest mushrooms and berries, and freshwater char. Presentations are elegant, in some cases emulating the upscale restaurants of Stockholm.

Lulviksvägen 1. ✆ 0920/20-00-00. Reservations recommended. Dinner fixed-price 3-course menu 244SEK ($32). AE, DC, MC, V. Daily 6–10pm. From Luleå's center, follow the signs to the airport and drive 5km (3 miles) south of town.

3 Arvidsjaur

699km (433 miles) N of Stockholm, 112km (69 miles) S of the Arctic Circle, 171km (106 miles) SW of Luleå

A modern community, Arvidsjaur nevertheless has an old Lappish center with well-preserved, cone-shape huts where reindeer are rounded up and marked in June and July. The city lies in a belt of coniferous forests bordering on the highland region; these forests alone would merit a visit.

Excellent skiing, an untouched wilderness with an abundance of wildlife, and good fishing at the Pite and Skellefte rivers are a few of this region's temptations.

ESSENTIALS

GETTING THERE   By Plane   Arvidsjaur can be reached by air from Stockholm, with daily departures in both directions. Flight time is 2 hours. For information and bookings, call **SAS** ✆ **0770/727-727.**

By Train   Arvidsjaur has rail links with Stockholm. Train schedules change depending on the time of year, so you should call for information at ✆ **0771/ 75-75-75.** Arvidsjaur is on the inland railway, a line that stretches for nearly 1,290km (800 miles), running between Kristinehamn in Värmland to Gällivare in Lapland. There are rail connections to the Northern Mainline from Stockholm up to the Finnish border.

The Lapps (Sami) in Sweden

The Lapps (or Sami), of whom 15,000 to 17,000 live in Sweden, have inhabited the area since ancient times. The area of Lapp settlement (known as Sapmi) extends over the entire Scandinavian Arctic region and stretches along the mountain districts on both sides of the Swedish-Norwegian border down to the northernmost part of Dalarna.

Many Lapps maintain links to their ancient culture, whereas others have completely assimilated. Some 2,500 still lead the nomadic life of their ancestors, herding reindeer and wearing traditional multicolored dress.

The language of the Lapps belongs to the Finno-Ugric group. A large part of Lapp literature has been published in northern Sami, which is spoken by approximately 75% of Lapps. As with all Arctic societies, oral literature has always played a prominent role. Among Lapps, this oral tradition takes the form of *yoiking,* a type of singing. (Once governments tried to suppress this, but now yoiking is enjoying a renaissance.) One of the classic works of Lapp literature is Johan Turi's *Tale of the Lapps,* first published in 1910.

Handicrafts are important in the Lapp economy. Several craft designers have developed new forms of decorative art, producing a revival in Lapp handicraft tradition.

Many members of the Sami community feel that the term *Lapp* has negative connotations; as a result, it's gradually being replaced by the indigenous minority's own name for itself, *sábme,* or other dialect variations. *Sami* seems to be the most favored English translation of *Lapp,* and the word is used increasingly.

By Bus   Weekend buses from Stockholm, with a change in Skellefteå (see chapter 11) can be booked through **Nyman & Schultz Travel Agency** by calling ✆ **0960/654-500.** For other bus connections in the area, including to Arjeplog, call ✆ **0960/103-07.**

By Car   Most motorists take the eastern coastal road of Sweden, E4, which runs through Umeå to Skellefteå. At Skellefteå, head inland and northwest along Route 94 into Arvidsjaur.

VISITOR INFORMATION   The **Arvidsjaur Tourist Bureau,** at Östra Skolgatan 18C, 93331 Arvidsjaur (✆ **0960/175-00;** fax 0960/136-87; www.arvidsjaurlappland.com), is open from June 15 to August 16 daily from 9:30am to 6pm. Otherwise, hours are Monday to Friday 8am to noon and 1 to 6pm.

SEEING THE SIGHTS

Places of interest in town include **Lapp Town** ★★ (✆ **0960/125-25**), in the center, with the world's largest preserved Lapp church village and more than 80 Lapp wooden huts and lodgings. Guided tours are offered daily at 5pm in July. Hours are noon to 5pm, and the fee is 30SEK ($3.90). Children up to 12 are admitted free.

You can also visit the **Glommersträsk Historical Museum** (📞 **0960/202-91**), a local heritage center. The farming estate here dates from the 1700s and consists of 12 buildings that contain a large collection of practical objects from the early colonization of the Lapp region. These include the region's first schoolroom from the 1840s, as well as a smithy. There is an on-site retail shop for handicrafts. Admission is 20SEK ($2.60). It is open from June 14 to August 13 Monday to Friday 10am to 4:30pm. Closed in winter.

EXPLORING THE AREA

Directly south of Arvidsjaur lies the exquisite, mountainous preservation region of **Vittjåkk-Akkanålke** ⭐, a forest reserve with hiking paths cut through its wild and beautiful reaches. The paths are 1.5 to 5km (1–3 miles) in length. Also contained within the nature preserve is **Lake Stenträsket,** which is known for its char fishing. In summer, you can rent boats to tour the lake. The summit of Akkanålke can be reached by car and offers a panoramic lookout perch.

Lappish souvenirs and handicrafts are available at **Anna-Lisas Souvenirbutik,** Stationsgatan 3 (📞 **0960/106-33**). Other souvenir stores in town are: **Handicraft Arvida,** Storgatan 17 (📞 **0960/133-20**); and **Lindmarks Slöjd & Snickeri,** Hedgatan 9 (📞 **0960/217-70**).

WHERE TO STAY & DINE

Laponia Hotel ⭐ The best-recommended and most substantial hotel in town was built in 1957 and has been renovated many times since, most recently in 2002. Guest rooms are comfortable, uncontroversial, outfitted the way you'd expect in an upscale motel, and filled with light from big windows. Each unit comes with a neatly tiled bathroom with a tub/shower. As a special feature, suites contain their own kitchenettes and sauna. The food at the hotel here is the best in town. You can savor both regional specialties of Lapland and international dishes. *Note:* The hotel also offers suites with a kitchen, and a bathroom with sauna and shower.

Storgatan 45, S-933 33 Arvidsjaur. 📞 **0960/555-00.** Fax 0960/555-99. www.hotell-laponia.se. 200 units. Mid-June to mid-Aug 780SEK ($101) double, from 1,380SEK ($179) suite; rest of year Mon–Thurs 1,270SEK ($165) double, from 1,870SEK ($243) suite; Fri–Sun 940SEK ($122) double, from 1,540SEK ($200) suite. Rates include breakfast. AE, DC, MC, V. Free parking. **Amenities:** Restaurant; bar; indoor heated pool; gym; spa; sauna; laundry service; dry cleaning; nonsmoking rooms; rooms for those w/limited mobility. *In room:* TV, dataport (in most), minibar.

EASY EXCURSIONS FROM ARVIDSJAUR

Arjeplog sits on the edge of high mountain country on a peninsula between the great lakes of Uddjaur and Hornavan. The highlands in this region are studded with excellent fishing waters (you can practically catch whitefish from the roadside). The church at Arjeplog was built in 1767 and contains a bridal crown (made from flowers and tree branches from the forest); legend says that it once was stolen by the Lapps but was found again up in the mountains. This city was colonized in the 16th century when silver mining started in Nasafjäll on the Norwegian border. Reindeer at that time carried the silver to Piteå for shipment. In **Aldorfstrom,** the silver village, you can still see some of the buildings from the old purifying plant. Today lead ore is mined in the "underwater mine" at Laisvall.

Guided visits to the area stop at **Galtispouda,** a mountain range outside Arjeplog, which offers a panoramic outlook over the surrounding lakes and mountains. The Arvidsjaur tourist board (see above) organizes excursions to the area from June 21 to August 6, departing from the tourist office Monday, Wednesday, and Friday at 11:15am, with a return by bus at 8:50pm. On Friday and Saturday the return to Arvidsjaur is by steam train, departing at 10pm. The cost is 550SEK ($72) for adults, and 275SEK ($36) for ages 6 to 16 (5 and under ride free). Visiting the silver museum at Arjeplog is another 50SEK ($6.50). To reach both Arjeplog and Galtispouda by car, drive northwest along Route 95.

4 Tärnaby & Hemavan

360km (223 miles) NE of Umeå, 328km (203 miles) W of Luleå, 440km (273 miles) N of Östersund, 1,008km (625 miles) N of Stockholm

Tärnaby was the birthplace of Ingmar Stenmark, double Olympic gold medalist and Sweden's greatest skier. Not surprisingly, Tärnaby also is the center of Sweden's most accessible alpine region, offering beautiful mountains and a chain of lakes. Hikers can strike out for Artfjället, Norra Storfjället, Mortsfjället, and Atoklinton, perhaps with hired guides. And Laxfjället, with its fine ski hills and gentle slopes, is nearby on the Blå Vägen (European Rd. 79).

Hemaven is the largest tourist resort in the area. Many paths lead toward Norra Storfjället, a small mountain visible from Hemavan. A delta formed by the River Ume is particularly rich in bird life.

The greatest trail is the **Kungsleden (Royal Trail),** running from Hemavan to Abisko for a distance of 338km (210 miles). This is one of the most fascinating trails in Europe.

ESSENTIALS

GETTING THERE   By Plane   Most visitors use the airport at Umeå rather than the one at Arvisjaur because of the greater frequency of flights. You can call **SAS** for flight information at Umeå (✆ **0770-727-727**) to see which flight is more convenient for you.

By Train   Two trains depart daily from Stockholm for the far northern rail junction of Storuman. Trains from Gothenburg headed for Storuman also are routed through Stockholm. From Storuman, it's necessary to go the rest of the way by bus (1½ hr. or more, depending on the weather). Call ✆ **0771/75-75-75** for rail schedules.

By Bus   From the rail junction at Storuman, five buses per day make the 126km (78-mile) run to Tärnaby. From the airport at Umeå, there are three or four buses a day, but it takes 5 hours. For schedules, call ✆ **0200/218-218.**

By Car   Take E4 north to Stockholm, transferring onto Route E75 at the junction to Östersund. From here, take Route 88 north to Storuman, then head northwest on E37 to Tärnaby. From Arvidsjaur, head southwest along Route 45 until you reach the junction with E12 heading west.

VISITOR INFORMATION   For information, **Turistinformation,** in the town center (✆ **0954/104-50**), is open from mid-June to mid-August Monday to Friday 8:30am to 7pm, Saturday and Sunday 10am to 6pm; off season, Monday to Friday 9am to 5pm.

EXPLORING THE AREA

Tärnaby and Hemavan may be tiny mountain villages, but they are popular destinations because they mark the end of the **Kungsleden Trail** ✦✦✦, one of the great hiking trails of Europe. The villages themselves are almost devoid of attractions but come as a welcome relief for those nearing the end of the trail. Most hikers begin their odyssey at Abisko (see "Abisko," later in this chapter) and end their journeys at Hemavan. However, you may prefer to go against the flow by starting at Hemavan and ending at Abisko.

Instead of overnighting at Hemavan, you can stay at Tärnaby, the little village nearby. It is much more attractive, with meadows whose midsummer wildflowers run up to the edge of the dark forests that surround the town.

The tourist office (see above) is staffed by helpful people who have the latest information on hiking and fishing in the area. Because conditions are constantly changing, depending on the weather and the season, it is wise to inquire here for advice before heading out into the wilderness on your own.

The town's most popular walk, which is signposted from the center, is across a series of meadows to **Laxfjället Mountain.** From the base of that mountain, you can look back for a panoramic view of Tärnaby. If the day is warm and sunny, you can follow the signs to the "beach" at **Lake Laisan.** Locals go swimming here in July, but if you're from somewhere like Florida, the waters might feel too cold for you.

WHERE TO STAY & DINE

Laisalidens Fjällhotell   This is the best hotel in the region and has a particularly accommodating staff. Its steep, sloping roof is designed to shed the winter's heavy snowfalls, and the dark, woodsy facade makes it look like a modern chalet. With windows opening onto views of the lake, this traditionally decorated mountain hotel offers pleasant but functional-looking guest rooms that are kept immaculately clean. The hotel arranges fishing trips as well as motorboat excursions to the nearby lakes. Built in 1953 and renovated in recent years, the hotel lies 20km (12 miles) west of Tärnaby, gloriously isolated amid trees and tundra. Bathrooms are very tiny, with shower stalls, toilets, and basic sinks. Simple Swedish food is served three times daily.

S-920 64 Tärnaby. ℂ **0954/21100.** Fax 0954/211-63. www.laisaliden.se. 16 units. 750SEK ($98) double. Rate includes breakfast. MC, V. Free parking. Bus: Vlå Vägen from Umeå. From the center of Tärnaby, follow Rte. 73 west for 20km (12 miles) until you come to the hotel. **Amenities:** Restaurant; bar; sauna; room service (7am–10pm); laundry service; dry cleaning. *In room:* TV.

Tärnaby Fjällhotell   This is the larger of the two hotels in the town center. Built in 1956 and renovated several times since, its rooms are comfortable and well maintained, with pastel colors and contemporary furnishings. All units contain private bathrooms furnished with either tubs or showers.

Östra Strandvägen 16, S-920 64 Tärnaby. ℂ **0954/104-20.** Fax 0954/106-27. www.hemavan.nu. 36 units. 660SEK ($86) double; summer 620SEK ($81) double. Rates include breakfast. AE, DC, MC, V. Free parking. **Amenities:** Restaurant; bar; gym; sauna; laundry service; dry cleaning. *In room:* TV.

5 Jokkmokk

198km (123 miles) NW of Luleå, 1,191km (738 miles) N of Stockholm, 204km (126 miles) S of Kiruna

This community on the Luleå River, just north of the Arctic Circle, has been a Sami trading and cultural center since the 17th century. With a population of 3,400 hearty souls, Jokkmokk (which means "bend in the river") is the largest settlement in the *kommun* (municipality). Bus routes link Jokkmokk with other villages in the area.

Who comes to Jokkmokk? Other than the summer tourists, visitors are mostly business travelers involved in some aspect of the timber industry or the hydroelectric power industry. Jokkmokk and the 12 hydroelectric plants that lie nearby produce as much as 25% of all the electricity used in Sweden. Most residents of the town were born here, except for a very limited number of urban refugees from Stockholm.

ESSENTIALS

GETTING THERE   By Plane   The nearest airport is in Luleå, 198km (123 miles) away (see "Getting There," in the "Luleå" section, earlier in this chapter, or call **SAS** at ℂ **0770/727-727**). From Luleå, you can take a bus for the final leg of the journey.

By Train   No trains run between Stockholm and Jokkmokk. However, three trains make the run from Stockholm to Murjek, a town lying 60km (37 miles) to the south of Jokkmokk. From Murjek, you can take one of three buses a day for the final lap into Jokkmokk.

By Bus   There is one scheduled bus per day from Luleå to Jokkmokk, which is timed to meet the plane's arrival. For information, call ℂ **0200/218218.**

By Car   From Luleå, take Route 97 northwest.

VISITOR INFORMATION   Contact the **Jokkmokk Turistbyrå,** at Stortorget 4 (ℂ **0971/222-50**), open from June to mid-August daily from 9am to 7pm, from mid-August to May Monday to Friday 8:30am to noon and 1 to 4pm.

SEEING THE SIGHTS

The Lapps (Sami) hold an **annual market** ★★★ here in early February, when they sell their local handicrafts. "The Great Winter Market" is a 400-year-old tradition. Held on the first weekend (Thurs–Sun) of February, it attracts some 30,000 people, not just to buy and sell, but also for the special experience of the place. If you're planning to come, you'll need to make hotel reservations a year in advance.

Salmon fishing is possible in the town's central lake. Locals jump in the river in summer to take a dip, but we suggest you watch from the sidelines unless you're a polar bear.

Karl IX decreed that the winter meeting place of the Jokkmokk Sami would be the site of a market and church. The first church, built in 1607, was known as the **Lapp Church.** A nearby hill, known as **Storknabben,** has a cafe from which, if the weather is clear, the midnight sun can be seen for about 20 days in midsummer.

Because Jokkmokk is the center of Sami culture in this area, an important establishment is the national Swedish Mountain and Sami Museum **Ájtte** ★★★, Kyrkogatan (ℂ **0971/170-70**), in the center of town. This museum (whose

---

Tips   A Quick Stop

If you're traveling from Luleå on Route 97 toward Jokkmokk, consider stopping at Boden. Founded in 1809, this is Sweden's oldest garrison town. After losing Finland to Russia, and fearful of a Russian invasion, Sweden built this fortress to protect its interior region. Visit the Garrionmuseet (Garrison Museum), which has exhibits on military history as well as uniforms and weapons used throughout Sweden's history.

Chillin' in Jokkmokk

Jokkmokk is one of the coldest places in Sweden in winter, with temperatures plunging below –30°F (–34°C) for days at a time. In the winter, the cold weather forces the Lapp Church to inter corpses in wall vaults until the spring thaw will permit burial in the ground.

Sami name translates to "storage hut") is one of the largest of its kind; its exhibits integrate nature and the cultures of the Swedish mountain region. A new part of the museum is the **Alpine Garden** (© **0971/10100**), which lies close to the museum on Lappstavägen. If you want to learn about the natural environment and the flora of the north of Sweden, this is the place to go. The mountain flora is easily accessible and beautifully arranged. There's also a restaurant and a gift shop. Museum admission is 50SEK ($6.50) for adults, free for children 17 and under. The museum is open year-round; in summer, Monday to Friday 9am to 7pm, and Saturday and Sunday 11am to 6pm; off season, it closes at 4pm.

A JOURNEY BACK IN TIME

Vuollerim   This 6,000-year-old winter settlement at the mouth of the Luleå River was created and used by a group of Stone Age people. They lived by hunting, fishing, and gathering berries and plants. They eventually abandoned the site, probably in search of better hunting grounds, and it remained untouched until 1983, when researchers from Umeå found this unique settlement, perhaps the best preserved in northern Europe. The Stone Age dwellings were equipped with a prehistoric heating system, and this winter village was populated by four to eight family groups. Diggings in the area have increased knowledge of the prehistory of northern Sweden. Visitors can see a full-size replica of the dwelling, and a cafe is surrounded by an exhibition of objects found during the excavations. A slide display offers a journey through thousands of years. A museum also includes other Stone Age exhibits.

Murjeksvägen 31. © **0976/101-65**. Admission 50SEK ($6.50). June–Sept Mon–Fri 9am–6pm; Oct–May Tues–Wed 10am–4pm. Take Rte. 97 toward Boden and Luleå 45km (28 miles) southeast of Jokkmokk.

OUTDOOR & ADVENTURE

Exploring conditions are optimal from mid-June to mid-August; you (and, unfortunately, the mosquitoes) will find the area most accessible at this time. The best way to tackle the region is to first consult the tourist office (see above). They will help you with maps and advice about how to see some of the best of the surrounding wilderness, and they will advise you about local conditions.

You can **hike** to the mighty **Muddus Fall** in the deep ravine of the Muddus River. Trips are conducted from June 2 to August 24 daily 9am to 5pm; they last about 8 hours and cover a distance of some 13km (8 miles). The price, including food, guide, and transportation, is 550SEK ($72) for adults, 200SEK ($26) for ages 7 to 15, and 150SEK ($20) for those 6 and under. For more information, call © **0971/122-20.**

At nearby **Lake Talvatissjön** you can catch Arctic char and rainbow trout (if you're lucky). Visit the tourist office for a *fiskekort* (fishing permit). Prices were not available at press time, but they'll probably be around $10. At the lake is a cleaning table for the fish, and a fireplace or grill in case you'd like to cook your catch.

SHOPPING

At **Jokkmoks Tenn,** Järnvägsgatan 19 (℃ **0971/554-20**), you will find the best collection of Sami traditional handicrafts. A workshop here is carried on as a family business. The best buys are in pewter objects and Lapp jewelry. If you'd like a selection of tough and durable clothing for winter, head for **Polstjärnan Atelje,** Hantverkaregatan 9 (℃ **0971/126-73**). At **Jokkmokks Stencenter,** Talvatis (℃ **0971/122-35**), rocks and minerals from the surrounding region are turned into beautiful jewelry and other items. Some of the offerings include mylonite, which is warm and colorful in red-black shades; unakite, in pink and green with flower patterns; quartzite, with various patterns and colors; gabbro, which is black with golden flakes of pyrite; and hornfels, in a soft brown, almost beige, color. You can tour the workshop here Monday through Friday in July from 10am to 6pm, and at other times by appointment.

WHERE TO STAY

Hotel Jokkmokk ⭐ _Finds_ The largest and best-appointed hotel in town was built in the mid-1980s just north of the edge of Lake Talvatis, near the town center. Designed in a modern format that includes simple, boxy lines and lots of varnished hardwoods, it offers clean, well-organized, and comfortable shelter against the sometimes-savage climate, and all the well-upholstered comforts of a big-city hotel. (Part of that feeling derives from the fact that some of its staff and managers are urban refugees from the Swedish capital, who moved here to get closer to the great outdoors.) Guest rooms have big windows overlooking the lake, the forest, and, in some cases, the lakeside road. All have fresh colors inspired by a Scandinavian springtime, and shower-only bathrooms with plenty of very welcome hot water. Six of the units are designated as "ladies' rooms"—especially feminine bedrooms adorned with pastels and florals. The hotel contains an indoor swimming pool, a sauna with an exercise area, a bar, and the best restaurant in town, which is recommended separately in "Where to Dine" (see below).

Box 85, Solgatan 455-96231, S-262 23 Jokkmokk. ℃ **0971/777-00.** Fax 0971/777-90. www.hoteljokkmokk.se. 75 units. Mid-June to mid-Aug 895SEK ($116) double; rest of year Mon–Thurs 1,495SEK ($194), Fri–Sun 895SEK ($116) double; 1,600SEK ($208) suites. Rates include buffet breakfast. AE, DC, MC, V. Free parking. **Amenities:** Restaurant; bar; indoor heated pool; gym; sauna; laundry service; dry cleaning; nonsmoking rooms; rooms for those w/limited mobility. _In room:_ TV, dataport.

Hotell Gästis ⭐⭐ This landmark hotel, dating from 1915, is in the exact center of the town, about 180m (590 ft.) from the rail station. In some respects, it has the qualities of a frontier-country hotel. It offers well-maintained rooms with modern furnishings and good beds, and small bathrooms equipped with shower units. Floors are either carpeted or covered in vinyl. The restaurant has won many awards and serves well-prepared meals, including continental dishes and _husmanskost_ (good home cooking). Entertainment and dancing are presented once a week. The sauna is free for all hotel guests.

Harrevägen 1, S-96 231 Jokkmokk. ℃ **0971/100-12.** Fax 0971/100-44. www.hotell-gastis.com. 27 units. 750SEK–995SEK ($98–$129) double; 900SEK–1,200SEK ($117–$156) triple. Rates include breakfast. AE, DC, MC, V. Free parking. **Amenities:** Restaurant; bar; sauna. _In room:_ TV, hair dryer.

WHERE TO DINE

The Restaurant in the Hotel Jokkmokk SWEDISH/LAPPISH There's not a great variety of restaurant options in Jokkmokk, but you'll find the best evening dining in town in this well-managed hotel dining room. Within a carpeted room with laminated ceiling beams and a sweeping row of windows overlooking the lake, you'll enjoy rich and flavorful specialties whose ingredients are found in the surrounding Lappish terrain. Specialties include a "Jokmokk pan" that consists of a mixture of cubed reindeer filet, mushrooms, onions, and potatoes, bound together in an herb-flavored cream sauce and served in a copper chafing dish brought directly to the table. Other unusual choices include local freshwater char with saffron sauce and mashed potatoes, and filet of elk with forest mushroom sauce.

Solgatan 24. (✆ **0971/553-20.** Reservations recommended. Main courses 125SEK–180SEK ($16–$23). AE, DC, MC, V. Daily 5–11pm.

6 Kvikkjokk

1,109km (688 miles) N of Stockholm, 97km (60 miles) W of Gällivare, 172km (107 miles) W of Luleå, 119km (74 miles) NW of Jokkmokk

Kvikkjokk was a silver-ore center in the 17th century, and many historical relics from that period can be seen in the area today. Today this mountain village is known as one of Lapland's most beautiful resorts and serves as the gateway to **Sarek National Park** ⍟⍟⍟, the largest wilderness area in Europe and one of the most representative of the highland regions. It's virtually inaccessible, almost entirely without trails, huts, or bridges. Nevertheless, the flora and fauna are fascinating, and the park as a whole is a richly rewarding experience for the dedicated outdoor adventurer.

ESSENTIALS

GETTING THERE   By Train & Bus   Take the train to Jokmokk (see earlier in this chapter), from which you must change to a bus to Kvikkjokk. For rail information and schedules, call (✆ **0771/75-75-75.** Two buses per day run between Jokmokk and Kvikkjokk, a distance of 119km (74 miles). Unfortunately, the buses don't always connect with train arrivals from Stockholm. For schedules, call (✆ **0200/218218.**

By Car   Take E4 north from Stockholm to Luleå, then head northwest along Route 97 through Boden to Jokmok. To get there from Jokmokk, drive north on Route 45. After passing the town of Vaikijaur, turn west on a secondary road, following the signs to Klubbudden. Continue west on this road, passing through the towns of Tjåmotis, Njavve, and Arrenjarka until you reach Kvikkjokk.

VISITOR INFORMATION   The tourist office at Jokmokk (see above) can provide data about the area.

EXPLORING THE WILDERNESS

The **Sarek National Park,** between the Stora and Lilla Luleälv, covers an area of 1,208 sq. km (471 sq. miles), with about 100 glaciers and 87 mountains rising more than 1,770m (5,806 ft.); eight are more than 1,950m (6,396 ft.). The most visited valley, **Rapadel** ⍟, opens onto Lake Laidaure. In winter, sled dogs pull people through this valley.

In 1909, Sweden established this nature reserve in the wilderness so that it could be preserved for future generations. To take a mountain walk through the entire park would take at least a week; most visitors stay only a day or 2. Although rugged and beautiful, Sarek is considered extremely difficult for even the most experienced of hikers. There is absolutely nothing here to aid the visitor—no designated hiking trails, no tourist facilities, no cabins or mountain huts, and no bridges over rivers (whose undertows, incidentally, are very dangerous). Mosquitoes can be downright treacherous, covering your eyes, nose, and ears. You should explore the park only if you hire an experienced guide. Contact a local hotel such as **Kvikkjokk Fjällstation,** below, for a recommendation.

Kvikkjokk, at the end of Route 805, is the starting or finishing point for many hikers using the **Kungsleden Trail.** Call the **Svenska Turistforeningen** at © **08/463-21-00** for information and also see "Abisko," later in this chapter. One- or 2-day outings can be made in various directions. Local guides also can lead you on an interesting boat trip (inquire at the hotel listed below). The boat will take you to a fascinating delta where the Tarra and Karnajokk rivers meet. The area also is good for canoeing.

WHERE TO STAY & DINE

Kvikkjokk Fjällstation Originally established in 1907 by the Swedish Touring Club, and enlarged with an annex in the 1960s, this mountain chalet offers simple, no-frills accommodations for hikers and rock-climbers. It's also the headquarters for a network of guides who operate canoe and hiking trips into the vast wilderness areas that fan out on all sides. Accommodations are functional, woodsy, and basic, and include eight double rooms, eight four-bed rooms, and two cabins with four beds each. There's a sauna, a plain restaurant, and access to canoe rentals and a variety of guided tours that depart at frequent intervals. The chalet is open only in summer. For information about the Kvikkmokk Fjällstation out of season, call the **tourist information office** in Jokkmokk (129km/80 miles away) at © **0971/222-50.**

S-962 02 Kvikkjokk. © **0971/210-22.** Fax 0971-210-39. 18 units, none with bathroom. 260SEK–400SEK ($34–$52) per person. AE, MC, V. Free parking. Closed Sept 19–Feb 15. **Amenities:** Restaurant; lounge; sauna; laundry service. *In room:* No phone.

7 Gällivare

97km (60 miles) N of the Arctic Circle, 1,198km (743 miles) N of Stockholm

As a city that is one of the most important sources of iron ore in Europe, Gällivare has a grim, industrial look. Traditionally, it has been a rather dour mining town, despite its location at the center of some of the great unspoiled wonders of Europe. The town had no involvement with resort-style sports until the Dundret Hotel (see "Where to Stay & Dine," below) began its high-energy marketing efforts.

This is a land of contrasts, from high mountain peaks to deep mines. We like to visit Gällivare mainly to explore some of the national parks, which range from a primeval forest at Muddus to panoramic terrain at Stora Sjöfjället. If you come in winter, the northern lights may persuade you to extend your visit.

ESSENTIALS

GETTING THERE By Plane There are two direct flights per day from Stockholm. There also are several commuter planes daily through Umeå to the Lapland Airport at Gällivare. Call **Swedline** (© **0495/249-065**) for information and schedules.

By Train The night train from Stockholm leaves about midday, allowing you to wake up in Gällivare in the morning in time for breakfast. For information and schedules, call © **0771/75-75-75.**

By Bus   The **Regional Express** has convenient daily runs that link Gällivare with Luleå, Ostersund, and Narvik in Norway. For information and schedules, call ℂ **0200/218218.**

By Car   From Jokkmokk, continue northeast along Route 45.

VISITOR INFORMATION   Tourist Information, Storgaan 16 (ℂ **0970/ 166-60**), is open Monday through Friday from 8am to 5pm.

FROM MOUNTAINS TO MINES

Many visitors, especially those from Stockholm, come for the winter skiing. Often national ski teams from abroad come here for training, as the town itself lies only a 10-minute drive from the ski slopes and trails. Snow is virtually guaranteed here earlier than anywhere else in Sweden—from late October to late April. In fact, the ski season is Sweden's longest—200 days of the year.

The Dundret Hotel (see "Where to Stay & Dine," below) owns all the lifts and controls access to the slopes and other ski-related infrastructures in town. Lift tickets cost 210SEK–240SEK ($27–$31) per day, or 500SEK–570SEK ($65–$74) for 3 days. (*Note:* These prices are inexpensive when compared to the alpine resorts farther south.)

If you follow Route 45 8km (5 miles) south of Gällivare, you'll arrive at **Dundret,** or Thunder Mountain. Many visitors come here to witness the spectacle of the midnight sun, best viewed from June 2 to July 12 from a table at the cafe on the summit, which is open daily in summer from 9pm to 1am. The **panoramic view** ★★ takes in the iron-ore mountain of Malmberget to the north and the peak of another mountain, Kebnekaise, to the northwest. You also can see the national parks of Sarek and Padjelanta to the west. Even the valley of the Lule River, with the mountains of Norway in the backdrop, can be viewed on a clear night.

Many visitors come here to take **mine tours,** which can be booked at the tourist office. Visitors can take two different tours, both offered only from June to August. One goes to an underground iron-ore mine Monday to Friday at 10am and 2pm, and costs 200SEK ($26); the other visits a copper mine Monday through Friday at 2pm, and costs 200SEK ($26). The latter tour always takes in **Kåkstan,** which is the shanty town in Malmberget, dating from 1888 when jobs were plentiful and wages high, but housing was scarce. As a result, the town of Malmberget came into being, with dwellings of every shape and size.

The iron mine tour of **Gruvtur** takes 3 hours and also visits the Gruvmuseet (mining museum), which displays artifacts from 250 years of mining. You also can visit various production sites and go underground to the ore face. The copper mine tour lasts 3½ hours, beginning at the shanty town and going on to an open-cast mine at Aitik. This is the largest copper mine still operating in Europe, and it's also Sweden's largest gold mine, producing 2 tons of gold annually.

EXPLORING THE NATIONAL PARKS

Many visitors come to Gällivare in the summer to explore the national parks. Various little unmarked roads (open in summer only) west of Gällivare will take you through the parks, but the best way to visit them is to ask the tourist office to pinpoint a tour route for you—a wonderful service that takes your time and stamina into account. They also can give you up-to-date road conditions, supply maps, answer questions, and advise you on the best ways to experience the parks.

If you plan serious hiking, write (they don't accept calls) the **National Council on Mountain Safety,** Fjällsäkerhetsrådet at Naturvardsverket, S-171 85, Solna.

MUDDUS NATIONAL PARK ★★★

Muddus, south of Gällivare, is one of Sweden's most spectacular parks. Fortunately, it also is the park most often recommended to beginners or less experienced hikers. It's always best to check locally before starting out on any exploration deep into the wilderness, but some general guidelines are as follows: During May and early June, the ground at Muddus is most often boggy and wet because of rapid snow melt. Conditions are best in July and early August, but keep in mind that summers are short and the weather conditions changeable. It can be hot and sunny at Muddus 1 hour and raining the next. By mid-August snow could be falling.

Essentially, Muddus consists of marshland and forest (mostly pine) in the area between Gällivare and Jokkmokk. It's worth exploring some of its 48,000 hectares (118,560 acres), which house bears, moose, otters, wolverines, and many bird species. In summer, you may spot grazing reindeer or perhaps a whooper swan. The Muddusjokk River flows through the park, providing a panoramic 42m (140-ft.) waterfall. Trails also cross the park; they're well marked and lead visitors to the most scenic spots.

If you have time only to sample the park's beauty and don't plan extensive in-depth penetration of the forest, you can explore the western edges of Muddus, which skirt Route 45 as it goes north from Gällivare. The best approach is to leave Route 45 at Liggadammen. Even if you don't have a car, several buses per day in summer run from Gällivare to Liggadammen. Once here you'll see a trail leading to Skaite. You can follow this trail for a couple of hours, and once at Skaite, you can take an extensive hiking trail that stretches for 50km (31 miles). This well-marked trail has cabins along the way, plus a campsite by Muddus Falls, which is the most beautiful part of this national park.

STORA SJÖFÄLLET & PADJELANTA ★★★

Stora Sjöfället, along with Padjelanta National Park, is Europe's largest national park. Padjelanta demands more mountain hiking experience than Stora Sjöfället. The forests here contain many of the same species as the alpine area, but there also are blue hare, moose, fox, ermines, squirrels, otters, martens, and lynx. The most common fish are trout, alpine char, grayling, burbot, and whitefish. Reindeer breeding is carried on throughout the year in both parks, with about 125 reindeer breeders owning a total of 25,000 animals. During spring, summer, and autumn, most Lapps live in these mountains at about seven settlements, which include Ritjem and Kutjaure.

Lake Virihaure ★★★ in Padjelanta National Park is often called Sweden's most beautiful lake. Both parks contain marked hiking trails, and overnight accommodations are available in cabins—mainly Lapp huts and cottages. Good hiking equipment, including a tent, is advisable if you're planning a long hike through either park. Huts are just basic cabins with a roof and four walls—you'll have to bring a sleeping bag. They generally have summer-only toilets. Cottages vary but may have beds (you provide your own sleeping bag) and cooking facilities. They also have toilets (but a shower is rare). Hikers usually just crash at huts, but cottages should be reserved. Call the **Swedish Touring Club** (✆ 08/463-21-00) before you go.

You can **fish** in Padjelanta with a permit (contact any tourist office), but not in Stora Sjöfället.

WHERE TO STAY & DINE

Dundret ✦ *Kids*   Although Gällivare contains about a half-dozen other hotels and guesthouses, this is the only one that caters to ecology lovers, sports enthusiasts, and anyone interested in direct, firsthand exposure to Lapland's great outdoors. It dates from the 1920s, when some mountain huts on nearby peaks were the site of ski competitions for national athletic groups, but the main building as you'll see it today was constructed in the 1950s, with frequent improvements and enlargements ever since. Known fondly by the staff as Björn Fälten (the Bear Trap), it's the longest log-built building in Europe, with all the idiosyncratic and rustic touches you'd expect.

Since it was founded, many of the developments at this resort have involved the construction and maintenance of 90 cottages, each of them built of wood and outfitted in a rustic style appropriate to the far north. Each has a kitchen, holds up to four people, and receives a minimum of time and attention from the staff once the occupants have checked in. Preferable are the conventional hotel rooms; each receives daily maid service and is outfitted in a cozy, modern style that includes views over the surrounding wilderness, lots of heat and warmth, and comfortable chairs, beds, and small sofas. Bathrooms (with showers in both cottages and hotel rooms) are very compact, but they are well kept with up-to-date plumbing.

P.O. Box 82, S-982 21 Gällivare. © **0970/145-60.** Fax 0970/148-27. www.dundret.se. 35 units; plus 90 self-catering cottages with kitchen. 1,460SEK ($190) double; rate includes breakfast. 915SEK–1,375SEK ($119–$179) 4-bed cottage, with linens; breakfast 65SEK ($8.45) extra per person. A 1-time final cleaning fee costs 400SEK–600SEK ($52–$78), regardless of the length of your stay in a cottage. AE, DC, MC, V. From Gällivare's center, drive 3.2km (2 miles) north, following the signs for Jokkmokk. **Amenities:** Restaurant; indoor heated pool; fitness center; sauna; children's center; laundry service; dry cleaning; nonsmoking rooms; winter sports; snowboarding; chair lift. *In room:* TV.

⎛ *Moments* **A Winter Wonderland**
_____

At **Dundret** (see above), one of the leading resorts of the north, the first chair lift, inaugurated in 1955, was also the first in Sweden. It was rebuilt in 1978 and supplemented with another since then; both lead to at least a dozen well-maintained downhill slopes of varying degrees of difficulty. Six of these slopes are illuminated for use throughout the long, dark winter. There's also a small-scale ski jump, a health and fitness center with a limited array of spa facilities, and a very attractive log-sided room that contains a heated indoor pool; facilities for snowboarding; and Snowland, a child-care and entertainment facility designed to interest and amuse young children, presumably while their parents take time out for themselves. (A regular sight here are snow bears, inspired by the characters at Disney, who ride with young children in motorized sleighs.) Kiosks and sports shops rent and sell ski equipment and accessories. The staff is adept at arranging snow-scooter safaris, ice fishing, dog team trips, junkets on sleighs pulled by reindeer, overnight stays in a Lapp tent, and outdoor barbecues, regardless of the season. They also can arrange for visits to remote mountain streams where you can catch graylings. The schools of graylings found in this part of Sweden are the largest concentration of this type of fish in Europe.

8 Kiruna

193km (120 miles) N of Jokkmokk, 1,317km (817 miles) N of Stockholm

Covering more than 4,800 sq. km (1,872 sq. miles), Kiruna is the largest (in terms of geography) city in the world. Its extensive boundaries incorporate both Kebnekaise Mountain and Lake Torneträsk. This northernmost town in Sweden lies at about the same latitude as Greenland. The midnight sun can be seen here from mid-May to mid-July.

ESSENTIALS

GETTING THERE   By Plane   SAS (℃ **0770/727-727**) flies twice daily from Stockholm (flight time: 95 min.).

Train   Two or three trains per day make the 16-hour trip to Gällivare, a major rail junction. From here, you can change trains to Kiruna, a trip of 1½ hours. For schedules and information, phone ℃ **0771/75-75-75.**

By Bus   There's also daily bus service between Gällivare and Kiruna. Contact **Länstrafiken** at ℃ **0926/756-80.**

By Car   From Gällivare, continue northwest along E10.

VISITOR INFORMATION   Contact the **Kiruna Turistbyrå,** Lars Janssons Vagen 17 (℃ **0980/188-80; www.lappland.se**), open from June 15 to August 20 Monday to Friday 8:30am to 8pm, Saturday and Sunday 8:30am to 6pm; from August 21 to June 14 Monday to Friday 8:30am to 5pm, Saturday 8:30am to 2pm.

SEEING THE SIGHTS

Kiruna, which emerged at the turn of the 20th century, owes its location to the nearby deposits of iron ore. Guided tours of the mines are offered year-round (children 6 and under are not permitted on these tours). Visitors are taken through an underground network of tunnels and chambers. For details on the tours, contact the tourist office.

Southeast of the railroad station, the tower of the **Stadshus** (℃ **0980/70-496**) dominates Kiruna. The building was designed by Arthur von Schmalensee and inaugurated in 1963. A carillon of 23 bells rings out at noon and 6pm daily. This cast-iron tower was designed by Bror Markland and features unusual door handles of reindeer horn and birch. The interior draws upon materials from around the world: a mosaic floor from Italy, walls of handmade brick from the Netherlands, and pine from the American Northwest. Note also the hand-knotted hanging entitled *Magic Drum from Rautas,* a stunning work by artist Sven Xet Erixon. The upper part of the hanging depicts the midnight sun. Inside you'll find an art collection and some Sami handicraft exhibits. It's open June through August Monday through Friday from 9am to 6pm, and Saturday and Sunday from 10am to 6pm; September through May Monday through Friday from 10am to 5pm.

A short walk up the road will take you to the **Kiruna Kyrka** ✮✮, Kirkogatan 8 (℃ **0980/678-12**), open Monday through Friday from 9am to 6pm, Saturday and Sunday from 11am to 4:45pm. This church was constructed like a stylized Sami tent in 1912 (indeed, the dark timber interior does evoke a Lapp hut), with an origami design of rafters and wood beams. Sweden's architects on several occasions have voted it as their country's most beautiful building. Gustaf Wickman designed this unusual church, which has a free-standing bell tower supported by 12 props. Christian Eriksson designed the gilt bronze statues standing sentinel around the roofline. They represent such states of mind as shyness, arrogance, trust, melancholy, and love. Above the main door of the church is a relief depicting groups of Lapps beneath the clouds of heaven. This, too, is Eriksson's creation. The altarpiece by Prince Eugen evokes Paradise as a Tuscan landscape, a rather inappropriate image for this part of the world. Eriksson also created the cross depicting Lapps praying and, at its base, a metal sculpture entitled *St. George and the Dragon.*

You also can visit **Hjalmar Lundbohmsgården** (© **0980/701-10**), the official museum of the city of Kiruna. It's situated in a manor house built in 1899 by the city's founder and owner of most of the region's iron mines, Hjalmar Lundbohm. Many of the museum's exhibits deal with the city's origins in the late 19th century, the economic conditions in Europe that made its growth possible, and the personality of the entrepreneur who persuaded thousands of Swedes to move north to work in the mines. It's open June through August Monday to Friday from 10am to 6pm; off season, you must phone ahead for opening hours, which could be any day of the week between the hours of 8am and 4pm. Admission is 20SEK ($2.60) for adults, 15SEK ($1.95) for children 7 to 15, free for children under 7.

VISITING SWEDEN'S HIGHEST MOUNTAIN

Eighty kilometers (50 miles) away from the commercial center of town, the highest mountain in Sweden, **Kebnekaise Mountain** ☆☆, rises 2,090m (6,856 ft.) above sea level. This is a trip best made from late June to mid-August; from mid-August to September, weather conditions can prohibit the trip. To reach the mountain, take a bus to **Aroksjokk** village from the bus stop in Kiruna's center (no phone). Ask for schedules at the train station next door, where someone is usually on duty, or check with the Kiruna Tourist Office. From **Aroksjokk** village, a motorboat will take you to the Lapp village of **Nikkaluokta.** From here, it's a 21km (13-mile) hike (including another short boat trip) to the foot of the mountain. The trail is signposted at various points and runs along streams, and through meadows and pinewoods. Some of the Sami in the village of Nikkaluokta will offer you their services as guides on the hike; negotiate the fee depending on the time of the year and the number of your party. You do not have to seek them out; once you arrive at Nikkaluokta, they will come to you, eager to assist. The Samis can also arrange overnight stays and hikes or boating trips. The Swedish Touring Club has a mountain station at Kebnekaise, and the station guide here can arrange group hikes to the summit (requiring about 4 hr. for the ascent). It's a fairly easy climb for those in good physical shape; no mountaineering equipment is necessary. It also is possible to ski on Kebnekaise mountain in winter; it's best to consult the tourist board for more information.

SHOPPING

About 4km (2½ miles) north of Kiruna along highway E10 is a showcase of Lappish artifacts, **Mattarahkka** (© **0980/191-91**). Established in 1993, it's a log house capped proudly with the red, blue, yellow, and green Sami flag. The site includes workshops where visitors can watch traditional Sami products (knives, leather knapsacks, hats, gloves, and tunics) being made. Many of the items are for sale. The interior includes a simple cafe. The site is open from late June to August daily 10am to 6pm; off season Monday to Friday noon to 6pm.

(Finds   The Ice Hotel

Since the late 1980s, the most unusual, and most impermanent, hotel in Sweden is re-created early every winter on the frozen steppes near the iron mines of Jukkasjärvi, 200km (124 miles) north of the Arctic Circle. Here, the architect Yngve Bergqvist, financed by a group of friends who (not surprisingly) developed the original concept over bottles of vodka in an overheated sauna, uses jackhammers, bulldozers, and chainsaws to fashion a 60-room hotel out of 4,000 tons of densely packed snow and ice. The basic design is that of an igloo, but with endless amounts of whimsical sculptural detail thrown in as part of the novelty. Like Conrad Hilton's worst nightmare, the resulting "hotel" will inevitably buckle, collapse, and then vanish during the spring thaws. Despite its temporary state, during the long and frigid darkness of north Sweden's midwinter, it attracts a steady stream of engineers, theatrical designers, sociologists, and the merely curious, who avail themselves of timely activities in Sweden's far north: dogsled and snowmobile rides, cross-country skiing, and shimmering views of the aurora borealis. On the premises are an enormous reception hall, a multimedia theater, two saunas, and an ice chapel appropriate for simple meditation, weddings, and baptisms.

Available for occupancy (temperatures permitting) between mid-December and sometime in March, the hotel resembles an Arctic cross between an Arabian casbah and a medieval cathedral. Minarets are formed by dribbling water for about a week onto what eventually becomes a slender and soaring pillar of ice. Domes are formed igloo-style out of ice blocks arranged in a curved-roof circle. Reception halls boast rambling vaults supported by futuristic-looking columns of translucent ice, and sometimes whimsical sculptures whose sense of the absurd heightens a venue that visitors describe as surreal. Some of these are angled in ways that amplify the weak midwinter daylight that filters through panes of (what else?) chainsawed ice.

Purists quickly embrace the structure as the perfect marriage of architecture and environment; sensualists usually admire it hastily before heading off to warmer climes and other, more conventional hotels.

WHERE TO STAY

In addition to the hotels listed below, **Jukkasjärvi Wärdshus och Hembygdsgård** 𝒻 at Jukkasjärvi rents accommodations (see "Where to Dine," below).

Hotel Kebne och Kaisa   Located next to the police station on the main road passing through Kiruna (airport buses stop at the door), this hotel consists of two separate buildings, both constructed around 1911 and renovated in 2004. The rooms are modern and comfortable, each decorated in an international style. Each unit has a well-maintained tub/shower. All rooms are nonsmoking. The hotel also operates one of the best restaurants in Kiruna.

What's the most frequently asked question on the lips of virtually everyone who shows up? "Is it comfortable?" The answer is: "not particularly," although a stay probably will enhance your appreciation of the (warm and modern) comforts of conventional housing. Upon arrival, guests are issued thermal jumpsuits of "beaver nylon" whose air-lock cuffs are designed to help the wearer survive temperatures as low as –8°F (–22°C). Beds are fashioned from blocks of chiseled ice lavishly draped, Eskimo-style, with reindeer skins. Guests keep warm with insulated body bags that were developed for walks on the moon. Other than a temporary escape into the hotel's sauna, be prepared for big chills: Room temperatures remain cold enough to keep the walls from melting. Some claim that this exposure will bolster your immune system so that it can better fight infections when you return to your usual environment.

The interior decor is, as you'd expect, hyperglacial, and loaded with insights into what the world might look like if an atomic war drove civilization underground to confront its stark and frigid destiny. Most rooms resemble a setting from a scary 1950s sci-fi flick, sometimes with an icy version of a pair of skin-draped Adirondack chairs pulled up to the surreal glow of an electric fireplace that emits light but, rather distressingly, no heat. Throughout there's an endearing decorative reliance on whatever bas-reliefs and curios its artisans may have decided to chisel into the ice.

There's lots of standing up at the long countertop crafted from ice that doubles as a bar. What should you drink? Swedish vodka, of course, that's dyed a (frigid) shade of blue and served in cups crafted from ice. Vodka never gets any colder than this.

Interested in this holiday on ice? Contact the **Ice Hotel,** Marknadsvägen 63, S-981 91 Jukkasjärvi, Sweden (*C* **0980/668-00;** fax 0980/ 668-90). Doubles cost from 2,800SEK ($364) and suites 3,800SEK ($494) per day, including breakfast. Heated cabins, located near the ice palace, are available for 2,800SEK ($364) per night, double. Toilets are available in a heated building next door.

From Kiruna, head east immediately along Route E10 until you come to a signpost marked JUKKASJÄRVI and follow this tiny road northeast for about 2.5km (1½ miles).

Konduktogrsatan 7, S-981 34 Kiruna. *C* **0980/123-80.** Fax 0980/681-81. www.hotellkebne.com. 54 units. June 15–Aug 15 700SEK ($91) double; Aug 16–June 14 Sun–Thurs 1,245SEK ($162) double, Fri–Sat 696SEK ($90) double. Rates include buffet breakfast. AE, DC, MC, V. Free parking. **Amenities:** Restaurant; bar; sauna; room service (7am–midnight); laundry service; dry cleaning; solarium. *In room:* TV, dataport, safe.

Scandic Hotel Ferrum (★)   Run by the Scandic chain, this hotel is named after the iron ore *(ferrum)* for which Kiruna is famous. The six-story hotel was built in 1967 and is one of the tallest buildings in town. Functional and standardized in design, it's one of your best bets for lodging and food. It has two well-run restaurants, Reenstierna and Mommas; a steakhouse; plus a cocktail bar and a small casino. The rooms are modern and comfortably furnished with excellent beds and neatly kept bathrooms with tub/showers. Rooms are available for people with disabilities and for guests with allergies.

Lars Janssongatan 15, S-981 31 Kiruna. ℰ **0980/39-86-00.** Fax 0980/39-86-11. www.scandichotels.com. 171 units. 1,540SEK–1,840SEK ($200–$239) double; 2,400SEK ($312) suite. Rates include buffet breakfast. AE, DC, MC, V. Parking 85SEK ($11). Closed Dec 23–26. **Amenities:** 2 restaurants; bar; lounge; casino; gym; sauna; laundry service; dry cleaning; nonsmoking rooms; solarium. *In room:* TV, dataport, hair dryer, trouser press.

Vinter Hotell Palatset   This hotel occupies what originally was built in 1904 as a private home for a prosperous entrepreneur in the iron-ore industry. Radically renovated and upgraded in 1989 and 1990, it includes the much-improved main house, a 1950s-era annex containing 4 of the hotel's 20 rooms, a sauna/solarium complex, and a bar with an open fireplace. There's also a dining room, frequented mostly by other residents of the hotel, that serves rib-sticking Swedish food. Rooms are high-ceilinged, dignified-looking, and outfitted with hardwood floors, comfortable modern furniture, and good beds. Bathrooms are quite small, each with a shower. All rooms are nonsmoking.

P.O. Box 18, Järnvägsgatan 18, S-981 21 Kiruna. ℰ **0980/677-70.** Fax 0980/130-50. www.kiruna.se/~vinterp. 20 units. Mid-June to mid-Aug and Fri–Sat year-round 840SEK ($109) double; rest of year 1,360SEK ($177) double. The hotel also has 4 rooms in the annex that are 690SEK ($90) mid-June to mid-Aug and Fri–Sat year-round; rest of year 960SEK ($125). Rates include buffet breakfast. AE, DC, MC, V. Free parking. **Amenities:** Restaurant; bar; sauna; room service (7am–midnight); laundry service; dry cleaning. *In room:* TV, dataport, hair dryer.

WHERE TO DINE

Jukkasjärvi Wärdshus och Hembygdsgård ⭐ *Finds* SWEDISH   Set 16km (10 miles) east of the center of Kiruna, this is the best independent restaurant in the district, and the one that's frequently cited as a culinary beacon in the rest of Swedish Lapland. Set within what was built in the 1850s as a clapboard-sided retirement home for aging and ailing Lapps, it contains room for 80 diners at a time, and a venue that takes far-northern cuisine very, very seriously. Menu items are devoted to local ingredients and include Arctic char with apple cider sauce, filet of reindeer with Arctic shiitake mushrooms, fresh-caught Arctic salmon with lemon sauce, and a succulent filet of beef with garlic-flavored yogurt sauce. Expect wild berries (especially cloudberries), herring (many varieties), dried and smoked meats, reindeer in season, and mushrooms from the fields, along with salted fish.

On the premises is a separate building that's responsible for renting about 45 cottages, each with a kitchen; no maid or maintenance service is associated with the rental. The cottages rent, year-round, for 550SEK ($72) per day, for between one and four occupants.

Jukkasjärvi, Marknadsvägen 63, S-981 91 Kiruna. ℰ **0980-668-00.** Reservations recommended. Fixed-price lunch 105SEK ($14); main courses 180SEK–250SEK ($23–$33). AE, DC, MC, V.

9 Abisko

86km (53 miles) NW of Kiruna, 1,467km (910 miles) N of Stockholm

Any resort north of the Arctic Circle is a curiosity; Abisko, on the southern shore of Lake Torneträsk, encompasses a scenic valley, a lake, and an island. An elevator takes passengers to Mount Nuolja (Njulla). Nearby is the protected Abisko National Park, containing remarkable flora, including orchids.

Moments Northernmost Golf in the World

Here's how to achieve one-upmanship on your golfing pals back home: You can play at the northernmost golf course in the world. The **Arctic Golf Course** has only 9 holes, occupying a terrain of mostly thin-soiled tundra with a scattering of birch forest. It is open only from mid-June to mid-August. During that limited period, golfers can play 24 hours per day, as the course is lit by the midnight sun. For more information, contact Björkliden Arctic Golf Club, Kvarnbacksvägen 28, Bromma S-168 74 (© 08/5648-8830). Bromma is a suburb of Stockholm.

ESSENTIALS

GETTING THERE   By Train & Bus   You can get a train to Kiruna (see earlier in this chapter). From here, there are both bus and rail links into Abisko. For train information, call © **0771/75-75-75.** For bus information, call **Länstrafiken** at © **0926/756-80.**

By Car   From Kiruna, continue northwest on E10 into Abisko.

VISITOR INFORMATION   Contact the tourist office in Kiruna (see earlier in this chapter).

EXPLORING THE AREA

Abisko National Park ★★ (© **0980/40-200**), established in 1903, is situated around the Abiskojokk River, including the mouth of the river where it flows into Lake Torneträsk. This is a typical alpine valley with a rich variety of flora and fauna. The highest mountain is Slåttatjåkka, 1,170m (3,838 ft.) above sea level. Slightly shorter Njulla, which rises 1,140m (3,739 ft.), has a cable car. The name *Abisko* is a Lapp word meaning "ocean forest." The park's proximity to the Atlantic gives it a maritime character, with milder winters and cooler summers than the more continentally influenced areas east of the Scandes or Caledonian mountains.

Abisko is more easily accessible than **Vadvetjåkka National Park,** the other, smaller park in the area. Three sides of Vadvetjåkka Park are bounded by water that is difficult to wade through, and the fourth side is rough terrain with treacherously slippery bogs and steep precipices fraught with rock slides. Established in 1920, it lies northwest of Lake Torneträsk, with its northern limits at the Norwegian border. It's composed of mountain precipices and large tracts of bog and delta. It also has rich flora, along with impressive brook ravines. Its highest mountain is Vadvetjåkka, with a southern peak at 1,095m (3,592 ft.) above sea level.

Abisko is one of the best centers for watching the **midnight sun,** which can be seen from June 13 to July 4. It's also the start of the longest marked trail in the world, the Kungsleden.

Kungsleden (Royal Trail) ★★★ may just prove to be the hike of a lifetime; this approximately 338km (210-mile) trail journeys through Abisko National Park to Riksgränsen on the Norwegian frontier, cutting through Sweden's highest mountain (Kebnekaise) on the way. Properly fortified and with adequate camping equipment, including a sleeping bag and food, you can walk these trails, which tend to be well maintained and clearly marked. Cabins and rest stops (local guides refer to them as "fell stations") are spaced a day's hike

(13–21km/8–13 miles) apart, so you'll have adequate areas to rest between bouts of trekking and hill climbing. These huts provide barely adequate shelter from the wind, rain, snow, and hail in case the weather turns turbulent, as it so often does in this part of the world. At most of the stops, you cook your own food and clean up before leaving. Most lack running water, although there are some summer-only toilets. At certain points, the trail crosses lakes and rivers; boats are provided to help you get across. The trail actually follows the old nomadic paths of the Lapps. Those with less time or energy will find the trail broken up into several smaller segments.

The trail is long but relatively easy to walk along. All the streams en route are traversed by bridges. In places where the ground is marshy, it has been overlaid with wooden planks. In summer, locals operate boat services on some of the lakes you'll pass. Often they'll rent you a rowboat or canoe from a makeshift kiosk or collapsible tent that's dismantled and hauled away after the first frost.

During the summer, the trail is not as isolated as you may think. It is, in fact, the busiest hiking trail in Sweden, and adventurers from all over the world traverse it. The trail is most crowded in July, when the weather is most reliable.

For maps and more information about this adventure, contact the local tourist office or the **Svenska Turistförening,** the Swedish Touring Club, P.O. Box 25, S101 20 Stockholm (© 08/463-21-00).

WHERE TO STAY & DINE

Abisko Turiststation Owned by the Swedish Touring Club since 1910, this big, modern hotel, about 450m (1,476 ft.) from the bus station, offers accommodations in the main building, in the annex, and within 28 cabins. Each cabin is made up of two apartments suitable for up to six occupants, and each unit features a kitchen and a private bathroom with a shower unit. From the hotel you can see the lake and the mountains. The staff is helpful in providing information about excursions. The rooms are basic but reasonably comfortable, and some offer exceptional views.

S-98107 24 Abisko. © **0980/402-00.** Fax 0980/401-40. www.abisko.nu. 77 units, 43 with bathroom; plus 56 cabin apts. 780SEK ($101) double without bathroom; 910SEK–1,220SEK ($118–$159) double with bathroom. Rates include breakfast. Cabin apt 1,080SEK ($140) per night or 7,560SEK ($983) per week up to 6 occupants. Breakfast not included. AE, MC, V. Free parking. Closed Sept 20–Feb 28. **Amenities:** Restaurant; bar. *In room:* No phone.

CROSSING THE BORDER TO NORWAY

Because Abisko is close to the Norwegian border, you may want to cross into Norway (don't forget your passport!) after your tour of Swedish Lapland. If so, just take E10 west across the border toward Narvik. From Kiruna, trains and buses go to the hamlet of Rigsgränsen, the last settlement in Sweden, before continuing for the final, short leg to Narvik. Schedules depend entirely on the weather; for buses, call © **0200/218218;** for trains, © **0771/75-75-75.** However, if you'd like to return to Stockholm, follow E10 east toward the coast, then head south on E4 to the capital city.

Appendix:
Sweden in Depth

Roughly the size of California, Sweden has some 280,000 sq. km (109,200 sq. miles) of landmass, bordering Finland to its northeast and Norway to its west. As the northern end creeps over the Arctic Circle, the southern third of Sweden juts into the Baltic Sea. This southern tier is the site of most of the population; much of the north is uninhabited and occupies one of the last great wildernesses of Europe.

Known for its warm summers and bitterly cold winters, Sweden is a land of lakes and forests, mountains and meadows. Because of generally poor soil and a rocky landscape, Swedes have turned to mining, steel production, and forestry to spur their economy.

Swedes are known for their almost mystical love of nature. Although they travel in winter to escape the cold, they are known as their own greatest tourists when the all-too-brief summer arrives. Many Swedes have second homes in remote parts of the country.

Many visitors heading for history- and monument-rich France or Italy mistakenly think Sweden lacks attractions. This is not the case. Sweden possesses 1,140 historic fortresses, 2,500 open-air runic stones, and 25,000 protected Iron Age graveyards, and the Stockholm area alone has 10 royal castles.

As in parts of the American West, you'll encounter one thing in Sweden that is not always available in other parts of Europe: the wide-open yonder. Space characterizes Sweden's vast forests, mountains, and national parks. Sometimes you can travel for miles without encountering another soul.

Stockholm is, of course, the major target of nearly all visitors. More than 7 centuries old, it is a regal place, filled with everything from the winding cobbled streets of its medieval district to the marble, glass, and granite of its high-rises in the commercial center. It is a city of serenity, of beautiful buildings, countless shopping opportunities, and sightseeing galore. And no other European capital has such a dramatic landscape as Stockholm's 24,000 islands, skerries, and islets. It is a city designed to delight.

As many other world capitals decay and seem long past their prime, Stockholm grows better with age. No longer as provincial as it was even 15 years ago, today Stockholm is lively, vibrant, and filled with nightlife and great restaurants, along with a sophisticated, savvy population enjoying one of the world's highest standards of living.

But Sweden only begins in Stockholm. At least two other major cities merit exploration: Gothenburg and Malmö. Gothenburg enjoys a dramatic landscape along Sweden's craggy western coastline; this major seaport is filled with tree-lined boulevards, restaurants, museums, endless shopping, elegant buildings, and nightclubs. North of Gothenburg you encounter sleepy fishing harbors in rocky coves and offshore islands where city folk come in summer to retreat.

Southwestern Malmö boasts one of northern Europe's most attractive medieval centers, and also is a good base for exploring the ancient university city of Lund, with its mass of students, a revered 12th-century Romanesque cathedral, medieval streets, and numerous museums.

However grand the cities may be, any native Swede will tell you that the countryside is the chief reason to visit. Our favorite destinations, the folkloric provinces of Dalarna and Värmland, form Sweden's heartland. Filled with forests and vast lakes, this is the landscape described in the country's greatest literature. Some towns, especially around Lake Siljan, still look as they did in the Middle Ages. Folk dances and music festivals keep the summer lively.

The ancient province of Skåne in the southwest is called the château country because of all the French-like castles that still dot its landscape of undulating fields and curving, rocky coastline. In spring, black windmills and white churches pose against a background of yellow rape, crimson poppies, and lush green meadows.

For sheer scenic drama, nothing equals Lapland, that remote and isolated region of Europe in the north, home to the Lapps (or Sami) and their reindeer herds. It's a domain of truly awesome proportions. Birch-clad valleys and sprawling woodlands of pine give way to waterfalls, roaring river rapids, mountain plateaus, and fens covered with moss. The numerous rivers of the region snake down from the mountains to spill out into the Gulf of Bothnia, and the locals have long ago accepted and adapted to the harsh lifestyle imposed on them by the weather. Unspoiled nature under the midnight sun is a potent attraction.

Finally, there is the island of Gotland in the Baltic, which knew its heyday in Viking times. This land of beaches, spas, and sailing has a warmer climate than the rest of Sweden. Some 100 churches and chapels still remain on the island, and its capital of Visby is one of the oldest cities of Sweden. Its Old Town wall stretches for over 3km (1¾ miles) and is capped by 44 towers. Crenellated turrets and long, thin, arched windows evoke the Middle Ages.

Sweden is a country where you can enjoy history and urban pleasures, but the nation's heart and soul can be found in its vast landscapes. From a summer wilderness fragrant with fields of orchids and traversed by wild elk, to the dark wintry landscape dotted by husky sleds and paraskiing, Sweden provides a stunning vacation experience.

1 Sweden Today

Sweden is one of the most paradoxical nations on earth. An essentially conservative country, it is nonetheless a leader in social welfare, prison reform, and equal opportunity for women.

Despite trouble maintaining its once bustling economy, Sweden has long enjoyed some of the highest wages and the best standard of living in Europe. There may be trouble in paradise, but compared with the rest of the world, Sweden is better off than most other nations.

This is a land where the urbane and the untamed are said to live harmoniously. With a population density of only 48 people per square mile, there's ample space for all of Sweden's nine million residents. About 85% of Sweden's citizens live in the southern half of the country. The north is populated by Sweden's two chief minority groups: the Sami (Lapp) and the Finnish-speaking people of the northeast. Among the cities, Stockholm is the political capital, with a population of 1,435,000; Gothenburg, the automobile-manufacturing center, has 704,000; and Malmö, the port city, has 458,000.

Once home to an ethnically homogenous society, Sweden has experienced a vast wave of immigration in the past several years. Today more than 10% of Sweden's residents are immigrants or the children of immigrants. Much of this influx is from other Scandinavian countries. Because of Sweden's strong stance on human rights, it also has become a major destination for political and social refugees from Africa and the Middle East. A vast number of immigrants seeking asylum come from the former Yugoslavia.

Sweden's government is a constitutional monarchy supported by a parliamentary government. The royal family functions primarily in a ceremonial capacity. The actual ruling body is a one-chamber parliament, whose members are popularly elected for 3-year terms. The present government is headed by a Social Democrat, Goeran Persson. Because of Sweden's location in the Baltic, it has been active in promoting peace among the warring Baltic states. The country is an active member of the United Nations and was admitted as a full member to the European Union in 1995.

Like other European countries, Sweden's policy of cradle-to-grave welfare has been threatened in recent years. The main topic of debate in the Social Democrat–dominated parliament is how to sustain Sweden's generous welfare system while putting a halt to ever-increasing taxes, currently at 59%. At this time, the state provides health insurance along with many generous family benefits, including an allowance for care providers, 15 months paid parental leave after the birth of a child (divided between both parents), tax-free child allowances, and education stipends for children. When a Swede reaches retirement at age 65, he or she is entitled to a hefty pension that rises with inflation.

Education plays an important role in Sweden. Schools are run by various municipalities, providing free tuition, books, and lunches. Although attendance is mandatory for only 9 years, 90% of Swedes pursue some form of higher education. Adult education and university study are funded by the state.

Sweden's advanced level of education coincides with its high-tech industrial economy. Although in years past Sweden's economy was based on agriculture, in the latter half of the 20th century and post-millennium, industry has become predominant, employing nearly 80% of all Swedish workers. More than 50% of Sweden's exports are composed of heavy machinery including cars, trucks, and telecommunications equipment. Companies such as Saab and Volvo (bought by Ford Motor Co.) produce vehicles familiar throughout the world. Despite Sweden's industrial milieu, the country manages to produce some 80% of its own food.

Although such a highly industrialized nation depends on its factories, Sweden has enacted stringent environmental policies. The task of monitoring the country's environment is the responsibility of local governments. Each of Sweden's 286 municipalities has the right to limit pollutant emissions in its own sector.

The environment has always played an integral role in the lives of Swedes. Sweden has 20 national parks; although these wilderness areas are not regulated by law, Sweden's policy of free access entitles citizens to unlimited admission at no charge.

Another important element is Sweden's strong focus on culture. Over the past 25 years, Swedes have turned their attention to music. Today young people are purchasing more recorded music and attending more live concerts than they were even a decade ago. Book reading is on the rise (more than 9,000 titles are published in Sweden every year, and Swedes traditionally have had a literacy rate of over 99%), museum attendance has increased, and there's greater interest in the media. The average Swede spends 6 hours per day immersed in some form of mass media (newspapers, magazines, television, radio, and so forth).

Increasingly, Sweden is being pressed to drop its neutrality and to join an expanding NATO. Although it firmly resists that pressure, Sweden has, nonetheless, taken part in Bosnian peacekeeping. Although Sweden has been a member of the European Union since 1995, polls today indicate that it would reject membership if a new election were held.

There is a certain nostalgia sweeping Sweden today, a desire to return to the way life used to be when Sweden was one of the three or four richest countries in the world.

As Sweden moves even deeper into the 21st century, its problems continue. For example, businesses can't grow because it's too expensive to hire people. Observers have noted that young Swedes are starting to think internationally, and some of them are leaving Sweden to take positions elsewhere in the global economy. "The people leaving are the very people that Sweden needs the most," one Swedish businessman lamented to the press.

2 The Natural Environment

Sweden stretches about 1,600km (992 miles) from north to south, but it's sparsely populated, with a disproportionate amount of territory lying above the Arctic Circle. Sweden is one of the countries located farthest from the equator. From north to south, Sweden lies at roughly the same latitude as Alaska. Forests cover more than half the land; Sweden is a heavily industrialized nation and less than 10% of its land is used for agriculture.

Sweden can be divided into three main regions: the mountainous northern zone of Norrland; Svealand, the lake-filled, hilly region of central Sweden; and Götaland, the broad plateau in southern Sweden, home of most of the country's agricultural enterprises.

Did You Know?

- Sweden ranks second after Finland in coffee consumption per capita worldwide. In 1993, the Swedes consumed 76.8 million kilograms of roasted coffee, an average of roughly three to five cups per person, per day.
- Counting all the inlets, promontories, and islands, Sweden has a coastal strip 7,500km (4,650 miles) long—one-fifth of the Earth's circumference.
- A survey showed that a large percentage of Americans confuse Sweden and Switzerland.
- Half the couples living together in Sweden are unmarried.
- Sweden has contributed two words to international gastronomy: smörgåsbord (smorgasbord in English) and *Absolut.*
- The world's longest smorgasbord was prepared in Sweden, stretching for 718m (2,355 ft.).
- James Joyce, F. Scott Fitzgerald, George Orwell, Marcel Proust, and Aldous Huxley *did not* win Sweden's Nobel Prize for literature.
- Sweden is one of the five nations that established colonies in North America.

Sweden has more than 100,000 lakes, including Vänern, the largest in western Europe. About 9% of the countryside is covered by lakes, which play an important role in transporting goods from the Baltic ports to cities throughout Sweden and the rest of Scandinavia. Canals link many of these lakes to the sea. The most important of these is the Göta Canal. Constructed in the 19th century, this 600km-long (372-mile) canal links Gothenburg in the west to Stockholm in the east. Some 195km (121 miles) of canals were constructed to connect the various lakes and rivers that make up this waterway.

Sweden's rivers tend to be short and to empty into one of the numerous lakes. They're used for short-haul transportation, linking the network of lakes, but especially for providing hydroelectric power to fuel the many factories scattered throughout the countryside. The most important rivers are the Pite, the Lule, and the Indal.

Sweden's expansive seacoast is more than 2,500km (1,550 miles) long. The west is bounded by the Kattegat and the Skagerrak, and the east by the Gulf of Bothnia and the Baltic Sea. Numerous small islands and reefs dot the eastern and southwestern coasts. If all the inlets and islands were included, the coastline of Sweden would measure 7,500km (4,650 miles). Öland and Gotland, Sweden's largest, most populated islands, are situated in the Baltic Sea, off the eastern coast.

Sweden is a center for alpine activities, including skiing, hiking, and glacier walking—most of which take place in the mountainous regions of Norrland. This far-northern area is home to many of the country's highest peaks, including its highest mountain, Kebnekaise, at 2,080m (6,822 ft.).

The flora of Sweden varies with the region. There are five rather disparate zones, each supporting a distinct array of plant life: the tundra in the north, coniferous forests below the timber line, central Sweden's birch forests, coniferous forests in the south, and the beech and oak zones found in the southern regions.

Animal life also differs depending on the region. The countryside teems with bears, elk, reindeer, fox, wolves, and otters. Numerous game birds also make their home in Sweden's expansive forests.

3 History 101

THE VIKINGS Although documented by little other than legend, the Viking age (roughly A.D. 700–1000) is the epoch that has most captured the attention of the world. Up to then, Sweden had been relatively isolated, although travelers from the south brought some artifacts from different civilizations.

The base of Viking power at the time was the coastal regions around and to the north of what today is Stockholm. Either as plunderers, merchants, or slave traders—perhaps a combination of all three—Swedish Vikings maintained contact with the

Dateline

- 829 Christianity is introduced by St. Anskar.
- 1008 Pagan Viking king Olaf Skottkonung converts to Christianity.
- 1130–56 King Sverker unites the lands of Svear and Gotar, the heart of today's modern nation.
- 1160 King Eric IX presides over a Christian country and becomes patron saint of Sweden.
- 1248 Birger Jarl abolishes serfdom and founds Stockholm.
- 1319 Magnus VII of Norway unites Sweden with Norway.

continues

East, both Russia and Constantinople, and with parts of western Europe, including Britain and Ireland. Swedish Vikings joined their brother Vikings in Norway and Denmark in pillaging, trading with, or conquering parts of Ireland and the British Isles, their favorite targets.

CHRISTIANITY & THE MIDDLE AGES

With the aid of missions sent from Britain and northern Germany, Christianity gradually made headway, having been introduced in 829 by St. Anskar, a Frankish missionary. It did not become widespread, however, until the 11th century. In 1008 Olaf Skottkonung, the ruler of a powerful kingdom in northern Sweden, converted to Christianity, but later in the century, the religion came into confusion, with civil wars and a pagan reaction against the converting missionaries.

Ruling from 1130 to 1156, King Sverker united the lands of Svear and Gotar, which later became the heart of modern Sweden. A strong centralized government developed under this king.

Christianity finally became almost universally accepted under Eric IX, who ruled until 1160. He led a crusade to Finland and later became the patron saint of Sweden. By 1164, his son, Charles VII, had founded the first archbishopric at Uppsala. The increasing influence of this new religion led to the death of the Viking slave trade, and many Vikings turned to agriculture as the basis of their economy. A landowning aristocracy eventually arose.

Sweden's ties with the Hanseatic ports of Germany grew stronger, and trade with other Baltic ports flourished at the city of Visby on the island of Gotland. Sweden traded in copper, pelts, iron, and butter, among other products.

Sweden's greatest medieval statesman was Birger Jarl, who ruled from

- **1350** Black Death sweeps across Sweden.
- **1389** Margaretha rules Sweden, Norway, and Denmark by the Union of Kalmar.
- **1523** Gustavus Vasa founds the Vasa Dynasty.
- **1598** Sigismund deposed after brief union of thrones of Sweden and Poland.
- **1600–11** Karl IX leads Sweden into ill-fated wars with Denmark, Russia, and Poland.
- **1611** Gustavus II Adolphus ascends to the throne; presides over ascension of Sweden as a great European power.
- **1648** Treaty of Westphalia grants Sweden the possessions of Stettin, Bremen, and West Pomerania.
- **1654** Queen Christina abdicates the Swedish throne.
- **1655–97** Long reign of Charles XI renews Sweden's strength.
- **1718** Killed in battle, Charles XII, leader of the Great Northern War, presides over demise of Swedish empire.
- **1746–92** Gustavus III revives the absolute power of the monarchy.
- **1809** Napoleon names Jean Bernadotte as heir to the throne of Sweden.
- **1889** The Social Democratic Party is formed.
- **1905** Sweden grants independence to Norway.
- **1909** Suffrage for all men is achieved.
- **1921** Suffrage for women and an 8-hour workday are established.
- **1940** Sweden declares its neutrality in World War II.
- **1946** Sweden joins the United Nations.
- **1953** Dag Hammarskjöld becomes secretary-general of the United Nations.
- **1973** Karl XVI Gustaf ascends the throne.
- **1986** Olof Palme, prime minister and leader of the Social Democrats, is assassinated.
- **1992** Sweden faces currency crisis.
- **1994** Refugees and the welfare system strain Sweden's budget.
- **1995** Along with Finland and Austria, Sweden is granted full membership in the European Union.

1248 to 1266; during his reign, he abolished serfdom and founded Stockholm. When his son, Magnus Laduläs, became king in 1275, he granted extensive power to the Catholic Church and founded a hereditary aristocracy.

AN INTRANORDIC UNION

Magnus VII of Norway (1316–74) was only 3 years old when he was elected to the Swedish throne, but his election signaled a recognition of the benefits of increased cooperation within the Nordic world. During his reign, there emerged distinct social classes, including the aristocracy, the Catholic clergy (which owned more than 20% of the land), peasant farmers and laborers, and a commercial class of landowners, foresters, mine-owners, and merchants. The fortunes and power of this last group were based on trade links with a well-organized handful of trading cities (the Hanseatic League) scattered throughout Germany and along the Baltic coastline. As trade increased, these cities (especially Visby, on the island of Gotland) and their residents flourished, and the power of the Hanseatic League grew.

In 1350, the Black Death arrived in Sweden, decimating the population. This proved to be the greatest catastrophe experienced by the Western world up to that time. Imported from Asia after wreaking havoc in China and Turkistan, it is thought to have spread to Sweden through trade with Britain. The plague seriously hindered Sweden's development, although the country didn't suffer as much as nations such as England.

In 1389, the Swedish aristocracy, fearing the growing power of the Germans within the Hanseatic League, negotiated for an intra-Nordic union with Denmark and the remaining medieval fiefdoms in Norway and Finland. The birth process of this experimental union began in the Swedish city of Kalmar, which gave its name in 1397 to the brief but farsighted Union of Kalmar. A leading figure in its development was the Danish queen Margaretha, who was already queen of Denmark and Norway when the aristocracy of Sweden offered her the throne in 1389. Despite the ideals of the union, it collapsed after about 40 years because of a revolt by merchants, miners, and peasants in defense of Sweden's trade links with the Hanseatic League, coupled with power struggles between Danish and Swedish nobles.

Although the union was a failure, one of its legacies was the establishment—partly as a compromise among different political factions—of a Riksdag (parliament) made up of representatives from various towns and regions; the peasant classes also had some limited representation.

Queen Margaretha's heir (her nephew, Eric of Pomerania; 1382–1459) became the crowned head of three countries (Norway, Denmark, and Sweden). He spent most of his reign fighting with the Hanseatic League. Deposed in 1439, he was replaced by Christopher of Bavaria, whose early death in 1448 led to a major conflict and the eventual dissolution of the Kalmar Union. The Danish king, Christian II, invaded Stockholm in 1520, massacred the leaders who opposed him, and established an unpopular reign; there was much civil disobedience until the emergence of the Vasa dynasty, which expelled the Danes.

- 1996 Social Democrat Goeran Persson, Sweden's finance minister, is elected prime minister.
- 1997 World headlines link Sweden to past sterilization programs and Nazi gold.
- 1998 Social Democrats remain in power on pledge to continue huge welfare programs.
- 2000 The 24 billion SEK ($3 billion) Øresund bridge links Denmark and Sweden for the first time.
- 2002 Sweden okays adoption rights to same-sex families.

THE VASA DYNASTY   In May 1520, a Swedish nobleman, Gustavus Vasa, returned from captivity in Denmark and immediately began to plan for the military expulsion of the Danes from Sweden. In 1523 he captured Stockholm from its Danish rulers, won official recognition for Swedish independence, and was elected king of Sweden.

In a power struggle with the Catholic Church, he confiscated most Church-held lands (vastly increasing the power of the state overnight) and established Lutheranism as the national religion. He commissioned a complete translation of the Bible and other religious works into Swedish, and forcefully put down local uprisings in the Swedish provinces. He established the right of succession for his offspring and decreed that his son, Eric XIV, would follow him as king (which he did in 1543).

Although at first Eric was a wise ruler, his eventual downfall was in part due to his growing conflicts with Swedish noblemen and a marriage to his unpopular mistress, Karin Mansdotter. (Previously, he had unsuccessfully negotiated marriage with the English queen, Elizabeth I.) Eric eventually went insane before being replaced by Johan III.

The next 50 years were marked by Danish plots to regain control of Sweden and Swedish plots to conquer Poland, Estonia, and the Baltic trade routes leading to Russia. A dynastic link to the royal families of Poland led to the ascension of Sigismund (son of the Swedish king Johan III) in Warsaw. When his father died, Sigismund became king of both Sweden and Poland simultaneously. His Catholicism, however, was opposed by Sweden, which expelled him in 1598. He was followed by Karl (Charles) IX (1566–1632), who led Sweden into a dangerous and expensive series of wars with Denmark, Russia, and its former ally, Poland.

By 1611, as Sweden was fighting simply to survive, Gustavus II Adolphus (1594–1632) ascended the throne. Viewed today as a brilliant politician and military leader, he was one of the century's most stalwart Protestants at a time when political alliances often were formed along religious lines. After organizing an army composed mainly of farmers and field hands (financed by money from the Falun copper mines), he secured Sweden's safety and with his armies penetrated as far south as Bavaria. He died fighting against the Hapsburg emperor's Catholic army near the city of Lützen in 1632.

When he died, his heir and only child, Christina (1626–89), was 6 years old. During her childhood, power was held by the respected Swedish statesman Axel Oxenstierna, who continued the Thirty Years' War in Germany for another 16 years. It finally concluded with the Treaty of Westphalia in 1648. Christina, who did not want to pursue war and had converted to Catholicism (against the advice of her counselors), abdicated the throne in 1654 in favor of her cousin, Charles X Gustav (1622–60).

After his rise to power, Charles X expelled the Danes from many of Sweden's southern provinces, establishing the Swedish borders along the approximate lines of today. He also invaded and conquered Poland (1655–56), but his territorial ambitions were thwarted by a national uprising. He later defeated the Danes (1657–58), and at the time of his death, Sweden was ringed by enemies. Charles X was succeeded by Charles XI (1655–97), whose reign was fiscally traumatic. The endless wars with Denmark (and other kingdoms in northern Germany) continued. However, an even greater problem was the growing power of wealthy Swedish nobles, who had amassed (usually through outright purchase from the cash-poor monarchy) an estimated 72% of Sweden's land. In a bitter and acrimonious process, Charles redistributed the land into approximately equal shares held by the monarchy, the nobles, and Sweden's independent farmers. The position of small landowners has remained secure in Sweden ever since, although the absolute monarch gained increased power. With Charles's new-found wealth, he greatly strengthened the country's military power.

Charles XII (1682–1718) came to the throne at the age of 4 with his mother, the queen, as regent. Denmark, Poland, and Russia allied themselves against Sweden in the Great Northern War, which broke out in 1700. Charles invaded Russia but was defeated; he escaped to Turkey, where he remained a prisoner for 4 years. In 1714, he returned to Sweden to continue fighting but was killed in 1718. Charles XII presided over the collapse of the Swedish empire.

Under Frederick I (1676–1751), Sweden regained some of its former prestige. The chancellor, Count Arvid Horn (1664–1742), had real power. He formed an alliance with England, Prussia, and France against Russia. The *Hattar* (Hats) and *Mossorna* (Caps) were the two opposing parties in the Riksdag then, and the Hats began a war with Russia in 1741. The conflict continued through the reign of the next king, Adolphus Frederick (1710–71). Although he initiated many reforms, encouraged the arts, and transformed the architectural landscape of Stockholm, Gustavus III (1746–92) revived the absolute power of the monarchy, perhaps as a reaction against the changes effected by the French Revolution. He was assassinated by a group of fanatical noblemen while attending a ball at the opera.

THE 19TH CENTURY   The next king was Gustavus IV (1778–1837). Because he hated Napoleon, Gustavus IV led Sweden into the Third Coalition against France (1805–07). For his efforts, he lost Stralsund and Swedish Pomerania; in the wars against Russia and Denmark, Sweden lost Finland in 1808. The next year, following an uprising, Gustavus IV was overthrown and died in exile.

A new constitution was written in 1808, granting the Riksdag equal power with the king. Under these provisions, Charles XIII (1748–1818), the uncle of the deposed king, became the new monarch.

Napoleon arranged for his aide, Jean Bernadotte (1763–1844), to become heir to the Swedish throne. Bernadotte won a war with Denmark, forcing that country to cede Norway to Sweden (1814). Upon the death of Charles, Bernadotte became king of Sweden and Norway, ruling as Charles XIV. During his reign, Sweden adopted a policy of neutrality, and the royal line that he established is still on the throne today. Charles XIV was succeeded by his son, Oscar I (1799–1859), who introduced many reforms, including freedom of worship and of the press.

The Industrial Revolution of the 19th century changed the face of Sweden. The Social Democratic Party was launched in 1889, leading to a universal suffrage movement. All males acquired the right to vote in 1909.

THE 20TH CENTURY   Norway declared its independence in 1905 and Sweden accepted the secession. Sweden adhered to a policy of neutrality during World War I, although many Swedes were sympathetic to the German cause. Many Swedish volunteers enlisted in the White Army during the Russian Revolution of 1917.

In 1921, women gained the right to vote, and an 8-hour workday was established. The Social Democratic Party continued to grow in power, and after 1932 a welfare state was instituted.

Although Sweden offered weapons and volunteers to Finland during its Winter War against the Soviet Union in 1939, it declared its neutrality during World War II. Sweden evoked long-lived resentment from its neighbor, Norway, whose cities were leveled by the Nazi troops that had been granted free passage across Swedish territory. Under heavy Allied threats against Sweden in 1943 and 1944, Nazi troop transports through the country eventually were halted. Throughout the war, Sweden accepted many impoverished and homeless refugees. The rescue attempts of Hungarian Jews led by Swedish businessman and diplomat Raoul Wallenberg have been recounted in books and films.

Sweden joined the United Nations in 1946 but refused to join NATO in 1949. Rather more disturbing was Sweden's decision to return to the Soviet Union many German and Baltic refugees who had opposed Russia during the war. They were presumably killed on Stalin's orders.

Dag Hammarskjöld, as secretary-general of the United Nations in 1953, did much to help Sweden regain the international respect that it had lost because of its wartime policies. In 1961, toward the end of his second 5-year term, he was killed in an airplane crash.

Sweden continued to institute social reforms in the 1950s and 1960s, including the establishment of a national health service.

At only 27 years old, Karl XVI Gustaf became king of Sweden in 1973, following the death of his grandfather, Gustaf VI Adolf (the king's father had been killed in an airplane crash when the king was still a child). In 1976, he married Silvia Sommerlath, who was born in Germany. King Karl XVI Gustaf and Queen Silvia have three children.

The Social Democrats ruled until 1976, when they were toppled by a Center/Liberal/Moderate coalition. The Social Democrats returned in 1982 but lost their majority in 1985 and had to rely on Communist support to enact legislation.

The leader of their party since 1969, Olof Palme was prime minister until his assassination outside a movie theater in Stockholm in 1986. A pacifist, he was a staunch critic of the United States, especially during the Vietnam War. In spite of an arrest, the murder has not been satisfactorily resolved.

Following the assassination of Olof Palme, vice prime minister Ingvar Carlsson was shoehorned into power, in accordance with provisions within the Social Democratic Party's bylaws. There he remained as an honest but dull caretaker until the end of Palme's elected term, devoted to promoting the party platforms of bountiful social benefits coupled with staggeringly high taxes.

In the early 1990s, Sweden faced some of the most troubling economic problems in recent memory, foremost of which was slow economic growth. Inflation was severe. In 1992, the government, then led by Conservative Prime Minister Carl Bildt, experienced a currency crisis that made headlines around the world. In September 1994, the Social Democrats, again spearheaded by Ingvar Carlsson, were returned to office after a brief interim of Conservative rule. The election brought the proportion of women in the Swedish Parliament to 41%, the highest in the world.

In 1995, Sweden, along with Finland and Austria, was granted full membership in the European Union, thereby providing a context for much-needed economic growth. In 1996, Prime Minister Carlsson, citing advanced age and a growing distaste for public life (in which he was the butt of many jokes that compared his appearance to that of an old shoe), retired midway through the elected term of his party.

> **Fun Fact** **There's Something About the Swedes**
>
> The Swedes are responsible for inventing much that has changed modern life, including the safety match, alternating current, the milk separator, the refrigerator, the vacuum cleaner, and the ball bearing. And of course, there's the zipper (which has led to all sorts of interesting situations all over the world).

Following well-established parliamentary procedures, fellow Social Democrat Goeran Persson took his place. A highly capable former finance minister, Persson appealed to Swedes with a platform that advocated cutting taxes and curtailing government spending. Despite personal talent, Persson has been judged as a capable but remote administrator whose most visible drawback is a chilly, somewhat arrogant personal style that has provoked murmurs of discontent among some members of the Swedish electorate.

Just as its own image as one of the most progressive nations on earth was being questioned, a chilling chapter from Sweden's past was revealed in 1997. Sweden had as many as 60,000 of its citizens sterilized, some involuntarily, from 1935 to 1976. The ideas behind the sterilization program had similarities to Nazi ideas of racial superiority. Singled out were those judged to be inferior, flawed by bad eyesight, mental retardation, and otherwise "undesirable" racial characteristics. The state wanted to prevent these genetic characteristics from being passed on. This law wasn't overturned until 1976. The respected newspaper *Dagens Nyheter* stirred national debate and worldwide headlines when it ran a series of articles about the former program, and at press time, Sweden had decided to pay reparations to those affected by the program.

As if this weren't bad enough, Sweden's once-lustrous reputation received more battering in 1997 with revelations of wartime iron exports that fed Hitler's military machine and of postwar Swedish hoarding of German gold, much of it looted from Nazi victims, which it received in payment for the metal.

In an election in September 1998, Social Democrats, still led by Goeran Persson, remained in power on a pledge to increase spending on the country's huge welfare program. The party secretary of the Moderates, Gunner Hokmark, found little comfort in the election, claiming, "It puts Swedes in a left lock that is stronger than any other country of Europe."

POST-MILLENNIUM   The government presently spends 46% of the gross national product on welfare, more than any other industrialized country. The income taxes required to support this public outlay take 59% of the pay of people. Employers pay up to 41% of employee remuneration into social security and pension plans. The former Communist Party now is called the Left Party, and it has steadily been growing in approval with voters.

In May 2000, Sweden, for the first time in its history, became physically linked with the continent by the Øresund Bridge. Construction on the 16km (10-mile) motor and railway link began in 1995. Both Queen Margrethe of Denmark and King Carl Gustaf of Sweden inaugurated the span that links the Scandinavian peninsula with Europe.

The bridge gives the island of Zealand (the eastern part of Denmark) and Scania (the southern part of Sweden) a shared bridge, serving some 3.5 million inhabitants in the area.

The Øresund region, which encompasses parts of both Sweden and Denmark, is the largest domestic market in Northern Europe—larger than Stockholm and equal in size to Berlin, Hamburg, and Amsterdam combined. Built at a cost of 24 billion SEK ($3 billion), it is the largest combined rail and road tunnel in the world. The price of a one-way fare in a passenger car is 240SEK ($30).

In theory, a vehicle now can travel in roughly a straight line from the Arctic coast of Norway to the Mediterranean shores of Spain. For centuries, it has been a dream to link the continent from its northern tip to its southern toe. The "Øresund Fixed Link" spans the icy Øresund Sound between the cities of Copenhagen and Malmö.

In 2002 Sweden again became one of the world leaders in advanced social legislation when parliament voted to let same-sex couples adopt children. Under the new bill, gays registered in a legal partnership, allowed in Sweden since 1995, can be considered joint adoptive parents. One of the partners will also be able to adopt the child of another.

Sweden is hardly viewed as a Banana Republic where its leaders are routinely assassinated. However, violence against public officials has come to Scandinavia. One of the most recent attacks occurred on September 11, 2003, when Ann Lindh, Sweden's minister for foreign affairs, was stabbed and mortally wounded while on a personal errand. She stood as a role model for many younger women and a representative of a modern, outward-looking Swede.

4 Famous Swedes

Ingmar Bergman (b. 1918)   Sweden's greatest film director made his debut in 1938 as an amateur director at a theater in Stockholm. His first feature film, *Crisis,* was released in 1945, but it wasn't until the 1950s that he became world famous. He made such highly acclaimed films as *The Seventh Seal, Wild Strawberries,* and *Cries and Whispers,* all hailed as classics. In three decades he directed more than 40 films, each dealing with a universal theme such as human isolation.

Ingrid Bergman (1916–82)   One of the world's finest stage and screen actresses always predicted that, in spite of her impressive achievements, her obituaries would carry the headlines "Star of Casablanca Dies." And so they did. An unknown, she left Sweden for Hollywood to make *Intermezzo,* which was followed by such great films as *Gaslight* (her first Oscar), *For Whom the Bell Tolls, Notorious,* and *Anastasia.* She embodied virtue in such films as *The Bells of St. Mary's* and *Joan of Arc,* which led to a massive outcry against her when she left her Swedish husband and child to marry the Italian film director Roberto Rossellini. She was even condemned in the U.S. Senate. Sixteen years later, she made a powerful comeback; *Murder on the Orient Express* brought her a third and final Oscar.

Baron Jons Jakob Berzelius (1779–1848)   Born in Vaversunda Sorgård in Sweden, Berzelius studied chemistry and medicine, graduating from Uppsala in 1802. He was named a member of the Royal Academy of Sciences in 1808, becoming secretary for life there in 1818. In 1835, King Charles XIV made him a baron. His many books on chemistry include *Theory of Chemical Proportions and Chemical Action of Electricity* in 1844. He was one of the fathers of modern chemistry, developing a system of chemical symbols and atomic weights of the elements.

Ikea Style

One of the most famous manufacturers of household furniture and housewares in the world is Ikea, a company founded after World War II whose stores are sprawling warehouses filled with a cornucopia of modern furniture and household accessories that show the good life *à la Suèdoise*. Their trademark style involves ample amounts of birch trim and birch veneer, sometimes accented with black, always presented in a "less is more" format that shows the virtues of thrift, simple lines, and efficiency. From the core of two megastores, set to the north and south of Stockholm, respectively, a series of other outlets have sprung up around the world. Vital to the organization's self-image is the presence of a cafeteria serving all-Swedish food. They provide cost-conscious refreshments and pick-me-ups that fortify shoppers (and those who merely crave *frikadeller* [meatballs]), at budget prices.

Björn Borg (b. 1956)   At 17 years of age, this world-famous tennis player was on world-class circuits. Beginning in 1976, he won five consecutive Wimbledon singles titles. With his long hair, headband, and superbly elastic legs, he personified an era in tennis. Borg was able to help Sweden win the first Davis Cup Trophy against Czechoslovakia in 1975, making him a national hero in his homeland. With 62 singles titles to his name, Borg is remembered for his sheer athleticism on the court and his ice-cool temperament under pressure.

Charles XII (1682–1718)   The oldest son of Charles XI of Sweden and Ulrika Eleanora of Denmark, this king is one of the most famous ever to emerge from Sweden. Following his father on the throne, he became an absolute monarch in 1697 at the age of 15. In 1700, the Great Northern War broke out as Sweden faced Denmark, Poland, and Russia. He crushed the forces of Peter the Great in 1701 but eventually lost to the Russian army in 1709 and was forced into exile in Turkey. Returning to Sweden in 1714, he invaded Norway 4 years later, where he was fatally shot in the head.

Queen Christina (1626–89)   Christina became queen of Sweden at the age of 6, when she ruled under regents. Ironically, she is best remembered for two events: her abdication in 1654 and a Greta Garbo film, *Queen Christina*. Born in a palace in Stockholm on December 8, 1626, she was the daughter of King Gustavus II Adolphus and Maria Eleanora of Brandenburg. Taught philosophy by Descartes, Christina established a school system in Sweden, helped bring about the first Swedish newspaper, and improved industry. Her favorite residence was Riario Palace in Rome, where she lived with her lover, Decio Cardinal Azzolino, to whom she left everything in her will. She was buried at St. Peter's in Rome. The Vatican Library holds her entire collection of books.

Stefan Bengt Edberg (b. 1966)   Today a well-paid spokesman for Adidas, in 1988 Edberg became the first Swede since Borg to win the Wimbledon singles title. He went on to win again in 1990 and followed that by winning the U.S. Open in 1991 and again in 1992. He lives in England and France, and remains one of the world's most admired tennis players.

Volvo Versus ABBA

In the late 1970s, money generated by ABBA was second only to that of Volvo in terms of total exports from Sweden.

John Ericsson (1803–89)   Sweden's most famous inventor played a decisive role in the Civil War in the United States. He was born in Långbanshyttan, Sweden, on July 31, 1803, and by 1820 had joined the Swedish Army. Ericsson's marine propeller, by 1843, had shown itself superior to the paddle wheel. His warship, *Monitor*, on May 9, 1862, defeated the Confederacy's *Merrimac*, saving the Yankee fleet and earning the inventor world renown. Although he moved to the United States and played a part in its turbulent history, he specified that he be buried on Swedish soil. After Ericsson's death in the United States on March 8, 1889, his body was transported to Sweden on the American armored cruiser *Baltimore* with full honors.

Greta Garbo (1905–90)   One of the "fabulous faces" of the 20th century, Garbo was a screen actress of legendary charm who, after coming to MGM in 1925, launched a career that was to include such screen classics as *Anna Christie* (her first talkie), *Grand Hotel, Camille,* and *Ninotchka.* She played opposite some of the biggest male stars in film history—often with her lover, John Gilbert. ("I would rather spend an hour with Fleka than a lifetime with any other woman," he said of her.) Born Greta Gustafsson on September 18, 1905, in the city slums of Stockholm at Blekingegatan 32 (now a restaurant), she got her start as a *Tvålflicka* ("soap lather girl") in a barbershop, and later modeled hats at PUB Department store. In Hollywood she abdicated as screen queen in 1941. "They dug my grave. I play no more bad womens." Her most famous address was a seven-room apartment overlooking the East River in New York where she lived under the pseudonym Miss Harriet Brown.

Dag Hammarskjöld (1905–61)   In 1936, Hammarskjöld became undersecretary in the Ministry of Finance and later president of the board controlling the Bank of Sweden. After serving as minister of state, he was named secretary-general of the United Nations, where he presided over bitter Cold War disputes. He was unanimously re-elected for another 5 years in 1957. He met crisis after crisis, notably over the Suez Canal. His decision to send United Nations troops to the Belgian Congo was bitterly denounced by the Soviet Union, which demanded his resignation; he refused. He was posthumously awarded the Nobel Peace Prize.

John Hanson (1721–83)   A colonial Swede, this "first president of the United States" was born in Mulberry Grove, Maryland, and in time became a plantation owner with some 100 black slaves. In 1781, when Maryland became the last of 13 colonies to ratify the Articles of Confederation, the Continental Congress unanimously elected John Hanson the first president of the United States in a Congress assembled for a 12-month term—8 years before George Washington was elected. During his 1-year term (1781–82), he established the Department of State, War, Navy, and Treasury; set up a national judiciary, a national bank, and a post office; and formed a cabinet. He died in his sleep a year after leaving office. Virtually unknown, ignored, or forgotten by most Americans, he is still remembered in Maryland on April 14, John Hanson Day, and by lobbyists who want to make that date a national holiday. A life-size statue of Hanson stands in the rotunda of the Capitol building in Washington.

Charles John (1763–1844)   Born as Jean Bernadotte in Paul, France, he launched his military career by joining the French army in 1790. Meeting and becoming friends with Napoleon in 1797, Bernadotte later became his bitter enemy. He married Napoleon's ex-fiancée, Desirée Clary, in 1798 (the Marlon Brando film *Desirée* was based on these events). In 1803, Bernadotte became minister to the United States, and in 1810 he was asked to become prince of Sweden to replace Charles XIII upon his death. Charles John allied with Russia, Great Britain, and Prussia to take Norway from Denmark and to fight Napoleon. The Danes were defeated in 1813 in the Battle of Leipzig, and Charles John took control of Norway.

Selma Lagerlöf (1858–1940)   The towering woman writer of her country, the novelist was called "specifically Swedish and undeniably universal" by Paul Valery. Her works, including *The Saga of Gösta Berling* and *The Wonderful Adventures of Nils,* have been translated into 40 languages. In 1909 she won the Nobel Prize for literature, and in 1914 became the first female member of the Swedish Academy. At 75 she published her last collection of short stories and was at work on a novel when she died at her beloved Mårbacka, outside Karlstad (open to the public).

Jenny Lind (1820–87)   "The Swedish Nightingale" was born the daughter of a lace manufacturer in Stockholm and went from there to captivate the hearts of the world with her music. She also captured the heart of Hans Christian Andersen (but didn't want it). Launched in opera in 1837, she appeared in France and England before her 2-year triumphant tour of the United States, at which time she was engaged to P. T. Barnum. Settling in England after her 1852 marriage to Otto Goldschmidt, she appeared in oratorios and concerts there, eventually becoming a professor of music. Her last public appearance was at Düsseldorf, Germany, on January 20, 1870, singing an oratorio composed by her husband. She died on November 2, 1887, at Malvern, England.

Astrid Lindgren (1907–2002)   This children's book writer enjoyed international fame as the creator of Pippi Longstocking (Pippi Långssstrump). Her works are still published around the world in various languages, and it's estimated that she sold six million copies. She conceived of this red-haired, rambunctious heroine in 1944 as a present to her daughter. In 1949, a Hamburg-based publisher acquired Continental rights and launched Lindgren and Pippi into international stardom. Her writings earned her a position as one of Sweden's most honored writers. In 1993, she won the UNESCO International Book Award.

Carolus Linnaeus (or Carl von Linné) (1707–78)   The great Swedish botanist compiled *Species Plantarum* (Plant Species), a definitive catalogue of plants, in 1753. Nicknamed "the little botanist" at the age of 8, he began the modern system of botanical nomenclature. Linnaeus was born at South Rashult, Sweden, on May 23, 1707. At Uppsala University, he was given a chair of botany in 1742. The Linnaeus Garden at Uppsala is open to the public. Here he received a "Patent of Nobility" and the new name Carl von Linné. After suffering an apoplectic attack, he died on January 20, 1778, and was buried at the University of Uppsala Cathedral.

Swedish Yankees

Waves of Swedes came to the United States in the 19th century and rushed to embrace Americanisms and the English language. Perhaps because they blend in so well, the descendants of those immigrants are among the least noticeable, least self-asserting national groups in the country today. Despite their assimilation, Swedish immigrants have had an influence as profound as that of any other national group.

The Swedes first settled in North America in 1638, when the colony of New Sweden was established at the mouth of the Delaware River. The settlement was captured by the Dutch 17 years later, and the settlers evacuated to New Amsterdam, the town that became New York. Famous Swedes who left their mark included Capt. Jonas Bronck, whose homestead still bears a version of his name—the Bronx. Later, during the American Revolution, came such ideologues as Count Axel von Fersen (who reportedly had a tryst or two with Marie Antoinette) and John Mårtensson (John Morton), one of the signers of the Declaration of Independence. Sweden, lacking a base in the New World and eager to undermine Britain (one of its most powerful maritime rivals), was the first country to sign a trade agreement with the fledgling United States.

Fascination with the New World overcame Sweden's population in earnest in 1846, and waves of Swedes set out to seek health, wealth, religious freedom, and a land of their own. During a 5-year period beginning in 1868, five annual crops failed in Sweden, leading to the migration of at least 100,000 people. Between 1846 and 1873, a total of 1.5 million Swedes emigrated to North America—a figure that's especially impressive considering that Sweden's entire population was only around 4 million. The drain on the country's human resources was disastrous. Of all European countries, only Ireland lost a larger proportion of its population to emigration.

It's noteworthy that Sweden's high literacy rate, which endured despite the famine that affected many immigrants, helped Swedes to assimilate in the New World. In some regions of the Midwest, Swedes tended to settle together, but there were never any urban ghettos inhabited mainly by Swedes.

The first, and among the best-publicized, group of Swedish immigrants was a 1,500-member religious sect known as Jansonists (Erikjansare) whose leader, Erik Jansson, founded a colony in Illinois known as Bishop's Hill. Conceived as a utopia where all goods and property would be shared in common, it attracted national journalistic attention until an enraged disciple, furious at the refusal of the group's leader to allow his wife to leave the community, shot Jansson. Jansson's disciples, who believed he was immortal and would soon be resurrected, scattered throughout the Midwest and eventually established their own farms.

Carl Milles (1875–1955)   The most distinguished Swedish sculptor of the 20th century was born in Uppsala and studied in Paris, where he won recognition. He was greatly influenced by Rodin and sculpted in an Impressionistic style, mainly in clay, wood, and stone. He worked in Sweden until 1930 but from then on lived in the United States, where he became an American citizen and executed many notable commissions, including "Meeting of the Water" in St. Louis. His later works, exhibited from Chicago to New York, had a simplified quality that was both expressive and dramatic.

Alfred Nobel (1833–96)   This 19th-century Swedish industrialist and creator of prizes that bear his name was the inventor of dynamite, which, although used in war, has played an important role in the industrial development of the world. He studied explosives and in 1867 was given a British patent for dynamite. He constructed and perfected detonators and amassed a great fortune, amounting to $9.2 million upon his death, which he stipulated go as prizes "to those who have conferred the greatest benefit on mankind."

Olof Palme (1927–86)   The former prime minister of Sweden ironically became better known upon his death. Leaving a cinema with his wife, he was mysteriously gunned down on a street. A controversial leader, Palme was a leader of the so-called Socialist International, consisting of Social Democratic parties, and was particularly active in the Third World. His vehement attacks on the United States at the time of the Vietnam War led to acrid exchanges with Washington. To the end, he was a great champion of the welfare society.

August Strindberg (1849–1912)   Son of a steamship agent and a former waitress, Strindberg had an unhappy childhood, as related in his autobiography *The Son of a Servant* in 1889. But in time he was to become the country's greatest playwright, exerting a profound influence on international drama. A freelance journalist and later a librarian, he tried many professions before publishing his widely acclaimed novel *The Red Room,* written in 1879. Between stormy marriages, he wrote many plays, including *The Father* (1887) and *Miss Julie* (1888). He died of cancer on May 14, 1912, in Stockholm and was ignored in death as in life by the Swedish Academy.

Emanuel Swedenborg (1688–1772)   Son of a bishop in Skåra, who was a major religious figure in Sweden, Swedenborg became a scientist, philosopher, and theologian. He studied in Uppsala and went to England to pursue his interest in natural sciences. Influenced by Descartes, he published many philosophical and psychological works in the 1720s and 1730s, in which he saw the world as subject to mechanical laws. He was concerned with the source and structure of matter, concluding finally that the soul is material, as reported in his *Regnum Animale.* His theological insights had great influence on Dostoyevsky, Emerson, Balzac, Ezra Pound, and others; many congregations in the United States take Swedenborg's writings as their doctrinal basis. His *Journal of Dreams* is still widely read.

Mai Zetterling (1926–94)   One of Europe's busiest female film directors, Zetterling died while filming *The Woman Who Cleaned the World,* which she had written. Born in Vasteras to a working-class family, she first became famous as an actress in the film *Torment* (1947), written by Ingmar Bergman. She appeared opposite such stars as Danny Kaye in *Knock on Wood* (1954) and Peter Sellers in *Only Two Can Play* (1961). In the 1960s and 1970s, she turned to directing such films as *Night Games* (1966) and *Of Seals and Men* (1979). She also wrote short stories, novels, and children's books.

Anders Zorn (1860–1920)   A renowned painter, sculptor, and member of the Association of Artists, founded in the 19th century. His famous works include *Midsummer Nights' Dance* and *Young Girls Bathing*. His works can be seen in Dalarna, Stockholm, and Chicago.

5 The Swedish Chef

The fame of the *smörgåsbord* (smorgasbord) is justly deserved. Using a vast array of dishes—everything from Baltic herring to smoked reindeer—the smorgasbord can be eaten either as hors d'oeuvres or as a meal in itself.

One cardinal rule of the smorgasbord: Don't mix fish and meat dishes. It is customary to begin with *sill* (herring), prepared in many ways. Herring usually is followed by other treats from the sea (jellied eel, smoked fish, and raw pickled salmon); then diners proceed to the cold meat dishes, such as baked ham or liver paste, which are accompanied by vegetable salads. Hot dishes, often Swedish meatballs, come next and are backed up by cheese and crackers, and sometimes a fresh fruit salad.

The smorgasbord is not served as often in Sweden as many visitors seem to believe, as it requires time-consuming preparation. Many Swedish families reserve it for special occasions. In lieu of the 40-dish smorgasbord, some restaurants have taken to serving a plate of *assietter* (hors d'oeuvres). One of the tricks for enjoying smorgasbord is timing. It's best to go early, when dishes are fresh. Late arrivals may be more fashionable, but the food often is stale.

The average times for meals in Sweden are generally from 8 to 11am for the standard continental breakfast, noon to 2:30pm for lunch, and as early as 5:30pm for dinner to around 8 or 8:30pm (many restaurants in Stockholm are open to midnight—but don't count on this in the small villages).

A Swedish breakfast at your hotel might consist of cheese, ham, sausage, egg, bread, and perhaps *filmjölk,* a kind of sour-milk yogurt. **Smörgas,** the famous Swedish open-face sandwich, like the Danish *smørrebrød* and Norwegian *smørbrød,* is a slice of buttered bread with something on top. It is eaten for breakfast or any time during the day, and you'll find it at varying prices, depending on what you order and where you order it.

Unless you decide to have smorgasbord (never served in the evening) at lunch, you'll find that the Swedes do not go in for lavish spreads in the middle of the day. The usual luncheon order consists of one course, as you'll observe on menus, especially in larger towns. Dinner menus are for complete meals, with appetizer, main course and side dishes, and dessert included.

Generally, Swedish chefs tend to be far more expert with **fish dishes** (freshwater pike and salmon are star choices) than with meat courses. The Swedes go stark raving mad at the sight of *kraftor* (crayfish), in season from mid-August to mid-September. This succulent, dill-flavored delicacy is eaten with the fingers, and much of the fun is the elaborate ritual surrounding its consumption.

A platter of thin **pancakes,** served with lingonberries (comparable to cranberries), is the traditional Thursday-night dinner in Sweden. It often is preceded by yellow split-pea soup seasoned with pork. It's good any night of the week—but somehow better on Thursday.

Swedish cuisine used to be deficient in fresh vegetables and fruits, and relied heavily on canned goods, but this is no longer true. Potatoes are the staff of life, but fresh salads have long peppered the landscape, especially in big cities.

The calorie-laden Swedish pastry—the mainstay of the *konditori* (cafeteria)—is tempting and fatal to weight-watchers.

DRINKS   **Kaffe** (coffee) is the universal drink in Sweden, although tea (taken straight) and milk also are popular. The water is perfectly safe to drink all over Sweden. Those who want a reprieve from alcohol might find the fruit-flavored **Pommac** a good soft-drink beverage, but Coca-Cola is ubiquitous.

The state monopoly, Systembolaget, controls the sale of alcoholic beverages. Licensed restaurants may sell alcohol after noon only (1pm on Sun).

Schnapps or aquavit, served icy cold, is a superb Swedish drink, often used to accompany smorgasbord. The run-of-the-mill Swedish **beer** (pilsner) has only a small amount of alcohol. All restaurants serve *lättol* (light beer) and *folköl*, a somewhat stronger brew. Swedish vodka, or **brännvin,** is made from corn and potatoes and flavored with different spices. All brännvin is served ice cold in schnapps glasses. Keep in mind that aquavit is much stronger than it looks, and Sweden has strictly enforced rules about drinking and driving. Most Swedes seem to drink their liquor straight. But mixed drinks, especially in urban areas, are now more commonplace. Either way, the drink prices are sky-high.

Index

See also Accommodations and Restaurant indexes, below.

Galerie Kvinnfolki (Gotland), 265
Gallerian (Stockholm), 115
Gallerian (Västerås), 132
Gällivare, 21, 342, 358–361
Galtispouda, 351
Gamla Gefle (Gävle), 318
Gamla Rådhuset (Lidköping), 280–281
Gamla Stan (Old Town; Stockholm), 57–58
  accommodations, 72–73
  restaurants, 84–87
  shopping, 110
  sights and attractions, 93, 96, 97, 99–100
  walking tours, 109
    self-guided, 103–106
Gamla Stan (Old Town; Västerås), 133
Gamlia (Umeå), 8
Gamla Uppsala, 7, 127
Gammelgården (Rättvik), 313
Gammelstad (Old Town; Luleå), 347
Gammelstads Kyrka (Luleå), 347
Gammlia (Umeå), 337
Garbo, Greta, 50, 58, 112, 116, 158, 206, 381, 382
Gärdslösa (Öland), 254
Gävle, 316–321
Gävleborg County Museum (Gävle), 318–319
Gay and lesbian travelers
  Gothenburg, 158
  information and resources, 29–30
  Stockholm, 118–119
Gay Pride Week, 30
Gay Switchboard, 30
Geocity (Stockholm), 113
Germany, ferries from, 43
Gillblad's (Gothenburg), 155
Giovanni's Room, 30
Glass and crystal
  buying, 233
  Helsingborg, 182
  Malmö, 192
  Stockholm, 113
  Växjö, 231–234
Glassware, Kalmar, 225
Glimmingehus (near Simrishamn), 210
Global Refunds, 53
Globen (Stockholm Globe Arena), 109
Glommersträsk Historical Museum (Arvidsjaur), 351
Glömminge Krukmarkeri (Öland), 257

Goda Hopp, 167
Golf, 5, 23–24
  Båstad, 173
  Halland, 165
  Lapland, 344
  Öland, 251
  Söderhamn, 322
  Stockholm, 109
Gondolen (Stockholm), 121
Göta Älv, 6
Göta Canal, 6, 271–274, 287
Göta Canal Steamship Company, 274
Göta Källare (Stockholm), 119
Götaland, 15
Götaplatsen (Gothenburg), 137, 150–151
Göta River, 274, 275
  Älvsborg Bridge (Gothenburg), 138
Göteborg Maritima Centrum (Gothenburg), 151
Göteborgs Konstmuseum (Gothenburg), 9, 151
Göteborgskortet (Gothenburg Card), 138
Göteborgsoperan (Gothenburg Opera House), 156
Gothenburg, 1–2, 136–176, 369
  accommodations, 140–145
  architectural highlights, 153
  area code, 139
  arriving in, 136
  business hours, 139
  consulates, 139
  currency exchange, 139
  dentists, 139
  doctors, 139
  easy excursions to the Bohuslän Coast & Halland, 158–176
  emergencies, 139
  eyeglasses, 139
  gay nightlife, 158
  for kids, 153
  laundry and dry cleaning, 139
  layout of, 137–138
  liquor laws, 139
  luggage storage and lockers, 139
  nightlife, 156–158
  organized tours, 154
  parks and gardens, 152
  pharmacy, 139
  photographic supplies, 140
  picnic fare, 147
  police, 140

  post office, 140
  radio and TV stations, 140
  restaurants, 145–149
  shopping, 154–156
  sights and attractions, 150–154
  transit information, 140
  transportation, 138
  visitor information, 137
Gotland, 2, 250, 260–270
  accommodations, 265–267
  exploring by car, 262
  shopping, 265
  sights and attractions, 262, 264–265
  southern, 269–270
  traveling to, 260–261
Gotlands Fornsal (Visby), 264, 265
GoToMyPC, 36
Granberget, 308
Gran Building (Sundsvall), 328
Grand Hotel (Stockholm), 108
Gränna, 240–243
Grännaberger (Gränna Mountain), 240
The Great Winter Market (Jokkmokk), 354
Greta (Gothenburg), 158
Gripsholm Castle, 129
Gröna Lunds Tivoli (Stockholm), 117
Grönsakstorget/Kungstorget (Gothenburg), 154
Gruvtur, 359
Guest Apartment (Stockholm), 93
Guldhedens Vattentorn (Gothenburg), 150
Gunnarssons Träfigurer (Stockholm), 114
Gustaf Wasa, 6
Gustav Adolfs Torg (Gothenburg), 138
Gustav Adolfs Torg (Stockholm), 103, 106
Gustavus IV, 377
Gustavus Vasa, 126, 129, 225, 242, 244, 273, 314, 376
Gustav Vasa, King, 9, 132, 134, 243, 244

H abo Kyrka, 285
Hägnan Museum (Luleå), 347
Halland, 165–176
Hallands Väderö, 172–173

Restaurants

FROMMER'S® COMPLETE TRAVEL GUIDES

Alaska
Alaska Cruises & Ports of Call
American Southwest
Amsterdam
Argentina & Chile
Arizona
Atlanta
Australia
Austria
Bahamas
Barcelona, Madrid & Seville
Beijing
Belgium, Holland & Luxembourg
Bermuda
Boston
Brazil
British Columbia & the Canadian Rockies
Brussels & Bruges
Budapest & the Best of Hungary
Calgary
California
Canada
Cancún, Cozumel & the Yucatán
Cape Cod, Nantucket & Martha's Vineyard
Caribbean
Caribbean Ports of Call
Carolinas & Georgia
Chicago
China
Colorado
Costa Rica
Cruises & Ports of Call
Cuba
Denmark
Denver, Boulder & Colorado Springs
England
Europe
Europe by Rail
European Cruises & Ports of Call

Florence, Tuscany & Umbria
Florida
France
Germany
Great Britain
Greece
Greek Islands
Halifax
Hawaii
Hong Kong
Honolulu, Waikiki & Oahu
India
Ireland
Italy
Jamaica
Japan
Kauai
Las Vegas
London
Los Angeles
Maryland & Delaware
Maui
Mexico
Montana & Wyoming
Montréal & Québec City
Munich & the Bavarian Alps
Nashville & Memphis
New England
Newfoundland & Labrador
New Mexico
New Orleans
New York City
New York State
New Zealand
Northern Italy
Norway
Nova Scotia, New Brunswick & Prince Edward Island
Oregon
Ottawa
Paris
Peru

Philadelphia & the Amish Country
Portugal
Prague & the Best of the Czech Republic
Provence & the Riviera
Puerto Rico
Rome
San Antonio & Austin
San Diego
San Francisco
Santa Fe, Taos & Albuquerque
Scandinavia
Scotland
Seattle
Shanghai
Sicily
Singapore & Malaysia
South Africa
South America
South Florida
South Pacific
Southeast Asia
Spain
Sweden
Switzerland
Texas
Thailand
Tokyo
Toronto
Turkey
USA
Utah
Vancouver & Victoria
Vermont, New Hampshire & Maine
Vienna & the Danube Valley
Virgin Islands
Virginia
Walt Disney World® & Orlando
Washington, D.C.
Washington State

FROMMER'S® DOLLAR-A-DAY GUIDES

Australia from $50 a Day
California from $70 a Day
England from $75 a Day
Europe from $85 a Day
Florida from $70 a Day
Hawaii from $80 a Day

Ireland from $80 a Day
Italy from $70 a Day
London from $90 a Day
New York City from $90 a Day
Paris from $90 a Day
San Francisco from $70 a Day

Washington, D.C. from $80 a Day
Portable London from $90 a Day
Portable New York City from $90 a Day
Portable Paris from $90 a Day

FROMMER'S® PORTABLE GUIDES

Acapulco, Ixtapa & Zihuatanejo
Amsterdam
Aruba
Australia's Great Barrier Reef
Bahamas
Berlin
Big Island of Hawaii
Boston
California Wine Country
Cancún
Cayman Islands
Charleston
Chicago
Disneyland®
Dominican Republic
Dublin

Florence
Frankfurt
Hong Kong
Las Vegas
Las Vegas for Non-Gamblers
London
Los Angeles
Los Cabos & Baja
Maine Coast
Maui
Miami
Nantucket & Martha's Vineyard
New Orleans
New York City
Paris

Phoenix & Scottsdale
Portland
Puerto Rico
Puerto Vallarta, Manzanillo & Guadalajara
Rio de Janeiro
San Diego
San Francisco
Savannah
Vancouver
Vancouver Island
Venice
Virgin Islands
Washington, D.C.
Whistler

FROMMER'S® NATIONAL PARK GUIDES

Algonquin Provincial Park
Banff & Jasper
Family Vacations in the National
  Parks

Grand Canyon
National Parks of the American
  West
Rocky Mountain

Yellowstone & Grand Teton
Yosemite & Sequoia/Kings
  Canyon
Zion & Bryce Canyon

FROMMER'S® MEMORABLE WALKS

Chicago
London

New York
Paris

San Francisco

FROMMER'S® WITH KIDS GUIDES

Chicago
Las Vegas
New York City

Ottawa
San Francisco
Toronto

Vancouver
Walt Disney World® & Orlando
Washington, D.C.

SUZY GERSHMAN'S BORN TO SHOP GUIDES

Born to Shop: France
Born to Shop: Hong Kong,
  Shanghai & Beijing

Born to Shop: Italy
Born to Shop: London

Born to Shop: New York
Born to Shop: Paris

FROMMER'S® IRREVERENT GUIDES

Amsterdam
Boston
Chicago
Las Vegas
London

Los Angeles
Manhattan
New Orleans
Paris
Rome

San Francisco
Seattle & Portland
Vancouver
Walt Disney World®
Washington, D.C.

FROMMER'S® BEST-LOVED DRIVING TOURS

Austria
Britain
California
France

Germany
Ireland
Italy
New England

Northern Italy
Scotland
Spain
Tuscany & Umbria

THE UNOFFICIAL GUIDES®

Beyond Disney
California with Kids
Central Italy
Chicago
Cruises
Disneyland®
England
Florida
Florida with Kids
Inside Disney

Hawaii
Las Vegas
London
Maui
Mexico's Best Beach Resorts
Mini Las Vegas
Mini Mickey
New Orleans
New York City
Paris

San Francisco
Skiing & Snowboarding in the
  West
South Florida including Miami &
  the Keys
Walt Disney World®
Walt Disney World® for
  Grown-ups
Walt Disney World® with Kids
Washington, D.C.

SPECIAL-INTEREST TITLES

Athens Past & Present
Cities Ranked & Rated
Frommer's Best Day Trips from London
Frommer's Best RV & Tent Campgrounds
  in the U.S.A.
Frommer's Caribbean Hideaways
Frommer's China: The 50 Most Memorable Trips
Frommer's Exploring America by RV
Frommer's Gay & Lesbian Europe
Frommer's NYC Free & Dirt Cheap

Frommer's Road Atlas Europe
Frommer's Road Atlas France
Frommer's Road Atlas Ireland
Frommer's Wonderful Weekends from
  New York City
The New York Times' Guide to Unforgettable
  Weekends
Retirement Places Rated
Rome Past & Present

Travel Tip: He who finds the best hotel deal has more to spend on facials involving knobbly vegetables.

Hello, the Roaming Gnome here. I've been nabbed from the garden and taken round the world. The people who took me are so terribly clever. They find the best offerings on Travelocity. For very little cha-ching. And that means I get to be pampered and exfoliated till I'm pink as a bunny's doodah.

***
** travelocity®

1-888-TRAVELOCITY / travelocity.com / America Online Keyword: Travel

Travel Tip: Make sure there's customer service for any change of plans — involving friendly natives, for example.

One can plan and plan, but if you don't book with the right people you can't seize le moment and canoodle with the poodle named Pansy. I, for one, am all for fraternizing with the locals. Better yet, if I need to extend my stay and my gnome nappers are willing, it can all be arranged through the 800 number at, oh look, how convenient, the lovely company coat of arms.

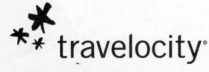

travelocity®